Medieval & Renaissance Literary Studies

The Divorce Tracts of John Milton

Texts and Contexts

edited by Sara J. van den Berg
& W. Scott Howard

DUQUESNE UNIVERSITY PRESS
Pittsburgh, Pennsylvania

Published in the United States of America by
Duquesne University Press
600 Forbes Avenue
Pittsburgh, Pennsylvania 15282

Library of Congress Cataloging-in-Publication Data

Milton, John, 1608–1674.
The divorce tracts of John Milton : texts and contexts / edited by Sara J. van den Berg and W. Scott Howard.
p. cm.
Includes bibliographical references and index.
ISBN 978-0-8207-0440-1 (cloth : alk. paper)
1. Divorce—Early works to 1800. 2. Marriage—Early works to 1800. 3. Divorce—England—History—17th century—Sources. 4. Marriage—England—History—17th century—Sources. 5. Milton, John, 1608–1674—Political and social views. 6. Divorce in literature. 7. Marriage in literature. I. Van den Berg, Sara J. II. Howard, W. Scott. III. Milton, John, 1608–1674. Doctrine and discipline of divorce. IV. Title.
PR3569.V36 2010
824'.4—dc22

2010037573

∞ Printed on acid-free paper.

Contents

Acknowledgments

This project began when our students at the University of Washington, the University of Denver, and Saint Louis University wanted to read more of Milton's prose, especially his divorce tracts. This book is for them.

We are deeply grateful to past editors and commentators, especially Ernest Sirluck, Lowell W. Coolidge, and Arnold Williams, who prepared the second volume of the *Complete Prose Works of John Milton* for Yale University Press. Yale University Press allowed us to include many of their notes in this collection. Sharon Hampel deserves special thanks. She contributed the notes on Milton's debt to Hebrew law and learning that enrich our understanding of Milton's work. Special thanks are also due to Victor Castellani for his expertise with Greek and Latin sources, and to Peggy Keeran and Jennifer Bowers for their assistance with research strategies. We also wish to thank the editorial team at Duquesne University Press, especially Kathy Meyer, for their expertise in preparing this book for publication.

W. Scott Howard is very grateful to the University of Denver for support provided by the Division of Arts, Humanities, and Social Sciences and by research grants from the Professional Research Fund, the Faculty Research Fund, the Walter Rosenberry fund, and the Office of Internationalization; and for sabbaticals awarded in 2000, 2005, and 2009. Sara van den Berg is very grateful for support provided by Dean Donald G. Brennan and the College of Arts and Sciences, Saint Louis University; for a 2002 summer stipend from the National Endowment for the Humanities; for a Mellon Faculty Development Grant from Saint Louis University; and for a sabbatical awarded by Saint Louis University in 2007.

Portions of the introduction originally appeared as: Sara van den Berg's "Women, Children, and the Rhetoric of Milton's Divorce Tracts," *EMLS* 10, no. 1 (2004): 1–13; W. Scott Howard's "Milton's 'Divorcive' Liberties: Ecclesiastical, Domestic or Private, Civil, and Cosmological," *EMLS* 10, no. 1 (2004): 1–12; and the coauthored article, "G. M. Revealed: Printer of the First Attacks on *The Doctrine and Discipline of Divorce*," *Milton Quarterly* 38, no. 4 (2004): 242–52. We thank the editors of those journals for permission to incorporate revised passages from those essays in our introduction.

Sara van den Berg thanks John Shawcross, Michael Lieb, Helen Marlborough, Charles H. Parker, Stella Revard, Jonathan Sawday, Regina Schwartz, and Steven Zwicker for their help at key moments, and David Cormier for bracing discussions of Milton's prose. W. Scott Howard thanks John Shawcross, Annabel Patterson, Thomas Corns, Elizabeth Skerpan-Wheeler, Jameela Lares, Richard DuRocher, Nicholas von Maltzahn, and Nigel Smith.

This volume is dedicated to the memory of Albert C. Labriola, for his encouragement of this project and for his inestimable contributions to Milton scholarship.

A Note on the Texts

We have chosen to transcribe first editions of each text currently available through *Early English Books, Early English Books Online (EEBO),* http://eebo.chadwyck.com/home, and other specialized databases and library collections as noted below. Milton's divorce pamphlets have been lightly modernized in spelling and punctuation. The other contemporary documents are presented in their original form. Milton would have used the Geneva Bible. We have accordingly chosen to cite *The Geneva Bible: A Facsimile of the 1560 Edition* (Madison: University of Wisconsin Press, 1969). In citing the *Oxford English Dictionary* (*OED*), we follow the 2009 edition. We use the following abbreviations for Milton's works: YP for *The Complete Prose Works of John Milton,* 8 vols., ed. Don M. Wolfe et al. (New Haven: Yale University Press, 1953–82); *SP* for *John Milton: Selected Prose,* ed. C. A. Patrides (Columbia: University of Missouri Press, 1985); *PL* for *Paradise Lost,* ed. Alastair Fowler (London: Longman, 1971); and *CP* for *The Complete Poetry of John Milton,* ed. John Shawcross (New York: Doubleday, 1971).

Milton's Tracts, 1643–45

THE DOCTRINE AND DISCIPLINE OF DIVORCE: RESTORED TO THE GOOD OF BOTH SEXES, From the bondage of Canon Law, and other mistakes, to Christian freedom, guided by the Rule of Charity. Wherein also many places of Scripture have recovered their long-lost meaning. Seasonable to be now thought on in the Reformation intended (London, 1643). *Source:* Henry E. Huntington Library and Art Gallery, Wing 155:08; *EEBO.*

THE *Doctrine & Discipline* OF DIVORCE *Restored to the good of both Sexes, From the bondage of* CANON LAW, *and other mistakes, to the true meaning of Scripture in the Law and Gospel compared. Wherein also are set down the bad consequences of abolishing or condemning of Sin, that which the Law of God allows, and Christ abolished not. Now the second time revised and much augmented, In Two* BOOKS: *To the Parliament of England with the Assembly* (London, 1644). *Source:* British Library, Wing (2nd ed.), M2109, Thomason E.31[5]; *EEBO.*

THE JUDGEMENT OF MARTIN BUCER, CONCERNING DIVORCE, *Written to Edward the sixth, in his second Book of the Kingdom of Christ. And now Englished. Wherein a late Book restoring the Doctrine and Discipline of Divorce is here confirmed and justified by the authority of Martin Bucer* (London, 1644). *Source:* British Library, Wing (2nd ed.), B5270, Thomason E.4[19]; *EEBO.*

Tetrachordon: EXPOSITIONS UPON *The four chief places in Scripture, which treat of Marriage, or nullities in Marriage. Wherein the Doctrine and Discipline of Divorce, as was lately published, is confirmed by explanation of Scripture, by testimony of ancient Fathers, of civil laws in the Primitive Church, of famousest Reformed Divines, And lastly, by an intended Act of the Parliament and Church of England in the last year of* EDWARD *the Sixth* (London, 1645). *Source:* British Library, Wing (2nd ed.), M2184, Thomason E.271[12]; *EEBO.*

COLASTERION: A REPLY TO A NAMELESS ANSWER AGAINST *The Doctrine and Discipline of Divorce.* WHEREIN *The trivial Author of that Answer is discovered, the Licenser conferred with, and the Opinion which they traduce defended* (London, 1645). *Source:* British Library, Wing (2nd ed.), M2099, Thomason E.271[11]; *EEBO.*

Contemporary Pamphlets, 1644–45

William Prynne, *Twelve Considerable Serious Questions touching church government sadly propounded (out of a reall desire of unitie and tranquillity in church and state) to all sober-minded Christians, cordially affecting a speedy settled reformation, and brotherly Christian union in all our churches and denominations, now miserably wasted with civill unnatu[r]all warres, and deplorably lacerated with ecclesiasticall dissentions* (London, 1644). *Source:* Union Theological Seminary Library, New York, Wing P4117; *EEBO*.

Herbert Palmer, *The Glasse of Gods Providence Towards his Faithfull Ones. Held forth in a Sermon Preached to the two Houses of Parliament, at Margarets Westminster, Aug. 13.1644. being an extraordinary Day of Humiliation. Wherein is discovered the great failings that the best are liable unto; upon which God is provoked sometimes to take Vengeance. The whole is applied specially to a more carefull observation of our late Covenant, and particularly against the ungodly Toleration pleaded for under pretence of Liberty of Conscience* (London, 1644). *Source:* British Library, Wing (2nd ed.), P235; *EEBO*.

Anonymous, *An Answer to a Book, Intituled,* THE *Doctrine and Discipline* OF DIVORCE, OR, *A Plea for Ladies and Gentlewomen, and all other Maried Women against Divorce. Wherein, Both Sexes are vindicated from all bondage of Canon Law, and other mistakes whatsoever: And the unfound Principles of the Author are examined and fully confuted by authority of Holy Scripture, the Laws of this Land, and sound Reason* (London, 1644). *Source:* Henry E. Huntington Library and Art Gallery, Wing A3304; *EEBO*.

Daniel Featley, *Καταβαπτισταὶ κατάπτυστοι, The Dippers Dipt, or, The Anabaptists Duck'd and Plung'd over head and eares, at a Disputation in Southwark: together with a large and full discourse of their 1. Original. 2. Severall sorts. 3. Peculiar errours. 4. High attempts against the state. 5. Capitall Punishments, with an application to these times* (London, 1645). *Source:* Union Theological Seminary Library, N.Y. Wing F586, *EEBO*.

Introduction

Milton's Divorce Tracts and the Temper of the Times

Of all the controversial arguments Milton advanced in his poetry and prose, his justification of divorce was perhaps the most shocking to seventeenth century readers. The initial attacks (1644–45) came from eminent clergymen and one anonymous pamphleteer, and opposition would continue long after Milton's death. Not until the Divorce Reform Act (1969–73) would Parliament accept Milton's call for reform of marital law and legalize no-fault divorce on the ground of "irretrievable breakdown of the marital relationship"—or, to use Milton's words, "That indisposition, unfitness, or contrariety of mind, arising from a cause in nature unchangeable, hindring and ever likely to hinder the main benefits of conjugal society, which are solace and peace."[1] Milton also argued that divorce with the right to remarry (*a vinculo*)[2] should be the law in England as it was in the other Protestant nations of Europe, and that divorce should not be adjudicated in religious courts.

A proposal to permit divorce with the right to remarry had been rejected during the reign of Henry VIII. Although the king's divorce effected the separation of the Church of England from the Church of Rome, only England among Protestant nations retained the tradition of canon law and ecclesiastical courts to regulate marriage. Milton's tracts marked one extreme in the ensuing debate about divorce in early modern England, a debate that began the slow shift in English ideas about marriage from sacrament to secular contract. The issue of divorce was central to a larger debate about social values and policies. Milton's efforts to reform divorce law were grounded in his concept of liberty. As an institution, marriage linked the individual to the state, both in social practice and in the metaphorical framework of political theory. Advocating divorce disrupted that social paradigm. Milton's arguments for divorce as a Christian *doctrine and discipline* helped articulate a new paradigm of marriage as a private institution designed to foster personal spiritual growth.

The Divorce Tracts of John Milton: Texts and Contexts brings together for the first time in a single volume the complete texts of Milton's divorce pamphlets and four documents that represent the first responses to his argument. In a short span of 18 months, Milton published five tracts on divorce: *The Doctrine and Discipline of Divorce* (August 1, 1643), a much enlarged edition (February 2, 1644), *The Judgement of Martin Bucer* (August 6, 1644), *Tetrachordon* (March 4, 1644/45), and *Colasterion* (March 4, 1644/45).[3] Our collection is the first to include full-length presentations of both the 1643 and 1644 editions of *The Doctrine and Discipline of Divorce* as complete, separate works.[4] *The Complete Prose Works of John Milton,* the standard modern edition from Yale University Press, offers a hybrid document that combines the 1643 original version and the greatly expanded 1644 text of *The Doctrine and Discipline of Divorce.* The Yale editor, Lowell W. Coolidge, shows exactly which passages were added or omitted in 1644. The conflated text, however, is difficult to decipher, especially for readers not already familiar with the complexities of Milton's prose tracts. We present *The Divorce Tracts of John Milton: Texts and Contexts* as an accessible, lightly modernized text for interested readers in a variety of fields within and beyond seventeenth century literary studies.

This collection also provides the first modern transcription of *An Answer to a book, intituled, The doctrine and discipline of divorce, or, A plea for ladies and gentlewomen, and all other maried women against divorce* (1644). This anonymous pamphlet — the only full-length contemporary document to engage thoroughly with Milton's argument—elicited Milton's last divorce tract, *Colasterion* (1645). In addition to the whole text of *An Answer,* our volume includes selected passages from three other contemporary publications. Our transcriptions are arranged chronologically according to their appearance in print: William Prynne's *Twelve Considerable Serious Questions* (September 16, 1644); Herbert Palmer's *The Glasse of Gods Providence* (November 7, 1644); the anonymous tract, *An Answer* (November 14, 1644);[5] and Daniel Featley's *The Dippers Dipt* (February 7, 1645). Those are the four pamphlets to which Milton responded most clearly and directly in the pages of his divorce tracts.[6]

Tetrachordon presents Milton's response to Herbert Palmer and Daniel Featley; *Colasterion,* his counterattack on William Prynne and the author of *An Answer*. The degree to which Milton's opponents may have coordinated their attacks remains an open question. However, some connections underscore the importance of placing all five of Milton's divorce pamphlets within their immediate context of reception. *An Answer* was printed by George Miller, the same man who printed Herbert Palmer's *The Glasse of Gods Providence,* which had first been a major sermon preached before Parliament.[7] Palmer's attack on *The Doctrine and Discipline of Divorce* provoked Milton's response in *Tetrachordon. An Answer* and *The Glasse of Gods Providence* may have been designed as a tandem assault on Milton's ideas. Milton certainly intended a coordinated reply to his opponents when he published *Colasterion* and *Tetrachordon* on the same day. Juxtaposing the texts of Milton and his adversaries highlights the intensity of their arguments, and illustrates the contentious pamphlet warfare of the 1640s.

Each of Milton's five tracts is distinctive in its argument and its rhetoric. The first, *The Doctrine and Discipline of Divorce,* makes an impassioned plea for reform, offering vivid vignettes and images that convey the reality of unhappy marriage and the personal cost to spouses and children. The revised edition, almost twice as long, supplemented the emotional appeal with a stronger rhetorical structure. Milton set up chapters, each with a brief summary of the argument. He also added substantial sections about the relationship between Mosaic law, the Gospel, natural law, and the law of nations. He reinterpreted Pauline marital doctrine and emphasized that his call for English reform was congruent with the practice of continental reformers.

Milton's second tract, *The Judgement of Martin Bucer,* emphasized his nationalistic fervor. The tract is a translation of sections from *De regno Christi* (1557), which Bucer had written at Cambridge University. Milton believed that Bucer's arguments on behalf of Henry VIII supported his own theory that divorce could be a Christian "doctrine and discipline"—that is, principle and practice. "But this, I hope, will be enough to excuse me with the mere Englishman," Milton declares, "to be no forger of new and loose opinions." Bucer was not only a continental authority, but also someone whose arguments had been important in England. Moreover, even someone who knew only the English language ("the mere Englishman") had to respect his work: "Bucer wrote this tractate of divorce in England and for England." As a native, Milton believed he must do at least as much. Retranslating Bucer's text to make it more vivid and idiomatic, Milton hoped to revive the arguments of the original Protestant reformers, and thereby "to prevent this working mystery of ignorance and ecclesiastical thralldom, which under new shapes and disguises begins a-fresh to grow upon us."

Although Milton published *Tetrachordon* and *Colasterion* on the same day, it would be hard to imagine two works more different in rhetorical style and tone. Milton's rhetoric in *Tetrachordon* is stately and scholarly, as befits an address to the learned clergy. His rhetoric in *Colasterion,* on the other hand, more than matches the vituperation and snarling *ad hominem* blasts against Milton in *An Answer. Tetrachordon* was designed as a reply to Herbert Palmer, who had challenged Milton in *The Glasse of Gods Providence Towards His Faithfull Ones* (1644), to others who were "instigated to a hard censure" of his first tract, and also to those "judicious" parliamentarians who asked for a fuller explication of Scripture and additional citations of authorities. *Tetrachordon* explicates the four biblical passages that were the foundation of marital theory and the law prohibiting divorce: Genesis 1:27–28, Deuteronomy

24:1–2, Matthew 5:31–32, and 1 Corinthians 7:10–16. Milton offers an extended revisionary reading of these biblical texts in the spirit of the Augustinian "rule of charity" he had emphasized in *The Doctrine and Discipline of Divorce*. In *Colasterion,* on the contrary, he fights fire with fire, excoriating the anonymous pamphleteer who had attacked him in *An Answer to a book, intituled, The doctrine and discipline of divorce* (1644). Milton insistently restates the major points from his first tract and lashes out at the author of *An Answer* for failing to understand his arguments in the 1643 text.

Milton chose Greek titles that indicate the different rhetorical registers of the two works. *Tetrachordon,* a musical term, characterizes his attempt to bring four key tones, or verses, of the Hebrew Bible and the New Testament into harmony. *Colasterion,* on the other hand, refers to a place of punishment and to the punishing whip itself, indicating that Milton intends his tract as a place and a tool to punish his critic. *Colasterion* has generally been dismissed as a work unworthy of Milton, but those who would seek to understand the gender conflicts in Milton's works and in early modern England should pay close attention to the argument about wives in *An Answer* and *Colasterion.* The subtitle of *An Answer* casts the work as "a plea for ladies and gentlewomen, and all other maried women against divorce." In *Colasterion,* Milton rails against the claim that his argument would damage women.

At the time Milton wrote his divorce tracts, England observed canon law, which followed the biblical prohibition of divorce except in cases of adultery (the so-called Matthean exception). Marriage was considered a sacrament, binding for life, and the dissolution of a marriage for cruelty, desertion, or any reason except adultery usually resulted only in a permanent separation without the right to remarry (*a mensa et thoro*).[8] Divorce with the right to remarry was possible only if the marriage was invalid. Bigamy, inability to consent, refusal or inability to consummate a marriage, or close degrees of kinship were permissible grounds for annulment. A few members of the aristocracy sought divorce *a vinculo* through private bills in Parliament; middle-class people who were unhappily married often separated without benefit of law; and lower-class husbands were known to sell their wives. However, Milton lived in an England where marriage was in general a binding condition that ended only at the death of a spouse.

In his antiepiscopal tracts—such as *Of Reformation touching Church-Discipline* (1641) and *The Reason of Church-Government* (1642)—Milton argued for reform of the Church of England and resisted the authority of the bishops over the people. Under the influence of Presbyterian leaders, the Long Parliament appointed the Westminster Assembly to reform church government. In 1644, the Assembly drafted *A Directory for the publique worship of God, throughout the three kingdoms of England, Scotland, and Ireland,* to replace the *Book of Common Prayer* (1559), which was derided as papist by anti-Laudian Protestants. The Assembly then passed two ordinances in 1645. The first (in January) approved the use of the new directory; the second (in August) banned the use of the *Book of Common Prayer*. Regarding marriage, the *Directory* prohibited elaborate weddings, publishing banns, exchanging rings, ringing church bells, and other traditional celebrations. A couple need only exchange vows, without the blessing of a clergyman. As swiftly as those two ordinances were passed, however, the *Directory* was denounced by the majority of the population. Milton's divorce tracts (1643–45) may be rightly placed within this fraught context of ecclesiastical reform and an emerging desacramentalized, commonwealth model of marriage.

The Church of England's commitment to sacramental marriage represented one pole of opinion in England; radical sectarians who disavowed formal marriage, the opposite. None of the earlier declarations of reform in the British Isles mentioned divorce: not the *Scots Confession* (1560), the *Thirty-Nine Articles* (1563), or the Irish *Articles of Religion* (1615). By the 1640s, however, the central debate in England concerned whether the grounds for divorce should be expanded.

The debate centered on two biblical passages that outlined grounds for divorce: "fornication" (Matt. 19) and "desertion" (1 Cor. 7:1–16). The Presbyterian clergy debated how to define "fornication," and whether desertion as well as fornication could be grounds for divorce. William Perkins, in *The foundation of Christian religion* (1618), argued for a narrow definition, insisting that fornication designated "only the sin of adultery or... incest," but he held that a minister "may pronounce the marriage to be dissolved" in cases of desertion.[9] In *The Doctrine and Discipline of Divorce,* and more extensively in *Tetrachordon,* Milton enters the fray to argue for an expanded definition of "fornication." His 1643 tract cites John 8:3–11, in which "our Savior chose to use the word *fornication,* which word is found to signify other matrimonial transgressions... besides actual adultery." By interpreting the word "fornication" in the largest sense, Milton tries to argue that the grounds of divorce should be expanded to include more than physical infidelity. In *Tetrachordon,* he develops his interpretation of fornication at far greater length.

William Gouge, who chaired the Westminster Assembly committee on divorce, opposed any change. In *Of domesticall duties* (1634)—a text printed by George Miller for Edward Brewster—Gouge noted that continental Reformed churches permitted divorce and remarriage, but that "our church hath no such customs."[10] Milton, in the 1644 edition of *The Doctrine and Discipline of Divorce,* begins his prefatory letter to the Westminster Assembly with a contemptuous attack on custom.

Milton was the most vociferous advocate of divorce with the right to remarry, but he was not alone. William Ames, in *Conscience with the power and cases thereof* (1639), argued that divorce dissolves the marriage bond, so remarriage should be permitted. He further argued for an expanded definition of desertion, suggesting that a spouse who left the home might be considered "deserted" if "one party drive away the other with great fierceness and cruelty."[11] Ames followed Theodore Beza, the early continental reformer, who had argued, in 1582, that the Pauline concept of desertion should be construed broadly: "We know him also to be a deserter who does not refuse cohabitation, but obstinately demands impious conditions."[12]

In 1646, the Westminster Assembly voted to reaffirm the marital doctrine that divorce could be granted only in cases of adultery and then without the right to remarry. The debate continued, however, and 13 years after the *Westminster Confession* was adopted, Samuel Maresius argued (in 1659) that "Desertation is taken to be not only a determined and permanent withdrawal from the marital home and companionship, but an obstinate denial of the obligations of marriage, by intolerable cruelty...[or] by the acceptance of a mistress."[13]

The debate could be conducted in print because a new freedom of written expression became possible in the early 1640s. Strong feelings of resentment against the monarchy threatened the rule of Charles I, and in 1641 he sought to save his throne by abolishing the Star Chamber and its system of licensing. Indeed, Milton could publish his tracts only because censorship had been lifted. When Parliament reinstated the Licensing Order (1643), Milton protested in *Areopagitica* (1644). The title pages of Milton's divorce tracts suggest the unsettled condition of pamphlet rhetoric during these times. The first edition of *The Doctrine and Discipline of Divorce* was published without Milton's name; the printers were identified only by their initials: T. P. and M. S. (that is, Thomas Paine and Matthew Simmons). The title page of the second edition identified the author as J. M., but did not name the printer; the tract itself began with an open letter to Parliament signed by John Milton. In the preface to *Tetrachordon,* Milton discusses the issue of anonymous publication, insisting that he chose to put his name to his work despite the claims of his adversaries (such as Palmer and the anonymous author of *An Answer*) that he had not possessed the fortitude to claim responsibility for his bold arguments.

The freedom to publish was only one of the reforms sought by agitators (men and women) in the 1640s. Radical sects regarded all religious and social institutions as barriers to the freedom of the individual Christian citizen. The Diggers condemned private property, the Levellers attacked social hierarchy, the Ranters advocated radical free speech and action, and the Family of God advocated free love without the constraints of matrimony. Milton took care to avoid association with these radical ideas, and, in the preface to *Tetrachordon,* condemned Daniel Featley, who had linked Milton to radical Anabaptist doctrines of divorce. In "I did but prompt the age" (1645?)—one of two sonnets defending *Tetrachordon* from detractors—Milton mocks radicals who "bawl for freedom in thir senseles mood, / And still revolt when Truth would set them free. / Licence they mean, when they cry liberty."[14]

Milton's divorce tracts should be read in the context of the Westminster Assembly debates, the agitation for reform in society, and his own commitment to liberty.[15] Looking back on the turbulence of the 1640s, Milton would later argue, in *Second Defense of the English People* (1654), that his divorce tracts were intended to defend "real and substantial liberty; which is to be sought for not from without, but within."[16] He was at once radical and conservative. He did not want to abolish marriage, but sought to reform the social regulation of marriage to suit the needs of individual people. The divorce tracts call for change in the law based on Milton's belief in what he posited as "three species of liberty, without which it is scarcely possible to pass any life with comfort, namely, ecclesiastical, domestic or private, and civil" (*SP* 71). In this formulation, the domestic or private realm serves as the fulcrum for the subject's ecclesiastical and civil rights. Indeed, Milton reflects further on this latent epistemology of the "three species of liberty," more precisely defining the "domestic or private" sphere according to three matters: "whether the affair of marriage was rightly managed; whether the education of children was properly conducted; whether, lastly, we were to be allowed freedom of opinion" (*SP* 72). These reciprocal freedoms of marriage, education, and intellectual inquiry form a microcosm, within Milton's notion of domestic or private liberty, of the public spheres of agency granted to the individual. Milton's model for commonwealth liberty neither separates private from public realms nor simply elides their divisibility, but posits a rather paradoxical, inverse formulation: that domestic freedom, as the nexus of both ecclesiastical and civil rights, is always already socially contingent.

This epistemological inversion charges Milton's notions or "species" of liberty with transgressive energy and consequently grants the imagined subject of the early prose tracts increasing authority to reform public laws of custom on the basis of private apprehensions of unwritten divine laws of grace and charity as well as in accordance with the individual's apposite faculties of conscience and reason. Miltonic liberty is therefore inherently "divorcive"—free, that is, to overturn institutional laws that impede the subject's ability to engender and engage the inward (if irremediable) civil implications of their domestic freedom. Milton often strikes this paradoxical and vital ground in *The Doctrine and Discipline of Divorce;* for example, "Yet thus much I shall now insist on, that whatever the institution were, it could not be so enormous, nor so rebellious against both nature and reason, as to exalt itself above the end and person for whom it was instituted."

Annabel Patterson reflects that it is "a grave irony, nonetheless grave for being slightly comic, that Milton left us his thoughts on marriage primarily in four pamphlets advocating divorce."[17] It may seem less surprising to realize that Milton's notions about marriage should be encompassed by his arguments concerning divorce when the tracts are considered with regard to Milton's bold, capacious ideas about commonwealth liberty that emerged in the 1640s from the social movements for political and religious reform. The principle of liberty that informs Milton's arguments in the divorce tracts pertains as well to the larger body of his writings on ecclesiastical and civil reform. In his pamphlets from the 1640s—in particular, *Of Reformation touching Church-Discipline, The Doctrine and Discipline of Divorce,* and *The Tenure of Kings and Magistrates* (1649)—Milton's framework for the new forms of liberty that should be granted to Protestant English subjects stands most strongly within a cultural context of early seventeenth century debates about covenant theology and commonwealth government.

Just as Milton's species of liberty are inherently divorcive, his reformulation of the relationship between covenant and community hinges upon the inward ordinance of individual acts of nearly prophetic interpretation—the spirit of the law—that must not be subordinate to institutional practices, or custom—the letter of the law. Milton's idea of commonwealth subjectivity grants ecclesiastical and civil liberties on the condition that domestic liberty be made manifest according to the individual's private judgment of their duty to act within—and, if necessary, against—the public sphere.

Milton's arguments about commonwealth liberty feature divorce as a master trope, extending to his far-reaching claim, in *Doctrine and Discipline,* that "the world first rose out of chaos" by God's "divorcing command." *Paradise Lost* offers the most ambitious articulation of Milton's ideas touching upon what might be posited as cosmological liberty, which in turn provides an elegant solution to the *aporia* at the heart of the prose works that devise and defend an epistemology of the divorcive liberties (*PL* 7.239–41). If the "inward and irremediable disposition of man" must serve as the fulcrum for private acts of interpretation concerning the reformation and regulation of the church, the subject, and the state, then how and under what circumstances might that "inward and irremediable," private faculty be represented—that is, re-mediated—or made known within a public discourse informing the institution of law? Milton's tracts repeatedly encounter, but do not resolve, this conundrum, while his "higher argument" (*PL* 9.42) achieves a more dynamic accommodation of the spirit to the letter.

Individual acts of interpretation figure prominently in Milton's understanding of the new covenant, which grants to true believers a keen, singular insight into the spirit of the law. In *Christian Doctrine,* for example, Milton holds that "all true believers either prophesy or have within them the Holy Spirit, which is as good as having the gift of prophecy and dreams and visions" (YP 6:523–24). Thus he affirms that "on the evidence of scripture itself, all things are eventually to be referred to the Spirit and the unwritten word" (YP 6:590). If reading Scripture verges upon prophetic sight, then, for Milton, the work of interpreting and upholding the laws of existing social institutions turns upon an ethical imperative: that the individual subject must be granted the freedom of conscience as well as the reciprocal liberty to reform social discourse in accordance with their own reading of the spirit of the law.

Whereas Martin Luther and John Calvin both opposed matters of spirit to civil affairs, some seventeenth century English reformers, including Cornelius Burges, Stephen Marshall, Henry Parker, and Thomas Goodwin, were building new ecclesiastical and political contracts to install civil liberties within the scope of the commonwealth subject's private, spiritual agency.[18] In his *Commentary on Saint Paul's Epistle to the Galatians,* which Milton cites in *Christian Doctrine,* Luther insists that "in civil policy...nothing must be known as concerning the Gospel, conscience, grace, remission of sins, heavenly righteousness, or Christ himself, but Moses only, with the Law and the works thereof" (YP 6:538n31). Calvin, in book 3 of *Institutes of the Christian Religion,* offers the following precaution for upholding distinctions between spiritual and civil law: "We are not to misapply to the political order the gospel teaching on spiritual freedom, as if Christians were less subject, as concerns outward government, to human laws, because their consciences have been set free in God's sight."[19] In contrast, Milton and the reformers articulated a new epistemology in which the commonwealth subject's inward covenant with God may—especially during times of religious and political crisis—supersede the covenant with either church or state in order to redeem those institutions that must uphold the spirit of the law for the common good.

This epistemology of contingent covenants hinges upon Milton's key principle of liberty; while divorcive, such an understanding of religious, domestic, and civil transgression must accord with a constellation of faculties dwelling within the individual subject: grace, charity, conscience, and reason among the most pivotal. For example, in this celebrated passage from *Doctrine and Discipline,* the concept of divorce bridges all of Milton's major concerns with relationships among liberties (ecclesiastical, domestic or private, and civil), covenants, subjectivity and commonwealth government:

> He who marries, intends as little to conspire his own ruin as he that swears allegiance: and as a whole people is in proportion to an ill government, so is one man to an ill marriage. If they, against any authority, covenant, or statute, may by the sovereign edict of charity save not only their lives but honest liberties from unworthy bondage, as well may he against any private covenant, which he never entered to his mischief, redeem himself from unsupportable disturbances to

> honest peace and just contentment. And much the rather, for that to resist the highest magistrate though tyrannizing, God never gave us express allowance, only he gave us reason, charity, nature, and good example to bear us out; but in this economical misfortune thus to demean our selves, besides the warrant of those four great directors, which doth as justly belong hither, we have an express law of God, and such a law as whereof our Savior with a solemn threat forbid the abrogating. For no effect of tyranny can sit more heavy on the commonwealth than this household unhappiness on the family. And farewell all hope of true reformation in the State, while such an evil as this lies undiscerned or unregarded in the house.

In *Of Reformation,* Milton also figures the subject's liberty to contribute to the reformation of society in terms of divorcive agency. In opposition to prelacy, which (to follow Milton's metaphors) tyrannizes the subject's marriage to the church, common spiritual liberties must be defended first within the private sphere: "Well knows every wise Nation that their Liberty consists in manly and honest labours, in sobriety and rigorous honor to the Marriage Bed, which in both Sexes should be bred up from chast hopes to loyall Enjoyments" (*Of Reformation, SP* 97; YP 1:588). In opposition to the abuses of monarchic power by Charles I, common civil liberties must be guaranteed fundamentally within the domestic realm. Without the liberty of divorce at home, subjects suffer tyranny: "as wanting that power, which is the root and sourse of all liberty, to dispose and *oeconomize* in the Land which God hath giv'n them, as Maisters of Family in thir own house and free inheritance" (*Tenure, SP* 280; YP 3:237).

Upon what grounds does Milton ultimately justify these arguments for divorcive liberty? How and why exactly does he devise and defend his epistemology of covenants? The divorce tracts, as noted earlier, each repeatedly encounter a hermeneutic paradox: only the "inward and irremediable disposition of man"—that is, socially contingent domestic or private liberty—governs the transgressive interpretation of covenants; yet neither that inward disposition nor the reader's comparative and apposite acts of interpretation can be prescribed—that is, re-mediated (as such)—within forms of discursive reasoning. Milton's fundamental premise locates power not within the government but within the individual. The subject who calls for social change is transgressive, but society benefits when citizens challenge and seek to improve institutions and cultural practices. Milton's evaluation of divorce law, and his revisionary reading of the key biblical texts, remains deeply personal, verging at times on mysticism. There is "scarce any one saying in the Gospel," he writes, "but must be read with limitations and distinctions to be rightly understood; for Christ gives no full comments or continued discourses." Although Milton cites some authorities with approbation when they agree with his ideas, he does not cede his own interpretive authority to custom or a tradition of commentary. Every man must be his own priest, his own reader. God divorced to create whole things; his subjects must be separate in order to join with each other and with God.

Milton's arguments were rejected by his contemporaries, and he was often accused of agitating for marital reform only because of his own unhappy marriage and separation from Mary Powell. Milton had visited her family in June 1642 to collect a debt, and had returned home with a wife. She was much younger than Milton and seems to have found life with a schoolmaster and his charges quite stifling. After a few weeks, she returned to her parents' home. At the time Milton composed his tracts on divorce, he and his wife were still living apart. Mary would not return until 1645.

Although Milton protests that *The Doctrine and Discipline of Divorce* is "no mere amatorious novel," it contains a number of vignettes that seem to be loosely disguised bits of autobiography.[20] Early in his first divorce tract, Milton expresses sympathy for any husband and wife who are forced "to fadge together, and combine as they may to their unspeakable wearisomeness and despair." Writing for "the good of both sexes," Milton often focuses on mutual unhappiness and mutual failure, rather than merely blaming women. However, in a later vignette, Milton invites sympathy more for the husband than for the wife: "The soberest and best governed men are least practiced in these affairs; and who knows not that the bashful muteness of a virgin may oft-times hide all the un-liveliness and natural sloth which is really unfit for conversation...many who have spent their youth chastely, are in some things not so quick-sighted, while they haste too eagerly to light the nuptial torch." Two chapters later, Milton is even more hostile toward wives in describing the bitter disappointment of a man who "spent his youth without blame and laid up his chiefest earthly comforts in the enjoyment of a contented marriage," only to "find himself bound fast to an un-complying discord of nature, or, as it oft happens, to an image of earth and fleam."

However, Milton's tract does not always disparage women. Milton's marital experience underlies his reinterpretation of at least two biblical passages: the story of Jephthah, who "could not but oblige his conscience to be the sacrificer, or if not, the jailor of his innocent and only daughter"; and an incident in the book of Judges, "where the Levite's wife is said to have played the whore against him; which Josephus and the Septuagint, with the Chaldaean, interpret only of stubbornness and rebellion against her husband." Milton identifies with Jephthah, not with the daughter, in privileging conscience; yet by arguing that Jephthah mistook his own vow as the law, Milton treats this episode as a situation in which a daughter was needlessly harmed. Milton's reinterpretation of Judges seems more closely linked to his own marital situation, and can even be read as a kind of defense of Mary Powell. Milton rejects the usual condemnation of the Levite's wife: "And this I shall contribute, that had it been whoredom, she would have chosen any other place to run to, than to her father's house, it being so infamous for an Hebrew woman to play the harlot, and so opprobrious to the parents." This argument would certainly seem relevant to Milton's situation. Insofar as the Levite's wife is analogous to Mary Powell, Milton's interpretation labels the deserting woman's behavior without attacking her virtue.[21]

Whatever the precise circumstances of Milton's marriage and separation, the metaphorical language of his text conveys a deep sense of his idealism about married love, as well as his pain, disappointment, and loss. *The Doctrine and Discipline of Divorce* is saturated with metaphorical references to women's behavior, be it motherhood or prostitution. These references set up a positive and negative grid designed as an emotional substratum of Milton's argument. We read of "the womb of teeming Truth," on the one hand, and of Error as a Spenserian monstrous mother on the other. Custom, like Error, is a bad mother, nursing society (her young) with the bad milk of cultural junk food: "easy... to take and swallow down at pleasure; which proving but of bad nourishment in the concoction as it was heedless in the devouring, puffs up unhealthily a certain big face of pretended learning." Such men are "the brood of Belial, the draff of men," who will learn to their sorrow, he thunders, "that honest liberty is the greatest foe to dishonest licence."

Against Custom and Error Milton sets Truth and her teeming womb of ideas, but he gives her a problematic history: "Though this ill hap wait on her nativity, that she never comes into the world but like a bastard, to the ignominy of him that brought her forth; 'til Time, the midwife rather than the mother of Truth, have washed and salted the infant, declared her legitimate, and churched the father of his young Minerva, from the needless causes of his purgation." Truth is the child of a single speaker and can therefore be called "bastard." Later in the tract, Milton returns to this image of Truth as a bastard who has her "birth and beginning" from the "singular and private thoughts" of one person, but "in some age or other will find her witness, and shall be justified at last by her own children." Milton implies that his argument originated in his own circumstances, but that Time will wash and salt his Truth, purifying it of contaminating self-interest. Milton, like Zeus to Minerva, serves as mother/father of Truth—a mixing of gender that Fallon finds so common in Milton as to be a kind of marker of his thought.[22] Milton also reads Truth in the context of England, figured as good mother "teaching nations how to live," and the English language, figured as child of Truth. Milton reverts to a more negative female metaphor at the end of *Doctrine and Discipline* when he portrays the world as a fallen woman and condemns "the prostitute looseness of the times."

Most important is the chain of parents and children that Milton sets up in his metaphorical narrative of Truth. Although one goal of his tract is to argue that the purpose of marriage is not procreation but mutual companionship, the many positive and negative references to childbirth and children in this tract suggest the pain Milton must have felt when his own marriage failed and he had to face an apparently childless future. Milton's divorce tracts make the claim that marriage between unsuited or spiritually incompatible people is no marriage at all, and that in such cases both historical tradition and biblical precept sanction divorce, "especially if there be no children, and that there be mutual consent." The laws prohibiting divorce in all but a few cases were, he believed, oppressive: "For no effect of tyranny can sit more heavy on the commonwealth than this household unhappiness on the family."

Milton turns from metaphor to direct statement when he concludes that divorce should be a private act, requiring only that a husband avow that continuing the marriage would not serve "the good of husband, wife, or children." He then argues on behalf of women, declaring that a discreet divorce is preferable to a public proceeding for an honorable woman, so long as she is "not illiberally dealt with." He offers this summary of her interests: "for if she consent, wherein has the law to right her? or consent not, then is it either just, and so deserved, or if unjust, such in all likelihood was the divorcer, and to part from an unjust man is a happiness, and no injury to be lamented." Because Milton is arguing for divorce with the right to remarry, he looks forward as well, arguing for the rights and status of subsequent children: "And why should we not think them more holy than the offspring of a former ill-twisted wedlock, begotten only out of a bestial necessity, without any true love or contentment, or joy to their parents? So that in some sense we may call them the children of wrath and anguish, which will as little conduce to their sanctifying as if they had been bastards." As the offspring of marriage, children should properly be the sign of its truth. The children of an unhappy marriage are instead the sign of its falsity.

In *Tetrachordon,* Milton concerns himself not with metaphors and signs but with the real circumstances of people who are governed by biblical precept. He abandons metaphor in order to reinterpret the biblical texts that were foundational to Jewish and Christian marital law. These readings pay special attention to children. He glosses Genesis 1:28 early in *Tetrachordon,* arguing that "the desire of children is honest and pious," and he sympathizes with the plight of childless men: "But to dismiss a wife only for barrenness is hard: and yet in some the desire of children is so great, and so just, yea sometime so necessary, that to condemn such a one to a childless age, the fault apparently not being in him, might seem perhaps more strict than needed." Milton took care for the children of a first marriage. Indeed, in *Tetrachordon,* and even in *The Judgement of Martin Bucer,* he tries to defend their interests. When there are children, he argues, an unhappy marriage does special harm. The evil of an unhappy marriage "unavoidably will redound upon the children" because such an ill union "degenerates and disorders the best spirits, leaves them to unsettled imaginations and degraded hopes, careless of themselves." Glossing Deuteronomy 24:1–2, the Hebrew law of divorce, Milton asks "what love can there be to the unfortunate issue" of a "house of wrath":

> God therefore knowing how unhappy it would be for children to be born in such a family, gives this law either as a prevention, that being an unhappy pair they should not add to be unhappy parents, or else as a remedy, that if there be children, while they are fewest, they may follow either parent, as shall be agreed, or judged, from the house of hatred and discord to place of more holy and peaceable education.

Later, glossing 1 Corinthians 7 and the Pauline prohibition of divorce, Milton takes up the issue of mixed marriages, in which only one partner is Christian. In such cases, Milton contends that the Bible commands divorce to prevent "an irreligious seducement, feared both in respect of the believer himself and of his children in danger to be perverted by the misbelieving parent."

If the children themselves pose a threat to the Christian husband, Milton argues, citing Luke, chapter 14, they must be hated and forsaken. He admits that Paul's Epistle to the Corinthians holds a contrary view—"the unbelieving husband is sanctified by the wife, and the unbelieving wife is sanctified by the husband, else were your children unclean; but now they are holy"—but notes that even Paul offers an out: "But if the unbelieving depart, let him depart; a brother or a sister is not under bondage in such cases: but God hath called us to peace." God intends peace, not wrath, in or out of marriage. Finally, Milton cites the early Christian policies of Theodosius and Valentinian, who held that "a divorce mutually consented, might be suffered by the law, especially if there were no children, or if there were, careful provision was made."

In *Tetrachordon,* Milton veers away from evenhanded concern for both parties and frequently asserts the interest of the wronged and faultless husband.[23] We would note, in addition, that Milton casts off metaphor in favor of ever more direct comments about families. His argument is no longer legal but biblical, and rests on a reinterpretation of the foundational texts of Christian marital law. He repeatedly insists that wrath is the hallmark of an unhappy marriage, but his own rhetoric is, for the most part, temperate and dispassionate. Moreover, it seems clear that he was trying to keep his own personal circumstances out of the argument. There are no autobiographical vignettes in *Tetrachordon,* and his extensive dispassionate exegesis of the Pauline text that permitted divorce in cases of desertion precludes any focus on Mary Powell's desertion.

Milton's wrath explodes in *Colasterion,* a tract directed not at women but at the anonymous writer who dared attack *The Doctrine and Discipline of Divorce* by appealing to "Ladies and Gentlewomen, and all other Maried Women against Divorce."[24] Milton infers and then mocks the author's profession and social status: "I am sure none will guess him lower than an actual serving-man. This creature, for the story must on, (and what though he be the lowest person of an interlude, he may deserve a canvassing) transplanted himself, and to the improvement of his ages, and your better notice of his capacity, turned solicitor." Milton projects his self-righteous rage at this supposed "serving-man"—this "creature . . . turned solicitor"—to defend himself against the charge that he wrote against wives and for husbands. In this tract, however, Milton is more critical of women than in his earlier pamphlets. He displaces onto his anonymous antagonist the wrath he felt toward the failure of his own marriage and toward Mary Powell. It is only in *Colasterion* that Milton insists on the responsibility of a woman to be "a wife in some reasonable measure, willing and sufficient to perform the chief duties of her covenant." He further upholds the reasonableness of those expectations, mocking the accusation that he would have men abandon pregnant women and leave them portionless. For the first time, Milton indulges in vituperation, but his cascade of hostile adjectives and name-calling is always directed toward his antagonist, a man stupid, ignorant, willful, and—in a loaded term—"childish."

A bad argument is like a bad marriage, marked by rage, perturbation, bewilderment, and stubbornness. *Colasterion* is such a bad argument: Milton indulges in *ad hominem* attacks, answers ridicule with ridicule, and condescends to his opponent, mocking his argumentation as "silly conjectures" and his language as "the noisome stench of his rude slot." Throughout *The Doctrine and Discipline of Divorce,* Milton argued that good doctrine subordinates the body to the mind; he rejected church regulation of marriage because it was grounded in the needs and regulations of bodily desire, rather than in spiritual mutuality. In *Colasterion,* a grotesque rhetoric of the body erupts in metaphors of vituperation. A bad argument, like a bad marriage, gives grotesque prominence to the body.

Earlier in the divorce tracts, Milton argued that men need men for intellectual companionship but women for another kind of companionship, an intimacy free from constant competition and challenge. When Milton rejects the author of *An Answer* as a "mongrel" combination of serving-man and solicitor, he enacts a kind of rhetorical divorce. He wants to find a better antagonist, just as in arguing for divorce he wanted to be free to find a better wife. A better antagonist, like a better wife, will find Milton a better man:

> If any man equal to the matter shall think it appertains him to take in hand this controversy,...let him not, I entreat him, guess by the handling which meritoriously hath been bestowed on this object of

> contempt and laughter, that I account it any displeasure done me to be contradicted in print: but as it leads to the attainment of any thing more true, shall esteem it a benefit; and shall know how to return his civility and fair argument in such a sort, as he shall confess that to do so is my choice, and to have done thus was my chance.

The metaphors of maternity and childhood in *The Doctrine and Discipline of Divorce* and the grotesque images of the body in *Colasterion* express the hope and desire that motivate a marriage, and the shock, sorrow, and rage that mark its failure. Without that full scope of discourse, which includes personal feeling as well as intellectual reasoning, Milton would have left us with no sense of why his argument for marital reform really matters to him, and indeed to all parents and children.

Milton's personal circumstances, and the images that color his texts, are nonetheless subordinate to his rational argument about general circumstances and the law. The expanded edition of *The Doctrine and Discipline of Divorce* does not add a single metaphor or vignette or personal outburst, but repeatedly insists on the need to reconcile Law and Gospel, Hebrew and Christian texts, to prove the truth of his biblical interpretation. Reason, not rage or longing or grief, governs his argument. Milton reasons by analogy, and by Ramist principles of logic.

Milton's expanded focus on Law and Gospel in the 1644 edition of *The Doctrine and Discipline of Divorce* is clear even on the revised title page. In the 1643 edition he emphasized the rule of charity, seeking an audience tolerant of his new interpretation. In 1644, Milton prepares his readers for an argument both legal and theological. The second edition begins with a new introduction, addressing both Parliament and the Westminster Assembly, declaring that the whole argument will be based on "the good of man and the plain exigence of charity." This addition suggests that Milton was making a strategic decision to seek support from both groups. His attempt to diminish his opponents while expanding his audience is evident in the epigraph he added to the title page: "He that answereth a matter before he heareth it, it is folly and shame unto him" (Prov. 18:13). Milton rebukes those who attack his work for not reading it, while he suggests that debate requires mutual respect and attention and implies that his own text crafts a careful reply to his critics.

The first edition of *The Doctrine and Discipline of Divorce* outlines nine arguments justifying Christian divorce. The second edition, divided into two books, arranges those arguments into chapters. Most of the second book and many of the chapter titles shift the focus to the proper understanding of Law and Gospel. Mosaic law permitted divorce, while the Gospels prohibited it. Milton took on the task of reconciling the relevant biblical texts, both affirming Mosaic law and reading the Gospels as an extension, rather than a denial, of that law. Ernest Sirluck points out that Milton, in *The Reason of Church-Government,* had contrasted the "imperfect and obscure institution of the Law" to the "compleat and glorious ministration of the Gospell, which lookes on the Law, as on a childe" (YP 2:147). Now, rather than dismiss the Mosaic dispensation as a bow to the imperfect nature of the Jews or a sign of the immaturity of the Hebrew covenant, Milton argues that the dispensation reflects the perfect wisdom and mercy of God. Most of the additions in the first half of the 1644 tract amplify Milton's reading of Mosaic law to justify divorce, and develop his own reading of the Gospels to argue that the teachings of Christ are equally merciful and do not contradict Mosaic law. Milton also brings in other interpreters and historical practices to buttress his arguments, and tries to reconcile Law and Gospel first by splitting Christian laws into canon law, which he condemns, and "Christian imperial laws," which he finds more equitable.

It is in the second book of the 1644 edition that Milton makes his most substantial new arguments. The additions to this section of the tract probe the nature of law. He thinks of law as a covenant with God. Marriage is a human covenant. When Milton turns to "judicial law," he rejects the idea that it "should be either the shameless broker of our impunities or the intended instrument of our destruction." The faults of marriage, he argues, should be laid not on religious doctrine but on "man's unjust laws." Concluding his argument, in both editions of the tract, Milton regards it as "more wisdom and goodness to break that covenant seemingly and keep it really, than by compulsion of law to keep it seemingly and by compulsion of blameless nature to break it really." Law should not serve hatred or ignorant rigidity, and human beings should not be forced to "groan under the false imagination of a strictness never imposed from above."

In the final section of the 1644 tract, Milton argues that law must be superseded by conscience, and that the duty of the magistrate is only to make sure "that the condition of divorce be just and equal." The law is less important than unlocking the meaning of Christ's words with "the key of charity," so divorce is not a matter of law but of charity. Milton rejects "the iron manacles and fetters of law," which turn the golden chain of married love into a twisted rope of sand. His central argument is not that judicial law should conform to divine law, whether Mosaic or Christian. Instead, he relocates the site of law to interior conscience. It is conscience that must interpret and conform to the divine law revealed in Scripture.

In *Tetrachordon,* Milton replies to his learned opponents by offering a systematic reinterpretation of Scripture, breaking down key verses into words and phrases. At times, however, emotion overwhelms moderation. Commenting on Matthew 19:6 ("What therefore God hath joyned, let no man put asunder"), Milton poses a rhetorical question: "Shall we say that God hath joined error, fraud, unfitness, wrath, contention, perpetual loneliness, perpetual discord. Whatever lust, or wine, or witchery, threat, or enticement, avarice or ambition hath joined together, faithful with unfaithful, Christian with anti-Christian, hate with hate, or hate with love, shall we say this is God's joining?" Both the revised edition of *The Doctrine and Discipline of Divorce* and *Tetrachordon* illustrate a rhetoric of reconciliation governed by the Augustinian rule of charity. Milton argues that Christian divorce law should follow Hebrew precedent. He argues that the Bible should be read in a spirit of charity toward the men and women governed by its precepts. He cites scores of other authorities (from Erasmus, Luther, Melanchton and Beza to Wycliffe and other English reformers) to support his interpretations, lest anyone think he writes only his own "new and licentious" opinion. Milton also elaborates his discussion of the law of nature, using it to support his reading of Scripture and his arguments for human liberty.

Above all, insists Milton, charity is the fundamental obligation of husband and wife toward one another. Although his reading of Genesis clearly privileges the husband over the wife, other sections of *Tetrachordon* express a clear sense of the complexity of marriage and human relationships. It is adultery, he declares, if a man "shall put away his wife, that is a wife indeed, and not in name only." It is not sinful if a man "puts away by mutual consent, with all the considerations and respects of humanity and gentleness" a wife "whom, though he cannot love or suffer as a wife with that sincere affection that marriage requires, yet loves at least with that civility and goodness as not to keep her under a neglected and unwelcome residence." Where there is adultery, Milton rather surprisingly does not automatically call for divorce. It is not the crime of adultery that breaks a marriage, he declares, "but a perpetual unmeetness and unwillingness to all the duties of help, of love, and tranquility" that "is most contrary to the words and meaning of the institution." Adultery can be forgiven; moreover, "adultery does not exclude her other fitness, her other pleasingness; she may be otherwise both loving and prevalent, as many adulteresses be." It is "unfitness," not adultery, that "defrauds him of the whole contentment which is sought in wedlock." Milton also argues on behalf of a woman's right to remarry. The letter of the law during Milton's time, however, would forbid that right: "Be she never so wrongfully deserted or put away, as the law then suffered, if thus forsaken and expulsed she accept the refuge and protection of any honester man who would love her better, and give herself in marriage to him, by what the letter guides us, it shall be present adultery to them both." Milton condemns such literal practice as "harsh and cruel."

Not until the Divorce Reform Act of 1969–73 would English law permit divorce on the Miltonic grounds of irreparable breakdown of the marital relationship (that is, mutual incompatibility).

Nevertheless, the arguments and ideas Milton advanced in his five divorce pamphlets and other related writings across the span of his career—including, for example, his *Commonplace Book* (1635–47), *Second Defense of the English People* (1654), and the sonnets "A Book was writ," "I did but prompt the age," "On the New Forcers of Conscience," and "Meethought I saw my late espoused saint" (published 1673)—attest to the dynamic resilience he brought to bear on personal and public struggles for individuality and community in seventeenth century England. Those efforts engendered a diversified, robust context of responses that eventually prepared the ground for modern reform (see the appendix, "A Legacy of Reform, 1643–1973," for a selected list of those documents). That rich scope of engagement by varying degrees with Milton's ideas testifies to the ongoing importance of his arguments as the understanding of marriage shifted slowly from a religious and political paradigm designed to regulate procreation to a new model of marriage as a private institution intended to further the personal satisfaction of each party.

Although the first edition of Milton's *Doctrine and Discipline* had already sold out by the time of the second edition's release (which was not later than February 2, 1644), published responses to his tracts did not appear as soon as Milton may have wished. "In comparison with many other pamphlets of the period," according to Parker, "the sensational tractate on divorce appears phenomenally slow in finding a printed reaction, although it had a good sale from the start."[25] Between August 1, 1643 (the first edition's publication date), and February 1644, it appears that Milton's arguments elicited only loose talk, "opinion," and "odious inferences" from "men so lavishly traduced in me," as he reflects in the address to Parliament that introduces *The Judgement of Martin Bucer,* which was printed in London on August 6, 1644.

The first direct attack on Milton came on the Extraordinary Day of Humiliation, August 13, 1644, in a sermon preached before Parliament by the Reverend Herbert Palmer, "The Glasse of Gods Providence," which would appear in print on November 7. Palmer advocated the "*Extirpation of Heresie* and *Schisme,*...and such an *universall Toleration,* and pretended *Liberty of Conscience,"* and famously called *The Doctrine and Discipline of Divorce* a "*wicked booke…deserving to be burnt,* whose *Author* hath been so *impudent* as to *set his Name* to it."[26] Milton responded incisively to Palmer in his address "To the Parliament" that opens *Tetrachordon:*

> Yet that the author may be known to ground himself upon his own innocence and the merit of his cause, not upon the favor of a diversion or a delay to any just censure, but wishes rather he might see those his detractors at any fair meeting, as learned debatements are privileged with a due freedom under equal moderators, I shall here briefly single one of them (because he hath obliged me to it) who I persuade me having scarce read the book, nor knowing him who writ it, or at least feigning the latter, hath not forborne to scandalize him, unconferred with, unadmonished, undealt with by any pastorly or brotherly convincement, in the most open and invective manner, and at the most bitter opportunity that drift or set design could have invented.

Milton's remarks here appeal to the "learned debatements" of the members of Parliament on grounds that were personal, polemical, and political. Milton aimed to defend himself and his tracts against Palmer's incendiary remarks, but also needed to distinguish his arguments within and against a widening context of suspicion about radical reformers who relied upon "pretended *Liberty of Conscience*" to oppose "Churches Peace,…*sound Doctrine,* or the *Power of Godlinesse.*"[27] Palmer's sermon on August 13 before both houses of Parliament had fanned those flames. On August 26, the Committee for Printing—acting upon a petition submitted two days earlier by the Stationers' Company to the House of Commons—prepared an ordinance "diligently to inquire out the Authors, Printers, and Publishers, of the Pamphlet against the Immortality of the Soul, and concerning Divorce."[28] The outcome of that ordinance is not known.

William Prynne's *Twelve Considerable Serious Questions* posed the next challenge to Milton's *Doctrine and Discipline of Divorce* on or just before September 16, 1644. Prynne, one of the most prolific pamphleteers of the century, was well known for his fiery denunciations of deviant political, religious, and social reformers who pleaded their cause on the grounds of "*free liberty of conscienc*" [*sic*]. Echoing Palmer's sentiments, Prynne associates Milton's argument—"*divorce at pleasure, &c.*"—with other rebellious notions that were, in Prynne's view, as dangerous to the commonwealth as the monarchy.[29] In the opening pages of *Colasterion,* Milton would reply with characteristic acerbity:

> For what book hath he ever met with, as his complaint is, *Printed in the City,* maintaining either in the title, or in the whole pursuance, *Divorce at pleasure?* It is true, that to divorce upon extreme necessity, when through the perverseness or the apparent unfitness of either, the continuance can be to both no good at all but an intolerable injury and temptation to the wronged and the defrauded, to divorce then there is a book that writes it lawful. And that this law is a pure and wholesome national law, not to be withheld from good men because others likely enough may abuse it to their pleasure, cannot be charged upon that book, but must be entered a bold and impious accusation against God himself; who did not for this abuse withhold it from his own people.

Milton concludes this rejoinder by inviting Prynne to explain his reasoning in more clear, direct terms without "the gout and dropsy of a big margent"—that is, excessive biblical quotations swelling the margins of his text. Prynne would later respond sharply more than once to Milton's arguments for religious and political reform, but never again addressed Milton's arguments for divorce.[30]

The only contemporary full-length tract to engage with Milton's complete argument—*An Answer to a book, intituled, The doctrine and discipline of divorce, or, A plea for ladies and gentlewomen, and all other maried women against divorce* (November 14, 1644)—delivers a point-by-point refutation of Milton's framework. Our volume presents the first modern edition of this anonymous tract, which was printed by G. M., whom we have identified as George Miller (van den Berg and Howard 2004). Miller also printed Herbert Palmer's *Glasse of Gods Providence* and had sustained business relationships between 1642 and 1646 with Palmer, William Lee, Joseph Caryl (who licensed *An Answer*), and Giles Calvert (the preeminent radical publisher). Miller also served as an agent in Parliament's efforts to restrain the unlicensed print culture of the early 1640s. In one striking instance, Miller and Lee were both appointed by the Committee of Examinations in March 1642/43 to search for presses involved in publishing seditious pamphlets.[31] Miller may also have been summoned (in August 1644) to report to the Committee for Printing concerning the identity and whereabouts of authors, printers, and publishers of pamphlets on the subject of divorce.[32]

The fact that George Miller printed Palmer's *Glasse of Gods Providence* and the anonymous *An Answer* remains open to interpretation. Elizabeth Eisenstein claims that printers in seventeenth century England endorsed the ideas contained within the works they produced. Robert Darnton, on the contrary, concludes that printers were neutral businessmen.[33] Miller may have been indifferent to the content of the pamphlets, or he may have felt ambivalent about revealing his identity in these early challenges against Milton's first argument for divorce. Or, like Giles Calvert, Miller may have printed these assaults because of his own involvement in public debates about marital and divorce laws.[34] Calvert was clearly a niche publisher closely affiliated with the radical authors he promoted. George Miller had a much larger and more diverse business, so the case is somewhat tenuous for his direct involvement with criticism against Milton's argument for reform. Milton seems to have suspected collusion, though, between the author and the printer of *An Answer*. In *Colasterion* he assails the ignorance of his "ridiculous adversary," citing numerous errors in the text, unless they should be "scored upon the printer," whom he describes as the author's "deputy."

Because both *The Glasse of Gods Providence* and *An Answer* were printed by the same man, G. M., it is possible to speculate that there was a coordinated attack upon Milton by individuals who had different reasons for opposing the first edition of *The Doctrine and Discipline of Divorce*. *Colasterion* includes references to several antagonists. Milton begins by acknowledging "many rumours of confutations and convictions forthcoming against *The Doctrine and Discipline of Divorce*," then points directly to Herbert

Palmer's "by-blow from the pulpit." Milton then asserts that the 1643 *Doctrine and Discipline* "was answered...not by one, but by a pack of heads; of whom the chief [was]...an actual serving-man...turned solicitor [who]...conversed much with a stripling divine or two of those newly-fledged probationers that usually come scouting from the university." He further imputes cooperation between the serving-man and Joseph Caryl in their amplification of the hostile "buzz of such a drone's nest." As Stephen Dobranski demonstrates, writing and publishing were often "collaborative processes."[35] Between 1644 and 1645 Thomas Underhill used George Miller to print three sermons by Herbert Palmer, a Presbyterian who rejected Toleration; but Miller also worked extensively with Calvert, publisher of many Quaker texts and other radical works.

An Answer has been most readily available in William Riley Parker's indispensable casebook, *Milton's Contemporary Reputation,* which includes a photographic facsimile.[36] Like the other works included in this collection, *An Answer* is also available through *Early English Books* or *Early English Books Online (EEBO).* We know of only three extant copies: one in the British Library, another in the Huntington Library, and the privately owned copy that Parker used for his photographic facsimile.

The Huntington Library's copy of *An Answer* (shelfmark RB 46430) resides in a cluster of contemporary documents sewn together and enclosed (though not bound) within leather boards. A gold-leaf title (slightly faded) on the spine of this unbound "volume" reads, *Tracts By Milton and Relating to Him, 1641–1681.* No editor is listed, nor publisher or licenser. The book is not listed in *EEBO* or the Huntington catalogue, although it is searchable as a Bridgewater Library item (46429). The volume contains the 1643 edition of *The Doctrine and Discipline of Divorce* used by the Yale editors of Milton's prose, who designated it "the Bridgewater copy" (YP 2:218). The Bridgewater volume gathers together the following pamphlets: Milton's *Of Reformation Touching Church-Discipline* (1641); *An Argument or, Debate in Law of the Great Question Concerning the Militia,* by J. M. [John Marsh] (1642);

Tyrannicall-Government Anatomized: or, a Discourse Concerning Evil-Councellors. Being the Life and Death of John the Baptist, by George Buchanan (1642); Milton's *The Doctrine and Discipline of Divorce* (1643); the consequent *An Answer* (1644); Milton's *The Judgement of Martin Bucer* (1644), *Colasterion* (1645), *Tetrachordon* (1645), and *The Tenure of Kings and Magistrates* (1649), concluding with *Mr. John Milton's Character of the Long Parliament and Assembly of Divines in MDCXLI omitted in his other works and never before printed* (1681). All of these pamphlets appear to have been sewn together and then, at a later date, enclosed within the leather boards.

This unique volume may be the earliest example of an intentional gathering of Milton's writings on divorce and printed responses to his tracts. Further research into the Bridgewater Library may yield information that would more precisely date and explain this volume's origin; however, we suggest it is likely that these ten tracts were sewn together before the 1694, 1697, and 1698 collections of Milton's works,[37] none of which includes either all five of Milton's divorce pamphlets or *An Answer*. The act of gathering together Milton's divorce tracts and placing them squarely within a larger context of debate about commonwealth liberty underscores the relevance of Milton's arguments to the Westminster Assembly debates in the 1640s, and acknowledges *An Answer* as a key component in the development of Milton's ideas.

The abusive rhetoric employed by the authors of *An Answer* and *Colasterion* has not won many new readers for their dueling pamphlets, notwithstanding the coruscations of wit flashing across the pages. For example, in one memorable exchange, the serving-man begins:

> Your phrase is, *That such an imputation as would be cast upon the Law of God by this means, the rankest Polititian would think it shame and dis-worship that his lawes should be charged with any such thing.*
>
> Is this the fine language that your Book is commended for: Good your worship look a little upon your Rhetorick in this one piece, shall I say of nonsense: however I am sure it is contrary to all lawes and customes of speaking. *Rankest Polititian*. Wonderfull!

Not surprisingly, this critique of Milton's accommodation of the law of Moses to the new dispensation of Christ hit a nerve. Milton replies with remarkable intensity:

> And would you think to what a pride he swells in the contemplation of his rare stratagem, offering to carp at the language of a book, which yet he confesses to be generally commended; while himself will be acknowledged by all that read him, the basest and the hungriest endighter that could take the boldness to look abroad. Observe now the arrogance of a groom, how it will mount. I had written that common adultery is a thing which the rankest politician would think it shame and disworship that his law should countenance. First, it offends him that rankest should signify aught but his own smell; who that knows English would not understand me, when I say a rank serving man, a rank pettifogger, to mean a mere serving man, a mere and arrant pettifogger, who lately was so hardy as to lay aside his buckram-wallet and make himself a fool in print, with confuting books which are above him? Next, the word politician is not used to his maw, and thereupon he plays the most notorious hobby-horse, jesting and frisking in the luxury of his nonsense with such poor fetches to cog a laughter from us, that no antic hob-nail at a Morris but is more handsomely facetious.

Although some readers may wince at such vituperation, these volleys of insult are rather tame compared to the pamphlet-rhetoric of the times. By engaging in kind with his anonymous opponent—one demonstrably unfit for "apt and cheerfull conversation"—Milton stages in *Colasterion* a rhetorical and public divorce between the two pamphleteers.

An Answer certainly has many weaknesses in argument, but the tract scores more than a few direct hits on Milton's personality and, most strategically, on his idealistic notions about conversation, as Thomas Luxon demonstrates.[38] *An Answer* was the most complete response to Milton's 1643 tract, and provoked Milton to defend and elaborate, in *Colasterion,* several key points more clearly than he does in his other writings. Some of those key formulations include the following: that it is the duty of husband and wife to love one another; that peace and solace are the highest end of marriage; that marriage is "the mystery of joy"; and that marriage is "a civil ordinance made for man, not man for it." Most significantly, *Colasterion* contains the only explicit articulation in the divorce tracts of a principle very close to a *no-fault* clause: "Sometimes the fault is plainly not his who seeks divorce; sometimes it cannot be discerned whose fault it is; and therefore cannot in reason or equity be the matter of an absolute prohibition." Without the serving-man's challenge—no matter how base or reckless—we would not have *Colasterion* to complete the full development of Milton's contribution to public debate about divorce reform. Beyond those concerns, however, there are other reasons to find these dueling pamphlets interesting and enjoyable: the serving-man's lampooning of Milton's unremitting seriousness, and, on the other hand, Milton's vibrant metaphors and many neologisms, including "obtunding" and "opiniastrous."[39]

Echoing the incendiary, conservative remarks of Palmer and Prynne, Dr. Daniel Featley argues in *The Dippers Dipt* (February 7, 1645) against radical religious sects, especially the Anabaptists, with which he associates Milton's *Doctrine and Discipline:* "Witnesse a Tractate of Divorce, in which the bonds of mariage are let loose to inordinate lust, and putting away wives for many other causes besides that which our Saviour onely approveth, namely, in the case of Adultery."[40] Following his riposte to Palmer in *Tetrachordon,* Milton mocks Featley's accusations and reasoning:

> I must be forced to reckon that Doctor, who in a late equivocating treatise plausibly set afloat against the Dippers, diving the while himself with a more deep prelatical malignance against the present State and Church-government, mentions with ignominy the Tractate of Divorce; yet answers nothing, but instead thereof (for which I do not commend his marshalling) sets Moses also among the crew of his Anabaptists, as one who to a holy nation, the commonwealth of Israel, gave laws breaking the bonds of marriage to inordinate lust. These are no mean surges of blasphemy, not only dipping Moses the divine lawgiver, but dashing with a high hand against the justice and purity of God himself, as these ensuing Scriptures plainly and freely handled shall verify to the lancing of that old apostemated error. Him therefore I leave now to his repentance.

Although Featley did not retaliate in a new text, *The Dippers Dipt* appeared in seven editions: three in 1645; four others in 1646, 1647, 1651, and 1660.

Tetrachordon and *Colasterion* thus respectively frame Milton's four-point defense against his first opponents: Palmer and Featley, Prynne and the author of *An Answer*. Our volume offers a vivid presentation of that first round of pamphlet warfare. A cluster of documents published between 1645 and 1649 represents a widening context of engagement with and challenges against Milton's arguments (for a chronological listing of those seventeenth century texts, see the appendix). Although Milton did not reply within the pages of his divorce tracts to any of those contemporary, second-wave publications, many of them explicitly connect Milton's arguments to the burgeoning discourse of interrelated pamphlets on marriage and divorce reform. Milton's two sonnets, "I did but prompt the age to quit thir clogs" (1645) and "A book was writt of late call'd *Tetrachordon*" (1647), would address the temper of the times, but do not identify individual opponents or texts that directly challenged his divorce tracts.

Social historians (including John Witte Jr., Belinda Peters, and most notably Lawrence Stone) have traced a shift in the concept of marriage, throughout the early modern and modern eras, from a religious institution to a secular and a psychosocial contract.[41] Significant reform began in 1857, when adultery became a legal justification for divorce; that law, however, instated a double standard because a husband could sue for adultery but a wife could not. Full reform was finally enabled by a Church of England report, *Putting Asunder* (1966), which endorsed no-fault divorce. "The principle of breakdown might make secular divorce in some respects less offensive to Christian sentiment than it now is," the report contends. Rather than dissolve a sacred marriage, the state "would seem to say" that "this marriage relationship has so irretrievably disintegrated that it is no longer qualified to receive legal recognition: therefore recognition is withdrawn."[42] *Putting Asunder* severs church and state; the state withdraws legal recognition of a marriage but makes no attempt to cancel a sacrament.

The parliamentary debates that resulted in the Divorce Reform Act of 1969–73 were almost entirely secular. Debate focused mainly on the welfare of children and the cost to families and to society. No member of Parliament relied on biblical exegesis to endorse or oppose legal reforms, nor did any member explicitly refer to Milton's works. Those members who gave their view of marriage, however, echoed Milton's idea of mutual companionship and solace as its primary purpose. Other members emphasized the welfare of illegitimate children, defending them as Milton had defended the children of second marriages. Still others argued, as Milton had, that couples who sought divorce or separation were too often forced to accuse one of them of adultery (often falsely), and that legal reforms would reduce promiscuity and prostitution. Above all, advocates of reform declared, as Milton had, that a miserable marriage was no marriage at all.

The divorce tracts as a group, read together with the hostile polemics they occasioned, present a vivid example of the way pamphlet rhetoric shaped public opinion in the short period during the seventeenth century when censorship was lifted and London became, as Milton describes it in *Areopagitica,* a "mansion house of liberty:...there be pens and heads there, sitting by their studious lamps, musing, searching, revolving new notions and ideas wherewith to present, as with their homage and their fealty the approaching Reformation: others as fast reading, trying all things, assenting to the force of reason and convincement" (YP 2:554). Milton's readers across the centuries also enact the paradox of that liberty, as they endeavor to build social institutions designed to foster and yet inevitably restrain the individual's autonomy.

Both in content and in method, these texts are also important for our own culture and for the questions we ask of the past in order to address urgent contemporary issues. We live in what some might call a "culture of divorce," others a "culture of conflict." Milton's arguments that divorce could be "to the good of both sexes," based on religious belief as well as psychological insight and social idealism, make this often intimidating writer and his era accessible and compelling to contemporary readers. His claim for divorce on the basis of mutual incompatibility established the groundwork for the justification of divorce in late twentieth century Anglo-American law, but the effects, both beneficial and harmful, are all too familiar and remain a subject of controversy. In a 2003 *New Yorker* book review, for example, Rebecca Mead reflects at length upon Milton's argument in order to challenge jaded twenty-first century attitudes toward the institution of marriage.[43] In June 2010, the New York legislature was debating a law to permit no-fault divorce, and columnists in the *New York Times* debated the effect of such a law on women and children. Milton's rhetorical methods—from cogent advocacy to speculative commentary and poignant vignettes, from citation of authorities and carefully reasoned biblical exegesis to defensive vituperation—demonstrate the range of debate that marked the pamphlet warfare of his day and that endures in the media wrangling of our own.

Milton's Tracts, 1643–45

The Doctrine and Discipline of Divorce

Restored to the good of both Sexes, From the bondage of Canon Law, and other mistakes, to Christian freedom, guided by the Rule of Charity. Wherein also many places of Scripture have recovered their long-lost meaning. Seasonable to be now thought on in the Reformation intended.[1]

Matthew 13.52. ***Every Scribe instructed to the Kingdom of Heaven, is like the Master of a house which brings out of his treasury things old and new.***

London, Printed by T. P. and M. S.
In Goldsmiths Alley. 1643[2]

THE DOCTRINE AND DISCIPLINE OF *DIVORCE;* RESTORED TO THE GOOD OF BOTH SEXES.

Many men, whether it be their fate, or fond opinion, easily persuade themselves, if God would but be pleased a while to withdraw his just punishments from us, and to restrain what power either the devil or any earthly enemy has to work us woe, that then man's nature would find immediate rest and release from all evils. But verily they who think so, if they be such as have a mind large enough to take into their thoughts a general survey of human things, would soon prove themselves in that opinion far deceived. For though it were granted us by divine indulgence to be exempt from all that can be harmful to us from without, yet the perverseness of our folly is so bent, that we should never desist hammering out of our own hearts, as it were out of a flint, the seeds and sparkles of new miseries to our selves, 'til all were in a blaze again. And no marvel if out of our own hearts, for they are evil,[3] but even out of those things which God meant us, either for a principal good or a pure contentment, we are still hatching and contriving upon our selves matter of continual sorrow and perplexity. What greater good to man than that revealed rule, whereby God vouchsafes to show us how he would be worshiped? And yet that not rightly understood, became the cause that once a famous man in Israel could not but oblige his conscience to be the sacrificer, or if not, the jailor of his innocent and only daughter.[4] And was the cause oft-times that armies of valiant men have given up their throats to a heathenish enemy on the Sabbath day, fondly thinking their defensive resistance to be as then a work unlawful.[5] What thing more instituted to the solace and delight of man than marriage? And yet the misinterpreting of some Scripture directed mainly against the abusers of the law for divorce given them by Moses[6] has changed the blessing of matrimony not seldom into a familiar and co-inhabiting mischief; at least into a drooping and disconsolate household captivity, without refuge or redemption. So ungoverned and so wild a race doth superstition run us from one extreme of abused liberty into the other of unmerciful restraint. For although God in the first ordaining of marriage[7] taught us to what end he did it, in words expressly implying the apt and cheerful conversation of man with woman, to comfort and refresh him against the evil of solitary life, not mentioning the purpose of generation 'til afterwards, as being but a secondary end in dignity, though not in necessity; yet now, if any two be but once handed in the Church,[8] and have tasted in any sort of the nuptial bed, let them find themselves never so mistaken in their dispositions through any error, concealment, or misadventure, that through their different tempers, thoughts, and constitutions, they can neither be to one another a remedy against loneliness, nor live in any union or contentment all their days, yet they shall, so they be but found suitably weaponed to the least possibility of sensual enjoyment, be made, in spite of *antipathy,* to fadge together,[9] and combine as they may to their unspeakable wearisomeness and despair of all sociable delight in the ordinance which God established to that very end. What a calamity is this, and as the wise man, if he were alive, would sigh out in his own phrase, what a *sore evil is this under the sun!*[10] All which we can refer justly to no other author than the canon law and her adherents, not consulting with charity, the interpreter and guide of our faith, but resting in the mere element of the text; doubtless by the policy of the devil to make that gracious ordinance become unsupportable, that what with men not daring to venture upon wedlock, and what with men wearied out of it, all inordinate license might abound. It was for many ages that marriage lay in disgrace with most of the ancient doctors, as a work of the flesh, almost a defilement, wholly denied to priests, and the second time dissuaded to all, as he that reads Tertullian or Jerome[11] may see at large. Afterwards it was thought so sacramental[12] that no adultery could dissolve it; yet there remains a burden on it as heavy as the other two were disgraceful or superstitious, and of as much iniquity, crossing a law not only written by Moses, but charactered in us by nature, of more antiquity and deeper ground than marriage itself; which law is to force nothing against the faultless proprieties of nature:[13] yet that this may be disingenuously done, our Savior's words touching divorce are as it were congealed into a stony rigor, inconsistent both with his doctrine and his office, and that which he preached only to the conscience is by canonical tyranny snatched into the compulsive censure of a judicial court, where laws are imposed even against the venerable and secret power of nature's impression to love what ever cause be found to loath.[14] Which is a heinous barbarism both against the honor of marriage, the dignity of man and his soul, the goodness of Christianity, and all the humane respects of civility. Notwithstanding that some of the wisest and gravest among the Christian Emperors,[15] who had about them, to consult with, those of the Fathers then living,[16] who for their learning and holiness of life are still with us in great store have made their statutes and edicts concerning this debate far more easy and relenting in many necessary cases wherein the canon is inflexible. And Hugo Grotius,[17] a man of these times, one of the best learned, seems not obscurely to adhere in his persuasion to the equity of those imperial decrees in his notes upon the evangelists, much allaying the outward roughness of the text, which has for the most part been too immoderately expounded; and excites the diligence of others to enquire further into this question, as containing many points which have not yet been explained. By which, and by my own apprehension of what public duty each man owes, I conceive myself exhorted among the rest to communicate such thoughts as I have, and offer them now in this general labor of reformation to the candid view both of Church and magistrate; especially because I see it the hope of good men that those irregular and un-spiritual courts have spun their utmost date in this land; and some better course must now be constituted. He therefore that by adventuring shall be so happy as with success to ease and set free the minds of ingenuous and apprehensive men from this needless thralldom, he that can prove it lawful and just to claim the performance of a fit and matchable conversation—no less essential to the prime scope of marriage than the gift of bodily conjunction—or else to have an equal plea of divorce as well as for that corporal deficiency;[18] he that can but lend us the clue that winds out this labyrinth of servitude to such a reasonable and expedient liberty as this, deserves to be reckoned among the public benefactors of civil and humane life, above the inventors of wine and oil; for this is a far dearer, far nobler, and more desirable cherishing to man's life, unworthily exposed to sadness and mistake, which he shall vindicate. Not that license and levity and un-consented breach of faith should herein be countenanced, but that some conscionable and tender pity might be had of those who have unwarily, in a thing they never practiced before, made themselves the bondmen of a luckless and helpless matrimony. In which argument he whose courage can serve him to give the first onset, must look for two several oppositions: the one from those who, having sworn themselves to long custom and the letter of the text, will not out of the road; the other from those whose gross and vulgar apprehensions conceit but low of matrimonial purposes, and in the work of male and female think they have all. Nevertheless, it shall be here sought by due ways to be made appear, that those words of God in the institution promising a meet help against loneliness,[19] and those words of Christ, *that his yoke is easy and his burden light,*[20] were not spoken in vain; for if the knot of marriage may in no case be dissolved but for adultery, all the burdens and services of the law are not so intolerable. This only is desired of them who are minded to judge hardly of thus maintaining, that they would be still and hear all out, nor think it equal to answer deliberate reason with sudden heat and noise; remembering this, that many truths now of reverend esteem and credit had their birth and beginning once from singular and private thoughts while the most of men were otherwise possessed, and had the fate at first to be generally exploded and exclaimed on by many violent opposers; yet I may err perhaps in soothing myself that this present truth revived, will deserve to be not ungently received on all hands; in that it undertakes the cure of an inveterate disease crept into the best part of humane society: and to do this with no smarting corrosive, but with a smooth and pleasing lesson, which received has the virtue to soften and dispel rooted and knotty sorrows, and without enchantment or spell used, has regard at once both to serious pity and upright honesty; that tends to the redeeming and restoring of none but such as are the object of compassion, having in an ill hour hampered themselves to the utter dispatch of all their most beloved comforts and repose for this life's term. But if we shall obstinately dislike this new overture of unexpected ease and recovery, what remains but to deplore the forwardness of our hopeless condition, which neither can endure the estate we are in, nor admit of remedy either sharp or sweet. Sharp we our selves distaste; and sweet, under whose hands we are, is scrupled and suspected as too luscious. In such a posture Christ found the Jews, who were neither won with the austerity of John the Baptist, and thought it too much license to follow freely the charming pipe of him who sounded and proclaimed liberty and relief to all distresses: yet Truth in some age or other will find her witness, and shall be justified at last by her own children.[21]

To remove therefore if it be possible, this great and sad oppression, which through the strictness of a literal interpreting has invaded and disturbed the dearest and most peaceable estate of household society, to the overburdening, if not the overwhelming of many Christians' better worth than to be so deserted of the Church's considerate care, this position shall be laid down, first proving, then answering what may be objected either from Scripture or light of reason:

That indisposition, unfitness, or contrariety of mind, arising from a cause in nature unchangeable, hindering and ever likely to hinder the main benefits of conjugal society, which are solace and peace, is a greater reason of divorce than natural frigidity, especially if there be no children, and that there be mutual consent.[22]

For all sense and reason and equity reclaims[23] that any law or covenant how solemn or straight so ever, either between God and man, or man and man, though of God's joining, should bind against a prime and principal scope of its own institution,[24] and of both or either party covenanting; neither can it be of force to engage a blameless creature to his own perpetual sorrow, mistaken for his expected solace, without suffering charity to step in and do a confessed good work of parting those whom nothing holds together but this of God's joining, falsely supposed against the express end of his own ordinance. And what his chief end was of creating woman to be joined with man, his own instituting words declare, and are infallible to inform us what is marriage and what is no marriage; unless we can think them set there to no purpose: *it is not good,* said he, *that man should be alone; I will make him a help meet for him.*[25] From which words so plain, less cannot be concluded, nor is by any learned interpreter, than that in God's intention a meet and happy conversation is the chiefest and the noblest end of marriage; for we find here no expression so necessarily implying carnal knowledge, as this prevention of loneliness to the mind and spirit of man. And indeed it is a greater blessing from God, more worthy so excellent a creature as man is, and a higher end to honor and sanctify the league of marriage, when the solace and satisfaction of the mind is regarded and provided for before the sensitive pleasing of the body. And with all generous persons married thus it is, that where the mind and person pleases aptly, there some un-accomplishment of the body's delight may be better borne with, than when the mind hangs off in an unclosing disproportion, though the body be as it ought; for there all corporal delight will soon become unsavory and contemptible. And the solitude of man, which God had namely and principally ordered to prevent by marriage, has no remedy, but lies under a worse condition than the loneliest single life; for in single life the absence and remoteness of a helper might inure him to expect his own comforts out of himself or to seek with hope; but here the continual sight of his deluded thoughts without cure must needs be to him, if especially his complexion[26] incline him to melancholy, a daily trouble and pain of loss in some degree like that which reprobates feel.[27] Lest therefore so noble a creature as man should be shut up incurably under a worse evil by an easy mistake in that ordinance which God gave him to remedy a less evil, reaping to himself sorrow while he went to rid away solitude, it cannot avoid to be concluded, that if the woman be naturally so of disposition, as will not help to remove, but help to increase that same God-forbidden loneliness which will in time draw on with it a general discomfort and dejection of mind, not beseeming either Christian profession or moral conversation, unprofitable and dangerous to the commonwealth, when the household estate, out of which must flourish forth the vigor and spirit of all public enterprises,[28] is so ill contented and procured at home, and cannot be supported; such a marriage can be no marriage whereto the most honest end is wanting: and the aggrieved person shall do more manly, to be extraordinary and singular in claiming the due right whereof he is frustrated, than to piece up his lost contentment by visiting the stews, or stepping to his neighbor's bed, which is the common shift in this misfortune; or else by suffering his useful life to waste away, and be lost under a secret affliction of an unconscionable size to human strength. How vain therefore is it, and how preposterous in the canon law to have made such careful provision against the impediment of carnal performance,[29] and to have had no care about the un-conversing inability of mind, so defective to the purest and most sacred end of matrimony: and that the vessel of voluptuous enjoyment must be made good to him that has taken it upon trust without any caution, when as the mind from whence must flow the acts of peace and love, a far more precious mixture than the quintessence of an excrement,[30] though it be found never so deficient and unable to perform the best duty of marriage in a cheerful and agreeable conversation, shall be thought good enough, how ever flat and melancholy it be, and must serve, though to the eternal disturbance and languishing of him that complains him. Yet wisdom and charity weighing God's own institution would think that the pining of a sad spirit wedded to loneliness should deserve to be freed, as well as the impatience of a sensual desire so providently relieved. This is read to us in the liturgy, that *we must not marry to satisfy the fleshly appetite, like brute beasts that have no understanding.*[31] But the canon so runs, as if it dreamt of no other matter than such an appetite to be satisfied: for if it happen that nature has stopped or extinguished the veins of sensuality, that marriage is annulled. But though all the faculties of the understanding and conversing part after trial appear to be so ill and so aversely met through nature's unalterable working, as that neither peace nor any sociable contentment can follow, that's as nothing, the contract shall stand as firm as ever, betide what will. What is this but secretly to instruct us, that however many grave reasons are pretended to the married life, yet that nothing indeed is thought worth regard therein but the prescribed satisfaction of an irrational heat; which cannot be but ignominious to the state of marriage, dishonorable to the undervalued soul of man, and even to Christian doctrine itself. While it seems more moved at the disappointing of an impetuous nerve[32] than at the ingenuous grievance of a mind unreasonably yoked; and to place more of marriage in the channel of concupiscence, than in the pure influence of peace and love, whereof the soul's lawful contentment is the only fountain.

But some are ready to object, that the disposition ought seriously to be considered before. But let them know again, that for all the wariness can be used, it may yet befall a discreet man to be mistaken in his choice: the soberest and best governed men are least practiced in these affairs; and who knows not that the bashful muteness of a virgin may oft-times hide all the un-liveliness and natural sloth which is really unfit for conversation; nor is there that freedom of access granted or presumed, as may suffice to a perfect discerning 'til too late: and where any indisposition is suspected, what more usual than the persuasion of friends, that acquaintance, as it increases, will amend all. And lastly, it is not strange though many who have spent their youth chastely, are in some things not so quick-sighted, while they haste too eagerly to light the nuptial torch; nor is it therefore that for a modest error a man should forfeit so great a happiness, and no charitable means to release him. Since they who have lived most loosely by reason of their bold accustoming, prove most successful in their matches, because their wild affections unsettling at will have been as so many divorces to teach them experience. When the sober man, honoring the appearance of modesty, and hoping well of every social virtue under that veil, may easily chance to meet, if not with a body impenetrable, yet often with a mind to all other due conversation inaccessible, and to all the more estimable and superior purposes of matrimony useless and almost lifeless: and what a solace, what a fit help such a consort would be through the whole life of a man, is less pain to conjecture than to have experience.

And that we may further see what a violent and cruel thing it is to force the continuing of those together whom God and nature in the gentlest end of marriage never joined, divers evils and extremities that follow upon such a compulsion shall here be set in view. Of evils the first and greatest is, that hereby a most absurd and rash imputation is fixed upon God and his holy laws, of conniving and dispensing with open and common adultery among his chosen people, a thing which the rankest politician would think it shame and dis-worship[33] that his laws should countenance; how and in what manner this comes to pass, I shall reserve, 'til the course of method brings on the unfolding of many Scriptures. Next the Law and Gospel are hereby made liable to more than one contradiction, which I refer also thither. Lastly, the supreme dictate of charity is hereby many ways neglected and violated. Which I shall forthwith address to prove. First we know St. Paul said, *It is better to marry than to burn.*[34] Marriage therefore was given as a remedy of that trouble: but what might this burning mean? Certainly not the mere motion of carnal lust, not the mere goad of a sensitive desire; God does not principally take care for such cattle.[35] What is it then but that desire which God put into Adam in Paradise before he knew the sin of incontinence; that desire which God saw it was not good that man should be left alone to burn in; the desire and longing to put off an unkindly solitude by uniting another body, but not without a fit soul to his in the cheerful society of wedlock. Which if it were so needed before the fall, when man was much more perfect in himself, how much more is it needed now against all the sorrows and casualties of this life to have an intimate and speaking help, a ready and reviving associate in marriage: whereof who misses by chancing on a mute and spiritless mate, remains more alone than before, and in a burning less to be contained than that which is fleshly and more to be considered as being more deeply rooted even in the faultless innocence of nature. As for that other burning, which is but as it were the venom of a lusty and overabounding concoction, strict life and labor with the abatement of a full diet may keep that low and obedient enough: but this pure and more inbred desire of joining to itself in conjugal fellowship a fit conversing soul (which desire is properly called love) *is stronger than death,* as the spouse of Christ thought, *many waters cannot quench it, neither can the floods drown it.*[36] This is that rational burning that marriage is to remedy, not to be allayed with fasting, nor with any penance to be subdued, which how can he assuage who by mishap has met the most unmeet and unsuitable mind? Who has the power to struggle with an intelligible flame, not in Paradise to be resisted, become now more ardent, by being failed of what in reason it looked for; and even then most unquenched, when the importunity of a provender burning is well enough appeased; and yet the soul has obtained nothing of what it justly desires. Certainly such a one forbidden to divorce, is in effect forbidden to marry, and compelled to greater difficulties than in a single life;

for if there be not a more human burning which marriage must satisfy, or else may be dissolved, than that of copulation, marriage cannot be honorable for the meet reducing and terminating of lust between two: seeing many beasts in voluntary and chosen couples live together as un-adulterously, and are as truly married in that respect. But all ingenuous men will see that the dignity and blessing of marriage is placed rather in the mutual enjoyment of that which the wanting soul needfully seeks, than of that which the plenteous body would joyfully give away. Hence it is that Plato in his festival discourse brings in Socrates relating what he feigned to have learned from the prophetess Diotima, how Love was the son of Penury, begot of Plenty in the garden of Jupiter.[37] Which divinely sorts with that which in effect Moses tells us, that Love was the son of Loneliness, begot in Paradise by that sociable and helpful aptitude which God implanted between man and woman toward each other.[38] The same also is that burning mentioned by St. Paul, whereof marriage ought to be the remedy; the flesh has other natural and easy curbs which are in the power of any temperate man. When therefore this original and sinless Penury or Loneliness of the soul cannot lay itself down by the side of such a meet and acceptable union as God ordained in marriage, at least in some proportion, it cannot conceive and bring forth Love, but remains utterly unmarried under a formal wedlock, and still burns in the proper meaning of St. Paul. Then enters Hate, not that Hate that sins, but that which only is natural dissatisfaction and the turning aside from a mistaken object:[39] if that mistake have done injury, it fails not to dismiss with recompense; for to retain still, and not be able to love, is to heap up more injury. Thence that wise and pious law of dismissal, Deuteronomy 24.1, took beginning; of which anon. He therefore who lacking of his due in the most native and human end of marriage, thinks it better to part than to live sadly and injuriously to that cheerful covenant (for not to be beloved and yet retained, is the greatest injury to a gentle spirit) he I say who therefore seeks to part, is one who highly honors the married life, and would not stain it: and the reasons which now move him to divorce, are equal to the best of those that could first warrant him to marry; for, as was plainly shown, both the hate which now diverts him and the loneliness which leads him still powerfully to seek a fit help, has not the least grain of a sin in it, if he be worthy to understand himself.

Thirdly, yet it is next to be feared, if he must be still bound without reason by a deaf rigor, that when he perceives the just expectance of his mind defeated, he will begin even against law to cast about where he may find his satisfaction more complete, unless he be a thing heroically virtuous, and that are not the common lump of men for whom chiefly the laws ought to be made, though not to their sins yet to their un-sinning weaknesses, it being above their strength to endure the lonely estate, which while they shunned, they are fallen into. And yet there follows upon this a worse temptation; for if he be such as has spent his youth without blame and laid up his chiefest earthly comforts in the enjoyment of a contented marriage, nor did neglect that furtherance which was to be obtained therein by constant prayers, when he shall find himself bound fast to an un-complying discord of nature, or, as it oft happens, to an image of earth and fleam,[40] with whom he looked to be the copartner of a sweet and gladsome society and sees withal that his bondage is now inevitable, though he be almost the strongest Christian, he will be ready to despair in virtue, and mutin[41] against divine providence: and this doubtless is the reason of those lapses and that melancholy despair which we see in many wedded persons, though they understand it not, or pretend other causes, because they know no remedy, and is of extreme danger; therefore when human frailty surcharged, is at such a loss, charity ought to venture much, and use bold medicine, lest an over-tossed faith endanger to shipwreck.

Fourthly, marriage is a covenant the very being whereof consists, not in a forced cohabitation and counterfeit performance of duties, but in unfeigned love and peace. Thence says Solomon in Ecclesiastes *live joyfully with the wife whom thou love, all thy days, for that is thy portion*.[42] How then, where we find it impossible to rejoice or to love, can we obey this precept? How miserably do we defraud ourselves of that comfortable portion which God gives us, by striving vainly to glue an error together which God and nature will not join; adding but more vexation and violence to that blissful society by our importunate superstition, that will not hearken to St. Paul 1 Corinthians 7, who, speaking of marriage and divorce, determines plain enough in general, that God therein *hath called us to peace* and not *to bondage*. Yes, God himself commands in his law more than once, and by his prophet Malachi, as Calvin and the best translations read, that *he who hates let him divorce;*[43] that is, he who cannot love, or delight. I cannot therefore be so diffident, as not securely to conclude, that he who can receive nothing of the most important helps in marriage, being thereby disenabled to return that duty which is his, with a clear and hearty countenance, and thus continues to grieve whom he would not, and is no less grieved, that man ought even for love's sake and peace to move divorce upon good and liberal conditions to the divorced. And it is a less breach of wedlock to part with wise and quiet consent betimes, than still to soil and profane that mystery of joy and union with a polluting sadness and perpetual distemper; for it is not the outward continuing of marriage that keeps whole that covenant, but whosoever does most according to peace and love, whether in marriage, or in divorce, he it is that breaks marriage least; it being so often written, that *love only is the fulfilling of every commandment.*[44]

Fifthly, as those priests of old were not to be long in sorrow, or if they were, they could not rightly execute their function; so every true Christian in a higher order of priesthood is a person dedicate to joy and peace, offering himself a lively sacrifice of praise and thanksgiving, and there is no Christian duty that is not to be seasoned and set off with cheerfulness; which in a thousand outward and intermitting crosses may yet be done well, as in this vale of tears, but in such a bosom affliction as this, which grinds the very foundations of his inmost nature, when he shall be forced to love against a possibility, and to use dissimulation against his soul in the perpetual and ceaseless duties of a husband, doubtless his whole duty of serving God must needs be blurred and tainted with a sad un-preparedness and dejection of spirit, wherein God has no delight.

Who sees not therefore how much more Christianly it would be to break by divorce that which is more broken by undue and forcible keeping, rather than *to cover the altar of the Lord with continual tears, so that he regards not the offering any more,* rather than that the whole worship of a Christian man's life should languish and fade away beneath the weight of an immeasurable grief and discouragement. And because some think the children of a second matrimony succeeding a divorce would not be a holy seed, why should we not think them more holy than the offspring of a former ill-twisted wedlock, begotten only out of a bestial necessity without any true love or contentment, or joy to their parents, so that in some sense we may call them the *children of wrath* and anguish, which will as little conduce to their sanctifying, as if they had been bastards; for nothing more than disturbance of mind suspends us from approaching to God. Such a disturbance especially as both assaults our faith and trust in God's providence, and ends, if there be not a miracle of virtue on either side, not only in bitterness and wrath, the canker of devotion, but in a desperate and vicious carelessness; when he sees himself without fault of his, trained by a deceitful bait into a snare of misery, betrayed by an alluring ordinance, and then made the thrall of heaviness and discomfort by an un-divorcing law of God, as he erroneously thinks, but of man's iniquity, as the truth is; for that God prefers the free and cheerful worship of a Christian, before the grievous and exacted observance of an unhappy marriage, besides that the general maxims of religion assure us, will be more manifest by drawing a parallel argument from the ground of divorcing an idolatress, which was, lest she should alienate his heart from the true worship of God: and what difference is there whether she pervert him to superstition by enticing sorcery, or disenable him in the whole service of God through the disturbance of her unhelpful and unfit society, and so drive him at last through murmuring and despair to thoughts of atheism; neither doth it lessen the cause of separating in that the one willingly allures him from the faith, the other perhaps unwillingly drives him; for in the account of God it comes all to one that the wife loses him a servant; and therefore by all the united force of the decalogue she ought to be disbanded,[45] unless we must set marriage above God and charity, which is a doctrine of devils no less than forbidding to marry.[46]

And here by the way to illustrate the whole question of divorce, before this treatise end, I shall not be reluctant to spend a few lines in hope to give a full resolve of that which is yet so much controverted, whether an idolatrous heretic ought to be divorced. To the resolving whereof we must first know that the Jews were commanded to divorce an unbelieving Gentile for two causes: first, because all other nations, especially the Canaanites were to them unclean; secondly, to avoid seduction. That other nations were to the Jews impure, even to the separating of marriage, will appear out of Exodus 34.16, Deuteronomy 7.3.6 compared with Ezra 9.2, also chapter 10.10, 11, Nehemiah 13.30. This was the ground of that doubt raised among the Corinthians by some of the circumcision:[47] whether an unbeliever were not still to be counted an unclean thing, so as that they ought to divorce from such a person. This doubt of theirs St. Paul removes by an evangelical reason, having respect to that vision of St. Peter, wherein the distinction of clean and unclean being abolished, all living creatures were sanctified to a pure and Christian use, and mankind especially, now invited by a general call to the covenant of grace.[48] Therefore said St. Paul, *the unbelieving wife is sanctified by the husband;*[49] that is, made pure and lawful to his use; so that he need not put her away for fear lest her unbelief should defile him; but that if he found her love still towards him, he might rather hope to win her. The second reason of that divorce was to avoid seduction, as is proven by comparing those places of the law to that which Ezra and Nehemiah did by divine warrant in compelling the Jews to forego their wives. And this reason is moral and perpetual in the rule of Christian faith without evasion. Therefore said the Apostle 2 Corinthians 6: *mis-yoke not together with infidels,* which is interpreted of marriage in the first place. And although the former legal pollution be now done off, yet there is a spiritual contagion in idolatry as much to be shunned; and though seduction were not to be feared, yet where there is no hope of converting, there always ought to be a certain religious aversion and abhorring, which can no way sort with marriage. Therefore said St. Paul, *what fellowship hath righteousness with unrighteousness? What communion hath light with darkness? What concord hath Christ with Belial? What part hath he that believes with an infidel?* And in the next verse but one he moralizes and makes us liable to that command of Isaiah, *wherefore come out from among them, and be you separate,* saith the Lord, *touch not the unclean thing, and I will receive you.* And this command thus gospelized to us, has the same force with that whereon Ezra grounded the pious necessity of divorcing.

Upon these principles I answer, that a right believer ought to divorce an idolatrous heretic, unless upon better hopes; however, that it is in the believer's choice to divorce or not.

The former part will be manifest thus: first, an apostate idolater whether husband or wife seducing was to die by the decree of God, Deuteronomy 13.6.9. That marriage therefore God himself disjoins. For others born idolaters the moral reason of their dangerous keeping, and the incommunicable antagony[50] that is between Christ and Belial, will be sufficient to enforce the commandment of those two inspired reformers, Ezra and Nehemiah, to put an idolater away as well under the Gospel.

The latter part, that although there be no seducement feared, yet if there be no hope given, the divorce is lawful, will appear by this: that idolatrous marriage is still hateful to God. Therefore still it may be divorced by the pattern of that warrant that Ezra had, and by the same everlasting reason: neither can any man give an account wherefore, if those whom God joins no man may separate, it should not follow, that whom he joins not but hates to join, those man ought to separate. But, said the lawyer, that which ought not have been done, once done, avails. I answer, this is but a crotchet of the law, but that brought against it, is plain Scripture. As for what Christ spoke concerning divorce, this is confessed by all knowing men, he meant only between them of the same faith. But what shall we say then to St. Paul, who seems to bid us not divorce an infidel willing to stay? We may safely say thus: that wrong collections have been hitherto made out of those words by modern divines. His drift, as was heard before, is plain: not to command our stay in marriage with an infidel, that had been a flat renouncing of the religious and moral law; but to inform the Corinthians that the body of an unbeliever was not defiling, if his desire to live in Christian wedlock showed any likelihood that his heart was opening to the faith: and therefore advises to forebear departure so long, 'til nothing have been neglected to set forward a conversion. This I say he advises, and that with certain cautions, not commands, if we can take up so much credit for him, as to get him believed upon his own word. For what is this else but his counsel in a thing indifferent, *to the rest speak I, not the Lord*. For though it be true that the Lord never spoke it, yet from St. Paul's mouth we should have taken it as a command, had not himself forewarned us, and disclaimed; which, notwithstanding if we shall still avouch to be a command, he palpably denying it, this is not to expound St. Paul, but to outface him. Neither doth it follow, but that the Apostle may interpose his judgment in a case of Christian liberty without the guilt of adding to God's word. How do we know marriage or single life to be of choice, but by such like words as these, *I speak this by permission, not of commandment, I have no command of the Lord, yet I give my judgment*. Why shall not the like words have leave to signify a freedom in this our present question, though Beza deny.[51] Neither is the Scripture hereby less inspired because St. Paul confesses to have written therein what he had not of command; for we grant that the Spirit of God led him thus to express himself to Christian prudence in a matter which God thought best to leave un-commanded. Beza therefore must be warily read when he taxes St. Augustine of blasphemy for holding that St. Paul spoke here as of a thing indifferent. But if it must be a command, I shall yet the more evince it to be a command that we should herein be left free: and that out of the Greek word used in the 12.v. which instructs us plainly, there must be a joint assent and good liking on both sides; he that will not deprave the text, must thus render it: *If a brother have an unbelieving wife, and she join in consent to dwell with him* (which cannot utter less to us than a mutual agreement) let him not put her away for the mere surmise of Judaic uncleanness; and the reason follows, for the body of an infidel is not polluted, neither to benevolence, nor to procreation. Moreover, this note of mutual complacency forbids all offer of seducement; which to a person of zeal cannot be attempted without great offence; if therefore seducement be feared, this place hinders not divorce. Another caution was put in this supposed command, of not bringing the believer into *bondage* hereby, which doubtless might prove extreme, if Christian liberty and conscience were left to the humor of a pagan staying at pleasure to play with, or to vex and wound with a thousand scandals and burdens, above strength to bear. If therefore the conceived hope of gaining a soul come to nothing, then charity commands that the believer be not wearied out with endless waiting under many grievances sore to his spirit, but that respect be had rather to the present suffering of a true Christian than the uncertain winning of an obdurate heretic. For this also must appertain to the precept, *let every man wherein he is called, therein abide with God,* v.24, that is, so walking in his inferior calling of marriage, as not by dangerous subjection to that ordinance, to hinder and disturb the higher calling of his Christianity. Last, whether this be a command or an advice, we must look that it be so understood as not to contradict the least point of moral religion that God has formerly commanded, otherwise what do we but set the moral law and the Gospel at civil war together: and who then shall be able to serve those two masters?

Now whether idolatry or adultery be the greatest violation of marriage, if any demand, let him thus consider, that among Christian writers touching matrimony, there are three chief ends thereof agreed on: Godly society, next civil, and thirdly, that of the marriage-bed. Of these the first in name to be the highest and most excellent, no baptized man can deny; nor that idolatry smites directly against this prime end, nor that such as the violated end is, such is the violation. But he who affirms adultery to be the highest breach, affirms the bed to be the highest of marriage, which is in truth a gross and boorish opinion, how common so ever; as far from the countenance of Scripture, as from the light of all clean philosophy, or civil nature. And out of question the cheerful help that may be in marriage toward sanctity of life, is the purest, and so the noblest end of that contract. But if the particular of each person be considered, then of those three ends which God appointed, that to him is greatest which is most necessary; and marriage is then most broken to him, when he utterly wants the fruition of that which he most sought therein, whether it were religious, civil, or corporal society. Of which wants to do him right by divorce only for the last and meanest, is a perverse injury, and the pretended reason of it as frigid as frigidity itself, which the code and canon are only sensible of.[52] Thus much of this controversy. I now return to the former argument. And having shown that disproportion, contrariety, or numbness of mind may justly be divorced, by proving already that the prohibition thereof opposes the express end of God's institution, suffers not marriage to satisfy that intellectual and innocent desire which God himself kindled in man to be the bond of wedlock, but only to remedy a sublunary[53] and bestial burning, which frugal diet without marriage would easily chasten. Next that it drives many to transgress the conjugal bed, while the soul wanders after that satisfaction which it had hope to end at home, but has missed. Or else it sits repining even to atheism; finding itself hardly dealt with, but misdeeming the cause to be in God's law, which is in man's unrighteous ignorance. I have shown also how it unties the inward knot of marriage, which is peace and love (if that can be untied which was never knit) while it aims to keep fast the outward formality; how it lets perish the Christian man, to compel impossibly the married man.

The sixth place declares this prohibition to be as respectless[54] of human nature, and therefore is not of God. He teaches that an unlawful marriage may be lawfully divorced. And that those who having thoroughly discerned each other's disposition which often cannot be until after matrimony, shall then find a powerful reluctance and recoil of nature on either side blasting all the content of their mutual society, that such persons are not lawfully married (to use the Apostle's words) *Say I these things as a man, or saith not the law also the same?* For it is written, Deuteronomy 22, *Thou shalt not sow thy vineyard with divers seeds, lest thou defile both.*

Thou shalt not plow with an ox and an ass together, and the like. I follow the pattern of St. Paul's reasoning: *Doth God care for asses and oxen,* how ill they yoke together, *or is it not said altogether for our sakes? For our sakes no doubt this is written.*[55] Yes the Apostle himself, in the afore-cited 2 Corinthians 6.14, alludes from that place of Deuteronomy to forbid mis-yoking marriage, as by the Greek word is evident, though he grants only one example of mis-matching with an infidel; yet next to that what can be a fouler incongruity, a greater violence to the reverend secret of nature, than to force a mixture of minds that cannot unite, and to sow the furrow of man's nativity with seed of two incoherent and uncombining dispositions. Surely if any noisomeness of body soon destroys the sympathy of mind to that work, much more will the antipathy of mind infuse itself into all the faculties and acts of the body, to render them invalid, unkindly, and even unholy against the fundamental law book of nature, which Moses never thwarts, but reverences. Therefore he commands us to force nothing against sympathy or natural order, no, not upon the most abject creatures, to show that such an indignity cannot be offered to man without an impious crime. And when he forbids all unmatchable and unmingling natures to consort, doubtless by all due consequence, if they chance through misadventure to be mis-coupled, he bids them part asunder, as persons whom God never joined.

Seventhly, the canon law and divines consent, that if either party be found contriving against another's life, they may be severed by divorce; for a sin against the life of marriage, is greater than a sin against the bed: the one destroys, the other but defiles. The same may be said touching those persons who being of a pensive nature and course of life, have summed up all their solace in that free and lightsome conversation which God and man intends in marriage: whereof when they see themselves deprived by meeting an unsociable consort, they often resent one another's mistake so deeply, that long it is not before grief ends one of them. When therefore this danger is foreseen, that the life is in peril by living together, what matter is it whether helpless grief or willful practice be the cause. This is certain, that the preservation of life is more worth than the compulsory keeping of marriage; and it is no less than cruelty to force a man to remain in that state as the solace of his life, which he and his friends know will be either the undoing or the disheartening of his life. And what is life without the vigor and spirit-full exercise of life? How can it be useful either to private or public employment? Shall it be therefore quite dejected, though never so valuable, and left to molder away in heaviness for the superstitious and impossible performance of an ill-driven bargain? Nothing more inviolable than vows made to God, yet we read in Numbers that if a wife had made such a vow, the mere will and authority of her husband might break it;[56] how much more may he break the error of his own bonds with an unfit and mistaken wife, to the saving of his welfare, his life—yes, his faith and virtue—from the hazard of over-strong temptations; for if man be lord of the Sabbath, to the curing of a fever, can he be less than lord of marriage in such important causes as these?

Eighthly, it is most sure that some even of those who are not plainly defective in body, yet are destitute of all other manageable gifts, and consequently have not the calling to marry; unless nothing be requisite thereto but a mere instrumental body; which to affirm is to that unanimous covenant a reproach: yet it is as sure that many such, not of their own desire, but by persuasion of friends, or not knowing themselves, do often enter into wedlock; where finding the difference at length between the duties of a married life, and the gifts of a single life; what unfitness of mind, what wearisomeness, what scruples and doubts to an incredible offence and displeasure are like to follow between, may be soon imagined: whom thus to shut up and immure in an unequal and mis-chosen match, is not a course that Christian wisdom and tenderness ought to use.[57] As for the custom that some parents and guardians have of forcing marriages, it will be better to say nothing of such a savage inhumanity, but only thus, that the law which gives not all freedom of divorce to any creature endued with reason so assassinated, is next in cruelty.

Ninthly, I suppose it will be allowed us that marriage is a human society, and that all human society must proceed from the mind rather than the body, else it would be but a kind of animal or beastly meeting; if the mind therefore cannot have that due company by marriage, that it may reasonably and humanly desire, that marriage can be no human society, but a certain formality; or an incorporation of little better than a brutish congress, and so in very wisdom and pureness to be dissolved.

But marriage is more than human, *the covenant of God,* Proverbs 2.17; therefore man cannot dissolve it. I answer, if it be more than human, so much the more it argues the chief society thereof to be in the soul rather than in the body, and the greatest breach thereof to be unfitness of mind rather than defect of body: for the body can have least affinity in a covenant more than human, so that the reason of dissolving holds good the rather. Again, I answer, that the Sabbath is a higher institution, a command of the first table,[58] for the breach whereof God has far more and more often testified his anger, than for divorces, which from Moses until after the captivity he never took displeasure at, nor then neither, if we mark the text; and yet as oft as the good of man is concerned, he not only permits, but commands to break the Sabbath. What covenant more contracted with God, and less in man's power, than the vow which has once passed his lips? Yet if it be found rash, if offensive, if unfruitful either to God's glory or the good of man, our doctrine forces not error and unwillingness irksomely to keep it, but counsels wisdom and better thoughts boldly to break it; therefore to enjoin the indissoluble keeping of a marriage found unfit against the good of man both soul and body, as has been evidenced, is to make an idol of marriage, to advance it above the worship of God and the good of man, to make it a transcendent command, above both the second and the first table, which is a most prodigious doctrine.

Next, whereas they cite out of the Proverbs, that it is *the covenant of God,* and therefore more than human, that consequence is manifestly false: for so the covenant which Zedechiah made with the infidel King of Babel, is called *the covenant of God,* Ezekiel 17.19, which would be strange to hear counted more than a human covenant. So every covenant between man and man, bound by oath, may be called the covenant of God, because God therein is attested. So of marriage he is the author and the witness; yet hence will not follow any divine astriction[59] more than what is subordinate to the glory of God and the main good of either party; for as the glory of God and their esteemed fitness one for the other, was the motive which led them both at first to think without other revelation that God had joined them together. So when it shall be found by their apparent unfitness, that their continuing to be man and wife is against the glory of God and their mutual happiness, it may assure them that God never joined them; who has revealed his gracious will not to set the ordinance above the man for whom it was ordained, not to canonize marriage either as a tyranness or a goddess over the enfranchised life and soul of man: for wherein can God delight, wherein be worshiped, wherein be glorified by the forcible continuing of an improper and ill-yoking couple? He that loved not to see the disparity of several cattle at the plow, cannot be pleased with any vast unmeetness in marriage. Where can be the peace and love which must invite God to such a house; may it not be feared that the not divorcing of such a helpless disagreement, will be the divorcing of God finally from such a place? But it is a trial of our patience they say. I grant it: but which of Job's afflictions were sent him with that law, that he might not use means to remove any of them if he could? And what if it subvert our patience and our faith too? Who shall answer for the perishing of all those souls perishing by stubborn expositions of particular and inferior precepts against the general and supreme rule of charity? They dare not affirm that marriage is either a sacrament or a mystery,[60] though all those sacred things give place to man, and yet they invest it with such an awful sanctity, and give it such adamantine chains to bind with, as if it were to be worshiped like some Indian deity, when it can confer no blessing upon us, but works more and more to our misery. To such teachers the saying of St. Peter at the council of Jerusalem will do well to be applied: *Why tempt ye God to put a yoke upon the necks* of Christian men, which neither the Jews, God's ancient people, *nor we are able to bear;* and nothing but unwary expounding has brought upon us. To these considerations this also may be added as no improbable conjecture: seeing that sort of men who follow Anabaptism, Familism, Antinomianism, and other *fanatic* dreams,[61] be such most commonly as are by nature addicted to religion, of life also not debauched, and that their opinions having full swing, do end in satisfaction of the flesh, it may be come with reason into the thoughts of a wise man, whether all this proceed not partly, if not chiefly, from the restraint of some lawful liberty, which ought to be given men, and is denied them. As from medicine we learn in menstrual bodies, where nature's current has been stopped, that the suffocation and upward forcing of some lower part, affects the head and inward sense with dotage and idle fancies. And on the other hand, whether the rest of vulgar men not so religiously professing do not give themselves much the more to whoredom and adulteries, loving the corrupt and venial discipline of clerical courts but hating to hear of perfect reformation, when as they foresee that then fornication shall be austerely censured, adultery punished, and marriage the appointed refuge of nature, though it hap to be never so incongruous and displeasing, must yet of force be worn out, when it can be to no other purpose but of strife and hatred, a thing odious to God. This may be worth the study of skillful men in theology, and the reason of things, and lastly to examine whether some undue and ill-grounded strictness upon the blameless nature of man be not the cause in those places where already reformation is, that the discipline of the Church so often and so unavoidably broken, is brought into contempt and derision. And if it be thus, let those who are still bent to hold this obstinate *literality* so prepare themselves as to share in the account for all these transgressions, when it shall be demanded at the last day by one who will scan and sift things with more than a literal wisdom of equity; for if these reasons be duly pondered, and that the Gospel is more jealous of laying on excessive burdens than ever the law was, lest the soul of a Christian which is inestimable, should be over-tempted and cast away, considering also that many properties of nature, which the power of regeneration itself never alters, may cause dislike of conversing even between the most sanctified, which continually grating in harsh tune together, may breed some jar and discord, and that end in rancor and strife, a thing so opposite both to marriage and to Christianity, it would perhaps be less scandalous to divorce a natural disparity than to link violently together an un-Christian dissension, committing two ensnared souls inevitably to kindle one another, not with the fire of love, but with a hatred *inconcileable,*[62] who were they dissevered would be straight friends in any other relation. But if an *alphabetical* servility[63] must be still urged, it may so fall out that the true Church may unwittingly use as much cruelty in forbidding to divorce, as the church of antichrist doth willfully in forbidding to marry.

But what are all these reasonings worth will some reply, when the words of Christ are plainly against all divorce except in case of fornication;[64] let us let such remember as a thing not to be denied, that all places of Scripture wherein just reason of doubt arises from the letter are to be expounded by considering upon what occasion every thing is set down, and by comparing other texts. The occasion which induced our Savior to speak of divorce was either to convince the extravagance of the Pharisees in that point, or to give a sharp and vehement answer to a tempting question. And in such cases that we are not to repose all upon the literal terms of so many words, many instances will teach us: wherein we may plainly discover how Christ meant not to be taken word for word, but like a wise physician, administering one excess against another to reduce us to a perfect mean. Where the Pharisees were strict, there Christ seems remiss; where they were too remiss, he saw it needful to seem most severe: in one place he censures an unchaste look to be adultery already committed;[65] another time he passes over actual adultery with less reproof than for an unchaste look;[66] not so heavily condemning secret weakness, as open malice. So here he may be justly thought to have given this rigid sentence against divorce, not to cut off all remedy from a good man who finds himself consuming away in a disconsolate and un-enjoined matrimony, but to lay a bridle upon the bold abuses of those over-weaning Rabbis; which he could not more effectually do, than by a countersway[67] of restraint curbing their wild exorbitance almost into the other extreme, as when we bow things the contrary way, to make them come to their natural straightness. And that this was the only intention of Christ is most evident if we attend but to his own words and protestation made in the same sermon, not many verses before he treats of divorcing, that he came not to abrogate from the law one jot or tittle, and denounces against them that shall so teach.[68] So that the question of divorce, following upon this his open profession, must needs confirm us that what ever else in the political law of more special relation to the Jews might cease to us, yet that of those precepts concerning divorce not one of them was repealed by the doctrine of Christ; for if these our Savior's words inveigh against all divorce, and condemn it as adultery, except it be for adultery, and be not rather understood against the abuse of those divorces permitted in the law, then is that law of Moses, Deuteronomy 24.1, not only repealed and wholly annulled against the promise of Christ and his known profession, not to meddle in matters judicial, but that which is more strange, the very substance and purpose of that law is contradicted and convinced both of injustice and impurity, as having authorized and maintained legal adultery by statute. Moses also cannot escape to be guilty of unequal and unwise decrees, punishing one act of secret adultery by death,[69] and permitting a whole life of open adultery by law. And albeit lawyers write that some political edicts, though not approved, are yet allowed to the scum of the people and the necessity of the times, these excuses have but a weak pulse: for first, we read, not that the scoundrel people, but the choicest, the wisest, the holiest of that nation have frequently used these laws, or such as these. Secondly, be it yielded, that in matters not very bad or impure, a human law giver may slacken something of that which is exactly good, to the disposition of the people and the times; but if the perfect, the pure, the righteous law of God, for so are all his statutes and his judgments, be found to have allowed smoothly without any certain reprehension, that which Christ afterward declares to be adultery, how can we free this law from the horrible indictment of being both impure, unjust, and fallacious. Neither will it serve to say this was permitted for the hardness of their hearts, in that sense as it is usually explained, for the law were then but a corrupt and erroneous schoolmaster,[70] teaching us to dash against a vital maxim of religion, by doing foul evil in hope of some uncertain good.[71] We cannot therefore with safety thus confine the free simplicity of our Savior's meaning to that which merely amounts from so many letters, inasmuch as it can consist neither with his former and cautionary words, nor with the scope of charity, commanding by his express commission in a higher strain. But all rather of necessity must be understood as only against the abuse of that wise and ingenious liberty which Moses gave, and to terrify a roving conscience from sinning under that pretext.

Others think to evade the matter by not granting any law of divorce, but only a dispensation, which is contrary to the words of Christ, who himself calls it a law, Mark 10.5.[72] But I answer, admitting it to be a dispensation, yet this is a certain rule, that so long as the cause remains, the dispensation ought. Let it be shown therefore either in the nature of the Gospel, or of man, why this dispensation should be made void. The Gospel indeed exhorts to highest perfection; but bears with weakest infirmity more than the law. The nature of man is as weak, and yet as hard: and that weakness and hardness as unfit, and as unteachable to be harshly dealt with as ever. Ay but, say they, there is a greater portion of spirit poured upon the Gospel which requires more perfect obedience. But that consequence is deceivable; for it is the law that is the exacter of our obedience even under the Gospel; how can it then exact concerning divorce, that which it never exacted before? The Gospel is a covenant revealing grace, not commanding a new morality, but assuring justification by faith only, contented if we endeavor to square our moral duty by those wise and equal Mosaic rules, which were as perfect, as strict, and as unpardonable to the Jews as to us; otherwise the law were unjust, giving grace of pardon without the Gospel, or if it give allowance without pardon, it would be dissolute and deceitful; saying in general, *do this and live,*[73] and yet deceiving and damning with obscure and hollow permissions. We find also by experience that the Spirit of God in the Gospel has been always more effectual in the illumination of our minds to the gift of faith, than in the moving of our wills to any excellence of virtue, either above the Jews or the Heathen. Hence those indulgences in the Gospel: *All cannot receive this saying: Every man hath his proper gift,* with strict charges not to lay on yokes which our Fathers could not bear.[74]

But this that Moses suffered for the hardness of their hearts he suffered not by that enacted dispensation, far be it, but by a mere accidental sufferance of undiscovered hypocrites, who made ill use of that law; for that God should enact a dispensation for hard hearts to do that whereby they must live in privileged adultery, however it go for the received opinion, I shall ever dissuade my self from so much hardihood as to believe. Certainly this is not the manner of God, whose pure eyes cannot behold, much less his perfect laws dispense with such impurity.[75] And if we consider well, we shall find that all dispensations are either to avoid worse inconveniences, or to support infirm consciences for a time. But that a dispensation should be as long lived as a law to tolerate adultery for hardness of heart, both sins perhaps of like degree, and yet this obdurate disease cannot be conceived how it is the more amended by this unclean remedy, is a notion of that extravagance from the sage principles of piety, that who considers thoroughly, cannot but admire how this has been digested all this while.[76] What may we do then to solve this seeming inconsistency? I must not dissemble that I am confident it can be done no other way than this.

Moses, Deuteronomy 24.1, established a grave and prudent law, full of moral equity, full of due consideration towards nature, that cannot be resisted; a law consenting with the laws of wisest men and civilest nations.[77] That when a man has married a wife, if it come to pass he cannot love her by reason of some displeasing natural quality or unfitness in her, let him write her a bill of divorce. The intent of which law undoubtedly was this: that if any good and peaceable man should discover some helpless disagreement or dislike either of mind or body, whereby he could not cheerfully perform the duty of a husband without the perpetual dissembling of offence and disturbance to his spirit, rather than to live uncomfortably and unhappily both to himself and to his wife, rather than to continue undertaking a duty which he could not possibly discharge, he might dismiss her whom he could not tolerably and so not conscionably retain. And this law the Spirit of God by the mouth of Solomon, Proverbs 30.21.23, testifies to be a good and a necessary law by granting it that to *dwell with a hated woman* (for *hated* the Hebrew word signifies) *is a thing that nature cannot endure.*[78] What follows then but that law must remedy what nature cannot undergo. Now that many licentious and hard-hearted men took hold of this law to cloak their bad purposes, is nothing strange to believe. And these were they, not for whom Moses made the law, God forbid, but whose hardness of heart taking ill advantage by this law he held it better to suffer as by accident, where it could not be detected, rather than good men should lose their just and lawful privileges of remedy. Christ therefore having to answer these tempting Pharisees, according as his custom was, not meaning to inform their proud ignorance what Moses did in the true intent of the law, which they had ill cited, suppressing the true cause for which Moses gave it, and extending it to every slight matter, tells them their own, what Moses was forced to suffer by their abuse of his law. Which is yet more plain if we mark that our Savior in the fifth of Matthew cites not the law of Moses, but the Pharisaical tradition falsely grounded upon that law.[79] And in those other places, chapter 19 and Mark 10, the Pharisees cite the law but conceal the wise and human reason there expressed; which our Savior corrects not in them, whose pride deserved not his instruction, only returns them what is proper to them: *Moses for the hardness of your heart suffered you,* that is, such as you, *to put away your wives;*[80] and *to you he wrote this precept*[81] for that cause, which (*to you*) must be read with an impression,[82] and understood limitedly of such as covered ill purposes under that law. For it was seasonable that they should hear their own unbounded license rebuked, but not seasonable for them to hear a good man's requisite liberty explained.[83] And to amaze them the more, because the Pharisees thought it no hard matter to fulfill the law, he draws them up to that inseparable institution which God ordained in the beginning before the fall, when man and woman were both perfect, and could have no cause to separate; just as in the same chapter[84] he stands not to contend with the arrogant young man who boasted his observance of the whole law, whether he had indeed kept it or not, but screws him up higher,[85] to a task of that perfection which no man is bound to imitate. And in like manner that pattern of the first institution he set before the opinionative Pharisees to dazzle them and not to bind us. For this is a solid rule, that every command given with a reason, binds our obedience no otherwise than that reason holds. Of this sort was that command in Eden: *therefore shall a man cleave to his wife, and they shall be one flesh;*[86] which we see is no absolute command, but with an inference, *therefore:* the reason then must be first considered, that our obedience be not mis-obedience. The first is, for it is not single, because the wife is to the husband *flesh of his flesh,* as in the verse going before. But this reason cannot be sufficient of itself; for why then should he for his wife leave his father and mother, with whom he is far *more flesh of flesh and bone of bone,* as being made of their substance. And besides it can be but a sorry and ignoble society of life, whose inseparable injunction depends merely upon flesh and bones. Therefore we must look higher, since Christ himself recalls us to the beginning, and we shall find that the primitive reason of never divorcing, was that sacred and not vain promise of God to remedy man's loneliness by *making him a help meet for him,*[87] though not now in perfection, as at first, yet still in proportion as things now are. And this is repeated verse 20, when all other creatures were fitly associated and brought to Adam as if the divine power had been in some care and deep thought, because *there was not yet found a help meet for man.* And can we so slightly depress the all-wise purpose of a deliberating God, as if his consultation had produced no other good for man but to join him with an accidental companion of propagation, which his sudden word had already made for every beast? Nay, a far less good to man it will be found, if she must at all adventures be fastened upon him individually.[88] And therefore even plain sense and equity, and, which is above them both, the all-interpreting voice of charity herself cries loud that this primitive reason, this consulted promise of God *to make a meet help,* is the only cause that gives authority to this command of not divorcing, to be a command. And it might be further added, that if the true definition of a wife were asked in good earnest, this clause of being *a meet help* would show it self so necessary, and so essential in that demonstrative argument, that it might be logically concluded: therefore she who naturally and perpetually is no meet help, can be no wife; which clearly takes away the difficulty of dismissing such a one.[89] Hence is manifest, that so much of the first institution as our Savior mentions, for he mentions not all, was but to quell and put to non-plus the tempting Pharisees; and to lay open their ignorance and shallow understanding of the Scriptures. For, said he, *have ye not read that he which made them at the beginning, made them male and female, and said, for this cause shall a man cleave to his wife?*[90] Which these blind usurpers of Moses chair could not gainsay: as if this single respect of male and female were sufficient against a thousand inconveniences and mischiefs to clog a rational creature to his endless sorrow unrelinquishably. What if they had thus answered, Master, if thou intend to make wedlock as inseparable as it was from the beginning, let it be made also a fit society, as God intended it, which we shall soon understand it ought to be, if thou recite the whole reason of the law. Doubtless our Savior had applauded their just answer. For then they had expounded this command of Paradise, even as Moses himself expounds it by his laws of divorce, that is, with due and wise regard had to the premises and reasons of the first command, according to which, without unclean and temporizing permissions he instructs us in this imperfect state what we may lawfully do about divorce.

But if it be thought that the disciples, offended at the rigor of Christ's answer, could yet obtain no mitigation of the former sentence pronounced to the Pharisees, it may be fully answered that our Savior continues the same reply to his disciples, as men leavened with the same customary license, which the Pharisees maintained, and displeased at the removing of a traditional abuse whereto they had so long not unwillingly been used: it was no time then to contend with their slow and prejudicial belief, in a thing wherein an ordinary measure of light in Scripture with some attention might afterwards inform them well enough.[91] After these considerations to take a law out of Paradise given in time of original perfection, and to take it barely without those just and equal inferences and reasons which mainly establish it, nor so much as admitting those needful and safe allowances wherewith Moses himself interprets it to the fallen condition of man, argues nothing in us but rashness and contempt of those means that God left us in his pure and chaste law, without which it will not be possible for us to perform the strict imposition of this command; or if we strive beyond our strength we shall strive to obey it otherwise than God commands it. And lamented experience daily teaches the bitter and vain fruits of this our presumption, forcing men in a thing wherein we are not able to judge either of their strength or their sufferance. Whom neither one vice nor other by natural addiction, but only marriage ruins, which doubtless is not the fault of that ordinance, for God gave it as a blessing, nor always of man's mis-choosing; it being an error above wisdom to prevent, as examples of wisest men so mistaken manifest. It is the fault therefore of a perverse opinion that will have it continued in despite of nature and reason, when indeed it was never truly joined. All those expositors upon the fifth of Matthew confess the law of Moses to be the law of the Lord, wherein no addition or diminution has place; yet coming to the point of divorce, as if they feared not to be called least in the Kingdom of Heaven,[92] any slight evasion will content them to reconcile those contradictions which they make between Christ and Moses, between Christ and Christ.

Some will have it no law, but the granted premises of another law following, contrary to the words of Christ, Mark 10.5, and all other translations of gravest authority, who render it in form of a law; agreeable to Malachi 2.16 as it is most anciently and modernly expounded.[93] Besides, the bill of divorce declares it to be orderly and legal. And what avails this to make the matter more righteous, if such an adulterous condition shall be mentioned to build a law upon without either punishment, or so much as forbidding; they pretend it is implicitly reproved in these words, Deuteronomy 24.4 *after she is defiled*. But who sees not that this defilement is only in respect of returning to her former husband after an intermixed marriage; else why was not the *defiling* condition first forbidden which would have saved the labor of this after law. Nor is it seemly or piously attributed to the justice of God and his known hatred of sin, that such a heinous fault as this through all the law should be only wiped with an implicit and oblique touch (which yet is falsely supposed) and that his peculiar people should be let wallow in adulterous marriages almost two thousand years for want of a direct law to prohibit them. It is rather to be confidently assumed that this was granted to apparent necessities, as being of unquestionable right and reason in the law of nature, in that it still passes without inhibition, even when greatest cause is given us to expect it should be directly forbidden. But it was not approved, so much the worse that it was allowed, as if sin had over-mastered the law of God, to conform her steady and straight rule to sin's crookedness, which is impossible. Besides, what needed a positive grant of that which was not approved? It restrained no liberty to him that could but use a little fraud; it had been better silenced, unless it were approved in some case or other.[94] Can we conceive without vile thoughts that the majesty and holiness of God could endure so many ages to gratify a stubborn people in the practice of a foul polluting sin, and could he expect they should abstain, he not signifying his mind in a plain command, at such time especially when he was framing their laws and them to all possible perfection? But they were to look back to the first institution, nay rather why was not that individual institution brought out of Paradise, as was that of the Sabbath, and repeated in the body of the law,[95] that men might have understood it to be a command? For that any sentence that bears the resemblance of a precept, set there so out of place in another world at such a distance from the whole law, and not once mentioned there, should be an obliging command to us, is very disputable, and perhaps it might be denied to be a command without further dispute. However, it commands not absolutely, as has been cleared, but only with reference to that precedent promise of God, which is the very ground of his institution; if that appear not in some tolerable sort, how can we affirm such a matrimony to be the same which God instituted! In such an accident it will best behoove our soberness to follow rather what moral Sinai prescribes equal to our strength, than fondly to think within our strength all that lost Paradise relates.

Another while it shall suffice them, that it was not a moral but a judicial law, and so was abrogated. Nay rather was not abrogated, because judicial: which law the ministry of Christ came not to deal with. And who put it in man's power to exempt, where Christ speaks in general of not abrogating *the least jot or tittle,* and in special not that of divorce, because it follows among those laws, which he promised expressly not to abrogate, but to vindicate from abusive traditions?[96] And if we mark the 31 verse of Matthew 5, he there cites not the law of Moses, but the licentious gloss which traduced the law; that therefore which he cited, that he abrogated, and not only abrogated but disallowed and flatly condemned, which could not be the law of Moses; for that had been foully to the rebuke of his great servant. To abrogate a law made with God's allowance, had been to tell us only that such a law was now to cease, but to refute it with an ignominious note of civilizing adultery, casts the reproof, which was meant only to the Pharisees even upon him who made the law. But yet if that be judicial which belongs to a civil court, this law is less judicial than nine of the ten Commandments; for antiquaries affirm that divorces proceeded among the Jews without knowledge of the magistrate, only with hands and seals under the testimony of some Rabbis to be then present.[97] And it was indeed a pure moral *economical* law, too hastily imputed of tolerating sin; being rather so clear in nature and reason, that it was left to a man's own arbitration to be determined between God and his own conscience. And that power which Christ never took from the master of family, but rectified only to a right and wary use at home: that power the undiscerning canonist has improperly usurped into his court-leet,[98] and be-scribbled with a thousand trifling impertinencies, which yet have filled the life of man with serious trouble and calamity. Yet grant it were of old a judicial law, it need not be the less moral for that, being conversant, as it is, about virtue or vice. And our Savior disputes not here the judicature, for that was not his office, but the morality of divorce, whether it be adultery or no. If therefore he touch the law of Moses' at all, he touches the moral part thereof; which is absurd to imagine that the covenant of grace should reform the exact and perfect law of works, eternal and immutable; or if he touch not the law at all, then is not the allowance thereof disallowed to us.

Others are so ridiculous as to allege that this license of divorcing was given them because they were so accustomed in Egypt.[99] As if an ill custom were to be kept to all posterity; for the dispensation is both universal and of time unlimited, and so indeed no dispensation at all; for the over-dated dispensation of a thing unlawful serves for nothing but to increase hardness of heart, and makes men but wax more incorrigible, which were a great reproach to be said of any law or allowance that God should give us. In these opinions it would be more religion to advise well, lest we make our selves more just than God, by censuring rashly that for sin which his unspotted law without rebuke allows, and his people without being conscious of displeasing him have used. And if we can think so of Moses, as that the Jewish obstinacy could compel him to write such impure permissions against the rule of God and his own judgment, doubtless it was his part to have protested publicly what straits he was driven to, and to have declared his conscience when he gave any law against his mind. For the law is the touchstone of sin and of conscience, must not be intermixed with corrupt indulgences; for then it loses the greatest praise it has, of being certain and infallible, not leading into error, as all the Jews were led by this connivance of Moses, if it were a connivance. But still they fly back to the primitive institution, and would have us re-enter Paradise against the sword that guards it.[100] Whom I again thus reply to, that the place in Genesis contains the description of a fit and perfect marriage, with an interdict of ever divorcing such a union; but where nature is discovered to have never joined indeed, but vehemently seeks to part, it cannot be there conceived that God forbids it; nay he commands it both in the law and in the prophet Malachi, which is to be our rule. And Perkins[101] upon this chapter of Matthew deals plainly, that our Savior here confutes not Moses law, but the false glosses that depraved the law; which being true, Perkins must needs grant that something then is left to that law which Christ found no fault with; and what can that be but the conscionable use of such liberty as the plain words import? So that by his own inference, Christ did not absolutely intend to restrain all divorces to the only cause of adultery. This therefore is the true scope of our Savior's will, that he who looks upon the law concerning divorce, should look also back upon the first institution, that he may endeavor what is most perfect: and he that looks upon the institution should not refuse as sinful and unlawful those allowances which God affords him in his following law, lest he make himself purer than his maker; and presuming above strength, slip into temptations irrecoverably. For this is wonderful, that in all those decrees concerning marriage, God should never once mention the prime institution to dissuade them from divorcing; and that he should forbid smaller sins as opposite to the hardness of their hearts, and let this adulterous matter of divorce pass ever unreproved. This is also to be marveled at, that seeing Christ did not condemn whatever it was that Moses suffered, and that thereupon the Christian magistrate permits usury and open stews, and here with us adultery to be so slightly punished which was punished by death to these hard-hearted Jews,[102] why we should strain thus at the matter of divorce, which may stand so much with charity to permit, and make no scruple to allow usury esteemed to be so much against charity.[103] But this it is to embroil ourselves against the righteous and all-wise judgments and statutes of God, which are not variable and contrary, as we would make them, one while permitting and another while forbidding, but are most constant and most harmonious each to other. For how can the uncorrupt and majestic law of God, bearing in her hand the wages of life and death, harbor such a repugnance within herself, as to require an unexempted and impartial obedience to all her decrees, either from us or from our mediator, and yet debase herself to falter so many ages with circumcised[104] adulteries, by unclean and slubbering permissions?

Yet Beza's opinion is that a politic law, but what politic law I know not, unless one of Machiavelli's, may regulate sin; may bear indeed, I grant, with imperfection for a time, as those canons of the Apostles did in ceremonial things.[105] But as for sin, the essence of it cannot consist with rule; and if the law fall[106] to regulate sin, and not to take it utterly away, it necessarily confirms and establishes sin. To make a regularity of sin by law, either the law must straiten sin into no sin, or sin must crook the law into no law. The judicial law can serve to no other end than to be the protector and champion of religion and honest civility, as is set down plainly, Romans 13,[107] and is but the arm of moral law, which can no more be separate from justice than justice from virtue. Their office also in a different manner steers the same course: the one teaches what is good by precept, the other un-teaches what is bad by punishment. But if we give way to politic dispensations of lewd uncleanness, the first good consequence of such a relax will be the justifying of papal stews,[108] joined with a toleration of epidemic whoredom. Justice must revolt from the end of her authority, and become the patron of that whereof she was created the punisher. The example of usury, which is commonly alleged, makes against the allegation which it brings, as I touched before. Besides, that usury, so much as is permitted by the magistrate and demanded with common equity, is neither against the word of God nor the rule of charity, as has been often discussed by men of eminent learning and judgment. There must be therefore some other example found out to show us wherein civil policy may with warrant from God settle wickedness by law, and make that lawful which is lawless. Although I doubt not but upon deeper consideration, that which is true in medicine will be found as true in policy: that as of bad pulses those that beat most in order are much worse than those that keep the most inordinate circuit, so of popular vices those that may be committed legally will be more pernicious than those that are left to their own course at peril, not under a stinted privilege to sin orderly and regularly, which is an implicit contradiction, but under due and fearless execution of punishment. The political law, since it cannot regulate vice, is to restrain it, by using all means to root it out; but if it suffer the weed to grow up to any pleasurable or contented height upon what pretext so ever, it fastens the root, it prunes and dresses vice, as if it were a good plant.[109] Lastly, if divorce were granted, as he says, not for men, but to release afflicted wives,[110] certainly it is not only a dispensation, but a most merciful law; and why it should not yet be in force, being wholly as needful, I know not what can be in cause but senseless cruelty.[111] Esteeming therefore to have asserted thus an injured law of Moses from the unwarranted and guilty name of a dispensation, to be again a most equal and requisite law, we have the word of Christ himself, that he came not to alter the least tittle of it; and signifies no small displeasure against him that shall teach to do so. On which relying, I shall not much waver to affirm, that those words which are made to intimate, as if they forbade all divorce but for adultery (though Moses have constituted otherwise), those words taken circumspectly, without regard to any precedent law of Moses or attestation of Christ himself, or without care to preserve those his fundamental and superior laws of nature and charity, to which all other ordinances give up their seals, are as much against plain equity, and the mercy of religion, as those words of *Take, eat, this is my body,* elementally understood, are against nature and sense.[112]

And surely the restoring of this degraded law has well recompensed the diligence was used, by enlightening us further to find out wherefore Christ took off the Pharisees from alleging the law, and referred them to the first institution, not condemning, altering, or abolishing this precept of divorce, which is plainly moral, for that were against his truth, his promise, and his prophetic office, but knowing how fallaciously they had cited and concealed the particular and natural reason of the law, that they might justify any froward reason of their own, he lets go that sophistry unconvinced, for that had been to teach them otherwise, which his purpose was not. And since they had taken a liberty which the law gave not, he amuses[113] and repels their tempting pride with a perfection of Paradise, which the law required not, not thereby to oblige our performance to that whereunto the law never enjoined the fallen estate of man. For if the first institution must make wedlock, what ever happen, inseparable to us, it must make it also as perfect, as rightly helpful, and as comfortable, as God promised it should be, at least in some degree; otherwise it is not equal or proportionate to the strength of man, that he should be reduced into such indissoluble bonds to his assured misery, if all the other conditions of that covenant be manifestly altered.

Next he saith, *they must be one flesh,* which, when all conjecturing is done, will be found to import no more but only to make legitimate and good the carnal act, which else might seem to have something of pollution in it: and infers thus much over, that the fit union of their souls be such as may even incorporate them to love and amity. But that can never be where no correspondence is of the mind; nay, instead of being one flesh, they will be rather two carcasses chained unnaturally together; or as it may happen, a living soul bound to a dead corpse, a punishment too like that inflicted by the tyrant Mezentius,[114] so little worthy to be received as that remedy of loneliness which God meant for us. Since we know it is not the joining of another body will remove loneliness, but the uniting of another compliable mind; and that it is no blessing but a torment, nay a base and brutish condition to be one flesh, unless where nature can in some measure fix a unity of disposition.[115]

Lastly, Christ himself tells who should not be put asunder, namely, those whom God has joined. A plain solution of this great controversy, if men would but use their eyes; for when is it that God may be said to join: when the parties and their friends consent? No surely, for that may concur to lewdest ends. Or is it when church rites are finished? Neither; for the efficacy of those depends upon the presupposed fitness of either party. Perhaps, after carnal knowledge? Least of all; for that may join persons whom neither law nor nature dares join. It is left, that only then, when the minds are fitly disposed, and enabled to maintain a cheerful conversation, to the solace and love of each other, according as God intended and promised in the very first foundation of matrimony, *I will make him a help meet for him;* for surely what God intended and promised, that only can be thought to be his joining, and not the contrary. So likewise the Apostle witnesses, 1 Corinthians 7.15, that in marriage *God hath called us to peace.* And doubtless in what respect he has called us to marriage, in that also he has joined us. The rest whom either disproportion or deadness of spirit, or something distasteful and averse in the immutable bent of nature renders un-conjugal, error may have joined, but God never joined against the meaning of his own ordinance. And if he joined them not, then is there no power above their own consent to hinder them from un-joining, when they cannot reap the soberest ends of being together in any tolerable sort. Neither can it be said properly that such twain were ever divorced, but only parted from each other, as two persons un-conjunctive and un-marriable together. But if, whom God has made a fit help, forwardness or private injuries has made unfit, that being the secret of marriage God can better judge than man, neither is man indeed fit or able to decide this matter; however it be, undoubtedly a peaceful divorce is a less evil, and less in scandal than a hateful hardhearted and destructive continuance of marriage in the judgment of Moses and of Christ, that justifies him in choosing the less evil, which if it were an honest and civil prudence in the law, what is there in the Gospel forbidding such a kind of legal wisdom, though we should admit the common expositors.[116]

Having thus unfolded those ambiguous reasons, with which Christ, as his wont was, gave to the Pharisees that came to sound him, such an answer as they deserved, it will not be uneasy[117] to explain the sentence itself that now follows: *Whosoever shall put away his wife, except it be for fornication, and shall marry another, commiteth adultery.*[118] First, therefore, I will set down what is observed by Grotius upon this point, a man of general learning. Next I produce what mine own thoughts gave me, before I had seen his annotations. Origen, says he, notes that Christ named adultery rather as one example of other like cases, than as one only exception. And that it is frequent, not only in human but in divine laws, to express one kind of fact, whereby other causes of like nature may have the like plea: as Exodus 2.1.18, 19, 20, 26, Deuteronomy 19.5; and from the maxims of civil law he shows that even in sharpest penal laws the same reason has the same right, and in gentler laws that from like causes to like the law interprets rightly. But it may be objected, he says, that nothing destroys the end of wedlock so much as adultery. To which he answers, that marriage was not ordained only for copulation, but for mutual help and comfort of life; and if we mark diligently the nature of our Savior's commands, we shall find that both their beginning and their end consists in charity: whose will is that we should so be good to others, as that we be not cruel to our selves. And hence it appears why Mark, and Luke, and St. Paul to the Corinthians mentioning this precept of Christ, add no exception: because exceptions that arise from natural equity are included silently under general terms. It would be considered therefore whether the same equity may not have place in other cases less frequent. Thus far he. From hence, is what I add: first, that this saying of Christ, as it is usually expounded, can be no law at all, that man for no cause should separate but for adultery, except it be a supernatural law, not binding us as we now are. Had it been the law of nature, either the Jews, or some other wise and civil nation would have pressed it; or let it be so, yet that law Deuteronomy 24.1 (whereby a man has leave to part, seeing that for just and natural cause discovered he cannot love) is a law more ancient and deeper engraved in blameless nature than the other. Therefore the inspired lawgiver Moses took care that this should be specified and allowed; the other he let vanish in silence, not once repeated in the volume of his law, even as the reason of it vanished with Paradise. Secondly, this can be no new command, for the Gospel enjoins no new morality, save only the infinite enlargement of charity, which in this respect is called the *new commandment* by St. John, as being the accomplishment of every command.[119] Thirdly, it is no command of perfection further than it partakes of charity, which is *the bond of perfection*.[120] Those commands therefore which compel us to self cruelty above our strength, so hardly will help forward to perfection, that they hinder and set backward in all the common rudiments of Christianity, as was proven. It being thus clear that the words of Christ can be no kind of command, as they are vulgarly taken, we shall now see in what sense they may be a command, and that an excellent one, the same with that of Moses, and no other. Moses had granted that only for a natural annoyance, defect, or dislike, whether in body or mind (for so the Hebrew words plainly note) which a man could not force himself to live with, he might give a bill of divorce, thereby forbidding any other cause wherein amendment or reconciliation might have place. This law the Pharisees depraving, extended to any slight contentious cause whatsoever. Christ therefore seeing where they halted,[121] urges the negative part of that law, which is necessarily understood (for the determinate permission of Moses binds them from further license) and checking their supercilious drift, declares that no accidental, temporary, or reconcilable offence, except fornication, can justify a divorce. He touches not here those natural and perpetual hindrances of society, which are not to be removed: for such, as they are aptest to cause an unchangeable offence, so are they not capable of reconcilement because not of amendment.[122] Thus is Moses' law here solidly confirmed, and those causes which he permitted, not a jot gainsaid. And that this is the true meaning of this place I prove also by no less an author than St. Paul himself, I Corinthians 7.10,11, upon which text interpreters agree that the Apostle only repeats the precept of Christ: where while he speaks of *the wife's reconcilement to her husband,* he puts it out of controversy, that our Savior meant only matters of strife and reconcilement; of which sort he would not that any difference should be the occasion of divorce, except fornication.[123]

But because we know that Christ never gave a judicial law, and that the word *fornication* is variously significant in Scripture, it will be much right done to our Savior's words, to consider diligently whether it be meant here that nothing but actual fornication, proven by witness, can warrant a divorce, for so our canon law judges. Nevertheless, as I find that Grotius on this place has observed, the Christian emperors, Theodosius the second and Justinian, men of high wisdom and reputed piety, decreed it to be a divorcive fornication if the wife attempted either against the knowledge, or obstinately against the will of her husband, such things as gave open suspicion of adultery: as the willful haunting of feasts, and invitations with men not of her near kindred, the lying forth of her house without probable cause, the frequenting of theaters against her husband's mind, her endeavor to prevent or destroy conception. Hence that of Jerome, *Where fornication is suspected, the wife may lawfully be divorced;* not that every motion of a jealous mind should be regarded, but that it should not be exacted to prove all things by the visibility of law witnessing, or else to hoodwink the mind. For the law is not able to judge of these things but by the rule of equity, and by permitting a wise man to walk the middle way of a prudent circumspection, neither wretchedly jealous, nor stupidly and tamely patient. To this purpose has Grotius in his notes. He shows also that fornication is taken in Scripture for such a continual headstrong behavior, as tends to plain contempt of the husband: and proves it out of Judges 19.2, where the Levite's wife is said to have played the whore against him; which Josephus and the Septuagint, with the Chaldean, interpret only of stubbornness and rebellion against her husband: and to this I add that Kimchi and the two other Rabbis who gloss the text, are in the same opinion. Ben Gersom reasons, that had it been whoredom, a Jew and a Levite would have disdained to fetch her again. And this I shall contribute, that had it been whoredom, she would have chosen any other place to run to, than to her father's house, it being so infamous for an Hebrew woman to play the harlot, and so opprobrious to the parents. Fornication then in this place of the Judges is understood for stubborn disobedience against the husband, and not for adultery. A sin of that sudden activity as to be already committed, when no more is done, but only looked unchastely: which yet I should be loath to judge worthy a divorce, though in our Savior's language it be called adultery.[124] Nevertheless when palpable and frequent signs are given, the law of God, Numbers 5, so far gave way to the jealousy of a man as that the woman set before the sanctuary with her head uncovered was adjured by the priest to swear whether she were false or no, and constrained to drink that *bitter water* with an undoubted *curse of rottenness and tympany*[125] to follow, unless she were innocent.[126] And the jealous man had not been guiltless before God, as seems by the last verse, if having such a suspicion in his head, he should neglect this trial; which if to this day it be not to be used, or be thought as uncertain of effect, as our antiquated law of Ordalium,[127] yet all equity will judge that many adulterous demeanors which are of lewd suspicion and example may be held sufficient to incur a divorce, though the act itself has not been proven. And seeing the generosity of our nation is so as to account no reproach more abominable than to be nicknamed the husband of an adulteress, that our law should not be as ample as the law of God to vindicate a man from that ignoble sufferance is our barbarous un-skillfulness, not considering that the law should be exasperated[128] according to our estimation of the injury. And if it must be suffered 'til the act be visibly proven, Solomon himself whose judgment will be granted to surpass the acuteness of any canonist, confesses, Proverbs 30.19.20, that for the act of adultery, it is as difficult to be found as the *track of an eagle in the air, or the way of a ship in the sea:* so that a man may be put to unmanly indignities, ere it be found out. This therefore may be enough to inform us, that divorcive adultery is not limited by our Savior to the utmost act, and that to be attested always by eye witness, but may be extended also to divers obvious actions, which either plainly lead to adultery, or give such presumption, whereby sensible men may suspect the deed to be already done. And this the rather may be thought, in that our Savior chose to use the word *fornication,* which word is found to signify other matrimonial transgressions of main breach to that covenant besides actual adultery.[129] Thus at length we see both by this and by other places, that there is scarce any one saying in the Gospel, but must be read with limitations and distinctions to be rightly understood; for Christ gives no full comments or continued discourses, but scatters the heavenly grain of his doctrine like pearl here and there, which requires a skillful and laborious gatherer, who must compare the words he finds with other precepts, with the end of every ordinance, and with the general *analogy* of evangelic doctrine: otherwise many particular sayings would be but strange repugnant riddles; and the Church would offend in granting divorce for frigidity, which is not here excepted with adultery, but by them added. And this was it undoubtedly which gave reason to St. Paul of his own authority, as he professes, and without command from the Lord, to enlarge the seeming construction of those places in the Gospel, by adding a case wherein a person deserted, which is something less than divorced, may lawfully marry again. And having declared his opinion in one case, he leaves a further liberty for Christian prudence to determine in cases of like importance, using words so plain as are not to be shifted off, *that a brother or a sister is not under bondage in such cases,* adding also, that *God hath called us to peace* in marriage. Now if it be plain that a Christian may be brought into unworthy *bondage,* and his religious *peace* not only interrupted now and then, but perpetually and finally hindered in wedlock by mis-yoking with a diversity of nature as well as of religion, the reasons of St. Paul cannot be made special to that one case of infidelity, but are of equal moment to a divorce, wherever Christian liberty and peace are without fault equally obstructed. That the ordinance which God gave to our comfort, may not be pinned upon us to our undeserved thralldom; to be cooped up as it were in mockery of wedlock, to a perpetual betrothed loneliness and discontent, if nothing worse ensue. There being nothing else of marriage left between such, but a displeasing and forced remedy against the sting of a brute desire: which fleshly accustoming[130] without the soul's union and commixture of intellectual delight, as it is rather a soiling than a fulfilling of marriage rites, so is it enough to debase the mettle of a generous spirit, and sinks him to a low and vulgar pitch of endeavor in all his actions, or, which is worse, leaves him in a despairing plight of abject and hardened thoughts: which condition rather than a good man should fall into, a man useful in the service of God and mankind, Christ himself has taught us to dispense with the most sacred ordinance of his worship, even for a bodily healing to dispense with that holy and speculative rest of Sabbath, much more than with the erroneous observance of an ill-knotted marriage, for the sustaining of an overcharged faith and perseverance.

And though bad causes would take license by this pretext, if that cannot be remedied, upon their conscience be it, who shall so do. This was that hardness of heart, and abuse of a good law which Moses was content to suffer, rather than good men should not have it at all to use needfully. And he who to run after one lost sheep left ninety-nine of his own flock at random in the wilderness,[131] would little perplex his thought for the obduring[132] of nine hundred and ninety such as will daily take worse liberties, whether they have permission or not. To conclude, as without charity God has given no commandment to men, so without it, neither can men rightly believe any commandment given. For every act of true faith, as well that whereby we believe the law, as that whereby we endeavor the law, is wrought in us by charity, according to that in the divine hymn of St. Paul, I Corinthians 13, *Charity believeth all things:* not as if she were so credulous, which is the exposition hitherto current, for that were a trivial praise; but to teach us that charity is the high governess of our belief, and that we cannot safely assent to any precept written in the Bible, but as charity commends it to us. Which agrees with that of the same Apostle to the Ephesians 4.14.15, where he tells us that the way to get a sure undoubted knowledge of things is to hold that for truth which accords most with charity. Whose unerring guidance and conduct having followed as a lodestar with all diligence and fidelity in this question, I trust, through the help of that illuminating spirit which has favored me, to have done no every day's work in asserting after many ages the words of Christ with other Scriptures of great concernment from burdensome remorseless obscurity, tangled with manifold repugnancies, to their native luster and consent between each other: hereby also dissolving tedious and Gordian difficulties which have hitherto molested the Church of God, and are now decided, not with the sword of Alexander, but with the immaculate hands of charity, to the unspeakable good of Christendom.[133] And let the extreme literalist sit down now and revolve[134] whether this in all necessity be not the due result of our Savior's words; or if he persist to be otherwise opinioned, let him well advise, lest thinking to grip fast the Gospel, he be found instead with the canon law in his fist: whose boisterous[135] edicts tyrannizing the blessed ordinance of marriage into the quality of a most unnatural and un-Christian yoke, have given the flesh this advantage to hate it, and turn aside, oft-times unwillingly, to all dissolute uncleanness, even 'til punishment itself is weary, and overcome by the incredible frequency of trading lust and uncontrolled adulteries. Yet men whose creed is custom, I doubt not but will be still endeavoring to hide the sloth of their own timorous capacities with this pretext, that for all this it is better to endure with patience and silence this affliction which God has sent. And I agree it is true, if this were exhorted and not enjoined; but withal it will be wisely done to be as sure as may be, that what man's iniquity has laid on, be not imputed to God's sending, lest under the color of an affected patience we detain ourselves at the gulf's mouth of many hideous temptations, not to be withstood without proper gifts, which, as

Perkins well notes, God gives not ordinarily, no not to most earnest prayers.[136] Therefore we pray, *lead us not into temptation,* a vain prayer, if having led our selves thither, we love to stay in that perilous condition. God sends remedies as well as evils; under which he who lies and groans, that may lawfully acquit himself, is accessory to his own ruin: nor will it excuse him, though he suffer through a sluggish fearfulness to search thoroughly what is lawful, for fear of disquieting the secure falsity of an old opinion. Who doubts not but that it may be piously said, to him who would dismiss frigidity, bear your trial, take it, as if God would have you live this life of continence. If he exhort this, I hear him as an angel, though he speak without warrant; but if he would compel me, I know him for Satan. To him who divorces an adulteress, piety might say: pardon her; you may show much mercy, you may win a soul. Yet the law both of God and man leaves it freely to him. For God loves not to plow out the heart of our endeavors with over-hard and sad tasks. God delights not to make a drudge of virtue, whose actions must be all elective and unconstrained. Forced virtue is as a bolt overshot: it goes neither forward nor backward, and does no good as it stands.[137] Seeing therefore that neither Scripture nor reason has laid this unjust austerity upon divorce, we may resolve that nothing else has wrought it, but that letter-bound servility of the canon doctors, supposing marriage to be a sacrament, and out of the art they have to lay unnecessary burdens upon all men, to make a fair show in the fleshly observance of matrimony, though peace and love with all other conjugal respects fare never so ill. And indeed the Papists who are the strictest forbidders of divorce, are the easiest libertines to admit of grossest uncleanness; as if they had a design by making wedlock a supportless[138] yoke, to violate it most, under color of preserving it most inviolable: and withal delighting, as their mystery[139] is, to make men the day-laborers of their own affliction, as if there were such a scarcity of miseries from abroad that we should be made to melt our choicest home blessings, and coin them into crosses, for want whereby to hold commerce with patience. If any therefore who shall happen to read this discourse, has been through misadventure ill engaged in this contracted evil here complained of, and finds the fits and workings of a high impatience frequently upon him, of all those wild words which men in misery think to ease themselves by uttering, let him not open his lips against the providence of Heaven, or tax the ways of God and his divine truth: for they are equal, easy, and not burdensome; nor do they ever cross the just and reasonable desires of men, nor involve this our portion of mortal life, into a necessity of sadness and malcontent, by laws commanding over the irreducible *antipathies* of nature sooner or later found, but allow us to remedy and shake off those evils into which human error has led us through the midst of our best intentions, and to support our incident extremities by that authentic precept of sovereign charity, whose grand commission is to do and to dispose over all the ordinances of God to man that love and truth may advance each other to everlasting. While we literally superstitious through customary faintness of heart, not venturing to pierce with our free thoughts into the full latitude of nature and religion, abandon ourselves to serve under the tyranny of usurped opinions, suffering those ordinances which were allotted to our solace and reviving, to trample over us and hale us into a multitude of sorrows which God never meant us. And where he set us in a fair allowance of way, with honest liberty and prudence to our guard, we never leave subtlizing and casuisting[140] until we have straightened and pared that liberal path into a razor's edge to walk on, between a precipice of unnecessary mischief on either side; and starting at every false alarm, we do not know which way to set a foot forward with manly confidence and Christian resolution, through the confused ringing in our ears of *panic* scruples and amazements.

Another act of papal encroachment it was, to pluck the power and arbitrament of divorce from the master of family, into whose hands God and the law of all nations had put it, and Christ so left it, preaching only to the conscience, and not authorizing a judicial court to toss about and divulge the unaccountable and secret reasons of disaffection between man and wife, as a thing most improperly answerable to any such kind of trial. But the Popes of Rome, perceiving the great revenue and high authority it would give them even over princes to have the judging and deciding of such a main consequence in the life of man as was divorce, wrought so upon the superstition of those ages, as to divest them of that right which God from the beginning had entrusted to the husband: by which means they subjected that ancient and naturally domestic prerogative to an external and unbefitting judicature. For although differences in divorce about dowries, jointures, and the like, besides the punishing of adultery, ought not to pass without referring, if need be, to the magistrate; yet for him to interpose his jurisdictive power upon the inward and irremediable disposition of man, to command love and *sympathy*, to forbid dislike against the guiltless instinct of nature, is not within the province of any law to reach, and were indeed an un-commodious rudeness, not a just power.[141] For if nature's resistless sway in love or hate be once compelled, it grows careless of itself, vicious, useless to friend, unserviceable and spiritless to the commonwealth. Which Moses rightly foresaw, and all wise lawgivers that ever knew man, what kind of creature he was. The Parliament also and clergy of England were not ignorant of this, when they consented that Harry the eighth might put away his Queen Anne of Cleves,[142] whom he could not like after he had been wedded half a year; unless it were that contrary to the proverb, they made a necessity of that which might have been a virtue in them to do.[143] For even the freedom and eminence of man's creation gives him to be a law in this matter to himself, being the head of the other sex which was made for him: whom therefore though he ought not to injure, yet neither should he be forced to retain in society to his own overthrow, nor to hear any judge therein above himself. It being also an unseemly affront to the sequestered and veiled modesty of that sex, to have her unpleasantness and other concealments bandied up and down, and aggravated in open court by those hired masters of tongue-fence.[144] Such uncomely exigencies it befell no less a majesty than Henry the eighth to be reduced to; who finding just reason in his conscience to forgo his brother's wife, after many indignities of being deluded, and made a boy of by those his two *cardinal* judges, was constrained at last for want of other proof that she had been carnally known by Prince Arthur, even to uncover the nakedness of that virtuous lady, and to recite openly the obscene evidence of his brother's chamberlain.[145] Yet it pleased God to make him see all the tyranny of Rome, by discovering this which they exercised over divorce; and to make him the beginner of a reformation to this whole Kingdom by first asserting into his *familiary*[146] power the right of just divorce. It is true, an adulteress cannot be shamed enough by any public proceeding: but that woman whose honor is not appeached[147] is less injured by a silent dismissal, being otherwise not illiberally dealt with, than to endure a clamoring debate of utter-less things, in a business of that civil secrecy and difficult discerning, as not to be over-much questioned by nearest friends. Which drew that answer from the greatest and worthiest Roman of his time, Paulus Emilius, being demanded why he would put away his wife for no visible reason, *This Shoe,* saith he, and held it out on his foot, *is a neat shoe, a new shoe, and yet none of ye know where it wrings me:*[148] much less by the unfamiliar cognizance of a feed gamester[149] can such a private difference be examined, neither ought it.

Lastly, all law is for some good that may be frequently attained without the admixture of a worse inconvenience; but the law forbidding divorce never attains to any good end of such prohibition, but rather multiplies evil. If it aim at the establishment of matrimony, we know that cannot thrive under a loathed and forced yoke, but is daily violated. If it seek to prevent the sin of divorcing, that lies not in the law to prevent; for he that would divorce and marry again, but for the law, has in the sight of God done it already. Civil or political sin it never was, neither in Jew nor Gentile, nor by any judicial intendment of Christ, only culpable as it transgresses the allowance of Moses in the inward man, which not any law but conscience only can evince.[150] The law can only look whether it be an injury to the divorced, which in truth it can be none, as a mere separation; for if she consent, wherein has the law to right her? Or consent not: then is it either just, and so deserved; or if unjust, such in all likelihood was the divorcer, and to part from an unjust man is a happiness, and no injury to be lamented. But suppose it be an injury, the law is not able to amend it, unless she think it other than a miserable redress to return back from whence she was expelled, or but entreated to be gone, or else to live apart still married without marriage, a married widow. Last, if it be to chasten the divorcer, what law punishes a deed which is not moral, but natural, a deed which cannot certainly be found to be an injury, or how can it be punished by prohibiting the divorce, but that the innocent must equally partake? So that we see the law can to no rational purpose forbid divorce, it can only take care that the conditions of divorce be not injurious.[151] But what? Shall then the disposal of that power return again to the master of family? Wherefore not? Since God there put it, and the presumptuous canon thence bereft it.[152] This only must be provided, that the ancient manner be observed in presence of the minister and other grave selected elders; who after they shall have admonished and pressed upon him the words of our Savior, and he shall have protested in the faith of the eternal Gospel, and the hope he has of happy resurrection, that otherwise than thus he cannot do, and thinks himself, and this his case not contained in that prohibition of divorce which Christ pronounced, the matter not being of malice, but of nature, and so not capable of reconciling, to constrain him further were to un-christen him, to unman him, to throw the mountain of Sinai upon him,[153] with the weight of the whole law to boot, flat against the liberty and essence of the Gospel, and yet nothing available either to the sanctity of marriage, the good of husband, wife, or children, nothing profitable either to Church or commonwealth. But this would bring in confusion. Be of good cheer, it would not: it wrought so little disorder among the Jews, that from Moses until after the captivity, not one of the prophets thought it worth rebuking; for that of Malachi well looked into, will appear to be, not against divorcing, but rather against keeping strange concubines, to the vexation of their Hebrew wives.[154] If therefore we Christians may be thought as good and tractable as the Jews were, and certainly the prohibitionists of divorce presume us to be better, then less confusion is to be feared for this among us, than was among them. If we be worse, or but as bad, which lamentable examples confirm we are, then have we more, or at least as much need of this permitted law, as they to whom God expressly gave it under a harsher covenant. Let not therefore the frailty of man go on thus inventing needless troubles to itself, to groan under the false imagination of a strictness never imposed from above, enjoining that for duty which is an impossible and vain overreaching. *Be not righteous overmuch,* is the counsel of Ecclesiastes, *why shouldst thou destroy thyself?*[155] Let us not be thus over-curious to strain at *atoms,*[156] and yet to stop every vent and cranny of permissive liberty; lest nature wanting those needful pores and breathing places which God has not debarred our weakness, either suddenly break out into some wide rupture of open vice and frantic heresy, or else inwardly fester with repining and blasphemous thoughts, under an unreasonable and fruitless rigor of unwarranted law. Against which evils nothing can more beseem the religion of the Church, or the wisdom of the State, than to consider timely and provide. And in so doing, let them not doubt but they shall vindicate the mis-reputed honor of God and his great lawgiver, by suffering him to give his own laws according to the condition of man's nature best known to him, without the insufferable imputation of dispensing legally with many ages of ratified adultery. They shall recover the mis-attended words of Christ to the sincerity of their true sense from manifold contradictions, and shall open them with the key of charity. Many helpless Christians they shall raise from the depth of sadness and distress, utterly unfitted, as they are, to serve God or man: many they shall reclaim from obscure and giddy sects, many regain from dissolute and brutish license, many from desperate hardness, if ever that were justly pleaded. They shall set free many daughters of Israel, not wanting much of her sad plight *whom Satan had bound eighteen years.*[157] Man they shall restore to his just dignity, and prerogative in nature, preferring the soul's free peace before the promiscuous draining of a carnal rage. Marriage from a perilous hazard and snare, they shall reduce to be a more certain haven and retirement of happy society; when they shall judge according to God and Moses, and how not then according to Christ? When they shall judge it more wisdom and goodness to break that covenant seemingly and keep it really, than by compulsion of law to keep it seemingly and by compulsion of blameless nature to break it really, at least if it were ever truly joined. The vigor of discipline they may then turn with better success upon the prostitute looseness of the times, when men finding in themselves the infirmities of former ages, shall not be constrained above the gift of God in them, to unprofitable and impossible observances never required from the civilest, the wisest, the holiest nations, whose other excellencies in moral virtue they never yet could equal. Last of all, to those whose mind still is to maintain textual restrictions, whereof the bare sound cannot consist sometimes with humanity, much less with charity, I would ever answer by putting them in remembrance of a command above all commands, which they seem to have forgot, and who spoke it; in comparison whereof this, which they so exalt, is but a petty and subordinate precept. *Let them go* therefore with whom I am loath to couple them, yet they will needs run into the same blindness with the Pharisees, *let them go* therefore and consider well what this lesson means, *I will have mercy and not sacrifice;*[158] for on that *saying all the law and prophets depend,*[159] much more the Gospel whose end and excellence is mercy and peace. Or if they cannot learn that, how will they hear this, which yet I shall not doubt to leave with them as a conclusion: that God the Son has put all other things under his own feet; but his commandments he has left all under the feet of charity.[160]

The end.

***Omitted pa.* 19. *lin.* 28.** Whom thus to shut up and immure together, the one with a mis-chosen mate, the other in a mistaken calling, is not a course, & etc.[161]

***Omitted pa.* 24. *lin.* 22.** Uncertain good. This only text not to be matched again throughout the whole Scripture: whereby God in his perfect law should seem to have granted to the hard hearts of his holy people under his own hand a civil immunity and free charter to live and die in a long successive adultery, under a covenant of works, 'til the Messiah, and then that indulgent permission to be strictly denied by a covenant of grace; besides the incoherence of such a doctrine cannot, must not be thus interpreted to the raising of a paradox never known until then, only hanging by the twined thread of one doubtful Scripture, against so many other rules and leading principles of religion, of justice, and purity of life. For what could be granted more either to the fear or to the lust of any tyrant or politician[162] than this authority of Moses thus expounded, which opens him a way at will to dam up justice, and not only to admit of any Romish or Austrian dispenses,[163] but to enact a statute of that which he dares not seem to approve, even to legitimate vice, to make sin itself a free citizen of the commonwealth, pretending only these or these plausible reasons? And well he might, all the while that Moses shall be alleged to have done as much without showing any reason at all. Yet this could not enter into the heart of David, Psalm 94.20, how any such authority as endeavors *to fashion wickedness by law,* should derive itself from God. And Isaiah lays *woe upon them that decree unrighteous decrees,* 10.1. Now which of these two is the better lawgiver, and which deserves most a woe: he that gives out an edict singly unjust, or he that confirms to generations a fixed and unmolested impunity of that which is not only held to be unjust, but also unclean, and both in a high degree, not only as they themselves affirm, an injurious expulsion of one wife, but also an unclean freedom by more than a patent to wed another adulterously? How can we therefore with safety thus dangerously confine the free simplicity of our Savior's meaning to that which merely amounts from so many letters, when therefore it can consist neither with his former and cautionary words, nor with other more pure and holy principles, nor finally with the scope of charity? & etc.[164]

The Doctrine & Discipline of Divorce

Restored to the good of both Sexes, From the bondage of canon law, and other mistakes, to the true meaning of Scripture in the Law and Gospel compared.[1] Wherein also are set down the bad consequences of abolishing or condemning of Sin, that which the Law of God allows, and Christ abolished not.[2] Now the second time revised and much augmented, In Two books:[3] To the Parliament of *England* with the Assembly. The Author *J. M.*

Matth. 13. 52. *Every Scribe instructed to the Kingdome of Heaven is like the Master of a house which bringeth out of his treasury things new and old.*

Prov. 18. 13. *He that answereth a matter before he heareth it, it is folly and shame unto him.*[4]

***London,* Imprinted in the year 1644.**

TO THE PARLIAMENT OF ENGLAND, with the Assembly.[5]

If it were seriously asked, and it would be no untimely question, renowned Parliament, select Assembly, who of all teachers and masters that have ever taught hath drawn the most disciples after him, both in religion and in manners, it might be not untruly answered, 'Custom.' Though virtue be commended for the most persuasive in her theory, and conscience in the plain demonstration of the spirit finds most evincing, yet whether it be the secret of divine will, or the original blindness we are born in, so it happens for the most part that custom still is silently received for the best instructor. Except it be, because the method is so glib and easy, in some manner like to that vision of Ezekiel,[6] rolling up her sudden book of implicit knowledge, for him that will, to take and swallow down at pleasure; which proving but of bad nourishment in the concoction[7] as it was heedless in the devouring, puffs up unhealthily a certain big face of pretended learning, mistaken among credulous men for the wholesome habit of soundness and good constitution, but is indeed no other than that swollen visage of counterfeit knowledge and literature, which not only in private mars our education, but also in public is the common climber into every chair, where either religion is preached, or law reported, filling each estate of life and profession with abject and servile principles, depressing the high and heaven-born spirit of man far beneath the condition wherein either God created him or sin hath sunk him. To pursue the allegory, Custom being but a mere face, as Echo is a mere voice, rests not in her unaccomplishment until by secret inclination she incorporate herself with Error, who being a blind and serpentine body without a head,[8] willingly accepts what he wants and supplies what her incompleteness went seeking. Hence it is, that Error supports Custom, Custom countenances Error; and these two between them would persecute and chase away all truth and solid wisdom out of human life, were it not that God, rather than man, once in many ages, calls together the prudent and religious counsels of men, deputed to repress the encroachments and to work off the inveterate blots and obscurities wrought upon our minds by the subtle insinuating of Error and Custom; who with the numerous and vulgar train of their followers make it their chief design to envy and cry down the industry of free reasoning, under the terms of humour and innovation,[9] as if the womb of teeming Truth were to be closed up, if she presume to bring forth aught that sorts not with their unchewed notions and suppositions. Against which notorious injury and abuse of man's free soul to testify and oppose the utmost that study and true labour can attain, heretofore the incitement of men reputed grave hath led me among others; and now the duty and the right of an instructed Christian calls me, through the chance of good or evil report, to be the sole advocate of a discountenanced truth: a high enterprise, Lords and Commons, a high enterprise and a hard, and such as every 7th son of a 7th son[10] does not venture on. Nor have I amidst the clamour of so much envy and impertinence whither to appeal but to the concourse of so much piety and wisdom here assembled, bringing in my hands an ancient and most necessary, most charitable, and yet most injured statute of Moses;[11] not repealed ever by him who only had the authority, but thrown aside with much inconsiderate neglect, under the rubbish of canonical ignorance, as once the whole law was by some such like conveyance in Josiah's time.[12] And he who shall endeavour the amendment of any old neglected grievance in Church or State, or in the daily course of life, if he be gifted with abilities of mind that may raise him to so high an undertaking, I grant he hath already much whereof not to repent him; yet let me aread him, not to be the foreman of any misjudged opinion, unless his resolutions be firmly seated in a square and constant mind, not conscious to itself of any deserved blame, and regardless of ungrounded suspicions. For this let him be sure he shall be boarded presently by the ruder sort, but not by discreet and well-nurtured men, with a thousand idle descants and surmises. Who when they cannot confute the least joint or sinew of any passage in the book; yet God forbid that truth should be truth, because they have a boisterous conceit of some pretences in the writer. But were they not more busy and inquisitive than the Apostle commends, they would hear him at least, *rejoicing so the truth be preached, whether of envy or other pretence whatsoever:*[13] for Truth is as impossible to be soiled by any outward touch, as the sunbeam; though this ill hap wait on her nativity, that she never comes into the world but like a bastard, to the ignominy of him that brought her forth; 'til Time, the midwife rather than the mother of Truth, have washed and salted the infant, declared her legitimate, and churched the father of his young Minerva, from the needless causes of his purgation.[14] Your selves can best witness this, worthy patriots,[15] and better will, no doubt, hereafter: for who among ye of the foremost that have travailed in her behalf to the good of Church or State, hath not been often traduced to be the agent of his own by-ends,[16] under pretext of reformation? So much the more I shall not be unjust to hope, that however infamy or envy may work in other men to do her fretful will against this discourse, yet that the experience of your own uprightness misinterpreted will put ye in mind to give it free audience and generous construction. What though the brood of Belial, the draff of men, to whom no liberty is pleasing but unbridled and vagabond lust without pale or partition, will laugh broad perhaps, to see so great a strength of Scripture mustering up in favour, as they suppose, of their debaucheries; they will know better when they shall hence learn that honest liberty is the greatest foe to dishonest licence.[17] And what though others, out of a waterish and queasy conscience, because ever crazy and never yet found, will rail and fancy to themselves that injury and licence is the best of this book? Did not the distemper of their own stomachs affect them with a dizzy megrim,[18] they would soon tie up their tongues and discern themselves, like that Assyrian Blasphemer,[19] all this while reproaching not man but the Almighty, the Holy One of Israel, whom they do not deny to have belawgiven[20] his own sacred people with this very allowance which they now call injury and licence, and dare cry shame on, and will do yet a while, 'til they get a little cordial sobriety to settle their qualming zeal. But this question concerns not us perhaps: indeed man's disposition, though prone to search after vain curiosities, yet when points of difficulty are to be discussed, appertaining to the removal of unreasonable wrong and burden from the perplexed life of our brother, it is incredible how cold, how dull, and far from all fellow-feeling we are, without the spur of self-concernment. Yet if the wisdom, the justice, the purity of God be to be cleared from foulest imputations, which are not yet avoided; if charity be not to be degraded and trodden down under a civil ordinance; if matrimony be not to be advanced like that exalted perdition written of to the Thessalonians, *above all that is called God,* or goodness, nay against them both;[21] then I dare affirm there will be found in the contents of this book that which may concern us all. You it concerns chiefly, Worthies in Parliament, on whom, as on our deliverers, all our grievances and cares, by the merit of your eminence and fortitude, are devolved. Me it concerns next, having with much labour and faithful diligence first found out, or at least with a fearless and communicative candor first published to the manifest good of Christendom, that which calling to witness every thing mortal and immortal I believe unfeignedly to be true. Let not other men think their conscience bound to search continually after truth, to pray for enlightening from above, to publish what they think they have so obtained, and debar me from conceiving my self tied by the same duties. Ye have now, doubtless, by the favour and appointment of God, ye have now in your hands a great and populous nation to reform; from what corruption, what blindness in religion, ye know well; in what a degenerate and fallen spirit from the apprehension of native liberty, and true manliness, I am sure ye find; with what unbounded licence rushing to whoredoms and adulteries, needs not long enquiry: insomuch that the fears which men have of too strict a discipline, perhaps exceed the hopes that can be in other, of ever introducing it with any great success. What if I should tell ye now of dispensations and indulgences, to give a little the reins, to let them play and nibble with the bait a while, a people as hard of heart as that Egyptian colony that went to Canaan.[22] This is the common doctrine that adulterous and injurious divorces were not connived only, but with eye open allowed of old for hardness of heart. But that opinion, I trust, by then this following argument hath been well read, will be left for one of the mysteries of an indulgent Antichrist, to farm out incest by, and those his other tributary pollutions.[23] What middle way can be taken, then, may some interrupt, if we must neither turn to the right, nor to the left, and that the people hate to be reformed? Mark then, Judges and Law-givers, and ye whose office it is to be our teachers, for I will utter now a doctrine, if ever any other, though neglected or not understood, yet of great and powerful importance to the governing of mankind. He who wisely would restrain the reasonable soul of man within due bounds must first himself know perfectly how far the territory and dominion extends of just and honest liberty. As little must he offer to bind that which God hath loosened, as to loosen that which he hath bound. The ignorance and mistake of this high point hath heaped up one huge half of all the misery that hath been since Adam. In the Gospel[24] we shall read a supercilious crew of masters, whose holiness, or rather whose evil eye, grieving that God should be so facile to man, was to set straiter[25] limits to obedience than God had set, to enslave the dignity of man, to put a garrison upon his neck of empty and over-dignified precepts; and we shall read our Savior never more grieved and troubled than to meet with such a peevish madness among men against their own freedom. How can we expect him to be less offended with us, when much of the same folly shall be found yet remaining where it least ought, to the perishing of thousands? The greatest burden in the world is superstition, not only of ceremonies in the Church but of imaginary and scarecrow sins at home. What greater weakening, what more subtle stratagem against our Christian warfare, when besides the gross body of real transgressions to encounter, we shall be terrified by a vain and shadowy menacing of faults that are not: when things indifferent[26] shall be set to over-front[27] us under the banners of sin, what wonder if we be routed, and by this art of our Adversary,[28] fall into the subjection of worst and deadliest offences? The superstition of the Papist is, *touch not, taste not,*[29] when God bids both; and ours is, *part not, separate not,* when God and charity both permits and commands. *Let all your things be done with charity,* saith St. Paul;[30] and his Master saith, *She is the fulfilling of the Law.*[31] Yet now a civil, an indifferent, a sometime dissuaded law of Marriage, must be forced upon us to fulfill, not only without charity but against her. No place in Heaven or Earth, except Hell, where charity may not enter: yet marriage, the ordinance of our solace and contentment, the remedy of our loneliness, will not admit now either of charity or mercy to come in and mediate, or pacify the fierceness of this gentle ordinance, the unremedied loneliness of this remedy. Advise ye well, supreme Senate, if charity be thus excluded and expulsed, how ye will defend the untainted honour of your own actions and proceedings. He who marries, intends as little to conspire his own ruin as he that swears allegiance: and as a whole people is in proportion to an ill government, so is one man to an ill marriage. If they, against any authority, covenant, or statute, may by the sovereign edict of charity save not only their lives but honest liberties from unworthy bondage, as well may he against any private covenant, which he never entered to his mischief, redeem himself from unsupportable disturbances to honest peace and just contentment. And much the rather, for that to resist the highest magistrate though tyrannizing, God never gave us express allowance, only he gave us reason, charity, nature, and good example to bear us out; but in this economical[32] misfortune thus to demean our selves, besides the warrant of those four great directors, which doth as justly belong hither, we have an express law of God, and such a law as whereof our Savior with a solemn threat forbid the abrogating.[33] For no effect of tyranny can sit more heavy on the commonwealth than this household unhappiness on the family. And farewell all hope of true reformation in the state, while such an evil as this lies undiscerned or unregarded in the house. On the redress whereof depends not only the spiritful and orderly life of our grown men but the willing and careful education of our children. Let this therefore be new examined, this tenure and freehold of mankind, this native and domestic charter given us by a greater Lord than that Saxon King the Confessor.[34] Let the statutes of God be turned over, be scanned anew, and considered not altogether by the narrow intellectuals of quotationists and commonplaces, but (as was the ancient right of Councils) by men of what liberal profession soever, of eminent spirit and breeding, joined with a diffuse and various knowledge of divine and human things; able to balance and define good and evil, right and wrong, throughout every state of life; able to show us the ways of the Lord straight and faithful as they are, not full of cranks and contradictions and pit-falling dispenses, but with divine insight and benignity measured out to the proportion of each mind and spirit, each temper and disposition created so different each from other, and yet by the skill of wise conducting, all to become uniform in virtue. To expedite these knots were worthy a learned and memorable synod; while our enemies expect to see the expectation of the Church tired out with dependencies and independencies how they will compound, and in what calends.[35] Doubt not, worthy Senators, to vindicate the sacred honour and judgment of Moses your predecessor, from the shallow commenting of scholastics and canonists. Doubt not after him to reach out your steady hands to the misinformed and wearied life of man to restore this his lost heritage into the household state; wherewith be sure that peace and love, the best subsistence of a Christian family, will return home from whence they are now banished; places of prostitution will be less haunted, the neighbour's bed less attempted, the yoke of prudent and manly discipline will be generally submitted to; sober and well-ordered living will soon spring up in the commonwealth. Ye have an author great beyond exception, Moses; and one yet greater, he who hedged in from abolishing every smallest jot and tittle of precious equity contained in that law, with a more accurate and lasting Masorah,[36] than either the synagogue of Ezra or the Galilean School at Tiberias hath left us.[37] Whatever else ye can enact will scarce concern a third part of the British name: but the benefit and good of this your magnanimous example will easily spread far beyond the banks of Tweed and the Norman Isles.[38] It would not be the first or second time since our ancient Druids, by whom the island was the cathedral of philosophy to France, left off their pagan rites, that England hath had this honour vouchsafed from Heaven, to give out reformation to the world. Who was it but our English Constantine[39] that baptized the Roman Empire? Who but the Northumbrian Willibrode, and Winifride of Devon,[40] with their followers, were the first Apostles of Germany? Who but Alcuin and Wicklef[41] our countrymen opened the eyes of Europe, the one in arts, the other in religion? Let not England forget her precedence of teaching nations how to live.

Know Worthies, know and exercise the privilege of your honoured country. A greater title I here bring ye than is either in the power or in the policy of Rome to give her monarchs; this glorious act will style ye the defenders of charity. Nor is this yet the highest inscription that will adorn so religious and so holy a defense as this. Behold here the pure and sacred law of God, and his yet purer and more sacred name offering themselves to you first, of all Christian Reformers, to be acquitted from the long-suffered ungodly attribute of patronizing adultery. Defer not to wipe off instantly these imputative blurs and stains cast by rude fancies upon the throne and beauty itself of inviolable holiness, lest some other people more devout and wise than we bereave us this offered immortal glory, our wonted prerogative, of being the first assertors in every great vindication. For me, as far as my part leads me, I have already my greatest gain, assurance, and inward satisfaction to have done in this nothing unworthy of an honest life, and studies well employed. With what event among the wise and right understanding handful of men, I am secure. But how among the drove of custom and prejudice this will be relished by such whose capacity, since their youth run ahead into the easy creek of a System or a Medulla,[42] sails there at will under the blown physiognomy of their unlaboured rudiments, for them, what their taste will be, I have also surety sufficient, from the entire league that hath been ever between formal ignorance and grave obstinacy. Yet when I remember the little that our Savior could prevail about this doctrine of charity against the crabbed textuists of his time, I make no wonder, but rest confident that whoso prefers either matrimony or other ordinance before the good of man and the plain exigence of charity, let him profess Papist or Protestant or what he will, he is no better than a Pharisee, and understands not the Gospel: whom as a misinterpreter of Christ I openly protest against, and provoke him to the trial of this truth before all the world. And let him bethink him withal how he will solder up the shifting flaws of his ungirded permissions, his venial and unvenial dispenses, wherewith the law of God pardoning and unpardoning hath been shamefully branded for want of heed in glossing, to have eluded and baffled out all faith and chastity from the marriage-bed of that holy seed, with politic and judicial adulteries. I seek not to seduce the simple and illiterate; my errand is to find out the choicest and the most learned, who have this high gift of wisdom to answer solidly or to be convinced. I crave it from the piety, the learning, and the prudence which is housed in this place. It might perhaps more fitly have been written in another tongue:[43] and I had done so, but that the esteem I have of my country's judgment, and the love I bear to my native language to serve it first with what I endeavour, made me speak it thus, ere I assay the verdict of outlandish[44] readers. And perhaps also here I might have ended nameless, but that the address of these lines chiefly to the Parliament of England might have seemed ungrateful not to acknowledge by whose religious care, unwearied watchfulness, courageous and heroic resolutions, I enjoy the peace and studious leisure to remain,

The honourer and attendant of their noble worth and virtues,

John Milton

THE DOCTRINE AND DISCIPLINE OF DIVORCE; RESTORED TO THE GOOD OF BOTH SEXES.

Book I

The Preface

That man is the occasion of his own miseries in most of those evils which he imputes to God's inflicting. The absurdity of our canonists in their decrees about divorce. The Christian imperial laws framed with more equity. The opinion of Hugo Grotius *and* Paulus Fagius.[45] *And the purpose in general of this discourse.*

Many men, whether it be their fate or fond opinion, easily persuade themselves, if God would but be pleased a while to withdraw his just punishments from us, and to restrain what power either the Devil or any earthly enemy hath to work us woe, that then man's nature would find immediate rest and releasement from all evils. But verily they who think so, if they be such as have a mind large enough to take into their thoughts a general survey of human things, would soon prove themselves in that opinion far deceived. For though it were granted us by divine indulgence to be exempt from all that can be harmful to us from without, yet the perverseness of our folly is so bent, that we should never lin[46] hammering out of our own hearts, as it were out of a flint, the seeds and sparkles of new misery to our selves, 'til all were in a blaze again. And no marvel if out of our own hearts, for they are evil;[47] but even out of those things which God meant us, either for a principal good or a pure contentment, we are still hatching and contriving upon our selves matter of continued sorrow and perplexity. What greater good to man than that revealed rule whereby God vouchsafes to show us how he would be worshipped? And yet that not rightly understood, became the cause that once a famous man in Israel could not but oblige his conscience to be the sacrificer, or if not, the jailer of his innocent and only daughter,[48] and was the cause oft-times that armies of valiant men have given up their throats to a heathenish enemy on the Sabbath-day, fondly thinking their defensive resistance to be as then a work unlawful.[49] What thing more instituted to the solace and delight of man than marriage? and yet the misinterpreting of some Scripture, directed mainly against the abusers of the law for divorce given by Moses,[50] hath changed the blessing of matrimony not seldom into a familiar and co-inhabiting mischief; at least into a drooping and disconsolate household captivity, without refuge or redemption. So ungoverned and so wild a race doth superstition run us, from one extreme of abused liberty into the other of unmerciful restraint. For although God in the first ordaining of marriage[51] taught us to what end he did it, in words expressly implying the apt and cheerful conversation of man with woman to comfort and refresh him against the evil of solitary life, not mentioning the purpose of generation 'til afterwards, as being but a secondary end in dignity, though not in necessity; yet now, if any two be but once handed in the Church,[52] and have tasted in any sort the nuptial bed, let them find themselves never so mistaken in their dispositions through any error, concealment, or misadventure, that through their different tempers, thoughts, and constitutions, they can neither be to one another a remedy against loneliness nor live in any union or contentment all their days, yet they shall, so they be but found suitably weaponed to the least possibility of sensual enjoyment, be made, spite of antipathy, to fadge together,[53] and combine as they may to their unspeakable wearisomeness, and despair of all sociable delight in the ordinance which God established to that very end. What a calamity is this, and as the wise man, if he were alive, would sigh out in his own phrase, *what a sore evil is this under the sun!*[54] All which we can refer justly to no other author than the canon law and her adherents, not consulting with charity, the interpreter and guide of our faith, but resting in the mere element[55] of the text; doubtless by the policy of the Devil to make that gracious ordinance become unsupportable, that what with men not daring to venture upon wedlock, and what with men wearied out of it, all inordinate licence might abound. It was for many ages that marriage lay in disgrace with most of the ancient doctors as a work of the flesh, almost a defilement, wholly denied to priests, and the second time dissuaded to all, as he that reads Tertullian or Jerome[56] may see at large. Afterwards it was thought so sacramental[57] that no adultery or desertion could dissolve it; and this is the sense of our canon courts in England to this day, but in no other reformed Church else;[58] yet there remains in them also a burden on it as heavy as the other two were disgraceful or superstitious, and of as much iniquity, crossing a law not only written by Moses but charactered in us by nature, of more antiquity and deeper ground than marriage itself, which law is to force nothing against the faultless proprieties of nature. Yet that this may be colourably done, our Savior's words touching divorce are as it were congealed into a stony rigour, inconsistent both with his doctrine and his office; and that which he preached only to the conscience is by canonical tyranny snatched into the compulsive censure of a judicial court, where laws are imposed even against the venerable and secret power of nature's impression, to love whatever cause be found to loathe.[59] Which is a heinous barbarism both against the honour of marriage, the dignity of man and his soul, the goodness of Christianity, and all the human respects of civility. Notwithstanding that some the wisest and gravest among the Christian emperors,[60] who had about them, to consult with, those of the Fathers then living;[61] who for their learning and holiness of life are still with us in great renown, have made their statutes and edicts concerning this debate far more easy and relenting in many necessary cases, wherein the canon is inflexible. And Hugo Grotius, a man of these times, one of the best learned, seems not obscurely to adhere in his persuasion of the equity of those imperial decrees in his notes upon the Evangelists, much allaying the outward roughness of the text, which hath for the most part been too immoderately expounded; and excites the diligence of others to inquire further into this question, as concerning many points that have not yet been explained. Which ever likely to remain intricate and hopeless upon the suppositions commonly stuck to, the authority of Paulus Fagius, one so learned and so eminent in England once, if it might persuade, would straight acquaint us with a solution of these differences, no less prudent than compendious. He, in his comment on the Pentateuch, doubted not to maintain that divorces might be as lawfully permitted by the magistrate to Christians as they were to the Jews. But because he is but brief, and these things of great consequence not to be kept obscure, I shall conceive it nothing above my duty, either for the difficulty or the censure that may pass thereon, to communicate such thoughts as I also have had, and do offer them now in this general labour of reformation to the candid view both of Church and magistrate, especially because I see it the hope of good men that those irregular and unspiritual courts have spun their utmost date in this land, and some better course must now be constituted. This therefore shall be the task and period[62] of this discourse to prove: first, that other reasons of divorce, besides adultery, were by the law of Moses, and are yet to be allowed by the Christian magistrate as a piece of justice, and that the words of Christ are not hereby contraried. Next, that to prohibit absolutely any divorce whatsoever, except those which Moses excepted, is against the reason of law, as in due place I shall show out of Fagius with many additions. He therefore who by adventuring shall be so happy as with success to light the way of such an expedient liberty and truth as this, shall restore the much-wronged and over-sorrowed state of matrimony, not only to those merciful and life-giving remedies of Moses, but as much as may be to that serene and blissful condition it was in at the beginning, and shall deserve of all apprehensive men (considering the troubles and distempers which for want of this insight have been so oft in kingdoms, in states and families) to be reckoned among the public benefactors of civil and human life above the inventors of wine and oil; for this is a far dearer, far nobler, and more desirable cherishing to man's life, unworthily exposed to sadness and mistake, which he shall vindicate. Not that licence, and levity, and unconsented breach of faith should herein be countenanced, but that some conscionable and tender pity might be had of those who have unwarily, in a thing they never practised before, made themselves the bondmen of a luckless and helpless matrimony. In which argument, he whose courage can serve him to give the first onset must look for two several oppositions: the one from those who having sworn themselves to long custom, and the letter of the text, will not out of the road; the other from those whose gross and vulgar apprehensions conceit but low of matrimonial purposes, and in the work of male and female think they have all. Nevertheless, it shall be here sought by due ways to be made appear that those words of God in the institution, promising a meet help against loneliness,[63] and those words of Christ, *That his yoke is easy, and his burden light,*[64] were not spoken in vain; for if the knot of marriage may in no case be dissolved but for adultery, all the burdens and services of the law are not so intolerable. This only is desired of them who are minded to judge hardly of thus maintaining, that they would be still, and hear all out, nor think it equal to answer deliberate reason with sudden heat and noise; remembering this, that many truths now of reverend esteem and credit had their birth and beginning once from singular and private thoughts, while the most of men were otherwise possessed, and had the fate at first to be generally exploded and exclaimed on by many violent opposers. Yet I may err perhaps in soothing myself, that this present truth revived will deserve on all hands to be not sinisterly received, in that it undertakes the cure of an inveterate disease crept into the best part of human society; and to do this with no smarting corrosive, but with a smooth and pleasing lesson, which received, hath the virtue to soften and dispel rooted and knotty sorrows, and without enchantment, if that be feared, or spell used, hath regard at once both to serious pity and upright honesty; that tends to the redeeming and restoring of none but such as are the object of compassion, having in an ill hour hampered themselves, to the utter dispatch of all their most beloved comforts and repose for this life's term. But if we shall obstinately dislike this new overture of unexpected ease and recovery, what remains but to deplore the frowardness of our hopeless condition, which neither can endure the estate we are in, nor admit of remedy either sharp or sweet. Sharp we ourselves distaste; and sweet, under whose hands we are, is scrupled and suspected as too luscious. In such a posture Christ found the Jews, who were neither won with the austerity of John the Baptist, and thought it too much licence to follow freely the charming pipe of him who sounded and proclaimed liberty and relief to all distresses. Yet Truth in some age or other will find her witness, and shall be justified at last by her own children.[65]

CHAP. I

The Position. Proved by the law of Moses. That law expounded and asserted to a moral and charitable use, first by Paulus Fagius, *next with other additions.*

To remove therefore, if it be possible, this great and sad oppression which through the strictness of a literal interpreting had invaded and disturbed the dearest and most peaceable estate of household society, to the over-burdening, if not the over-whelming of many Christians better worth than to be so deserted of the Church's considerate care, this position shall be laid down, first proving, then answering what may be objected either from Scripture or light of reason.

That indisposition, unfitness, or contrariety of mind, arising from a cause in nature unchangeable, hindering, and ever likely to hinder the main benefits of conjugal society, which are solace and peace, is a greater reason of divorce than natural frigidity, especially if there be no children, and that there be mutual consent.

This I gather from the law in Deut. 24. 1: *When a man hath taken a wife and married her, and it come to pass that she find no favour in his eyes, because he hath found some uncleanness in her, let him write her a bill of divorcement, and give it in her hand, and send her out of his house, &c.* This law, if the words of Christ may be admitted into our belief, shall never while the world stands, for him be abrogated.[66] First therefore I here set down what learned Fagius hath observed on this law. *The law of God,* said he, *permitted divorce for the help of human weakness. For every one that of necessity separates, cannot live single. That Christ denied divorce to his own, hinders not; for what is that to the unregenerate, who hath not attained such perfection? Let not the remedy be despised which was given to weakness. And when Christ saith, who marries the divorced commits adultery, it is to be understood if he had any plot in the divorce.* The rest I reserve until it be disputed, how the magistrate is to do herein. From hence we may plainly discern a twofold consideration of this law: first the end of the law-giver, and the proper act of the law, to command or to allow something just and honest, or indifferent. Secondly, his sufferance from some accidental result of evil by this allowance, which the law cannot remedy. For if this law have no other end or act but only the allowance of sin, though never to so good intention, that law is no law, but sin muffled in the robe of law, or law disguised in the loose garment of sin. Both which are two foul hypotheses, to save the phenomenon of our Savior's answer to the Pharisees about this matter.[67] And I trust anon by the help of an infallible guide to perfect such Prutenic tables as shall mend the astronomy of our wide expositors.[68]

The cause of divorce mentioned in the law, is translated *some uncleanness,* but in the Hebrew it sounds[69] *nakedness of ought, or any real nakedness:* which by all the learned interpreters is referred to the mind as well as the body.[70] And what greater nakedness or unfitness of mind than that which hinders ever the solace and peaceful society of the married couple; and what hinders that more than the unfitness and defectiveness of an unconjugal mind? The cause therefore of divorce expressed in the position cannot but agree with that described in the best and most equal sense of Moses' law. Which being a matter of pure charity, is plainly moral, and more now in force than ever, therefore surely lawful. For if under the law such was God's gracious indulgence, as not to suffer the ordinance of his goodness and favour through any error to be feared and stigmatized upon his servants to their misery and thralldom, much less will he suffer it now under the covenant of grace by abrogating his former grant of remedy and relief. But the first institution will be objected to have ordained marriage inseparable. To that a little patience until this first part have amply discoursed the grave and pious reasons of this divorsive law; and then I doubt not but with one gentle stroking to wipe away ten thousand tears out of the life of man. Yet thus much I shall now insist on, that whatever the institution were, it could not be so enormous, nor so rebellious against both nature and reason, as to exalt itself above the end and person for whom it was instituted.

CHAP. II

The first reason of this law grounded on the prime reason of matrimony. That no covenant whatsoever obliges against the main end both of itself and of the parties covenanting.

For all sense and equity reclaims[71] that any law or covenant, how solemn or straight soever, either between God and man, or man and man, though of God's joining, should bind against a prime and principal scope of its own institution,[72] and of both or either party covenanting; neither can it be of force to engage a blameless creature to his own perpetual sorrow, mistaken for his expected solace, without suffering charity to step in and do a confessed good work of parting those whom nothing holds together but this of God's joining, falsely supposed against the express end of his own ordinance. And what this chief end was of creating women to be joined with man, his own instituting words declare, and are infallible to inform us what is marriage, and what is no marriage, unless we can think them set there to no purpose: *It is not good,* saith he, *that man should be alone. I will make him a help-meet for him.*[73] From which words so plain, less cannot be concluded, nor is by any learned interpreter, than that in God's intention a meet and happy conversation[74] is the chiefest and the noblest end of marriage: for we find here no expression so necessarily implying carnal knowledge as this prevention of loneliness to the mind and spirit of man. To this, Fagius, Calvin, Pareus, Rivetus, as willingly and largely assent as can be wished.[75] And indeed it is a greater blessing from God, more worthy so excellent a creature as man is, and a higher end to honour and sanctify the league of marriage, whenas the solace and satisfaction of the mind is regarded and provided for before the sensitive pleasing of the body. And with all generous persons married thus it is, that where the mind and person pleases aptly, there some unaccomplishment of the body's delight may be better borne with, than when the mind hangs off in an unclosing disproportion though the body be as it ought; for there all corporeal delight will soon become unsavoury and contemptible. And the solitariness of man, which God had namely and principally ordered to prevent by marriage, hath no remedy, but lies under a worse condition than the loneliest single life; for in single life the absence and remoteness of a helper might inure him to expect his own comforts out of himself, or to seek with hope; but here the continual sight of his deluded thoughts without cure, must needs be to him, if especially his complexion[76] incline him to melancholy, a daily trouble and pain of loss, in some degree like that which reprobates feel.[77] Lest therefore so noble a creature as man should be shut up incurably under a worse evil by an easy mistake in that ordinance which God gave him to remedy a less evil, reaping to himself sorrow while he went to rid away solitariness, it cannot avoid to be concluded, that if the woman be naturally so of disposition as will not help to remove but help to increase that same God-forbidden loneliness, which will in time draw on with it a general discomfort and dejection of mind, not beseeming either Christian profession or moral conversation, unprofitable and dangerous to the commonwealth, when the household estate, out of which must flourish forth the vigour and spirit of all public enterprises,[78] is so ill contented and procured at home, and cannot be supported; such a marriage can be no marriage, whereto the most honest end is wanting. And the aggrieved person shall do more manly to be extraordinary and singular in claiming the due right whereof he is frustrated, than to piece up his lost contentment by visiting the stews,[79] or stepping to his neighbour's bed, which is the common shift in this misfortune, or else by suffering his useful life to waste away and be lost under a secret affliction of an unconscionable size to human strength. Against all which evils, the mercy of this Mosaic law was graciously exhibited.

CHAP. III

The ignorance and iniquity of canon law, providing all for the right of the body in marriage, but nothing for the wrongs and grievances of the mind. An objection, that the mind should be better looked to before contract, answered.

How vain therefore is it, and how preposterous in the canon law, to have made such careful provision against the impediment of carnal performance,[80] and to have had no care about the unconversing inability of mind, so defective to the purest and most sacred end of matrimony; and that the vessel of voluptuous enjoyment must be made good to him that has taken it upon trust, without any caution; whenas the mind, from whence must flow the acts of peace and love, a far more precious mixture than the quintessence of an excrement,[81] though it be found never so deficient and unable to perform the best duty of marriage in a cheerful and agreeable conversation, shall be thought good enough, however flat and melancholious it be, and must serve, though to the eternal disturbance and languishing of him that complains him. Yet wisdom and charity, weighing God's own institution, would think that the pining of a sad spirit wedded to loneliness should deserve to be freed, as well as the impatience of a sensual desire so providently relieved. It is read to us in the liturgy, that *we must not marry to satisfy the fleshly appetite, like brute beasts, that have no understanding:*[82] but the canon so runs, as if it dreamt of no other matter than such an appetite to be satisfied; for if it happen that nature hath stopped or extinguished the veins of sensuality, that marriage is annulled. But though all the faculties of the understanding and conversing part after trial appear to be so ill and so aversely met through nature's unalterable working, as that neither peace nor any sociable contentment can follow, 'tis as nothing; the contract shall stand as firm as ever, betide what will. What is this but secretly to instruct us, that however many grave reasons are pretended to the married life, yet that nothing indeed is thought worth regard therein but the prescribed satisfaction of an irrational heat? Which cannot be but ignominious to the state of marriage, dishonourable to the undervalued soul of man, and even to Christian doctrine itself; while it seems more moved at the disappointing of an impetuous nerve[83] than at the ingenuous[84] grievance of a mind unreasonably yoked; and to place more of marriage in the channel of concupiscence than in the pure influence of peace and love, whereof the soul's lawful contentment is the one only fountain.

But some are ready to object that the disposition ought seriously to be considered before. But let them know again, that for all the wariness can be used, it may yet befall a discreet man to be mistaken in his choice; and we have plenty of examples.[85] The soberest and best-governed men are least practised in these affairs; and who knows not that the bashful muteness of a virgin may ofttimes hide all the unliveliness and natural sloth which is really unfit for conversation; nor is there that freedom of access granted or presumed as may suffice to a perfect discerning 'til too late. And where any indisposition is suspected, what more usual than the persuasion of friends, that acquaintance as it increases will amend all? And lastly, it is not strange though many who have spent their youth chastely, are in some things not so quick-sighted, while they haste so eagerly to light the nuptial torch; nor is it therefore that for a modest error a man should forfeit so great a happiness, and no charitable means to release him. Since they who have lived most loosely by reason of their bold accustoming prove most successful in their matches, because their wild affections, unsettling at will, have been as so many divorces to teach them experience. Whenas the sober man honouring the appearance of modesty, and hoping well of every social virtue under that veil, may easily chance to meet, if not with a body impenetrable, yet often with a mind to all other due conversation inaccessible, and to all the more estimable and superior purposes of matrimony useless and almost lifeless; and what a solace, what a fit help such a consort would be through the whole life of a man, is less pain to conjecture than to have experience.

CHAP. IV

The second reason of this law, because without it, marriage as it happens oft is not a remedy of that which it promises, as any rational creature would expect. That marriage, if we pattern from the beginning, as our Savior bids, was not properly the remedy of lust, but the fulfilling of conjugal love and helpfulness.

And that we may further see what a violent cruel thing it is to force the continuing of those together, whom God and nature in the gentlest end of marriage never joined, divers evils and extremities that follow upon such a compulsion shall here be set in view. Of evils, the first and greatest is that hereby a most absurd and rash imputation is fixed upon God and his laws, of conniving and dispensing with open and common adultery among his chosen people, a thing which the rankest politician would think it shame and disworship[86] that his laws should countenance; how and in what manner that comes to pass, I shall reserve 'til the course of method brings on the unfolding of many Scriptures. Next, the Law and Gospel are hereby made liable to more than one contradiction, which I refer also thither. Lastly, the supreme dictate of charity is hereby many ways neglected and violated; which I shall forthwith address to prove. First, we know St. Paul saith, *It is better to marry than to burn.*[87] Marriage therefore was given as a remedy of that trouble; but what might this burning mean? Certainly not the mere motion of carnal lust, not the mere goad of a sensitive desire; God does not principally take care for such cattle.[88] What is it then but that desire which God put into Adam in Paradise before he knew the sin of incontinence; that desire which God saw it was not good that man should be left alone to burn in; the desire and longing to put off an unkindly solitariness by uniting another body, but not without a fit soul to his in the cheerful society of wedlock? Which if it were so needful before the fall, when man was much more perfect in himself, how much more is it needful now against all the sorrows and casualties of this life to have an intimate and speaking help, a ready and reviving associate in marriage? whereof who misses, by chancing on a mute and spiritless mate, remains more alone than before, and in a burning less to be contained than that which is fleshly, and more to be considered as being more deeply rooted even in the faultless innocence of nature. As for that other burning, which is but as it were the venom of a lusty and over-abounding concoction, strict life and labour, with the abatement of a full diet, may keep that low and obedient enough. But this pure and more inbred desire of joining to itself in conjugal fellowship a fit conversing soul (which desire is properly called love) is *stronger than death,* as the spouse of Christ thought; *many waters cannot quench it, neither can the floods drown it.*[89] This is that rational burning that marriage is to remedy, not to be allayed with fasting, nor with any penance to be subdued; which how can he assuage who by mishap hath met the most unmeet and unsuitable mind? Who hath the power to struggle with an intelligible flame, not in Paradise to be resisted, become now more ardent by being failed of what in reason it looked for; and even then most unquenched, when the importunity of a provender[90] burning is well enough appeased; and yet the soul hath obtained nothing of what it justly desires. Certainly such a one forbidden to divorce is in effect forbidden to marry, and compelled to greater difficulties than in a single life; for if there be not a more humane burning which marriage must satisfy, or else may be dissolved, than that of copulation, marriage cannot be honourable for the meet reducing and terminating lust between two; seeing many beasts in voluntary and chosen couples live together as unadulterously, and are as truly married in that respect. But all ingenuous men will see that the dignity and blessing of marriage is placed rather in the mutual enjoyment of that which the wanting soul needfully seeks, than of that which the plenteous body would joyfully give away. Hence it is that Plato in his festival discourse brings in Socrates relating what he feigned to have learnt from the prophetess Diotima, how Love was the son of Penury, begot of Plenty in the Garden of Jupiter.[91] Which divinely sorts with that which in effect Moses tells us, that Love was the son of Loneliness, begot in Paradise by that sociable and helpful aptitude which God implanted between man and woman toward each other.[92] The same also is that burning mentioned by St. Paul, whereof marriage ought to be the remedy; the flesh hath other natural[93] and easy curbs which are in the power of any temperate man. When therefore this original and sinless penury or loneliness of the soul cannot lay itself down by the side of such a meet and acceptable union as God ordained in marriage, at least in some proportion, it cannot conceive and bring forth love, but remains utterly unmarried under a formal wedlock and still burns in the proper meaning of St. Paul. Then enters hate, not that hate that sins, but that which only is natural dissatisfaction and the turning aside from a mistaken object;[94] if that mistake have done injury, it fails not to dismiss with recompense; for to retain still, and not be able to love, is to heap up more injury. Thence this wise and pious law of dismission now defended took beginning: he therefore who lacking of his due in the most native and humane end of marriage, thinks it better to part than to live sadly and injuriously to that cheerful covenant (for not to be beloved, and yet retained, is the greatest injury to a gentle spirit) he I say, who therefore seeks to part, is one who highly honours the married life and would not stain it: and the reasons which now move him to divorce are equal to the best of those that could first warrant him to marry; for, as was plainly shown, both the hate which now diverts him and the loneliness which leads him still powerfully to seek a fit help, hath not the least grain of a sin in it, if he be worthy to understand himself.

CHAP. V

The third reason of this law, because without it, he who hath happened where he find nothing but remediless offences and discontents, is in more and greater temptations than ever before.

Thirdly, yet it is next to be feared, if he must be still bound without reason by a deaf rigour, that when he perceives the just expectance of his mind defeated, he will begin even against law to cast about where he may find his satisfaction more complete, unless he be a thing heroically virtuous, and that are not the common lump of men, for whom chiefly the laws ought to be made; though not to their sins, yet to their unsinning weaknesses, it being above their strength to endure the lonely estate, which while they shunned, they are fallen into. And yet there follows upon this a worse temptation; for if he be such as hath spent his youth unblameably, and laid up his chiefest earthly comforts in the enjoyments of a contented marriage, nor did neglect that furtherance which was to be obtained therein by constant prayers, when he shall find himself bound fast to an uncomplying discord of nature, or, as it oft happens, to an image of earth and fleam,[95] with whom he looked to be the copartner of a sweet and gladsome society, and sees withal that his bondage is now inevitable; though he be almost the strongest Christian, he will be ready to despair in virtue, and mutin[96] against divine providence. And this doubtless is the reason of those lapses and that melancholy despair which we see in many wedded persons, though they understand it not, or pretend other causes, because they know no remedy, and is of extreme danger. Therefore when human frailty surcharged is at such a loss, charity ought to venture much, and use bold physic, lest an over-tossed faith endanger to shipwreck.

CHAP. VI

The fourth reason of this law, that God regards love and peace in the family more than a compulsive performance of marriage, which is more broke by a grievous continuance than by a needful divorce.

Fourthly, marriage is a covenant, the very being whereof consists not in a forced cohabitation and counterfeit performances of duties, but in unfeigned love and peace. And of matrimonial love, no doubt but that was chiefly meant, which by the ancient sages was thus parabled: that Love, if he be not twin-born, yet hath a brother wondrous like him, called Anteros;[97] whom while he seeks all about, his chance is to meet with many false and feigning desires that wander singly up and down in his likeness. By them in their borrowed garb, Love though not wholly blind, as poets wrong him, yet having but one eye, as being born an archer aiming, and that eye not the quickest in this dark region here below, which is not love's proper sphere, partly out of the simplicity and credulity which is native to him, often deceived, embraces and consorts him with these obvious and suborned[98] striplings, as if they were his mother's own sons; for so he thinks them, while they subtly keep themselves most on his blind side. But after a while, as his manner is, when soaring up into the high tower of his apogaeum,[99] above the shadow of the Earth, he darts out the direct rays of his then most piercing eyesight upon the impostures and trim disguises that were used with him, and discerns that this is not his genuine brother as he imagined. He has no longer the power to hold fellowship with such a personated[100] mate; for straight his arrows lose their golden heads and shed their purple feathers, his silken braids untwine and slip their knots,[101] and that original and fiery virtue given him by fate all on a sudden goes out, and leaves him undeified and despoiled of all his force, 'til finding Anteros at last, he kindles and repairs the almost faded ammunition of his Deity by the reflection of a coequal and homogeneal fire. Thus mine author sung it to me; and by the leave of those who would be counted the only grave ones, this is no mere amatorious novel[102] (though to be wise and skilful in these matters, men heretofore of greatest name in virtue, have esteemed it one of the highest arcs that human contemplation circling upwards can make from the glassy sea whereon he stands).[103] But this is a deep and serious verity, showing us that love in marriage cannot live nor subsist unless it be mutual; and where love cannot be, there can be left of wedlock nothing but the empty husk of an outside matrimony, as undelightful and unpleasing to God as any other kind of hypocrisy. So far is his command from tying men to the observance of duties which there is no help for, but they must be dissembled. If Solomon's advice be not over-frolic, *Live joyfully,* saith he, *with the wife whom thou lovest, all thy days, for that is thy portion.*[104] How then, where we find it impossible to rejoice or to love, can we obey this precept? How miserably do we defraud our selves of that comfortable portion which God gives us, by striving vainly to glue an error together, which God and nature will not join, adding but more vexation and violence to that blissful society by our importunate superstition, that will not hearken to St. Paul, 1 Cor. 7, who speaking of marriage and divorce, determines plain enough in general that God therein *hath called us to peace,* and not *to bondage.* Yea, God himself commands in his law more than once, and by his prophet Malachi, as Calvin and the best translations read, that *he who hates, let him divorce,*[105] that is, he who cannot love. Hence is it that the rabbis, and Maimonides famous among the rest in a book of his set forth by Buxtorsius, tells us, that *Divorce was permitted by Moses to preserve peace in marriage, and quiet in the family.*[106] Surely the Jews had their saving peace about them as well as we, yet care was taken that this wholesome provision for household peace should also be allowed them; and must this be denied to Christians? O perverseness! that the law should be made more provident of peace-making than the Gospel! that the Gospel should be put to beg a most necessary help of mercy from the law, but must not have it; and that to grind in the mill of an undelighted and servile copulation[107] must be the only forced work of a Christian marriage oft-times with such a yoke-fellow, from whom both love and peace, both nature and religion mourns[108] to be separated. I cannot therefore be so diffident as not securely to conclude that he who can receive nothing of the most important helps in marriage, being thereby disenabled to return that duty which is his with a clear and hearty countenance, and thus continues to grieve whom he would not, and is no less grieved, that man ought even for love's sake and peace to move divorce upon good and liberal conditions to the divorced. And it is a less breach of wedlock to part with wise and quiet consent betimes, than still to foil and profane that mystery of joy and union with a polluting sadness and perpetual distemper; for it is not the outward continuing of marriage that keeps whole that covenant, but whatsoever does most according to peace and love, whether in marriage or in divorce, he it is that breaks marriage least; it being so often written, that *Love only is the fulfilling of every Commandment.*[109]

CHAP. VII

The fifth reason, that nothing more hinders and disturbs the whole life of a Christian than a matrimony found to be incurably unfit, and doth the same in effect that an idolatrous match.

Fifthly, as those priests of old were not to be long in sorrow, or if they were, they could not rightly execute their function, so every true Christian in a higher order of priesthood is a person dedicate to joy and peace,[110] offering himself a lively sacrifice of praise and thanksgiving. And there is no Christian duty that is not to be seasoned and set off with cheerfulness,[111] which in a thousand outward and intermitting crosses may yet be done well, as in this vale of tears, but in such a bosom-affliction as this, crushing the very foundations of his inmost nature, when he shall be forced to love against a possibility, and to use a dissimulation against his soul in the perpetual and ceaseless duties of a husband, doubtless his whole duty of serving God must needs be blurred and tainted with a sad unpreparedness and dejection of spirit, wherein God has no delight. Who sees not therefore how much more Christianly it would be to break by divorce that which is more broken by undue and forcible keeping, rather than *to cover the altar of the Lord with continual tears, so that he regardeth not the offering any more;*[112] rather than that the whole worship of a Christian man's life should languish and fade away beneath the weight of an immeasurable grief and discouragement? And because some think the children of a second matrimony succeeding a divorce would not be a holy seed, it hindered not the Jews from being so; and why should we not think them more holy than the offspring of a former ill-twisted wedlock, begotten only out of a bestial necessity, without any true love or contentment, or joy to their parents? So that in some sense we may call them the children of wrath and anguish, which will as little conduce to their sanctifying as if they had been bastards. For nothing more than disturbance of mind suspends us from approaching to God, such a disturbance especially, as both assaults our faith and trust in God's providence and ends, if there be not a miracle of virtue on either side, not only in bitterness and wrath, the canker of devotion, but in a desperate and vicious carelessness, when he sees himself without fault of his, trained by a deceitful bait into a snare of misery, betrayed by an alluring ordinance, and then made the thrall of heaviness and discomfort by an undivorcing law of God, as he erroneously thinks, but of man's iniquity, as the truth is: for that God prefers the free and cheerful worship of a Christian, before the grievous and exacted observance of an unhappy marriage, besides that the general maxims of religion assure us, will be more manifest by drawing a parallel argument from the ground of divorcing an idolatress, which was, lest he should alienate his heart from the true worship of God; and what difference is there whether she perverts him to superstition by her enticing sorcery, or disenables him in the whole service of God through the disturbance of her unhelpful and unfit society, and so drive him at last, through murmuring and despair, to thoughts of atheism. Neither doth it lessen the cause of separating, in that the one willingly allures him from the faith, the other perhaps unwillingly drives him; for in the account of God it comes all to one, that the wife looses him a servant; and therefore by all the united force of the Decalogue she ought to be disbanded,[113] unless we must set marriage above God and charity, which is the doctrine of devils no less than forbidding to marry.[114]

CHAP. VIII

That an idolatrous heretic ought to be divorced after a convenient space given to hope of conversion. That place of I Cor. 7. restored from a twofold erroneous exposition, and that the common expositors flatly contradict the moral law.

And here by the way, to illustrate the whole question of divorce, ere this treatise end, I shall not be loath to spend a few lines in hope to give a full resolve of that which is yet so much controverted, whether an idolatrous heretic ought be divorced. To the resolving whereof we must first know that the Jews were commanded to divorce an unbelieving Gentile for two causes: first, because all other nations, especially the Canaanites, were to them unclean. Secondly, to avoid seducement. That other nations were to the Jews impure, even to the separating of marriage, will appear out of Exod. 34:16. Deut. 7:3, 6. compared with Ezra 9:2. also Chap. 10:10, 11. Nehem. 13:30. This was the ground of that doubt raised among the Corinthians by some of the circumcision:[115] whether an unbeliever were not still to be counted an unclean thing, so as that they ought to divorce from such a person. This doubt of theirs St. Paul removes by an evangelical reason, having respect to that vision of St. Peter, wherein the distinction of clean and unclean being abolished, all living creatures were sanctified to a pure and Christian use, and mankind especially, now invited by a general call to the covenant of grace.[116] Therefore saith St. Paul, *The unbelieving wife is sanctified by the husband;*[117] that is, made pure and lawful to his use, so that he need not put her away for fear lest her unbelief should defile him; but that if he found her love still towards him, he might rather hope to win her. The second reason of that divorce was to avoid seducement, as is proved by comparing those two places of the law to that which Ezra and Nehemiah did by divine warrant in compelling the Jews to forgo their wives. And this reason is moral and perpetual in the rule of Christian faith without evasion; therefore saith the Apostle, 2 Cor. 6: *misyoke not together with infidels,* which is interpreted of marriage in the first place. And although the former legal pollution be now done[118] off, yet there is a spiritual contagion in idolatry as much to be shunned; and though seducement were not to be feared, yet where there is no hope of converting, there always ought to be a certain religious aversation[119] and abhorring, which can no way sort with marriage: therefore saith S. Paul, *What fellowship hath righteousness with unrighteousness? what communion hath light with darkness? what concord hath Christ with Belial? what part hath he that believeth with an infidel?* And in the next verse but one he moralizes, and makes us liable to that command of Isaiah: *wherefore come out from among them, and be ye separate,* saith the Lord; *touch not the unclean thing, and I will receive ye.*[120] And this command thus gospelized to us, hath the same force with that whereon Ezra grounded the pious necessity of divorcing. Neither had he other commission for what he did, than such a general command in Deut. as this, nay not so direct as this; for he is bid there not to marry, but not bid to divorce, and yet we see with what a zeal and confidence he was the author of a general divorce between the faithful and unfaithful seed.[121] The Gospel is more plainly on his side, according to three of the Evangelists, than the words of the law; for where the case of divorce is handled with such a severity as was fittest to aggravate the fault of unbounded licence, yet still in the same chapter, when it comes into question afterwards whether any civil respect, or natural relation which is dearest, may be our plea to divide, or hinder or but delay our duty to religion, we hear it determined that father and mother, and wife also, is not only to be hated but forsaken, if we mean to inherit the great reward there promised. Nor will it suffice to be put off by saying we must forsake them only by not consenting or not complying with them, for that were to be done, and roundly too, though being of the same faith they should but seek out of a fleshly tenderness to weaken our Christian fortitude with worldly persuasions, or but to unsettle our constancy with timorous and softening suggestions: as we may read with what a vehemence Job, the most patient of men, rejected the desperate counsels of his wife;[122] and Moses, the meekest, being thoroughly offended with the profane speeches of Zippora, sent her back to her father.[123] But if they shall perpetually at our elbow seduce us from the true worship of God, or defile and daily scandalize our conscience by their hopeless continuance in misbelief, then even in the due progress of reason and that ever-equal proportion which justice proceeds by, it cannot be imagined that this cited place commands less than a total and final separation from such an adherent, at least that no force should be used to keep them together, while we remember that God commanded Abraham to send away his irreligious wife and her son for the offences which they gave in a pious family.[124] And it may be guessed that David for the like cause disposed of Michal in such a sort, as little differed from a dismission.[125] Therefore against reiterated scandals and seducements, which never cease, much more can no other remedy or retirement be found but absolute departure. For what kind of matrimony can that remain to be, what one duty between such can be performed as it should be from the heart, when their thoughts and spirits fly asunder as far as Heaven from Hell, especially if the time that hope should send forth her expected blossoms be past in vain? It will easily be true, that a father or a brother may be hated zealously, and loved civilly or naturally; for those duties may be performed at a distance, and do admit of any long absence. But how the peace and perpetual cohabitation of marriage can be kept, how that benevolent and intimate communion of body can be held with one that must be hated with a most operative hatred, must be forsaken and yet continually dwelt with and accompanied, he who can distinguish hath the gift of an affection very oddly divided and contrived; while others both just and wise, and Solomon among the rest, if they may not hate and forsake as Moses enjoins, and the Gospel imports, will find it impossible not to love otherwise than will sort with the love of God, whose jealousy brooks no corrival. And whether is more likely, that Christ bidding to forsake wife for religion, meant it by divorce as Moses meant it, whose law grounded on moral reason was both his office and his essence to maintain; or that he should bring a new morality into religion, not only new but contrary to an unchangeable command, and dangerously derogating from our love and worship of God? As if when Moses had bid divorce absolutely, and Christ had said, hate and forsake, and his Apostle had said, no communication with Christ and Belial; yet that Christ after all this could be understood to say, divorce not, no not for religion, seduce, or seduce not. What mighty and invisible Remora[126] is this in matrimony able to demur and to contemn all the divorcive engines in Heaven or Earth! Both which may now pass away if this be true, for more than many jots or tittles, a whole moral law is abolished. But if we dare believe it is not, then in the method of religion, and to save the honour and dignity of our faith, we are to retreat, and gather up our selves from the observance of an inferior and civil ordinance, to the strict maintaining of a general and religious command, which is written, *thou shalt make no covenant with them,* Deut. 7:2–3, and that covenant which cannot be lawfully made, we have directions and examples lawfully to dissolve. Also 2 Chron. 19:2, *shouldst thou love them that hate the Lord?* No, doubtless: for there is a certain scale of duties, there is a certain hierarchy of upper and lower commands, which for want of studying in right order, all the world is in confusion.

Upon these principles I answer, that a right believer ought to divorce an idolatrous heretic, unless upon better hopes; however, that it is in the believer's choice to divorce or not.

The former part will be manifest thus: first, that an apostate idolater, whether husband or wife seducing, was to die by the decree of God, Deut. 13:6, 9, that marriage therefore God himself disjoins. For others born idolaters, the moral reason of their dangerous keeping, and the incommunicable antagony[127] that is between Christ and Belial, will be sufficient to enforce the commandment of those two inspired reformers, Ezra and Nehemiah, to put an idolater away as well under the Gospel.

The latter part, that although there be no seducement feared, yet if there be no hope given, the divorce is lawful, will appear by this: that idolatrous marriage is still hateful to God, therefore still it may be divorced by the pattern of that warrant that Ezra had, and by the same everlasting reason. Neither can any man give an account wherefore, if those whom God joins no man can separate, it should not follow, that whom he joins not, but hates to join, those man ought to separate. But, saith the lawyer, that which ought not to have been done, once done avails. I answer, this is but a crotchet of the law, but that brought against it is plain Scripture. As for what Christ spoke concerning divorce, 'tis confessed by all knowing men, he meant only between them of the same faith. But what shall we say then to St. Paul, who seems to bid us not divorce an infidel willing to stay? We may safely say thus, that wrong collections have been hitherto made out of those words by modern divines. His drift, as was heard before, is plain: not to command our stay in marriage with an infidel—that had been a flat renouncing of the religious and moral law—but to inform the Corinthians that the body of an unbeliever was not defiling if his desire to live in Christian wedlock showed any likelihood that this heart was opening to the faith; and therefore advises to forbear departure so long 'til nothing have been neglected to set forward a conversion. This I say he advises, and that with certain cautions, not commands, if we can take up so much credit for him as to get him believed upon his own word. For what is this else but his counsel in a thing indifferent, *to the rest speak I, not the Lord.* For though it be true that the Lord never spoke it, yet from St. Paul's mouth we should have took it as a command, had not himself forewarned us, and disclaimed, which notwithstanding if we shall still avouch to be a command, he palpably denying it, this is not to expound St. Paul but to outface him. Neither doth it follow, but that the

Apostle may interpose his judgment in a case of Christian liberty without the guilt of adding to God's word. How do we know marriage or single life to be of choice, but by such like words as these: *I speak this by permission, not of commandment; I have no command of the Lord, yet I give my judgment.* Why shall not the like words have leave to signify a freedom in this our present question, though Beza deny?[128] Neither is the Scripture hereby less inspired because St. Paul confesses to have written therein what he had not of command; for we grant that the Spirit of God led him thus to express himself to Christian prudence, in a matter which God thought best to leave uncommanded. Beza therefore must be warily read, when he taxes St. Austin of blasphemy for holding that St. Paul spoke here as of a thing indifferent. But if it must be a command, I shall yet the more evince it to be a command that we should herein be left free, and that out of the Greek word used in the 12 v.[129] which instructs us plainly there must be a joint assent and good liking on both sides. He that will not deprave the text must thus render it: *if a brother have an unbelieving wife, and she join in consent to dwell with him* (which cannot utter less to us than a mutual agreement) let him not put her away for the mere surmise of Judaical uncleanness; and the reason follows, for the body of an infidel is not polluted, neither to benevolence nor to procreation. Moreover, this note of mutual complacency forbids all offer of seducement, which to a person of zeal cannot be attempted without great offence. If therefore seducement be feared, this place hinders not divorce. Another caution was put in this supposed command, of not bringing the believer into bondage hereby, which doubtless might prove extreme if Christian liberty and conscience were left to the humor of a pagan staying at pleasure to play with, and to vex and wound with a thousand scandals and burdens above strength to bear. If therefore the conceived hope of gaining a soul come to nothing, then charity commands that the believer be not wearied out with endless waiting under many grievances sore to his spirit, but that respect be had rather to the present suffering of a true Christian than the uncertain winning of an obdurate heretic. The counsel we have from St. Paul to hope, cannot countermand the moral and evangelic charge we have from God to fear seducement, to separate from the misbeliever, the unclean, the obdurate. The Apostle wishes us to hope, but does not send us a wool-gathering after vain hope; he saith, *how knowest thou, O Man, whether thou shalt save thy wife?* that is, 'til he try all due means, and set some reasonable time to himself, after which he may give over washing an Ethiope, if he will hear the advice of the Gospel. *Cast not pearls before swine,* saith Christ himself. *Let him be to thee as a Heathen. Shake the dust off thy feet.*[130] If this be not enough, hate and forsake what relation soever. And this also that follows must appertain to the precept, *let every man wherein he is called, therein abide with God,* v.24, that is, so walking in his inferior calling of marriage, as not by dangerous subjection to that ordinance to hinder and disturb the higher calling of his Christianity. Last, and never too oft remembered, whether this be a command or an advice, we must look that it be so understood as not to contradict the least point of moral religion that God hath formerly commanded. Otherwise what do we but set the moral law and the Gospel at civil war together? and who then shall be able to serve these two masters?

CHAP. IX

That adultery is not the greatest breach of matrimony; that there may be other violations as great.

Now whether idolatry or adultery be the greatest violation of marriage, if any demand let him thus consider, that among Christian writers touching matrimony, there be three chief ends thereof agreed on: godly society, next civil, and thirdly, that of the marriage-bed. Of these the first in name to be the highest and most excellent, no baptized man can deny, nor that idolatry smites directly against this prime end; nor that such as the violated end is, such is the violation. But he who affirms adultery to be the highest breach, affirms the bed to be the highest of marriage, which is in truth a gross and boorish opinion, how common soever, as far from the countenance of Scripture as from the light of all clean philosophy or civil nature. And out of question the cheerful help that may be in marriage toward sanctity of life is the purest and so the noblest end of that contract. But if the particular of each person be considered, then of those three ends which God appointed, that to him is greatest which is most necessary; and marriage is then most broken to him when he utterly wants the fruition of that which he most sought therein, whether it were religious, civil or corporeal society. Of which wants, to do him right by divorce only for the last and meanest is a perverse injury, and the pretended reason of it as frigid as frigidity itself, which the Code and canon are only sensible of.[131] Thus much of this controversy. I now return to the former argument. And having shown that disproportion, contrariety or numbness of mind may justly be divorced, by proving already the prohibition thereof opposes the express end of God's institution, suffers not marriage to satisfy that intellectual and innocent desire which God himself kindled in man to be the bond of wedlock, but only to remedy a sublunary[132] and bestial burning, which frugal diet, without marriage, would easily chasten. Next, that it drives many to transgress the conjugal bed, while the soul wanders after that satisfaction which it had hope to find at home, but hath missed. Or else it sits repining even to atheism, finding itself hardly dealt with, but misdeeming the cause to be in God's law, which is in man's righteous ignorance. I have shown also how it unties the inward knot of marriage, which is peace and love (if that can be untied which was never knit) while it aims to keep fast the outward formality; how it lets perish the Christian man, to compel impossibly the married man.

CHAP. X

The sixth reason of this law, that to prohibit divorce sought for natural causes, is against nature.

The sixth place declares this prohibition to be as respectless[133] of human nature as it is of religion, and therefore is not of God. He teaches that an unlawful marriage may be lawfully divorced. And that those who having thoroughly discerned each other's disposition, which oft-times cannot be 'til after matrimony, shall then find a powerful reluctance and recoil of nature on either side, blasting all the content of their mutual society, that such persons are not lawfully married (to use the Apostle's words) *say I these things as a man, or saith not the law also the same?* for it is written, Deut. 22, *thou shalt not sow thy vineyard with different seeds, lest thou defile both. Thou shalt not plow with an ox and an ass together;* and the like. I follow the pattern of St. Paul's reasoning; *doth God care for asses and oxen,* how ill they yoke together, *or is it not said altogether for our sakes? for our sakes no doubt this is written.*[134] Yea the Apostle himself, in the forecited 2 Cor. 6:14, alludes from that place of Deut. to forbid misyoking marriage, as by the Greek word is evident, though he instance but in one example of mismatching with an infidel. Yet next to that, what can be a fouler incongruity, a greater violence to the reverend secret of nature, than to force a mixture of minds that cannot unite, and to sow the sorrow of man's nativity with seed of two incoherent and uncombining dispositions. Which act being kindly and voluntary, as it ought, the Apostle in the language he wrote called *Eunoia,* and the Latins, *Benevolence,*[135] intimating the original thereof to be in the understanding and the will; if not, surely there is nothing which might more properly be called a *malevolence* rather, and is the most injurious and unnatural tribute that can be extorted from a person endued with reason, to be made pay out the best substance of his body, and of his soul too, as some think, when either for just and powerful causes he cannot like, or from unequal causes finds not recompence. And that there is a hidden efficacy of love and hatred in man as well as in other kinds, not moral but natural, which though not always in the choice yet in the success of marriage will ever be most predominant, besides daily experience, the author of Ecclesiasticus, whose wisdom hath set him next the Bible,[136] acknowledges, 13.16: *A Man,* saith he, *will cleave to his like*. But what might be the cause, whether each one's allotted genius or proper star, or whether the supernal influence of schemes and angular aspects, or this elemental crasis[137] here below, whether all these jointly or singly meeting friendly, or unfriendly in either party, I dare not, with the men I am likest to clash, appear so much a philosopher as to conjecture.[138] The ancient proverb in Homer less abstruse entitles this work of leading each like person to his like, peculiarly to God himself,[139] which is plain enough also by his naming of a meet or like help in the first espousal instituted. And that every woman is meet for every man, none so absurd as to affirm. Seeing then there is a twofold seminary or stock in nature from whence are derived the issues of love and hatred, distinctly flowing through the whole mass of created things, and that God's doing ever is to bring the due likenesses and harmonies of his works together, except when out of two contraries met to their own destruction, he moulds a third existence; and that it is error, or some evil angel which either blindly or maliciously hath drawn together in two persons ill embarked in wedlock the sleeping discords and enmities of nature lulled on purpose with some false bait, that they may wake to agony and strife, later than prevention could have wished, if from the bent of just and honest intentions beginning what was begun and so continuing, all that is equal, all that is fair and possible hath been tried, and no accommodation likely to succeed, what folly is it still to stand combating and battering against invincible causes and effects, with evil upon evil, 'til either the best of our days be lingered out, or ended with some speeding sorrow. The wise Ecclesiasticus advises rather, 37:27, *My son, prove thy soul in thy life, see what is evil for it, and give not that unto it.* Reason he had to say so; for if the noisomeness or disfigurement of body can soon destroy the sympathy of mind to wedlock duties, much more will the annoyance and trouble of mind infuse itself into all the faculties and acts of the body, to render them invalid, unkindly, and even unholy against the fundamental law-book of nature, which Moses never thwarts but reverences. Therefore he commands us to force nothing against sympathy or natural order, no not upon the most abject creatures, to show that such an indignity cannot be offered to man without any impious crime. And certainly those divine meditating words of finding out a meet and like help to man have in them a consideration of more than the indefinite likeness of womanhood; nor are they to be made waste paper on, for the dullness of canon-divinity, no, nor those other allegoric precepts of beneficence fetch out of the closet of nature to teach us goodness and compassion in not compelling together unmatchable societies, or if they meet through mischance, by all consequence to disjoin them, as God and nature signifies and lectures to us not only by those recited decrees but even by the first and last of all his visible works, when by his divorcing command the world first rose out of chaos, nor can be renewed again out of confusion, but by the separating of unmeet consorts.

CHAP. XI

The seventh reason, that sometimes continuance in marriage may be evidently the shortening or endangering of life to either party, both law and divinity concluding that life is to be preferred before marriage, the intended solace of life.

Seventhly, the canon-law and divines consent, that if either party be found contriving against another's life, they may be severed by divorce; for a sin against the life of marriage is greater than a sin against the bed: the one destroys, the other defiles it. The same may be said touching those persons who, being of a pensive nature and course of life, have summed up all their solace in that free and lightsome conversation which God and man intends in marriage: whereof when they see themselves deprived by meeting an unsociable consort, they oft-times resent one another's mistake so deeply, that long it is not ere grief end one of them. When therefore this danger is foreseen, that the life is in peril by living together, what matter is it whether helpless grief or willful practice be the cause? This is certain, that the preservation of life is more worth than the compulsory keeping of marriage; and it is no less than cruelty to force a man to remain in that state at the solace of his life, which he and his friends know will be either the undoing or the disheartening of his life. And what is life without vigour and spiritual exercise of life? how can it be useful either to private or public employment? Shall it therefore be quite dejected, though never so valuable, and left to moulder away in heaviness for the superstitious and impossible performance of an ill-driven bargain? Nothing more inviolable than vows made to God; yet we read in Numbers, that if a wife had made such a vow, the mere will and authority of her husband might break it.[140] How much more then may he break the error of his own bonds with an unfit and mistaken wife to the saving of his welfare, his life, yea his faith and virtue from the hazard of over-strong temptations? For if man be Lord of the Sabbath to the curing of a fever,[141] can he be less than Lord of marriage in such important causes as these?

CHAP. XII

The eighth reason, it is probable, or rather certain, that every one who happens to marry, hath not the calling; and therefore upon unfitness found and considered, force ought not to be used.

Eighthly, it is most sure that some even of those who are not plainly defective in body are yet destitute of all other marriageable gifts, and consequently have not the calling to marry, unless nothing be requisite thereto but a mere instrumental body, which to affirm is to that unanimous covenant a reproach; yet it is as sure that many such, not of their own desire but by the persuasion of friends, or not knowing themselves, do often enter into wedlock; where finding the difference at length between the duties of a married life and the gifts of a single life, what unfitness of mind, what wearisomeness, what scruples and doubts to an incredible offence, and displeasure are like to follow between, may be soon imagined; whom thus to shut up and immure together, the one with a mischosen mate, the other in a mistaken calling, is not a course that Christian wisdom and tenderness ought to use. As for the custom that some parents and guardians have of forcing marriages, it will be better to say nothing of such a savage inhumanity, but only this: that the law which gives not all freedom of divorce to any creature endued with reason, so assassinated, is next in cruelty.

CHAP. XIII

The ninth reason, because marriage is not a mere carnal coition, but a human society, where that cannot reasonably be had, there can be no true matrimony. Marriage compared with all other covenants and vows warrantably broken for the good of man.

Marriage the Papists' sacrament, and unfit marriage the Protestants' idol.

Ninthly, I suppose it will be allowed us that marriage is a human society, and that all human society must proceed from the mind rather than the body, else it would be but a kind of animal or beastish meeting. If the mind therefore cannot have that due company by marriage that it may reasonably and humanly desire, that marriage can be no human society but a certain formality or gilding over of little better than a brutish congress, and so in very wisdom and pureness to be dissolved.

But marriage is more than human, *the covenant of God,* Prov. 2:17; therefore man cannot dissolve it. I answer, if it be more than human, so much the more it argues the chief society thereof to be in the soul rather than in the body, and the greatest breach thereof to be unfitness of mind rather than defect of body: for the body can have least affinity in a covenant more than human, so that the reason of dissolving holds good the rather. Again, I answer, that the Sabbath is a higher institution, a command of the first table,[142] for the breach whereof God hath far more and oftener testified his anger than for divorces, which from Moses to Malachi he never took displeasure at, nor then neither if we mark the text; and yet as oft as the good of man is concerned, he not only permits but commands to break the Sabbath. What covenant more contracted with God, and less in man's power, than the vow which hath once past his lips? yet if it be found rash, if offensive, if unfruitful either to God's glory or the good of man, our doctrine forces not error and unwillingness irksomely to keep it, but counsels wisdom and better thoughts boldly to break it. Therefore, to enjoin the indissoluble keeping of a marriage found unfit against the good of man both soul and body, as hath been evidenced, is to make an idol of marriage, to advance it above the worship of God and the good of man, to make it a transcendent command above both the second and first table, which is a most prodigious doctrine.

Next, whereas they cite out of the Proverbs, that it is *the covenant of God,* and therefore more than human, that consequence is manifestly false; for so the covenant which Zedekiah made with the infidel King of Babel, is called *the covenant of God,* Ezek. 17:19, which would be strange to hear counted more than a human covenant. So every covenant between man and man, bound by oath, may be called the covenant of God, because God therein is attested. So of marriage he is the author and the witness; yet hence will not follow any divine astriction[143] more than what is subordinate to the glory of God and the main good of either party: for as the glory of God and their esteemed fitness one for the other was the motive which led them both at first to think without other revelation that God had joined them together, so when it shall be found by their apparent unfitness, that their continuing to be man and wife is against the glory of God and their mutual happiness, it may assure them that God never joined them, who hath revealed his gracious will not to set the ordinance above the man for whom it was ordained, not to canonize marriage either as a tyranness or a goddess over the enfranchised life and soul of man. For wherein can God delight, wherein be worshiped, wherein be glorified by the forcible continuing of an improper and ill-yoking couple? He that loved not to see the disparity of several cattle at the plow, cannot be pleased with vast unmeetness in marriage. Where can be the peace and love which must invite God to such a house? May it not be feared that the not divorcing of such a helpless disagreement will be the divorcing of God finally from such a place? But it is a trial of our patience, they say. I grant it; but which of Job's afflictions were sent him with that law that he might not use means to remove any of them if he could? and what if it subvert our patience and our faith too? Who shall answer for the perishing of all those souls, perishing by stubborn expositions of particular and inferior precepts against the general and supreme rule of charity? They dare not affirm that marriage is either a sacrament or a mystery,[144] though all those sacred things give place to man, and yet they invest it with such an awful sanctity, and give such adamantine chains to bind with, as if it were to be worshiped like some Indian deity, when it can confer no blessing upon us, but works more and more to our misery. To such teachers the saying of St. Peter at the Council of Jerusalem will do well to be applied:[145] *why tempt ye*

God to put a yoke upon the necks of Christian men, which neither the Jews, God's ancient people, *nor we are able to bear;* and nothing but unwary expounding hath brought upon us.

CHAP. XIV

Considerations concerning Familism, Antinomianism, and why it may be thought that such opinions may proceed from the undue restraint of some just liberty, than which no greater cause to contemn discipline.

To these considerations this also may be added as no improbable conjecture, seeing that sort of men who follow Anabaptism, Familism, Antinomianism, and other fanatic dreams[146] (if we understand them not amiss)[147] be such most commonly as are by nature addicted to religion, of life also not debauched, and that their opinions having full swing do end in satisfaction of the flesh, it may come with reason into the thoughts of a wise man, whether all this proceed not partly, if not chiefly, from the restraint of some lawful liberty which ought to be given men and is denied them. As by physic we learn in menstruous bodies, where nature's current hath been stopped, that the suffocation and upward forcing of some lower part affects the head and inward sense with dotage and idle fancies. And on the other hand, whether the rest of vulgar men not so religiously professing, do not give themselves much the more to whoredom and adulteries, loving the corrupt and venial discipline of clergy-courts, but hating to hear of perfect reformation; whenas they foresee that then fornication shall be austerely censured, adultery punished, and marriage the appointed refuge of nature, though it hap to be never so incongruous and displeasing, must yet of force be worn out, when it can be to no other purpose but of strife and hatred, a thing odious to God. This may be worth the study of skillful men in theology and the reason of things. And lastly, to examine whether some undue and ill-grounded strictness upon the blameless nature of man be not the cause in those places where already reformation is, that the discipline of the Church, so often and so unavoidably broken, is brought into contempt and derision. And if it be thus, let those who are still bent to hold this obstinate literality so prepare themselves as to share in the account for all these transgressions, when it shall be demanded at the last day by One who will scan and shift things with more than a literal wisdom of equity. For if these reasons be duly pondered, and that the Gospel is more jealous of laying on excessive burdens than ever the law was, lest the soul of a Christian, which is inestimable, should be over-tempted and cast away; considering also that many properties of nature, which the power of regeneration itself never alters, may cause dislike of conversing, even between the most sanctified; which continually grating in harsh tune together, may breed some jar and discord, and that end in rancor and strife, a thing so opposite both to marriage and to Christianity, it would perhaps be less scandal to divorce a natural disparity than to link violently together an unchristian dissension, committing two ensnared souls inevitably to kindle one another, not with the fire of love, but with a hatred inconcileable,[148] who, were they dissevered, would be strait friends in any other relation. But if an alphabetical servility[149] must be still urged, it may so fall out, that the true Church may unwittingly use as much cruelty in forbidding to divorce, as the Church of Antichrist doth willfully in forbidding to marry.

The Second Book

CHAP. I

The ordinance of Sabbath and marriage compared. Hyperbole no infrequent figure in the Gospel. Excess cured by contrary excess. Christ neither did nor could abrogate the law of divorce, but only reprove[150] *the abuse thereof.*

Hitherto the position undertaken hath been declared, and proved by a law of God, that law proved to be moral, and unabolishable for many reasons equal, honest, charitable, just, annexed thereto. It follows now that those places of Scripture which have a seeming to revoke the prudence of Moses, or rather that merciful decree of God, be forthwith explained and reconciled. For what are all these reasonings worth, will some reply, whenas the words of Christ are plainly against all divorce, except in case of fornication.[151] To whom he whose mind were to answer no more but this, *except also in case of charity,* might safely appeal to the more plain words of Christ in defence of so excepting. *Thou shalt do no manner of work,* saith the commandment of the Sabbath.[152] Yes, saith Christ, works of charity. And shall we be more severe in paraphrasing the considerate and tender Gospel than he was in expounding the rigid and peremptory law? What was ever in all appearance less made for man, and more for God alone, than the Sabbath? yet when the good of man comes into the scales, we hear that voice of infinite goodness and benignity, that *Sabbath was made for man, not man for Sabbath.*[153] What thing ever was more made for man alone and less for God than marriage? And shall we load it with a cruel and senseless bondage utterly against both the good of man and the glory of God? Let whoso will now listen, I want neither pall nor mitre, I stay neither for ordination nor induction, but in the firm faith of a knowing Christian, which is the best and truest endowment of the keys,[154] I pronounce the man who shall bind so cruelly a good and gracious ordinance of God hath not in that the Spirit of Christ. Yet that every text of Scripture seeming opposite may be attended with a due exposition, this other part ensues, and makes account to find no slender arguments for this assertion out of those very Scriptures which are commonly urged against it.

First therefore let us remember, as a thing not to be denied, that all places of Scripture wherein just reason of doubt arises from the latter, are to be expounded by considering upon what occasion every thing is set down, and by comparing other texts. The occasion which induced our Savior to speak of divorce was either to convince the extravagance of the Pharisees in that point or to give a sharp and vehement answer to a tempting question. And in such cases, that we are not to repose all upon the literal terms of so many words many instances will teach us: wherein we may plainly discover how Christ meant not to be taken word for word, but like a wise physician, administering one excess against another, to reduce us to a perfect mean. Where the Pharisees were strict, there Christ seems remiss; where they were too remiss, he saw it needful to seem most severe. In one place he censures an unchaste look to be adultery already committed;[155] another time he passes over actual adultery with less reproof than for an unchaste look,[156] not so heavily condemning secret weakness as open malice. So here he may be justly thought to have given this rigid sentence against divorce, not to cut off all remedy from a good man who finds himself consuming away in a disconsolate and unenjoined matrimony, but to lay a bridle upon the bold abuses of those overweaning Rabbis; which he could not more effectually do than by a countersway[157] of restraint curbing their wild exorbitance almost into the other extreme, as when we bow things the contrary way to make them come to their natural straightness. And that this was the only intention of Christ is most evident if we attend but to his own words and protestation made in the same sermon, not many verses before he treats of divorcing, that he came not to abrogate from the law one jot or tittle, and denounces against them that shall so teach.[158]

But St. Luke, the verse immediately before going that of divorce, inserts the same caveat,[159] as if the latter could not be understood without the former; and as a witness to produce against this our willful mistake of abrogating, which must needs confirm us that whatever else in the political law of more special relation to the Jews might cease to us, yet that of those precepts concerning divorce, not one of them was repealed by the doctrine of Christ, unless we have vowed not to believe his own cautious and immediate profession. For if these our Savior's words inveigh against all divorce and condemn it as adultery, except it be for adultery, and be not rather understood against the abuse of those divorces permitted in the law, then is that law of Moses, Deut. 24:1. not only repealed and wholly annulled, against the promise of Christ and his known profession not to meddle in matters judicial, but that which is more strange, the very substance and purpose of that law is contradicted and convinced both of injustice and impurity, as having authorized and maintained legal adultery by statute. Moses also cannot escape to be guilty of unequal and unwise decrees, punishing one act of secret adultery by death[160] and permitting a whole life of open adultery by law. And albeit lawyers write that some political edicts, though not approved, are yet allowed to the scum of the people and the necessity of the times, these excuses have but a weak pulse. For first we read, not that the scoundrel people but the choicest, the wisest, the holiest of that nation have frequently used these laws, or such as these, in the best and holiest times. Secondly, be it yielded that in matters not very bad or impure a human lawgiver may slacken something of that which is exactly good to the disposition of the people and the times; but if the perfect, the pure, the righteous law of God, for so are all his statutes and his judgments, be found to have allowed smoothly, without any certain reprehension, that which Christ afterward declares to be adultery, how can we free this law from the horrible indictment of being both impure, unjust, and fallacious?

CHAP. II

How divorce was permitted for hardness of heart, cannot be understood by the common exposition. That the law cannot permit, much less enact, a permission of sin.

Neither will it serve to say this was permitted for the hardness of their hearts, in that sense as it is usually explained; for the law were then but a corrupt and erroneous school-master,[161] teaching us to dash against a vital maxim of religion by doing foul evil in hope of some certain good. This only text not to be matched again throughout the whole Scripture, whereby God in his perfect law should seem to have granted to the hard hearts of his holy people under his own hand a civil immunity and free charter to live and die in a long successive adultery under a covenant of works 'til the Messiah, and then that indulgent permission to be strictly denied by a covenant of grace, besides the incoherence of such a doctrine cannot, must not be thus interpreted, to the raising of a paradox never known 'til then, only hanging by the twined thread of one doubtful Scripture, against so many other rules and leading principles of religion, of justice, and purity of life. For what could be granted more either to the fear or to the lust of any tyrant or politician[162] than this authority of Moses thus expounded; which opens him a way at will to dam up justice, and not only to admit of any Romish or Austrian dispenses,[163] but to enact a statute of that which he dares not seem to approve, even to legitimate vice, to make sin itself, the ever alien and vassal sin, a free citizen of the commonwealth, pretending only these or these plausible reasons? And well he might, all the while that Moses shall be alleged to have done as much without showing any reason at all. Yet this could not enter into the heart of David, Psal. 94:20, how any such authority as endeavours *to fashion wickedness by a law* should derive itself from God. And Isaiah lays *woe upon them that decree unrighteous decrees,* chap. 10:1. Now which of these two is the better law-giver, and which deserves most a woe: he that gives out an edict singly unjust, or he that confirms to generations a fixed and unmolested impunity of that which is not only held to be unjust but also unclean, and both in a high degree, not only as they themselves affirm, an injurious expulsion of one wife, but also an unclean freedom by more than a patent to wed another adulterously? How can we therefore with safety thus dangerously confine the free simplicity of our Savior's meaning to that which merely amounts from so many letters, whenas it can consist neither with his former and cautionary words, nor with other more pure and holy principles, nor finally with the scope of charity, commanding by his express commission in a higher strain. But all rather of necessity must be understood as only against the abuse of that wise and ingenuous liberty which Moses gave, and to terrify a roving conscience from sinning under that pretext.

CHAP. III

That to allow sin by law is against the nature of law, the end of the law-giver, and the good of the people. Impossible therefore in the law of God. That it makes God the author of sin, more than any thing objected by the Jesuits or Arminians against predestination.

But let us further examine upon what consideration a law of licence could be thus given to a holy people for the hardness of heart. I suppose all will answer, that for some good end or other. But here the contrary shall be proved. First, that many ill effects but no good end of such a sufferance can be shown; next, that a thing unlawful can for no good end whatever be either done or allowed by a positive law. If there were any good end aimed at, that end was then good either as to the law, or to the lawgiver licensing, or as to the person licensed. That it could not be the end of the law, whether moral or judicial, to license a sin, I prove easily out of Rom. 5:20, *The law entered, that the offence might abound;* that is, that sin might be made abundantly manifest to be heinous and displeasing to God, that so his offered grace might be the more esteemed. Now if the law, instead of aggravating and terrifying sin, shall give out licence, it foils itself, and turns recreant from its own end. It forestalls the pure grace of Christ, which is through righteousness, with impure indulgences, which are through sin. And instead of discovering sin, for *by the law is the knowledge thereof,* saith St. Paul,[164] and that by certain and true light for men to walk in safety, it holds out false and dazzling fires to stumble men, or like those miserable flies[165] to run into with delight and be burnt. For how many souls might easily think that to be lawful which the law and magistrate allowed them? Again, we read 1 Tim. 1:5, *the end of the commandment is charity out of a pure heart, and of a good conscience, and of faith unfained.* But never could that be charity to allow a people what they could not use with a pure heart, but with conscience and faith both deceived, or else despised. The more particular end of the judicial law is set forth to us clearly, Rom. 13, *that God hath given to that law a sword not in vain, but to be a terror to evil works, a revenge to execute wrath upon him that doth evil.* If this terrible commission should but forbear to punish wickedness, were it other to be accounted than partial and unjust? but if it begin to write indulgence to vulgar uncleanness, can it do more to corrupt and shame the end of its own being? Lastly, if the law allow sin, it enters into a kind of covenant with sin; and if it do, there is not a greater sinner in the world than the law itself. The law, to use an allegory something different from that in Philo Judaeus concerning Amalek, though haply more significant, the law is the Israelite, and hath this absolute charge given it, Deut. 25, *to blot out the memory of sin, the Amalekite, from under Heaven, not to forget it.* Again, the law is the Israelite, and hath this express repeated command *to make no covenant with* Sin, *the Canaanite,*[166] but to expel him, lest he prove a snare. And to say truth, it were too rigid and reasonless to proclaim such an enmity between man and man, were it not the type of a greater enmity between law and sin. I speak even now, as if sin were condemned in a perpetual villenage[167] never to be free by law, never to be manumitted;[168] but sure sin can have no tenure by law past all atonement: both diagonial contraries,[169] as much allowing one another as day and night together in one hemisphere. Or if it be possible that sin with his[170] darkness may come to composition, it cannot be without a foul eclipse and twilight to the law, whose brightness ought to surpass the noon. Thus we see how this unclean permission defeats the sacred and glorious end both of the moral and judicial law.

As little good can the lawgiver propose to equity by such a lavish remissness as this: if to remedy hardness of heart, Paraeus and other divines confess,[171] it more increases by this liberty than is lessened. And how is it probable that their hearts were more hard in this, that it should be yielded to, than in any other crime? Their hearts were set upon usury, and are to this day, no nation more; yet that which was the endamaging only of their estates was narrowly forbid; this which is thought the extreme injury and dishonour of their wives and daughters, with the defilement also of themselves, is bounteously allowed. Their hearts were as hard under their best Kings to offer in high places, though to the true God. Yet that, but a small thing, is strictly forewarned; this, accounted a high offence against one of the greatest moral duties, is calmly permitted and established. How can it be evaded but that the heavy censure of Christ should fall worse upon this lawgiver of theirs than upon all the scribes and Pharisees? For they did but omit judgment and mercy to trifle in mint and cumin, yet all according to law;[172] but this their law-giver, altogether as punctual in such niceties, goes marching on to adulteries through the violence of divorce by law against law. If it were such a cursed act of Pilate, a subordinate judge to Caesar, over-swayed by those hard hearts with much ado to suffer one transgression of law but once,[173] what is it then with less ado to publish a law by transgression for many ages? Did God for this come down and cover the Mount of Sinai with his glory, uttering in thunder those his sacred ordinances out of the bottomless treasures of his wisdom and infinite pureness, to patch up an ulcerous and rotten commonwealth with strict and stern injunctions to wash the skin and garments for every unclean touch, and such easy permission given to pollute the soul with adulteries by public authority without disgrace or question? No, it had been better that man had never known law or matrimony, than that such foul iniquity should be fastened upon the Holy One of Israel, the Judge of all the Earth, and such a piece of folly as Beelzebub[174] would not commit, to divide against himself and prevent his own ends; or if he to compass more mischief might yield perhaps to feign some good deed, yet that God should enact a licence of certain evil for uncertain good against his own glory and pureness is abominable to conceive. And as it is destructive to the end of law, and blasphemous to the honour of the law-giver licensing, so it is as pernicious to the person licensed. If a private friend admonish not, the Scripture saith, *he hates his brother, and lets him perish;*[175] but if he soothe him and allow him in his faults, the Proverbs teach us *he spreads a net for his neighbour's feet, and works ruin.*[176] If the magistrate or prince forget to administer due justice and restrain not sin, Eli himself could say *it made the Lord's people to transgress.*[177] But if he countenance them against law by his own example, what havoc it makes both in religion and virtue among the people may be guessed by the anger it brought upon Hophni and Phineas not to be appeased *with sacrifice nor offering for ever.*[178] If the law be silent to declare sin, the people must needs generally go astray, for the Apostle himself saith, *he had not known lust but by the law;*[179] and surely such a nation seems not to be under the illuminating guidance of God's law, but under the horrible doom rather of such as despise the Gospel: *he that is filthy, let him be filthy still.*[180] But where the law itself gives a warrant for sin, I know not what condition of misery to imagine miserable enough for such a people, unless that portion of the wicked, or rather of the damned, on whom God threatens in 11 Psalm, *to rain snares:* but that questionless cannot be by any law, which the Apostle saith *is a ministry ordained of God for our good,*[181] and not so many ways and in so high a degree to our destruction, as we have now been graduating.[182] And this is all the good can come to the person licensed in his hardness of heart.

I am next to mention that, which because it is a ground in divinity, Rom. 3, will save the labour of demonstrating, unless her given axioms be more doubted than in other arts (although it be no less firm in the precepts of philosophy) that a thing unlawful can for no good whatsoever be done, much less allowed by a positive law. And this is the matter why interpreters upon that passage in Hosea will not consent it to be a true story that the prophet took a harlot to wife,[183] because God, being a pure Spirit, could not command a thing repugnant to his own nature, no not for so good an end as to exhibit more to the life a wholesome and perhaps a converting parable to many an Israelite. Yet that he commanded the allowance of adulterous and injurious divorces for hardness of heart, a reason obscure and in a wrong sense, they can very savourily[184] persuade themselves; so tenacious is the leaven of an old conceit. But they shift it: he permitted only. Yet silence in the law is consent, and consent is accessory; why then is not the law being silent, or not active against a crime, accessory to its own conviction, itself judging? For though we should grant that it approves not, yet it wills; and the lawyer's maxim is, that *the will compelled is yet the will.* And though Aristotle in his *Ethics* call this a mixed action, yet he concludes it to be voluntary and inexcusable, if it be evil. How justly then might human law and philosophy rise up against the righteousness of Moses, if this be true which our vulgar divinity fathers upon him, yea upon God himself, not silently and only negatively to permit, but in his law to divulge a written and general privilege to commit and persist in unlawful divorces with a high hand, with security and no ill fame: for this is more than permitting or conniving, this is maintaining; this is warranting, this protecting, yea this is doing evil, and such an evil as that reprobate law-giver did, whose lasting infamy is engraven upon him like a surname, *he who made Israel to sin.*[185] This is the lowest pitch contrary to God that public fraud and injustice can descend.

If it be affirmed that God, as being Lord, may do what he will, yet we must know that God hath not two wills, but one will, much less two contrary. If he once willed adultery should be sinful and to be punished with death, all his omnipotence will not allow him to will the allowance that his holiest people might as it were by his own antinomy, or counter-statute, live unreproved in the same fact as he himself esteemed it, according to our common explainers. The hidden ways of his providence we adore and search not, but the law is his revealed will, his complete, his evident and certain will; herein he appears to us as it were in human shape, enters into covenant with us, swears to keep it, binds himself like a just law-giver to his own prescriptions, gives himself to be understood by men, judges and is judged, measures and is commensurate to right reason, cannot require less of us in one cantle of his law than in another; his legal justice cannot be so fickle and so variable, sometimes like a devouring fire,[186] and by and by connivent[187] in the embers, or, if I may so say, oscitant[188] and supine. The vigor of his law could no more remit, than the hallowed fire on his altar could be let go out.[189] The lamps that burned before him might need snuffing, but the light of his law never. Of this also more beneath, in discussing a solution of Rivetus.

The Jesuits, and that sect among us which is named of Arminius,[190] are wont to charge us of making God the author of sin, in two degrees especially, not to speak of his permissions: 1. Because we hold that he hath decreed some to damnation, and consequently to sin, say they; next, because those means which are of saving knowledge to others, he makes to them an occasion of greater sin. Yet considering the perfection wherein man was created, and might have stood, no decree necessitating his free will, but subsequent, though not in time yet in order to causes which were in his own power, they might methinks be persuaded to absolve both God and us. Whenas the doctrine of Plato and Chrysippus, with their followers, the Academics and the Stoics, who knew not what a consummate and most adorned Pandora was bestowed upon Adam to be the nurse and guide of his arbitrary happiness and perseverance, I mean his native innocence and perfection, which might have kept him from being our true Epimetheus,[191] and though they taught of virtue and vice to be both the gift of divine destiny, they could yet give reasons not invalid to justify the councils of God and fate from the insulsity[192] of mortal tongues: that man's own free will self-corrupted is the adequate and sufficient cause of his disobedience besides fate; as Homer also wanted not to express, both in his *Iliad* and *Odyssey*. And Manilius the poet, although in his fourth book he tells of some *created both to sin and punishment,* yet without murmuring, and with an industrious cheerfulness, he acquits the Deity. They were not ignorant in their heathen lore, that it is most God-like to punish those who of his creatures became his enemies with the greatest punishments; and they could attain also to think that the greatest when God himself throws a man farthest from him; which then they held he did, when he blinded, hardened, and stirred up his offenders to finish and pile up their desperate work since they had undertaken it. To banish forever into a local Hell, whether in the air or in the center, or in that uttermost and bottomless gulf of chaos, deeper from holy bliss than the world's diameter multiplied, they thought not a punishing so proper and proportionate for God to inflict as to punish sin with sin. Thus were the common sort of Gentiles wont to think, without any wry thoughts cast upon divine governance. And therefore Cicero, not in his Tuscan or Campanian retirements among the learned wits of that age, but even in the Senate to a mixed auditory (though he were sparing otherwise to broach his philosophy among statists and lawyers) yet as to this point both in his oration against Piso, and in that which is about the answers of the soothsayers against Clodius, he declares it publicly as no paradox to common ears, that God cannot punish man more, nor make him more miserable, than still by making him more sinful. Thus we see how in this controversy the justice of God stood upright even among heathen disputers. But if any one be truly and not pretendedly zealous for God's honour, here I call him forth before men and angels to use his best and most advised skill, lest God more unavoidably than ever yet, and in the guiltiest manner, be made the author of sin: if he shall not only deliver over and incite his enemies by rebuke to sin as a punishment, but shall by patent under his own broad seal allow his friends whom he would sanctify and save, whom he would unite to himself, and not disjoin, whom he would correct by wholesome chastening, and not punish as he doth the damned by lewd sinning, if he shall allow these in his law the perfect rule of his own purest will, and our most edified conscience, the perpetrating of an odious and manifold sin without the least contesting. 'Tis wondered how there can be in God a secret and revealed will; and yet what wonder, if there be in man two answerable causes. But here there must be two revealed wills grappling in a fraternal war with one another without any reasonable cause apprehended. This cannot be less than to engraft sin into the substance of the law, which law is to provoke sin by crossing and forbidding, not by complying with it. Nay this is, which I tremble in uttering, to incarnate sin into the unpunishing and well-pleased will of God. To avoid these dreadful consequences that tread upon the heels of those allowances to sin, will be a task of far more difficulty than to appease those minds which perhaps out of a vigilant and wary conscience except against[193] predestination. Thus finally we may conclude, that a law wholly giving licence cannot upon any good consideration be given to a holy people for hardness of heart in the vulgar sense.

CHAP. IV

That if divorce be no command, no more is marriage. That divorce could be no dispensation if it were sinful. The solution of Rivetus, *that God dispensed by some unknown way, ought not to satisfy a Christian mind.*

Others think to evade the matter by not granting any law of divorce, but only a dispensation, which is contrary to the words of Christ, who himself calls it a law, Mark 10.5. Or if we speak of a command in the strictest definition, then marriage itself is no more a command than divorce, but only a free permission to him who cannot contain.[194] But as to dispensation, I affirm the same as before of the law, that it can never be given to the allowance of sin. God cannot give it, neither in respect of himself nor in respect of man. Not in respect of himself, being a most pure essence, the just avenger of sin; neither can he make that cease to be a sin which is in itself unjust and impure, as all divorces they say were, which were not for adultery. Not in respect of man, for then it must be either to his good or to his evil. Not to his good: for how can that be imagined any good to a sinner, whom nothing but rebuke and due correction can save, to hear the determinate oracle of divine law louder than any reproof dispensing and providing for the impunity and convenience of sin; to make that doubtful, or rather lawful, which the end of the law was to make most evidently hateful. Nor to the evil of man can a dispense be given; for if *the law were ordained unto life,* Rom. 7:10, how can the same God publish dispenses against that law, which must needs be unto death? Absurd and monstrous would that dispense be, if any judge or law should give it a man to cut his own throat, or to damn himself. Dispense therefore presupposes full pardon, or else it is not a dispense but a most baneful and bloody snare. And why should God enter covenant with a people to be holy, as *the command is holy, and just, and good,* Rom. 7:12, and yet suffer an impure and treacherous dispense to mislead and betray them under the vizard of law to a legitimate practice of uncleanness? God is no covenant-breaker; he cannot do this.

Rivetus, a diligent and learned writer, having well weighed what hath been written by those founders of dispense and finding the small agreement among them, would fain work himself aloof these rocks and quick-sands, and thinks it best to conclude that God certainly did dispense, but by some way to us unknown, and so to leave it. But to this I oppose, that a Christian by no means ought rest himself in such an ignorance whereby so many absurdities will straight reflect both against the purity, justice, and wisdom of God, the end also both of Law and Gospel, and the comparison of them both together. God indeed in some ways of his providence is high and secret, past finding out; but in the delivery and execution of his law, especially in the managing of a duty so daily and so familiar as this is whereof we reason, hath plain enough revealed himself, and requires the observance thereof not otherwise than to the law of nature and equity imprinted in us seems correspondent. And he hath taught us to love and to extol his laws, not only as they are his, but as they are just and good to every wise and sober understanding. Therefore Abraham, even to the face of God himself, seemed to doubt of divine justice, if it should swerve from the irradiation wherewith it had enlightened the mind of man and bound itself to observe its own rule: *Wilt thou destroy the righteous with the wicked? that be far from thee; shall not the Judge of the Earth do right?*[195] Thereby declaring, that God hath created righteousness in right itself, against which he cannot do. So David, Psalm. 119, *the testimonies which thou hast commanded are righteous and very faithful; thy word is very pure, therefore thy servant loves it.*[196] Not only then for the author's sake, but for its own purity. *He is faithful,* saith St. Paul, *he cannot deny himself;*[197] that is, he cannot deny his own promises, cannot but be true to his own rules. How should we imitate him else, to *be perfect as he is perfect?*[198] If at pleasure he can dispense with golden poetic ages of such pleasing licence, as in the fabled reign of old Saturn, and this perhaps before the law might have some covert,[199] but under such an undispensing covenant as Moses made with them, and not to tell us why and wherefore, indulgence cannot give quiet to the breast of an intelligent man. We must be resolved how the law can be pure and perspicuous, and yet throw a polluted skirt over these Eleusinian Mysteries,[200] that no man can utter what they mean: worse in this than the worst obscenities of heathen superstition, for their filthiness was hid, but the mystic reason thereof known to their sages. But this Jewish imputed filthiness was daily and open, but the reason of it is not known to our divines. We know of no design the Gospel can have to impose new righteousness upon works, but to remit the old by faith without works, if we mean justifying works.[201] We know no mystery our Savior could have to lay new bonds upon marriage in the covenant of grace which himself had loosened to the severity of law. So that Rivetus may pardon us if we cannot be contented with his non-solution to remain in such a peck of uncertainties and doubts, so dangerous and ghastly to the fundamentals of our faith.

CHAP. V

What a dispensation is.

Therefore, to get some better satisfaction, we must proceed to inquire as diligently as we can what a dispensation is, which I find to be either properly so called, or improperly. Improperly so called, is rather a particular and exceptive law, absolving and disobliging from a more general command for some just and reasonable cause. As Numb. 9, they who were unclean or in a journey had leave to keep the Passover in the second month, but otherwise ever in the first. As for that in Leviticus of marrying the brother's wife, it was a penal statute rather than a dispense; and commands nothing injurious or in it self unclean, only prefers a special reason of charity before an institutive decency, and perhaps is meant for lifetime only, as is expressed beneath in the prohibition of taking two sisters. What other edict of Moses, carrying but the semblance of a law in any other kind, may bear the name of a dispense, I have not readily to instance. But a dispensation most properly is some particular accident rarely happening, and therefore not specified in the law but left to the decision of charity, even under the bondage of Jewish rites, much more under the liberty of the Gospel. Thus did *David enter into the house of God, and did eat the shewbread,*[202] *he and his followers, which was* ceremonially *unlawful.*[203] Of such dispenses as these it was that Verdune the French divine so gravely disputed in the Council of Trent against Friar Adrian, who held that the Pope might dispense with any thing. *It is a fond persuasion,* saith Verdune, *that dispensing is a favour; nay, it is as good distributive justice as what is most, and the priest sins if he gives it not, for it is nothing else but a right interpretation of law.* Thus far that I can learn touching this matter wholesomely decreed. But that God, who is the giver of every good and perfect gift, James 1[204] should give out a rule and directory to sin by, should enact a dispensation as long-lived as a law whereby to live in privileged adultery for hardness of heart, and yet this obdurate disease cannot be conceived how it was the more amended by this unclean remedy, is the most deadly and scorpion-like gift[205] that the enemy of mankind could have given to any miserable sinner, and is rather such a dispense as that was which the serpent gave to our first parents. God gave quails in his wrath,[206] and kings in his wrath,[207] yet neither of these things evil in themselves; but that he whose eyes cannot behold impurity, should in the book of his holy covenant, his most unpassionate law, give licence and statute for uncontrolled adultery, although it go for the received opinion,

I shall ever dissuade my soul from such a creed, such an indulgence as the shop of Antichrist never forged a baser.

CHAP. VI

That the Jew had no more right to this supposed dispense than the Christian hath, and rather not so much.

But if we must needs dispense, let us for a while so far dispense with truth as to grant that sin may be dispensed; yet there will be copious reason found to prove that the Jew had no more right to such a supposed indulgence than the Christian, whether we look at the clear knowledge wherein he lived, or the strict performance of works whereto he was bound. Besides visions and prophecies, they had the law of God, which in the Psalms and Proverbs is chiefly praised for sureness and certainty, both easy and perfect to the enlightening of the simple.[208] How could it be so obscure then, or they so sottishly blind in this plain moral and household duty? They had the same precepts about marriage. Christ added nothing to their clearness, for that had argued them imperfect; he opens not the law, but removes the Pharisaic mists raised between the law and the people's eyes. The only sentence which he adds, *What God hath joined let no man put asunder,*[209] is as obscure as any clause fetched out of Genesis, and hath increased a yet undecided controversy of clandestine marriages.[210] If we examine over all his sayings, we shall find him not so much interpreting the law with his words, as referring his own words to be interpreted by the law, and oftener obscures his mind in short, and vehement, and compact sentences, to blind and puzzle them the more who would not understand the law. The Jews therefore were as little to be dispensed with for lack of moral knowledge as we.

Next, none I think will deny but that they were as much bound to perform the law as any Christian. That severe and rigorous knife not sparing the tender foreskin of any male infant, to carve upon his flesh the mark of that strict and pure covenant whereinto he entered, might give us to understand enough against the fancy of dispensing.[211] St. Paul testifies that every *circumcised man is a debtor to the whole law,* Gal. 5, or else *circumcision is in vain,*

Rom, 2:25. How vain then, and how preposterous must it needs be to exact a circumcision of the flesh from an infant unto an outward sign of purity, and to dispense an uncircumcision in the soul of a grown man to an inward and real impurity? How vain again was that law to impose tedious expiations for every slight sin of ignorance and error, and to privilege without penance or disturbance an odious crime whether of ignorance or obstinacy? How unjust also inflicting death and extirpation for the mark of circumstantial pureness omitted, and proclaiming all honest and liberal indemnity to the act of a substantial impureness committed, making void the covenant that was made against it? Thus if we consider the tenor of the law, to be circumcised and to perform all, not pardoning so much as the scapes[212] of error and ignorance, and compare this with the condition of the Gospel, Believe and be baptized,[213] I suppose it cannot be long ere we grant that the Jew was bound as strictly to the performance of every duty as was possible, and therefore could not be dispensed with more than the Christian, perhaps not so much.

CHAP. VII

That the Gospel is more apt to dispense than the law. Paraeus *answered.*

If then the law will afford no reason why the Jew should be more gently dealt with than the Christian, then surely the Gospel can afford as little why the Christian should be less gently dealt with than the Jew. The Gospel indeed exhorts to highest perfection, but bears with weakest infirmity more than the law. Hence those indulgences, *all cannot receive this saying, every man hath his proper gift,* with express charges not to *lay on yokes which our fathers could not bear.*[214] The nature of man still is as weak, and yet as hard; and that weakness and hardness as unfit and as unteachable to be harshly used as ever. Ay but, saith Paraeus, there is a greater portion of spirit poured upon the Gospel, which requires from us more perfect obedience. I answer, this does not prove that the law therefore might give allowance to sin more than the Gospel; and if it were not sin, we know it the work of the spirit to *mortify our corrupt desires and evil concupiscence;*[215] but not to root up our natural affections and disaffections, moving to and fro even in wisest men upon just and necessary reasons, which were the true ground of that Mosaic dispense, and is the utmost extent of our pleading. What is more or less perfect we dispute not, but what is sin or no sin. And in that I still affirm the law required as perfect obedience as the Gospel; besides, that the prime end of the Gospel is not so much to exact our obedience, as to reveal grace and the satisfaction of our disobedience. What is now exacted from us, it is the accusing law that does it, even yet under the Gospel, but cannot be more extreme to us now than to the Jews of old; for the law ever was of works, and the Gospel ever was of grace.

Either then the law by harmless and needless dispenses, which the Gospel is now made to deny, must have anticipated and exceeded the grace of the Gospel, or else must be found to have given politic and superficial graces without real pardon, saying in general, do this and live, and yet deceiving and damning under-hand with unsound and hollow permissions, which is utterly abhorring from the end of all law, as hath been showed. But if those indulgences were safe and sinless, out of tenderness and compassion, as indeed they were, and yet shall be abrogated by the Gospel, then the law, whose end is by rigour to magnify grace, shall itself give grace and pluck a fair plume from the Gospel; instead of hastening us thither, alluring us from it. And whereas the tenor of the law was a servant to amplify and illustrate the mildness of grace, now the unmildness of evangelic grace shall turn servant, to declare the grace and mildness of the rigorous law. The law was harsh to extol the grace of the Gospel, and now the Gospel by a new affected strictness of her own shall extenuate the grace which herself offers. For by exacting a duty which the law dispensed, if we perform it, then is grace diminished, by how much performance advances, unless the Apostle argue wrong;[216] if we perform it not, and perish for not performing, then are the conditions of grace harder than those of rigour. If through faith and repentance we perish not, yet grace still remains the less by requiring that which rigour did not require, or at least not so strictly. Thus much therefore to Paraeus, that if the Gospel require more perfect obedience than the law as a duty, it exalts the law and debases itself, which is dishonourable to the work of our redemption. Seeing therefore that all the causes of any allowance that the Jews might have remain as well to the Christians, this is a certain rule, that so long as the causes remain the allowance ought. And having thus at length inquired the truth concerning law and dispense, their ends, their uses, their limits, and in what manner both Jew and Christian stand liable to the one or capable of the other, we may safely conclude that to affirm the giving of any law or law-like dispense to sin for hardness of heart is a doctrine of that extravagance[217] from the sage principles of piety, that whoso considers thoroughly cannot but admire how this hath been digested all this while.

CHAP. VIII

The true sense how Moses suffered divorce for hardness of heart.

What may we do then to salve this seeming inconsistence? I must not dissemble that I am confident it can be done no other way than this:

Moses, Deut. 24.1. established a grave and prudent law, full of moral equity, full of due consideration towards nature, that cannot be resisted, a law consenting with the laws of wisest men and civilest nations; that when a man hath married a wife, if it come to pass that he cannot love her by reason of some displeasing natural quality or unfitness in her, let him write her a bill of divorce. The intent of which law undoubtedly was this: that if any good and peaceable man should discover some helpless disagreement or dislike either of mind or body whereby he could not cheerfully perform the duty of a husband without the perpetual dissembling of offence and disturbance to his spirit, rather than to live uncomfortably and unhappily both to himself and to his wife, rather than to continue undertaking a duty which he could not possibly discharge, he might dismiss her whom he could not tolerably and so not conscionably retain. And this law the Spirit of God by the mouth of Solomon, Prov. 30:21, 23, testifies to be a good and a necessary law, by granting it that *a hated woman* (for so the Hebrew word signifies, rather than odious, though it come all to one) *that a hated woman, when she is married, is a thing that the Earth cannot bear.*[218] What follows then but that the charitable law must remedy what nature cannot undergo? Now that many licentious and hard-hearted men took hold of this law to cloak their bad purposes is nothing strange to believe. And these were they, not for whom Moses made the law, God forbid, but whose hardness of heart taking ill advantage by this law, he held it better to suffer as by accident, where it could not be detected, rather than good men should lose their just and lawful privilege of remedy. Christ therefore having to answer these tempting Pharisees, according as his custom was, not meaning to inform their proud ignorance what Moses did in the true intent of the law, which they had ill cited, suppressing the true cause for which Moses gave it, and extending it to every slight matter, tells them their own, what Moses was forced to suffer by their abuse of his law. Which is yet more plain if we mark that our Savior in Mat. 5 cites not the law of Moses, but the pharisaical tradition falsely grounded upon that law.[219] And in those other places, chap. 19. and Mark 10, the Pharisees cite the law but conceal the wise and human reason there expressed; which our Savior corrects not in them, whose pride deserved not his instruction, only returns them what is proper to them: *Moses for the hardness of your heart suffered you,* that is such as you, *to put away your wives;* and *to you he wrote this precept* for this cause, which (to you) must be read with an impression,[220] and understood limitedly of such as covered ill purposes under that law. For it was seasonable that they should hear their own unbounded licence rebuked, but not seasonable for them to hear a good man's requisite liberty explained. But us he hath taught better, if we have ears to hear. He himself acknowledged it to be a law, Mark 10, and being a law of God, it must have an undoubted *end of charity, which may be used with a pure heart, a good conscience, and faith unfained,* as was heard It cannot allow sin, but is purposely to resist sin, as by the same chapter to Timothy appears. There we learn also, *that the law is good, if a man use it lawfully.*[221] Out of doubt then there must be a certain good in this law, which Moses willingly allowed, and there might be an unlawful use made thereof by hypocrites; and that was it which was unwillingly suffered, foreseeing it in general but not able to discern it in particulars. Christ therefore mentions not here what Moses and the law intended, for good men might know that by many other rules; and the scornful Pharisees were not fit to be told, until they could employ that knowledge they had less abusively. Only he acquaints them with what Moses by them was put to suffer.

CHAP. IX

The words of the institution how to be understood; and of our Savior's answer to his disciples.

And to entertain a little their overweening arrogance as best befitted, and to amaze them yet further, because they thought it no hard matter to fulfill the law, he draws them up to that inseparable institution which God ordained in the beginning before the fall, when man and woman were both perfect and could have no cause to separate; just as in the same chapter he stands not to contend with the arrogant young man who boasted his observance of the whole law, whether he had indeed kept it or not, but screws him up higher to a task of that perfection which no man is bound to imitate.[222] And in like manner that pattern of the first institution he set before the opinionative Pharisees, to dazzle them, and not to bind us. For this is a solid rule: that every command given with reason binds our obedience no otherwise than that reason holds. Of this sort was that command in Eden: *therefore shall a man cleave to his wife, and they shall be one flesh;*[223] which we see is no absolute command, but with an inference. Therefore the reason then must be first considered, that our obedience be not mis-obedience. The first is, for it is not single, because the wife is to the husband *flesh of his flesh,* as in the verse going before. But this reason cannot be sufficient of itself: for why then should he for his wife leave his father and mother, with whom he is far *more flesh of flesh, and bone of bone,* as being made of their substance? And besides, it can be but a sorry and ignoble society of life whose inseparable injunction depends merely upon flesh and bones. Therefore we must look higher, since Christ himself recalls us to the beginning, and we shall find that the primitive reason of never divorcing, was that sacred and not vain promise of God to remedy man's loneliness by *making him a meet help for him,*[224] though not now in perfection, as at first, yet still in proportion as things now are. And this is repeated verse 20, when all other creatures were fitly associated and brought to Adam, as if the divine power had been in some care and deep thought, because *there was not yet found an help-meet for man.* And can we so slightly depress the all-wise purpose of a deliberating God, as if his consultation had produced no other good for man but to join him with an accidental companion of propagation, which his sudden word had already made for every beast? Nay, a far less good to man it will be found, if she must at all adventures be fastened upon him individually.[225] And therefore even plain sense and equity, and, which is above them both, the all-interpreting voice of charity herself cries loud that this primitive reason, this consulted promise of God *to make a meet help,* is the only cause that gives authority to this command of not divorcing, to be a command. And it might be further added, that if the true definition of a wife were asked in good earnest, this clause of being *a meet help* would show itself so necessary, and so essential in that demonstrative argument, that it might be logically concluded therefore she who naturally and perpetually is no meet help can be no wife, which clearly takes away the difficulty of dismissing of such a one. If this be not thought enough, I answer yet further, that marriage, unless it mean a fit and tolerable marriage, is not inseparable neither by nature nor institution. Not by nature, for then those Mosaic divorces had been against nature, if separable and inseparable be contraries, as who doubts they be; and what is against nature is against law, if soundest philosophy abuse us not. By this reckoning Moses should be most unmosaic, that is most illegal, not to say most unnatural. Nor is it inseparable by the first institution; for then no second institution of the same law for so many causes could dissolve it, it being most unworthy a human (as Plato's judgment is in the fourth book of his *Laws*) much more a divine lawgiver, to write two several decrees upon the same thing. But what could Plato have deemed if one of these were good, and the other evil to be done? Lastly, suppose it be inseparable by institution, yet in competition with higher things, as religion and charity in mainest matters, and when the chief end is frustrate for which it was ordained, as hath been shown, if still it must remain inseparable, it holds a strange and lawless propriety from all other works of God under Heaven. From these many considerations, we may safely gather that so much of the first institution as our Savior mentions, for he mentions not all, was but to quell and put to nonplus the tempting Pharisees, and to lay open their ignorance and shallow understanding of the Scriptures. For, saith he, *Have ye not read that he which made them at the beginning, made them male and female, and said, for this cause shall a man cleave to his wife?*[226] which these blind usurpers of Moses' chair could not gainsay, as if this single respect of male and female were sufficient against a thousand inconveniences and mischiefs to clog a rational creature to his endless sorrow unrelinquishably, under the guileful superscription of his intended solace and comfort. What if they had thus answered, 'Master, if thou mean to make wedlock as inseparable as from the beginning, let it be made a fit society, as God meant it, which we shall soon understand it ought to be, if thou recite the whole reason of the law.' Doubtless our Savior had applauded their just answer. For then they had expounded his command of Paradise, even as Moses himself expounds it by his laws of divorce, that is, with due and wise regard to the premises and reasons of the first command; according to which, without unclean and temporizing permissions, he instructs us in this imperfect state what we may lawfully do about divorce.

But if it be thought that the disciples, offended at the rigour of Christ's answer, could yet obtain no mitigation of the former sentence pronounced to the Pharisees, it may be fully answered that our Savior continues the same reply to his disciples, as men leavened with the same customary licence which the Pharisees maintained, and displeased at the removing of a traditional abuse whereto they had so long not unwillingly been used. It was no time then to contend with their slow and prejudicial belief in a thing wherein an ordinary measure of light in Scripture, with some attention, might afterwards inform them well enough. And yet, ere Christ had finished this argument, they might have picked out of his own concluding words an answer more to their minds, and in effect the same with that which hath been all this while entreating audience. *All men,* saith he, *cannot receive this saying, save they to whom it is given; he that is able to receive it, let him receive it.*[227] What saying is this which is left to a man's choice to receive, or not receive? What but the married life? Was our Savior so mild and so favourable to the weakness of a single man, and is he turned on the sudden so rigourous and inexorable, to the distresses and extremities of an ill-wedded man? Did he so graciously give leave to change the better single life for the worse married life? Did he open so to us this hazardous and accidental door of marriage to shut upon us like the gate of death, without retracting or returning, without permitting to change the worst, most insupportable, most unchristian mischance of marriage for all the mischiefs and sorrows that can ensue, being an ordinance which was especially given as a cordial and exhilarating cup of solace, the better to bear our other crosses and afflictions? Questionless this was a hard-heartedness of divorcing, worse than that in the Jews, which they say extorted the allowance from Moses, and is utterly dissonant from all the doctrine of our Savior. After these considerations, therefore, to take a law out of Paradise given in time of original perfection, and to take it barely without those just and equal inferences and reasons which mainly establish it, nor so much as admitting those needful and safe allowances wherewith Moses himself interprets it to the fallen condition of man, argues nothing in us but rashness and contempt of those means that God left us in his pure and chaste law, without which it will not be possible for us to perform the strict imposition of this command; or if we strive beyond our strength, we shall strive to obey it otherwise than God commands it. And lamented experience daily teaches the bitter and vain fruits of this our presumption, forcing men in a thing wherein we are not able to judge either of their strength or of their sufferance. Whom neither one vice nor other by natural addiction, but only marriage ruins, which doubtless is not the fault of that ordinance, for God gave it as a blessing, nor always of man's mischoosing, it being an error above wisdom to prevent, as examples of wisest men so mistaken manifest. It is the fault therefore of a perverse opinion that will have it continued in despite of nature and reason, when indeed it was never truly joined. All those expositors upon the first of Matthew confess the law of Moses to be the law of the Lord, wherein no addition or diminution hath place; yet coming to the point of divorce, as if they feared not to be called least in the Kingdom of Heaven, any slight evasion will content them, to reconcile those contradictions which they make between Christ and Moses, between Christ and Christ.

CHAP. X

The vain shift of those who make the law of divorce to be only the premises of a succeeding law.

Some will have it no law, but the granted premises of another law following,[228] contrary to the words of Christ, Mark 10:5, and all other translations of gravest authority, who render it in form of a law, agreeable to Mal. 2:16 as it is most anciently and modernly expounded. Besides, the bill of divorce, and the particular occasion therein mentioned, declared it to be orderly and legal. And what avails this to make the matter more righteous, if such an adulterous condition shall be mentioned to build a law upon without either punishment or so much a forbidding? They pretend it is implicitly reproved in these words, Deut. 24:4, *after she is defiled;* but who sees not that this defilement is not only in respect of returning to her former husband after an intermixed marriage? Else why was not the defiling condition first forbidden, which would have saved the labour of this after-law? Nor is it seemly or piously attributed to the justice of God and his known hatred of sin, that such a heinous fault as this through all the law should be only whipped with an implicit and oblique touch (which yet is falsely supposed); and that his peculiar people should be let wallow in adulterous marriages almost two thousand years for want of a direct law to prohibit them. 'Tis rather to be confidently assumed that this was granted to apparent necessities, as being of unquestionable right and reason in the law of nature, in that it still passes without inhibition even when the greatest cause is given to us to expect it should be directly forbidden.

CHAP. XI

The other shift of saying divorce was permitted by law, but not approved. More of the institution.

But it was not approved. So much the worse that it was allowed: as if sin had overmastered the word of God to conform her steady and straight rule to sin's crookedness, which is impossible. Besides, what needed a positive grant of that which was not approved? It restrained no liberty to him that could but use a little fraud; it had been better silenced unless it were approved in some case or other. But still it was not approved. Miserable excusers! He who doth evil that good may come thereby, approves not what he doth; and yet the grand rule forbids him, and counts his damnation just if he do it.[229] The sorceress Medea did not approve her own evil doings, yet looked not to be excused for that.[230] And it is the constant opinion of Plato in *Protagoras,* and other of his Dialogues agreeing with that proverbial sentence among the Greeks, that *No man is wicked willingly;* which also the Peripatetics do rather distinguish than deny.[231] What great thank then if any man, reputed wise and constant, will neither do nor permit others under his charge to do that which he approves not, especially in matter of sin? But for a judge, but for a magistrate, the shepherd of his people, to surrender up his approbation against law and his own judgment, to the obstinacy of his herd, what more un-judge-like, more un-magistrate-like, and in war more un-commander-like? Twice in a short time it was the undoing of the Roman State, first when Pompey, next when Marcus Brutus, had not magnanimity enough but to make so poor a resignation of what they approved, to what the boisterous tribunes and soldiers bawled for.[232] Twice it was the saving of two the greatest commonwealths in the world: of Athens by Themistocles at the sea fight of Salamis, of Rome by Fabius Maximus in the Punic War, for that these two matchless Generals had the fortitude at home against the rashness and the clamours of their own captains and confederates to withstand the doing or permitting of what they could not approve in their duty of their great command.[233] Thus far of civil prudence. But when we speak of sin, let us look again upon the old reverend Eli, who in his heavy punishment found no difference between the doing and permitting of what he did not approve.[234] If hardness of heart in the people may be an excuse, why then is Pilate branded through all memory? He approved not what he did, he openly protested, he washed his hands, and laboured not a little ere he would yield to the hard hearts of a whole people, both princes and plebeians, importuning and tumulting even to the fear of a revolt.[235] Yet is there any will undertake his cause? If therefore Pilate for suffering but one act of cruelty against law, though with much unwillingness testified, at the violent demand of a whole nation, shall stand so black upon record to all posterity, alas for Moses! What shall we say for him, while we are taught to believe he suffered not one act only both of cruelty and uncleanness in one divorce, but made it a plain and lasting law against law, whereby ten thousand acts accounted both cruel and unclean might be daily committed, and this without the least suit or petition of the people that we can read of.

And can we conceive without vile thoughts that the majesty and holiness of God could endure so many ages to gratify a stubborn people in the practice of a foul polluting sin? And could he expect they should abstain, he not signifying his mind in a plain command, at such time especially when he was framing their laws and them to all possible perfection? But they were to look back to the first institution; nay rather, why was not that individual institution brought out of Paradise, as was that of the Sabbath, and repeated in the body of the law,[236] that men might have understood it to be a command? For that any sentence that bears the resemblance of a precept, set there so out of place in another world, at such a distance from the whole law, and not once mentioned there, should be an obliging command to us, is very disputable, and perhaps it might be denied to be a command without further dispute.

However, it commands not absolutely, as hath been cleared, but only with reference to that precedent promise of God, which is the very ground of his institution; if that appear not in some tolerable sort, how can we affirm such a matrimony to be the same which God instituted? In such an accident it will best behoove our soberness to follow rather what moral Sinai prescribes equal to our strength, than fondly to think within our strength all that lost Paradise relates.

CHAP. XII

The third shift of them who esteem it a mere judicial law. Proved again to be a law of moral equity.

Another while it shall suffice them that it was not a moral but a judicial law, and so was abrogated, nay rather abrogated because judicial: which law the ministry of Christ came not to deal with. And who put it in man's power to exempt, where Christ speaks in general of not abrogating *the least jot or tittle,* and in special not that of divorce, because it follows among those laws which he promised expressly not to abrogate but to vindicate from abusive traditions. Which is most evidently to be seen in the 16th of Luke,[237] where this caution of not abrogating is inserted immediately, and not otherwise than purposely, when no other point of the law is touched but that of divorce. And if we mark the 31st verse of Mat. 5, he there cites not the law of Moses but the licentious gloss which traduced the law; that therefore which he cited, that he abrogated, and not only abrogated but disallowed and flatly condemned, which could not be the law of Moses, for that had been foully to the rebuke of his great servant. To abrogate a law made with God's allowance had been to tell us only that such a law was now to cease; but to refute it with an ignominious note of civilizing adultery casts the reproof, which was meant only to the Pharisees, even upon him who made the law. But yet if that be judicial which belongs to a civil court, this law is less judicial than nine of the ten commandments: for antiquaries affirm that divorces proceeded among the Jews without knowledge of the magistrate, only with hands and seals under the testimony of some rabbis to be then present.[238] Perkins, in a *Treatise of Conscience,* grants that what in the judicial law is of common equity binds also the Christian; and how to judge of this, prescribes two ways: if wise nations have enacted the same decree, or if it maintain the good of family, church, or commonwealth.[239] This therefore is a pure moral economical law, too hastily imputed of tolerating sin, being rather so clear in nature and reason that it was left to a man's own arbitrement to be determined between God and his own conscience, not only among the Jews but in every wise nation; the restraint whereof, who is not too thick-sighted, may see how hurtful and distractive it is to the house, the church, and commonwealth. And that power which Christ never took from the master of a family, but rectified only to a right and wary use at home, that power the undiscerning canonist hath improperly usurped in his court-leet,[240] and bescribbled with a thousand trifling impertinencies, which yet have filled the life of man with serious trouble and calamity. Yet grant it were of old a judicial law, it need not be the less moral for that, being conversant as it is about virtue or vice. And our Savior disputes not here the judicature, for that was not his office, but the morality of divorce, whether it be adultery or no. If therefore he touch the law of Moses at all, he touches the moral part thereof, which is absurd to imagine, that the covenant of grace should reform the exact and perfect law of works, eternal and immutable; or if he touch not the law at all, then is not the allowance thereof disallowed to us.

CHAP. XIII

The ridiculous opinion that divorce was permitted from the custom in Egypt. That Moses gave not this law unwillingly. Perkins *confesses this law was not abrogated.*

Others are so ridiculous as to allege that this licence of divorcing was given them because they were so accustomed in Egypt. As if an ill custom were to be kept to all posterity; for the dispensation is both universal and of time unlimited, and so indeed no dispensation at all. For the over-dated dispensation of a thing unlawful serves for nothing but to increase hardness of heart and makes men but wax more incorrigible, which were a great reproach to be said of any law or allowance that God should give us. In these opinions it would be more religion to advise well, lest we make our selves more just than God, by censuring rashly that for sin which his unspotted law without rebuke allows, and his people without being conscious of displeasing him have used. And if we can think so of Moses, as that the Jewish obstinacy could compel him to write such impure permissions against the word of God and his own judgment, doubtless it was his part to have protected publicly what straits he was driven to, and to have declared his conscience when he gave any law against his mind. For the law is the touchstone of sin and of conscience, and must not be intermixed with corrupt indulgences; for then it loses the greatest praise it has of being certain and infallible, not leading into error as all the Jews were led by this connivance of Moses, if it were a connivance. But still they fly back to the primitive institution, and would have us re-enter Paradise against the sword that guards it.[241] Whom I again thus reply to, that the place in Genesis contains the description of a fit and perfect marriage, with an interdict of ever divorcing such a union; but where nature is discovered to have never joined indeed, but vehemently seeks to part, it cannot be there conceived that God forbids it, nay, he commands it both in the law and in the prophet Malachi, which is to be our rule. And Perkins upon this chapter of Matthew deals plainly, that our Savior here confutes not Moses' law but the false glosses that depraved the law; which being true, Perkins must need grant that something then is left to that law which Christ found no fault with; and what can that be but the conscionable use of such liberty as the plain words import? So that by his own inference, Christ did not absolutely intend to restrain all divorces to the only cause of adultery. This therefore is the true scope of our Savior's will, that he who looks upon the law concerning divorce should also look back upon the institution, that he may endeavour what is most perfect; and he that looks upon the institution shall not refuse as sinful and unlawful those allowances which God affords him in his following law, lest he make himself purer than his Maker, and presuming above strength, slip into temptations irrecoverably. For this is wonderful, that in all those decrees concerning marriage, God should never once mention the prime institution to dissuade them from divorcing, and that he should forbid smaller sins as opposite to the hardness of their hearts and let this adulterous matter of divorce pass ever unreproved. This is also to be marveled, that seeing Christ did not condemn whatever it was that Moses suffered, and that thereupon the Christian magistrate permits usury and open stews, and here with us adultery to be so slightly punished which was punished by death to these hard-hearted Jews,[242] why we should strain thus at the matter of divorce, which may stand so much with charity to permit, and make no scruple ourselves against the righteous and all-wise judgments and statutes of God; which are not variable and contrarious, as we would make them, one while permitting and another while forbidding, but are most constant and most harmonious each to other. For how can the uncorrupt and majestic law of God, bearing in her hand the wages of life and death,[243] harbour such a repugnance within herself as to require an unexempted and impartial obedience to all the decrees, either from us or from our Mediator, and yet debase herself to falter so many ages with circumcised[244] adulteries by unclean and slubbering permissions?

CHAP. XIV

That Beza's *opinion of regulating sin by apostolic law*[245] *cannot be sound.*

Yet Beza's opinion is, that a politic law (but what politic law I know not, unless one of Machiavelli's) may regulate sin; may bear indeed, I grant, with imperfection for a time, as those canons of the Apostles did in ceremonial things.[246] But as for sin, the essence of it cannot consist with rule; and if the law fail to regulate sin, and not to take it utterly away, it necessarily confirms and establishes sin. To make a regularity of sin by law, either the law must straighten sin into no sin, or sin must crook the law into no law. The judicial law can serve to no other end than to be the protector and champion of religion and honest civility, as is set down plainly Rom. 13 and is but the arm of moral law, which can no more be separate from justice than justice from virtue. Their office also, in a different manner, steers the same course: the one teaches what is good by precept, the other unteaches what is bad by punishment. But if we give way to public dispensations of lewd uncleanness, the first good consequence of such a relax will be the justifying of papal stews,[247] joined with a toleration of epidemic whoredom. Justice must revolt from the end of her authority, and become the patron of that whereof she was created the punisher. The example of usury, which is commonly alleged, makes against the allegation which it brings, as I touched before. Besides that usury, so much as is permitted by the magistrate and demanded by common equity, is neither against the word of God nor the rule of charity, as hath been often discussed by men of eminent learning and judgment. There must be therefore some other example found out to show us wherein civil policy may with warrant from God settle wickedness by law, and make that lawful which is lawless. Although I doubt not but upon deeper consideration, that which is true in physic will be found as true in policy: that as of bad pulses those that beat most in order are much worse than those that keep the most inordinate circuit, so of popular vices those that may be committed legally will be more pernicious than those that are left to their own course at peril, not under a stinted privilege to sin orderly and regularly, which is an implicit contradiction, but under due and fearless execution of punishment. The political law, since it cannot regulate vice, is to restrain it by using all means to root it out. But if it suffer the weed to grow up to any pleasurable or contented height upon what pretext soever, it fastens the root, it prunes and dresses vice, as if it were a good plant. Let no man doubt therefore to affirm that it is not so hurtful or dishonourable to a commonwealth, nor so much to the hardening of hearts, when those worse faults pretended to be feared are committed by whoso dares under strict and executed penalty, as when those less faults tolerated for fear of greater, harden their faces, not their hearts only, under the protection of public authority. For what less indignity were this, than as if justice herself, the Queen of virtues[248] (descending from her sceptered royalty) instead of conquering should compound and treat with sin, her eternal adversary and rebel, upon ignoble terms? or as if the judicial law were like that untrusty steward in the Gospel, and instead of calling in the debts of his moral master should give out subtle and sly acquittances to keep himself from begging?[249] Or let us person[250] him like some wretched itinerary judge, who to gratify his delinquents before him would let them basely break his head, lest they should pull him from the bench and throw him over the bar. Unless we had rather think both moral and judicial, full of malice and deadly purpose, conspired to let the debtor Israelite, the seed of Abraham, run on upon a bankrupt score,[251] flattered with insufficient and ensnaring discharges, that so he might be haled to a more cruel forfeit for all the indulgent arrears which those judicial acquitments had engaged him in. No no, this cannot be, that the law, whose integrity and faithfulness is next to God, should be either the shameless broker of our impunities or the intended instrument of our destruction. The method of holy correction, such as became the commonwealth of Israel, is not to bribe sin with sin, to capitulate and hire out one crime with another; but with more noble and graceful severity than Popilius the Roman Legate used with Antiochus,[252] to limit and level out the direct way from vice to virtue, with straightest and exactest lines on either side, not winding or indenting so much as to the right hand of fair pretences. Violence indeed and insurrection may force the law to suffer what it cannot mend; but to write a decree in allowance of sin, as soon can the hand of justice rot off. Let this be ever concluded as a truth that will outlive the faith of those that seek to bear it down.

CHAP. XV

That divorce was not given for wives only, as Beza *and* Paraeus *write. More of the institution.*

Lastly, if divorce were granted, as Beza and others say, not for men, but to release afflicted wives,[253] certainly it is not only a dispensation but a most merciful law; and why it should not yet be in force, being wholly as needful, I know not what can be in cause but senseless cruelty. But yet, to say divorce was granted for relief of wives rather than of husbands is but weakly conjectured, and is manifestly the extreme shift of a huddled exposition. Whenas it could not be found how hardness of heart should be lessened by liberty of divorce, a fancy was devised to hide the flaw, by commenting that divorce was permitted only for the help of wives. Palpably uxorious! Who can be ignorant that woman was created for man, and not man for woman, and that a husband may be injured as insufferably in marriage as a wife? What an injury is it after wedlock not to be beloved? what to be slighted? what to be contended with in point of house-rule who shall be the head; not for any parity of wisdom, for that were something reasonable, but out of a female pride? *I suffer not,* saith St. Paul, *the woman to usurp authority over the man.*[254] If the Apostle could not suffer it, into what mould is he mortified that can? Solomon saith *that a bad wife is to her husband as rottenness to his bones, a continual dropping. Better dwell in the corner of the house-top, or in the wilderness,* than with such a one.[255] *Whoso hides her hides the wind, and one of the four mischiefs which the Earth cannot bear.*[256] If the Spirit of God wrote such aggravations as these, and (as may be guessed by these similitudes) counsels the man rather to divorce than to live with such a colleague, and yet on the other side expresses nothing of the wife's suffering with a bad husband, is it not most likely that God in his law had more pity towards man thus wedlocked than towards the woman that was created for another? The same spirit relates to us the course which the Medes and Persians took by occasion of Vashti, whose mere denial to come at her husband's sending lost her the being Queen any longer, and set up a wholesome law, *that every man should bear rule in his own house.*[257] And the divine relater shows us not the least sign of disliking what was done; how should he, if Moses long before was nothing less mindful of the honour and pre-eminence due to man. So that to say divorce was granted for woman rather than man, was but fondly invented. Esteeming therefore to have asserted thus an injured law of Moses from the unwarranted and guilty name of a dispensation to be again a most equal and requisite law, we have the word of Christ himself, that he came not to alter the least tittle of it; and signifies no small displeasure against him that shall teach to do so. On which relying, I shall not much waver to affirm that those words which are made to intimate as if they forbade all divorce but for adultery (though Moses have constituted otherwise) those words taken circumscriptly, without regard to any precedent law of Moses, or attestation of Christ himself, or without care to preserve those his fundamental and superior laws of nature and charity to which all other ordinances give up their seals, are as much against plain equity and the mercy of religion as those words of *Take, eat, this is my Body,* elementally understood, are against nature and sense.[258]

And surely the restoring of this degraded law hath well recompensed the diligence was used by enlightening us further to find out wherefore Christ took off the Pharisees from alleging[259] the law, and referred them to the first institution: not condemning, altering, or abolishing this precept of divorce, which is plainly moral, for that were against his truth, his promise, and his prophetic office; but knowing how fallaciously they had cited and concealed the particular and natural reason of the law that they might justify any froward reason of their own, he lets go that sophistry unconvinced, for that had been to teach them else, which his purpose was not. And since they had taken a liberty which the law gave not, he amuses[260] and repels their tempting pride with a perfection of Paradise, which the law required not; not thereby to oblige our performance to that whereto the law never enjoined the fallen estate of man: for if the first institution must make wedlock, whatever happen, inseparable to us, it must make it also as perfect, as meetly helpful and as comfortable as God promised it should be, at least in some degree; otherwise it is not equal or proportionable to the strength of man that he should be reduced into such indissoluble bonds to his assured misery, if all the other conditions of that covenant be manifestly altered.

CHAP. XVI

How to be understood that they must be one flesh; and how that those whom God hath joined, man should not sunder.

Next he saith, *they must be one flesh:* which, when all conjecturing is done, will be found to import no more but to make legitimate and good the carnal act, which else might seem to have something of pollution in it; and infers thus much over, that the fit union of their souls be such as may even incorporate them to love and amity. But that can never be where no correspondence is of the mind. Nay, instead of being one flesh, they will be rather two carcasses chained unnaturally together; or, as it may happen, a living soul bound to a dead corpse, a punishment too like that inflicted by the tyrant Mezentius,[261] so little worthy to be received as that remedy of loneliness which God meant us. Since we know it is not the joining of another body will remove loneliness, but the uniting of another compliable mind; and that it is no blessing but a torment, nay a base and brutish condition to be one flesh, unless where nature can in some measure fix a unity of disposition, the meaning therefore of these words, *For this cause shall a man leave his father and his mother, and shall cleave to his wife,* was first to show us the dear affection which naturally grows in every not unnatural marriage, even to the leaving of parents or other familiarity whatsoever. Next, it justifies a man in so doing, that nothing is done undutifully to father or mother. But he that should be here sternly commanded to cleave to his error, a disposition which to his he finds will never cement, a quotidian of sorrow and discontent in his house, let us be excused to pause a little, and bethink us every way round ere we lay such a flat solecism upon the gracious, and certainly not inexorable, not ruthless and flinty ordinance of marriage. For if the meaning of these words must be thus blocked up within their own letters from all equity and fair deduction, they will serve then well indeed their turn who affirm divorce to have been granted only for wives; whenas we see no word of this text binds women, but men only, what it binds. No marvel then if Salomith (sister to Herod) sent a writ of ease to Costobarus her husband, which (as Josephus there attests) was lawful only to men.[262] No marvel though Placidia, the sister of Honorius, threatened the like to Earl Constantius for a trivial cause, as Photius related from Olympiodorus.[263] No marvel any thing, if letters must be turned into palisadoes,[264] to stake out all requisite sense from entering to their due enlargement.

Lastly, Christ himself tells who should not be put asunder, namely, those whom God hath joined. A plain solution of this great controversy, if men would but use their eyes; for when is it that God may be said to join? when the parties and their friends consent? No surely, for that may concur to lewdest ends. Or is it when church-rites are finished? Neither; for the efficacy of those depends upon the presupposed fitness of either party. Perhaps after carnal knowledge? Least of all; for that may join persons whom neither law nor nature dares join. 'Tis left that only then, when the minds are fitly disposed and enabled to maintain a cheerful conversation, to the solace and love of each other, according as God intended and promised in the very first foundation of matrimony, *I will make him a help-meet for him;* for surely what God intended and promised, that only can be thought to be his joining, and not the contrary. So likewise the Apostle witnesses, 1 Cor. 7:15, that in marriage *God hath called us to peace*. And doubtless in what respect he hath called us to marriage, in that also he hath joined us. The rest, whom either disproportion or deadness of spirit or something distasteful and averse in the immutable bent of nature renders unconjugal, error may have joined, but God never joined against the meaning of his own ordinance. And if he joined them not, then is there no power above their own consent to hinder them from unjoining, when they cannot reap the soberest ends of being together in any tolerable sort. Neither can it be said properly that such twain were ever divorced, but only parted from each other, as two persons unconjunctive are unmarriable together. But if, whom God hath made a fit help, frowardness or private injuries hath made unfit, that being the secret of marriage, God can better judge than man; neither is man indeed fit or able to decide this matter. However it be, undoubtedly a peaceful divorce is a less evil and less in scandal than hateful, hard-hearted, and destructive continuance of marriage in the judgment of Moses and of Christ. That justifies him in choosing the less evil; which, if it were an honest and civil prudence in the law, what is there in the Gospel forbidding such a kind of legal wisdom, though we should admit the common expositors.[265]

CHAP. XVII

The sentence of Christ concerning divorce how to be expounded. What Grotius *hath observed. Other additions.*

Having thus unfolded those ambiguous reasons wherewith Christ (as his wont was) gave to the Pharisees that came to sound him such an answer as they deserved, it will not be uneasy[266] to explain the sentence itself that now follows: *Whosoever shall put away his wife, except it be for fornication, and shall marry another, commits adultery.*[267] First therefore, I will set down what is observed by Grotius upon this point, a man of general learning. Next, I produce what mine own thoughts gave me before I had seen his annotations. Origen, saith he, notes that Christ named adultery rather as one example of other like cases, than as one only exception; and that is frequent not only in human but in divine laws to express one kind of fact, whereby other causes of like nature may have the like plea, as Exod. 21:18, 19, 20, 26, Deut. 19:5. And from the maxims of civil law he shows that even in sharpest penal laws the same reason hath the same right; and in gentler laws, that from like causes to like the law interprets rightly. But it may be objected, saith he, that nothing destroys the end of wedlock so much as adultery. To which he answers, that marriage was not ordained only for copulation, but for mutual help and comfort of life; and if we mark diligently the nature of our Savior's commands, we shall find that both their beginning and their end consists in charity: whose will is that we should so be good to others as that we be not cruel to ourselves. And hence it appears why Mark and Luke, and St. Paul to the Corinthians, mentioning this precept of Christ, add no exception, because exceptions that arise from natural equity are included silently under general terms. It would be considered therefore whether the same equity may not have place in other cases less frequent. Thus far he. From hence is what I add: first, that this saying of Christ, as it is usually expounded, can be no law at all, that a man for no cause should separate but for adultery, except it be a supernatural law, not binding us as we now are.

Had it been the law of nature, either the Jews or some other wise and civil nation would have pressed it; or let it be so, yet that law, Deut. 24:1, whereby a man hath leave to part, whenas for just and natural cause discovered he cannot love, is a law more ancient and deeper engraven in blameless nature than the other. Therefore the inspired lawgiver Moses took care that this should be specified and allowed; the other he let vanish in silence, not once repeated in the volume of his law, even as the reason of it vanished with Paradise. Secondly, this can be no new command, for the Gospel enjoins no new morality, save only the infinite enlargement of charity, which in this respect is called the New Commandment by St. John, as being the accomplishment of every command.[268] Thirdly, it is no command of perfection further than it partakes of charity, which is *the bond of perfection*.[269] Those commands therefore which compel us to self-cruelty above our strength, so hardly will help forward to perfection, that they hinder and set backward in all the common rudiments of Christianity, as was proved. It being thus clear that the words of Christ can be no kind of command as they are vulgarly taken, we shall now see in what sense they may be a command, and that an excellent one, the same with that of Moses, and no other. Moses had granted, that only for a natural annoyance, defect, or dislike, whether in body or mind (for so the Hebrew word plainly notes) which a man could not force himself to live with, he might give a bill of divorce, thereby forbidding any other cause wherein amendment or reconciliation might have place. This law the Pharisees depraving, extended to any slight contentious cause whatsoever. Christ therefore seeing where they halted,[270] urges the negative part of the law, which is necessarily understood (for the determinate permission of Moses binds them from further licence), and checking their supercilious drift, declares that no accidental, temporary, or reconcilable offence (except fornication) can justify a divorce. He touches not here those natural and perpetual hindrances of society, whether in body or mind, which are not to be removed; for such, as they are aptest to cause an unchangeable offence, so are they not capable of reconcilement, because not of amendment: they do not break indeed, but they annihilate the bands of marriage more than adultery. For that fault committed argues not always a hatred either natural or incidental against whom it is committed; neither does it infer a disability of all future helpfulness, or loyalty, or living agreement, being once past and pardoned, where it can be pardoned. But that which naturally distastes, and *finds no favour in the eyes* of matrimony, can never be concealed, never appeased, never intermitted, but proves a perpetual nullity of love and contentment, a solitude and dead vacation[271] of all acceptable conversing. Moses therefore permits divorce, but in cases only that have no hands to join, and more need separating than adultery. Christ forbids it, but in matters only that may accord, and those less than fornication. Thus is Moses' law here plainly confirmed, and those causes which he permitted not a jot gainsaid. And that this is the true meaning of this place I prove by no less an author than St. Paul himself, 1 Cor. 7:10, 11, upon which text interpreters agree, that the Apostle only repeats the precept of Christ: where while he speaks of *the wife's reconcilement to her husband,* he puts it out of controversy that our Savior meant chiefly matters of strife and reconcilement, of which sort he would not that any difference should be the occasion of divorce except fornication. And that we may learn better how to value a grave and prudent law of Moses, and how unadvisedly we smatter with our lips when we talk of Christ's abolishing any judicial law of his great Father, except in some circumstances which are Judaical rather than judicial and need no abolishing but cease of themselves, I say again, that this recited law of Moses contains a cause of divorce greater beyond compare than that for adultery; and whoso cannot so conceive it, errs and wrongs exceedingly a law of deep wisdom for want of well fathoming. For let him mark, no man urges the just divorcing of adultery as it is a sin, but as it is an injury to marriage; and though it be but once committed, and that without malice, whether through importunity or opportunity, the Gospel does not therefore dissuade him who would therefore divorce; but that natural hatred, whenever it arises, is a greater evil in marriage than the accident of adultery, a greater defrauding, a greater injustice, and yet not blamable, he who understands not after all this representing, I doubt his will like a hard spleen draws faster than his understanding can sanguify.[272]

Nor did that man ever know or feel what it is to love truly, nor ever yet comprehend in his thoughts what the true intent of marriage is. And this also will be somewhat above his reach, but yet no less a truth for lack of his perspective, that as no man apprehends what vice is so well as he who is truly virtuous, no man knows Hell like him who converses most in Heaven, so there is none that can estimate the evil and the affliction of a natural hatred in matrimony unless he have a soul gentle enough and spacious enough to contemplate what is true love.

And the reason why men so disesteem this wise-judging law of God, and count hate, or *the not finding of favour* as it is there termed, a humourous, a dishonest, and slight cause of divorce, is because themselves apprehend so little of what true concord means. For if they did, they would be more just in their balancing between natural hatred and casual adultery: this being but a transient injury, and soon amended, I mean as to the party against whom the trespass is; but the other being an unspeakable and unremitting sorrow and offence, whereof no amends can be made, no cure, no ceasing but by divorce, which like a divine touch in one moment heals all, and like the word of God in one instant hushes outrageous tempests into a sudden stillness and peaceful calm.[273] Yet all this so great a good of God's own enlarging to us, is by the hard reins of them that sit us, wholly diverted and embezzled from us. Maligners of mankind! But who hath taught you to mangle thus, and make more gashes in the miseries of a blameless creature with the leaden daggers of your literal decrees, to whose ease you cannot add the tithe of one small atom but by letting alone your unhelpful surgery. As for such as think wandering concupiscence to be here newly and more precisely forbidden than it was before, if the Apostle can convince them, we know that we are to *know lust by the law,*[274] and not by the new discovery of the Gospel. The law of Moses knew what it permitted, and the Gospel knew what it forbid. He that under a peevish conceit of debarring concupiscence shall go about to make a novice of Moses (not to say a worse thing, for reverence sake) and such a one of God himself, as is a horror to think, to bind our Savior in the default of a downright promise breaking, and to bind the disunions of complaining nature in chains together and curb them with a canon bit, 'tis he that commits all the whoredom and adultery which himself adjudges, besides the former guilt so manifold that lies upon him. And if none of these considerations, with all their weight and gravity, can avail to the dispossessing him of his precious literalism, let some one or other entreat him but to read on in the same 19th of Matthew 'til he come to that place that says, *Some make themselves eunuchs for the Kingdom of Heaven's sake.* And if then he please to make use of Origen's knife, he may do well to be his own carver.[275]

CHAP. XVIII

Whether the words of our Savior be rightly expounded only of actual fornication to be the cause of divorce. The opinion of Grotius, *with other reasons.*

But because we know that Christ never gave a judicial law, and that the word fornication is variously significant in Scripture, it will be much right done to our Savior's words to consider diligently whether it be meant here that nothing but actual fornication proved by witness can warrant a divorce, for so our canon law judges. Nevertheless, as I find that Grotius on this place hath observed the Christian emperors, Theodosius the second and Justinian, men of high wisdom and reputed piety, decreed it to be a divorcive fornication if the wife attempted, either against the knowledge or obstinately against the will of her husband, such things as gave open suspicion of adulterizing, as the willful haunting of feasts, and invitations with men not of her near kindred, the lying forth of her house without probable cause, the frequenting of theatres against her husband's mind, her endeavour to prevent or destroy conception. Hence that of Jerome, *Where fornication is suspected, the wife may lawfully be divorced.* Not that every motion of a jealous mind should be regarded, but that it should not be exacted to prove all things by the visibility of law witnessing, or else to hoodwink the mind: for the law is not able to judge of these things but by the rule of equity and by permitting a wise man to walk the middle way of prudent circumspection, neither wretchedly jealous nor stupidly and tamely patient. To this purpose hath Grotius in his notes. He shows also that fornication is taken in Scripture for such a continual headstrong behaviour as tends to plain contempt of the husband, and proves it out of Judges 19:2, where the Levite's wife is said to have played the whore against him; which Josephus and the Septuagint, with the Chaldean, interpret only of stubbornness and rebellion against her husband; and to this I add, that Kimchi, and the two other rabbis who gloss the text, are in the same opinion. Ben Gersom reasons that had it been whoredom, a Jew and a Levite would have disdained to fetch her again. And this I shall contribute, that had it been whoredom, she would have chosen any other place to run to than to her father's house, it being so infamous for an Hebrew woman to play the harlot and so opprobrious to the parents. Fornication then in this place of the Judges is understood for stubborn disobedience against the husband, and not for adultery.[276] A sin of that sudden activity, as to be already committed when no more is done but only looked unchastely: which yet I should be loath to judge worthy a divorce, though in our Savior's language it be called adultery.[277] Nevertheless when palpable and frequent signs are given, the law of God, Num. 5, so far gave way to the jealousy of a man, as that the woman, set before the sanctuary with her head uncovered, was adjured by the priest to swear whether she were false or no, and constrained to drink that *bitter water* with an undoubted *curse of rottenness and tympany* to follow, unless she were innocent.[278] And the jealous man had not been guiltless before God, as seems by the last verse, if having such a suspicion in his head, he should neglect his trial; which if to this day it be not to be used, or be thought as uncertain of effect as our antiquated law of Ordalium,[279] yet all equity will judge that many adulterous demeanours, which are of lewd suspicion and example, may be held sufficient to incur a divorce though the act itself hath not been proved. And seeing the generosity of our nation is so as to account no reproach more abominable than to be nicknamed the husband of an adulteress, that our law should not be as ample as the law of God to vindicate a man from that ignoble sufferance, is our barbarous unskillfulness, not considering that the law should be exasperated[280] according to our estimation of the injury. And if it must be suffered 'til the act be visibly proved, Solomon himself, whose judgment will be granted to surpass the acuteness of any canonist, confesses, Proverbs 30:19, 20, that for the act of adultery it is as difficult to be found as the *track of an eagle in the air, or the way of a ship in the sea;* so that a man may be put to unmanly indignities ere it be found out. This therefore may be enough to inform us that divorcive adultery is not limited by our Savior to the utmost act, and that to be attested always by eye-witness, but may be extended also to divers obvious actions which either plainly lead to adultery or give such presumption whereby sensible men may suspect the deed to be already done. And this the rather may be thought, in that our Savior chose to use the word fornication, which word is found to signify other matrimonial transgressions of main breach to that covenant besides actual adultery. For that sin needed not the riddance of divorce, but of death by the law, which was active even 'til then by the example of the woman taken in adultery;[281] or if the law had been dormant, our Savior was more likely to have told them of their neglect than to have let a capital crime silently escape into a divorce; or if it be said his business was not to tell them what was criminal in the civil courts but what was sinful at the bar of conscience, how dare they then, having no other ground than these our Savior's words, draw that into the trial of law, which both by Moses and our Savior was left to the jurisdiction of conscience? But we take from our Savior, say they, only that it was adultery, and our law of itself applies the punishment. But by their leave that so argue, the great lawgiver of all the world, who knew best what was adultery, both to the Jew and to the Gentile appointed no such applying, and never likes when mortal men will be vainly presuming to outstrip his justice.

CHAP. XIX

Christ's manner of teaching. St. Paul *adds to the matter of divorce without command, to show the matter to be of equity, not of rigour. That the bondage of a Christian may be as much, and his peace as little, in some other marriages besides idolatrous. If those arguments therefore be good in that one case, why not in those other? Therefore the Apostle himself adds,* ἐντοῖστοιούτοις.[282]

Thus at length we see both by this and other places, that there is scarce any one saying in the Gospel but must be read with limitations and distinctions to be rightly understood; for Christ gives no full comments or continued discourses, but (as Demetrius the rhetorician phrases it) speaks oft in monosyllables, like a master scattering the heavenly grain of his doctrine like pearls here and there, which requires a skilful and laborious gatherer, who must compare the words he finds with other precepts,[283] with the end of every ordinance, and with the general analogy of evangelic doctrine; otherwise many particular sayings would be but strange repugnant riddles, and the Church would offend in granting divorce for frigidity, which is not here excepted with adultery but by them added. And this was it, undoubtedly, which gave reason to St. Paul of his own authority, as he professes, and without command from the Lord, to enlarge the seeming construction of those places in the Gospel by adding a case wherein a person deserted, which is something less than divorced, may lawfully marry again. And having declared his opinion in one case, he leaves a further liberty for Christian prudence to determine in cases of like importance, words so plain as not to be shifted off, that a brother or a sister is not under bondage in such cases; adding also, that God hath called us to peace in marriage. Now if it be plain that a Christian may be brought into unworthy bondage, and his religious peace not only interrupted now and then but perpetually and finally hindered in wedlock by misyoking with a diversity of nature as well as of religion, the reasons of St. Paul cannot be made special to that one case of infidelity, but are of equal moment to a divorce wherever Christian liberty and peace are without fault equally obstructed: that the ordinance which God gave to our comfort may not be pinned upon us to our undeserved thralldom, to be cooped up as it were in mockery of wedlock, to a perpetual betrothed loneliness and discontent, if nothing worse ensue. There being naught else of marriage left between such but a displeasing and forced remedy against the sting of a brute desire: which fleshly accustoming[284] without the soul's union and commixture of intellectual delight, as it is rather a soiling than a fulfilling of marriage-rites, so it is enough to abase the mettle of a generous spirit and sinks him to a low and vulgar pitch of endeavour in all his actions, or (which is worse) leaves him in a despairing plight of abject and hardened thoughts; which condition rather than a good man should fall into, a man useful in the service of God and mankind, Christ himself hath taught us to dispense with the most sacred ordinance of his worship, even for a bodily healing to dispense with that holy and speculative rest of Sabbath, much more then with the erroneous observance of an ill-knotted marriage, for the sustaining of an overcharged faith and perseverance.

CHAP. XX

The meaning of St. Paul, *that* Charity *believeth all things. What is to be said to the licence which is vainly feared will grow hereby. What to those who never have done prescribing patience in this case. The Papist most severe against divorce, yet most easy to all licence. Of all the miseries in marriage God is to be cleared, and the faults to be laid on man's unjust laws.*

And though bad causes would take licence by this pretext, if that cannot be remedied, upon their conscience be it who shall so do. This was that hardness of heart, and abuse of a good law, which Moses was content to suffer, rather than good men should not have it at all to use needfully. And he who to run after one lost sheep left ninety-nine of his own flock at random in the wilderness[285] would little perplex his thoughts for the obduring[286] of nine hundred and ninety such as will daily take worse liberties whether they have permission or not. To conclude, as without charity God hath given no commandment to men, so without it neither can men rightly believe any commandment given. For every act of true faith, as well that whereby we believe the law as that whereby we endeavour the law, is wrought in us by charity, according to that in the divine hymn of St. Paul, 1 Cor. 13, *Charity believeth all things;* not as if she were so credulous, which is the exposition hitherto current, for that were a trivial praise, but to teach us that charity is the high governess of our belief, and that we cannot safely assent to any precept written in the Bible but as charity commends it to us. Which agrees with that of the same Apostle to the Ephesians 4:14–15, where he tells us that the way to get a sure undoubted knowledge of things is to hold that for truth which accords most with charity. Whose unerring guidance and conduct having followed as a lodestar with all diligence and fidelity in this question, I trust, through the help of that illuminating spirit which hath favoured me, to have done no every day's work, in asserting after many ages the words of Christ with other Scriptures of great concernment from burdensome and remorseless obscurity, tangled with manifold repugnancies, to their native lustre and consent between each other; hereby also dissolving tedious and gordian difficulties which have hitherto molested the Church of God, and are now decided not with the sword of Alexander[287] but with the immaculate hands of charity, to the unspeakable good of Christendom. And let the extreme literalist sit down now and revolve[288] whether this in all necessity be not the due result of our Savior's words, or if he persist to be otherwise opinioned, let him well advise, lest thinking to grip fast the Gospel he be found instead with the canon law in his fist: whose boisterous[289] edicts tyrannizing the blessed ordinance of marriage into the quality of a most unnatural and un-Christianly yoke have given the flesh this advantage to hate it, and turn aside, oft-times unwillingly, to all dissolute uncleanness, even 'til punishment itself is weary of and overcome by the incredible frequency of trading lust[290] and uncontrolled adulteries. Yet men whose creed is custom, I doubt not but will be still endeavouring to hide the sloth of their own timorous capacities with this pretext, that for all this 'tis better to endure with patience and silence this affliction which God hath sent. And I agree 'tis true, if this be exhorted and not enjoined; but withal it will be wisely done to be as sure as may be, that what man's iniquity hath laid on be not imputed to God's sending, lest under the colour of an affected patience we detain our selves at the gulf's mouth of many hideous temptations, not to be withstood without proper gifts, which (as Perkins well notes) God gives not ordinarily, no not to most earnest prayers. Therefore we pray, *Lead us not into temptation*; a vain prayer, if having led our selves thither, we love to stray in that perilous condition. God sends remedies as well as evils, under which he who lies and groans, that may lawfully acquit himself, is accessory to his own ruin; nor will it excuse him, though he suffer, through a sluggish fearfulness to search thoroughly what is lawful, for fear of disquieting the secure falsity of an old opinion. Who doubts not but that it may be piously said to him who would dismiss his frigidity, "Bear your trial, take it as if God would have you live this life of continence"? If he exhort this, I hear him as an angel, though he spoke without warrant; but if he would compel me, I know him for Satan. To him who divorces an adulteress, Piety might say, 'Pardon her; you may show much mercy, you may win a soul.' Yet the law both of God and man leaves it freely to him; for God loves not to plow out the heart of our endeavours with over-hard and sad tasks. God delights not to make a drudge of virtue, whose actions must be all elective and unconstrained. Forced virtue is as a bolt overshot, it goes neither forward nor backward, and does no good as it stands. Seeing therefore that neither Scripture nor reason hath laid this unjust austerity upon divorce, we may resolve that nothing else hath wrought it but that letter-bound servility of the canon doctors, supposing marriage to be a sacrament, and out of the art they have to lay unnecessary burdens upon all men to make a fair show in the fleshly observance of matrimony, though peace and love with all other conjugal respects fare never so ill. And indeed the Papists, who were the strictest forbidders of divorce, are the easiest libertines to admit of grosser uncleanness; as if they had a design by making wedlock a supportless yoke,[291] to violate it most under colour of preserving it most inviolable; and withal delighting, as their mystery is,[292] to make men the day-labourers of their own afflictions, as if there were such a scarcity of miseries from abroad, that we should be made to melt our choicest home blessings and coin them into crosses, for want whereby to hold commerce with patience. If any therefore who shall hap to read this discourse hath been through misadventure ill engaged in this contracted evil here complained of, and finds the fits and workings of a high impatience frequently upon him, of all those wild words which men in misery think to ease themselves by uttering, let him not open his lips against the providence of Heaven, or tax the ways of God and his divine truth. For they are equal, easy, and not burdensome; nor do they ever cross the just and reasonable desires of men, nor involve this our portion of mortal life into a necessity of sadness and malcontent, by laws commanding over the irreducible antipathies of nature sooner or later found, but allow us to remedy and shake off those evils into which human error hath led us through the midst of our best intentions, and to support our incident extremities by that authentic precept of sovereign charity, whose grand commission is to do and to dispose over all the ordinances of God to man, that love and truth may advance each other to ever-lasting; while we, literally superstitious through customary faintness of heart, not venturing to pierce with our free thoughts into the full latitude of nature and religion, abandon ourselves to serve under the tyranny of usurped opinions, suffering those ordinances[293] which were allotted to our solace and reviving to trample over us and hale us into a multitude of sorrows, which God never meant us. And where he sets us in a fair allowance of way, with honest liberty and prudence to our guard, we never leave subtlizing and casuisting 'til we have straightened and pared that liberal path into a razor's edge to walk on, between a precipice of unnecessary mischief on either side; and starting at every false alarum, we do not know which way to set a foot forward with manly confidence and Christian resolution, through the confused ringing in our ears of panic scruples and amazements.

CHAP. XXI

That the matter of divorce is not to be tried by law, but by conscience, as many other sins are. The magistrate can only see that the condition of divorce be just and equal. The opinion of Fagius, *and the reasons of this assertion.*

Another act of papal encroachment it was, to pluck the power and arbitrement of divorce from the master of the family, into whose hands God and the law of all nations had put it, and Christ so left it, preaching only to the conscience, and not authorizing a judicial court to toss about and divulge the unaccountable and secret reasons of disaffection between man and wife, as a thing most improperly answerable to any such kind of trial. But the Popes of Rome, perceiving the great revenue and high authority it would give them even over princes, to have the judging and deciding of such a main consequence in the life of man as was divorce, wrought so upon the superstition of those ages as to divest them of that right which God from the beginning had entrusted to the husband: by which means they subjected that ancient and naturally domestic prerogative to an external and unbefitting judicature. For although differences in divorce about dowries, jointures, and the like, besides the punishing of adultery, ought not to pass without referring, if need be, to the magistrate, yet that the absolute and final hindering of divorce cannot belong to any civil or earthly power, against the will and consent of both parties, or of the husband alone, some reasons will be here urged as shall not need to decline the touch. But first I shall recite what hath been already yielded by others in favour of this opinion. Grotius and many more agree, that notwithstanding what Christ spoke therein to the conscience, the magistrate is not thereby enjoined aught against the preservation of civil peace, of equity, and of convenience. Among these Fagius is most remarkable, and gives the same liberty of pronouncing divorce to the Christian magistrate as the Mosaic had. *For whatever,* saith he, *Christ spoke to the regenerate, the judge hath to deal with the vulgar: if therefore any through hardness of heart will not be a tolerable wife to her husband, it will be lawful as well now as of old to pass the bill of divorce, not by private, but by public authority. Nor doth man separate and remove from perpetual vexation, and no small danger, those bodies whose minds are already separate, it being his office to procure peaceable and convenient living in the commonwealth, and being as certain also, that they so necessarily separated cannot all receive a single life.* And this I observe, that our divines do generally condemn separation of bed and board without the liberty of second choice;[294] if that therefore in some cases be most purely necessary, as who so blockish to deny, then is this also as needful. Thus far by others is already well stepped, to inform us that divorce is not a matter of law but of charity. If there remain a furlong yet to end the question, these following reasons may serve to gain it with any apprehension not too unlearned or too wayward. First, because oft-times the causes of seeking divorce reside so deeply in the radical and innocent affections of nature, as is not within the diocese of law to tamper with. Other relations may aptly enough be held together by a civil and virtuous love, but the duties of man and wife are such as are chiefly conversant in that love, which is most ancient and merely[295] natural; whose two prime statutes are to join itself to that which is good and acceptable and friendly, and to turn aside and depart from what is disagreeable, displeasing, and unlike. Of the two this latter is the strongest, and most equal[296] to be regarded; for although a man may often be unjust in seeking that which he loves, yet he can never be unjust or blamable in retiring from his endless trouble and distaste, whenas his tarrying can redound to no true content on either side. Hate is of all things the mightiest divider, nay is division itself. To couple hatred therefore, though wedlock try all her golden links and borrow to her aid all the iron manacles and fetters of law, it does but seek to twist a rope of sand, which was a task they say that posed the Devil.[297] And that sluggish fiend in Hell, Ocnus, whom the poems tell of, brought his idle cordage to as good effect, which never served to bind with but to feed the ass that stood at his elbow.[298] And that the restrictive law against divorce attains as little to bind any thing truly in a disjointed marriage, or to keep it bound, but serves only to feed the ignorance and definitive impertinence of a doltish canon, were no absurd allusion.[299] To hinder therefore those deep and serious regresses of nature in a reasonable soul parting from that mistaken help which he justly seeks in a person created for him, recollecting[300] himself from an unmeet help which was never meant, and to detain him by compulsion in such an unpredestined misery as this, is in diameter against[301] both nature and institution. But to interpose a jurisdictive power over the inward and irremediable disposition of man, to command love and sympathy, to forbid dislike against the guiltless instinct of nature, is not within the province of any law to reach, and were indeed an incommodious rudeness, not a just power: for that law may bandy with nature, and traverse her sage motions, was an error in Callicles the rhetorician, whom Socrates from high principles confutes in Plato's *Gorgias*.[302] If therefore divorce may be so natural, and that law and nature are not to go contrary; then to forbid divorce compulsively is not only against nature but against law.

Next, it must be remembered that all law is for some good that may be frequently attained without the admixture of a worse inconvenience; and therefore many gross faults, as ingratitude and the like, which are too far within the soul to be cured by constraint of law, are left only to be wrought on by conscience and persuasion. Which made Aristotle, in the 10th of his *Ethics* to Nicomachus, aim at a kind of division of law into private or persuasive, and public or compulsive. Hence it is that the law forbidding divorce never attains to any good end of such prohibition, but rather multiplies evil. For if nature's resistless sway in love or hate be once compelled, it grows careless of itself, vicious, useless to friends, unserviceable and spiritless to the commonwealth. Which Moses rightly foresaw, and all wise lawgivers that ever knew man, what kind of creature he was. The Parliament also and clergy of England were not ignorant of this, when they consented that Harry the 8th might put away his Queen Anne of Cleve, whom he could not like after he had been wedded half a year;[303] unless it were that, contrary to the proverb, they made a necessity of that which might have been a virtue in them to do. For even the freedom and eminence of man's creation gives him to be a law in this matter to himself, being the head of the other sex which was made for him;[304] whom therefore though he ought not to injure, yet neither should he be forced to retain in society to his own overthrow, nor to hear any judge therein above himself. It being also an unseemly affront to the sequestered and veiled modesty of that sex, to have her unpleasingness and other concealments bandied up and down, and aggravated in open court by those hired masters of tongue-fence.[305] Such uncomely exigencies it befell no less a Majesty than Henry the VIII to be reduced to, who finding just reason in his conscience to forgo his brother's wife, after many indignities of being deluded, and made a boy of by those his two cardinal judges,[306] was constrained at last, for want of other proof, that she had been carnally known by Prince Arthur, even to uncover the nakedness of that virtuous lady, and to recite openly the obscene evidence of his brother's chamberlain.[307] Yet it pleased God to make him see all the tyranny of Rome, by discovering this which they exercised over divorce, and to make him the beginner of a reformation to this whole Kingdom, by first asserting into his familiary power the right of just divorce. It is true, an adulteress cannot be shamed enough by any public proceeding; but that woman whose honour is not appeached,[308] is less injured by a silent dismission, being otherwise not illiberally dealt with, than to endure a clamouring debate of utterless things, in a business of that civil secrecy and difficult discerning, as not to be over-much questioned by nearest friends. Which drew that answer from the greatest and worthiest Roman of his time, Paulus Emilius, being demanded why he would put away his wife for no visible reason: *This shoe,* said he, and held it out on his foot, *is a neat shoe, a new shoe, and yet none of you know where it wrings me.*[309] Much less by the unfamiliar cognizance of a feed gamester[310] can such a private difference be examined, neither ought it.

Again, if law aim at the firm establishment and preservation of matrimonial faith, we know that cannot thrive under violent means, but is the more violated. It is not when two unfortunately met are by the canon forced to draw in that yoke an unmerciful day's work of sorrow 'til death unharness them, that then the law keeps marriage most unviolated and unbroken, but when the law takes order that marriage be accountant and responsible to perform that society, whether it be religious, civil, or corporeal, which may be conscionably required and claimed therein, or else to be dissolved if it cannot be undergone. This is to make marriage most indissoluble, by making it a just and equal dealer, a performer of those due helps which instituted the covenant, being otherwise a most unjust contract, and no more to be maintained under tuition[311] of law than the vilest fraud, or cheat, or theft that may be committed. But because this is such a secret kind of fraud or theft, as cannot be discerned by law but only by the plaintiff himself, therefore to divorce was never counted a political or civil offence neither to Jew nor Gentile, nor any judicial intention of Christ, further than could be discerned to transgress the allowance of Moses, which was of necessity so large, that it doth all one as if it sent back the matter undeterminable at law, and intractable by rough dealing to have instructions and admonitions bestowed about it by them whose spiritual office is to adjure and to denounce, and so left to the conscience. The law can only appoint the just and equal conditions of divorce, and is to look how it is an injury to the divorced, which in truth it can be none, as a mere separation; for if she consent, wherein has the law to right her? or consent not, then is it either just, and so deserved, or if unjust, such in all likelihood was the divorcer, and to part from an unjust man is a happiness, and no injury to be lamented. But suppose it be an injury, the law is not able to amend it, unless she think it other than a miserable redress to return back from whence she was expelled, or but entreated to be gone, or else to live apart still married without marriage, a married widow. Last, if it be to chasten the divorcer, what law punishes a deed which is not moral but natural, a deed which cannot certainly be found to be an injury? or how can it be punished by prohibiting the divorce, but that the innocent must equally partake both in the shame and in the smart? So that which way soever we look, the law can to no rational purpose forbid divorce; it can only take care that the conditions of divorce be not injurious. Thus then we see the trial of law how impertinent it is to this question of divorce, how helpless next, and then how hurtful.

CHAP. XXII

The last reason why divorce is not to be restrained by law, it being against the law of nature and of nations. The larger proof whereof referred to Mr. Selden's *book* De Jure Naturali & Gentium. *An objection of* Paraeus *answered. How it ought to be ordered by the Church. That this will not breed any worse inconvenience, nor so bad as is now suffered.*

Therefore the last reason why it should not be, is the example we have, not only from the noblest and wisest commonwealths, guided by the clearest light of human knowledge, but also from the divine testimonies of God himself, lawgiving in person to a sanctified people. That all this is true, whoso desires to know at large with least pains, and expects not here over-long rehearsals of that which is by others already so judiciously gathered, let him hasten to be acquainted with that noble volume written by our learned Selden, *Of the Law of Nature and of Nations*,[312] a work more useful and more worthy to be perused by whosoever studies to be a great man in wisdom, equity, and justice, than all those decretals and sumless sums[313] which the pontifical clerks have doted on, ever since that unfortunate mother famously sinned thrice, and died impenitent of her bringing into the world those two misbegotten infants, and for ever infants, Lombard and Gratian,[314] him the compiler of canon iniquity, the other the Tubalcain[315] of scholastic sophistry, whose overspreading barbarism hath not only infused their own bastardy upon the most fruitful part of human learning, not only dissipated and dejected the clear light of nature in us, and of nations, but hath tainted also the fountains of divine doctrine, and rendered the pure and solid law of God unbeneficial to us by their calumnious dunceries. Yet this law, which their unskillfulness hath made liable to all ignominy, the purity and wisdom of this law shall be the buckler of our dispute. Liberty of divorce we claim not, we think not, but from this law: the dignity, the faith, the authority thereof is now grown among Christians. O astonishment! a labour of no mean difficulty and envy to defend. That it should not be counted a faltering dispense, a flattering permission of sin, the bill of adultery, a snare, is the expense of all this apology. And all that we solicit is, that it may be suffered to stand in the place where God set it, amidst the firmament of his holy laws, to shine, as it was wont, upon the weaknesses and errors of men, perishing else in the sincerity of their honest purposes. For certain there is no memory of whoredoms and adulteries left among us now, when this warranted freedom of God's own giving is made dangerous and discarded for a scroll of licence. It must be your suffrages and votes, O Englishmen, that this exploded decree of God and Moses may escape and come off fair, without the censure of a shameful abrogating: which, if yonder sun ride sure, and mean not to break word with us tomorrow, was never yet abrogated by our Savior. Give sentence, if you please, that the frivolous canon may reverse the infallible judgment of Moses and his great Director. Or if it be the reformed writers whose doctrine persuades this rather, their reasons I dare affirm are all silenced, unless it be only this. Paraeus on the Corinthians would prove that hardness of heart in divorce is no more now to be permitted, but to be amerced[316] with fine and imprisonment. I am not willing to discover the forgettings of reverend men, yet here I must: what article or clause of the whole new covenant can Paraeus bring to exasperate the judicial law, upon any infirmity under the Gospel? (I say infirmity, for if it were the high hand of sin, the law as little would have endured it as the Gospel). It would not stretch to the dividing of an inheritance,[317] it refused to condemn adultery;[318] not that these things should not be done at law, but to show that the Gospel hath not the least influence upon judicial courts, much less to make them sharper and more heavy, lest of all to arraign before a temporal judge that which the law without summons acquitted. But, saith he, the law was the time of youth, under violent affections; the Gospel in us is mature age, and ought to subdue affections. True, and so ought the law too, if they be found inordinate, and not merely natural and blameless. Next I distinguish, that the time of the law is compared to youth and pupilage in respect of the ceremonial part, which led the Jews as children through corporeal and garish rudiments, until the fullness of time should reveal to them the higher lessons of faith and redemption. This is not meant of the moral part: therein it soberly concerned them not to be babies, but to be men in good earnest: the sad and awful majesty of the law was not to be jested with; to bring a bearded nonage with lascivious dispensations before that throne had been a lewd affront, as it is now a gross mistake. But what discipline is this, Paraeus, to nourish violent affections in youth, by cockering[319] and wanton indulgencies, and to chastise them in mature age with a boyish rod of correction? How much more coherent is it to Scripture, that the law as a strict schoolmaster should have punished every trespass without indulgence so baneful to youth, and that the Gospel should now correct that by admonition and reproof only, in free and mature age, which was punished with stripes in the childhood and bondage of the law?[320] What therefore it allowed then so fairly, much less is to be whipped now, especially in penal courts: and if it ought now to trouble the conscience, why did that angry accuser and condemner law reprieve it? So then, neither from Moses nor from Christ hath the magistrate any authority to proceed against it. But what? Shall then the disposal of that power return again to the master of a family? Wherefore not, since God there put it, and the presumptuous canon thence bereft it? This only must be provided, that the ancient manner be observed in the presence of the minister and other grave selected elders, who after they shall have admonished and pressed upon him the words of our Savior, and he shall have protested in the faith of the eternal Gospel, and the hope he has of happy resurrection, that otherwise than thus he cannot do, and thinks himself and this his case not contained in that prohibition of divorce which Christ pronounced, the matter not being of malice, but of nature, and so not capable of reconciling. To constrain him further were to unchristen him, to unman him, to throw the mountain of Sinai upon him, with the weight of the whole law to boot, flat against the liberty and essence of the Gospel, and yet nothing available either to the sanctity of marriage, the good of husband, wife, or children, nothing profitable either to church or commonwealth, but hurtful and pernicious in all these respects. But this will bring in confusion. Yet these cautious mistrusters might consider, that what they thus object lights not upon this book but upon that which I engage against them, the Book of God and Moses, with all the wisdom and providence which had forecast the worst of confusion that could succeed, and yet thought fit of such a permission. But let them be of good cheer, it wrought so little disorder among the Jews, that from Moses 'til after the captivity not one of the prophets thought it worth the rebuking; for that of Malachi well looked into will appear to be not against divorcing, but rather against keeping strange concubines, to the vexation of their Hebrew wives.[321] If therefore we Christians may be thought as good and tractable as the Jews were, and certainly the prohibiters of divorce presume us to be better, then less confusion is to be feared for this among us than was among them. If we be worse, or but as bad, which lamentable examples confirm we are, then have we more, or at least as much, need of this permitted law as they to whom God therefore gave it (as they say) under a harsher covenant. Let not therefore the frailty of man go on thus inventing needless troubles to itself, to groan under the false imagination of a strictness never imposed from above, enjoining that for duty which is an impossible and vain supererogating. *Be not righteous overmuch,* is the counsel of Ecclesiastes; *why shouldst thou destroy thyself?*[322] Let us not be thus over-curious to strain at atoms,[323] and yet to stop every vent and cranny of permissive liberty, lest nature wanting those needful pores and breathing-places which God hath not debarred our weakness, either suddenly break out into some wide rupture of open vice and frantic heresy, or else inwardly fester with repining and blasphemous thoughts, under an unreasonable and fruitless rigour of unwarranted law. Against which evils nothing can more beseem the religion of the Church, or the wisdom of the State, than to consider timely and provide. And in so doing let them not doubt but they shall vindicate the misreputed honour of God and his great lawgiver, by suffering him to give his own laws according to the condition of man's nature best known to him, without the insufferable imputation of dispensing legally with many ages of ratified adultery. They shall recover the misattended words of Christ to the sincerity of their true sense from manifold contradictions, and shall open them with the key of charity. Many helpless Christians they shall raise from the depth of sadness and distress, utterly unfitted as they are to serve God or man; many they shall reclaim from obscure and giddy sects, many regain from dissolute and brutish licence, many from desperate hardness, if ever that were justly pleaded. They shall set free many daughters of Israel, not wanting much of her sad plight *whom Satan had bound eighteen years.*[324] Man they shall restore to his just dignity and prerogative in nature, preferring the soul's free peace before the promiscuous draining of a carnal rage. Marriage, from a perilous hazard and snare, they shall reduce to be a more certain haven and retirement of happy society, when they shall judge according to God and Moses; and how not then according to Christ, when they shall judge it more wisdom and goodness to break that covenant seemingly, and keep it really, than by compulsion of law to keep it seemingly, and by compulsion of blameless nature to break it really, at least if it were ever truly joined. The vigour of discipline they may then turn with better success upon the prostitute looseness of the times, when men finding in themselves the infirmities of former ages, shall not be constrained above the gift of God in them, to unprofitable and impossible observances, never required from the civilest, the wisest, the holiest nations, whose other excellencies in moral virtue they never yet could equal. Last of all, to those whose mind is still to maintain textual restrictions, whereof the bare sound cannot consist sometimes with humanity, much less with charity, I would ever answer by putting them in remembrance of a command above all commands, which they seem to have forgot, and who spoke it; in comparison whereof, this which they so exalt is but a petty and subordinate precept. *Let them go therefore* with whom I am loath to couple them, yet they will needs run into the same blindness with the Pharisees; *let them go therefore* and consider well what this lesson means, *I will have mercy and not sacrifice;*[325] for on that *saying all the law and prophets depend,*[326] much more the Gospel, whose end and excellence is mercy and peace. Or if they cannot learn that, how will they hear this? which yet I shall not doubt to leave with them as a conclusion: that God the Son hath put all other things under his own feet, but his commandments he hath left all under the feet of charity.[327]

The Judgement of Martin Bucer, Concerning Divorce

Written to *Edward* the sixth, in his second Book of the Kingdom of Christ.[1] And now Englished.[2] Wherein a late Book restoring the *Doctrine and Discipline of Divorce* is here confirmed and justified by the authority of Martin Bucer. *To the Parliament of England.*

John 3.10. *Art thou a teacher of Israel, and know'st not these things?* Published by Authority.[3]

***London,* Printed by *Matthew Simmons,*[4] 1644.**

Testimonies of the high approbation Which learned men have given of Martin Bucer.

Simon Grynaeus, 1533[5]

Among all the Germans, I give the palm to Bucer for excellence in the Scriptures. Melancthon in human learning is wondrous fluent; but greater knowledge in the Scripture I attribute to Bucer, and speak it unfainedly.

John Calvin, 1539

Martin Bucer, a most faithful doctor of the Church of Christ, besides his rare learning and copious knowledge of many things, besides his clearness of wit, much reading, and other many and various virtues, wherein he is almost by none now living excelled, hath few equals, and excels most, hath this praise peculiar to himself, that none in this age hath used exacter diligence in the exposition of Scripture.

And a little beneath

Bucer is more large than to be read by over-busied men, and too high to be easily understood by unattentive men and of a low capacity.

Sir John Cheek,[6] *Tutor to K. Edward VI.* 1551

We have lost our master, than whom the world scarce held a greater, whether we consider his knowledge of true religion, or his integrity and innocence of life, or his incessant study of holy things, or his matchless labour of promoting piety, or his authority and amplitude of teaching, or whatever else was praise-worthy and glorious in him. *Script. Anglicana*. pag. 864.[7]

John Sturmius of Strasborrow[8]

No man can be ignorant what a great and constant opinion and estimation of Bucer there is in Italy, France, and England. Whence the saying of Quintilian hath oft come to my mind, that he hath well profited in eloquence whom Cicero pleases. The same say I of Bucer, that he hath made no small progress in Divinity whom Bucer pleases; for in his volumes, which he wrote very many, there is the plain impression to be discerned of many great virtues: of diligence, of charity, of truth, of acuteness of judgment, of learning. Wherein he hath a certain proper kind of writing, whereby he doth not only teach the reader but affects him with the sweetness of his sentences and with the manner of his arguing, which is so teaching and so logical that it may be perceived how learnedly he separates probable reasons from necessary, how forcibly he confirms what he has to prove, how sutt'ly[9] he refutes, not with sharpness but with truth.

Theodore Beza, on the portraiture of M. Bucer[10]

This is that countenance of Bucer, the mirror of mildness, tempered with gravity, to whom the City of Strasburgh owes the reformation of her Church. Whose singular learning and eminent zeal, joined with excellent wisdom, both his learned books and public disputations in the general Diets[11] of the Empire shall witness to all ages. Him the German persecution drove into England; where honourably entertained by Edward the sixth, he was for two years chief Professor of Divinity in Cambridge, with greatest frequency and applause of all learned and pious men until his death, 1551. *Bezae Icones.*[12]

Mr. Fox's Book of Martyrs, Vol. 3. p. 763[13]

Bucer, what by writing, but chiefly by reading and preaching openly, wherein being painful in the word of God he never spared himself nor regarded his health, brought all men into such an admiration of him, that neither his friends could sufficiently praise him nor his enemies in any point find fault with his singular life and sincere doctrine. A most certain token whereof may be his sumptuous burial at Cambridge, solemnized with so great an assistance of all the University that it was not possible to devise more to the setting out and amplifying of the same.

Dr. Pern, the Popish Vice-Chancellor of Cambridge, his adversary[14]

Cardinal Pool,[15] about the fourth year of Queen Mary, intending to reduce the University of Cambridge to Popery again, thought no way so effectual as to cause the bones of Martin Bucer and Paulus Fagius, which had been four years in the grave, to be taken up and burnt openly with their books, as knowing that those two worthy men had been of greatest moment to the reformation of that place from Popery, and had left such powerful seeds of their doctrine behind them as would never die, unless the men themselves were digged up and openly condemned for heretics by the University itself. This was put in execution, and Doctor Pern, Vice-Chancellor, appointed to preach against Bucer. Who, among other things, laid to his charge the opinions which he held of the marriage of priests, of divorcement, and of usury. But immediately after his sermon, or somewhat before, as the *Book of Martyrs* for a truth relates, Vol. 3. p. 770, the said Doctor Pern smiting himself on the breast, and in manner weeping, wished with all his heart that God would grant his soul might then presently depart and remain with Bucer's; for he knew his life was such, that if any man's soul were worthy of Heaven, he thought Bucer's in special to be most worthy. *Histor. de Combust. Buceri & Fagii.*[16]

Acworth the University Orator[17]

Soon after that Queen Elizabeth came to the crown, this condemnation of Bucer and Fagius by the Cardinal and his Doctors was solemnly repealed by the University and the memory of those two famous men celebrated in an oration by Acworth the University Orator, which is yet extant in the *Book of Martyrs,* Vol. 3. p. 773, and in Latin, *Scripta Anglic.* p. 936.

Nicholas Carre, a learned man; Walter Haddon, Master of the Requests to Queen Elizabeth; Matthew Parker, afterwards Primate of England, with other eminent men, in their funeral orations and sermons express abundantly how great a man Martin Bucer was, what an incredible loss England sustained in his death, and that with him died the hope of a perfect reformation for that age.[18] *Ibid.*

Jacobus Verheiden of Grave, in his Elegies Of famous Divines[19]

Though the name of Martin Luther be famous, yet thou Martin Bucer, for piety, learning, labor, care, vigilance, and writing, art not to be held inferior to Luther. Bucer was a singular instrument of God, so was Luther. By the death of this most learned and most faithful man, the Church of Christ sustained a heavy loss, as Calvin witnesseth. And they who are studious of Calvin are not ignorant how much he ascribes to Bucer; for thus he writes in a letter to Viretus: what a manifold loss befell the Church of God in the death of Bucer, as oft as I call to mind, I feel my heart almost rent asunder.

Peter Martyr Epist. to Conradus Hubertus[20]

He is dead, who hath overcome in many battles of the Lord. God lent us for a time this, our Father and our teacher, never enough praised. Death hath divided me from a most unanimous[21] friend, one truly according to mine own heart. My mind is over-pressed with grief, insomuch that I have no power to write more. I bid thee in Christ farewell, and wish thou mayst be able to bear the loss of Bucer better than I can bear it.

Testimonies given by learned men to Paulus Fagius, who held the same opinion with Martin Bucer concerning divorce

Paulus Fagius, born in the Palatinate, became most skillful in the Hebrew tongue. Being called to the ministry at Isna, he published many ancient and profitable Hebrew books, being aided in the expenses by a Senator of that city, as Origen sometime was by a certain rich man called Ambrosius. At length invited to Strasburgh, he there famously discharged the office of a teacher, until the same persecution drove him and Bucer into England, where he was preferred to a Professor's place in Cambridge and soon after died.

Melchior Adamus writes his life among the famous German Divines.

Sleidan and Thuanus[22] mention him with honour in their *History*. And *Verheiden* in his *Elegies*.

To the Parliament.

The Book which, among other great and high points of reformation, contains as a principal part thereof, this treatise here presented, Supreme Court of Parliament, was by the famous author Martin Bucer dedicated to Edward the sixth: whose incomparable youth doubtless had brought forth to the Church of England such a glorious manhood, had his life reached it, as would have left in the affairs of religion nothing without an excellent pattern for us now to follow. But since the secret purpose of divine appointment hath reserved no less perhaps than the just half of such a sacred work to be accomplished in this age, and principally, as we trust, by your successful wisdom and authority, religious Lords and Commons, what wonder if I seek no other, to whose exactest judgment and review I may commend these last and worthiest labours of this renowned teacher, whom living, all the pious nobility of those reforming times, your truest and best-imitated ancestors, reverenced and admired. Nor was he wanting to a recompence as great as was himself; when both at many times before, and especially among his last signs and prayers, testifying his dear and fatherly affection to the Church and realm of England, he sincerely wished in the hearing of many devout men that what he had in this his last book written to King Edward concerning discipline might have place in this Kingdom. His hope was then, that no calamity, no confusion, or deformity would happen to the commonwealth; but otherwise he feared, lest in the midst of all this ardency to know God, yet by the neglect of discipline, our good endeavours would not succeed. *These remarkable words of so godly and so eminent a man at his death, as they are related by a sufficient and well-known witness, who heard them, and inserted by Thuanus into his grave and serious History,*[23] *so ought they to be chiefly considered by that nation for those sake they were uttered, and more especially by that general council which represents the body of that nation. If therefore the book, or this part thereof, for necessary causes be now revived and recommended to the use of this undisciplined age, it hence appears that these reasons have not erred in the choice of a fit patronage for a discourse of such importance. But why the whole tractate is not here brought entire, but this matter of divorcement selected in particular, to prevent the full speed of some mis-interpreter, I hasten to disclose. First, it will be soon manifest to them who know what wise men should know, that the constitution and reformation of a commonwealth, if Ezra and Nehemiah*[24] *did not misreform, is, like a building, to begin orderly from the foundation thereof, which is marriage and the family, to set right first whatever is amiss therein. How can there else grow up a race of warrantable*[25] *men, while the house and home that breeds them is troubled and disquieted under a bondage, not of God's constraining with a natureless*[26] *constraint (if his most righteous judgments may be our rule) but laid upon us imperiously in the worst and weakest ages of knowledge by a canonical tyranny of stupid and malicious monks; who, having rashly vowed themselves to a single life which they could not undergo, invented new fetters to throw on matrimony, that the world thereby waxing more dissolute, they also in a general looseness might sin with more favour. Next, there being yet among many, such a strange iniquity and perverseness against all necessary divorce, while they will needs expound the words of our Savior, not duly by comparing other places, as they must do in the resolving of a hundred other Scriptures, but by persisting chiefly in the abrupt and Papistical way of a literal apprehension against the direct analogy of sense, reason, law, and Gospel, it therefore may well seem more than time to apply the sound and holy persuasions of this apostolic man to that part in us which is not yet fully dispossest of an error as absurd as most that we deplore in our blindest adversaries, and to let his authority and unanswerable reasons be vulgarly known, that either his name or the force of his doctrine may work a wholesome effect. Lastly, I find it clear to be the author's intention that this point of divorcement should be held and received as a most necessary and prime part of discipline in every Christian government. And therefore having reduced his model of reformation to fourteen heads, he bestows almost as much time about this one point of divorce as about all the rest; which also was the judgment of his heirs and learned friends in Germany, best acquainted with his meaning, who first publishing this his Book by Oporinus*[27] *at Basel (a city for learning and constancy in the true Faith, honourable among the first) added a special note in the title,* that there the reader should find the doctrine of divorce handled so solidly, and so fully, as scarce the like in a writer of that age. *And with this particular commendation they doubted not to dedicate the book, as a most profitable and exquisite discourse, to Christian the third, a worthy and pious King of Denmark, as the author himself had done before to our Edward the sixth. Yet did not Bucer in that volume only declare what his constant opinion was herein, but also in his commentary upon Matthew, written at Strasburgh divers years before, he treats distinctly and copiously the same argument in three several places, touches it also upon the 7th to the Romans, and promises the same solution more largely upon the 1st to the Corinthians, omitting no occasion to weed out this last and deepest mischief of the canon law, sown into the opinions of modern men against the laws and practice both of God's chosen people and the best primitive times. Wherein his faithfulness and powerful evidence prevailed so far with all the Church of Strasburgh that they published this doctrine of divorce as an article of their confession, after they had taught so eight and twenty years through all those times when that city flourished and excelled most, both in religion, learning, and government, under those first restorers of the Gospel there, Zellius, Hedio, Capito, Fagius, and those who incomparably then governed the commonwealth, Farrerus and Sturmius.*[28] *If therefore God in the former age found out a servant, and by whom he had converted and reformed many a city, by him thought good to restore the most needful doctrine of divorce from rigorous and harmful mistakes on the right hand, it can be no strange thing if in this age he stir up by whatsoever means whom it pleases him to take in hand and maintain the same assertion. Certainly if it be in man's discerning to sever providence from chance, I could allege many instances wherein there would appear cause to esteem of me no other than a passive instrument under some power and counsel higher and better than can be human, working to a general good in the whole course of this matter. For that I owe no light, or leading received from any man in the discovery of this truth, what time I first undertook it in* The Doctrine and Discipline of Divorce, *and had only the infallible grounds of Scripture to be my guide, he who tries the inmost heart, and saw with what severe industry and examination of myself I set down every period, will be my witness. When I had almost finished the first edition, I chanced to read in the notes of Hugo Grotius upon the 5th of Matthew, whom I straight understood inclining to reasonable terms in this controversy; and something he whispered rather than disputed about the law of charity, and the true end of wedlock.*[29] *Glad therefore of such an able assistant, however at much distance, I resolved at length to put off into this wild and calumnious world. For God, it seems, intended to prove me, whether I durst alone take up a rightful cause against a world of disesteem, and found I durst. My name I did not publish, as not willing it should sway the reader either for me or against me.*[30] *But when I was told that the style, which what it ails*[31] *to be so soon distinguishable I cannot tell, was known by most men, and that some of the clergy began to inveigh and exclaim on what I was credibly informed they had not read, I took it then for my proper season, both to show them a name that could easily contemn such an indiscreet kind of censure, and to reinforce the question with a more accurate diligence: that if any of them would be so good as to leave railing, and to let us hear so much of his learning and Christian wisdom as will be strictly demanded of him in his answering to this problem, care was had he should not spend his preparations against a nameless pamphlet.*[32] *By this time I had learnt that Paulus Fagius, one of the chief Divines in Germany, sent for by Frederic the Palatine to reform his Dominion,*[33] *and after that invited hither in King Edward's days to be a Professor of Divinity in Cambridge, was of the same opinion touching divorce which these men so lavishly traduced in me. What I found, I inserted where fittest place was, thinking sure they would respect so grave an author, at least to the moderating of their odious inferences. And having now perfected a second edition, I referred the judging thereof to your high and impartial sentence, honoured Lords and Commons. For I was confident, if anything generous, anything noble, and above the multitude, were left yet in the spirit of England, it could be nowhere sooner found, and nowhere sooner understood, than in that house of justice and true liberty where ye sit in council. Nor doth the event hitherto, for some reasons which I shall not here deliver, fail me of what I conceived so highly. Nevertheless, being far otherwise dealt with by some, of whose profession and supposed knowledge I had better hope, and esteemed the deviser of a new and pernicious paradox, I felt no difference within me from that peace and firmness of mind which is of nearest kind to patience and contentment: both for that I knew I had divulged a truth linked inseparably with the most fundamental rules of Christianity, to stand or fall together, and was not un-informed that divers learned and judicious men testified their daily approbation of the book. Yet at length it hath pleased God, who had already given me satisfaction in myself, to afford me now a means whereby I may be fully justified also in the eyes of men. When the book had been now the second time set forth well-nigh three months, as I best remember, I then first came to hear that Martin Bucer had written much concerning divorce; whom earnestly turning over, I soon perceived, but not without amazement, in the same opinion, confirmed with the same reasons which in that published book, without the help or imitation of any precedent writer, I had laboured out and laid together. Not but that there is some difference in the handling, in the order, and the number of arguments, but still agreeing in the same conclusion. So as I may justly gratulate mine own mind, with due acknowledgment of assistance from above, which led me, not as a learner, but as a collateral teacher, to a sympathy of judgment with no less a man than Martin Bucer. And he, if our things here below arrive him where he is, does not repent him to see that point of knowledge which he first, and with an unchecked freedom, preached to those more knowing times of England, now found so necessary, though what he admonished were lost out of our memory, yet that God doth now again create the same doctrine in another unwritten table, and raises it up immediately out of his pure oracle to the convincement of a perverse age, eager in the reformation of names and ceremonies, but in realities as traditional and as ignorant as their forefathers. I would ask now the foremost of my profound accusers, whether they dare affirm that to be licentious, new, and dangerous, which Martin Bucer so often and so urgently avouched to be most lawful, most necessary, and most Christian, without the least blemish to his good name, among all the worthy men of that age, and since, who testify so highly of him? If they dare, they must then set up an arrogance of their own against all those churches and saints who honoured him without this exception. If they dare not, how can they now make that licentious doctrine in another, which was never blamed or confuted in Bucer, or in Fagius? The truth is, there will be due to them for this their unadvised rashness, the best donative*[34] *that can be given them: I mean a round reproof, now that where they thought to be most magisterial, they have displayed their own want, both of reading and of judgment. First, to be so unacquainted in the writings of Bucer, which are so obvious*[35] *and so useful in their own faculty; next, to be so caught in a prejudicating*[36] *weakness, as to condemn that for lewd which (whether they knew or not) these elect servants of Christ commended for lawful, and for new that which was taught by these almost the first and greatest authors of reformation, who were never taxed for so teaching, and dedicated without scruple to a royal pair of the first reforming Kings in Christendom, and confessed in the public confession of a most orthodoxal Church and State in Germany. This is also another fault which I must tell them: that they have stood now almost this whole year clamouring afar off, while the book hath been twice printed, twice bought up, and never once vouchsafed a friendly conference with the author, who would be glad and thankful to be shown an error, either by private dispute or public answer, and could retract, as well as wise men before him; might also be worth the gaining, as one who heretofore hath done good service to the Church by their own confession. Or if he be obstinate, their confutation would have rendered him without excuse, and reclaimed others of no mean parts who incline to his opinion. But now their work is more than doubled; and how they will hold up their heads against the sudden aspect of these two great and reverend Saints whom they have defamed, how they will make good the censuring of that, for a novelty of licence, which Bucer constantly taught to be a pure and holy law of Christ's Kingdom, let them advise. For against these my adversaries, who before the examining of a propounded truth in a fit time of reformation, have had the conscience to oppose naught else but their blind reproaches and surmises, that a single innocence might not be oppressed and overborn by a crew of mouths, for the restoring of a law and doctrine falsely and unlearnedly reputed new and scandalous, God, that I may ever magnify and record this his goodness, hath unexpectedly raised up as it were from the dead more than one famous light of the first reformation to bear witness with me, and to do me honour in that very thing wherein these men thought to have blotted me, and hath given them the proof of a capacity which they despised, running equal and authentic*[37] *with some of their chiefest masters unthought of, and in a point of sagest moment. However, if we know at all when to ascribe the occurrences of this life to the work of a special providence, as nothing is more usual in the talk of good men, what can be more like to a special providence of God, than in the first reformation of England, that this question of divorce, as a main thing to be restored to just freedom, was written, and seriously commended to Edward the sixth, by a man called from another country to be the instructor of our nation; and now in this present renewing of the Church and commonwealth, which we pray may be more lasting, that the same question should be again treated and presented to this Parliament, by one enabled to use the same reasons without the least sight or knowledge of what was done before. It were no trespass, Lords and Commons, though something of less note were attributed to the ordering of a heavenly power; this question therefore of such prime concernment both to Christian and civil welfare, in such an extraordinary manner, not recovered, but plainly twice born to these latter ages, as from a divine hand I tender to your acceptance and most considerate thoughts. Think not that God raised up in vain a man of greatest authority in the Church to tell a trivial and licentious tale in the ears of that good Prince,*[38] *and to bequeath it as his last will and testament, nay rather as the testament and royal law of Christ to this nation; or that it should of itself after so many years, as it were in a new field where it was never sown, grow up again as a vicious plant in the mind of another, who had spoke honestest things to the nation, though he knew not that what his youth then reasoned without a pattern had been heard already and well allowed from the gravity and worth of Martin Bucer; 'til meeting with the envy of men ignorant in their own undertaken calling, God directed him to the forgotten writings of this faithful evangelist, to be his defense and warrant against the gross imputation of broaching licence. Ye are now in the glorious way to high virtue, and matchless deeds, trusted with a most inestimable trust, the asserting of our just liberties. Ye have a nation that expects now, and from mighty sufferings aspires to be the example of all Christendom to a perfectest reforming. Dare to be as great, as ample, and as eminent in the fair progress of your noble designs as the full and goodly stature of truth and excellence itself; as unlimited by petty precedents and copies, as your unquestionable calling from Heaven gives ye power to be. What are all our public immunities and privileges worth? And how shall it be judged that we fight for them with minds worthy to enjoy them, if we suffer ourselves in the meanwhile not to understand the most important freedom that God and Nature hath given us in the family, which no wise nation ever wanted 'til the Popery and superstition of some former ages attempted to remove and alter divine and most prudent laws for human and most imprudent canons: whereby good men in the best portion of their lives, and in that ordinance of God which entitles them from the beginning to most just and requisite contentments, are compelled to civil indignities, which by the law of* Moses *bad men were not compelled to? Be not bound about and straitened in the spacious wisdom of your free spirits by the scanty and unadequate*[39] *and inconsistent principles of such as condemn others for adhering to traditions, and are themselves the prostrate worshippers of custom and of such a tradition as they can deduce from no antiquity, but from the rudest and thickest barbarism of Antichristian times. But why do I anticipate the more acceptable and prevailing voice of learned Bucer himself, the pastor of nations? And O that I could set him living before ye in that doctoral chair, where once the learnedest of England thought it no disparagement to sit at his feet! He would be such a pilot, and such a Father to ye, as ye would soon find the difference of his hand and skill upon the helm of reformation. Nor do I forget that faithful associate of his labours, Paulus Fagius; for these their great names and merits, how precious soever, God hath now joined with me necessarily, in the good or evil report of this doctrine which I leave with you. It was written to a religious King of this land; written earnestly, as a main matter wherein this Kingdom needed a reform, if it purposed to be the Kingdom of Christ; written by him, who if any, since the days of* Luther, *merits to be counted the Apostle of our Church; whose unwearied pains and watching for our sakes, as they spent him quickly here among us, so did they, during the shortness of his life, incredibly promote the Gospel throughout this realm. The authority, the learning, the godliness of this man consulted with, is able to out-balance all that the lightness of a vulgar opposition can bring to counterpoise. I leave him also as my complete surety and testimonial, if truth be not the best witness to itself, that what I formerly presented to your reading on this subject was good, and just, and honest, not licentious. Not that I have now more confidence by the addition of these great authors to my party, for what I wrote was not my opinion but my knowledge, even then when I could trace no footstep in the way I went; nor that I think to win upon your apprehensions with numbers and with names, rather than with reasons; yet certainly the worst of my detractors will not except against so good a bail of my integrity and judgment as now appears for me. They must else put in the fame of Bucer and of Fagius, as my accomplices and confederates, into the same indictment; they must dig up the good name of these prime worthies (if their names could be ever buried) they must dig them up and brand them as the Papists did their bodies; and those their pure unblamable spirits, which live not only in Heaven but in their writings, they must attaint*[40] *with new attaintures, which no Protestant ever before aspersed them with. Or if perhaps we may obtain to get our appeachment*[41] *new drawn a writ of error, not of libertism, that those two principal leaders of reformation may not now come to be sued in a bill of licence, to the scandal of our Church,*[42] *the brief result will be, that for the error, if their own works be not thought sufficient to defend them, there lives yet, who will be ready in a fair and christianly discussive way to debate and sift this matter to the utmost ounce of learning and religion in him that shall lay it as an error, either upon Martin Bucer, or any other of his opinion. If this be not enough to qualify*[43] *my traducers, and that they think it more for the wisdom of their virulence not to recant the injuries they have bespoke me, I shall not for much more disturbance than they can bring me intermit*[44] *the prosecution of those thoughts which may render me best serviceable, either to this age, or if it so happen, to posterity: following the fair path which your illustrious exploits, honoured Lords and Commons, against the breast of tyranny have opened, and depending so on your happy successes in the hopes that I have conceived either of myself, or of the nation, as must needs conclude me, who most affectionately wishes and awaits the prosperous issue of your noble and valorous counsels.*

JOHN MILTON.

THE JUDGEMENT OF *MARTIN BUCER* TOUCHING *DIVORCE*. Taken out of the second Book entitled *Of the Kingdom of Christ* written by *Martin Bucer* to *Edward* the Sixth, King of *England*.

CHAP. XV

The 7th law of the sanctifying and ordering of marriage.[45]

Besides these things, Christ our King and his churches require from your Sacred Majesty that you would take upon you the just care of marriages. For it is unspeakable how many good consciences are hereby entangled, afflicted, and in danger, because there are no just laws, no speedy way constituted according to God's word, touching this holy society and fountain of mankind. For seeing matrimony is a civil thing,[46] men, that they may rightly contract, inviolably keep, and not without extreme necessity dissolve marriage, are not only to be taught by the doctrine and discipline of the Church, but also are to be acquitted, aided, and compelled by laws and judicature[47] of the commonwealth. Which thing pious Emperors acknowledging, and therein framing themselves to the law of nations, gave laws both of contracting and preserving, and also where an unhappy need required, of divorcing marriages. As may be seen in the *Code of Justinian,* the 5th Book, from the beginning through twenty-four titles. And in the Authentic of *Justinian* the 22d, and some others.[48]

But the Antichrists[49] of Rome, to get the imperial power into their own hands, first by fraudulent persuasion, afterwards by force, drew to themselves the whole authority of determining and judging as well in matrimonial causes as in most other matters. Therefore it hath been long believed that the care and government thereof doth not belong to the civil magistrate. Yet where the Gospel of Christ is received, the laws of Antichrist[50] should be rejected. If therefore Kings and governors take not this care by the power of law and justice to provide that marriages be piously contracted, religiously kept, and lawfully dissolved if need require, who sees not what confusion and trouble is brought upon this holy society; and what a rack[51] is prepared, even for many of the best consciences, while they have no certain laws to follow, no justice to implore, if any intolerable thing happen. And how much it concerns the honour and safety of the commonwealth, that marriages, according to the will of Christ, be made, maintained, and not without just cause dissolved, who understands not? For unless that first and holiest society of man and woman be purely constituted, that household discipline may be upheld by them according to God's law, how can we expect a race of good men? Let your Majesty therefore know that this is your duty, and in the first place, to reassume to yourself the just ordering of matrimony, and by firm laws to establish and defend the religion of this first and divine society among men, as all wise law-givers of old, and Christian Emperors have carefully done.

The two next chapters, because they chiefly treat about the degrees of consanguinity and affinity, I omit; only setting down a passage or two concerning the judicial laws of Moses, how fit they be for Christians to imitate rather than any other.

CHAP. XVII. toward the end

I confess that we, being free in Christ, are not bound to the civil laws of Moses in every circumstance; yet seeing no laws can be more honest, just, and wholesome than those which God himself gave, who is eternal Wisdom and Goodness, I see not why Christians, in things which no less appertain to them, ought not to follow the laws of God rather than of any men.[52] We are not to use circumcision, sacrifice, and those bodily washings prescribed to the Jews; yet by these things we may rightly learn with what purity and devotion both Baptism and the Lord's Supper should be administered and received. How much more is it our duty to observe diligently what the Lord hath commanded, and taught by the examples of his people concerning marriage, whereof we have the use no less than they?

And because this same worthy author hath another passage to this purpose, in his Comment upon Matthew, Chap. 5. 19. I here insert it from p. 46.

Since we have need of civil laws, and the power of punishing, it will be wisest not to contemn those given by Moses; but seriously rather to consider what the meaning of God was in them, what he chiefly required, and how much it might be to the good of every nation if they would borrow thence their manner of governing the commonwealth; yet freely all things and with the Spirit of Christ. For what Solon, or Plato, or Aristotle, what lawyers or Caesars could make better laws than God? And it is no light argument, that many magistrates at this day do not enough acknowledge the Kingdom of Christ, though they would seem most Christian, in that they govern their states by laws so diverse from those of Moses.

The 18th *chapter I only mention as determining a thing not here in question, that marriage without consent of parents ought not to be held good; yet with this qualification fit to be known.*

That if parents admit not the honest desires of their children but shall persist to abuse the power they have over them, they are to be mollified by admonitions, entreaties, and persuasions, first of their friends and kindred, next of the church-elders. Whom if still the hard parents refuse to hear, then ought the magistrate to interpose his power, lest any by the evil mind of their parents be detained from marriage longer than is meet, or forced to an unworthy match: in which case the Roman laws also provided. *C. de nupt.* l. 11, 13, 26.[53]

CHAP. XIX

Whether it may be permitted to revoke the promise of marriage.

Here ariseth another question concerning contracts, when they ought to be unchangeable: for religious Emperors decreed that the contract was not indissoluble until the spouse were brought home and the solemnities performed. They thought it a thing unworthy of divine and human equity, and the due consideration of man's infirmity in deliberating and determining, when space is given to renounce other contracts of much less moment which are not yet confirmed before the magistrate, to deny that to the most weighty contract of marriage, which requires the greatest care and consultation. Yet lest such a covenant should be broken for no just cause, and to the injury of that person to whom marriage was promised, they decreed a fine, that he who denied marriage to whom he had promised, and for some cause not approved by the judges, should pay the double of that pledge which was given at making sure, or as much as the judge should pronounce might satisfy the damage or the hindrance of either party. It being most certain, that oft-times after contract, just and honest causes of departing from promise come to be known and found out, it cannot be other than the duty of pious Princes to give men the same liberty of unpromising in these causes as pious Emperors granted, especially where there is only a promise and not carnal knowledge. And as there is no true marriage between them who agree not in true consent of mind, so it will be the part of godly magistrates to procure that no matrimony be among their subjects but what is knit with love and consent.[54] And though your Majesty be not bound to the imperial laws,[55] yet it is the duty of a Christian King to embrace and follow whatever he knows to be any where piously and justly constituted, and to be honest, just, and well-pleasing to his people. But why in God's law and the examples of his saints nothing hereof is read, no marvel, seeing his ancient people had power, yea a precept, that whoso could not bend his mind to the true love of his wife should give her a bill of divorce and send her from him, though after carnal knowledge and long dwelling together. This is enough to authorize a godly Prince in that indulgence which he gives to the changing of a contract: both because it is certainly the invention of Antichrist, that the promise of marriage *de praesenti,* as they call it,[56] should be indissoluble, and because it should be a Prince's care that matrimony be so joined as God ordained: which is, that every one should love his wife with such a love as Adam expressed to Eve. So as we may hope that they who marry may become one flesh, and one also in the Lord.

CHAP. XX

Concerns only the celebration of marriage.

CHAP. XXI

The means of preserving marriage holy and pure.

Now since there ought not to be less care that marriage be religiously kept than that it be piously and deliberately contracted, it will be meet that to every church be ordained certain grave and godly men who may have this care upon them: to observe whether the husband bear himself wisely toward the wife, loving, and inciting her to all piety and the other duties of this life; and whether the wife be subject to her husband, and study to be truly a meet help to him, as first to all godliness so to every other use of life. And if they[57] shall find each to other failing of their duty, or the one long absent from the other without just and urgent cause, or giving suspicion of irreligious and impure life, or of living in manifest wickedness, let it be admonished them in time. And if their authority be contemned,[58] let the names of such contemners be brought to the magistrate, who may use punishment to compel such violators of marriage to their duty, that they may abstain from all probable suspicion of transgressing; and if they admit of suspected company, the magistrate is to forbid them; whom they not therein obeying, are to be punished as adulterers, according to the law of *Justinian, Authent.* 117. For if holy wedlock, the fountain and seminary of good subjects, be not vigilantly preserved from all blots and disturbances, what can be hoped, as I said before, of the springing up of good men, and a right reformation of the commonwealth? We know it is not enough for Christians to abstain from foul deeds, but from the appearance and suspicion thereof.

CHAP. XXII

Of lawful divorce, what the ancient churches have thought.

Now we shall speak about that dissolving of matrimony which may be approved in the sight of God, if any grievous necessity require. In which thing the Roman Antichrists have knit many a pernicious entanglement to distressed consciences. For that they might here also exalt themselves above God, as if they would be wiser and chaster than God himself is, for no cause, honest or necessary, will they permit a final divorce; in the meanwhile, whoredoms and adulteries, and worse things than these, not only tolerating in themselves and others, but cherishing, and throwing men headlong into these evils. For although they also disjoin married persons from board and bed, that is, from all conjugal society and communion, and this not only for adultery, but for ill usage, and matrimonial duties denied, yet they forbid those thus parted to join in wedlock with others, but, as I said before, any dishonest associating they permit. And they pronounce the bond of marriage to remain between those whom they have thus separated. As if the bond of marriage, God so teaching and pronouncing, were not such a league as binds the married couple to all society of life and communion in divine and human things; and so associated keeps them. Something indeed out of the later Fathers they may pretend for this their tyranny, especially out of Austin[59] and some others, who were much taken with a preposterous admiration of single life. Yet though these Fathers, from the words of Christ not rightly understood, taught that it was unlawful to marry again while the former wife lived, whatever cause there had been either of desertion or divorce, yet if we mark the custom of the Church, and the common judgment which both in this time and afterward prevailed, we shall perceive that neither these Fathers did ever cast out of the Church any one for marrying after a divorce, approved by the imperial laws.

Nor only the first Christian Emperors, but the latter also, even to Justinian, and after him, did grant for certain causes approved by judges to make a true divorce; which made and confirmed by law, it might be lawful to marry again: which if it could not have been done without displeasing Christ and his Church, surely it would not have been granted by Christian Emperors, nor had the Fathers then winked at those doings in the Emperors. Hence ye may see that Jerome also, though zealous of single life more than enough, and such a condemner of second marriage though after the death of either party, yet forced by plain equity defended Fabiola, a noble matron of Rome, who having refused her husband for just causes was married to another.[60] For that the sending of a divorce to her husband was not blame-worthy, he affirms, because the man was heinously vicious; and that if an adulterous wife may be discarded, an adulterous husband is not to be kept. But that she married again while yet her husband was alive, he defends in that the Apostle[61] hath said, *It is better to marry than to burn;* and that young widows should marry, for such was Fabiola, and could not remain in widowhood.

But some one will object that Jerome there adds, *Neither did she know the vigour of the Gospel, wherin all cause of marrying is debarred from women while their husbands live; and again, while she avoided many wounds of Satan, she received one ere she was aware.* But let the equal[62] reader mind also what went before: *because,* saith he, soon after the beginning, *there is a rock and storm of slanderers opposed against her, I will not praise her converted, unless I first absolve her guilty.* For why does he call them slanderers who accused Fabiola of marrying again, if he did not judge it a matter of Christian equity and charity to pass by and pardon that fact, though in his own opinion he held it a fault? And what can this mean: *I will not praise her, unless I first absolve her.* For how could he absolve her, but by proving that Fabiola, neither in rejecting her vicious husband, nor in marrying another, had committed such a sin as could be justly condemned? Nay, he proves both by evident reason and clear testimonies of Scripture that she avoided sin.[63]

This also is hence understood, that *Jerome* by the vigor of the Gospel meant that height and perfection of our Savior's precept which might be remitted to those that burn; for he adds, *But if she be accused in that she remained not unmarried, I shall confess the fault, so I may relate the necessity.* If then he acknowledged a necessity, as he did, because she was young and could not live in widowhood, certainly he could not impute her second marriage to her much blame. But when he excuses her out of the word of God, does he not openly declare his thoughts that the second marriage of Fabiola was permitted her by the Holy Ghost himself, for the necessity which she suffered, and to shun the danger of fornication, though she went somewhat aside from the vigor of the Gospel?[64] But if any urge that Fabiola did public penance for her second marriage, which was not imposed but for great faults, 'tis answered, she was not enjoined to this penance but did it of her own accord, *and not 'til after her second husband's death.* As in the time of Cyprian[65] we read that many were wont to do voluntary penance for small faults, which were not liable to excommunication.

CHAP. XXIII

That marriage was granted by the ancient Fathers, even after the vow of single life. I omit his testimonies out of Cyprian, Gelasius, Epiphanius,[66] *contented only to relate what he thence collects to the present purpose.*

Some will say, perhaps, wherefore all this concerning marriage after vow of single life, whenas the question was of marriage after divorce? For this reason, that they whom it so much moves, because some of the Fathers thought marriage after any kind of divorce to be condemned of our Savior, may see that this conclusion follows not. The Fathers thought all marriage after divorce to be forbidden of our Savior; therefore they thought such marriage was not to be tolerated in a Christian. For the same Fathers judged it forbidden to marry after vow; yet such marriages they neither dissolved nor excommunicated. For these words of our Savior, and of the Holy Ghost, stood in their way: *All cannot receive this saying, but they to whom it is given. Every one hath his proper gift from God, one after this manner, another after that. It is better to marry than to burn. I will that younger widows marry;* and the like.

So there are many canons and laws extant, whereby priests, if they married, were removed from their office. Yet is it not read that their marriage was dissolved, as the Papists now-a-days do, or that they were excommunicated; nay expressly they might communicate as laymen. If the consideration of human infirmity, and those testimonies of divine Scripture which grant marriage to every one that wants it, persuaded those Fathers to bear themselves so humanely toward them who had married with breach of vow to God, as they believed, and with divorce of that marriage wherein they were in a manner joined to God, who doubts but that the same Fathers held the like humanity was to be afforded to those who after divorce and faith broken with men, as they thought, entered into a second marriage? For among such are also found no less weak, and no less burning.

CHAP. XXIV

Who of the ancient Fathers granted marriage after divorce.

This is clear both by what hath been said, and by that which Origen relates of certain Bishops in his time, *Homil. 7.* in Matth. *I know some,* saith he, *which are over churches, who without Scripture have permitted the wife to marry while her former husband lived. And did this against Scripture, which saith, The wife is bound to her husband so long as he lives; and she shall be called an adultress, if, her husband living, she take another man; yet did they not permit this without cause, perhaps for the infirmity of such as had not continence they permitted evil to avoid worse.* Ye see Origen and the doctors of his age, not without all cause, permitted women after divorce to marry, though their former husbands were living; yet writes that they permitted against Scripture. But what cause could they have to do so, unless they thought our Savior in his precepts of divorce had so forbidden, as willing to remit such perfection to his weaker ones, cast into danger of worse faults?

The same thought Leo, Bishop of Rome,[67] *Ep. 85.* to the African Bishops of Mauritania Caesariensis, wherein complaining of a certain priest, who divorcing his wife, or being divorced by her, as other copies have it, had married another, neither dissolves the matrimony nor excommunicates him, only unpriests him. The Fathers therefore, as we see, did not simply and wholly condemn marriage after divorce.[68]

But as for me, this remitting of our Savior's precepts, which these ancients allow to the infirm in marrying after vow and divorce, I can in no ways admit; for whatsoever plainly consents not with the commandment cannot, I am certain, be permitted, or suffered in any Christian: for Heaven and Earth shall pass away, but not a tittle from the commands of God among them who expect life eternal. Let us therefore consider, and weigh the words of our Lord concerning marriage and divorce, which he pronounced both by himself and by his Apostle, and let us compare them with other oracles of God; for whatsoever is contrary to these, I shall not persuade the least tolerating thereof. But if it can be taught to agree with the word of God, yea, to be commanded that most men may have permission given to them to divorce and marry again, I must prefer the authority of God's word before the opinion of Fathers and Doctors, as they themselves teach.[69]

CHAP. XXV

The words of our Lord, and of the Holy Ghost by the Apostle Paul concerning divorce are explained.

But the words of our Lord, and of the Holy Ghost, out of which Austin and some others of the Fathers think it concluded that our Savior forbids marriage after any divorce, are these: Mat. v.31, 32. *It hath been said,* &c. And Mat. xix.7, *They say unto him, why did Moses then command?* &c. and Mark x. and Luke xvi. Rom. vii.1, 2, 3, and I Cor. vii.10–11.[70] Hence therefore they conclude that all marriage after divorce is called adultery; which to commit, being no ways to be tolerated in any Christian, they think it follows that second marriage is in no case to be permitted either to the divorcer or to the divorced.

But that it may be more fully and plainly perceived what force is in this kind of reasoning, it will be the best course to lay down certain grounds whereof no Christian can doubt the truth.[71] First, it is a wickedness to suspect that our Savior branded that for adultery which himself, in his own law which he came to fulfill and not to dissolve, did not only permit but also command; for by him, the only mediator, was the whole law of God given. But that by this law of God marriage was permitted after any divorce is certain by Deut. xxiv.1.

CHAP. XXVI

That God in his law did not only grant but also command divorce to certain men.

Deut. xxiv.1. *When a man hath taken a wife,* &c.[72] But in Mal. 2:15, 16. is read the Lord's command to put her away whom a man hates, in these words: *Take heed to your spirit, and let none deal injuriously against the wife of his youth. If he hate, let him put away, saith the Lord God of Israel. And he shall hide thy violence with his garment,* that marries her divorced by thee, *saith the Lord of hosts;* but *take heed to your spirit, and do no injury.* By these testimonies of the divine law, we see that the Lord did not only permit, but also expressly and earnestly commanded his people, by whom he would that all holiness and faith of marriage covenant should be observed, that he who could not induce his mind to love his wife with a true conjugal love might dismiss her that she might marry to another.

CHAP. XXVII

That what the Lord permitted and commanded to his ancient people concerning divorce belongs also to Christians.

Now what the Lord permitted to his first-born people, that certainly he could not forbid to his own among the Gentiles, whom he made coheirs and into one body with his people; nor could he ever permit, much less command aught that was not good for them, at least so used as he commanded. For being God, he is not changed as man. Which thing who seriously considers, how can he imagine that God would make that wicked to them that believe, and serve him under grace, which he granted and commanded to them that served him under the law, whenas the same causes require the same permission. And who that knows but human matters, and loves the truth, will deny that many marriages hang as ill together now as ever they did among the Jews? So that such marriages are liker to torments than true marriages.[73] As therefore the Lord doth always succor and help the oppressed, so he would ever have it provided for injured husbands and wives, that under pretence of the marriage-bond, they be not sold to perpetual vexations, instead of the loving and comfortable marriage-duties. And lastly, as God doth always detest hypocrisy and fraud, so neither doth he approve that among his people, that should be counted marriage wherein none of those duties remain whereby the league of wedlock is chiefly preserved. What inconsiderate neglect then of God's law is this, that I may not call it worse, to hold that Christ our Lord would not grant the same remedies both of divorce and second marriage to the weak, or to the evil, if they will needs have it so, but especially to the innocent and wronged; whenas the same urgent causes remain as before, when the discipline of the Church and magistrate hath tried what may be tried.

CHAP. XXVIII

That our Lord Christ intended not to make new laws of marriage and divorce, or of any civil matters.

It is agreed by all who determine of the Kingdom and offices of Christ by the holy Scriptures,[74] as all godly men ought to do, that our Savior upon Earth took not on him either to give new laws in civil affairs or to change the old. But it is certain that matrimony and divorce are civil things. Which the Christian Emperors knowing, gave conjugal laws, and reserved the administration of them to their own courts; which no true ancient Bishop ever condemned.

Our Savior came to preach repentance and remission. Seeing therefore those who put away their wives without any just cause were not touched with conscience of the sin, through misunderstanding of the law, he recalled them to a right interpretation, and taught that the woman in the beginning was so joined to the man that there should be a perpetual union both in body and spirit: where this is not, the matrimony is already broke, before there be yet any divorce made, or second marriage.

CHAP. XXIX

That it is wicked to strain the words of Christ beyond their purpose. This is his third axiom, whereof there needs no explication here.

CHAP. XXX

That all places of Scripture about the same thing are to be joined, and compared, to avoid contradictions.[75]

This he demonstrates at large out of sundry places in the Gospel, and principally by that precept against swearing,[76] which compared with many places of the law and prophets is a flat contradiction of them all, if we follow superstitiously the letter. Then having repeated briefly his four axioms, he thus proceeds.

These things thus pre-admonished, let us inquire what the undoubted meaning is of our Savior's words, and enquire according to the rule which is observed by all learned and good men in their expositions: that praying first to God, who is the only opener of our hearts, we may first with fear and reverence consider well the words of our Savior touching this question. Next, that we may compare them with all other places of Scripture treating of this matter, to see how they consent with our Savior's words and those of his Apostle.

CHAP. XXXI

This chapter disputes against Austin and the Papists, who deny second marriage even to them who divorce in case of adultery; which because it is not controverted among true Protestants, but that the innocent person is easily allowed to marry, I spare the translating.

CHAP. XXXII

That a manifest adultress ought to be divorced, and cannot lawfully be retained in marriage by any true Christian.
This though he prove sufficiently, yet I let pass, because this question was not handled in The Doctrine and Discipline of Divorce; to which book I bring so much of this treatise as runs parallel.

CHAP. XXXIII

That adultery is to be punished by death.
This chapter also I omit for the reason last alleged.

CHAP. XXXIV

That it is lawful for a wife to leave an adulterer, and to marry another husband. This is generally granted, and therefore excuses me the writing out.

CHAP. XXXV

Places in the writings of the Apostle Paul touching divorce explained.

Let us consider the answers of the Lord given by the Apostle severally. Concerning the first, which is Rom. vii. 1, *Know ye not, brethren, for I speak to them that know the law,* &c. Ver. 2, *The woman is bound by the law to her Husband so long as he liveth.*[77] Here it is certain that the Holy Ghost had no purpose to determine aught of marriage or divorce, but only to bring an example from the common and ordinary law of wedlock, to show that as no covenant holds either party being dead, so now that we are not bound to the law but to Christ our Lord, seeing that through him we are dead to sin and to the law; and so joined to Christ that we may bring forth fruit in him from a willing godliness, and not by the compulsion of law whereby our sins are more excited and become more violent. What therefore the Holy Spirit here speaks of matrimony, cannot be extended beyond the general rule.

Besides it is manifest that the Apostle did allege the law of wedlock, as it was delivered to the Jews; for, saith he, I speak to them that know the law. They knew no law of God but that of Moses, which plainly grants divorce for several reasons. It cannot therefore be said that the Apostle cited this general example out of the law to abolish the several exceptions of that law which God himself granted by giving authority to divorce.

Next, when the Apostle brings an example out of God's law concerning man and wife it must be necessary that we understand such for man and wife, as are so indeed according to the same law of God; that is, who are so disposed as that they are both willing and able to perform the necessary duties of marriage not those who under a false title of marriage, keep themselves mutually bound to injuries and disgraces; for such twain are nothing less than lawful man and wife.[78]

The like answer is to be given to all the other places both of the Gospel and the Apostle, that whatever exception may be proved out of God's law be not excluded from those places. For the Spirit of God doth not condemn things formerly granted and allowed where there is like cause and reason. Hence Ambrose, upon that place, I Cor. vii.15, *A brother or a sister is not under bondage in such cases,*[79] thus expounds: *The reverence of marriage is not due to him who abhors the author of marriage, nor is that marriage ratified which is without devotion to God; he sins not therefore who is put away for God's cause, though he join himself to another. For the dishonor of the Creator dissolves the right of matrimony to him who is deserted, that he be not accused, though marrying to another. The faith of wedlock is not to be kept with him who departs, that he might not hear the God of Christians to be the author of wedlock. For if Ezra caused the misbelieving wives and husbands to be divorced, that God might be appeased, and not offended, though they took others of their own faith, how much more shall it be free, if the misbeliever depart, to marry one of our own religion. For this is not to be counted matrimony, which is against the law of God.*

Two things are here to be observed toward the following discourse, which truth itself and the force of God's word hath drawn from this holy man. For those words are very large: *Matrimony is not ratified without devotion to God.* And *the dishonour of the Creator dissolves the right of matrimony.* For devotion is far off, and dishonour is done to God by all who persist in any wickedness and heinous crime.

CHAP. XXXVI

That although it seem in the Gospel as if our Savior granted divorce only for adultery, yet in very deed he granted it for other causes also.

Now is to be dealt with this question, Whether it be lawful to divorce and marry again for other causes besides adultery, since our Savior expressed that only. To this question, if we retain our principles already laid and must acknowledge it to be a cursed blasphemy if we say that the words of God do contradict one another, of necessity we must confess that our Lord did grant divorce, and marriage after that, for other causes besides adultery, notwithstanding what he said in Matthew. For first, they who consider but only that place, I Cor. vii[80] which treats of believers and misbelievers matched together, must of force confess that our Lord granted just divorce, and second marriage in the cause of desertion, which is other than the cause of fornication. And if there be one other cause found lawful, then is it most true that divorce was granted not only for fornication.

Next, it cannot be doubted, as I showed before, by them to whom it is given to know God and his judgments out of his own word, but that, what means of peace and safety God ever granted and ordained to his elected people, the same he grants and ordains to men of all ages who have equally need of the same remedies. And who, that is but a knowing man, dares say there be not husbands and wives now to be found in such a hardness of heart that they will not perform either conjugal affection, or any requisite duty thereof, though it be most deserved at their hands.

Neither can anyone defer to confess but that God, whose property it is to judge the cause of them that suffer injury, hath provided for innocent and honest persons wedded, how they might free themselves by lawful means of divorce from the bondage and iniquity of those who are falsely termed their husbands or their wives. This is clear out of *Deut.* 24.1, *Malach.* 2, *Matth.* 19, I *Cor.* 7, and out of those principles which the Scripture everywhere teaches: That God changes not his mind, dissents not from himself, is no accepter of persons; but allows the same remedies to all men oppressed with the same necessities and infirmities; yet requires that we should use them. This he will easily perceive, who considers these things in the Spirit of the Lord.

Lastly, it is most certain that the Lord hath commanded us to obey the civil laws every one of his own commonwealth, if they be not against the laws of God.

CHAP. XXXVII

For what causes divorce is permitted by the civil law
ex l. consensu Codic. de repudiis.

It is also manifest that the law of Theodosius and Valentinian, which begins *Consensu,* &c. touching divorce, and many other decrees of pious Emperors agreeing herewith, are not contrary to the word of God; and therefore may be recalled into use by any Christian Prince or commonwealth; nay, ought to be with due respect had to every nation. For whatsoever is equal and just, that in every thing is to be sought and used by Christians. Hence it is plain that divorce is granted by divine approbation, both to husbands and to wives, if either party can convict the other of these following offences before the magistrate.

If the husband can prove the wife to be an adultress, a witch, a murderess, to have bought or sold to slavery any one freeborn, to have violated sepulchers, committed sacrilege, favoured thieves and robbers, desirous of feasting with strangers, the husband not knowing, or not willing, if she lodge forth without a just and probable cause, or frequent theatres and sights, he forbidding, if she be privy with those that plot against the State, or if she deal falsely, or offer blows. And if the wife can prove her husband guilty of any those forenamed crimes, and frequent the company of lewd women in her sight, or if he beat her, she had the like liberty to quit herself; with this difference, that the man after divorce might forthwith marry again, the woman not 'til a year after, lest she might chance to have conceived.

CHAP. XXXVIII

An exposition of those places wherein God declares
the nature of holy wedlock.

Now to the end it may seem that this agrees with the divine law, the first institution of marriage is to be considered, and those texts in which God established the joining of male and female and described the duties of them both. When God had determined to make woman, and give her as a wife to man, he spake thus,

Gen. 2:18: *It is not good for man to be alone, I will make him a help-meet for him. And Adam said,* but in the Spirit of God, v. 23–24, *This is now bone of my bone, and flesh of my flesh. Therefore shall a man leave his father and mother, and shall cleave to his wife, and they shall be one flesh.*

To this first institution did Christ recall his own; when answering the Pharisees, he condemned the licence of unlawful divorce. He taught therefore by his example, that we, according to this first institution, and what God hath spoken thereof, ought to determine what kind of covenant marriage is, how to be kept, and how far; and lastly, for what causes to be dissolved. To which decrees of God these also are to be joined, which the Holy Ghost hath taught by his Apostle, that neither the husband nor the wife *hath power of their own body, but mutually each of either's.* That *the husband shall love the wife as his own body, yea as Christ loves his Church; and that the wife ought to be subject to her husband, as the Church is to Christ.*

By these things the nature of holy wedlock is certainly known; whereof if only one be wanting in both or either party, and that either by obstinate malevolence or too deep inbred weakness of mind, or lastly, through incurable impotence of body, it cannot then be said that the covenant of matrimony holds good between such; if we mean that covenant which God instituted and called marriage, and that whereof only it must be understood that our Savior said, *Those whom God hath joined, let no man separate.*[81]

And hence is concluded, that matrimony requires continual cohabitation and living together, unless the calling of God be otherwise evident; which union if the parties themselves disjoin either by mutual consent, or one against the other's will depart, the marriage is then broken. Wherein the Papists, as in other things, oppose themselves against God, while they separate for many causes from bed and board, and yet will have the bond of matrimony remain, as if this covenant could be other than the conjunction and communion not only of bed and board but of all other living and helpful duties. This we may see in these words: *I will make him a help-meet for him: bone of his bone, and flesh of his flesh. For this cause shall he leave father and mother, and cleave to his wife, and they twain shall be one flesh.* By which words, who discerns not that God requires of them both so to live together, and to be united not only in body but in mind also, with such an affection as none may be dearer and more ardent among all the relations of mankind, nor of more efficacy to the mutual offices of love and loyalty. They must communicate and consent in all things both divine and human, which have any moment to well and happy living. The wife must honour and obey her husband, as the Church honours and obeys Christ her head. The husband must love and cherish his wife, as Christ his Church. Thus they must be to each other, if they will be true man and wife in the sight of God, whom certainly the churches ought to follow in their judgment. Now the proper and ultimate end of marriage is not copulation, or children, for then there was not true matrimony between Joseph and Mary the Mother of Christ, nor between many holy persons more; but the full and proper and main end of marriage is the communicating of all duties, both divine and human, each to other with utmost benevolence and affection.

CHAP. XXXIX

The properties of a true and Christian marriage more distinctly repeated.

By which definition we may know that God esteems and reckons upon these four necessary properties to be in every true marriage. 1. That they should live together, unless the calling of God require otherwise for a time. 2. That they should love one another to the height of dearness, and that in the Lord, and in the communion of true religion. 3. That the husband bear himself as the head and preserver of his wife, instructing her to all godliness and integrity of life; that the wife also be to her husband a help, according to her place, especially furthering him in the true worship of God, and next in all the occasion of civil life. And 4. That they defraud not each other of conjugal benevolence, as the Apostle commands, I Cor. 7. Hence it follows, according to the sentence of God, which all Christians ought to be ruled by, that between those who, either through obstinacy or helpless inability, cannot or will not perform these repeated duties, between those there can be no true matrimony, nor ought they to be counted man and wife.

CHAP. XL

Whether those crimes recited chap. 37 out of the civil law dissolve matrimony in God's account.

Now if a husband or wife be found guilty of any of those crimes, which by the law *consensu* are made causes of divorce, 'tis manifest that such a man cannot be the head and preserver of his wife, nor such a woman be a meet help to her husband, as the divine law in true wedlock requires; for these faults are punished either by death, or deportation, or extreme infamy, which are directly opposite to the covenant of marriage. If they deserve death, as adultery and the like,[82] doubtless God would not that any should live in wedlock with them whom he would not have to live at all. Or if it be not death, but the incurring of notorious infamy, certain it is neither just, nor expedient, nor meet that an honest man should be coupled with an infamous woman, nor an honest matron with an infamous man. The wise Roman Princes had so great regard to the equal honour of either wedded person that they counted those marriages of no force which were made between the one of good repute and the other of evil note. How much more will all honest regard of Christian expedience and comeliness beseem and concern those who are set free and dignified in Christ, than it could the Roman Senate, or their sons, for whom that law was provided.

And this all godly men will soon apprehend, that he who ought to be the head and preserver not only of his wife, but also of his children and family, as Christ is of his Church, had need be one of honest name; so likewise the wife, which is to be the meet help of an honest and good man, the mother of an honest offspring and family. The glory of the man, even as the man is the glory of Christ, should not be tainted with ignominy; as neither of them can avoid to be, having been justly appeached[83] of those forenamed crimes, and therefore cannot be worthy to hold their place in a Christian family. Yea, they themselves turn out themselves and dissolve that holy covenant. And they who are true brethren and sisters in the Lord are no more in bondage to such violators of marriage.

But here the patrons of wickedness and dissolvers of Christian discipline will object that it is the part of man and wife to bear one another's cross, whether in calamity or infamy, that they might gain each other, if not to a good name, yet to repentance and amendment. But they who thus object, seek the impunity of wickedness, and the favour of wicked men, not the duties of true charity; which prefers public honesty before private interest, and had rather the remedies of wholesome punishment appointed by God should be in use, than that by remissness, the licence of evil doing should increase. For if they who, by committing such offences, have made void the holy knot of marriage, be capable of repentance, they will be sooner moved when due punishment is executed on them than when it is remitted.

We must ever beware, lest in contriving what will be best for the soul's health of delinquents, we make ourselves wiser and discreeter than God. He that religiously weighs his oracles concerning marriage cannot doubt that they who have committed the foresaid transgressions have lost the right of matrimony, and are unworthy to hold their dignity in an honest and Christian family.

But if any husband or wife see such signs of repentance in their transgressor, as that they doubt not to regain them by continuing with them and partaking of their miseries and attaintures, they may be left to their own hopes and their own mind, saving ever the right of Church and commonwealth, that it receive no scandal by the neglect of due severity, and their children no harm by this invitation to licence and want of good education.

From all these considerations, if they be thought on, as in the presence of God and out of his word, any one may perceive, who desires to determine of these things by the Scripture, that those causes of lawful divorce, which the most religious Emperors Theodosius and Valentinian set forth in the forecited place, are according to the law of God and the prime institution of marriage. *And were still more and more straitened, as the Church and State of the Empire still more and more corrupted and degenerated.*[84] Therefore pious Princes and commonwealths both may and ought establish them again, if they have a mind to restore the honour, sanctity, and religion of holy wedlock to their people, and disentangle many consciences from a miserable and perilous condition to a chaste and honest life.

To those recited causes wherefore a wife might send a divorce to her husband, Justinian added four more, *Constit.* 117. And four more, for which a man might put away his wife. Three other causes were added in the *Code de repudiis, l. Jubemus.* All which causes are so clearly contrary to the first intent of marriage, that they plainly dissolve it. *I set them not down, being easy to be found in the body of the civil law.*[85]

It was permitted also by Christian Emperors that they who would divorce by mutual consent might without impediment. Or if there were any difficulty at all in it, the law expresses the reason, that it was only in favour of the children; so that if there were none, the law of those godly Emperors made no other difficulty of a divorce by consent.[86] Or if any were minded without consent of the other to divorce, and without those causes which have been named, the Christian Emperors laid no other punishment upon them than that the husband wrongfully divorcing his wife should give back her dowry and the use of that which was called *donatio propter nuptias;*[87] or if there were no dowry nor no donation, that he should then give her the fourth part of his goods. The like penalty was inflicted on the wife departing without just cause. But that they who were once married should be compelled to remain so ever against their wills was not exacted. Wherein those pious Princes followed the law of God in Deut. xxiv.1 and his express charge by the prophet Malachi to dismiss from him the wife whom he hates. For God never meant in marriage to give to man a perpetual torment instead of a meet help. Neither can God approve that to the violation of this holy league (which is violated as soon as true affection ceases and is lost) should be added murder, which is already committed by either of them who resolvedly hates the other, as I showed out of I John 15: *Whoso hateth his brother is a murderer.*[88]

CHAP. XLI

Whether the husband or wife deserted may marry to another.

The wife's desertion of her husband, the Christian Emperors plainly decreed to be a just cause of divorce, whenas they granted him the right thereof if she had but lain out one night against his will without probable cause. But of the man deserting his wife they did not so determine. Yet if we look into the word of God, we shall find that he who though but for a year without just cause forsakes his wife, and neither provides for her maintenance nor signifies his purpose of returning and goodwill towards her, whenas he may, hath forfeited his right in her so forsaken. For the Spirit of God speaks plainly, that both man and wife have such power over one another's person as that they cannot deprive each other of living together, but by consent, and for a time.

Hither may be added, that the Holy Spirit grants desertion to be a cause of divorce in those answers given to the Corinthians concerning a brother or sister deserted by a misbeliever.[89] *If he depart, let him depart, a brother or a sister is not under bondage in such cases.* In which words, who sees not that the Holy Ghost openly pronounced that the party without cause deserted is not bound for another's willful desertion.

But some will say, that this is spoken of a misbeliever departing. But I beseech ye, doth not he reject the faith of Christ in his deeds, who rashly breaks the holy covenant of wedlock instituted by God? And besides this, the Holy Spirit does not make the misbelieving of him who departs, but the departing of him who misbelieves, to be the just cause of freedom to the brother and sister.

Since therefore it will be agreed among Christians, that they who depart from wedlock without just cause do not only deny the faith of matrimony but of Christ also, whatever they profess with their mouths, it is but reason to conclude that the party deserted is not bound in case of causeless desertion, but that he may lawfully seek another consort, if it be needful to him, toward a pure and blameless conversation.[90]

CHAP. XLII

That impotence of body, leprosy, madness, &c. are just causes of divorce.

Of this, because it was not disputed in *The Doctrine and Discipline of Divorce,* him that would know further I commend to the Latin original.

CHAP. XLIII

That to grant divorce for all the causes which have been hitherto brought, disagrees not from the words of Christ, naming only the cause of adultery.

Now we must see how these things can stand with the words of our Savior, who seems directly to forbid all divorce except it be for adultery. To the understanding whereof, we must ever remember this: That in the words of our Savior there can be no contrariety. That his words and answers are not to be stretched beyond the question proposed. That our Savior did not there purpose to treat of all the causes for which it might be lawful to divorce and marry again; *for then that in the Corinthians of marrying again without guilt of adultery could not be added.*[91] That it is not good for that man to be alone, who hath not the special gift from above. That it is good for every such one to be married, that he may shun fornication.

With regard to these principles, let us see what our Lord answered to the tempting Pharisees about divorce and second marriage, and how far his answer doth extend.

First, no man who is not very contentious will deny that the Pharisees asked our Lord whether it were lawful to put away such a wife as was truly, and according to God's law, to be counted a wife; that is, such a one as would dwell with her husband, and both would and could perform the necessary duties of wedlock tolerably. But she who will not dwell with her husband is not put away by him, but goes of herself; and she who denies to be a meet help, or to be so hath made herself unfit by open misdemeanors, or through incurable impotencies cannot be able, is not by the law of God to be esteemed a wife, as hath been shown both from the first institution and other places of Scripture. Neither certainly would the Pharisees propound a question concerning such an unconjugal wife; *for their depravation*[92] *of the law had brought them to that pass, as to think a man had right to put away his wife for any cause, though never so slight.*[93] Since therefore it is manifest that Christ answered the Pharisees concerning a fit and meet wife according to the law of God, whom he forbid to divorce for any cause but fornication, who sees not that it is a wickedness so to wrest and extend that answer of his, as if it forbade to divorce her who hath already forsaken, or hath lost the place and dignity of a wife, by deserved infamy, *or hath undertaken to be that which she hath not natural ability to be.*[94]

This truth is so powerful, that it hath moved the Papists to grant their kind of divorce for other causes besides adultery, as for ill usage, and the not performing of conjugal duty; and to separate from bed and board for these causes, which is as much divorce as they grant for adultery.

But some perhaps will object, that though it be yielded that our Lord granted divorce not only for adultery, yet it is not certain that he permitted marriage after divorce, unless for that only cause. I answer, first, that the sentence of divorce and second marriage is one and the same. So that when the right of divorce is evinced to belong not only to the cause of fornication, the power of second marriage is also proved to be not limited to that cause only; and that most evidently, whenas the Holy Ghost, I Cor. 7.[95] so frees the deserted party from bondage, as that he may not only send a just divorce in case of desertion, but may seek another marriage.

Lastly, seeing God will not that any should live in danger of fornication and utter ruin for the default of another, and hath commanded the husband to send away with a bill of divorce her whom he could not love, it is impossible that the charge of adultery should belong to him who for lawful causes divorces and marries, or to her who marries after she hath been unjustly rejected, or to him who receives her without all fraud to the former wedlock. For this were a horrid blasphemy against God, so to interpret his words as to make him dissent from himself; for who sees not a flat contradiction in this, to enthrall[96] blameless men and women to miseries and injuries under a false and soothing title of marriage, and yet to declare by his Apostle that a brother or sister is not under bondage in such cases. No less do these two things conflict with themselves: to enforce the innocent and faultless to endure the pain and misery of another's perverseness, or else to live in unavoidable temptation; and to affirm elsewhere that he lays on no man the burden of another man's sin, nor doth constrain any man to the endangering of his soul.

CHAP. XLIV

That to those also who are justly divorced, second marriage ought to be permitted.

This although it be well proved, yet because it concerns only the offender, I leave him to search out his own charter himself in the author.

CHAP. XLV

That some persons are so ordained to marriage as that they cannot obtain the gift of continence, no not by earnest prayer; and that therein every one is to be left to his own judgment and conscience, and not to have a burden laid upon him by any other.

CHAP. XLVI

The words of the Apostle concerning the praise of single life unfolded.

These two chapters not so immediately debating the right of divorce, I chose rather not to insert.

CHAP. XLVII

The conclusion of this treatise.

These things, most renowned King, I have brought together, both to explain for what causes the unhappy, but sometimes most necessary help of divorce ought to be granted, according to God's word, by Princes and rulers: as also to explain how the words of Christ do consent with such a grant. I have been large indeed both in handling those oracles of God, and in laying down those certain principles, which he who will know what the mind of God is in this matter must ever think on and remember. But if we consider what mist and obscurity hath been poured out by Antichrist upon this question, and how deep this pernicious contempt of wedlock, and admiration of single life, even in those who are not called thereto, hath sunk into many men's persuasions, I fear lest all that hath been said be hardly enough to persuade such that they would cease at length to make themselves wiser and holier than God himself, in being so severe to grant lawful marriage, and so easy to connive at all, not only whoredoms but deflowerings and adulteries. Whenas among the people of God, no whoredom was to be tolerated.

Our Lord Jesus Christ, who came to destroy the works of Satan, send down his Spirit upon all Christians, and principally upon Christian Governors both in Church and commonwealth (for of the clear judgment of your royal Majesty I nothing doubt, revolving the Scripture so often as ye do) that they may acknowledge how much they provoke the anger of God against us, whenas all kind of unchastity is tolerated, fornications and adulteries winked at, but holy and honourable wedlock is oft withheld by the mere persuasion of Antichrist, from such as without this remedy cannot preserve themselves from damnation! For none who hath but a spark of honesty will deny that Princes and states ought to use diligence toward the maintaining of pure and honest life among all men, without which all justice, all fear of God, and true religion decays.

And who knows not that chastity and pureness of life can never be restored, or continued in the commonwealth, unless it be first established in private houses, from whence the whole breed of men is to come forth. To effect this, no wise man can doubt that it is necessary for Princes and magistrates first with severity to punish whoredom and adultery; next to see that marriages be lawfully contracted, and in the Lord; then that they be faithfully kept; and lastly, when that unhappiness urges, that they be lawfully dissolved, and other marriage granted, according as the law of God, and of nature, and Constitutions of pious Princes have decreed; as I have shown both by evident authorities of Scripture, together with the writings of the ancient Fathers and other testimonies. Only the Lord grant that we may learn to prefer his ever just and saving Word before the comments of Antichrist, too deeply rooted in many, and the false and blasphemous exposition of our Savior's words. *Amen.*

The end.

A Post-script

Thus far Martin Bucer; whom, where I might without injury to either part of the cause, I deny not to have epitomized;[97] in the rest observing a well-warranted rule, not to give an inventory of so many words but to weigh their force. I could have added that eloquent and right Christian discourse written by Erasmus on this argument, not disagreeing in effect from Bucer. But this, I hope, will be enough to excuse me with the mere Englishman,[98] to be no forger of new and loose opinions. Others may read him in his own phrase on the first to the Corinthians, and ease me who never could delight in long citations, much less in whole traductions, whether it be natural disposition or education in me, or that my mother bore me a speaker of what God made mine own, and not a translator. There be others also whom I could reckon up, of no mean account in the Church (and Peter Martyr among the first), who are more than half our own in this controversy. But this is a providence not to be slighted, that as Bucer wrote this tractate of divorce in England and for England, so Erasmus professes he begun here among us the same subject, especially out of compassion, for the need he saw this nation had of some charitable redress herein; and seriously exhorts others to use their best industry in the clearing of this point, wherein custom hath a greater sway than verity. That therefore which came into the mind of these two admired strangers to do for England, and in a touch of highest prudence which they took to be not yet recovered from monastic superstition, if I a native am found to have done for mine own country, altogether suitably and conformly to their so large and clear understanding, yet without the least help of theirs, I suppose that henceforward among conscionable and judicious persons it will no more be thought to my discredit, or at all to this nation's dishonour.

And if these their books, the one shall be printed often with best allowance in most religious cities, the other with express authority of Leo the tenth, a Pope, shall for the propagating of truth be published and republished though against the received opinion of that church, and mine containing but the same thing shall in a time of reformation, a time of free speaking, free writing, not find a permission to the press, I refer me to wisest men, whether truth be suffered to be truth, or liberty to be liberty now among us, and be not again in danger of new fetters and captivity after all our hopes and labours lost, and whether learning be not (which our enemies too prophetically feared) in the way to be trodden down again by ignorance. Whereof while time is, out of the faith owing to God and my country, I bid this Kingdom beware; and doubt not but God, who hath dignified this Parliament already to so many glorious degrees, will also give them (which is a singular blessing) to inform themselves rightly in the midst of an unprincipled age and to prevent this working mystery of ignorance and ecclesiastical thralldom, which under new shapes and disguises begins a-fresh to grow upon us.

The end.

Tetrachordon[1]

EXPOSITIONS UPON **The four chief places in Scripture, which treat of Marriage, or nullities in Marriage. On: Genesis 1:27, 28. compared and explained by Genesis 2:18, 23, 24. Deuteronomy 24:1, 2. Matthew 5:31, 32. with Matthew 19: from the 3rd verse to the 11th. 1 Corinthians 7: from the 10th to the 16th. Wherein the Doctrine and Discipline of Divorce, as was lately published, is confirmed by explanation of Scripture, by testimony of ancient Fathers, of civil laws in the Primitive Church, of famousest Reformed Divines, And lastly, by an intended Act of the Parliament and Church of England in the last year of** EDWARD **the Sixth.**

By the former Author *J. M.*

σκαοῖσι <μὲν γὰρ> καινὰ προσφέρων σοφὰ
δόξεις ἀχρεῖος κοὐ σοφὸς πεφυκέναι·
τῶν δ’ αὖ δοκούντων εἰδέναι τι ποικίλον
κρείσσων νομισθεὶς ἐν πόλει λυπρὸς φανῇ.

Euripid. Medea.[2]

***London:* Printed in the year: 1645**[3]

To the Parliament.

That which I knew to be the part of a good magistrate, aiming at true liberty through the right information[4] *of religious and civil life, and that which I saw, and was partaker of, your vows and solemn covenants,*[5] *Parliament of England, your actions also manifestly tending to exalt the truth, and to depress the tyranny of error, and ill custom, with more constancy and prowess than ever yet any, since that Parliament which put the first scepter of this Kingdom into his hand whom God and extraordinary virtue made their Monarch, were the causes that moved me, one else not placing much in the eminence of a dedication, to present your high notice with a discourse, conscious to itself of nothing more than of diligence, and firm affection to the public good. And that ye took it so as wise and impartial men, obtaining so great power and dignity, are wont to accept, in matters both doubtful and important, what they think offered them well meant, and from a rational ability, I had no less than to persuade me. And on that persuasion am returned, as to a famous and free port, myself also bound by more than a maritime law,*[6] *to expose as freely what fraughtage*[7] *I conceive to bring of no trifles. For although it be generally known, how and by whom ye have been instigated to a hard censure of that former book entitled* The Doctrine and Discipline of Divorce, *an opinion held by some of the best among reformed writers without scandal or confutement, though now thought new and dangerous by some of our severe Gnostics,*[8] *whose little reading, and less meditating, holds ever with hardest obstinacy that which it took up with easiest credulity, I do not find yet that aught, for the furious incitements which have been used, hath issued by your appointment that might give the least interruption or disrepute either to the author, or to the book. Which he who will be better advised than to call your neglect, or connivance at a thing imagined so perilous, can attribute it to nothing more justly than to the deep and quiet stream of your direct and calm deliberations, that gave not way either to the fervent rashness or the immaterial gravity of those who ceased not to exasperate without cause. For which uprightness and incorrupt refusal of what ye were incensed to, Lords and Commons (though it were done to justice, not to me, and was a peculiar demonstration how far your ways are different from the rash vulgar)*[9] *besides those allegiances of oath and duty which are my public debt to your public labors, I have yet a store of gratitude laid up which cannot be exhausted; and such thanks perhaps they may live to be, as shall more than whisper to the next ages. Yet that the author may be known to ground himself upon his own innocence and the merit of his cause, not upon the favor of a diversion or a delay to any just censure, but wishes rather he might see those his detractors at any fair meeting, as learned debatements are privileged with a due freedom under equal moderators, I shall here briefly single one of them (because he hath obliged me to it) who I persuade me having scarce read the book, nor knowing him who writ it, or at least feigning the latter, hath not forborne to scandalize him, unconferred with, unadmonished, undealt with by any pastorly or brotherly convincement, in the most open and invective manner, and at the most bitter opportunity that drift or set design could have invented.*[10] *And this, whenas the canon law, though commonly most favoring the boldness of their priests, punishes the naming or traducing of any person in the pulpit, was by him made no scruple.*[11] *If I shall therefore take license by the right of nature, and that liberty wherein I was born, to defend myself publicly against a printed calumny, and do willingly appeal to those judges to whom I am accused, it can be no immoderate or unallowable course of seeking so just and needful reparations. Which I had done long since, had not these employments, which are now visible, deferred me. It was preached before ye, Lords and Commons, in August last upon a special day of humiliation,*[12] *that* there was a wicked book abroad, *and ye were taxed of sin that it was yet uncensured,* the Book deserving to be burnt, *and* impudence *also was charged upon the author, who durst* set his name to it, and dedicate it to your selves. *First, Lords and Commons, I pray to that God, before whom ye then were prostrate, so to forgive ye those omissions and trespasses which ye desire most should find forgiveness, as I shall soon show to the world how easily ye absolve yourselves of that which this man calls your sin, and is indeed your wisdom, and your nobleness, whereof to this day ye have done well not to repent. He terms it* a wicked Book, *and why but* for allowing other causes of divorce, than Christ and his Apostles mention, *and with the same censure condemns of wickedness not only Martin Bucer,*[13] *that elect instrument of reformation, highly honored and had in reverence by Edward the sixth and his whole Parliament, whom also I had published in English by a good providence, about a week before this calumnious digression was preached; so that if he knew not Bucer then, as he ought to have known, he might at least have known him some months after, ere the sermon came in print, wherein notwithstanding he persists in his former sentence, and condemns again of wickedness, either ignorantly or willfully, not only Martin Bucer, and all the choicest and holiest of our reformers, but the whole Parliament and Church of England in those best and purest times of Edward the sixth.*[14] *All which I shall prove with good evidence at the end of these explanations. And then let it be judged and seriously considered with what hope the affairs of our religion are committed to one among others, who hath now only left him which of the twain he will choose, whether this shall be his palpable ignorance, or the same wickedness of his own book, which he so lavishly imputes to the writings of other men; and whether this of his, that thus peremptorily defames and attaints of wickedness unspotted churches, unblemished Parliaments, and the most eminent restorers of Christian doctrine, deserve not to be burnt first. And if his heat had burst out only against the opinion, his wonted passion had no doubt been silently borne with wonted patience. But since against the charity of that solemn place and meeting it served him further to inveigh opprobriously against the person, branding him with no less than impudence only for setting his name to what he had written, I must be excused not to be so wanting to the defense of an honest name, or to the reputation of those good men who afford me their society, but to be sensible of such a foul endeavored disgrace, not knowing aught either in mine own deserts, or the laws of this land, why I should be subject, in such a notorious and illegal manner, to the intemperances of this man's preaching choler.*[15] *And indeed to be so prompt and ready in the midst of his humbleness to toss reproaches of this bulk and size, argues as if they were the weapons of his exercise, I am sure not of his ministry, or of that day's work. Certainly to subscribe my name at what I was to own, was what the State had ordered and requires. And he who lists*[16] *not to be malicious, would call it ingenuity, clear conscience, willingness to avouch what might be questioned, or to be better instructed. And if God were so displeased with those, Isaiah 58 who* on the solemn fast were wont to smite with the fist of wickedness, *it could be no sign of his own humiliation accepted, which disposed him to smite so keenly with a reviling tongue. But if only to have writ my name must be counted impudence, how doth this but justify another, who might affirm with as good warrant, that the late discourse of* Scripture and Reason, *which is certain to be chiefly his own draught,*[17] *was published without a name, out of base fear, and the sly avoidance of what might follow to his detriment, if the party at Court should hap to reach him. And I, to have set my name where he accuses me to have set it, am so far from recanting, that I offer my hand also if need be, to make good the same opinion which I there maintain, by inevitable consequences drawn parallel from his own principal arguments in that of* Scripture and Reason: *which I shall pardon him, if he can deny without shaking his own composition to pieces. The* impudence *therefore, since he weighed so little what a gross revile that was to give his equal, I send him back again for a phylactery*[18] *to stitch upon his arrogance, that censures not only before conviction so bitterly without so much as one reason given, but censures the Congregation of his Governors to their faces, for not being so hasty as himself to censure.*

And whereas my other crime is, that I addressed the dedication of what I had studied to the Parliament, how could I better declare the loyalty which I owe to that supreme and majestic tribunal, and the opinion which I have of the high-entrusted judgement and personal worth assembled in that place. With the same affections therefore, and the same addicted[19] *fidelity, Parliament of England, I here again have brought to your perusal on the same argument these following expositions of Scripture. The former book, as pleased some to think who were thought judicious, had of reason in it to a sufficiency; what they required was that the Scriptures there alleged might be discussed more fully. To their desires, thus much further hath been labored in the Scriptures. Another sort also who wanted more authorities, and citations, have not been here unthought of. If all this attain not to satisfy them, as I am confident that none of those our great controversies at this day hath had a more demonstrative explaining, I must confess to admire what it is, for doubtless it is not reason nowadays that satisfies, or suborns the common credence of men, to yield so easily, and grow so vehement in matters much more disputable and far less conducing to the daily good and peace of life. Some whose necessary shifts have long inured them to cloak the defects of their unstudied years, and hatred now to learn, under the appearance of a grave solidity, which estimation they have gained among weak perceivers, find the ease of slighting what they cannot refute, and are determined, as I hear, to hold it not worth the answering. In which number I must be forced to reckon that Doctor,*[20] *who in a late equivocating treatise plausibly set afloat against the Dippers,*[21] *diving the while himself with a more deep prelatical*[22] *malignance against the present State and Church-government, mentions with ignominy the* Tractate of Divorce; *yet answers nothing, but instead thereof (for which I do not commend his marshalling) sets Moses also among the crew of his Anabaptists, as one who to a holy nation, the commonwealth of Israel, gave laws* breaking the bonds of marriage to inordinate lust. *These are no mean surges of blasphemy, not only dipping Moses the divine lawgiver, but dashing with a high hand against the justice and purity of God himself, as these ensuing Scriptures plainly and freely handled shall verify to the lancing of that old apostemated*[23] *error. Him therefore I leave now to his repentance.*

Others, which is their courtesy, confess that wit and parts may do much to make that seem true which is not (as was objected to Socrates by them who could not resist his efficacy, that he ever made the worst cause seem the better)[24] *and thus thinking themselves discharged of the difficulty, love not to wade further into the fear of a convincement. These will be their excuses to decline the full examining of this serious point. So much the more I press it and repeat it, Lords and Commons, that ye beware while time is, ere this grand secret, and only art of ignorance affecting tyranny, grow powerful, and rule among us. For if sound argument and reason shall be thus put off, either by an undervaluing silence, or the masterly censure of a railing word or two in the pulpit, or by rejecting the force of truth as the mere cunning of eloquence and sophistry, what can be the end of this, but that all good learning and knowledge will suddenly decay. Ignorance, and illiterate presumption, which is yet but our disease, will turn at length into our very constitution, and prove the hectic evil of this age: worse to be feared, if it get once to reign over us, than any Fifth Monarchy.*[25] *If this shall be the course, that what was wont to be a chief commendation and the ground of other men's confidence in an author, his diligence, his learning, his elocution whether by right, or by ill meaning granted him, shall be turned now to a disadvantage and suspicion against him, that what he writes, though unconfuted, must therefore be mistrusted, therefore not received for the industry, the exactness, the labor in it, confessed to be more than ordinary, as if wisdom had now forsaken the thirsty and laborious inquirer to dwell against her nature with the arrogant and shallow babbler, to what purpose all those pains and that continual searching required of us by Solomon to the attainment of understanding?*[26] *Why are men bred up with such care and expense to a life of perpetual studies, why do yourselves with such endeavor seek to wipe off the imputation of intending to discourage the progress and advance of learning? He therefore whose heart can bear him to the high pitch of your noble enterprises, may easily assure himself that the prudence and far-judging circumspectness of so grave a magistracy sitting in Parliament, who have before them the prepared and purposed act of their most religious predecessors to imitate in this question,*[27] *cannot reject the clearness of these reasons, and these allegations both here and formerly offered them; nor can over-look the necessity of ordaining more wholesomely and more humanly in the casualties of divorce than our laws have yet established: if the most urgent and excessive grievances happening in domestic life be worth the laying to heart, which, unless charity be far from us, cannot be neglected. And that these things both in the right constitution and in the right reformation of a commonwealth call for speediest redress, and ought to be the first considered, enough was urged in what was prefaced to that monument of Bucer which I brought to your remembrance, and the other time before. Henceforth, except new cause be given, I shall say less and less. For if the law make not timely provision, let the law, as reason is, bear the censure of those consequences which her own default now more evidently produces. And if men want*[28] *manliness to expostulate the right of their due ransom and to second their own occasions, they may sit hereafter and bemoan themselves to have neglected through faintness the only remedy of their sufferings, which a seasonable and well-grounded speaking might have purchased them. And perhaps in time to come, others will know how to esteem what is not every day put into their hands, when they have marked events and better weighed how hurtful and unwise it is to hide a secret and pernicious rupture under the ill counsel of bashful silence. But who would distrust aught, or not be ample in his hopes of your wise and Christian determinations? who have the prudence to consider, and should have the goodness like gods, as ye are called, to find out readily, and by just law to administer those redresses which have of old, not without God ordaining, been granted to the adversities of mankind, ere they who needed were put to ask. Certainly, if any other have enlarged his thoughts to expect from this government so justly undertaken, and by frequent assistances from Heaven so apparently upheld, glorious changes and renovations both in Church and State, he among the foremost might be named, who prays that the fate of England may tarry for no other deliverers.*

John Milton

Tetrachordon, Expositions upon the four chief places in Scripture which treat of marriage, or nullities in marriage

Gen. 1.27: *So God created man in his own image, in the image of God created he him; male and female created he them.*

Gen. 1.28: *And God blessed them, and God said unto them, Be fruitful, &c.*

Gen. 2.18: *And the Lord God said, It is not good that man should be alone, I will make him a help-meet for him.*

Gen. 2.23: *And Adam said, This is now bone of my bones, and flesh of my flesh; she shall be called Woman, because she was taken out of Man.*

Gen. 2.24: *Therefore shall a man leave his father and his mother, and shall cleave unto his wife, and they shall be one flesh.*

Gen. 1.27

[*So God created man in his own image.*] To be informed aright in the whole history of marriage, that we may know for certain, not by a forced yoke but by an impartial definition, what marriage is, and what is not marriage, it will undoubtedly be safest, fairest, and most with our obedience, to inquire, as our Savior's direction is, how it was in the beginning. And that we begin so high as man created after God's own image, there want not earnest causes. For nothing nowadays is more degenerately forgotten than the true dignity of man, almost in every respect, but especially in this prime institution of matrimony, wherein his native pre-eminence ought most to shine. Although if we consider that just and natural privileges men neither can rightly seek, nor dare fully claim, unless they be allied to inward goodness and steadfast knowledge, and that the want of this quells them to a servile sense of their own conscious unworthiness, it may save the wondering why in this age many are so opposite both to human and to Christian liberty, either while they understand not or envy others that do; contenting, or rather priding themselves in a specious humility and strictness bred out of low ignorance that never yet conceived the freedom of the Gospel, and is therefore by the Apostle to the Colossians ranked with no better company than will-worship and the mere show of wisdom.[29] And how injurious herein they are, if not to themselves yet to their neighbors, and not to them only but to the all-wise and bounteous grace offered us in our redemption, will orderly appear.

[*In the Image of God created he him.*] It is enough determined, that this image of God wherein man was created, is meant wisdom, purity, justice, and rule over all creatures. All which being lost in Adam, was recovered with gain by the merits of Christ. For albeit our first parent had lordship over sea, and land, and air, yet there was a law without him, as a guard set over him. But Christ, having cancelled the handwriting of ordinances which was against us, Coloss. 2.14, and interpreted the fulfilling of all through charity, hath in that respect set us over law, in the free custody of his love, and left us victorious under the guidance of his living Spirit, not under the dead letter;[30] to follow that which most edifies, most aids, and furthers a religious life, makes us holiest and likest to his immortal Image, not that which makes us most conformable and captive to civil and subordinate precepts, whereof the strictest observance may oft-times prove the destruction not only of many innocent persons and families, but of whole nations. Although indeed no ordinance human or from Heaven can bind against the good of man; so that to keep them strictly against that end, is all one with to break them. Men of most renowned virtue have sometimes by transgressing most truly kept the law; and wisest magistrates have permitted and dispensed it; while they looked not peevishly at the letter but with a greater spirit at the good of mankind, if always not written in the characters of law yet engraven in the heart of man by a divine impression. This heathens could see, as the well-read in story can recount of Solon and Epaminondas, whom Cicero in his first book of invention nobly defends. *All law,* saith he, *we ought to refer to the common good, and interpret by that, not by the scroll of letters. No man observes law for law's sake, but for the good of them for whom it was made.*[31] The rest might serve well to lecture these times, deluded through belly-doctrines[32] into a devout slavery. The Scripture also affords us David in the shewbread,[33] Hezekiah in the Passover,[34] sound and safe transgressors of the literal command, which also dispensed not seldom with itself; and taught us on what just occasions to do so until our Savior, for whom that great and God-like work was reserved, redeemed us to a state above prescriptions by dissolving the whole law into charity. And have we not the soul to understand this, and must we against this glory of God's transcendent love towards us be still the servants of literal indictment?

[*Created he him.*] It might be doubted why he saith, *In the image of God created he him,* not them, as well as *male and female* them; especially since that image might be common to them both, but male and female could not, however the Jews fable and please themselves with the accidental concurrence of Plato's wit, as if man at first had been created hermaphrodite:[35] but then it must have been male and female created he him. So, had the image of God been equally common to them both, it had no doubt been said, In the image of God created he them. But St. Paul ends the controversy by explaining that the woman is not primarily and immediately the image of God, but in reference to the man. The head of the woman, saith he, 1 Cor. 11, is the man: he the image and glory of God, she the glory of the man; he not for her, but she for him.[36] Therefore his precept is, *Wives be subject to your husbands as is fit in the Lord,* Coloss. 3.18. *In everything,* Eph. 5.24. Nevertheless man is not to hold her as a servant, but receives her into a part of that empire which God proclaims him to, though not equally, yet largely, as his own image and glory: for it is no small glory to him, that a creature so like him should be made subject to him. Not but that particular exceptions may have place, if she exceed her husband in prudence and dexterity, and he contentedly yield, for then a superior and more natural law comes in, that the wiser should govern the less wise, whether male or female. But that which far more easily and obediently follows from this verse, is that, seeing woman was purposely made for man, and he her head, it cannot stand before the breath of this divine utterancc, that man the portraiture of God, joining to himself for his intended good and solace an inferior sex, should so become her thrall, whose willfulness or inability to be a wife frustrates the occasional end of her creation, but that he may acquit himself to freedom by his natural birthright and that indelible character of priority[37] which God crowned him with. If it be urged that sin hath lost him this, the answer is not far to seek: that from her the sin first proceeded, which keeps her justly in the same proportion still beneath. She is not to gain by being first in the transgression that man should further lose to her, because already he hath lost by her means. Oft it happens that in this matter he is without fault, so that his punishment herein is causeless; and God hath the praise in our speeches of him, to sort his punishment in the same kind with the offence. Suppose he erred; it is not the intent of God or man to hunt an error so to the death with a revenge beyond all measure and proportion. But if we argue thus, *this affliction is befallen him for his sin, therefore he must bear it, without seeking the only remedy,* first it will be false that all affliction comes for sin, as in the case of Job, and of the man born blind, John 9.3, was evident; next, by that reason, all miseries coming for sin, we must let them all lie upon us like the vermin of an Indian Catharist,[38] which his fond[39] religion forbids him to molest. Were it a particular punishment inflicted through the anger of God upon a person, or upon a land, no law hinders us in that regard, no law but bids us remove it if we can; much more if it be a dangerous temptation withal; much more yet, if it be certainly a temptation and not certainly a punishment, though a pain. As for what they say we must bear with patience, to bear with patience and to seek effectual remedies implies no contradiction. It may no less be for our disobedience, our unfaithfulness, and other sins against God, that wives become adulterous to the bed; and questionless we ought to take the affliction as patiently as Christian prudence would wish; yet hereby is not lost the right of divorcing for adultery. No you say, because our Savior excepted that only. But why, if he were so bent to punish our sins and try our patience in binding on us a disastrous marriage, why did he except adultery? Certainly to have been bound from divorce in that case also had been as plentiful a punishment to our sins, and not too little work for the patientest. Nay, perhaps they will say it was too great a sufferance: and with as slight a reason, for no wise man but would sooner pardon the act of adultery once and again committed by a person worth pity and forgiveness, than to lead a wearisome life of unloving and unquiet conversation with one who neither affects nor is affected, much less with one who exercises all bitterness, and would commit adultery too, but for envy lest the persecuted condition should thereby get the benefit of his freedom. 'Tis plain therefore, that God enjoins not this supposed strictness of not divorcing either to punish us, or to try our patience.

Moreover, if man be the image of God, which consists in holiness, and woman ought in the same respect to be the image and companion of man, in such wise to be loved as the Church is beloved of Christ, and if, as God is the head of Christ and Christ the head of man, so man is the head of woman,[40] I cannot see by this golden dependence of headship and subjection, but that piety and religion is the main tie of Christian matrimony. So as if there be found between the pair a notorious disparity either of wickedness or heresy, the husband by all manner of right is disengaged from a creature, not made and inflicted on him to the vexation of his righteousness; the wife also, as her subjection is terminated in the Lord, being herself the redeemed of Christ, is not still bound to be the vassal of him who is the bond-slave of Satan: she being now neither the image nor the glory of such a person, nor made for him, nor left in bondage to him, but hath recourse to the wing of charity and protection of the Church, unless there be a hope on either side. Yet such a hope must be meant, as may be a rational hope, and not an endless servitude. Of which hereafter.

But usually it is objected, that if it be thus, then there can be no true marriage between misbelievers and irreligious persons. I might answer, let them see to that who are such; the Church hath no commission to judge those without, I Cor. 5. But this they will say perhaps, is but penuriously[41] to resolve a doubt. I answer therefore, that where they are both irreligious, the marriage may be yet true enough to them in a civil relation. For there are left some remains of God's image in man, as he is merely man; which reason God gives against the shedding of man's blood, Genesis 9:6, as being made in God's image, without expression whether he were a good man or a bad to exempt the slayer from punishment. So that in those marriages where the parties are alike void of religion, the wife owes a civil homage and subjection, the husband owes a civil loyalty. But where the yoke is mis-yoked, heretic with faithful, godly with ungodly, to the grievance and manifest endangering of a brother or sister, reasons of a higher strain than matrimonial bear sway; unless the Gospel instead of freeing us debase itself to make us bondmen, and suffer evil to control good.

[*Male and female created he them.*] This contains another end of matching man and woman, being the right and lawfulness of the marriage-bed; though much inferior to the former end of her being his image and help in religious society. And who of weakest insight may not see that this creating of them male and female cannot in any order of reason, or Christianity, be of such moment against the better and higher purposes of their creation as to enthrall husband or wife to duties or to sufferings unworthy and unbeseeming the image of God in them? Now whenas not only men, but good men, do stand upon their right, their estimation, their dignity in all other actions and deportments[42] with warrant enough and good conscience, as having the image of God in them, it will not be difficult to determine what is unworthy and unseemly for a man to do or suffer in wedlock; and the like proportionally may be found for woman, if we love not to stand disputing below the principles of humanity. He that said *Male and female created he them,* immediately before that said also in the same verse, *In the image of God created he him,* and redoubled it, that our thoughts might not be so full of dregs as to urge this poor consideration of *male and female* without remembering the nobleness of that former repetition; lest when God sends a wise eye to examine our trivial glosses, they be found extremely to creep upon the ground: especially since they confess that what here concerns marriage is but a brief touch, only preparative to the institution which follows more expressly in the next chapter; and that Christ so took it, as desiring to be briefest with them who came to tempt him, account shall be given in due place.

Verse 28. *And God blessed them, and God said unto them, be fruitful, and multiply, and replenish the Earth, &c.*

This declares another end of matrimony, the propagation of mankind; and is again repeated to Noah and his sons.[43] Many things might be noted on this place not ordinary, nor unworth the noting; but I undertook not a general comment. Hence therefore we see the desire of children is honest and pious, if we be not less zealous in our Christianity than Plato was in his heathenism; who in the sixth of his *Laws,* counts offspring therefore desirable, that we may leave in our stead sons of our sons, continual servants of God: a religious and prudent desire, if people knew as well what were required to breeding as to begetting; which desire perhaps was a cause why the Jews hardly could endure a barren wedlock, and Philo in his book of special laws esteems him only worth pardon that sends not barrenness away.[44] Carvilius, the first recorded in Rome to have sought divorce, had it granted him for the barrenness of his wife, upon his oath that he married to the end he might have children; as Dionysius and Gellius are authors.[45] But to dismiss a wife only for barrenness is hard: and yet in some the desire of children is so great, and so just, yea sometime so necessary, that to condemn such a one to a childless age, the fault apparently not being in him, might seem perhaps more strict than needed. Sometimes inheritances, crowns, and dignities are so interested and annexed in their common peace and good to such or such lineal descent, that it may prove a great moment both in the affairs of men and religion to consider thoroughly what might be done herein, notwithstanding the waywardness of our school doctors.[46]

Gen. 2.18

And the Lord said, It is not good that man should be alone; I will make him a help-meet for him.

Verse 23. *And Adam said, &c.* **Verse 24.** *Therefore shall a man leave, &c.*

This second chapter is granted to be a commentary on the first, and these verses granted to be an exposition of that former verse, *Male and female created he them,* and yet when this male and female is by the explicit words of God himself here declared to be not meant other than a fit help and meet society, some who would engross to themselves the whole trade of interpreting will not suffer the clear text of God to do the office of explaining itself.

[*And the Lord God said It is not good.*] A man would think that the consideration of who spake should raise up the attention of our minds to inquire better, and obey the purpose of so great a Speaker. For as we order the business of marriage, that which he here speaks is all made vain; and in the decision of matrimony, or not matrimony, nothing at all regarded. Our presumption hath utterly changed the state and condition of this ordinance: God ordained it in love and helpfulness to be indissoluble, and we in outward act and formality to be a forced bondage; so that being subject to a thousand errors in the best men, if it prove a blessing to any it is of mere accident, as man's law hath handled it, and not of institution.

[*It is not good for man to be alone.*] Hitherto all things that have been named were approved of God to be very good. Loneliness is the first thing which God's eye named not good: whether it be a thing, or the want of something, I labor not; let it be their tendance, who have the art to be industriously idle. And here *alone* is meant alone without woman; otherwise Adam had the company of God himself, and angels to converse with; all creatures to delight him seriously, or to make him sport. God could have created him out of the same mould a thousand friends and brother Adams to have been his consorts, yet for all this 'til Eve was given him, God reckoned him to be alone.

[*It is not good.*] God here presents himself like to a man deliberating; both to show us that the matter is of high consequence, and that he intended to found it according to natural reason, not impulsive command, but that the duty should arise from the reason of it, not the reason be swallowed up in a reasonless duty. *Not good,* was as much to Adam before his fall as not pleasing, not expedient; but since the coming of sin into the world, to him who hath not received the continence, it is not only not expedient to be alone, but plainly sinful. And therefore he who willfully abstains from marriage, not being supernaturally gifted, and he who by making the yoke of marriage unjust and intolerable causes men to abhor it, are both in a diabolical sin, equal to that of Antichrist who forbids to marry.[47] For what difference at all whether he abstain men from marrying, or restrain them in a marriage happening totally discommodious, distasteful, dishonest and pernicious to him without the appearance of his fault? For God does not here precisely say, I make a female to this male, as he did briefly before; but expounding himself here on purpose, he saith, because it is not good for man to be alone, I make him therefore a meet help. God supplies the privation of not good, with the perfect gift of a real and positive good; it is man's perverse cooking[48] who hath turned this bounty of God into a scorpion, either by weak and shallow constructions, or by proud arrogance and cruelty to them who neither in their purposes nor in their actions have offended against the due honor of wedlock.

Now whereas the Apostle's speaking in the Spirit, I Cor. 7, pronounces quite contrary to this word of God, *It is good for a man not to touch a woman,* and God cannot contradict himself, it instructs us that his commands and words, especially such as bear the manifest title of some good to man, are not to be so strictly wrung as to command without regard to the most natural and miserable necessities of mankind. Therefore the Apostle adds a limitation in the 26 verse of that chapter for the present necessity it is good; which he gives us doubtless as a pattern how to reconcile other places by the general rule of charity.

[*For man to be alone.*] Some would have the sense hereof to be in respect of procreation only; and Austin[49] contests that manly friendship in all other regards had been a more becoming solace for Adam than to spend so many secret years in an empty world with one woman. But our writers[50] deservedly reject this crabbed opinion, and defend that there is a peculiar[51] comfort in the married state, beside the genial bed, which no other society affords. No mortal nature can endure, either in the actions of religion or study of wisdom, without sometime slackening the cords of intense thought and labor; which lest we should think faulty, God himself conceals us not his own recreations before the world was built: *I was,* saith the eternal wisdom, *daily his delight, playing always before him.*[52] And to him indeed wisdom is as a high tower of pleasure, but to us a steep hill, and we toiling ever about the bottom: he executes with ease the exploits of his omnipotence, as easy as with us it is to will; but no worthy enterprise can be done by us without continual plodding and wearisomeness to our faint and sensitive abilities. We cannot therefore always be contemplative, or pragmatical abroad, but have need of some delightful intermissions, wherein the enlarged soul may leave off a while her severe schooling; and like a glad youth in wandering vacancy, may keep her holidays to joy and harmless pastime: which as she cannot well do without company, so in no company so well as where the different sex, in most resembling unlikeness and most unlike resemblance, cannot but please best and be pleased in the aptitude of that variety. Whereof lest we should be too timorous, in the awe that our flat sages would form us and dress us, wisest Solomon among his gravest Proverbs[53] countenances a kind of ravishment and erring fondness in the entertainment of wedded leisures; and in the Song of Songs, which is generally believed even in the jolliest expressions to figure the spousals of the church with Christ, sings of a thousand raptures between those two lovely ones far on the hither side of carnal enjoyment. By these instances, and more which might be brought, we may imagine how indulgently God provided against man's loneliness: that he approved it not, as by himself declared not good; that he approved the remedy thereof, as of his own ordaining, consequently good. And as he ordained it, so doubtless proportionably to our fallen estate he gives it; else were his ordinance at least in vain, and we for all his gifts still empty handed. Nay, such an unbounteous giver we should make him, as in the fables Jupiter was to Ixion: giving him a cloud instead of Juno; giving him a monstrous issue by her, the breed of centaurs, a neglected and unloved race,[54] the fruits of a delusive[55] marriage; and lastly giving him her with a damnation to that wheel in Hell, from a life thrown into the midst of temptations and disorders. But God is no deceitful giver, to bestow that on us for a remedy of loneliness, which if it bring not a sociable mind as well as a conjunctive[56] body leaves us no less alone than before, and if it bring a mind perpetually averse and disagreeable betrays us to a worse condition than the most deserted loneliness. God cannot in the justice of his own promise and institution so unexpectedly mock us by forcing that upon us, as the remedy of solitude, which wraps us in a misery worse than any wilderness, as the Spirit of God himself judges, Prov. 19:13, especially knowing that the best and wisest men amidst the sincere and most cordial designs of their heart do daily err in choosing. We may conclude therefore, seeing orthodoxall expositors confess to our hands that by loneliness is not only meant the want of copulation, and that man is not less alone by turning in a body to him, unless there be within it a mind answerable, that it is a work more worthy the care and consultation of God to provide for the worthiest part of man, which is his mind, and not unnaturally to set it beneath the formalities and respects of the body, to make it a servant of its own vassal, I say we may conclude that such a marriage, wherein the mind is so disgraced and vilified below the body's interest, and can have no just or tolerable contentment, is not of God's institution, and therefore no marriage. Nay in concluding this, I say we conclude no more than what the common expositors themselves give us, both in that which I have recited and much more hereafter. But the truth is, they give us in such a manner as they who leave their own mature positions like the eggs of an ostrich in the dust; I do but lay them in the sun; their own pregnancies hatch the truth; and I am taxed of novelties and strange producements, while they, like that inconsiderate bird, know not that these are their own natural breed.[57]

[*I will make him a help meet for him.*] Here the heavenly institutor, as if he labored, not to be mistaken by the supercilious hypocrisy of those that love to master their brethren, and to make us sure that he gave us not now a servile yoke but an amiable knot, contents not himself to say, I will make him a wife, but resolving to give us first the meaning before the name of a wife, saith graciously, *I will make him a help meet for him.* And here again, as before, I do not require more full and fair deductions than the whole consent of our divines usually raise from this text: that in matrimony there must be first a mutual help to piety, next to civil fellowship of love and amity, then to generation, so to household affairs, lastly the remedy of incontinence.[58] And commonly they reckon them in such order, as leaves generation and incontinence to be last considered. This I amaze me at, that though all the superior and nobler ends both of marriage and of the married persons be absolutely frustrate, the matrimony stirs not, loses no hold, remains as rooted as the center; but if the body bring but in a complaint of frigidity, by that cold application only, this adamantine[59] Alp of wedlock has leave to dissolve, which else all the machinations of religious or civil reason at the suit of a distressed mind, either for divine worship or human conversation violated, cannot unfasten. What courts of concupiscence[60] are these, wherein fleshly appetite is heard before right reason, lust before love or devotion? They may be pious Christians together, they may be loving and friendly, they may be helpful to each other in the family, but they cannot couple: that shall divorce them, though either party would not. They can neither serve God together, nor one be at peace with the other, nor be good in the family one to other, but live as they were dead, or live as they were deadly enemies in a cage together; 'tis all one, they can couple: they shall not divorce 'til death, no though this sentence be their death. What is this, besides tyranny, but to turn nature upside down, to make both religion and the mind of man wait upon the slavish errands of the body, and not the body to follow either the sanctity or the sovereignty of the mind unspeakably wronged, and with all equity complaining? What is this but to abuse the sacred and mysterious bed of marriage to be the compulsive sty of an ingrateful and malignant lust, stirred up only from a carnal acrimony,[61] without either love or peace, or regard to any other thing holy or human.[62] This I admire how possibly it should inhabit thus long in the sense of so many disputing theologians, unless it be the lowest lees[63] of a canonical infection liver-grown to their sides; which perhaps will never uncling, without the strong abstersive[64] of some heroic magistrate, whose mind, equal to his high office, dares lead him both to know and do without their frivolous case-putting. For certain he shall have God and this institution plainly on his side. And if it be true both in divinity and law, that consent alone, though copulation never follow, makes a marriage, how can they dissolve it for the want of that which made it not, and not dissolve it for that not continuing which made it, and should preserve it in love and reason, and difference it from a brute conjugality.

[*Meet for him.*] The original here is more expressive than other languages word for word can render it; but all agree effectual conformity of disposition and affection to be hereby signified; which God as it were not satisfied with the naming of a help, goes on describing *another self, a second self, a very self itself.*[65] Yet now there is nothing in the life of man, through our misconstruction, made more uncertain, more hazardous and full of chance than this divine blessing with such favorable significance here conferred upon us: which if we do but err in our choice, the most unblamable error that can be, err but one minute, one moment after those mighty syllables pronounced which take upon them to join Heaven and Hell together unpardonably 'til death pardon, this divine blessing that looked but now with such a humane smile upon us, and spoke such gentle reason, straight vanishes like a fair sky and brings on such a scene of cloud and tempest as turns all to shipwrack without haven or shore but to a ransomless captivity. And then they tell us it is our sin, but let them be told again, that sin through the mercy of God hath not made such waste upon us as to make utterly void to our use any temporal benefit, much less any so much availing to a peaceful and sanctified life, merely for a most incident error which no weariness can certainly shun. And wherefore serves our happy redemption, and the liberty we have in Christ, but to deliver us from calamitous yokes not to be lived under without the endangerment of our souls, and to restore us in some competent measure to a right in every good thing both of this life and the other. Thus we see how treatably[66] and distinctly God hath here taught us what the prime ends of marriage are: mutual solace and help. That we are now, upon the most irreprehensible[67] mistake in choosing, defeated and defrauded of all this original benignity,[68] was begun first through the snare of Antichristian canons long since obtruded upon the Church of Rome and not yet scoured off by reformation, out of a lingering vain-glory that abides among us to make fair shows in formal ordinances, and to enjoin continence and bearing of crosses in such a garb as no Scripture binds us, under the thickest arrows of temptation, where we need not stand. Now we shall see with what acknowledgment and assent Adam received this new associate, which God brought him.

Verse 23. *And Adam said This is now bone of my bones, and flesh of my flesh, she shall be called Woman, because she was taken out of Man.*

That there was a nearer alliance between Adam and Eve, than could be ever after between man and wife, is visible to any. For no other woman was ever molded out of her husband's rib, but of mere strangers for the most part they come to have that consanguinity[69] which they have by wedlock. And if we look nearly upon the matter, though marriage be most agreeable to holiness, to purity and justice, yet is it not a natural, but a civil and ordained relation. For if it were in nature, no law or crime could disannul it, to make a wife, or husband, otherwise than still a wife or husband, but only death; as nothing but that can make a father no father, or a son no son. But divorce for adultery or desertion, as all our churches agree but England, not only separates, but nullifies and extinguishes the relation itself of matrimony, so that they are no more man and wife; otherwise the innocent party could not marry elsewhere, without the guilt of adultery; next, were it merely natural, why was it here ordained more than the rest of moral law to man in his original rectitude, in whose breast all that was natural or moral was engraven without external constitutions and edicts. Adam therefore in these words does not establish an indissoluble bond of marriage in the carnal ligaments of flesh and bones; for if he did, it would belong only to himself in the literal sense, every one of us being nearer in flesh of flesh, and bone of bones to our parents than to a wife. They therefore were not to be left for her in that respect. But Adam, who had the wisdom given him to know all creatures, and to name them according to their properties, no doubt but had the gift to discern perfectly that which concerned him much more, and to apprehend at first sight the true fitness of that consort which God provided him. And therefore spake in reference to those words which God pronounced before: as if he had said, this is she by whose meet help and society I shall no more be alone; this is she who was made my image, even as I the image of God, not so much in body, as in unity of mind and heart. And he might as easily know what were the words of God, as he knew so readily what had been done with his rib while he slept so soundly. He might well know, if God took a rib out of his inside to form of it a double good to him, he would far sooner disjoin it from his outside to prevent a treble mischief to him; and far sooner cut it quite off from all relation for his undoubted ease, than nail it into his body again, to stick forever there a thorn in his heart. Whenas nature teaches us to divide any limb from the body to the saving of his fellows, though it be the maiming and deformity of the whole, how much more is it her doctrine to sever by incision, not a true limb so much, though that be lawful, but an adherent, a sore, the gangrene of a limb, to the recovery of a whole man. But if in these words we shall make Adam to erect a new establishment of marriage in the mere flesh, which God so lately had instituted and founded in the sweet mild familiarity of love and solace and mutual fitness, what do we but use the mouth of our general parent, the first time it opens, to an arrogant opposition and correcting of God's wiser ordinance. These words therefore cannot import any thing new in marriage, but either that which belongs to Adam only, or to us in reference only to the instituting words of God which made a meet help against loneliness. Adam spake like Adam the words of flesh and bones, the shell and rind of matrimony; but God spake like God, of love solace and meet help, the soul both of Adam's words and of matrimony.

Verse 24. *Therefore shall a man leave his father and his mother, and shall cleave unto his wife; and they shall be one flesh.*

This verse, as our common heed expounds it, is the great knot-tier, which hath undone by tying, and by tangling, millions of guiltless consciences: this is that grisly porter, who having drawn men and wisest men by subtle allurement within the train of an unhappy matrimony, claps the dungeon gate upon them, as irrecoverable as the grave. But if we view him well, and hear him with not too hasty and prejudicant[70] ears, we shall find no such terror in him. For first, it is not here said absolutely without all reason he shall cleave to his wife, be it to his weal or to his destruction as it happens, but he shall do this upon the premises and considerations of that meet help and society before mentioned. *Therefore he shall cleave to his wife,* no otherwise a wife, than a fit help. He is not bid to leave the dear cohabitation of his father, mother, brothers and sisters, to link himself inseparably with the mere carcass of a marriage, perhaps an enemy. This joining particle *Therefore* is in all equity, nay in all necessity of construction, to comprehend first and most principally what God spake concerning the inward essence of marriage in his institution: that we may learn how far to attend what Adam spake of the outward materials thereof in his approbation. For if we shall bind these words of Adam only to a corporeal meaning, and that the force of this injunction upon all us his sons to live individually with any woman which hath befallen us in the most mistaken wedlock shall consist not in those moral and relative causes of Eve's creation but in the mere anatomy of a rib, and that Adam's insight concerning wedlock reached no further, we shall make him as very an idiot as the Socinians[71] make him; which would not be reverently done of us. Let us be content to allow our great forefather so much wisdom, as to take the instituting words of God along with him into this sentence, which if they be well minded will assure us that flesh and ribs are but of a weak and dead efficacy to keep marriage united where there is no other fitness. The rib of marriage, to all since Adam, is a relation much rather than a bone; the nerves and sinews thereof are love and meet help. They knit not every couple that marries, and where they knit they seldom break, but where they break, which for the most part is where they never truly joined, to such at the same instant both flesh and rib cease to be in common; so that here they argue nothing to the continuance of a false or violated marriage, but must be led back to receive their meaning from those institutive words of God which give them all the life and vigor they have.

[*Therefore shall a man leave his father, &c.*] What to a man's thinking more plain by this appointment, that the fatherly power should give place to conjugal prerogative? Yet it is generally held by reformed writers against the Papist, that though in persons at discretion the marriage in itself be never so fit, though it be fully accomplished with benediction, board and bed, yet the father not consenting, his main will without dispute shall dissolve all. And this they affirm only from collective reason, not any direct law; for that in Exod. 22:17, which is most particular, speaks that a father may refuse to marry his daughter to one who hath deflowered her, not that he may take her away from one who hath soberly married her. Yet because the general honor due to parents is great, they hold he may, and perhaps hold not amiss. But again, when the question is of harsh and rugged parents who defer to bestow their children seasonably, they agree jointly that the Church or magistrate may bestow them, though without the father's consent: and for this they have no express authority in Scripture. So that they may see by their own handling of this very place, that it is not the stubborn letter must govern us, but the divine and softening breath of charity which turns and winds the dictate of every positive command and shapes it to the good of mankind. Shall the outward accessory of a father's will wanting, rend the fittest and most affectionate marriage in twain after all nuptial consummations, and shall not the want of love and the privation of all civil and religious concord, which is the inward essence of wedlock, do as much to part those who were never truly wedded? Shall a father have this power to vindicate his own willful honor and authority to the utter breach of a most dearly-united marriage, and shall not a man in his own power have the permission to free his soul, his life, and all his comfort of life from the disaster of a no-marriage? Shall fatherhood, which is but man, for his own pleasure dissolve matrimony, and shall not matrimony, which is God's ordinance, for its own honor and better conservation, dissolve itself, when it is wrong and not fitted to any of the chief ends which it owes us?

[*And they shall be one flesh.*] These words also infer that there ought to be an individuality in marriage, but without all question presuppose the joining causes. Not a rule yet that we have met with, so universal in this whole institution, but hath admitted limitations and conditions according to human necessity. The very foundation of matrimony, though God laid it so deliberately, *that it is not good for man to be alone,* holds not always, if the Apostle can secure us. Soon after we are bid leave father and mother, and cleave to a wife, but must understand the father's consent withal, else not. *Cleave to a wife,* but let her be a wife, let her be a meet help, a solace, not a nothing, not an adversary, not a desertrice;[72] can any law or command be so unreasonable as to make men cleave to calamity, to ruin, to perdition? In like manner here, *They shall be one flesh;* but let the causes hold, and be made really good, which only have the possibility to make them one flesh. We know that flesh can neither join nor keep together two bodies of itself; what is it then must make them one flesh but likeness, but fitness of mind and disposition, which may breed the spirit of concord, and union between them? If that be not in the nature of either, and that there has been a remediless mistake, as vain we go about to compel them into one flesh as if we undertook to weave a garment of dry sand. It were more easy to compel the vegetable and nutritive power of nature to assimilations and mixtures which are not alterable each by other, or force the concoctive stomach to turn that into flesh which is so totally unlike that substance as not to be wrought on. For as the unity of mind is nearer and greater than the union of bodies, so doubtless is the dissimilitude greater and more dividual, as that which makes between bodies all difference and distinction. Especially whenas besides the singular and substantial differences of every soul, there is an intimate quality of good or evil through the whole progeny of Adam, which like a radical heat, or mortal chillness, joins them, or disjoins them irresistibly. In whom therefore either the will or the faculty is found to have never joined, or now not to continue so, 'tis not to say, they shall be one flesh, for they cannot be one flesh. God commands not impossibilities; and all the ecclesiastical glue that liturgy or laymen can compound is not able to solder us two such incongruous natures into the one flesh of a true beseeming marriage. Why did Moses then set down their uniting into one flesh? And I again ask, why the Gospel so oft repeats the eating of our Savior's flesh, the drinking of his blood?

That we are one body with him, the members of his body, flesh of his flesh, and bone of his bone, Ephesians 5:30. Yet lest we should be Capernaitans,[73] as we are told there that the flesh profiteth nothing, so we are told here, if we be not as deaf as adders, that this union of the flesh proceeds from the union of a fit help and solace. We know that there was never a more spiritual mystery than this Gospel taught us under the terms of body and flesh; yet nothing less intended than that we should stick there. What a stupidness then is it, that in marriage, which is the nearest resemblance of our union with Christ, we should deject our selves to such a sluggish and underfoot philosophy as to esteem the validity of marriage merely by the flesh, though never so broken and disjointed from love and peace, which only can give a human qualification to that act of the flesh and distinguish it from bestial. The text therefore uses this phrase, that *they shall be one flesh,* to justify and make legitimate the rites of marriage bed; which was not unneedful, if for all this warrant, they were suspected of pollution by some sects of philosophy, and religions of old, and latelier among the Papists, and other heretics elder than they. Some think there is a high mystery in those words, from that which Paul saith of them, Ephesians 5:32, *This is a great mystery, but I speak of Christ and the Church:* and thence they would conclude marriage to be inseparable. For me, I dispute not now whether matrimony be a mystery or no; if it be of Christ and his Church, certainly it is not meant of every ungodly and miswedded marriage, but then only mysterious when it is a holy, happy, and peaceful match. But when a saint is joined with a reprobate, or both alike, wicked with wicked, fool with fool, a he drunkard with a she, when the bed hath been nothing else for twenty years or more but an old haunt of lust and malice mixed together, no love, no goodness, no loyalty, but counterplotting and secret wishing one another's dissolution, this is to me the greatest mystery in the world, if such a marriage as this can be the mystery of aught, unless it be the mystery of iniquity:[74] according to that which Pareus cites out of Chrysostom,[75] that a bad wife is a help for the devil, and that like may be said of a bad husband. Since therefore none but a fit and pious matrimony can signify the union of Christ and his church, there cannot hence be any hindrance of divorce to that wedlock wherein there can be no good mystery. Rather it might to a Christian conscience be matter of finding itself so much less satisfied than before, in the continuance of an unhappy yoke, wherein there can be no representation either of Christ or of his church.

Thus having inquired the institution how it was in the beginning, both from the I chap. of Gen. where it was only mentioned in part, and from the second, where it was plainly and evidently instituted, and having attended each clause and word necessary, with a diligence not drowsy, we shall now fix with some advantage and by a short view backward gather up the ground we have gone, and sum up the strength we have, into one argumentative head, with that organic force that logic proffers us. All arts acknowledge that then only we know certainly when we can define; for definition is that which refines the pure essence of things from the circumstance. If therefore we can attain in this our controversy to define exactly what marriage is, we shall soon learn when there is a nullity thereof, and when a divorce.

The part therefore of this chapter which hath been here treated doth orderly and readily resolve itself into a definition of marriage, and a consectary[76] from thence. To the definition these words chiefly contribute: *It is not good, &c. I will make, &c.* Where the consectary begins this connection, *Therefore* informs us, *Therefore shall a Man, &c.* Definition is decreed by logicians to consist only of causes constituting the essence of a thing. What is not therefore among the causes constituting marriage must not stay in the definition. Those causes are concluded to be matter, and, as the artist calls it, form.[77] But inasmuch as the same thing may be a cause more ways than one, and that in relations and institutions which have no corporeal subsistence but only a respective being, the form by which the thing is what it is, is oft so slender and undistinguishable that it would soon confuse, were it not sustained by the efficient and final causes which concur to make up the form invalid otherwise of itself, it will be needful to take in all the four causes into the definition. First therefore the material cause of matrimony is man and woman; the author and efficient, God and their consent; the internal form and soul of this relation is conjugal love arising from a mutual fitness to the final causes of wedlock, help and society in religious, civil and domestic conversation, which includes as an inferior end the fulfilling of natural desire, and specifical increase; these are the final causes both moving the efficient, and perfeting the form. And although copulation be considered among the ends of marriage yet the act thereof in a right esteem can no longer be matrimonial, then it is an effect of conjugal love. When love finds itself utterly unmatched, and justly vanishes, nay rather cannot but vanish, the fleshly act indeed may continue, but not holy, not pure, not beseeming the sacred bond of marriage; being at best but an animal excretion, but more truly worse and more ignoble than that mute kindlyness[78] among the herds and flocks: in that proceeding as it ought from intellective principles, it participates of nothing rational, but that which the field and the fold equals. For in human actions the soul is the agent, the body in a manner passive. If then the body do out of sensitive force what the soul complies not with, how can man, and not rather something beneath man, be thought the doer.

But to proceed in the pursuit of an accurate definition, it will avail us something, and whet our thoughts, to examine what fabric hereof others have already reared. Pareus on Gen. defines marriage to be *an indissoluble conjunction of one man and one woman to an individual*[79] *and intimate conversation, and mutual benevolence, &c.*[80] Wherein is to be marked his placing of intimate conversation before bodily benevolence; for bodily is meant, though indeed benevolence rather founds will than body. Why then shall divorce be granted for want of bodily performance, and not for want of fitness to intimate conversation, whenas corporeal benevolence cannot in any human fashion be without this? Thus his definition places the ends of marriage in one order, and esteems them in another. His tautology also of indissoluble and individual is not to be imitated; especially since neither indissoluble nor individual hath aught to do in the exact definition, being but a consectary flowing from thence, as appears by plain Scripture, *Therefore shall a Man leave, &c.* For marriage is not true marriage by being individual, but therefore individual if it be true marriage. No argument but causes enter the definition; a consectary is but the effect of those causes. Besides, that marriage is indissoluble is not catholickly[81] true; we know it dissoluble for adultery and for desertion by the verdict of all reformed churches. Dr. Ames[82] defines it *an individual conjunction of one man and one woman, to communion of body and mutual society of life.* But this perverts the order of God, who in the institution places meet help and society of life before communion of body. And vulgar estimation undervalues beyond comparison all society of life and communion of mind beneath the communion of body; granting no divorce but to the want or miscommunicating of that. Hemingius,[83] an approved author, Melanchton's scholar, and who, next to Bucer and Erasmus,[84] writes of divorce most like a divine, thus comprises, *Marriage is a conjunction of one man and one woman lawfully consenting, into one flesh, for mutual help's sake, ordained of God.* And in his explanation stands punctually[85] upon the conditions of consent, that it be not in any main matter deluded, as being the life of wedlock, and no true marriage without a true consent. *Into one flesh* he expounds into one mind, as well as one body, and makes it the formal cause:[86] Herein only missing, while he puts the effect into his definition instead of the cause which the text affords him. For *one flesh* is not the formal essence of wedlock, but one end, or one effect of *a meet help,* the end oft-times being the effect and fruit of the form, as logic teaches; else many aged and holy matrimonies, and more eminently that of Joseph and Mary,[87] would be no true marriage. And that maxim generally received would be false, *that consent alone, though copulation never follow, makes the marriage.*[88] Therefore to consent lawfully into one flesh is not the formal cause of matrimony, but only one of the effects. The civil lawyers, and first Justinian[89] or Tribonian,[90] defines matrimony *a conjunction of man and woman containing individual accustom of life.* Wherein first, individual is not so bad as indissoluble put in by others: and although much cavil might be made in the distinguishing between indivisible and individual, yet the one taken for possible, the other for actual, neither the one nor the other can belong to the essence of marriage, especially when a civilian defines by which law marriage is actually divorced for many causes, and with good leave, by mutual consent. Therefore where *conjunction* is said, they who comment[91] the *Institutes* agree that conjunction of mind is by the law meant, not necessarily conjunction of body. That law then had good reason attending to its own definition, that divorce should be granted for the breaking of that conjunction which it holds necessary, sooner than for the want of that conjunction which it holds not necessary. And whereas Tuningus[92] a famous lawyer excuses individual as the purpose of marriage, not always the success, it suffices not. Purpose is not able to constitute the essence of a thing. Nature herself, the universal mother, intends nothing but her own perfection and preservation, yet is not the more indissoluble for that. The *Pandects* out of Modestinus,[93] though not define, yet well describe marriage: *the conjunction of male and female, the society of all life, the communion of divine and human right;* which Bucer also imitates on the fifth to the *Ephesians*. But it seems rather to comprehend the several ends of marriage than to contain the more constituting cause that makes it what it is.

That I therefore among others (for who sings not Hylas[94]) may give as well as take matter to be judged on, it will be looked I should produce another definition than these which have not stood the trial. Thus then I suppose that marriage by the natural and plain order of God's institution in the text may be more demonstratively and essentially defined. Marriage is a divine institution joining man and woman in a love fitly disposed to the helps and comforts of domestic life. A divine institution. This contains the prime efficient cause of marriage. As for consent of parents and guardians, it seems rather a concurrence than a cause: for as many that marry are in their own power as not; and where they are not their own, yet are they not subjected beyond reason. Now though efficient causes are not requisite in a definition, yet divine institution hath such influence upon the form, and is so a conserving cause of it, that without it the form is not sufficient to distinguish matrimony from other conjunctions of male and female, which are not to be counted marriage. *Joining man and woman in a love, &c.* This brings in the parties consent; until which be, the marriage hath no true being. When I say *consent,* I mean not error, for error is not properly consent. And why should not consent be here understood with equity and good to either part, as in all other friendly covenants, and not be strained and cruelly urged to the mischief and destruction of both? Neither do I mean that singular act of consent which made the contract: for that may remain, and yet the marriage not true nor lawful; and that may cease, and yet the marriage both true and lawful, to their sin that break it. So that either as no efficient at all, or but a transitory, it comes not into the definition. That consent I mean which is a love fitly disposed to mutual help and comfort of life. This is that happy form of marriage naturally arising from the very heart of divine institution in the text, in all the former definitions either obscurely, and under mistaken terms expressed, or not at all. This gives marriage all her due, all her benefits, all her being, all her distinct and proper being. This makes a marriage not a bondage, a blessing not a curse, a gift of God not a snare. Unless there be a love, and that love born of fitness, how can it last? unless it last, how can the best and sweetest purposes of marriage be attained, and they not attained, which are the chief ends, and with a lawful love constitute the formal cause it self of marriage, how can the essence thereof subsist, how can it be indeed what it goes for? Conclude therefore by all the power of reason, that where this essence of marriage is not, there can be no true marriage; and the parties either one of them or both are free, and without fault, rather by a nullity than by a divorce, may betake them to a second choice if their present condition be not tolerable to them. If any shall ask, why *domestic* in the definition? I answer, that because both in the Scriptures, and in the gravest poets and philosophers, I find the properties and excellencies of a wife set out only from domestic virtues; if they extend further, it diffuses them into the notion of some more common duty than matrimonial.

Thus far of the definition; the consectary[95] which flows from thence, and altogether depends thereon, is manifestly brought in by this connective particle *Therefore,* and branches itself into a double consequence: first, individual society, *therefore shall a man leave father and mother;* secondly, conjugal benevolence, *and they shall be one flesh.* Which as was shown, is not without cause here mentioned, to prevent and to abolish the suspect of pollution in that natural and undefiled act. These consequences therefore cannot either in religion, law, or reason be bound, and posted upon mankind to his sorrow and misery, but receive what force they have from the meetness of help and solace which is the formal cause and end of that definition that sustains them. And although it be not for the majesty of Scripture to humble herself in artificial theorems, and definitions, and corollaries, like a professor in the schools, but looks to be analyzed and interpreted by the logical industry of her disciples and followers, and to be reduced by them, as oft as need is, into those sciential[96] rules which are the implements of instruction, yet Moses, as if foreseeing the miserable work that man's ignorance and pusillanimity[97] would make in this matrimonious business, and endeavoring his utmost to prevent it, condescends in this place to such a methodical and school-like way of defining, and consequencing, as in no place of the whole law more.

Thus we have seen, and if we be not contentious may know, what was marriage in the beginning, to which in the Gospel we are referred, and what from hence to judge of nullity or divorce. Here I esteem the work done; in this field the controversy decided; but because other places of Scripture seem to look adversely upon this our decision, although indeed they keep all harmony with it, and because it is a better work to reconcile the seeming diversities of Scripture than the real dissentions of nearest friends, I shall assay in three following discourses to perform that office.

Deut. 24.1, 2

1. *When a man hath taken a wife, and married her, and it come to pass that she find no favor in his eyes, because he hath found some uncleanness in her, then let him write her a bill of divorcement, and give it in her hand, and send her out of his house.*

2. *And when she is departed out of his house, she may go and be another man's wife.*

That which is the only discommodity of speaking in a clear matter, the abundance of argument that presses to be uttered, and the suspense of judgment what to choose, and how in the multitude of reason to be not tedious, is the greatest difficulty which I expect here to meet with. Yet much hath been said formerly concerning this law in *The Doctrine of Divorce;* whereof I shall repeat no more than what is necessary. Two things are here doubted: first, and that but of late, whether this be a law or no; next, what this reason of uncleanness might mean for which the law is granted. That it is a plain law no man ever questioned, 'til Vatablus[98] within these hundred years professed Hebrew at Paris, a man of no religion, as Beza[99] deciphers him. Yet some there be who follow him, not only against the current of all antiquity, both Jewish and Christian, but the evidence of Scripture also, Malach. 2:16, *Let him who hateth put away saith the Lord God of Israel.* Although this place also hath been tampered with, as if it were to be thus rendered, *The Lord God saith, that he hateth putting away.* But this new interpretation rests only in the authority of Junius;[100] for neither Calvin,[101] nor Vatablus himself, nor any other known divine so interpreted before. And they of best note who have translated the Scripture since, and Diodati[102] for one, follow not his reading. And perhaps they might reject it, if for nothing else, for these two reasons: First, it introduces in a new manner the person of God speaking less majestic than he is ever wont. When God speaks by his prophet, he ever speaks in the first person, thereby signifying his majesty and omni-presence. He would have said, I hate putting away, saith the Lord; and not sent word by *Malachi* in a sudden fallen style, *The Lord God saith that he hateth putting away:* that were a phrase to shrink the glorious omnipresence of God speaking into a kind of circumscriptive absence. And were as if a herald in the atchievement[103] of a king should commit the indecorum to set his helmet sideways and close, not full-faced and open in the posture of direction and command. We cannot think therefore that this last prophet would thus in a new fashion absent the person of

God from his own words, as if he came not along with them. For it would also be wide from the proper scope of his place: he that reads attentively will soon perceive, that God blames not here the Jews for putting away their wives, but for keeping strange concubines, to the profaning of Juda's holiness and the vexation of their Hebrew wives, verse 11 and 14, *Judah hath married the daughter of a strange God,* and exhorts them rather to put their wives away whom they hate, as the law permitted, than to keep them under such affronts. And it is received that this prophet lived in those times of Ezra and Nehemiah (nay by some is thought to be Ezra himself) when the people were forced by these two worthies to put their strange wives away.[104] So that what the story of those times, and the plain context of the 11 verse, from whence this rebuke begins, can give us to conjecture of the obscure and curt Ebraisms that follow, this prophet does not forbid putting away, but forbids keeping, and commands putting away according to God's law, which is the plainest interpreter both of what God will and what he can best suffer. Thus much evinces that God there commanded divorce by Malachi, and this confirms that he commands it also here by Moses.

I may the less doubt to mention by the way an author, though counted apocryphal, yet of no small account for piety and wisdom, the author of *Ecclesiasticus*. Which book, begun by the grandfather of that Jesus who is called the Son of Sirach, might have been written in part not much after the time when Malachi lived, if we compute by the reign of Ptolemaeus Euergetes.[105] It professes to explain the law and the prophets; and yet exhorts us to divorce for incurable causes, and to cut off from the flesh those whom it there describes, Ecclesiastic. 25. 26. Which doubtless that wise and ancient writer would never have advised, had either Malachi so lately forbidden it, or the law by a full precept not left it lawful. But I urge not this for want of better proof; our Savior himself allows divorce to be a command, Mark 10:3, 5. Neither do they weaken this assertion who say it was only a sufferance, as shall be proved at large in that place of Matthew. But suppose it were not a written law they never can deny it was a custom, and so effect nothing.

For the same reasons that induce them why it should not be a law, will straiten them as hard why it should be allowed a custom. All custom is either evil or not evil. If it be evil, this is the very end of lawgiving, to abolish evil customs by wholesome laws, unless we imagine Moses weaker than every negligent and startling[106] politician. If it be, as they make this of divorce to be, a custom against nature, against justice, against charity, how, upon this most impure custom tolerated, could the God of pureness erect a nice and precise law, that the wife married after divorce could not return to her former husband, as being defiled? What was all this following niceness worth, built upon the lewd foundation of a wicked thing allowed? In few words then, this custom of divorce either was allowable or not allowable. If not allowable, how could it be allowed? If it were allowable, all who understand law will consent, that a tolerated custom hath the force of a law, and is indeed no other but an unwritten law, as Justinian calls it, and is as prevalent as any written statute.[107] So that their shift of turning this law into a custom wheels about, and gives the onset upon their own flanks; not disproving, but concluding it to be the more firm law, because it was without controversy a granted custom, as clear in the reason of common life as those given rules whereon Euclides[108] builds his propositions.

Thus being every way a law of God, who can without blasphemy doubt it to be a just and pure law? Moses continually disavows the giving them any statute, or judgment, but what he learnt of God;[109] of whom also in his song he saith, Deut. 32, *He is the rock, his work is perfect, all his ways are judgment, a God of truth and without iniquity, just and right is he.* And David testifies, the judgments of the Lord *are true and righteous altogether.* Not partly right and partly wrong, much less wrong altogether, as divines of nowadays dare censure them. Moses again, of that people to whom he gave this law, saith, Deut. 14, *Ye are the children of the Lord your God, the Lord hath chosen thee to be a peculiar people to himself above all the nations upon the Earth, that thou should keep all his Commandments; and be high in praise, in name, and in honor, holy to the Lord, chap. 26.* And in the fourth, *Behold*

I have taught you statutes and judgments, even as the Lord my God commanded me; keep therefore and do them. For this is your wisdom and your understanding in the sight of nations that shall hear all these statutes and say, surely this great nation is a wise and understanding people. For what nation is there so great, who hath God so nigh to them? And what nation that hath statutes and judgments so righteous as all this law which I set before you this day?[110] Thus whether we look at the purity and justice of God himself, the jealousy of his honor among other nations, the holiness and moral perfection which he intended by his law to teach this people, we cannot possibly think how he could endure to let them slug[111] and grow inveterately wicked, under base allowances and whole adulterous lives by dispensation. They might not eat, they might not touch an unclean thing; to what hypocrisy then were they trained up, if by prescription of the same law, they might be unjust, they might be adulterous for term of life? forbid to soil their garments with a coy[112] imaginary pollution, but not forbid, but countenanced and animated by law to soil their souls with deepest defilements. What more unlike to God, what more like that God should hate, than that his law should be so curious to wash vessels and vestures, and so careless to leave unwashed, unregarded, so foul a scab of Egypt in their souls? What would we more? The Statutes of the Lord are all pure and just: and if all, then this of divorce.

[*Because he hath found some uncleanness in her.*] That we may not esteem this law to be a mere authorizing of license, as the Pharisees took it, Moses adds the reason, *for some uncleanness found*. Some heretofore have been so ignorant as to have thought that this *uncleanness* means adultery. But Erasmus, who for having writ an excellent treatise of divorce, was wrote against by some burly standard divine perhaps of Cullen, or of Lovain,[113] who calls himself Phimostomus,[114] shows learnedly out of the Fathers, with other testimonies and reasons, that *uncleanness* is not here so understood, defends his former work, though new to that age and perhaps counted licentious, and fears not to engage all his fame on the argument. Afterward, when expositors began to understand the Hebrew text, which they had not done of many ages before, they translated word for word not *uncleanness,* but *the nakedness of any thing;* and considering that nakedness is usually referred in Scripture to the mind as well as to the body, they constantly expound it any defect, annoyance, or ill quality in nature, which to be joined with, makes life tedious, and such company worse than solitude. So that here will be no cause to vary from the general consent of exposition, which gives us freely that God permitted divorce for whatever was unalterably distasteful, whether in body or mind. But with this admonishment, that if the Roman law, especially in contracts and dowries, left many things to equity with these cautions, *ex fide bona, quod aequius melius erit, ut inter bonos bene agier,*[115] we will not grudge to think that God intended not license here to every humor, but to such remediless grievances as might move a good, and honest, and faithful man then to divorce, when it can no more be peace or comfort to either of them continuing thus joined. And although it could not be avoided but that men of hard hearts would abuse this liberty, yet doubtless it was intended as all other privileges in law are: to good men principally, to bad only by accident. Also that the sin was not in the permission, nor simply in the action of divorce (for then the permitting also had been sin) but only in the abuse. But that this law should, as it were, be wrung from God and Moses, only to serve the hard-heartedness and the lust of injurious men, how remote it is from all sense, and law, and honesty, and therefore surely from the meaning of Christ, shall abundantly be manifest in due order.

Now although Moses needed not to add other reason of this law than that one there expressed, yet to these ages wherein canons, and Scotisms,[116] and Lumbard[117] laws have dulled and almost obliterated the lively sculpture of ancient reason and humanity, it will be requisite to heap reason upon reason, and all little enough to vindicate the whiteness and the innocence of this divine law from the calumny it finds at this day, of being a door to license and confusion. Whenas indeed there is not a judicial point in all Moses consisting of more true equity, high wisdom, and God-like pity than this law; not derogating but preserving the honor and peace of marriage, and exactly agreeing with the sense and mind of that institution in Genesis.

For first, if marriage be but an ordained relation, as it seems not more, it cannot take place above the prime dictates of nature; and if it be of natural right, yet it must yield to that which is more natural, and before it by eldership and precedence in nature. Now it is not natural that Hugh marries Beatrice, or Thomas Rebecca, being only a civil contract, and full of many chances but that these men seek them meet helps, that only is natural; and that they espouse them such, that only is marriage. But if they find them neither fit helps, nor tolerable society, what thing more natural, more original and first in nature than to depart from that which is irksome, grievous, actively hateful, and injurious even to hostility, especially in a conjugal respect, wherein antipathies are invincible, and where the forced abiding of the one can be no true good, no real comfort to the other. For if he finds no contentment from the other, how can he return it from himself, or no acceptance, how can he mutually accept? What more equal, more pious, than to untie a civil knot for a natural enmity held by violence from parting, to dissolve an accidental conjunction of this or that man and woman, for the most natural and most necessary disagreement of meet from unmeet, guilty from guiltless, contrary from contrary? It being certain that the mystical and blessed unity of marriage can be no way more unhallowed and profaned than by the forcible uniting of such disunions and separations. Which if we see oft-times they cannot join or piece up to a common friendship, or to a willing conversation in the same house, how should they possibly agree to the most familiar and united amity of wedlock? Abraham and Lot,[118] though dear friends and brethren in a strange country, chose rather to part asunder than to infect their friendship with the strife of their servants. Paul and Barnabas,[119] joined together by the Holy Ghost to a spiritual work, thought it better to separate when once they grew at variance. If these great saints joined by nature, friendship, religion, high providence, and revelation, could not so govern a casual difference, a sudden passion, but must in wisdom divide from the outward duties of a friendship, or a colleagueship in the same family, or in the same journey, lest it should grow to a worse division, can anything be more absurd and barbarous than that they whom only error, casualty, art, or plot hath joined, should be compelled, not against a sudden passion but against the permanent and radical discords of nature, to the most intimate and incorporating duties of love and embracement, therein only rational and human as they are free and voluntary, being else an abject and servile yoke, scarce not brutish. And that there is in man such a peculiar sway of liking or disliking in the affairs of matrimony, is evidently seen before marriage among those who can be friendly, can respect each other, yet to marry each other would not for any persuasion. If then this unfitness and disparity be not 'til after marriage discovered, through many causes, and colors, and concealments that may overshadow, undoubtedly it will produce the same effects, and perhaps with more vehemence, that such a mistaken pair would give the world to be unmarried again. And their condition Solomon to the plain justification of divorce expresses, Prov. 30:21, 23, where he tells us of his own accord that a *hated,* or a *hateful* woman, *when she is married, is a thing for which the Earth is disquieted, and cannot bear it:* thus giving divine testimony to this divine law, which bids us nothing more than is the first and most innocent lesson of nature, to turn away peaceably from what afflicts and hazards our destruction, especially when our staying can do no good and is exposed to all evil.

Secondly, it is unjust that any ordinance, ordained to the good and comfort of man, where that end is missing, without his fault, should be forced upon him to an unsufferable misery and discomfort, if not commonly ruin. All ordinances are established in their end; the end of law is the virtue, is the righteousness of law. And therefore him we count an ill expounder who urges law against the intention thereof. The general end of every ordinance, of every severest, every divinest, even of Sabbath is the good of man, yea his temporal good not excluded. But marriage is one of the benignest ordinances of God to man, whereof both the general and particular end is the peace and contentment of man's mind, as the institution declares. Contentment of body they grant, which if it be defrauded, the plea of frigidity shall divorce. But here lies the fathomless absurdity: that granting this for bodily defect, they will not grant it for any defect of the mind, any violation of religious or civil society. Whenas, if the argument of Christ be firm against the ruler of the synagogue, Luke 13, *Thou hypocrite, doth not each of you on the Sabbath-day loosen his ox or his ass from the stall, and lead him to watering, and should not I unbind a daughter of Abraham from this bond of Satan,*[120] it stands as good here. Ye have regard in marriage to the grievance of body, should you not regard more the grievances of the mind, seeing the soul as much excels the body as the outward man excels the ass, and more, for that *animal* is yet a living creature, perfect in itself, but the body without the soul is a mere senseless trunk. No ordinance therefore given particularly to the good both spiritual and temporal of man, can be urged upon him to his mischief, and if they yield this to the unworthier part, the body, where about are they in their principles, that they yield it not to the more worthy, the mind of a good man?

Thirdly, as no ordinance, so no covenant, no not between God and man, much less between man and man, being as all are, intended to the good of both parties, can hold to the deluding or making miserable of them both. For equity is understood in every covenant, even between enemies, though the terms be not expressed. If equity therefore made it, extremity may dissolve it. But marriage, they use to say, is the Covenant of God. Undoubted: and so is any covenant frequently called in Scripture, wherein God is called to witness. The covenant of friendship between David and Jonathan is called the Covenant of the Lord, I Sam. 20. The Covenant of Zedekiah with the King of Babel, a covenant to be doubted whether lawful or no, yet in respect of God invoked thereto is called the *Oath, and the Covenant of God,* Ezek. 17. Marriage also is called the *Covenant of God,* Prov. 2:17. Why, but as before, because God is the witness thereof, Mal. 2:14. So that this denomination adds nothing to the covenant of marriage, above any other civil and solemn contract; nor is it more indissoluble for this reason than any other against the end of its own ordination; nor is any vow or oath to God exacted with such a rigor, where superstition reigns not. For look how much divine the covenant is, so much the more equal; so much the more to be expected that every article thereof should be fairly made good, no false dealing, or unperforming should be thrust upon men without redress, if the covenant be so divine. But faith they say must be kept in covenant, though to our damage. I answer, that only holds true where the other side performs, which failing, he is no longer bound. Again, this is true when the keeping of faith can be of any use or benefit to the other. But in marriage, a league of love and willingness, if faith be not willingly kept, it scarce is worth the keeping; nor can be any delight to a generous mind with whom it is forcibly kept. And the question still supposes the one brought to an impossibility of keeping it as he ought, by the other's default; and to keep it formally, not only with a thousand shifts and dissimulations but with open anguish, perpetual sadness and disturbance, no willingness, no cheerfulness, no contentment, cannot be any good to a mind not basely poor and shallow with whom the contract of love is so kept. A covenant therefore brought to that pass, is on the unfaulty side without injury dissolved.

Fourthly, the law is not to neglect men under greatest sufferances, but to see covenants of greatest moment most faithfullest performed. And what injury comparable to that sustained in a frustrate and false-dealing marriage, to lose, for another's fault against him, the best portion of his temporal comforts, and of his spiritual too, as it may fall out? It was the law, that for man's good and quiet reduced things to propriety which were at first in common; how much more law-like were it to assist nature in disappropriating that evil which by continuing proper becomes destructive. But he might have bewared. So he might in any other covenant, wherein the law does not constrain error to so dear a forfeit. And yet in these matters wherein the wisest are apt to err, all the wariness that can be oft-times nothing avails. But the law can compel the offending party to be more duteous. Yes, if all these kind of offences were fit in public to be complained on, or being compelled were any satisfaction to a mate not sottish[121] or malicious. And these injuries work so vehemently, that if the law remedy them not, by separating the cause when no way else will pacify, the person not relieved betakes him either to such disorderly courses or to such a dull dejection as renders him either infamous, or useless to the service of God and his Country. Which the law ought to prevent as a thing pernicious to the commonwealth; and what better prevention than this which *Moses* used?

Fifthly, the law is to tender the liberty and the human dignity of them that live under the law, whether it be the man's right above the woman, or the woman's just appeal against wrong and servitude. But the duties of marriage contain in them a duty of benevolence, which to do by compulsion against the soul, where there can be neither peace, nor joy, nor love, but an enthrallment to one who either cannot, or will not be the mutual in the godliest and the civilest ends of that society, is the ignoblest and the lowest slavery that a human shape can be put to. This law therefore justly and piously provides against such an unmanly task of bondage as this. The civil law, though it favored the setting free of a slave, yet if he proved ungrateful to his patron, reduced him to a servile condition.[122] If that law did well to reduce from liberty to bondage for an ingratitude not the greatest, much more became it the law of God to enact the restorement of a free-born man from an unpurposed and unworthy bondage to a rightful liberty for the most unnatural fraud and ingratitude that can be committed against him. And if that civilian Emperor in his title of *Donations*[123] permit the giver to recall his gift from him who proves unthankful towards him, yea, though he had subscribed and signed in the deed of the gift, not to recall it though for this very cause of ingratitude, with much more equity doth Moses permit here the giver to recall no petty gift, but the gift of himself from one who most injuriously and deceitfully uses him against the main ends and conditions of his giving himself, expressed in God's institution.

Sixthly, although there be nothing in the plain words of this law that seems to regard the afflictions of a wife, how great so ever, yet expositors determine, and doubtless determine rightly, that God was not uncompassionate of them also in the framing of this law. For should the rescript[124] of Antoninus[125] in the civil law give release to servants flying for refuge to the Emperor's statue, by giving leave to change their cruel masters,[126] and should God, who in his law also is good to injured servants by granting them their freedom in divers cases, not consider the wrongs and miseries of a wife which is no servant? Though herein the counter-sense of our divines, to me, I must confess seems admirable, who teach that God gave this as a merciful law, not for man whom he here names, and to whom by name he gives this power, but for the wife whom he names not, and to whom by name he gives no power at all. For certainly if man be liable to injuries in marriage, as well as woman, and man be the worthier person, it were a preposterous law to respect only the less worthy: her whom God made for marriage, and not him at all for whom marriage was made.[127]

Seventhly, the law of marriage gives place to the power of parents: for we hold that consent of parents not had may break the wedlock, though else accomplished. It gives place to masterly power, for the master might take away from an Hebrew servant the wife which he gave him, Exodus 21:4. If it be answered, that the marriage of servants is no matrimony: 'tis replied that this in the ancient Roman law is true, not in the Mosaic. If it be added, she was a stranger, not an Hebrew, therefore easily divorced, it will be answered that strangers not being Canaanites, and they also being converts, might be lawfully married, as Rahab was.[128] And her conversion is here supposed; for an Hebrew master could not lawfully give a heathen wife to an Hebrew servant. However, the divorcing of an Israelitish woman was as easy by the law as the divorcing of a stranger, and almost in the same words permitted, Deuteronomy 24 and 21:14. Lastly, it gives place to the right of war, for a captive woman lawfully married, and afterwards not beloved, might be dismissed, only without ransom, Deut. 21. If marriage be dissolved by so many exterior powers, not superior, as we think, why may not the power of marriage itself for its own peace and honor dissolve itself? Where the persons wedded be free persons, why may not a greater and more natural power complaining dissolve marriage? For the ends why matrimony was ordained are certainly and by all logic above all the ordinance itself, why may not that dissolve marriage without which that institution hath no force at all? For the prime ends of marriage are the whole strength and validity thereof, without which matrimony is like an idol, nothing in the world.

But those former allowances were all for hardness of heart. Be that granted, until we come where to understand it better: if the law suffer thus far the obstinacy of a bad man, is it not more righteous here to do willingly what is but equal, to remove in season the extremities of a good man?

Eighthly, if a man had deflowered a virgin, or brought an ill name on his wife that she came not a virgin to him, he was amerced[129] in certain shekels of silver,[130] and bound never to divorce her all his days, Deut. 22, which shows that the law gave no liberty to divorce where the injury was palpable; and that the absolute forbidding to divorce was in part the punishment of a deflowerer and a defamer. Yet not so but that the wife questionless might depart when she pleased. Otherwise this course had not so much righted her, as delivered her up to more spite and cruel usage. This law therefore doth justly distinguish the privilege of an honest and blameless man in the matter of divorce from the punishment of a notorious offender.

Ninthly, suppose it might be imputed to a man that he was too rash in his choice and why he took not better heed; let him now smart, and bear his folly as he may, although the law of God, that terrible law, do not thus upbraid the infirmities and unwilling mistakes of man in his integrity. But suppose these and the like proud aggravations of some stern hypocrite, more merciless in his mercies than any literal law in the vigor of severity, must be patiently heard; yet all law, and God's law especially, grants everywhere to error easy remitments,[131] even where the utmost penalty exacted were no undoing. With great reason therefore and mercy doth it here not torment an error, if it be so, with the endurance of a whole life lost to all household comfort and society, a punishment of too vast and huge dimension for an error, and the more unreasonable for that the like objection may be opposed against the plea of divorcing for adultery: he might have looked better before to her breeding under religious parents; why did he not more diligently inquire into her manners, into what company she kept? every glance of her eye, every step of her gait would have prophesied adultery, if the quick scent of these discerners had been took along; they had the divination to have foretold you all this, as they have now the divinity to punish an error inhumanly. As good reason to be content, and forced to be content with your adulteress, if these objectors might be the judges of human frailty. But God more mild and good to man, than man to his brother, in all this liberty given to divorcement, mentions not a word of our past errors and mistakes, if any were, which these men objecting from their own inventions prosecute with all violence and iniquity. For if the one be to look so narrowly what he takes, at the peril of ever keeping, why should not the other be made as wary what is promised, by the peril of losing? for without those promises the treaty of marriage had not proceeded. Why should his own error bind him, rather than the other's fraud acquit him? Let the buyer beware, saith the old law-beaten termer. Belike then there is no more honesty nor ingenuity in the bargain of a wedlock than in the buying of a colt. We must it seems drive it on as craftily with those whose affinity we seek, as if they were a pack of sale-men and complotters.[132] But the deceiver deceives himself in the unprosperous marriage, and therein is sufficiently punished. I answer, that the most of those who deceive are such as either understand not or value not the true purposes of marriage; they have the prey they seek, not the punishment. Yet say it prove to them some cross, it is not equal that error and fraud should be linked in the same degree of forfeiture, but rather that error should be acquitted, and fraud bereaved his morsel,[133] if the mistake were not on both sides; for then on both sides the acquitment will be reasonable if the bondage be intolerable: which this law graciously determines, not unmindful of the wife, as was granted willingly to the common expositors, though beyond the letter of this law, yet not beyond the spirit of charity.[134]

Tenthly, marriage is a solemn thing, some say a holy, the resemblance of Christ and his church;[135] and so indeed it is where the persons are truly religious. And we know all sacred things not performed sincerely as they ought, are no way acceptable to God in their outward formality; and that wherein it differs from personal duties, if they be not truly done, the fault is in ourselves. But marriage to be a true and pious marriage is not in the single power of any person; the essence whereof, as of all other covenants is in relation to another, the making and maintaining causes thereof are all mutual, and must be a communion of spiritual and temporal comforts. If then either of them cannot or obstinately will not be answerable in these duties, so as that the other can have no peaceful living, or enduring the want of what he justly seeks, and sees no hope, then straight from that dwelling love, which is the soul of wedlock, takes his flight, leaving only some cold performances of civil and common respects; but the true bond of marriage, if there were ever any there, is already burst like a rotten thread. Then follows dissimulation, suspicion, false colors, false pretences and worse than these, disturbance, annoyance, vexation, sorrow, temptation even in the faultless person, weary of himself, and of all action public or domestic; then comes disorder, neglect, hatred, and perpetual strife, all these the enemies of holiness and Christianity, and every one persisted in, a remediless violation to matrimony. Therefore God, who hates all feigning and formality where there should be all faith and sincereness, and abhors the inevitable discord where there should be greatest concord, when through another's default, faith and concord cannot be, counts it neither just to punish the innocent with the transgressor, nor holy, nor honorable for the sanctity of marriage, that should be the union of peace and love, to be made the commitment and close fight of enmity and hate. And therefore doth in this law what best agrees with his goodness, loosening a sacred thing to peace and charity rather than binding it to hatred and contention; loosening only the outward and formal tie of that which is already inwardly and really broken, or else was really never joined.

Eleventhly, one of the chief matrimonial ends is said to seek a holy seed;[136] but where an unfit marriage administers continual cause of hatred and distemper, there, as was heard before, cannot choose but much unholiness abide. Nothing more unhallows a man, more unprepares him to the service of God in any duty, than a habit of wrath and perturbation, arising from the importunity of troublous causes never absent. And where the household stands in this plight, what love can there be to the unfortunate issue, what care of their breeding, which is of main conducement to their being holy. God therefore knowing how unhappy it would be for children to be born in such a family, gives this law either as a prevention, that being an unhappy pair they should not add to be unhappy parents, or else as a remedy, that if there be children, while they are fewest, they may follow either parent, as shall be agreed, or judged, from the house of hatred and discord to a place of more holy and peaceable education.

Twelfthly, all law is available to some good end, but the final prohibition of divorce avails to no good end, causing only the endless aggravation of evil; and therefore this permission of divorce was given to the Jews by the wisdom and fatherly providence of God; who knew that law cannot command love, without which matrimony hath no true being, no good, no solace, nothing of God's instituting, nothing but so sordid and so low, as to be disdained of any generous person. Law cannot enable natural inability either of body, or mind, which gives the grievance. It cannot make equal those inequalities, it cannot make fit those unfitnesses. And where there is malice more than defect of nature, it cannot hinder ten thousand injuries, and bitter actions of despite too subtle and too unapparent for law to deal with. And while it seeks to remedy mere outward wrongs, it exposes the injured person to other more inward and more cutting. All these evils unavoidably will redound upon the children, if any be, and the whole family. It degenerates and disorders the best spirits, leaves them to unsettled imaginations and degraded hopes, careless of themselves, their household and their friends, unactive to all public service, dead to the commonwealth; wherein they are by one mishap, and no willing trespass of theirs, outlawed from all the benefits and comforts of married life and posterity. It confers as little to the honor and inviolable keeping of matrimony, but sooner stirs up temptations and occasions to secret adulteries and unchaste roving. But it maintains public honesty. Public folly, rather who shall judge of public honesty? The law of God, and of most ancientest Christians, and all civil nations, or the illegitimate law of monks and canonists,[137] the most malevolent, most inexperienced, most incompetent judges of matrimony?

These reasons, and many more that might be alleged, afford us plainly to perceive both what good cause this law had to do for good men in mischances, and what necessity it had to suffer accidentally the hard-heartedness of bad men, which could not certainly discover, or discovering could not subdue, no nor endeavor to restrain without multiplying sorrow to them, for whom all was endeavored. The guiltless therefore were not deprived their needful redresses, and the hard hearts of others unchastisable in those judicial courts, were so remitted there, as bound over to the higher session[138] of conscience.

Notwithstanding all this, there is a loud exception against this law of God, nor can the holy author save his law from this exception, that it opens a door to all license and confusion. But this is the rudest, I was almost saying the most graceless objection, and with the least reverence to God and Moses, that could be devised: This is to cite God before man's tribunal, to arrogate a wisdom and holiness above him. Did not God then foresee what event of license or confusion could follow? Did not he know how to ponder these abuses with more prevailing respects, in the most even balance of his justice and pureness, 'til these correctors came up to show him better? The law is, if it stir up sin any way, to stir it up by forbidding, as one contrary excites another, Romans 7:7; but if it once come to provoke sin by granting license to sin, according to laws that have no other honest end but only to permit the fulfilling of obstinate lust, how is God not made the contradicter of himself? No man denies that best things may be abused; but it is a rule resulting from many pregnant experiences, that what doth most harm in the abusing, used rightly doth most good. And such a good to take away from honest men, for being abused by such as abuse all things, is the greatest abuse of all. That the whole law is no further useful than as a man uses it lawfully, St. Paul teaches I Timothy 1:8. And that Christian liberty may be used for an occasion to the flesh, the same Apostle confesses, Galatians 5:13, yet thinks not of removing it for that, but bids us rather *stand fast in the liberty wherewith Christ hath freed us, and not be held again in the yoke of bondage.*[139] The very permission which Christ gave to divorce for adultery may be foully abused by any whose hardness of heart can either feign adultery, or dares commit, that he may divorce. And for this cause the Pope, and hitherto the Church of England, forbid all divorce from the bond of marriage, though for openest adultery. If then it be righteous to hinder for the fear of abuse, that which God's law notwithstanding that caution hath warranted to be done, doth not our righteousness come short of Antichrist, or do we not rather herein conform our selves to his unrighteousness in this undue and unwise fear? For God regards more to relieve by this law the just complaints of good men than to curb the license of wicked men, to the crushing withal and the overwhelming of his afflicted servants. He loves more that his law should look with pity upon the difficulties of his own, than with rigor upon the boundless riots of them who serve another master, and hindered here by the strictness will break another way to worse enormities. If this law therefore have many good reasons for which God gave it, and no intention of giving scope to lewdness, but as abuse by accident comes in with every good law, and every good thing, it cannot be wisdom in us, while we can content us with God's wisdom, nor can be purity, if his purity will suffice us, to except against this law as if it fostered license. But if they affirm this law had no other end but to permit obdurate lust because it would be obdurate, making the law of God intentionally to proclaim and enact sin lawful, as if the will of God were become sinful, or sin stronger than his direct and law-giving will, the men would be admonished to look well to it, that while they are so eager to shut the door against license they do open a worse door to blasphemy. And yet they shall be here further shown their iniquity; what more foul and common sin among us than drunkenness, and who can be ignorant, that if the importation of wine and the use of all strong drink were forbid, it would both clean rid the possibility of committing that odious vice, and men might afterwards live happily and healthfully, without the use of those intoxicating liquors. Yet who is there the severest of them all that ever propounded to lose his sack,[140] his ale, toward the certain abolishing of so great a sin? Who is there of them, the holiest, that less loves his rich canary[141] at meals, though it be fetched from places that hazard the religion of them who fetch it, and though it make his neighbor drunk out of the same tun?[142] While they forbid not therefore the use of that liquid merchandise, which forbidden would utterly remove a most loathsome sin, and not impair either the health or the refreshment of mankind, supplied many other ways, why do they forbid a law of God, the forbidding whereof brings into an excessive bondage oft-times the best of men, and betters not the worse? He to remove a national vice will not pardon his cups, nor think it concerns him to forbear the quaffing of that outlandish grape in his unnecessary fullness, though other men abuse it never so much, nor is he so abstemious as to intercede with the magistrate that all matter of drunkenness be banished the commonwealth, and yet for the fear of a less inconvenience unpardonably requires of his brethren in their extreme necessity, to debar themselves the use of God's permissive law, though it might be their saving, and no man's endangering the more. Thus this peremptory strictness we may discern of what sort it is, how unequal and how unjust.

But it will breed confusion. What confusion it would breed, God himself took the care to prevent in the fourth verse of this chapter, that the divorced being married to another might not return to her former husband. And Justinian's law counsels the same in his title of *Nuptials*.[143] And what confusion else can there be in separation, to separate, upon extreme urgency, the religious from the irreligious, the fit from the unfit, the willing from the willful, the abused from the abuser? Such a separation is quite contrary to confusion. But to bind and mix together holy with atheist, heavenly with hellish, fitness with unfitness, light with darkness, antipathy with antipathy, the injured with the injurer, and force them into the most inward nearness of a detested union, this doubtless is the most horrid, the most unnatural mixture, the greatest confusion that can be confused.

Thus by this plain and Christian Talmud[144] vindicating the law of God from irreverent and unwary expositions, I trust, where it shall meet with intelligible perusers, some stay at least of men's thoughts will be obtained, to consider these many prudent and righteous ends of this divorcing permission. That it may have, for the great author's sake, hereafter some competent allowance to be counted a little purer than the prerogative of a legal and public ribaldry, granted to that holy seed. So that from hence we shall hope to find the way still more open to the reconciling of those places which treat this matter in the Gospel. And thither now, without interruption, the course of method brings us.

Tetrachordon,
Matt. 5.31, 32

31. *It hath been said whosoever shall put away his wife, let him give her a writing of divorcement.*

32. *But I say unto you that whosoever shall put away his wife, &c.*

Matt. 19.3, 4, &c

3 *And the Pharisees also came unto him tempting him, &c.*

[*It hath been said.*] What hitherto hath been spoke upon the law of God touching matrimony or divorce, he who will deny to have been argued according to reason and all equity of Scripture, I cannot edify how, or by what rule of proportion that man's virtue calculates, what his *elements*[145] are, nor what his *analytics*.[146] Confidently to those who have read good books, and to those whose reason is not an illiterate book to themselves, I appeal, whether they would not confess all this to be the commentary of truth and justice were it not for these recited words of our Savior. And if they take not back that which they thus grant, nothing sooner might persuade them that Christ here teaches no new precept, and nothing sooner might direct them to find his meaning, than to compare and measure it by the rules of nature and eternal righteousness, which no written law extinguishes, and the Gospel least of all. For what can be more opposite and disparaging to the covenant of love, of freedom, and of our manhood in grace, than to be made the yoking pedagogue of new severities, the scribe of syllables and rigid letters, not only grievous to the best of men, but different and strange from the light of reason in them, save only as they are fain to stretch and distort their apprehensions for fear of displeasing the verbal straightness of a text, which our own servile fear gives us not the leisure to understand aright. If the law of Christ shall be written in our hearts, as was promised to the Gospel, Jeremiah 31:33, how can this in the vulgar and superficial sense be a law of Christ, so far from being written in our hearts that it injures and disallows not only the free dictates of nature and moral law but of charity also and religion in our hearts. Our Savior's doctrine is, that the end and the fulfilling of every command is charity; no faith without it, no truth without it, no worship, no works pleasing to God but as they partake of charity. He himself sets us an example, breaking the solemnest and strictest ordinance of religious rest, and justified the breaking, not to cure a dying man, but such whose cure might without danger have been deferred.[147] And wherefore needs must the sick man's bed be carried home on that day by his appointment, and why were the disciples who could not forbear on that day to pluck the corn so industriously defended, but to show us that, if he preferred the slightest occasions of man's good before the observing of highest and severest ordinances, he gave us much more easy leave to break the intolerable yoke of a never well-joined wedlock for the removing of our heaviest afflictions. Therefore it is that the most evangelic precepts are given us in proverbial forms, to drive us from the letter, though we love ever to be sticking there. For no other cause did Christ assure us that whatsoever things we bind or slacken on Earth are so in Heaven, but to signify that the Christian arbitrament of charity is supreme decider of all controversy and supreme resolver of all Scripture; not as the Pope determines for his own tyranny, but as the church ought to determine for its own true liberty. Hence Eusebius,[148] not far from the beginning of his history, compares the state of Christians to that of Noah and the Patriarchs before the law. And this indeed was the reason why apostolic tradition in the ancient church was counted nigh equal to the written word, though it carried them at length awry, for want of considering that tradition was not left to be imposed as law but to be a pattern of that Christian prudence and liberty which holy men by right assumed of old: which truth was so evident that it found entrance even into the Council of Trent[149] when the point of tradition came to be discussed. And Marinaro,[150] a learned Carmelite,[151] for approaching too near the true cause that gave esteem to tradition, that is to say, the difference between the Old and New Testament, the one punctually prescribing written law, the other guiding by the inward spirit, was reprehended by

Cardinal *Pole*[152] as one that had spoken more worthy a German colloquy[153] than a general council. I omit many instances, many proofs and arguments of this kind, which alone would compile a just volume, and shall content me here to have shown briefly that the great and almost only commandment of the Gospel is to command nothing against the good of man, and much more no civil command against his civil good. If we understand not this, we are but cracked cymbals,[154] we do but tinkle, we know nothing, we do nothing, all the sweat of our most toilsome obedience will but mock us. And what we suffer superstitiously returns us no thanks. Thus medicining our eyes we need not doubt to see more into the meaning of these our Savior's words than many who have gone before us.

[*It hath been said, whosoever shall put away his wife.*] Our Savior was by the doctors of his time suspected of intending to dissolve the law. In this chapter, he wipes off this aspersion upon his accusers and shows how they were the law-breakers. In every commonwealth when it decays, corruption makes two main steps; first when men cease to do according to the inward and uncompelled actions of virtue, caring only to live by the outward constraint of law, and turn the simplicity of real good into the craft of seeming so by law. To this hypocritical honesty was Rome declined in that age wherein Horace lived, and discovered it to Quintius:

> Whom do we count a good man, whom but he
> Who keeps the laws and statutes of the Senate,
> Who judges in great suits and controversies,
> Whose witness and opinion wins the cause;
> But his own house, and the whole neighborhood
> Sees his foul inside through his whited skin.[155]

The next declining is, when law becomes now too strait for the secular manners, and those too loose for the cincture of law. This brings in false and crooked interpretations to eke out law, and invents the subtle encroachment of obscure traditions hard to be disproved. To both these descents the Pharisees themselves were fallen. Our Savior therefore shows them both where they broke the law, in not marking the divine intent thereof but only the letter, and where they depraved the letter also with sophistical expositions. This law of divorce they had depraved both ways. First, by teaching that to give a bill of divorce was all the duty which that law required, whatever the cause were. Next, by running to divorce for any trivial, accidental cause, whenas the law evidently stays in the grave causes of natural and immutable dislike. *It hath been said,* saith he, Christ doth not put any contempt or disesteem upon the law of Moses by citing it so briefly; for in the same manner God himself cites a law of greatest caution, Jeremiah 3:1, *They say if a man put away his wife, shall he return to her again, &c.* Nor doth he more abolish it than the law of swearing, cited next with the same brevity, and more appearance of contradicting. For divorce hath an exception left it, but we are charged there, as absolutely as words can charge us, *not to swear at all:* yet who denies the lawfulness of an oath, though here it be in no case permitted? And what shall become of his solemn protestation not to abolish one law, or one tittle[156] of any law, especially of those which he mentions in this chapter? And that he meant more particularly the not abolishing of Mosaic divorce is beyond all cavil manifest in Luke 16:17–18, where this clause against abrogating is inserted immediately before the sentence against divorce, as if it were called thither on purpose to defend the equity of this particular law against the foreseen rashness of common textuaries, who abolish laws as the rabble demolish images, in the zeal of their hammers oft violating the sepulchers of good men; like Pentheus in the tragedies, they see that for Thebes[157] which is not, and take that for superstition, as these men in the heat of their annulling perceive not how they abolish right, and equal, and justice, under the appearance of judicial. And yet are confessing all the while, that these sayings of Christ stand not in contradiction to the law of Moses but to the false doctrine of the Pharisees raised from thence; that the law of God is perfect, not liable to additions or diminutions; and Pareus accuses the Jesuit Maldonatus[158] of greatest falsity for limiting the perfection of that law only to the rudeness of the Jews. He adds, *that the law promiseth life to the performers thereof; therefore needs not perfecter precepts, than such as bring to life;*

that *if the corrections of Christ stand opposite, not to the corruptions of the Pharisees, but to the law itself of God, the heresy of Manes would follow, one God of the Old Testament and another of the New. That Christ saith not here except your righteousness exceed the righteousness of Moses's law, but of the scribes and Pharisees.*[159] That all this may be true, whither is common sense flown asquint if we can maintain that Christ forbid the Mosaic divorce utterly, and yet abolished not the law that permits it? For if the conscience only were checked, and the law not repealed, what means the fanatic boldness of this age, that dares tutor Christ to be more strict than he thought fit? Ye shall have the evasion, it was a judicial law. What could infancy and slumber have invented more childish? Judicial or not judicial, it was one of those laws expressly which he forewarned us with protestation, that his mind was not to abrogate; and if we mark the steerage of his words, what course they hold, we may perceive that what he protested not to dissolve (that he might faithfully and not deceitfully remove a suspicion from himself) was principally concerning the judicial law; for of that sort are all these here which he vindicates, except the last. Of the ceremonial law he told them true, that nothing of it should pass *until all were fulfilled.*[160] Of the moral law he knew the Pharisees did not suspect he meant to nullify that: for so doing would soon have undone his authority, and advanced theirs. Of the judicial law therefore chiefly this apology was meant: for how is that fulfilled longer than the common equity thereof remains in force? And how is this our Savior's defense of himself not made fallacious, if the Pharisees chief fear be lest he should abolish the judicial law, and he to satisfy them protests his good intention to the moral law. It is the general grant of divines that what in the judicial law is not merely judicial, but reaches to human equity in common, was never in the thought of being abrogated. If our Savior took away aught of law, it was the burdensome[161] of it, not the ease of burden; it was the bondage, not the liberty of any divine law that he removed: this he often professed to be the end of his coming. But what if the law of divorce be a moral law, as most certainly it is fundamentally, and hath been so proved in the reasons thereof. For though the giving of a bill may be judicial, yet the act of divorce is altogether conversant in good and evil, and so absolutely moral. So far as it is good, it never can be abolished being moral; so far as it is simply evil it never could be judicial, as hath been shewen at large in *The Doctrine of Divorce,* and will be reassumed anon. Whence one of these two necessities follow, that either it was never established or never abolished. Thus much may be enough to have said on this place. The following verse will be better unfolded in the 19. chapter, where it meets us again, after a large debatement on the question between our Savior and his adversaries.

Matt. 19.3, 4, &c

Verse 3. *And the Pharisees came unto him tempting him, and saying unto him.*

[*Tempting him.*] The manner of these men coming to our Savior, not to learn but to tempt him, may give us to expect that their answer will be such as is fittest for them, not so much a teaching as an entangling. No man, though never so willing or so well enabled to instruct, but if he discern his willingness and candor made use of to entrap him will suddenly draw in himself, and laying aside the facile vein of perspicuity will know his time to utter clouds and riddles; if he be not less wise than that noted fish,[162] whenas he should be not unwiser than the serpent. Our Savior at no time expressed any great desire to teach the obstinate and unteachable Pharisees; but when they came to tempt him, then least of all. As now about the liberty of divorce, so another time about the punishment of adultery[163] they came to sound him, and what satisfaction got they from his answer, either to themselves or to us, that might direct a law under the Gospel, new from that of Moses, unless we draw his absolution of adultery into an edict. So about the tribute, who is there can pick out a full solution, what and when we must give to Caesar, by the answer which he gave the Pharisees?[164] If we must give to Caesar that which is Caesar's, and all be Caesar's which hath his image, we must either new stamp our coin or we may go new stamp our foreheads with the superscription of slaves instead of freemen. Besides, it is a general precept, not only of

Christ but of all other sages, not to instruct the unworthy and the conceited who love tradition more than truth, but to perplex and stumble them purposely with contrived obscurities. No wonder then if they who would determine of divorce by this place have ever found it difficult, and unsatisfying through all the ages of the church, as Austin[165] himself and other great writers confess. Lastly it is manifest to be the principal scope of our Savior, both here and in the 5. of Matthew, to convince the Pharisees of what they being evil did licentiously, not to explain what others being good and blameless men might be permitted to do in case of extremity. Neither was it seasonable to talk of honest and conscientious liberty among them who had abused legal and civil liberty to uncivil license. We do not say to a servant what we say to a son; nor was it expedient to preach freedom to those who had transgressed in wantonness. When we rebuke a prodigal, we admonish him of thrift, not of magnificence or bounty. And to school a proud man we labor to make him humble, not magnanimous. So Christ to retort these arrogant inquisitors their own, took the course to lay their haughtiness under a severity which they deserved; not to acquaint them, or to make them judges either of the just man's right and privilege or of the afflicted man's necessity. And if we may have leave to conjecture, there is a likelihood offered us by Tertullian in his 4. against Marcion,[166] whereby it may seem very probable that the Pharisees had a private drift of malice against our Savior's life in proposing this question; and our Savior had a peculiar aim in the rigor of his answer, both to let them know the freedom of his spirit and the sharpness of his discerning. *This I must now show,* saith Tertullian, *whence our Lord deduced this sentence, and which way he directed it, whereby it will more fully appear that he intended not to dissolve Moses.* And thereupon tells us, that the vehemence of this our Savior's speech was chiefly darted against Herod and Herodias. The story is out of Josephus;[167] Herod had been a long time married to the daughter of Aretas, King of Petra, 'til happening on his journey toward Rome to be entertained at his brother Philip's house, he cast his eye unlawfully and unguestlike upon Herodias there, the wife of Philip, but daughter of Aristobulus their common brother, and durst make words of marrying her his niece from his brother's bed. She assented, upon agreement he should expel his former wife. All was accomplished, and by the Baptist rebuked with the loss of his head. Though doubtless that stayed not the various discourses of men upon the fact, which while the Herodian flatterers, and not a few perhaps among the Pharisees endeavored to defend by wresting the law, it might be a means to bring the question of divorce into a hot agitation among the people, how far Moses gave allowance. The Pharisees therefore, knowing our Savior to be a friend of John the Baptist, and no doubt but having heard much of his Sermon in the Mount, wherein he spake rigidly against the license of divorce, they put him this question, both in hope to find him a contradicter of Moses and a condemner of Herod, so to ensnare him within compass of the same accusation which had ended his friend; and our Savior so orders his answer, as that they might perceive Herod and his adulteress only not named, so lively it concerned them both what he spake. No wonder then if the sentence of our Savior sounded stricter than his custom was: which his conscious attempters doubtless apprehended sooner than his other auditors. Thus much we gain from hence to inform us, that what Christ intends to speak here of divorce, will be rather the forbidding of what we may not do herein passionately and abusively, as *Herod* and *Herodias* did, than the discussing of what herein we may do reasonably and necessarily.

[*Is it lawful for a man to put away his wife.*][168] It might be rendered more exactly from the Greek, *to loosen or to set free;* which though it seem to have milder signification than the two Hebrew words commonly used for divorce, yet interpreters have noted that the Greek also is read in the Septuagint, for an act which is not without constraint. As when Achish drove from his presence David, counterfeiting madness, Psal. 34. The Greek word is the same with this here, *to put away.* And Erasmus quotes Hilary,[169] rendering it by an expression not so soft. Whence may be doubted whether the Pharisees did not state this question in the strict right of the man, not tarrying for the wife's consent. And if our Savior answer directly according to what was asked in the term of putting away, it may be questionable whether the rigor of his sentence did not forbid only such putting away as is without mutual consent, in a violent and harsh manner, or without any reason but will, as the Tetrarch did. Which might be the cause that those Christian emperors feared not in their constitutions to dissolve marriage by mutual consent: in that our Savior seems here, as the case is most likely, not to condemn all divorce but all injury and violence in divorce. But no injury can be done to them who seek it, as the *Ethics* of Aristotle[170] sufficiently prove. True it is, that an unjust thing may be done to one though willing, and so may justly be forbidden: But divorce being in itself no unjust or evil thing, but only as it is joined with injury, or lust, injury it cannot be at law, if consent be, and Aristotle err not. And lust it may as frequently not be, while charity hath the judging of so many private grievances in a misfortuned wedlock, which may pardonably seek a redemption. But whether it be or not, the law cannot discern or examine lust, so long as it walks from one lawful term to another, from divorce to marriage, both in themselves indifferent. For if the law cannot take hold to punish many actions apparently covetous, ambitious, ingrateful, proud, how can it forbid and punish that for lust, which is but only surmised so, and can no more be certainly proved in the divorcing now than before in the marrying. Whence if divorce be no unjust thing but through lust, a cause not discernable by law as law is wont to discern in other cases, and can be no injury where consent is, there can be nothing in the equity of law why divorce by consent may not be lawful: leaving secrecies to conscience, the thing which our Savior here aims to rectify, not to revoke the statutes of Moses. In the meanwhile the word *to put away,* being in the Greek *to loosen or dissolve,* utterly takes away that vain papistical distinction of divorce from bed and divorce from bond, evincing plainly that Christ and the Pharisees mean here that divorce which finally dissolves the bond, and frees both parties to a second marriage.

[*For every cause.*] This the Pharisees held, that for every cause they might divorce, for every accidental cause and quarrel of difference that might happen. So both Josephus[171] and Philo,[172] men who lived in the same age, explain; and the Syriac translator,[173] whose antiquity is thought parallel to the Evangelists themselves, reads it conformably *upon any occasion or pretence*. Divines also generally agree that thus the Pharisees meant. Cameron, a late writer much applauded, commenting this place not undiligently, affirms that the Greek preposition *κατὰ* translated unusually (*for*) hath a force in it implying the suddenness of those Pharisaic divorces; and that their question was to this effect, *whether for any cause, whatever it chanced to be, straight as it rose, the divorce might be lawful*. This he freely gives, whatever moved him, and I as freely take, nor can deny his observation to be acute and learned. If therefore we insist upon the word of *putting away*, that it imports a constraint without consent, as might be insisted, and may enjoy what Cameron[174] bestows on us, that for every cause is to be understood *according as any cause may happen*, with a relation to the speediness of those divorces, and that Herodian act especially, as is already brought us, the sentence of our Savior will appear nothing so strict a prohibition as hath been long conceived, forbidding only to divorce for casual and temporary causes, that may be soon ended or soon remedied; and likewise forbidding to divorce rashly, and on the sudden heat, except it be for adultery. If these qualifications may be admitted, as partly we offer them, partly are offered them by some of their own opinion, and that where nothing is repugnant why they should not be admitted, nothing can wrest them from us, the severe sentence of our Savior will straight unbend the seeming frown into that gentleness and compassion which was so abundant in all his actions, his office and his doctrine, from all which otherwise it stands off at no mean distance.

Verse 4. *And he answered and said unto them, have ye not read that he which made them at the beginning, made them male and female?*

Verse 5. *And said, for this cause shall a man leave father and mother, and shall cleave to his wife, and they twain shall be one flesh?*

Verse 6. *Wherefore they are no more twain but one flesh, what therefore God hath joined together, let no man put asunder.*

[4. and 5. *Made them male and female, and said, for this cause, &c.*] We see it here undeniably, that the law which our Savior cites to prove that divorce was forbidden is not an absolute and tyrannical command without reason, as nowadays we make it little better, but is grounded upon some rational cause not difficult to be apprehended, being in a matter which equally concerns the meanest and the plainest sort of persons in a household life. Our next way then will be to inquire if there be not more reasons than one, and if there be, whether this be the best and chiefest. That we shall find by turning to the first institution, to which Christ refers our own reading; he himself having to deal with treacherous assailants, uses brevity, and lighting on the first place in Genesis that mentions any thing tending to marriage in the first chapter, joins it immediately to the 24 verse of the 2 chapter, omitting all the prime words between, which create the institution, and contain the noblest and purest ends of matrimony, without which attained, that conjunction hath nothing in it above what is common to us with beasts. So likewise beneath in this very chapter, to the young man who came not tempting him but to learn of him, asking him which commandments he should keep, he neither repeats the first table, nor all the second, nor that in order which he repeats. If here then being tempted, he desire to be the shorter and the darker in his conference, and omit to cite that from the second of Genesis, which all divines confess is a commentary to what he cites out of the first, the *making them Male and Female;* what are we to do but to search the institution ourselves, and we shall find there his own authority giving other manner of reasons why such firm union is to be in matrimony, without which reasons their being male and female can be no cause of joining them inseparably: for if it be, then no adultery can sever. Therefore the prohibition of divorce depends not upon this reason here expressed to the Pharisees, but upon the plainer and more eminent causes omitted here and referred to the institution; which causes not being found in a particular and casual matrimony, this sensitive and materious[175] cause alone can no more hinder a divorce against those higher and more human reasons urging it than it can alone without them to warrant a copulation, but leaves arbitrary to those who in their chance of marriage find not why divorce is forbid them but why it is permitted them; and find both here and in Genesis, that the forbidding is not absolute but according to the reasons there taught us, not here. And that our Savior taught them no better, but uses the most vulgar, most animal and corporeal argument to convince them, is first to show us, that as through their licentious divorces they made no more of marriage than as if to marry were no more than to be male and female, so he goes no higher in his confutation; deeming them unworthy to be talked with in a higher strain, but to be tied in marriage by the mere material cause thereof, since their own license testified that nothing matrimonial was in their thought but to be male and female. Next it might be done to discover the brute ignorance of these carnal doctors who, taking on them to dispute of marriage and divorce, were put to silence with such a slender opposition as this, and outed from their hold with scarce one quarter of an argument. That we may believe this, his entertainment of the young man soon after may persuade us. Whom, though he came to preach eternal life by faith only, he dismisses with a salvation taught him by his works only. On which place *Pareus* notes *that this man was to be convinced by a false persuasion; and that Christ is wont otherwise to answer hypocrites, otherwise those that are docible.*[176] Much rather then may we think that, in handling these tempters, he forgot not so to frame his prudent ambiguities and concealments as was to the troubling of those peremptory disputants most wholesome. When therefore we would know what right there may be, in ill accidents, to divorce, we must repair thither where God professes to teach his servants by the prime institution, and not where we see him intending to dazzle sophisters. We must not read *he made them male and female* and not understand he made them more intendedly a meet help to remove the evil of being alone. We must take both these together, and then we may infer completely as from the whole cause why a man shall cleave to his wife, and they twain shall be one flesh. But if the full and chief cause why we may not divorce be wanting here, this place may skirmish with the rabbis while it will, but to the true Christian it prohibits nothing beyond the full reason of its own prohibiting, which is best known by the institution.

[Verse 6. *Wherefore they are no more twain, but one flesh.*] This is true in the general right of marriage but not in the chance medley of every particular match. For if they who were once undoubtedly one flesh yet become twain by adultery, then sure they who were never one flesh rightly, never helps meet for each other according to the plain prescript of God, may with less ado than a volume be concluded still twain. And so long as we account a magistrate no magistrate if there be but a flaw in his election, why should we not much rather count a matrimony no matrimony if it cannot be in any reasonable manner according to the words of God's institution?

[*What therefore God hath joined, let no man put asunder.*] But here the Christian prudence lies to consider what God hath joined. Shall we say that God hath joined error, fraud, unfitness, wrath, contention, perpetual loneliness, perpetual discord. Whatever lust, or wine, or witchery, threat, or enticement, avarice or ambition hath joined together, faithful with unfaithful, Christian with anti-Christian, hate with hate, or hate with love, shall we say this is God's joining?

[*Let not man put asunder.*] That is to say, what God hath joined; for if it be, as how oft we see it may be, not of God's joining, and his law tells us he joins not unmatchable things, but hates to join them as an abominable confusion, then the divine law of Moses puts them asunder, his own divine will in the institution puts them asunder, as oft as the reasons be not extant for which God ordained their joining. Man only puts asunder when his inordinate desires, his passion, his violence, his injury makes the breach: not when the utter want of that which lawfully was the end of his joining, when wrongs, and extremities, and unsupportable grievances compel him to disjoin. When such as Herod and the Pharisees divorce beside law, or against law, then only man separates, and to such only this prohibition belongs. In a word, if it be unlawful for man to put asunder that which God hath joined, let man take heed it be not detestable to join that by compulsion which God hath put asunder.

Verse 7. *They say unto him, why did Moses then command to give a writing of divorcement, and to put her away?*

Verse 8. *He saith unto them, Moses because of the hardness of your hearts suffered you to put away your wives, but from the beginning it was not so.*

[*Moses because of the hardness of your hearts suffered you.*] Hence the divinity now current argues that this judicial Moses is abolished. But suppose it were so, though it hath been proved otherwise, the firmness of such right to divorce as here pleads is fetched from the prime institution, does not stand or fall with the judicial Jew, but is as moral as what is moralest. Yet as I have shown positively that this law cannot be abrogated, both by the words of our Savior pronouncing the contrary and by that unabolishable equity which it conveys to us, so I shall now bring to view those appearances of strength which are levied from this text to maintain the most gross and massy paradox that ever did violence to reason and religion, bred only under the shadow of these words, to all other piety or philosophy strange and insolent, that God by act of law drew out a line of adultery almost two thousand years long, although to detect the prodigy[177] of this surmise, the former book set forth on this argument hath already been copious. I shall not repeat much, though I might borrow of mine own, but shall endeavor to add something either yet untouched or not largely enough explained. First, it shall be manifest that the common exposition cannot possibly consist with Christian doctrine; next, a truer meaning of this our Savior's reply shall be left in the room. The received exposition is, that God though not approving did enact a law to permit adultery by divorcement simply unlawful. And this conceit they feed with fond supposals that have not the least footing in Scripture. As that the Jews learned this custom of divorce in Egypt, and therefore God would not unteach it them 'til Christ came, but let it stick as a notorious botch of deformity in the midst of his most perfect and severe law. And yet he saith, Levit. the 18, *after the doings of Egypt ye shall not do*. Another while they invent a slander (as what thing more bold than teaching ignorance when he shifts to hide his nakedness) that the Jews were naturally to their wives the cruelest men in the world: would poison, brain, and do I know not what, if they might not divorce. Certain, if it were a fault heavily punished to bring an evil report upon the land which God gave, what is it to raise a groundless calumny against the people which God made choice of? But that this bold interpretament, how commonly soever sided with, cannot stand a minute with any competent reverence to God or his law, or his people, nor with any other maxim of religion, or good manners, might be proved through all the heads and topics of argumentation; but I shall willingly be as concise as possible. First the law, not only the moral but the judicial, given by Moses is just and pure; for such is God who gave it. *Hearken O Israel,* saith Moses, Deut. 4, *unto the statutes and the judgments which I teach you, to do them, that ye may live, &c. Ye shall not add unto the word which I command you, neither shall ye diminish aught from it, that ye may keep the commandments of the Lord your God which I command you.* And onward in this chapter, *Behold I have taught you statutes and judgments, even as the Lord my God commanded me. Keep therefore and do them, for this is your wisdom and your understanding. For what nation hath God so nigh unto them, and what nation hath statutes and judgments so righteous as all this law which I set before ye this day.* Is it imaginable there should be among these a law which God allowed not, a law giving permissions laxative[178] to unmarry a wife and marry a lust, a law to suffer a kind of tribunal adultery? Many other scriptures might be brought to assert the purity of this judicial law, and many I have alleged before; this law therefore is pure and just. But if it permit, if it teach, if it defend that which is both unjust and impure, as by the common doctrine it doth, what think we? The three general doctrines of Justinian's law are *To live in honesty, to hurt no man, to give every one his due.*[179] Shall the Roman civil law observe these three things as the only end of law, and shall a statute be found in the civil law of God enacted simply and totally against all these three precepts of nature and morality?

Secondly, the gifts of God are all perfect, and certainly the law is of all his other gifts one of the perfetest. But if it give that outwardly which it takes away really, and give that seemingly which, if a man take it, wraps him into sin and damns him, what gift of an enemy can be more dangerous and destroying than this.

Thirdly, Moses everywhere commends his laws, prefers them before all of other nations, and warrants them to be the way of life and safety to all that walk therein, Levit. 18. But if they contain statutes which God approves not, and train men unwitting to commit injustice and adultery under the shelter of law, if those things be sin, and death sin's wages, what is this law but the snare of death?

Fourthly, The statutes and judgments of the Lord, which without exception are often told us to be such as doing we may live by them, are doubtless to be counted the rule of knowledge and of conscience. *For I had not known lust,* saith the Apostle, *but by the law.*[180] But if the law come down from the state of her incorruptible majesty to grant lust his boon, palpably it darkens and confounds both knowledge and conscience; it goes against the common office of all goodness and friendliness, which is at least to counsel and admonish; it subverts the rules of all sober education, and is itself a most negligent and debauching tutor.

Fifthly, if the law permit a thing unlawful, it permits that which elsewhere it hath forbid; so that hereby it contradicts itself, and transgresses itself. But if the law become a transgressor, it stands guilty to itself, and how then shall it save another; it makes a confederacy with sin, how then can it justly condemn a sinner? and thus reducing itself to the state of neither saving nor condemning, it will not fail to expire, solemnly ridiculous.

Sixthly, the prophets in Scripture declare severely against the decreeing of that which is unjust, Psal. 94: 20, Isaiah the 10th. But it was done, they say, for hardness of heart; to which objection the Apostle's rule, *not to do evil that good may come thereby,*[181] gives an invincible repulse: and here especially, where it cannot be shown how any good came by doing this evil, how rather more evil did not hereon abound; for the giving way to hardness of heart hardens the more, and adds more to the number. God to an evil and adulterous generation would not grant a sign,[182] much less would he for their hardness of heart pollute his law with adulterous permission. Yea, but to permit evil is not to do evil. Yes, it is in a most eminent manner to do evil: where else are all our grave and faithful sayings, that he whose office is to forbid and forbids not, bids, exhorts, encourages. Why hath God denounced his anger against parents, masters, friends, magistrates neglectful of forbidding what they ought, if law, the common father, master, friend, and perpetual magistrate, shall not only forbid, but enact, exhibit, and uphold with countenance and protection a deed every way dishonest, whatever the pretence be. If it were of those inward vices, which the law cannot by outward constraint remedy but leaves to conscience and persuasion, it had been guiltless in being silent; but to write a decree of that which can be no way lawful, and might with ease be hindered, makes law by the doom of law itself accessory in the highest degree.

Seventhly, it makes God the direct author of sin, for although he be not made the author of what he silently permits in his providence, yet in his law, the image of his will, when in plain expression he constitutes and ordains a fact utterly unlawful, what wants he to authorize it, and what wants that to be the author?

Eighthly, to establish by law a thing wholly unlawful and dishonest, is an affirmation was never heard of before in any law, reason, philosophy, or religion, 'til it was raised by inconsiderate glossists[183] from the mistake of this text. And though the civilians have been contented to chew this opinion after the canon had subdued them, yet they never could bring example or authority either from divine writ, or human learning, or human practice in any nation or well-formed republic, but only from the customary abuse of this text. Usually they allege the Epistle of Cicero to Atticus, wherein Cato is blamed for giving sentence to the scum of Romulus, as if he were in Plato's commonwealth. Cato could have called some great one into judgment for bribery; Cicero as the time stood, advised against it. Cato, not to endammage[184] the public treasury would not grant to the Roman knights that the Asian taxes might be farmed them at a less rate; Cicero wished it granted.[185] Nothing in all this will be like the establishing of a law to sin. Here are no laws made, here only the execution of law is craved might be suspended: between which and our question is a broad difference. And what if human lawgivers have confessed they could not frame their laws to that perfection which they desired? We hear of no such confession from *Moses* concerning the laws of God, but rather all praise and high testimony of perfection given them. And although man's nature cannot bear exactest laws, yet still within the confines of good it may and must; so long as less good is far enough from altogether evil. As for what they instance of usury, let them first prove usury to be wholly unlawful, as the law allows it; which learned men as numerous on the other side will deny them. Or if it be altogether unlawful, why is it tolerated more than divorce? He who said *divorce not,* said also *lend hoping for nothing again,* Luke 6:35. But then they put it, that trade could not stand, and so to serve the commodity of insatiable trading usury shall be permitted, but divorce, the only means oft-times to right the innocent and outrageously wronged, shall be utterly forbid. This is egregious doctrine, and for which one day charity will much thank them. Beza not finding how to salve this perplexity, and Cameron since him, would secure us; although the latter confesses that to *permit a wicked thing by law, is a wickedness which God abhors; yet to limit sin, and prescribe it a certain measure, is good.* First, this evasion will not help here. For this law bounded no man: he might put away whatever found not favor in his eyes. And how could it forbid to divorce whom it could not forbid to dislike, or command to love. If these be the limits of law to restrain sin, who so lame a sinner but may hop over them more easily than over those Romulean circumscriptions, not as Remus did with hard success,[186] but with all indemnity. Such a limiting as this were not worth the mischief that accompanies it. This law therefore not bounding the supposed sin, by permitting enlarges it, gives it enfranchisement. And never greater confusion than when law and sin move their landmarks, mix their territories, and correspond, have intercourse, and traffic together. When law contracts a kindred and hospitality with transgression, becomes the godfather of sin, and names it lawful; when sin revels and gossips within the arsenal of law, plays and dandles the artillery of justice that should be bent against her, this is a fair limitation indeed. Besides it is an absurdity to say that law can measure sin, or moderate sin; sin is not a predicament[187] to be measured and modified, but is always an excess. The least sin that is, exceeds the measure of the largest law that can be good, and is as boundless as that vacuity beyond the world. If once it square to the measure of law, it ceases to be an excess, and consequently ceases to be a sin; or else law conforming itself to the obliquity of sin, betrays itself to be not straight, but crooked, and so immediately no law. And the improper conceit of moderating sin by law will appear, if we can imagine any lawgiver so senseless as to decree that so far a man may steal, and thus far be drunk, that moderately he may cozen, and moderately commit adultery. To the same extent it would be as pithily absurd to publish that a man may moderately divorce, if to do that be entirely naught. But to end this moot, the law of Moses is manifest to fix no limit therein at all, or such at least as impeaches the fraudulent abuser no more than if it were not set; only requires the dismissive writing without other caution, leaves that to the inner man and the bar of conscience. But it stopped other sins. This is as vain as the rest, and dangerously uncertain: the contrary to be feared rather, that one sin admitted courteously by law opened the gate to another. However, evil must not be done for good. And it were a fall to be lamented, and an indignity unspeakable, if law should become tributary to Sin, her slave, and forced to yield up into his hands her awful minister Punishment, should buy out her peace with Sin for sin, paying as it were her so many Philistian foreskins[188] to the proud demand of Transgression. But suppose it any way possible to limit sin, to put a girdle about that chaos; suppose it also good: yet if to permit sin by law be an abomination in the eyes of God, as Cameron acknowledges, the evil of permitting will eat out the good of limiting. For though sin be not limited, there can but evil come out of evil; but if it be permitted and decreed lawfully by divine law, of force then sin must proceed from the infinite good, which is a dreadful thought. But if the restraining of sin, by this permission being good as this author testifies, be more good than the permission of more sin by the restraint of divorce, and that God, weighing both these like two ingots[189] in the perfect scales of his justice and providence, found them so, and others coming without authority from God shall change this counterpoise, and judge it better to let sin multiply by setting a judicial restraint upon divorce, which Christ never set, than to limit sin by this permission, as God himself thought best to permit it, it will behoove them to consult betimes whether these their balances be not false and abominable. And this their limiting that which God loosened, and their loosening the sins that he limited, which they confess was good to do, and were it possible to do by law, doubtless it would be most morally good; and they so believing, as we hear they do, and yet abolishing a law so good and moral, the limiter of sin, what are they else but contrary to themselves? For they can never bring us to that time wherein it will not be good to limit sin, and they can never limit it better than so as God prescribed in his law.

Others conceive it a more defensible retirement to say this permission to divorce sinfully for hardness of heart was a dispensation. But surely they either know not, or attend not to what a dispensation means. A dispensation is for no long time, is particular to some persons rather than general to whole people, always hath charity the end, is granted to necessities and infirmities, not to obstinate lust. This permission is another creature, hath all those evils and absurdities following the name of a dispensation, as when it was named a law; and is the very Antarctic pole against charity, nothing more adverse, ensnaring and ruining those that trust in it or use it; so lewd and criminous as never durst enter into the head of any politician, Jew, or proselyte, 'til they became the apt scholars of this canonistic exposition. Aught in it that can allude in the least manner to charity or goodness, belongs with more full right to the Christian under grace and liberty than to the Jew under law and bondage. To Jewish ignorance it could not be dispensed without a horrid imputation laid upon the law, to dispense foully instead of teaching fairly; like that dispensation that first polluted Christendom with idolatry, permitting to laymen images instead of books and preaching. Sloth or malice in the law would they have this called? But what ignorance can be pretended for the Jews, who had all the same precepts about marriage that we now: for Christ refers all to the institution. It was as reasonable for them to know then as for us now, and concerned them alike: for wherein hath the Gospel altered the nature of matrimony? All these considerations, or many of them, have been further amplified in *The Doctrine of Divorce*. And what Rivetus[190] and Pareus[191] hath objected or given over as past cure hath been there discussed. Whereby it may be plain enough to men of eyes, that the vulgar exposition of a permittance by law to an entire sin, whatever the color may be, is an opinion both ungodly, unpolitic, unvirtuous, and void of all honesty and civil sense. It appertains therefore to every zealous Christian both for the honor of God's laws, and the vindication of our Savior's words, that such an irreligious depravement no longer may be soothed and flattered through custom, but with all diligence and speed solidly refuted, and in the room a better explanation given; which is now our next endeavor.

[*Moses suffered you to put away, &c.*] Not commanded you, says the common observer, and therefore cared not how soon it were abolished, being but suffered; herein declaring his annotation to be slight and nothing law prudent. For in this place *commanded and suffered* are interchangeably used in the same sense both by our Savior and the Pharisees. Our Savior who here saith *Moses suffered you,* in the 10 of Mark saith *Moses wrote you this command*. And the Pharisees who here say *Moses commanded,* and would mainly have it a command, in that place of Mark say *Moses suffered,* which had made against them in their own mouths if the word of *suffering* had weakened the command. So that *suffered* and *commanded* is here taken for the same thing on both sides of the controversy, as Cameron also and others on this place acknowledge. And lawyers know that all the precepts of law are divided into obligatory and permissive, containing either what we must do or what we may do; and of this latter sort are as many precepts as of the former, and all as lawful. Tutelage, an ordainment than which nothing more just, being for the defense of orphans, the *Institutes* of Justinian say *is given and permitted by the civil law:* and *to parents it is permitted to choose and appoint by will the guardians of their children.* What more equal, and yet the civil law calls this *permission.* So likewise to *manumise,*[192] to adopt, to make a will, and to be made an heir is called *permission* by law. Marriage itself, and this which is already granted, to divorce for adultery, obliges no man, is but a permission by law, is but suffered. By this we may see how weakly it hath been thought that all divorce is utterly unlawful, because the law is said to *suffer* it: whenas to suffer is but the legal phrase denoting what by law a man may do or not do.

[*Because of the hardness of your hearts.*] Hence they argue that therefore he allowed it not; and therefore it must be abolished. But the contrary to this will sooner follow, that because he suffered it for a cause, therefore in relation to that cause he allowed it. Next, if he in his wisdom and in the midst of his severity allowed it for hardness of heart, it can be nothing better than arrogance and presumption to take stricter courses against hardness of heart than God ever set an example, and that under the Gospel which warrants them to no judicial act of compulsion in this matter, much less to be more severe against hardness of extremity than God thought good to be against hardness of heart. He suffered it, rather than worse inconveniences. These men, wiser as they make themselves, will suffer the worst and heinousest inconveniences to follow, rather than they will suffer what God suffered, although they can know when they please that Christ spoke only to the conscience, did not judge on the civil bench but always disavowed it. What can be more contrary to the ways of God than these their doings? If they be such enemies to hardness of heart, although this groundless rigor proclaims it to be in themselves, they may yet learn, or consider that hardness of heart hath a twofold acception in the Gospel. One, when it is in a good man taken for infirmity, and imperfection, which was in all the Apostles, whose weakness only, not utter want of belief, is called hardness of heart, Mark 16. Partly for this hardness of heart, the imperfection and decay of man from original righteousness, it was that God suffered not divorce only, but all that which by civilians is termed *the secondary law of nature and of nations.* He suffered his own people to waste and spoil and slay by war, to lead captives, to be some masters, some servants, some to be princes, others to be subjects; he suffered propriety to divide all things by several possession, trade and commerce, not without usury; in his commonwealth some to be undeservedly rich, others to be undeservingly poor. All which 'til hardness of heart came in, was most unjust; whenas prime nature made us all equal, made us equal coheirs by common right and dominion over all creatures. In the same manner, and for the same cause, he suffered divorce as well as marriage, our imperfect and degenerate condition of necessity requiring this law among the rest, as a remedy against intolerable wrong and servitude above the patience of man to bear. Nor was it given only because our infirmity, or if it must be so called, hardness of heart could not endure all things, but because the hardness of another's heart might not inflict all things upon an innocent person, whom far other ends brought into a league of love and not of bondage and indignity. If therefore we abolish divorce as only suffered for hardness of heart, we may as well abolish the whole law of nations, as only suffered for the same cause; it being shown us by Saint Paul 1 Cor. 6 that the very seeking of a man's right by law, and at the hands of a worldly magistrate, is not without the hardness of our hearts. *For why do ye not rather take wrong,* saith he, *why suffer ye not rather yourselves to be defrauded?* If nothing now must be suffered for hardness of heart, I say the very prosecution of our right by way of civil justice can no more be suffered among Christians for the hardness of heart wherewith most men pursue it. And that would next remove all our judicial laws, and this restraint of divorce also in the number; which would more than half end the controversy. But if it be plain that the whole juridical law and civil power is only suffered under the Gospel for the hardness of our hearts, then wherefore should not that which Moses suffered be suffered still by the same reason?

In a second signification, hardness of heart is taken for a stubborn resolution to do evil. And that God ever makes any law purposely to such, I deny: for he vouchsafes not to enter covenant with them, but as they fortune to be mixed with good men and pass undiscovered; much less that he should decree an unlawful thing only to serve their licentiousness. But that God suffers this reprobate hardness of heart I affirm, not only in this law of divorce but throughout all his best and purest commandments. He commands all to worship in singleness of heart according to all his ordinances, and yet suffers the wicked man to perform all the rites of religion hypocritically and in the hardness of his heart. He gives us general statutes and privileges in all civil matters, just and good of themselves, yet suffers unworthiest men, to use them and by them to prosecute their own right, or any color of right, though for the most part maliciously, covetously, rigorously, revengefully. He allowed by law the discreet father and husband to forbid, if he thought fit, the religious vows of his wife or daughter, Num. 30, and in the same law suffered the hard-heartedness of impious and covetous fathers or husbands abusing this law to forbid their wives or daughters in their offerings and devotions of greatest zeal. If then God suffer hardness of heart equally in the best laws as in this of divorce, there can be no reason that for this cause this law should be abolished. But other laws, they object, may be well used, this never. How often shall I answer both from the institution of marriage, and from other general rules in Scripture, that this law of divorce hath many wise and charitable ends besides the being suffered for hardness of heart, which is indeed no end but an accident happening through the whole law; which gives to good men right and to bad men who abuse right under false pretences, gives only sufferance. Now although Christ express no other reasons here but only what was suffered, it nothing follows that this law had no other reason to be permitted but for hardness of heart. The Scripture seldom or never in one place sets down all the reasons of what it grants or commands, especially when it talks to enemies and tempters. Saint Paul permitting marriage, 1 Corinthians 7:2, seems to permit even that also for hardness of heart only, lest we should run into fornication; yet no intelligent man thence concludes marriage allowed in the Gospel only to avoid an evil because no other end is there expressed. Thus *Moses* of necessity suffered many to put away their wives for hardness of heart; but enacted the law of divorce doubtless for other good causes, not for this only sufferance. He permitted not divorce by law as an evil, for that was impossible to divine law, but permitted by accident the evil of them who divorced against the law's intention undiscoverably. This also may be thought not improbably, that Christ stirred up in his Spirit against these tempting Pharisees, answered them in a certain form of indignation usual among good authors; whereby the question or the truth is not directly answered, but something which is fitter for them, who ask, to hear. So in the ecclesiastical stories one demanding how God employed himself before the world was made, had answer: that he was making Hell for curious questioners.[193] Another (and Libanius the Sophist as I remember) asking in derision some Christian, what the carpenter, meaning our Savior, was doing, now that Julian so prevailed, had it returned him, that the carpenter was making a coffin for the apostate.[194] So Christ, being demanded maliciously why Moses made the law of divorce, answers them in a vehement scheme,[195] not telling them the cause why he made it, but what was fittest to be told them, that *for the hardness of their hearts* he suffered them to abuse it. And albeit Mark say not he suffered you, but *to you he wrote this precept;* Mark may be warrantably expounded by Matthew the larger. And whether he suffered, or gave precept, being all one as was heard, it changes not the trope of indignation, fittest account for such askers. Next for the hardness of *your hearts to you he wrote this precept,* infers not therefore for this cause only he wrote it, as was paralleled by other Scriptures. Lastly, it may be worth the observing, that Christ speaking to the Pharisees does not say in general that for hardness of heart he gave this precept, but you he suffered, and to you he gave this precept for your hardness of heart. It cannot be easily thought that Christ here included all the children of Israel under the person of these tempting Pharisees but that he conceals wherefore he gave the better sort of them this law, and expresses by saying emphatically *To you* how he gave it to the worser, such as the Pharisees best represented, that is to say for the hardness of your hearts: as indeed to wicked men and hardened hearts he gives the whole law and the Gospel also, to harden them the more. Thus many ways it may orthodoxally be understood how God or Moses suffered such as the demanders were, to divorce for hardness of heart; whereas the vulgar expositor, beset with contradictions and absurdities round and resolving at any peril to make an exposition of it, as there is nothing more violent and boisterous than a reverend ignorance in fear to be convicted, rushes brutely and impetuously against all the principles both of nature, piety, and moral goodness, and in the fury of his literal expounding overturns them all.

[*But from the beginning it was not so.*] Not how from the beginning do they suppose, that men might not divorce at all, not necessarily, not deliberately except for adultery, but that some law, like canon law, presently attached them both before and after the flood, 'til stricter Moses came, and with law brought license into the world? That were a fancy indeed to smile at. Undoubtedly as to point of judicial law, divorce was more permissive from the beginning before Moses than under Moses. But from the beginning, that is to say, by the institution in Paradise, it was not intended that matrimony should dissolve for every trivial cause as you Pharisees accustom. But that it was not thus suffered from the beginning ever since the race of men corrupted, and laws were made, he who will affirm must have found out other antiquities than are yet known. Besides we must consider now, what can be so as from the beginning, not only what should be so. In the beginning, had men continued perfect, it had been just that all things should have remained as they began to Adam and Eve. But after that the sons of men grew violent and injurious, it altered the lore of justice, and put the government of things into a new frame. While man and woman were both perfect each to other, there needed no divorce; but when they both degenerated to imperfection, and oft-times grew to be an intolerable evil each to other, then law more justly did permit the alienating of that evil which mistake made proper than it did the appropriating of that good which nature at first made common. For if the absence of outward good be not so bad as the presence of a close evil, and that propriety, whether by covenant or possession, be but the attainment of some outward good, it is more natural and righteous that the law should sever us from an intimate evil than appropriate any outward good to us from the community of nature. The Gospel indeed, tending ever to that which is perfetest, aimed at the restorement of all things as they were in the beginning. And therefore all things were in common to those primitive Christians in the Acts, which Ananias and Sapphira[196] dearly felt. That custom also continued more or less 'til the time of Justin Martyr, as may be read in his second *Apology,* which might be writ after that act of communion perhaps some forty years above a hundred.[197] But who will be the man that shall introduce this kind of commonwealth, as Christianity now goes? If then marriage must be as in the beginning, the persons that marry must be such as then were, the institution must make good, in some tolerable sort, what it promises to either party. If not, it is but madness to drag this one ordinance back to the beginning, and draw down all other to the present necessity and condition far from the beginning, even to the tolerating of extortions and oppressions. Christ only told us that from the beginning it was not so; that is to say, not so as the Pharisees manured[198] the business; did not command us that it should be forcibly so again in all points as at the beginning, or so at least in our intentions and desires, but so in execution as reason and present nature can bear. Although we are not to seek, that the institution itself from the first beginning was never but conditional, as all covenants are: because thus and thus, therefore so and so; if not thus, then not so. Then moreover was perfetest to fulfill each law in itself; now is perfetest in this estate of things, to ask of charity how much law may be fulfilled: else the fulfilling oft-times is the greatest breaking. If any therefore demand which is now most perfection, to ease an extremity by divorce, or to enrage and fester it by the grievous observance of a miserable wedlock, I am not destitute to say which is most perfection (although some who believe they think favorably of divorce, esteem it only venial to infirmity). Him I hold more in the way to perfection who forgoes an unfit, ungodly, and discordant wedlock, to live according to peace and love, and God's institution in a fitter choice, than he who debars himself the happy experience of all godly, which is peaceful conversation in his family, to live a contentious and un-Christian life not to be avoided, in temptations not to be lived in, only for the false keeping of a most unreal nullity, a marriage that hath no affinity with God's intention, a daring phantasm, a mere toy of terror awing weak senses, to the lamentable superstition of ruining themselves; the remedy whereof God in his law vouchsafes us. Which not to dare use, he warranting, is not our perfection, is our infirmity, our little faith, our timorous and low conceit of charity; and in them who force us, it is their masking pride and vanity to seem holier and more circumspect than God. So far is it that we need impute to him infirmity, who thus divorces: since the rule of perfection is not so much that which was done in the beginning, as that which now is nearest to the rule of charity. This is the greatest, the perfetest, the highest commandment.

Verse 9. *And I say unto you, whoso shall put away his wife, except it be for fornication, and shall marry another, committeth adultery; and whoso marrieth her which is put away, doth commit adultery.*

[*And I say unto you.*] That this restrictive denouncement of Christ contradicts and refutes that permissive precept of Moses, common expositors themselves disclaim; and that it does not traverse from the closet of conscience to the courts of civil or canon law, with any Christian rightly commenced requires not long evincing. If Christ then did not here check permissive Moses, nor did reduce matrimony to the beginning more than all other things, as the reason of man's condition could bear, we would know precisely what it was which he did, and what the end was of his declaring thus austerely against divorce. For this is a confessed oracle in law, that he who looks not at the intention of a precept, the more superstitious he is of the letter, the more he misinterprets. Was it to shame Moses? That had been monstrous. Or all those purest ages of Israel, to whom the permission was granted? That were as incredible. Or was it that he who came to abrogate the burden of law, not the equity, should put this yoke upon a blameless person, to league himself in chains with a begirting[199] mischief, not to separate 'til death? He who taught us that no man puts a piece of new cloth upon an old garment, nor new wine into old bottles, that he should sew this patch of strictness upon the old apparel of our frailty, to make a rent more incurable, whenas in all other amendments his doctrine still charges, that regard be had to the garment, and to the vessel, what it can endue; this were an irregular and single piece of rigor, not only sounding disproportion to the whole Gospel, but outstretching the most rigorous nerves of law and rigor itself. No other end therefore can be left imaginable of this excessive restraint, but to bridle those erroneous and licentious postillers[200] the Pharisees; not by telling them what may be done in necessity, but what censure they deserve who divorce abusively, which their Tetrarch[201] had done. And as the offence was in one extreme, so the rebuke, to bring more efficaciously to a rectitude and mediocrity, stands not in the middle way of duty but in the other extreme. Which art of powerful reclaiming, wisest men have also taught in their ethical precepts and gnomologies;[202] resembling it, as when we bend a crooked wand the contrary way; not that it should stand so bent, but that the overbending might reduce it to a straightness by its own reluctance. And as the physician cures him who hath taken down poison, not by the middling temper of nourishment but by the other extreme of antidote, so Christ administers here a sharp and corrosive sentence against a foul and putrid license; not to eat into the flesh, but into the sore. And knowing that our divines through all their comments make no scruple, where they please, to soften the high and vehement speeches of our Savior, which they call hyperboles, why in this one text should they be such crabbed Masorites[203] of the letter, as not to mollify a transcendence of literal rigidity which they confess to find often elsewhere in his manner of delivery, but must make their exposition here such an obdurate Cyclops, to have but one eye for this text, and that only open to cruelty and enthrallment, such as no divine or human law before ever heard of. No, let the foppish canonist, with his fardel[204] of matrimonial cases, go and be vendible[205] where men be so unhappy as to cheapen him: the words of Christ shall be asserted from such elemental notaries, and resolved by the now-only lawgiving mouth of charity; which may be done undoubtedly by understanding them as follows.

[*Whosoever shall put away his wife.*] That is to say, shall so put away as the propounders of this question, the Pharisees, were wont to do, and covertly defended Herod for so doing; whom to rebuke, our Savior here mainly intends, and not to determine all the cases of divorce, as appears by Saint Paul.[206] Whosoever shall put away, either violently without mutual consent for urgent reasons, or conspiringly by plot of lust, or cunning malice, shall put away for any sudden mood, or contingency of disagreement, which is not daily practice but may blow soon over and be reconciled, except it be fornication; whosoever shall put away rashly, as his choler prompts him, without due time of deliberating, and think his conscience discharged only by the bill of divorce given and the outward law satisfied; whosoever lastly shall put away his wife, that is a wife indeed, and not in name only, such a one who both can and is willing to be a meet help toward the chief ends of marriage both civil and sanctified, except fornication be the cause, that man, or that pair, commit adultery. Not he who puts away by mutual consent, with all the considerations and respects of humanity and gentleness without malicious or lustful drift. Not he who after sober and cool experience, and long debate within himself, puts away whom, though he cannot love or suffer as a wife with that sincere affection that marriage requires, yet loves at least with that civility and goodness as not to keep her under a neglected and unwelcome residence, where nothing can be hearty, and not being, it must needs be both unjoyous and injurious to any perceiving person so detained, and more injurious than to be freely and upon good terms dismissed. Nor doth he put away adulterously who complains of causes rooted in immutable nature: utter unfitness, utter disconformity, not concilable because not to be amended without a miracle. Nor he who puts away an unquenchable vexation from his bosom, and flies an evil than which a greater cannot befall human society. Nor he who puts away with the full suffrage and applause of his conscience, not relying on the written bill of law but claiming by faith and fullness of persuasion the rights and promises of

God's institution, of which he finds himself in a mistaken wedlock defrauded. Doubtless this man hath bail enough to be no adulterer giving divorce for these causes.

[*His Wife.*] This word is not to be idle here, a mere word without a sense, much less a fallacious word signifying contrary to what it pretends, but faithfully signifies a wife, that is, a comfortable help and society, as God instituted; does not signify deceitfully under this name an intolerable adversary, not a helpless, unaffectionate and sullen mass, whose very company represents the visible and exactest figure of loneliness itself. Such an associate he who puts away, divorces not a wife but disjoins a nullity which God never joined, if she be neither willing nor to her proper and requisite duties sufficient, as the words of God institute her. And this also is Bucer's explication of this place.[207]

[*Except it be for fornication, or saving for the cause of fornication, as Mat. 5.*] This declares what kind of causes our Savior meant: fornication being no natural and perpetual cause, but only accidental and temporary, therefore shows that head of causes from whence it is excepted to be meant of the same sort. For exceptions are not logically deduced from a diverse kind, as to say whoso puts away for any natural cause except fornication, the exception would want salt. And if they understand it, whoso for any cause whatever, they cast[208] themselves; granting divorce for frigidity, a natural cause of their own allowing, though not here expressed, and for desertion without infidelity, whenas he who marries, as they allow him for desertion, deserts as well as is deserted, and finally puts away for another cause besides adultery. It will with all due reason therefore be thus better understood: whoso puts away for any accidental and temporary causes, except one of them, which is fornication. Thus this exception finds out the causes from whence it is excepted to be of the same kind, that is casual, not continual.

[*Saving for the cause of fornication.*] The New Testament, though it be said originally writ in Greek, yet hath nothing near so many Atticisms as Hebraisms, and Syriacisms,[209] which was the majesty of God, not filing[210] the tongue of Scripture to a Gentilish *idiom,* but in a princely manner offering to them as to Gentiles and foreigners grace and mercy, though not in foreign words yet in a foreign style that might induce them to the fountains; and though their calling were high and happy, yet still to acknowledge God's ancient people their betters, and that language the metropolitan language. He therefore who thinks to scholiaze[211] upon the Gospel, though Greek, according to his Greek analogies, and hath not been auditor to the oriental dialects, shall want in the heat of his analysis no accommodation to stumble. In this place, as the 5 of Mat. reads it, *saving for the cause of fornication,* the Greek, such as it is, sounds it, except for the *word, report, speech, or proportion* of fornication. In which regard with other inducements, many ancient and learned writers have understood this exception as comprehending any fault equivalent and proportional to fornication. But truth is, the Evangelist here Hebraizes,[212] taking *word* or *speech* for *cause* or *matter* in the common eastern phrase, meaning perhaps no more than if he had said for fornication, as in this 19th chapter. And yet the word is found in the 5th of Exodus also signifying proportion; where the Israelites are commanded to do their tasks, *the matter of each day in his day.* A task we know is a proportion of work not doing the same thing absolutely every day, but so much. Whereby it may be doubtful yet, whether here be not excepted not only fornication itself, but other causes equipollent[213] and proportional to fornication. Which very word also to understand rightly, we must of necessity have recourse again to the Hebrew. For in the Greek and Latin sense by fornication is meant the common prostitution of body for sale. So that they who are so exact for the letter, shall be dealt with by the *Lexicon,* and the *Etymologicon* too if they please, and must be bound to forbid divorce for adultery also, until it come to open whoredom and trade, like that for which Claudius divorced Messalina.[214] Since therefore they take not here the word fornication in the common significance, for an open exercise in the stews,[215] but grant divorce for one single act of privatest adultery, notwithstanding that the word speaks a public and notorious frequency of fact, not without price, we may reason with as good leave, and as little straining to the text, that our Savior on set purpose chose this word fornication, improperly applied to the lapse of adultery, that we might not think ourselves bound from all divorce except when that fault hath been actually committed. For the language of Scripture signifies by fornication (and others besides St. Austin so expounded it)[216] not only the trespass of body nor perhaps that between married persons, unless in a degree or quality as shameless as the bordello, but signifies also any notable disobedience, or intractable carriage of the wife to the husband, as Judges 19:2, whereof at large in *The Doctrine of Divorce,* l. 2. c. 18. Secondly signifies the apparent alienation of mind not to idolatry (which may seem to answer the act of adultery) but far on this side to any point of will-worship, though to the true God; sometimes it notes the love of earthly things or worldly pleasures, though in a right believer, sometimes the least suspicion of unwitting idolatry. As Num. 15:39, willful disobedience to any the least of God's commandments is called fornication. Psal. 73:26, 27. A distrust only in God, and withdrawing from that nearness of zeal and confidence which ought to be, is called fornication. We may be sure it could not import thus much less than idolatry in the borrowed metaphor between God and man, unless it signified as much less than adultery in the ordinary acception between man and wife. Add also that there was no need our Savior should grant divorce for adultery, it being death by law, and law then in force. Which was the cause why Joseph sought to put away his betrothed wife privately,[217] lest he should make her an example of capital punishment, as learnedest expounders affirm, Herod being a great zealot of the Mosaic law, and the Pharisees great masters of the text, as the woman taken in adultery doubtless had cause to fear. Or if they can prove it was neglected, which they cannot do, why did our Savior shape his answer to the corruption of that age, and not rather tell them of their neglect? If they say he came not to meddle with their judicatures, much less then was it in his thought to make them new ones, or that divorce should be judicially restrained in a stricter manner by these his words, more than adultery judicially acquitted by those his words to the adulteress. His sentence doth no more by law forbid divorce here, than by law it doth absolve adultery there. To them, therefore, who have drawn this yoke upon Christians from his words thus wrested, nothing remains but the guilt of a presumption and perverseness which will be hard for them to answer. Thus much that the word fornication is to be understood as the language of Christ understands it, for a constant alienation and disaffection of mind, or for the continual practice of disobedience and crossness from the duties of love and peace, that is in sum, when to be a tolerable wife is either naturally not in their power, or obstinately not in their will; and this opinion also is St. Austin's, lest it should hap to be suspected of novelty. Yet grant the thing here meant were only adultery, the reason of things will afford more to our assertion than did the reason of words. For why is divorce unlawful but only for adultery? Because, say they, that crime only breaks the matrimony. But this, I reply, the institution itself gainsays: for that which is most contrary to the words and meaning of the institution, that most breaks the matrimony. But a perpetual unmeetness and unwillingness to all the duties of help, of love, and tranquility is most contrary to the words and meaning of the institution; that therefore much more breaks matrimony than the act of adultery though repeated. For this, as it is not felt, nor troubles him who perceives it not, so being perceived may be soon repented, soon amended, soon, if it can be pardoned, may be redeemed with the more ardent love and duty in her who hath the pardon. But this natural unmeetness both cannot be unknown long, and ever after cannot be amended, if it be natural, and will not, if it be far gone obstinate. So that wanting aught in the instant to be as great a breach as adultery, it gains it in the perpetuity to be greater. Next, adultery does not exclude her other fitness, her other pleasingness; she may be otherwise both loving and prevalent,[218] as many adulteresses be. But in this general unfitness or alienation she can be nothing to him that can please. In adultery nothing is given from the husband, which he misses, or enjoys the less, as it may be subtly given; but this unfitness defrauds him of the whole contentment which is sought in wedlock. And what benefit to him, though nothing be given by the stealth of adultery to another, if that which there is to give, whether it be solace or society, be not such as may justly content him? And so not only deprives him of what it should give him, but gives him sorrow and affliction, which it did not owe him. Besides, is adultery the greatest breach of matrimony in respect of the offence to God, or of the injury to man? If in the former, then other sins may offend God more, and sooner cause him to disunite his servant from being one flesh with such an offender. If in respect of the latter, other injuries are demonstrated therein more heavy to man's nature than the iterated act of adultery. God therefore in his wisdom would not so dispose his remedies as to provide them for the less injuries and not allow them for the greater. Thus is won both from the word fornication and the reason of adultery, that the exception of divorce is not limited to that act but enlarged to the causes above specified.

[*And whoso marrieth her which is put away, doth commit adultery.*] By this clause alone, if by nothing else, we may assure us, that Christ intended not to deliver here the whole doctrine of divorce but only to condemn abuses. Otherwise to marry after desertion, which the Apostle and the reformed churches at this day permit, is here forbid as adultery. Be she never so wrongfully deserted or put away, as the law then suffered, if thus forsaken and expulsed she accept the refuge and protection of any honester man who would love her better, and give herself in marriage to him, by what the letter guides us, it shall be present adultery to them both. This is either harsh and cruel, or all the church's teaching as they do the contrary are loose and remiss; besides that the Apostle himself stands deeply fined in a contradiction against our Savior. What shall we make of this? What rather the common interpreter can make of it, for they be his own markets, let him now try; let him try which way he can wind in his Vertumnian[219] distinctions and evasions, if his canonical gabardine[220] of text and letter do not now sit too close about him and pinch his activity; which if I err not, hath here hampered itself in a spring fit for those who put their confidence in alphabets.[221] Spanheim,[222] a writer of evangelic doubts, comes now and confesses that our Savior's words *are to be limited beyond the limitation there expressed and excepted beyond their own exception,* as not speaking of what happened rarely, but what most commonly. Is it so rare, Spanheim, to be deserted, or was it then so rare to put away injuriously, that a person so hatefully expelled should to the heaping of more injury be turned like an infectious thing out of all married fruition upon pain of adultery, as not considerable to the brevity of this half sentence? Of what then speaks our Savior? Of *that collusion,* saith he, *which was then most frequent among the Jews of changing wives and husbands, through inconstancy and unchaste desires.* Colluders yourselves, as violent to this law of God by your unmerciful binding as the Pharisees by their unbounded loosening! Have thousands of Christian souls perished as to this life, and God knows what hath betided their consciences, for want of this healing explanation, and is it now at last obscurely drawn forth only to cure a scratch, and leave the main wound spouting? *Whosoever puts away his wife except for fornication commits adultery:* that shall be spoke of all ages, and all men, though never so justly otherwise moved to divorce. In the very next breath, *and whoso marries her which is put away, commiteth adultery:* the men are new and miraculous, they tell you now *you are to limit it to that age when it was in fashion to chop matrimonies; and must be meant of him who puts away with his wife's consent through the lightness and lewdness of them both.* But what rule of logic, or indeed of reason, is our commission to understand the *antecedent* one way and the *consequent* another, for in that habitude this whole verse may be considered; or at least to take the parts of a *copulat axiom,* both absolutely affirmative, and to say that first is absolutely true, the other not, but must be limited to a certain time and custom: which is no less than to say they are both false. For in this compound axiom, be the parts never so many, if one of them do but falter and be not equally absolute and general, the rest are all false. If therefore, that *he who marries her which is put away commits adultery* be not generally true, neither is it generally true that *he commits adultery who puts away for other cause then fornication.* And if the marrying her which is put away must be understood limited, which they cannot but yield it must, with the same limitation must be understood the putting away. Thus doth the common exposition confound itself and justify this which is here brought: that our Savior, as well in the first part of this sentence as in the second, prohibited only such divorces as the Jews then made through malice or through plotted license, not those which are for necessary and just causes; where charity and wisdom disjoins, that which not God but error and disaster joined.

And there is yet to this our exposition a stronger siding friend than any can be an adversary, unless Saint Paul be doubted, who repeating a command concerning divorce, I Cor. 7, which is agreed by writers to be the same with this of our Savior, and appointing that the *wife remain unmarried, or be reconciled to her husband,* leaves it infallible that our Savior spake chiefly against putting away for casual and choleric[223] disagreements, or any other cause which may with human patience and wisdom be reconciled, not hereby meaning to hale and dash together the irreconcilable aversations of nature, nor to tie up a faultless person like a parricide,[224] as it were into one sack with an enemy, to be his causeless tormenter and executioner the length of a long life. Lastly, let this sentence of Christ be understood how it will, yet that it was never intended for a judicial law to be enforced by the magistrate, besides that the office of our Savior had no such purpose in the Gospel, this latter part of the sentence may assure us: *and whoso marrieth her which is put away, commits adultery*. Shall the exception for adultery belong to this clause or not? If not, it would be strange that he who marries a woman really divorced for adultery, as Christ permitted, should become an adulterer by marrying one who is now no other man's wife, himself being also free, who might by this means reclaim her from common whoredom. And if the exception must belong hither, then it follows that he who marries an adulteress divorced, commits no adultery; which would soon discover to us what an absurd and senseless piece of injustice this would be to make a civil statute of in penal courts: whereby the adulteress put away may marry another safely, and without a crime to him that marries her, but the innocent and wrongfully divorced shall not marry again without the guilt of adultery both to herself and to her second husband. This saying of Christ therefore cannot be made a temporal law, were it but for this reason. Nor is it easy to say what coherence there is at all in it from the letter, to any perfect sense not obnoxious to some absurdity, and seems much less agreeable to whatever else of the Gospel is left us written; doubtless by our Savior spoken in that fierceness and abstruse intricacy, first to amuse[225] his tempters, and admonish in general the abusers of that Mosaic law; next, to let Herod know a second knower of his unlawful act, though the Baptist were beheaded; last, that his disciples and all good men might learn to expound him in this place, as in all other his precepts, not by the written letter but by that unerring paraphrase of Christian love and charity, which is the sum of all commands, and the perfection.

Verse 10. *His Disciples say unto him, if the case of the man be so with his wife, it is not good to marry.*

This verse I add, to leave no objection behind unanswered: for some may think, if this our Savior's sentence be so fair, as not commanding aught that patience or nature cannot brook, why then did the disciples murmur and say *it is not good to marry*. I answer that the disciples had been longer bred up under the Pharisaean doctrine than under that of Christ, and so no marvel though they yet retained the infection of loving old licentious customs; no marvel though they thought it hard they might not for any offence that thoroughly angered them divorce a wife as well as put away a servant, since it was but giving her a bill, as they were taught. Secondly, it was no unwonted thing with them not to understand our Savior in matters far easier. So that be it granted their conceit of this text was the same which is now commonly conceived, according to the usual rate of their capacity then, it will not hurt a better interpretation. But why did not Christ seeing their error inform them? for good cause; it was his professed method not to teach them all things at all times, but each thing in due place and season. Christ said, Luke 22, that *he who had no sword should sell his garment and buy one;* the disciples took it in a manifest wrong sense, yet our Savior did not there inform them better. He told them it was easier for a camel to go through a needle's eye than a rich man in at Heaven gate.[226] They were amazed exceedingly; he explained himself to mean of those who trust in riches, Mark 10. *They were amazed then out of measure,* for so Mark relates it; as if his explaining had increased their amazement, in such a plain case, and which concerned so nearly their calling to be informed in. Good reason therefore, if Christ at that time did not stand amplifying, to the thick prejudice and tradition wherein they were, this question of more difficulty and less concernment to any perhaps of them in particular. Yet did he not omit to sow within them the seeds of a sufficient determining, against the time that his promised Spirit should bring all things to their memory. He had declared in their hearing not long before, how distant he was from abolishing the law itself of divorce; he had referred them to the institution; and after all this, gives them a set answer, from which they might collect what was clear enough, that *all men cannot receive all sayings,* Matthew 19:11. If such regard be had to each man's receiving of marriage or single life, what can arise that the same Christian regard should not be had in most necessary divorce? All which instructed both them and us, that it beseemed his disciples to learn the deciding of this question, which hath nothing new in it, first by the institution, then by the general grounds of religion, not by a particular saying here or there, tempered and leveled only to an incident occasion, the riddance of a tempting assault. For what can this be but weak and shallow apprehension, to forsake the standard principles of institution, faith, and charity; then to be blank and various at every occurrence in Scripture, and in a cold spasm of scruple to rear peculiar doctrines upon the place that shall bid the gray authority of most unchangeable and sovereign rules to stand by and be contradicted. Thus to this evangelic precept of famous difficulty, which for these many ages weakly understood, and violently put in practice, hath made a shambles rather than an ordinance of matrimony, I am firm a truer exposition cannot be given. If this or that argument here used please not every one, there is no scarcity of arguments; any half of them will suffice. Or should they all fail, as truth itself can fail as soon, I should content me with the institution alone to wage this controversy, and not distrust to evince. If any need it not, the happier; yet Christians ought to study earnestly what may be another's need. But if, as mortal mischances are, some hap to need it, let them be sure they abuse not, and give God his thanks, who hath revived this remedy, not too late for them, and scoured off an inveterate misexposition from the Gospel: a work not to perish by the vain breath or doom of this age. Our next industry shall be, under the same guidance, to try with what fidelity that remaining passage in the Epistles touching this matter, hath been commented.

1 Cor. 7.10, &c

10. *And unto the married I command, &c.*

11. *And let not the husband put away his wife.*

This intimates but what our Savior taught before, that divorce is not rashly to be made, but reconcilement to be persuaded and endeavored, as oft as the cause can have to do with reconcilement and is not under the dominion of blameless nature; which may have reason to depart though seldomest and last from charitable love, yet sometimes from friendly, and familiar, and something oftner from conjugal love, which requires not only moral but natural causes to the making and maintaining, and may be warrantably excused to retire from the deception of what it justly seeks and the ill requitals which unjustly it finds. For Nature hath her zodiac also, keeps her great annual circuit over human things as truly as the sun and planets in the firmament; hath her anomalies,[227] hath her obliquities[228] in ascensions and declinations, accesses and recesses, as blamelessly as they in Heaven; and sitting in her planetary orb with two reins in each hand, one strait, the other loose, tempers the course of minds as well as bodies to several conjunctions and oppositions, friendly or unfriendly aspects, consenting oftest with reason but never contrary.[229] This in the effect no man of meanest reach but daily sees; and though to every one it appear not in the cause, yet to a clear capacity, well nurtured with good reading and observation, it cannot but be plain and visible. Other exposition therefore than hath been given to former places that give light to these two summary verses will not be needful, save only that these precepts are meant to those married who differ not in religion.

[*But to the rest speak I, not the Lord; if any brother hath a wife that believeth not, and she be pleased to dwell with him, let him not put her away.*] Now follows what is to be done if the persons wedded be of a different faith. The common belief is, that a Christian is here commanded not to divorce if the infidel please to stay, though it be but to vex, or to deride, or to seduce the Christian. This doctrine will be the easy work of a refutation. The other opinion is, that a Christian is here conditionally permitted to hold wedlock with a misbeliever only upon hopes limited by Christian prudence, which without much difficulty shall be defended. That this here spoken by Paul, not by the Lord, cannot be a command, these reasons avouch. First, the law of Moses, Exod. 34:16, Deut. 7:3, 6, interpreted by Ezra and Nehemiah, two infallible authors, commands to divorce an infidel not for the fear only of a ceremonious defilement but of an irreligious seducement, feared both in respect of the believer himself and of his children in danger to be perverted by the misbelieving parent, Nehem. 13:24.26. And Peter Martyr thought this a convincing reason.[230] If therefore the legal pollution vanishing have abrogated the ceremony of this law, so that a Christian may be permitted to retain an infidel without uncleanness, yet the moral reason of divorcing stands to eternity, which neither Apostle nor angel from Heaven can countermand. All that they reply to this is their human warrant that God will preserve us in our obedience to this command against the danger of seducement. And so undoubtedly he will, if we understand his commands aright; if we turn not this evangelic permission into a legal, and yet illegal, command; if we turn not hope into bondage, the charitable and free hope of gaining another into the forced and servile temptation of losing ourselves: but more of this beneath. Thus these words of Paul, by common doctrine made a command, are made a contradiction to the moral law.

Secondly, not the law only, but the Gospel from the law, and from itself, requires even in the same chapter, where divorce between them of one religion is so narrowly forbid, rather than our Christian love should come into danger of backsliding, to forsake all relations how near soever, and the wife expressly, with promise of a high reward, Matthew 19:29. And he who hates not father or mother, wife or children hindering his Christian course, much more if they despise or assault it, cannot be a disciple, Luke 14:26. How can the Apostle then command us to love and continue in that matrimony which our Savior bids us hate and forsake? They can as soon teach our faculty of respiration to contract and to dilate itself at once, to breathe and to fetch breath in the same instant, as teach our minds how to do such contrary acts as these towards the same object, and as they must be done in the same moment. For either the hatred of her religion and her hatred to our religion will work powerfully against the love of her society, or the love of that will by degrees flatter out all our zealous hatred and forsaking and soon ensnare us to un-Christianly compliances.

Thirdly, in marriage there ought not only to be a civil love, but such a love as Christ loves his church; but where the religion is contrary without hope of conversion, there can be no love, no faith, no peaceful society (they of the other opinion confess it) nay there ought not to be, further than in expectation of gaining a soul; when that ceases, we know God hath put an enmity between the seed of the woman and the seed of the serpent. Neither should *we love them that hate the Lord,* as the prophet told Jehosaphat, 2 Chron. 19. And this Apostle himself, in another place, warns us *that we be not unequally yoked with infidels,* II Corinthians 6:14, for that there can be no fellowship, no communion, no concord between such. Outward commerce and civil intercourse cannot perhaps be avoided; but true friendship and familiarity there can be none. How vainly therefore, not to say how impiously, would the most inward and dear alliance of marriage or continuance in marriage be commanded where true friendship is confessed impossible. For, say they, we are forbid here to marry with an infidel, not bid to divorce. But to rob the words thus of their full sense will not be allowed them: it is not said, enter not into yoke, but *be not unequally yoked,* which plainly forbids the thing in present act, as well as in purpose; and his manifest conclusion is, not only that *we should not touch,* but that having touched, *we should come out from among them, and be separate,* with the promise of a blessing thereupon that *God will receive us, will be our Father, and we his sons and daughters,* verse 17, 18. Why we should stay with an infidel after the expense of all our hopes, can be but for a civil relation; but why we should depart from a seducer, setting aside the misconstruction of this place, is from a religious necessity of departing. The worse cause therefore of staying (if it be any cause at all, for civil government forces it not) must not overtop the religious cause of separating, executed with such an urgent zeal and such a prostrate humiliation by Ezra and Nehemiah. What God hates to join, certainly he cannot love should continue joined: it being all one in matter of ill consequence, to marry or to continue married with an infidel, save only so long as we wait willingly and with a safe hope. Saint Paul therefore citing here a command of the *Lord Almighty,* for so he terms it, that we should *separate,* cannot have bound us with that which he calls his own whether command or counsel that we should not separate.

Which is the fourth reason, for he himself takes care lest we should mistake him, [*But to the rest speak I not the Lord.*] If the Lord spake not, then man spake, it and man hath no Lordship to command the conscience: yet modern interpreters will have it a command, maugre[231] St. Paul himself; they will make him a prophet like Caiaphas,[232] to speak the word of the Lord, not thinking, nay denying to think; though he disavow to have received it from the Lord his word shall not be taken, though an Apostle, he shall be borne down in his own Epistle by a race of expositors who presume to know from whom he spake, better than he himself. Paul deposes that the Lord speaks not this, they, that the Lord speaks it. Can this be less than to brave him with a full faced contradiction? Certainly to such a violence as this, for I cannot call it an expounding, what a man should answer I know not, unless that if it be their pleasure next to put a gag into the Apostle's mouth, they are already furnished with a commodious audacity toward the attempt. Beza would seem to shun the contradictory by telling us that the Lord spake it not in person, as he did the former precept.[233] But how many other doctrines doth St. Paul deliver which the Lord spake not in person, and yet never used this preamble but in things indifferent? So long as we receive him for a messenger of God, for him to stand sorting sentences what the Lord spake in person, and what he not the Lord in person, would be but a chill trifling, and his readers might catch an ague the while. But if we shall supply the grammatical ellipsis regularly, and as we must in the same tense, all will be then clear; for we cannot supply it thus, to the rest I speak, the Lord spake not, but I speak, the Lord speaks not. If then the Lord neither spake in person, nor speaks it now, the Apostle testifying both, it follows duly that this can be no command. Forsooth the fear is, lest this not being a command, would prove an evangelic counsel, and so make way for supererogations.[234] As if the Apostle could not speak his mind in things indifferent, as he doth in four or five several places of this chapter with the like preface of not commanding, but that the doubted inconvenience of supererogating must needs rush in. And how adds it to the word of the Lord (for this also they object) whenas the Apostle by his Christian prudence guides us in the liberty which God hath left us to, without command? Could not the Spirit of God instruct us by him what was free, as well as what was not? But what need I more, when Cameron an ingenuous writer and in high esteem, solidly confutes the surmise of a command here, and among other words hath these: that *when Paul speaks as an Apostle, he uses this form,* The Lord saith, not I verse 10, *but as a private man he saith,* I speak, not the Lord. And thus also all the prime Fathers, Austin, Jerome, and the rest understood this place.

Fifthly, the very stating of the question declares this to be no command: if any brother hath an unbelieving wife, and she be pleased to dwell with him, let him not put her away. For the Greek word *συνευδοκεῖ* does not imply only her being pleased to stay, but his being pleased to let her stay; it must be a consent of them both. Nor can the force of this word be rendered less, without either much negligence or iniquity of him that otherwise translates it. And thus the Greek Church also and their synods understood it, who best knew what their own language meant, as appears by Matthaeus Monachus, an author set forth by Leunclavius,[235] and of antiquity perhaps not inferior to Balsamon,[236] who writes upon the canons of the Apostles: this author in his chap *That marriage is not to be made with heretics* thus recites the second canon of the 6 Synod: *As to the Corinthians, Paul determines, if the believing wife choose to live with the unbelieving husband, or the believing husband with the unbelieving wife,* mark, saith he, *how the Apostle here condescends, if the believer please to dwell with the unbeliever; so that if he please not, out of doubt the marriage is dissolved. And I am persuaded it was so in the beginning, and thus preached.* And thereupon gives an example of one, who though not deserted, yet by the decree of Theodotus the Patriarch[237] divorced an unbelieving wife. What therefore depends in the plain state of this question on the consent and well liking of them both, must not be a command. Lay next the latter end of the 11 verse to the twelfth (for wherefore else is logic taught us) in a discreet axiom, as it can be no other by the phrase, *the Lord saith, let not the husband put away his wife. But I say, let him not put away a misbelieving wife.* This sounds as if, by the judgment of Paul, a man might put away any wife but the misbelieving; or else the parts are not discreet, or dissentanie,[238] for both conclude not putting away, and consequently in such a form the proposition is ridiculous. Of necessity therefore, the former part of this sentence must be conceived as understood, and silently granted, that although the Lord command to divorce an infidel, yet I, not the Lord, command you? No, but give my judgment, that for some evangelic reasons a Christian may be permitted not to divorce her. Thus while we reduce the brevity of St. Paul to a plainer sense, by the needful supply of that which was granted between him and the Corinthians, the very logic of his speech extracts him confessing that the Lord's command lay in a seeming contrariety to this his counsel; and that he meant not to thrust out a command of the Lord by a new one of his own, as one nail drives another, but to release us from the rigor of it by the right of the Gospel, so far forth as a charitable cause leads us on in the hope of winning another soul without the peril of losing our own. For this is the glory of the Gospel: to teach us that *the end of the commandment is charity,* I Tim. 1, not the drudging out a poor and worthless duty forced from us by the tax and taile[239] of so many letters. This doctrine therefore can be no command, but it must contradict the moral law, the Gospel, and the Apostle himself both elsewhere and here also even in the act of speaking.

If then it be no command, it must remain to be a permission, and that not absolute, for so it would be still contrary to the law, but with such a caution as breaks not the law, but as the manner of the Gospel is, fulfils it through charity. The law had two reasons. The one was ceremonial, the pollution that all Gentiles were to the Jews; this the vision of Peter had abolished, Acts 10, and cleansed all creatures to the use of a Christian.[240] The Corinthians understood not this, but feared lest dwelling in matrimony with an unbeliever they were defiled. The Apostle discusses that scruple with an evangelic reason, showing them that although God heretofore under the law, not intending the conversion of the Gentiles, except some special ones, held them as polluted things to the Jew, yet now purposing to call them in, he hath purified them from that legal uncleanness wherein they stood, to use and to be used in a pure manner.

For saith he, *the unbelieving husband is sanctified by the wife, and the unbelieving wife is sanctified by the husband, else were your children unclean; but now they are holy*. That is, they are sanctified to you from that legal impurity which you so fear; and are brought into a near capacity to be holy, if they believe, and to have free access to holy things. In the meantime, as being God's creatures, a Christian hath power to use them according to their proper use; inasmuch as now *all things to the pure are become pure*. In this legal respect, therefore, ye need not doubt to continue in marriage with an unbeliever. Thus others also expound this place, and Cameron especially.[241] This reason warrants us only what we may do without fear of pollution, does not bind us that we must. But the other reason of the law to divorce an infidel was moral, the avoiding of enticement from the true faith. This cannot shrink; but remains in as full force as ever, to save the actual Christian from the snare of a misbeliever. Yet if a Christian full of grace and spiritual gifts, finding the misbeliever not frowardly affected, fears not a seducing but hopes rather a gaining, who sees not that this moral reason is not violated by not divorcing, which the law commanded to do, but better fulfilled by the excellence of the Gospel working through charity. For neither the faithful is seduced, and the unfaithful is either saved, or with all discharge of love and evangelic duty sought to be saved. But contrary wise, if the infirm Christian shall be commanded here against his mind, against his hope, and against his strength, to dwell with all the scandals, the household persecutions, or alluring temptations of an infidel, how is not the Gospel by this made harsher than the law, and more yoking? Therefore the Apostle ere he deliver this other reason why we need not in all haste put away an infidel, his mind misgiving him lest he should seem to be the imposer of a new command, stays not for method, but with an abrupt speed inserts the declaration of their liberty in this matter.

But if the unbelieving depart, let him depart; a brother or a sister is not under bondage in such cases: but God hath called us to peace.

[*But if the unbelieving depart.*] This cannot be restrained to local departure only; for who knows not that an offensive society is worse than a forsaking. If his purpose of cohabitation be to endanger the life, or the conscience, Beza himself is half persuaded that this may purchase to the faithful person the same freedom that a desertion may; and so Gerard[242] and others whom he cites. If therefore he depart in affection; if he depart from giving hope of his conversion; if he disturb, or scoff at religion, seduce, or tempt, if he rage; doubtless not the weak only but the strong may leave him, if not for fear yet for the dignity's sake of religion, which cannot be liable to all base affronts merely for the worshipping of a civil marriage. I take therefore *departing* to be as large as the negative of being well pleased: that is, if he be not pleased for the present to live lovingly, quietly, inoffensively, so as may give good hope; which appears well by that which follows.

[*A brother or a sister is not under bondage in such cases.*] If St. Paul provide seriously against the bondage of a Christian, it is not the only bondage to live unmarried for a deserting infidel. But to endure his presence intolerably, to bear indignities against his religion in words or deeds, to be wearied with seducements, to have idolatries and superstitions ever before his eyes, to be tormented with impure and profane conversation, this must needs be bondage to a Christian. Is this left all unprovided for, without remedy, or freedom granted? Undoubtedly no, for the Apostle leaves it further to be considered with prudence what bondage a brother or sister is not under, not only in this case but as he speaks himself plurally, *in such cases.*

[*But God hath called us to peace.*] To peace, not to bondage, not to brabbles[243] and contentions with him who is not pleased to live peaceably, as marriage and Christianity requires. And where strife arises from a cause hopeless to be allayed, what better way to peace than by separating that which is ill joined. It is not divorce that first breaks the peace of a family, as some fondly comment on this place, but it is peace already broken, which, when other cures fail, can only be restored to the faultless person by a necessary divorce. And St. Paul here warrants us to seek peace, rather than remain in bondage. If God hath called us to peace, why should we not follow him, why should we miserably stay in perpetual discord under a servitude not required?

[*For what knowest thou O wife, whether thou shalt save thy husband, &c.*] St. Paul having thus cleared himself, not to go about the mining or our Christian liberty, not *to cast a snare upon us,* which to do he so much hated, returns now to the second reason of that law: to put away an infidel for fear of seducement, which he does not here contradict with a command now to venture that; but if neither the infirmity of the Christian nor the strength of the unbeliever be feared, but hopes appearing that he may be won, he judges it no breaking of that law, though the believer be permitted to forbear divorce, and can abide, without the peril of seducement, to offer the charity of a salvation to wife or husband, which is the fulfilling, not the transgressing, of that law, and well worth the undertaking with much hazard and patience. For what knowest thou whether thou shalt save thy wife, that is, 'til all means convenient and possible with discretion and probability, as human things are, have been used. For Christ himself sends not our hope on pilgrimage to the world's end,[244] but sets it bounds beyond which we need not wait on a brother, much less on an infidel. If after such a time we may count a professing Christian no better than a heathen, after less time perhaps we may cease to hope of a heathen that he will turn Christian. Otherwise, to bind us harder than the law, and tell us we are not under bondage, is mere mockery. If 'til the unbeliever please to part, we may not stir from the house of our bondage, then certain this our liberty is not grounded in the purchase of Christ but in the pleasure of a miscreant. What knows the loyal husband whether he may not save the adulteress, he is not therefore bound to receive her. What knows the wife but she may reclaim her husband who hath deserted her? Yet the reformed churches do not enjoin her to wait longer than after the contempt of an ecclesiastical summons. Beza himself here befriends us with a remarkable speech, *what could be firmly constituted in human matters, if under pretence of expecting grace from above, it should be never lawful for us to seek our right.* And yet in other cases not less reasonable to obtain a most just and needful remedy by divorce, he turns the innocent party to a task of prayers beyond the multitude of beads and rosaries, to beg the gift of chastity in recompense of an injurious marriage. But the Apostle is evident enough, *we are not under bondage,* trusting that he writes to those who are not ignorant what bondage is, to let supercilious determiners cheat them of their freedom. God hath called us to peace, and so doubtless hath left in our hands how to obtain it seasonably, if it be not our own choice to sit ever like novices wretchedly servile.

Thus much the Apostle on this question between Christian and Pagan, to us now of little use; yet supposing it written for our instruction as it may be rightly applied, I doubt not but that the difference between a true believer and a heretic, or any one truly religious either deserted or seeking divorce from any one grossly erroneous or profane, may be referred hither. For St. Paul leaves us here the solution not of this case only, which little concerns us, but of *such like cases,* which may occur to us. For where the reasons directly square, who can forbid why the verdict should not be the same? But this the common writers allow us not. And yet from this text, which in plain words gives liberty to none, unless deserted by an infidel, they collect the same freedom though the desertion be not for religion, which, as I conceive, they need not do, but may without straining reduce it to the cause of fornication. For first they confess that desertion is seldom without a just suspicion of adultery; next it is a breach of marriage in the same kind, and in some sort worse: for adultery though it give to another, yet it bereaves not all; but the deserter wholly denies all right, and makes one flesh twain, which is counted the absolutest breach of matrimony, and causes the other, as much as in him lies, to commit sin by being so left. Nevertheless, those reasons which they bring of establishing by this place the like liberty from any desertion are fair and solid; and if the thing be lawful, and can be proved so, more ways than one, so much the safer. Their arguments I shall here recite, and that they may not come idle, shall use them to make good the like freedom to divorce for other causes; and that we are not more under bondage to any heinous default against the main ends of matrimony, than to a desertion. First they allege that to I Tim. 5:8, *If any provide not for those of his own house, he hath denied the faith, and is worse than an infidel.* But a deserter, say they, *can have no care of them who are most his own, therefore the deserted party is not less to be righted against such a one than against an infidel.* With the same evidence I argue that man or wife who hates in wedlock is perpetually unsociable, unpeaceful, or unduteous, either not being able or not willing to perform what the main ends of marriage demand in help and solace, cannot be said to care for who should be dearest in the house, therefore is worse than an infidel in both regards: either in undertaking a duty which he cannot perform, to the undeserved and unspeakable injury of the other party so defrauded and betrayed, or not performing what he hath undertaken, whenas he may or might have, to the perjury of himself more irreligious than heathenism. The blameless person therefore hath as good a plea to sue out his delivery from this bondage as from the desertion of an infidel, since most writers cannot but grant that desertion is not only a local absence but an intolerable society; or if they grant it not, the reasons of St. Paul grant it, with as much leave as they grant to enlarge a particular freedom from paganism into a general freedom from any desertion. Secondly, they reason from the likeness of either fact, *the same loss redounds to the deserted by a Christian as by an infidel, the same peril of temptation.* And I in like manner affirm that if honest and free persons may be allowed to know what is most to their own loss, the same loss and discontent, but worse disquiet with continual misery and temptation resides in the company, or better called the persecution of an unfit or an unpeaceable consort, than by his desertion. For then the deserted may enjoy himself at least. And he who deserts is more favorable to the party whom his presence afflicts, than that importunate thing which is and will be ever conversant before the eyes a loyal and individual vexation. As for those who still rudely urge it no loss to marriage, no desertion, so long as the flesh is present and offers a benevolence that hates, or is justly hated, I am not of that vulgar and low persuasion to think such forced embracements as these worth the honor or the humanity of marriage, but far beneath the soul of a rational and free-born man. Thirdly they say, *it is not the infidelity of the deserter, but the desertion of the infidel from which the Apostle gives this freedom;* and I join, that the Apostle could as little require our subjection to an unfit and injurious bondage present as to an infidel absent. To free us from that which is an evil by being distant, and not from that which is an inmate, and in the bosom evil, argues an improvident and careless deliverer. And thus all occasions, which way soever they turn, are not unofficious to administer something which may conduce to explain or to defend the assertion of this book touching divorce. I complain of nothing, but that it is indeed too copious to be the matter of a dispute, or a defense, rather to be yielded, as in the best ages, a thing of common reason, not of controversy. What have I left to say? I fear to be more elaborate in such perspicuity as this, lest I should seem not to teach, but to upbraid the dullness of an age; not to commune with reason in men, but to deplore the loss of reason from among men: this only, and not the want of more to say, is the limit of my discourse.

[*Who among the fathers have interpreted the words of Christ concerning divorce, as is here interpreted; and what the civil law of Christian emperors in the primitive church determined.*]

Although testimony be in logic an argument rightly called *inartificial,*[245] and doth not solidly fetch the truth by multiplicity of authors, nor argue a thing false by the few that hold so, yet seeing most men from their youth so accustom as not to scan reason nor clearly to apprehend it, but to trust for that the names and numbers of such as have got, and many times undeservedly, the reputation among them to know much, and because there is a vulgar[246] also of teachers, who are as blindly by whom they fancy led, as they lead the people, it will not be amiss for them who had rather list themselves under this weaker sort, and follow authorities, to take notice that this opinion which I bring, hath been favored, and by some of those affirmed, who in their time were able to carry what they taught, had they urged it, through all Christendom; or to have left it such a credit with all good men, as they who could not boldly use the opinion would have feared to censure it. But since by his appointment on whom the times and seasons wait, every point of doctrine is not fatal to be thoroughly sifted out in every age, it will be enough for me to find that the thoughts of wisest heads heretofore, and hearts no less reverenced for devotion, have tended this way, and contributed their lot in some good measure towards this which hath been here attained. Others of them, and modern especially, have been as full in the assertion, though not so full in the reason; so that either in this regard, or in the former, I shall be manifest in a middle fortune to meet the praise or dispraise of being something first. But I defer not what I undertook to show, that in the church both primitive and reformed, the words of Christ have been understood to grant divorce for other causes than adultery; and that the word *fornication* in marriage hath a larger sense than that commonly supposed.

Justin Martyr in his first *Apology,*[247] written within 50 years after St. John died, relates a story which Eusebius transcribes, that a certain matron of Rome, the wife of a vicious husband, herself also formerly vicious, but converted to the faith, and persuading the same to her husband, at least the amendment of his wicked life, upon his not yielding to her daily entreaties and persuasions in this behalf, procured by law to be divorced from him. This was neither for adultery nor desertion, but as the relation says, *esteeming it an ungodly thing to be the consort of bed with him, who against the law of nature and of right sought out voluptuous ways.* Suppose he endeavored some unnatural abuse, as the Greek admits that meaning. It cannot yet be called adultery. It therefore could be thought worthy of divorce no otherwise than as equivalent, or worse; and other vices will appear in other respects as much divorcive. Next, 'tis said her friends advised her to stay a while; and what reason gave they? Not because they held unlawful what she purposed, but because they thought she might longer yet hope his repentance. She obeyed, 'til the man going to Alexandria, and from thence reported to grow still more impenitent, not for any adultery or desertion, whereof neither can be gathered, but saith the Martyr, and speaks it like one approving, *lest she should be partaker of his unrighteous and ungodly deeds, remaining in wedlock, the communion of bed and board with such a person, she left him by a lawful divorce.* This cannot but give us the judgment of the church in those pure and next to Apostolic times. For how else could the woman have been permitted, or here not reprehended; and if a wife might then do this without reproof, a husband certainly might no less, if not more.

Tertullian in the same Age, writing his 4th book against Marcion witnesses *that Christ by his answer to the Pharisees protected the constitution of Moses as his own, and directed the institution of the creator,* for I alter not his Carthaginian phrase;[248] he excused rather than destroyed the constitution of Moses. I say he forbid conditionally, if any one therefore put away, that he may marry another. So that if he prohibited conditionally, then not wholly; and what he forbade not wholly, he permitted otherwise where the cause ceases for which he prohibited: that is, when a man makes it not the cause of his putting away merely that he may marry again. Christ teaches not contrary to Moses; the justice of divorce hath Christ the asserter. He would not have marriage separate, nor kept with ignominy, permitting then a divorce, and guesses that this vehemence of our Savior's sentence was chiefly bent against Herod, as was cited before. Which leaves it evident how Tertullian interpreted this prohibition of our Savior; for whereas the text is, *whosoever putteth away, and marrieth another,* wherefore should Tertullian explain it, *whosoever putteth away that he may marry another,* but to signify his opinion that our Savior did not forbid divorce from an unworthy yoke, but forbid the malice or the lust of a needless change and chiefly those plotted divorces then in use.

Origen in the next century testifies[249] to have known certain who had the government of churches in his time, who permitted some to marry while yet their former husbands lived, and excuses the deed as done *not without cause, though without Scripture,* which confirms that cause not to be adultery; for how then was it against Scripture that they married again. And a little beneath, for I cite his 7th homily on Matthew, saith he, *To endure faults worse than adultery and fornication seems a thing unreasonable,* and disputes therefore that Christ did not speak by way of precept, but as it were expounding. By which, and the like speeches, Origen declares his mind far from thinking that our Savior confined all the causes of divorce to actual adultery.

Lactantius,[250] of the age that succeeded, speaking of this matter in the 6th of his *Institutions,* hath these words: *But lest any think he may circumscribe divine precepts, let this be added, that all misinterpreting, and occasion of fraud, or death may be removed, he commits adultery who marries the divorced wife, and, besides the crime of adultery, divorces a wife that he may marry another.* To divorce and marry another, and to divorce that he may marry another, are two different things; and imply that Lanctantius thought not this place the forbidding of all necessary divorce but such only as proceeded from the wanton desire of a future choice, not from the burden of a present affliction.

About this time the Council of Eliberis in Spain[251] decreed the husband excommunicate, *if he kept his wife being an adulteress; but if he left her, he might after ten years be received into communion, if he retained her any while in his house after the adultery known.* The council of Neocaesarea[252] in the year 314 decreed, that if the wife of any Laic[253] were convicted of adultery, that man could not be admitted into the ministry: if after ordination it were committed, he was to divorce her; if not, he could not hold his ministry. The Council of Nantes[254] condemned in seven years' penance the husband that would reconcile with an adulteress. But how proves this that other causes may divorce? It proves thus: there can be but two causes why these councils enjoined so strictly the divorcing of an adulteress, either as an offender against God, or against the husband. In the latter respect they could not impose on him to divorce, for every man is the master of his own forgiveness; who shall hinder him to pardon the injuries done against himself? It follows therefore that the divorce of an adulteress was commanded by these three councils, as it was a sin against God; and by all consequence they could not but believe that other sins as heinous might with equal justice be the ground of a divorce.

Basil in his 73rd rule, as Chamier[255] numbers it, thus determines that divorce ought not to be, unless for adultery, *or the hindrance to a godly life.* What doth this but proclaim aloud more causes of divorce than adultery, if by other sins besides this, in wife or husband, the godliness of the better person may be certainly hindered and endangered.

Epiphanius,[256] no less ancient, writing against heretics, and therefore should himself be orthodoxal above others, acquaints us in his second book, Tom. 1, not that his private persuasion was, but that the whole church in his time generally thought other causes of divorce lawful besides adultery, as comprehended under that name: if, saith he, *a divorce happen for any cause, either fornication, or adultery, or any heinous fault, the word of God blames not either the man or wife marrying again, nor cuts them off from the congregation, or from life, but bears with the infirmity; not that he may keep both wives, but that leaving the former he may be lawfully joined to the latter, the holy word, and the holy Church of God commiserates this man, especially if he be otherwise of good conversation, and live according to God's law.* This place is clearer than exposition, and needs no comment.

Ambrose[257] on the 16th of Luke, teaches *that all wedlock is not God's joining:* and to the 19th of Pro. that a *wife is prepared of the Lord,* as the old Latin translates it; he answers that the septuagint renders it, *a wife is fitted by the Lord, and tempered to a kind of harmony; and where that harmony is there God joins; where it is not, there dissension reigns, which is not from God, for God is love.* This he brings to prove the marrying of Christian with Gentile to be no marriage, and consequently divorced without sin; but he who sees not this argument how plainly it serves to divorce any untenable or untunable matrimony, sees little. On the Ist to the Cor. 7, he grants a woman may leave her husband not for only fornication, *but for apostasy, and inverting nature, though not marry again; but the man may:* here are causes of divorce assigned other than adultery. And going on, he affirms *that the cause of God is greater than the cause of matrimony; that the reverence of wedlock is not due to him who hates the author thereof; that no matrimony is firm without devotion to God; that dishonor done to God acquits the other being deserted from the bond of matrimony; that the faith of marriage is not to be kept with such.* If these contorted sentences be aught worth, it is not the desertion that breaks what is broken, but the impiety; and who then may not for that cause better divorce, than tarry to be deserted? Or these grave sayings of St. *Ambrose* are but knacks.[258]

Jerome on the 19th of Matthew explains, that for the cause of fornication or the *suspicion thereof a man may freely divorce.* What can breed that suspicion but sundry faults leading that way? By Jerome's consent, therefore, divorce is free not only for actual adultery but for any cause that may incline a wise man to the just suspicion thereof.

Austin also must be remembered among those who hold that this instance of fornication gives equal inference to other faults equally hateful, for which to divorce; and therefore in his books to Pollentius he disputes that *infidelity, as being a greater sin than adultery, ought so much the rather cause a divorce.* And on the Sermon in the Mount, under the name of fornication will have idolatry or any harmful superstition contained, which are not thought to disturb matrimony so directly as some other obstinacies and disaffections, more against the daily duties of that covenant, and in the eastern tongues not unfrequently called fornication, as hath been shown. *Hence is understood,* saith he, *that not only for bodily fornication, but for that which draws the mind from God's law, and foully corrupts it, a man may without fault put away his wife, and a wife her husband, because the Lord excepts the cause of fornication, which fornication we are constrained to interpret in a general sense.* And in the first book of his *Retractions,* chap. 16, he retracts not this his opinion, but commends it to serious consideration and explains that he counted not there all sin to be fornication, but the more detestable sort of sins. The cause of fornication therefore is not in this discourse newly interpreted to signify other faults infringing the duties of wedlock, besides adultery.

Lastly, the Council of Agatha[259] in the year 506. can. 25 decreed, that *if laymen who divorced without some great fault, or giving no probable cause, therefore divorced, that they might marry some unlawful person, or some other man's, if before the provincial Bishops were made acquainted, or judgment past, they presumed this, excommunication was the penalty.* Whence it follows, that if the cause of divorce were some great offence, or that they gave probable causes for what they did, and did not therefore divorce that they might presume with some unlawful person, or what was another man's, the censure of church in those days did not touch them.

Thus having alleged enough to show after what manner the primitive church for above 500 years understood our Savior's words touching divorce, I shall now with a labor less dispersed, and sooner dispatched, bring under view what the civil law of those times constituted about this matter. I say the civil law, which is the honor of every true civilian to stand for, rather than to count that for law which the pontificial canon had enthralled them to, and instead of interpreting a generous and elegant law made them the drudges of a blockish rubric.

Theodosius and Valentinian,[260] pious emperors both, ordained that as by consent lawful marriages were made, so by consent, but not without the bill of divorce, they might be dissolved; and to dissolve was the more difficult, only in favor of the children. We see the wisdom and piety of that age, one of the purest and learnedest since Christ, conceived no hindrance in the words of our Savior, but that a divorce mutually consented might be suffered by the law, especially if there were no children, or if there were, careful provision was made. And further saith that law (supposing there wanted the consent of either) *we design the causes of divorce by this most wholesome law; for as we forbid the dissolving of marriage without just cause, so we desire that a husband or a wife distressed by some adverse necessity, should be freed, though by an unhappy, yet a necessary relief.* What dram of wisdom or religion (for charity is truest religion) could there be in that knowing age, which is not virtually summed up in this most just law? As for those other Christian emperors, from Constantine the first of them, finding the Roman law in this point so answerable to the Mosaic, it might be the likeliest cause why they altered nothing to restraint, but if aught, rather to liberty, for the help and consideration of the weaker sex, according as the Gospel seems to make the wife more equal to her husband in these conjugal respects than the law of Moses doth. Therefore *if a man were absent from his wife four years, and in that space not heard of, though gone to war in the service of the Empire,* she might divorce, and marry another, by the edict of Constantine to Dalmatius, *Co. l.* 5. *tit.* 17. And this was an age of the church both ancient and cried up still for the most flourishing in knowledge and pious government since the Apostles. But to return to this law of Theodosius, with this observation by the way, that still as the church corrupted, as the clergy grew more ignorant, and yet more usurping on the magistrate, who also now declined, so still divorce grew more restrained; though certainly if better times permitted the thing that worse times restrained, it would not weakly argue that the permission was better and the restraint worse. This law therefore of Theodosius, wiser in this than the most of his successors, though not wiser than God and Moses, reduced the causes of divorce to a certain number which by the judicial law of God and all recorded humanity were left before to the breast of each husband, provided that the dismiss was not without reasonable conditions to the wife. But this was a restraint not yet come to extremes. For besides adultery, and that not only actual but suspected by many signs there set down, any fault equally punishable with adultery or equally infamous might be the cause of a divorce. Which informs us how the wisest of those ages understood that place in the Gospel, whereby not the pilfering of a benevolence was considered as the main and only breach of wedlock, as is now thought, but the breach of love and peace, a more holy union than that of the flesh; and the dignity of an honest person was regarded, not to be held in bondage with one whose ignominy was infectious. To this purpose was constituted *Cod.* l. 5. *tit.* 17. and *Authent collat.* 4. *tit.* 1. *Novell.* 22, where Justinian added three causes more. In the 117 *Novell* most of the same causes are allowed, but the liberty of divorcing by consent is repealed: but by whom? By Justinian, not a wiser, not a more religious emperor than either of the former, but noted by judicious writers for his fickle head in making and unmaking laws; and how Procopius, a good historian[261] and a counselor of state then living, deciphers him in his other actions, I willingly omit. Nor was the church then in better case, but had the corruption of a 100 declining year swept on it when the statute of consent was called in; which as I said, gives us every way more reason to suspect this restraint more than that liberty: which therefore in the reign of Justin, the succeeding emperor was recalled, *Novell.* 140, and established with a preface more wise and Christianly than for those times, declaring the necessity to restore that Theodosian law if no other means of reconcilement could be found. And by whom this law was abrogated, or how long after, I do not find; but that those other causes remained in force as long as the Greek empire subsisted, and were assented to by that church, is to be read in the canons and edicts compared by Photius the Patriarch,[262] with the avertiments of Balsamon and Matthaeus Monachus thereon.

But long before those days, Leo,[263] the son of Basilius Macedo reigning about the year 886 and for his excellent wisdom surnamed the Philosopher, constituted *that in the case of madness the husband might divorce after three years, the wife after 5. Constitut. Leon. 111, 112.* This declares how he expounded our Savior, and derived his reasons from the institution, which in his preface with great eloquence are set down; whereof a passage or two may give some proof, though better not divided from the rest. *There is not,* saith he, *a thing more necessary to preserve mankind, than the help given him from his own rib; both God and nature so teaching us: which being so, it was requisite that the providence of law, or if any other care be to the good of man, should teach and ordain those things which are to the help and comfort of married persons, and confirm the end of marriage purposed in the beginning, not those things which afflict and bring perpetual misery to them.* Then answers the objection that they are one flesh: *if matrimony had held so as God ordained it, he were wicked that would dissolve it. But if we respect this in matrimony, that it be contracted to the good of both, how shall he, who for some great evil feared, persuades not to marry though contracted, not persuade to unmarry, if after marriage a calamity befall? Should we bid beware lest any fall into an evil, and leave him helpless who by human error is fallen therein? This were as if we should use remedies to prevent a disease, but let the sick die without remedy.* The rest will be worth reading in the author.

And thus we have the judgment first of primitive Fathers, next of the imperial law not disallowed by the universal church in ages of her best authority, and lastly, of the whole Greek Church and civil state, incorporating their canons and edicts together, that divorce was lawful for other causes equivalent to adultery, contained under the word fornication. So that the exposition of our Savior's sentence here alleged hath all these ancient and great asserters, is therefore neither new nor licentious, as some would persuade the commonalty; although it be nearer truth that nothing is more new than those teachers themselves, and nothing more licentious than some known to be, whose hypocrisy yet shames not to take offence at this doctrine for license; whenas indeed they fear it would remove license, and leave them but few companions.

[*That the Pope's canon law encroaching upon civil magistracy abolished all divorce even for adultery. What the reformed divines have recovered; and that the famousest of them have taught according to the assertion of this book.*]

But in these western parts of the empire it will appear almost unquestionable that the cited law of Theodosius and Valentinian stood in force until the blindest and corruptest times of Popedom displaced it. For, that the volumes of Justinian never came into Italy, or beyond Illyricum, is the opinion of good antiquaries. And that only manuscript thereof found in Apulia, by Lotharius the Saxon, and given to the state of Pisa for their aid at sea against the Normans of Sicily, was received as a rarity not to be matched. And although the Goths, and after them the Lombards and Franks, who over-run the most of Europe, except this island (unless we make our Saxons and Normans a limb of them) brought in their own customs, yet that they followed the Roman laws in their contracts and marriages, Agathias[264] the historian is alleged. And other testimonies relate that Alaricus and Theodoric[265] their kings writ their statutes out of this *Theodosian Code,* which hath the recited law of divorce. Nevertheless while the monarchs of Christendom were yet barbarous, and but half-Christian, the Popes took this advantage of their weak superstition to raise a corpulent[266] law out of the canons and decretals[267] of audacious priests; and presumed also to set this in the front; *that the constitutions of princes are not above the constitutions of clergy, but beneath them.* Using this very instance of divorce as the first prop of their tyranny; by a false consequence drawn from a passage of Ambrose upon Luke, where he saith, *though man's law grant it, yet God's law prohibits it.* Whence Gregory the Pope,[268] writing to Theoctista, infers that ecclesiastical courts cannot be dissolved by the magistrate. A fair conclusion from a double error. First, in saying that the divine law prohibited divorce, for what will he make of Moses? Next, supposing that it did, how will it follow, that whatever Christ forbids in his evangelic precepts should be hauled into a judicial constraint against the pattern of a divine law? Certainly the Gospel came not to enact such compulsions. In the meanwhile we may note here that the restraint of divorce was one of the first fair seeming pleas which the Pope had to step into secular authority, and with his Antichristian rigor to abolish the permissive law of Christian princes conforming to a sacred lawgiver. Which if we consider, this papal and unjust restriction of divorce need not be so dear to us, since the plausible restraining of that was in a manner the first loosening of Antichrist and as it were the substance of his eldest horn.[269] Nor do we less remarkably owe the first means of his fall here in England to the contemning of that restraint by Henry 8, whose divorce he opposed. Yet was not that rigor executed anciently in spiritual courts until Alexander the third,[270] who trod upon the neck of Frederic Barbarossa the Emperor,[271] and summoned our Henry 2 into Normandy about the death of Becket.[272] He it was, that the worthy author may be known, who first actually repealed the imperial law of divorce, and decreed this tyrannous decree, that matrimony for no cause should be dissolved, though for many causes it might separate; as may be seen *Decret. Gregor.* l. 4. *tit.* 19 and in other places of the canonical tomes.[273] The main good of which invention, wherein it consists, who can tell? But that it hath one virtue incomparable, to fill all Christendom with whoredoms and adulteries beyond the art of Balaams[274] or of devils. Yet neither can these, though so perverse, but acknowledge that the words of Christ under the name of fornication allow putting away for other causes than adultery both from *bed and board,* but not from the *bond;* their only reason is, because marriage they believe to be a sacrament.[275] But our divines who would seem long since to have renounced that reason, have so forgot themselves as yet to hold the absurdity, which but for that reason, unless there be some mystery of Satan in it, perhaps the Papist would not hold. Tis true, we grant divorce for actual and proved adultery, and not for less than many tedious and unrepairable years of desertion, wherein a man shall lose all his hope of posterity, which great and holy men have bewailed, ere he can be righted; and then perhaps on the confines of his old age, when all is not worth the while. But grant this were seasonably done; what are these two cases to many other which afflict the state of marriage as bad, and yet find no redress? What hath the soul of man deserved, if it be in the way of salvation, that it should be mortgaged thus, and may not redeem itself according to conscience out of the hands of such ignorant and slothful teachers as these, who are neither able nor mindful to give due tendance to that precious cure which they rashly undertake; nor have in them the noble goodness to consider these distresses and accidents of man's life, but are bent rather to fill their mouths with tithe and oblation.[276] Yet if they can learn to follow as well as they can seek to be followed, I shall direct them to a fair number of renowned men, worthy to be their leaders, who will commend to them a doctrine in this point wiser than their own, and if they be not impatient, it will be the same doctrine which this treatise hath defended.

Wicklef,[277] that Englishman honored of God to be the first preacher of a general reformation to all Europe, was not in this thing better taught of God, than to teach among his chiefest recoveries of truth that divorce is lawful to the Christian for many other causes equal to adultery. This book indeed, through the poverty of our libraries I am forced to cite from Arnisaeus of Halberstad[278] on the rite of marriage, who cites it from Corasius of Toulouse,[279] *c.* 4. *Cent. Sct.* and he from Wicklef, *l.* 4. *Dial. c,* 21. So much the sorrier, for that I never looked into an author cited by his adversary upon this occasion but found him more conducible to the question than his quotation rendered him.

Next, Luther,[280] how great a servant of God, in his book of conjugal life quoted by Gerard out of the Dutch,[281] allows divorce for the obstinate denial of conjugal duty; and *that a man may send away a proud Vashti, and marry an Esther in her stead.*[282] It seems, if this example shall not be impertinent, that Luther meant not only the refusal of benevolence but a stubborn denial of any main conjugal duty; or if he did not, it will be evinced from what he allows. For out of question, with men that are not barbarous, love and peace and fitness will be yielded as essential to marriage as corporeal benevolence. *Though I give my body to be burnt,* saith St. Paul, *and have not charity, it profits me nothing.*[283] So though the body prostitute itself to whom the mind affords no other love or peace, but constant malice and vexation, can this bodily benevolence deserve to be called a marriage between Christians and rational creatures?

Melanchton, the third great luminary of reformation in his book *Concerning Marriage* grants divorce for cruel usage, and danger of life, urging the authority of that Theodosian law which he esteems written with the grave deliberation of godly men; and that they who reject this law, and think it disagreeing from the Gospel, understand not the difference of Law and Gospel; that the magistrate ought not only to defend life but to succor the weak conscience, lest broke with grief and indignation, it relinquish prayer and turn to some unlawful thing.[284] What if this heavy plight of despair arise from other discontents in wedlock which may go to the soul of a good man more than the danger of his life, or cruel using, which a man cannot be liable to? Suppose it be ingrateful usage, suppose it be perpetual spite and disobedience, suppose a hatred, shall not the magistrate free him from this disquiet which interrupts his prayers, and disturbs the course of his service to God and his country all as much, and brings him such a misery as that he more desires to leave his life than fears to lose it? Shall not this equally concern the office of civil protection, and much more the charity of a true church to remedy?

Erasmus, who for learning was the wonder of his age, both in his notes on Matthew and on the first to the Corinthians in a large and eloquent discourse, and in his answer to Phimostomus, a Papist, maintains (and no Protestant then living contradicted him)[285] that the words of Christ comprehend many other causes of divorce under the name of fornication.

Bucer (whom our famous Dr. Rainolds[286] was wont to prefer before Calvin) in his comment on Matthew and in his second book, *Of the Kingdom of Christ,* treats of divorce at large to the same effect, as is written in *The Doctrine and Discipline of Divorce* lately published, and the translation is extant: whom lest I should be thought to have wrested to mine own purpose, take something more out of his 49th chap., which I then for brevity omitted. *It will be the duty of pious princes, and all who govern church or commonwealth, if any, whether husband or wife, shall affirm their want of such who either will, or can tolerably perform the necessary duties of married life, to grant that they may seek them such, and marry them; if they make it appear that such they have not.* This book he wrote here in England, where he lived the greatest admired man, and this he dedicated to Edward the sixth.

Fagius,[287] ranked among the famous divines of Germany, whom Frederic, at that time the Palatine, sent for to be the reformer of his Dominion, and whom afterwards England sought to, and obtained of him to come and teach her, differs not in this opinion from Bucer, as his notes on the *Chaldee paraphrast* well testify.

The whole Church of Strasburgh[288] in her most flourishing time, when Zellius, Hedio, Capito, and other great divines taught there, and those two renowned magistrates Farrerus and Sturmius[289] governed that commonwealth and academy to the admiration of all Germany, hath thus in the 21st Article: *We teach that if according to the word of God, yea or against it, divorces happen, to do according to God's word, Deut. 24.1. Mat. 19. 1 Cor. 7. and the observations of the primitive church, and the Christian constitution of pious Caesars.*[290]

Peter Martyr[291] seems in word our easy adversary, but is indeed for us: toward which though it be something when he saith of this opinion, *that it is not wicked, and can hardly be refuted,* this which follows is much more. *I speak not here,* saith he, *of natural impediments, which may so happen, that the matrimony can no longer hold;* but adding, that he often wondered how the ancient and most Christian Emperors established those laws of divorce, and neither Ambrose, who had such influence upon the laws of Theodosius, nor any of those holy Fathers found fault, nor any of the churches, why the magistrates of this day should be so loath to constitute the same. Perhaps they fear an inundation of divorces, which is not likely, whenas we read not either among the Hebrews, Greeks, or Romans, that they were much frequent where they were most permitted. If they judge Christian men worse than Jews or pagans, they both injure that name and by this reason will be constrained to grant divorces the rather, because it was permitted as a remedy of evil. For who would remove the medicine while the disease is yet so rife?[292] This being read both in his commonplaces, and on the first to the Corinthians, with what we shall relate more of him yet ere the end, sets him absolutely on this side. Not to insist that in both these, and other places of his commentaries, he grants divorce not only for desertion but for the seducement and scandalous demeanor of a heretical consort.

Musculus,[293] a divine of no obscure fame, distinguishes between the religious and the civil determination of divorce; and leaving the civil wholly to the lawyers, pronounces a conscionable divorce for impotence not only natural, but accidental, if it be durable. His equity, it seems, can enlarge the words of Christ to one cause more than adultery; why may not the reason of another man as wise, enlarge them to another cause?

Gualter of Zuric,[294] a well-known judicious commentator, in his Homilies on Matthew, allows divorce for *leprosy, or any other cause which renders unfit for wedlock,* and calls this rather *a nullity of marriage than a divorce.* And who that is not himself a mere body can restrain all the unfitness of marriage only to a corporeal defect?

Hemingius,[295] an author highly esteemed, and his works printed at Geneva, writing of divorce, confesses that learned men *vary in this question, some granting three causes thereof, some five, others many more;* he himself gives us six, *adultery, desertion, inability, error, evil-usage, and impiety,* using argument *that Christ under one special contains the whole kind, and under the name and example of fornication, he includes other causes equipollent.*[296] This discourse he wrote at the request of many who had the judging of these causes in Denmark and Norway, who by all likelihood followed his advice.

Hunnius,[297] a Doctor of Wittenberg, well known in both Divinity and other arts, on the 19th of Mat. affirms *that the exception of fornication expressed by our Savior excludes not other causes equaling adultery, or destructive to the substantials of matrimony; but was opposed to the custom of the Jews who made divorce for every light cause.*

Felix Bidenbachius,[298] an eminent divine in the Dutchy of Wirtemberg, affirms *that the obstinate refusal of conjugal due is a lawful cause of divorce,* and gives an instance *that the consistory of that state so judged.*

Gerard cites Harbardus, an author not unknown,[299] and Arnisaeus cites Wigandus,[300] both yielding divorce *in case of cruel usage;* and another author, who testifies *to have seen, in a dukedom of Germany, marriages disjoined for some implacable enmities arising.*

Beza, one of the strictest against divorce, denies it not *for danger of life from a heretic, or importunate solicitation to do aught against religion;* and counts it *all one whether the heretic desert, or would stay upon intolerable conditions*. But this decision well examined will be found of no solidity. For Beza would be asked why, if God so strictly exact our stay in any kind of wedlock, we had not better stay and hazard a murdering for religion at the hand of a wife, or husband, as he and others enjoin us to stay and venture it for all other causes but that? And why a man's life is not as well and warrantably saved by divorcing from an orthodox murderer as a heretical? Again, if desertion be confessed by him to consist not only in the forsaking but in the insufferable conditions of staying, a man may as well deduce the lawfulness of divorcing from any intolerable conditions (if his grant be good that we may divorce thereupon from a heretic) as he can deduce it lawful to divorce from any deserter by finding it lawful to divorce from a deserting infidel. For this is plain, if Saint Paul's permission to divorce an infidel deserter infer it lawful for any malicious desertion, then doth Beza's definition of a deserter transfer itself with like facility from the cause of religion to the cause of malice, and proves it as good to divorce from him who intolerably stays as from him who purposely departs; and leaves it as lawful to depart from him who urgently requires a wicked thing, though professing the same religion, as from him who urges a heathenish or superstitious compliance in a different faith. For if there be such necessity of our abiding, we ought rather to abide the utmost for religion than for any other cause, seeing both the cause of our stay is pretended our religion to marriage, and the cause of our suffering is supposed our constant marriage to religion. Beza therefore, by his own definition of a deserter, justifies a divorce from any wicked or intolerable conditions rather in the same religion than in a different.

Aretius,[301] a famous divine of Bern, approves many causes of divorce in his *Problems,* and adds, *that the laws and consistories of Switzerland approve them also.* As first, *adultery, and that not actual only, but intentional;* alleging Matthew 5: *Whosoever looketh to lust, hath committed adultery already in his heart. Whereby,* saith he, *our Savior shows that the breach of matrimony may be not only by outward act, but by the heart and desire; when that hath once possessed, it renders the conversation intolerable, and commonly the fact follows.* Other causes to the number of nine or ten, consenting in most with the imperial laws, may be read in the author himself, who avers them *to be grave and weighty.* All these are men of name in divinity, and to these if need were, might be added more. Nor have the civilians been all so blinded by the canon as not to avouch the justice of those old permissions touching divorce.

Alciat of Milan,[302] a man of extraordinary wisdom and learning, in the sixth book of his *Parerga,* defends those imperial laws, *not repugnant to the Gospel, as the church then interpreted.* For, saith he, *the ancients understood him separate by man, whom passions and corrupt affections divorced, not, if the provincial Bishops first heard the matter, and judged, as the Council of Agatha declares;* and on some part of the Code he names Isidorus Hispalensis,[303] the first computer of canons, *to be in the same mind.* And in the former place gives his opinion *that divorce might be more lawfully permitted than usury.*

Corasius, recorded by Helvicus,[304] among the famous lawyers, hath been already cited of the same judgment.

Wesembechius,[305] a much-named civilian, in his comment on this law defends it, and affirms *that our Savior excluded not other faults equal to adultery; and that the word fornication signifies larger among the Hebrews than with us, comprehending every fault which alienates from him to whom obedience is due, and that the primitive church interpreted so.*

Grotius,[306] yet living, and of prime note among learned men, retires plainly from the canon to the ancient civility, yea, to the Mosaic law, as being most just and undeceivable. On the 5th of Matt. he saith, *that Christ made no civil laws, but taught us how to use law: that the law sent not a husband to the judge about this matter of divorce, but left him to his own conscience; that Christ therefore cannot be thought to send him; that adultery may be judged by a vehement suspicion; that the exception of adultery seems an example of other like offences; proves it from the manner of speech, the maxims of law, the reason of charity, and common equity.*

These authorities without long search I had to produce, all excellent men, some of them such as many ages had brought forth none greater. Almost the meanest of them might deserve to obtain credit in a singularity; what might not then all of them joined in an opinion so consonant to reason? For although some speak of this cause, others of that, why divorce may be, yet all agreeing in the necessary enlargement of that textual straitness, leave the matter to equity, not to literal bondage, and so the opinion closes. Nor could I have wanted more testimonies, had the cause needed a more solicitous inquiry. But herein the satisfaction of others hath been studied, not the gaining of more assurance to mine own persuasion: although authorities contributing reason withal, be good confirmation and a welcome. But God, I solemnly attest him, withheld from my knowledge the consenting judgment of these men so late, until they could not be my instructors but only my unexpected witnesses to partial men, that in this work I had not given the worst experiment of an industry joined with integrity and the free utterance though of an unpopular truth. Which yet to the people of England may, if God so please, prove a memorable informing; certainly a benefit which was intended them long since by men of highest repute for wisdom and piety, Bucer and Erasmus. Only this one authority more, whether in place or out of place, I am not to omit; which if any can think a small one, I must be patient: it is no smaller than the whole assembled authority of England, both Church and State; and in those times which are on record for the purest and sincerest that ever shone yet on the reformation of this island, the time of Edward the 6th. That worthy Prince having utterly abolished the canon law out of his dominions, as his father did before him, appointed by full vote of

Parliament a committee of two and thirty chosen men, divines and lawyers, of whom Cranmer the Archbishop,[307] Peter Martyr, and Walter Haddon[308] (not without the assistance of Sir John Cheeke[309] the King's tutor, a man at that time counted the learnedest of Englishmen, and for piety not inferior) were the chief, to frame anew some ecclesiastical laws, that might be in stead of what was abrogated. The work with great diligence was finished, and with as great approbation of that reforming age was received; and had been doubtless, as the learned Preface thereof testifies, established by act of Parliament, had not the good King's death so soon ensuing, arrested the further growth of religion also, from that season to this. Those laws, thus founded on the memorable wisdom and piety of that religious Parliament and synod, allow divorce and second marriage *not only for adultery or desertion but for any capital enmity or plot laid against the other's life, and likewise for evil and fierce usage*. Nay, the 12th chapter of that title by plain consequence declares, *that lesser contentions, if they be perpetual, may obtain divorce,* which is all one really with the position by me held in the former treatise published on this argument, herein only differing, that there the cause of perpetual strife was put for example in the unchangeable discord of some natures; but in these laws, intended us by the best of our ancestors, the effect of continual strife is determined no unjust plea of divorce, whether the cause be natural or willful. Whereby the wariness and deliberation from which that discourse proceeded will appear, and that God hath aided us to make no bad conclusion of this point, seeing the opinion which of late hath undergone ill censures among the vulgar hath now proved to have done no violence to Scripture, unless all these famous authors alleged have done the like, nor hath affirmed aught more than what indeed the most nominated Fathers of the church both ancient and modern are expectedly affirming, the laws of God's peculiar[310] people and of primitive Christendom found to have practiced, reformed churches and states to have imitated, and especially the most pious church-times of this Kingdom to have framed and published, and but for sad hindrances in the sudden change of religion had enacted by Parliament. Henceforth let them who condemn the assertion of this book for new and licentious, be sorry; lest, while they think to be of the graver sort, and take on them to be teachers, they expose themselves rather to be pledged[311] up and down, by men who intimately know them, to the discovery and contempt of their ignorance and presumption.

The End.

Errata.[312]
Pag. 57. *lin.* 16. *and by them to prosecute, no comma between.*
Pag. 88. *lin.* 3. Basilius Macedo, *no comma between.* [98].

Colasterion[1]

A Reply to a nameless[2] answer against *The Doctrine and Discipline of Divorce.* wherein The trivial Author of that Answer is discovered, the Licenser conferred with, and the Opinion which they traduce defended

By the former Author, *J. M.*

Prov. 26:5. *Answer a Fool according to his folly, lest he bee wise in his own conceit.*

Printed in the Year, 1645.

Colasterion: A Reply to a nameless Answer against *The Doctrine and Discipline of Divorce.*

After many rumours of confutations and convictions forthcoming against *The Doctrine and Discipline of Divorce,* and now and then a by-blow from the pulpit, feathered with a censure strict indeed, but how true, more beholden to the authority of that devout place which it borrowed to be uttered in, than to any sound reason which it could oracle, while I still hoped as for a blessing to some piece of diligence, or learned discretion come from them, it was my hap at length, lighting on a certain parcel of queries,[3] that seek and find not, to find not seeking, at the tail of Anabaptist, Antinomian, Heretical, Atheistic Epithets, a jolly[4] slander called *Divorce at pleasure.* I stood awhile and wondered, what we might do to a man's heart, or what anatomy use, to find in it sincerity; for all our wonted marks every day fail us, and where we thought it was, we see it is not, for alter and change residence it cannot sure. And yet I see no good of body or of mind secure to a man for all his past labours, without perpetual watchfulness and perseverance. Whenas one above others, who hath suffered much and long in the defence of truth, shall after all this give her cause to leave him so destitute and so vacant of her defence as to yield his mouth to be the common road of truth and falsehood, and such falsehood as is joined with a rash and heedless calumny of his neighbour.[5] For what book hath he ever met with, as his complaint is, *Printed in the City,* maintaining either in the title, or in the whole pursuance, *Divorce at pleasure?* It is true, that to divorce upon extreme necessity, when through the perverseness or the apparent unfitness of either, the continuance can be to both no good at all but an intolerable injury and temptation to the wronged and the defrauded, to divorce then there is a book that writes it lawful. And that this law is a pure and wholesome national law, not to be withheld from good men because others likely enough may abuse it to their pleasure, cannot be charged upon that book, but must be entered a bold and impious accusation against God himself; who did not for this abuse withhold it from his own people. It will be just, therefore, and best for the reputation of him who in his *Subitanes*[6] hath thus censured, to recall his sentence. And if out of the abundance of his volumes, and the readiness of his quill, and the vastness of his other employments, especially in the great audit for accounts, he can spare us aught to the better understanding of this point, he shall be thanked in public; and what hath offended in the book shall willingly submit to his correction. Provided he be sure not to come with those old and stale suppositions, unless he can take away clearly what that discourse hath urged against them, by one who will expect other arguments to be persuaded the good health of a sound answer than the gout and dropsy of a big margent, littered and overlaid with crude and huddled quotations.[7] But as I still was waiting, when these light-armed refuters would have done pelting at their three lines uttered with a sage delivery of no reason but an impotent and worse than Bonner-like[8] censure to burn that which provokes them to a fair dispute, at length a book was brought to my hands, entitled *An Answer to The Doctrine and Discipline of Divorce.* Gladly I received it, and very attentively composed myself to read; hoping that now some good man had vouchsafed the pains to instruct me better than I could yet learn out of all the volumes which for this purpose I had visited. Only this I marvelled, and other men have since, whenas I, in a subject so new to this age, and so hazardous to please, concealed not my name, why this author, defending that part which is so creeded[9] by the people, would conceal his.[10] But ere I could enter three leaves into the pamphlet (for I defer the pleasant rudeness, which by the licenser's leave I met with afterwards) my satisfaction came in abundantly, that it could be nothing why he durst not name himself but the guilt of his own wretchedness. For first, not to speak of his abrupt and bald beginning, his very first page notoriously betrays him an illiterate and arrogant presumer in that which he understands not, bearing us in hand as if he knew both Greek and Hebrew, and is not able to spell it; which had he been, it had been either written as it ought or scored upon the printer. If it be excused as the carelessness of his deputy, be it known, the learned author himself is inventoried and summed up to the utmost value of his livery-cloak. Whoever he be, though this to some may seem a slight contest, I shall yet continue to think that man full of other secret injustice, and deceitful pride, who shall offer in public to assume the skill, though it be but of a tongue which he hath not, and would catch his readers to believe of his ability, that which is not in him. The licenser indeed, as his authority now stands, may license much; but if these Greek orthographies were of his licensing, the boys at school might reckon with him at his grammar. Nor did I find that his want of the pretended languages alone, but accompanied with such a low and home-spun expression of his mother-English all along, without joint or frame, as made me ere I knew further of him, often stop and conclude that this author could for certain be no other than some mechanic. Nor was the style flat and rude, and the matter grave and solid, for then there had been pardon; but so shallow and so unwary was that also, as gave sufficiently the character of a gross and sluggish, yet a contentious and overweening pretender. For first, it behooving him to show, as he promises, what divorce is, and what the true doctrine and discipline thereof, and this being to do by such principles and proofs as are received on both sides, he performs neither of these; but shows it first from the Judaical practice, which he himself disallows, and next from the practice of canon law, which the book he would confute utterly rejects, and all laws depending thereon; which this puny clerk calls the laws of England, and yet pronounces them by an ecclesiastical judge: as if that were to be accounted the law of England, which depends on the Popery of England; or if it were, this Parliament he might know hath now damned that judicature.[11] So that whether his meaning were to inform his own party, or to confute his adversary, instead of showing us the true doctrine and discipline of divorce, he shows us nothing but his own contemptible ignorance. For what is the Mosaic law to his opinion? And what is the canon, utterly now antiquated, either to that, or to mine? Ye see already what a faithful definer we have of him. From such a wind egg[12] of definition as this, they who expect any of his other arguments to be well hatched, let them enjoy the virtue of their worthy champion. But one thing more I observed, a singular note of his stupidity, and that his trade is not to meddle with books, much less with confutations; whenas *The Doctrine of Divorce* had now a whole year been published the second time, with many arguments added, and the former ones bettered and confirmed, this idle pamphlet comes reeling forth against the first edition only, as may appear to any by the pages quoted; which put me in mind of what by chance I had notice of to this purpose the last summer, as nothing so serious but happens oft-times to be attended with ridiculous accident: it was then told me that *The Doctrine of Divorce* was answered, and the *Answer* half printed against the first edition, not by one, but by a pack of heads;[13] of whom the chief, by circumstance, was intimated to me, and since ratified to be no other, if any can hold laughter, and I am sure none will guess him lower than an actual servingman. This creature, for the story must on, (and what though he be the lowest person of an interlude, he may deserve a canvassing) transplanted himself, and to the improvement of his ages, and your better notice of his capacity, turned solicitor. And having conversed much with a stripling divine or two of these newly-fledged probationers that usually come scouting from the university and lie here no lame legers[14] to pop into the Bethesda of some knight's chaplainship,[15] where they bring grace to his good cheer but no peace or benediction else to his house; these made the champarty,[16] he contributed the law, and both joined in the divinity. Which made me intend, following the advice also of friends, to lay aside the thought of misspending a reply to the buzz of such a drones' nest. But finding that it lay, whatever was the matter, half a year after unfinished in the press, and hearing for certain that a divine of note,[17] out of his goodwill to the opinion, had taken it into his revise, and something had put out, something put in, and struck it here and there with a clove of his own calligraphy to keep it from tainting: and farther, when I saw the stuff, though very coarse and threadbare, garnished and trimly faced with the commendations of a licenser,[18] I resolved, so soon as leisure granted me the recreation, that my man of law should not altogether lose his soliciting. Although I impute a share of the making to him whose name I find in the approbation, who may take, as his mind serves him, this reply. In the mean while it shall be seen, I refuse no occasion, and avoid no adversary, either to maintain what I have begun, or to give it up for better reason.

To begin then with the licenser and his censure. For a licenser is not contented now to give his single Imprimatur, but brings his chair into the title-leaf; there sits and judges up or judges down what book he pleases: If this be suffered, what worthless author or what cunning printer will not be ambitious of such a stale[19] to put off the heaviest gear; which may in time bring in round fees to the licenser, and wretched misleading to the people. But to the matter: he approves *the publishing of this book, to preserve the strength and honour of marriage against those sad breaches and dangerous abuses of it.* Belike then the wrongful suffering of all those sad breaches and abuses in marriage to a remediless thraldom, *is the strength and honour of marriage;* a boisterous and bestial strength, a dishonourable honour, an infatuated doctrine, worse than the *salvo jure*[20] of tyrannizing, which we all fight against. Next he saith, that *common discontents make these breaches in unstaid minds, and men given to change.* His words may be apprehended, as if they disallowed only to divorce for common discontents, in unstaid minds, having no cause but a desire of change, and then we agree. But if he take all discontents on this side adultery to be common, that is to say, not difficult to endure, and to affect only unstaid minds, it might administer just cause to think him the most unfit man that could be, to offer at a comment upon Job;[21] as seeming by this to have no more true sense of a good man in his afflictions than those Edomitish[22] friends had, of whom Job complains and against whom God testifies his anger. Shall a man of your own coat, who hath espoused his flock, and represents Christ more in being the true husband of his congregation than an ordinary man doth in being the husband of his wife, and yet this representment is thought a chief cause why marriage must be inseparable; shall this spiritual man ordinarily for the increase of his maintenance, or any slight cause, forsake that wedded cure of souls, that should be dearest to him, and marry another and another? And shall not a person wrongfully afflicted, and persecuted even to extremity, forsake an unfit, injurious, and pestilent mate, tied only by a civil and fleshly covenant? If you be a man so much hating change, hate that other change; if yourself be not guilty, counsel your brethren to hate it; and leave to be the supercilious judge of other man's miseries and changes, that your own be not judged. The reasons of your licensed pamphlet, you say, are good; they must be better than you own then. I shall wonder else how such a trivial fellow was accepted and commended to be the confuter of so dangerous an opinion as ye give out mine.

Now therefore to your attorney, since no worthier an adversary makes his appearance, nor this neither his appearance, but lurking under the safety of his nameless obscurity; such as ye turn him forth at the postern I must accept him, and in a better temper than Ajax do mean to scourge this ram for ye 'til I meet with his Ulysses.[23]

He begins with law,[24] and we have it of him as good, cheap as any huckster at law, newly set up, can possibly afford, and as impertinent; but for that he hath received his handsel.[25] He presumes also to cite the civil law, which I perceive, by his citing, never came within his dormitory;[26] yet what he cites makes but against himself.

His second thing therefore, is to refute the adverse position, and very methodically, three pages before he sets it down; and sets his own in the place, *that disagreement of mind or disposition, though showing itself in much sharpness, is not by the law of God or man a just cause of divorce.*

To this position I answer: that it lays no battery[27] against mine, no nor so much as faces it, but tacks about long ere it come near, like a harmless and respectful confutement. For I confess that disagreement of mind or disposition, though in much sharpness, is not always a just cause of divorce; for much may be endured. But what if the sharpness be much more than his much? To that point it is our mishap we have not here his grave decision. He that will contradict the position which I alleged, must hold that no disagreement of mind or disposition can divorce, though shown in most sharpness; otherwise he leaves a place for equity to appoint limits, and so his following arguments will either not prove his own position, or not disprove mine.

His first argument, all but what hobbles to no purpose, is this: *Where the Scripture commands a thing to be done, it appoints when, now, and for what, as in the case of death or excommunication. But the Scripture directs not what measure of disagreement or contrariety may divorce. Therefore, the Scripture allows not any divorce for disagreement.*

Answer. First, I deny your major;[28] the Scripture appoints many things, and yet leaves the circumstance to man's discretion, particularly in your own examples. Excommunication is not taught when, and for what to be, but left to the Church. How could the licenser let pass this childish ignorance, and call it good? Next, in matters of death, the laws of England, whereof you have intruded to be an opiniastrous[29] sub-advocate, and are bound to defend them, conceive it not enjoined in Scripture, when or for what cause they shall put to death, as in adultery, theft, and the like. Your minor also is false, for the Scripture plainly sets down for what measure of disagreement a man may divorce, Deut. 24:1. Learn better what that phrase means, *if she find no favour in his eyes.*

Your second argument, without more tedious fumbling, is briefly thus: *If diversity in religion, which breeds a greater dislike than any natural disagreement, may not cause a divorce, then may not the lesser disagreement: but diversity of religion may not; ergo.*

Answer. First, I deny in the major, that diversity of religion breeds a greater dislike to marriage duties, than natural disagreement. For between Israelite or Christian and infidel, more often hath been seen too much love: but between them who perpetually clash in natural contrarieties, it is repugnant that there should be ever any married love or concord. Next, I deny your minor, that it is commanded not to divorce in diversity of religion, if the infidel will stay: for that place in St. Paul[30] commands nothing, as that book at large affirmed, though you over-skipped it.

Secondly, if it do command, it is but with condition that the infidel be content and well-pleased to stay, which cuts off the supposal of any great hatred or disquiet between them, seeing the infidel had liberty to depart at pleasure; and so this comparison avails nothing.

Your third argument is from Deut. 22, *If a man hate his wife, and raise an ill report that he found her no virgin*; if this were false, *he might not put her away,* though hated never so much.

Answer. This was a malicious hatred, bent against her life, or to send her out of doors without her portion. Such a hater loses by due punishment that privilege, Deut. 24:1, to divorce for a natural dislike; which though it could not love conjugally, yet sent away civilly, and with just conditions. But doubtless the wife in that former case had liberty to depart from her false accuser, lest his hatred should prove mortal; else that law, peculiarly made to right the woman, had turned to her greatest mischief.

Your fourth argument: *One Christian ought to bear the infirmities of another, but chiefly of his wife.*

Answer. I grant infirmities, but not outrages, nor perpetual defraudments of truest conjugal society, not injuries and vexations as importunate as fire. Yet to endure very much, might do well an exhortation, but not a compulsive law. For the Spirit of God himself, by Solomon, declares that such a consort *the Earth can-*

not bear, and better dwell in a corner of the house-top, or in the wilderness.[31] Burdens may be borne, but still with consideration to the strength of an honest man complaining. Charity indeed bids us forgive our enemies, yet doth not force us to continue friendship and familiarity with those friends who have been false or unworthy towards us; but is contented in our peace with them, at a fair distance. Charity commands not the husband to receive again into his bosom the adulterous wife, but thinks it enough if he dismiss her with a beneficent and peaceful dismissal. No more doth charity command; nor can her rule compel, to retain in nearest union of wedlock one whose other grossest faults, or disabilities to perform what was covenanted, are the just causes of as much grievance and dissension in a family as the private act of adultery. Let not therefore, under the name of fulfilling charity, such an unmerciful and more than legal yoke be padlocked upon the neck of any Christian.

Your fifth argument: *If the husband ought to love his wife, as Christ his Church, then ought she not to be put away for contrariety of mind.*

Answer. This similitude turns against him: for if the husband must be as Christ to the wife, then must the wife be as the Church to her husband. If there be a perpetual contrariety of mind in the Church toward Christ, Christ himself threatens to divorce such a spouse, and hath often done it. If they urge this was no true church, I urge again that was no true wife.

His sixth argument is from Mat. 5:32, which he expounds after the old fashion, and never takes notice of what I brought against that exposition; let him therefore seek his answer there. Yet can he not leave this argument, but he must needs first show us a curvet[32] of his madness, holding out an objection, and running himself upon the point. *For,* saith he, *if Christ except no cause but adultery, then all other causes, as frigidity, incestuous marriage, &c. are no causes of divorce; and answers, that the speech of Christ holds universally as he intended it; namely, to condemn such divorce as was groundlessly practiced among the Jews, for every cause which they thought sufficient, not checking the law of consanguinities or affinities, or forbidding other cause which makes marriage void, ipso facto.*

Answer. Look to it now, you be not found taking fees on both sides; for if you once bring limitations to the universal words of Christ, another will do as much with as good authority; and affirm that neither did he check the law, Deut. 24:1, nor forbid the causes that make marriage void actually; which if any thing in the world doth, unfitness doth, and contrariety of mind; yea, more than adultery, for that makes not the marriage void, not much more unfit, but for the time, if the offended party forgive. But unfitness and contrariety frustrates and nullifies for ever, unless it be a rare chance, all the good and peace of wedded conversation; and leaves nothing between them enjoyable, but a prone and savage necessity, not worth the name of marriage, unaccompanied with love. Thus much his own objection hath done against himself.

Argument 7th. He insists, *That man and wife are one flesh, therefore must not separate.* But must be sent to look again upon the 35th page of that book, where he might read an answer, which he stirs not. Yet can he not abstain, but he must do us another pleasure ere he goes; although I call the common pleas to witness, I have not hired his tongue, whatever men may think by his arguing. For besides adultery, he excepts other causes which dissolve the union of being one flesh, either directly or by consequence. If only adultery be excepted by our Savior, and he voluntarily can add other exceptions that dissolve that union, both directly and by consequence, these words of Christ, the main obstacle of divorce, are open to us by his own invitation to include whatever causes dissolve that union of flesh, either directly or by consequence. Which, 'til he name other causes more likely, I affirm to be done soonest by unfitness and contrariety of mind; for that induces hatred, which is the greatest dissolver both of spiritual and corporeal union, turning the mind, and consequently the body, to other objects. Thus our doughty adversary, either directly or by consequence, yields us the question with his own mouth; and the next thing he does, recants it again.

His 8th argument shivers in the uttering, and he confesses to be not over-confident of it; but of the rest it may be sworn he is.

St. Paul, I Cor. 7, saith that *the married have trouble in the flesh;* therefore we must bear it, though never so intolerable.

I answer, if this be a true consequence, why are not all troubles to be borne alike? Why are we suffered to divorce adulteries, desertions, or frigidities? Who knows not that trouble and affliction is the decree of God upon every state of life? Follows it therefore, that though they grow excessive and insupportable, we must not avoid them? If we may in all other conditions, and not in marriage; the doom of our suffering ties us not by the trouble, but by the bond of marriage; and that must be proved inseparable from other reasons, not from this place. And his own confession declared the weakness of this argument, yet his ungoverned arrogance could not be dissuaded from venting it.

His 9th argument is, *That a husband must love his wife as himself; therefore he may not divorce for any disagreement, no more than he may separate his soul from his body.*

I answer: if he love his wife as himself, he must love her so far as he may preserve him to her in a cheerful and comfortable manner, and not so as to ruin himself by anguish and sorrow, without any benefit to her. Next, if the husband must love his wife as himself, she must be understood a wife in some reasonable measure, willing and sufficient to perform the chief duties of her covenant, else by the hold of this argument, it would be his great sin to divorce either for adultery or desertion. The rest of this will run circuit with the union of one flesh, which was answered before. And that to divorce a relative and metaphorical union of two bodies into one flesh cannot be likened in all things to the dividing of that natural union of soul and body into one person, is apparent of itself.

His last argument he fetches *from the inconveniences that would follow upon this freedom of divorce, to the corrupting of men's minds and the overturning of all human society.*

But for me, let God and Moses answer this blasphemer, who dares bring in such a foul indictment against the divine law. Why did God permit this to his people the Jews, but that the right and good which came directly thereby was more in his esteem than the wrong and evil which came by accident? And for those weak supposes of infants that would be left in their mother's belly (which must needs be good news for chambermaids to hear a serving man grown so provident for great bellies) and portions and jointures likely to incur embezzlement hereby, the ancient civil law instructs us plentifully how to award, which our profound opposite knew not, for it was not in his tenures.[33]

His arguments are spun; now follows the chaplain with his antiquities, wiser if he had refrained, for his very touching aught that is learned soils it, and lays him still more and more open, a conspicuous gull. There being both Fathers and Councils more ancient, wherewith to have served his purpose better than with what he cites, how may we do to know the subtle drift that moved him to begin first with the twelfth Council of Toledo? I would not undervalue the depth of his notion; but perhaps he had heard that the men of Toledo had store of good blade mettle, and were excellent at cutling.[34] Who can tell but it might be the reach of his policy, that these able men of decision would do best to have the prime stroke among his testimonies in deciding this cause? But all this craft avails him not; for seeing they allow no cause of divorce but fornication, what do these keen doctors here, but cut him over the sinews with their Toledo's, for holding in the precedent page other causes of divorce besides, both directly and by consequence. As evil doth that Saxon Council, next quoted, bestead him. For if it allow divorce precisely for no cause but fornication, it thwarts his own exposition; and if it understand fornication largely, it sides with whom he would confute. However, the authority of that synod can be but small, being under Theodorus, the Canterbury Bishop, a Grecian Monk of Tarsus, revolted from his own church to the Pope. What have we next? The civil law stuffed in between two Councils, as if the code had been some synod; for that he understood himself in this quotation is incredible; where the law, Cod. l. 3. tit. 38. leg. 11, speaks not of divorce, but against the dividing of possessions to divers heirs, whereby the married servants of a great family were divided, perhaps into distant countries and colonies: father from son, wife from husband, sore against their will. Somewhat lower he confesses *that the civil law allows many reasons of divorce, but the canon law decrees otherwise;* a fair credit to his cause! And I amaze me, though the fancy of this doubt be as obtuse and sad as any mallet, how the Licenser could sleep out all this, and suffer him to uphold his opinion by canons and Gregorical decretals; a law which not only his adversary but the whole reformation of this Church and State hath branded and rejected. As ignorantly, and too ignorantly to deceive any reader but an unlearned, he talks of Justin Martyr's apology, not telling us which of the twain; for that passage in the beginning of his first, which I have cited elsewhere, plainly makes against him. So doth Tertullian, cited next, and next Erasmus, the one against Marcion, the other in his *Annotations on Matthew,* and to the Corinthians. And thus ye have the list of his choice antiquities, as pleasantly chosen as ye would wish from a man of his handy vocation, puffed up with no luck at all, above the stint of his capacity.

Now he comes to the position which I set down whole; and like an able textman slits it into four, that he may the better come at it with his barber-surgery and his sleeves turned up. Wherein first, he denies *that any disposition, unfitness, or contrariety of mind is unchangeable in nature, but that by the help of diet and physic it may be altered.*

I mean not to dispute philosophy with this pork, who never read any. But I appeal to all experience, though there be many drugs to purge these redundant humours and circulations, that commonly impair health and are not natural, whether any man can with the safety of his life bring a healthy constitution into physic with this design, to alter his natural temperament and disposition of mind. How much more vain and ridiculous would it be, by altering and rooting up the grounds of nature, which is most likely to produce death or madness, to hope the reducing of a mind to this or that fitness, or two disagreeing minds to a mutual sympathy? Suppose they might, and that with great danger of their lives and right senses, alter one temperature,[35] how can they know that the succeeding disposition will not be as far from fitness and agreement? They would perhaps change melancholy into sanguine; but what if phlegm and choler in as great a measure come instead? The unfitness will be still as difficult and troublesome.[36] But lastly, whether these things be changeable or not, experience teaches us, and our position supposes, that they seldom do change in any time commensurable to the necessities of man, or convenient to the ends of marriage. And if the fault be in the one, shall the other live all his days in bondage and misery for another's perverseness or immedicable disaffection? To my friends, of which may fewest be so unhappy, I have a remedy, as they know, more wise and manly to prescribe; but for his friends and followers (of which many may deserve justly to feel themselves the unhappiness which they consider not in others) I send them by his advice to sit upon the stool and strain, 'til their cross dispositions and contrarieties of mind shall change to a better correspondence, and to a quicker apprehension of common sense and their own good.

His second reason is as heedless, *because that grace may change the disposition, therefore no indisposition may cause divorce.*

Answer. First, it will not be deniable that many persons, gracious both, may yet happen to be very unfitly married to the great disturbance of either. Secondly, what if one have grace, the other not, and will not alter, as the Scriptures testify there be of those, in whom we may expect a change when *the black-a-moor changes his colour, or the leopard his spots,* Jer. 13:23. Shall the gracious therefore dwell in torment all his life for the ungracious? We see that holiest precepts, than which there can no better physic be administered to the mind of man, and set on with powerful preaching, cannot work this cure, no not in the family, not in the wife of him that preaches day and night to her. What an unreasonable thing it is, that men, and clergymen especially, should exact such wondrous changes in another man's house, and are seen to work so little in their own.

To the second point of the position, that this unfitness hinders the main ends and benefits of marriage; he answers, *if I mean the unfitness of choler, or sullen disposition, that soft words, according to Solomon, pacify wrath.*

But I reply, that the saying of Solomon is a proverb, frequently true, not universally, as both the event shows, and many other sentences written by the same author, particularly of an evil woman,

Prov. 21:9, 19, and in other chapters, that she is better shunned than dwelt with, and a desert is preferred before her society. What need the Spirit of God put this choice into our heads, if soft words could always take effect with her? How frivolous is not only this disputer, but he that taught him thus and let him come abroad.

To his second answer I return this, that although there be not easily found such an antipathy as to hate one another like a toad or poison; yet that there is oft such a dislike in both, or either, to conjugal love, as hinders all the comfort of matrimony, scarce any can be so simple as not to apprehend. And what can be that favour, found or not found, in the eyes of the husband, but a natural liking or disliking; whereof the law of God, Deut. 24, bears witness, as of an ordinary accident, and determines wisely and divinely thereafter. And this dissatisfaction happening to be in the one, not without the unspeakable discomfort of the other, must he be left like a thing consecrated to calamity, and despair without redemption?

Against the third branch of the position, he denies *that solace and peace, which is contrary to discord and variance, is the main end of marriage*. What then? He will have it *the solace of male and female*. Came this doctrine out of some school, or some sty? Who but one forsaken of all sense and civil nature, and chiefly of Christianity, will deny that peace, contrary to discord, is the calling and the general end of every Christian, and of all his actions, and more especially of marriage, which is the dearest league of love, and the dearest resemblance of that love which in Christ is dearest to his Church? How then can peace and comfort, as it is contrary to discord, which God hates to dwell with, not be the main end of marriage? Discord then we ought to fly, and to pursue peace, far above the observance of a civil covenant already broken, and the breaking daily iterated on the other side. And what better testimony than the words of the institution itself, to prove that a conversing solace and peaceful society is the prime end of marriage, without which no other help or office can be mutual, beseeming the dignity of reasonable creatures, that such as they should be coupled in the rites of nature by the mere compulsion of lust, without love or peace, worse than wild beasts. Nor was it half so wisely spoken as some deem, though Austin[37] spoke it, that if God had intended other than copulation in marriage, he would for Adam have created a friend, rather than a wife, to converse with, and our own writers blame him for this opinion: for which and the like passages concerning marriage, he might be justly taxed of rusticity[38] in these affairs. For this cannot but be with ease conceived, that there is one society of grave friendship and another amiable and attractive society of conjugal love, besides the deed of procreation, which of itself soon cloys, and is despised, unless it be cherished and re-incited with a pleasing conversation. Which if ignoble and swinish minds cannot apprehend, shall such merit therefore to be the censurers of more generous and virtuous spirits?

Against the last point of the position, to prove that contrariety of mind is not a greater cause of divorce than corporal frigidity, he enters into such a tedious and drawling tale of burning, and burning, and lust and burning, that the dull argument itself burns too for want of stirring; and yet all this burning is not able to expel the frigidity of his brain. So long therefore as that cause in the position shall be proved a sufficient cause of divorce, rather than spend words with this fleamy clod of an antagonist more than of necessity, and a little merriment, I will not now contend whether it be a greater cause than frigidity or no.

His next attempt is upon the arguments which I brought to prove the position. And for the first, not finding it of that structure as to be scaled with his short ladder, he retreats with a bravado, that it deserves no answer. And as I much wonder what the whole book deserved, to be thus troubled and solicited by such a paltry solicitor. I would he had not cast the gracious eye of his duncery upon the small deserts of a pamphlet, whose every line meddled with, uncases him to scorn and laughter.

That which he takes for the second argument, if he look better, is no argument, but an induction to those that follow. Then he stumbles that I should say, the gentlest ends of marriage, confessing that he understands it not. And I believe him heartily: for how should he, a serving man both by nature and by function, an idiot by breeding, and a solicitor by presumption, ever come to know or feel within himself what the meaning is of gentle? He blames it for a neat phrase, for nothing angers him more than his own proper contrary. Yet altogether without art sure he is not; for who could have devised to give us more briefly a better description of his own servility?

But what will become now of the business I know not; for the man is suddenly taken with a lunacy of law, and speaks revelations out of *The Attorneys Academy*,[39] only from a lying spirit: for he says, that *where a thing is void ipso facto, there needs no legal proceeding to make it void;* which is false, for marriage is void by adultery or frigidity, yet not made void without legal proceeding. Then asks my opinion of John-a-Noaks and John-a-Stiles.[40] And I answer him, that I for my part think John Dory[41] was a better man than both of them: for certainly they were the greatest wranglers that ever lived, and have filled all our law-books with the obtunding[42] story of their suits and trials.

After this he tells a miraculous piece of antiquity, how two *Romans, Titus and Sempronius, made feoffments*,[43] at *Rome* sure, and *levied fines* by the common law. But now his fit of law past, yet hardly come to himself, he maintains, that if marriage be void, as being neither of God nor nature, there needs no legal proceeding to part it, and I tell him that offends not me. *Then,* quoth he, *this is nothing to your book, being The Doctrine and Discipline of Divorce*. But that I deny him; for all discipline is not legal, that is to say, juridical, but some is personal, some economical, and some ecclesiastical. Lastly, if I prove that contrary dispositions are joined neither of God nor nature, and so the marriage void, he will give me the controversy. I have proved it in that book to any wise man, and without more ado the institution proves it.

Where I answer an objection usually made, that the disposition ought to be known before marriage, and show how difficult it is to choose a fit consort and how easy to mistake, the servitor would know what I mean by conversation, declaring his capacity nothing refined since his law-puddering, but still the same it was in the pantry and at the dresser. Shall I argue of conversation with this hoyden,[44] to go and practice at his opportunities in the larder?[45] To men of quality I have said enough; and experience confirms by daily example that wisest, most sober, most just men are sometimes miserably mistaken in their choice. Whom to leave thus without remedy, tossed and tempested in a most unquiet sea of afflictions and temptations, I say is most un-Christianly.

But he goes on to untruss my arguments, imagining them his master's points.[46] Only in the passage following, I cannot but admire the ripeness and the pregnance of his native treachery, endeavouring to be more a fox than his wit will suffer him. Whereas I briefly mentioned certain heads of discourse, which I referred to a place more proper according to my method, to be treated there at full with all their reasons about them, this brain-worm[47] against all the laws of dispute will needs deal with them here. And as a country hind, sometimes ambitious to show his betters that he is not so simple as you take him, and that he knows his advantages, will teach us a new trick to confute by. And would you think to what a pride he swells in the contemplation of his rare stratagem, offering to carp at the language of a book, which yet he confesses to be generally commended; while himself will be acknowledged by all that read him, the basest and the hungriest endighter[48] that could take the boldness to look abroad. Observe now the arrogance of a groom, how it will mount. I had written that common adultery is a thing which the rankest politician would think it shame and disworship that his law should countenance. First, it offends him that rankest should signify aught but his own smell; who that knows English would not understand me, when I say a rank serving man, a rank pettifogger, to mean a mere serving man, a mere and arrant pettifogger, who lately was so hardy as to lay aside his buckram-wallet and make himself a fool in print, with confuting books which are above him? Next, the word politician is not used to his maw, and thereupon he plays the most notorious hobby-horse, jesting and frisking in the luxury of his nonsense with such poor fetches to cog a laughter from us, that no antic hob-nail at a Morris but is more handsomely facetious.

Concerning that place Deut. 24:1, which he saith to be the main pillar of my opinion, though I rely more on the institution[49] than on that: these two pillars I do indeed confess are to me as those two in the porch of the temple, Jachin and Boaz,[50] which names import establishment and strength; nor do I fear who can shake them. The exposition of Deut., which I brought, is the received exposition, both ancient and modern, by all learned men, unless it be a monkish Papist here and there. And the gloss which he and his obscure assistant would persuade us to, is merely new and absurd, presuming out of his utter ignorance in the Hebrew, to interpret these words of the text: first, in a mistaken sense of uncleanness, against all approved writers; secondly, in a limited sense, whenas the original speaks without limitation, some uncleanness or any. And it had been a wise law indeed to mean itself particular, and not to express the case which this acute Rabbi hath all this while been hooking for; whereby they who are most partial to him may guess that something is in this doctrine which I allege, that forces the adversary to such a new and strained exposition: wherein he does nothing for above four pages but founder himself to and fro in his own objections; one while denying that divorce was permitted, another while affirming that it was permitted for the wife's sake, and after all, distrusts himself. And for his surest retirement, betakes him to those old suppositions: that Christ abolished the Mosaic law of divorce; that the Jews had not sufficient knowledge in this point, through the darkness of the dispensation of heavenly things; that under the plenteous grace of the Gospel, we are tied by cruelest compulsion to live in marriage 'til death, with the wickedest, the worst, the most persecuting mate. These ignorant and doting surmises he might have read confuted at large, even in the first edition, but found it safer to pass that part over in silence. So that they who see not the sottishness of this his new and tedious exposition, are worthy to love it dearly.

His explanation done, he charges me with a *wicked gloss, and almost blasphemy,* for saying that Christ in teaching meant not always to be taken word for word; but like a wise physician, administering one excess against another to reduce us to a perfect mean. Certainly to teach us were not dishonest method: Christ himself hath often used hyperboles in his teaching; and gravest authors, both Aristotle in the second of his *Ethics to Nichomachus,* and Seneca in his seventh *de Beneficiis,* advise us to stretch out the line of precept oft-times beyond measure, that while we tend further, the mean might be the easier attained. And whoever comments that 5th of Matthew, when he comes to the *turning of cheek after cheek to blows,* and the *parting both with cloak and coat,*[51] if any please to be the rifler, will be forced to recommend himself to the same exposition, though this chattering law-monger be bold to call it wicked. Now note another precious piece of him; *Christ,* saith he, *doth not say that an unchaste look is adultery, but the lusting after her;* as if the looking unchastely could be without lusting. This gear is licensed for good reason: *Imprimatur.*

Next he would prove that the speech of Christ is not uttered in excess against the Pharisees. First, *because he speaks it to his disciples,* Mat. 5, which is false, for he spake it to the multitude, as by the first verse is evident, among which in all likelihood were many Pharisees, but out of doubt, all of them Pharisean disciples and bred up in their doctrine; from which extremes of error and falsity, Christ throughout his whole sermon labours to reclaim the people. Secondly, saith he, *because Christ forbids not only putting away, but marrying her who is put away.* Acutely, as if the Pharisees might not have offended as much in marrying the divorced, as in divorcing the married. The precept may bind all, rightly understood; and yet the vehement manner of giving it may be occasioned only by the Pharisees.

Finally, he winds up his text with much doubt and trepidation; for it may be his trenchers were not scraped, and that which never yet afforded corn of savour to his noddle, the salt-seller was not rubbed: and therefore in this haste *easily granting, that his answers fall foul upon each other,* and praying you would not think *he writes as a prophet, but as a man,* he runs to the black jack,[52] fills his flagon, spreads the table, and serves up dinner.

After waiting and voiding,[53] he thinks to void my second argument, and the contradictions that will follow both in the Law and Gospel, if the Mosaic law were abrogated by our Savior and a compulsive prohibition fixed instead; and sings his old song, that the Gospel counts unlawful that which the law allowed, instancing in circumcision, sacrifices, washings. But what are these ceremonial things to the changing of a moral point in household duty, equally belonging to Jew and Gentile? Divorce was then right, now wrong; then permitted in the rigourous time of law, now forbidden by law, even to the most extremely afflicted, in the favourable time of grace and freedom. But this is not for an unbuttoned fellow to discuss in the garret at his tressle,[54] and dimension of candle by the snuff; which brought forth his scullionly paraphrase on St. Paul, whom he brings in, discoursing such idle stuff to the maids and widows as his own servile inurbanity forbears not to put into the Apostle's mouth, of the soul's conversing; and this he presumes to do, being a bayard,[55] who never had the soul to know what conversing means, but as his provender and the familiarity of the kitchen schooled his conceptions.

He passes to the third argument, like a boar in a vineyard, doing naught else, but still as he goes champing and chewing over what I could mean by this chimera of a fit conversing soul, notions and words never made for those chops; but like a generous wine, only by over-working the settled mud of his fancy, to make him drunk, and disgorge his vileness the more openly. All persons of gentle breeding (I say gentle, though this barrow grunts at the word) I know will apprehend, and be satisfied in what I spoke, how unpleasing and discontenting the society of body must needs be between those whose minds cannot be sociable. But what should a man say more to a snout in this pickle? What language can be low and degenerate enough?

The fourth argument which I had was, that marriage being a covenant, the very being whereof consists in the performance of unfeigned love and peace, if that were not tolerably performed, the covenant became broke and revocable. Which how can any, in whose mind the principles of right reason and justice are not cancelled, deny? For how can a thing subsist, when the true essence thereof is dissolved? Yet this he denies, and yet in such a manner as alters my assertion; for he puts in, *though the main end be not attained in full measure;* but my position is, if it be not tolerably attained, as throughout the whole discourse is apparent.

Now for his reasons: *Heman found not that peace and solace which is the main end of communion with God; should he therefore break off that communion?*[56]

I answer, that if Heman found it not, the fault was certainly his own. But in marriage it happens far otherwise: sometimes the fault is plainly not his who seeks divorce; sometimes it cannot be discerned whose fault it is; and therefore cannot in reason or equity be the matter of an absolute prohibition.

His other instance declares what a right handicrafts man he is of petty cases, and how unfit to be aught else at highest but a hackney of the law. I change houses with a man; it is supposed I do it for my own ends; I attain them not in this house; I shall not therefore go from my bargain.[57] How without fear might the young Charinus in *Andria* now cry out, what likeness can be here to a marriage?[58] In this bargain was no capitulation, but the yielding of possession to one another, wherein each of them had his several end apart. In marriage there is a solemn vow of love and fidelity each to other. This bargain is fully accomplished in the change; in marriage the covenant still is in performing. If one of them perform nothing tolerably, but instead of love abound in disaffection, disobedience, fraud, and hatred; what thing in the nature of a covenant shall bind the other to such a perdurable mischief? Keep to your problems of ten groats, these matters are not for pragmatics and folk-mooters[59] to babble in.

Concerning the place of Paul, *that God hath called us to peace,* I Cor. 7 and therefore certainly, if anywhere in this world, we have a right to claim it reasonably in marriage, 'tis plain enough in the sense which I gave, and confessed by Paraeus and other orthodox divines, to be a good sense, and this answerer doth not weaken it. The other place, *that he who hateth, may put away,* which, if I show him, he promises to yield the whole controversy, is besides Deut. 24:1, Deut. 21:14, and before this, Exod. 21:8. Of Malachi, I have spoken more in another place; and say again, that the best interpreters, all the ancient and most of the modern, translate it as I cite it, and very few otherwise, whereof perhaps Junius is the chief.

Another thing troubles him, that marriage is called the mystery of joy. Let it still trouble him; for what hath he to do either with joy or with mystery? He thinks it frantic divinity to say, it is not the outward continuance of marriage that keeps the covenant of marriage whole; but whosoever doth most according to peace and love, whether in marriage or divorce, he breaks marriage least. If I shall spell it to him, *he breaks marriage least* is to say, he dishonours not marriage; for *least* is taken in the Bible, and other good authors, for *not at all.* And a particular marriage a man may break, if for a lawful cause, and yet not break, that is, not violate, or dishonour the ordinance of marriage. Hence these two questions that follow are left ridiculous; and the maids at Aldgate,[60] whom he flouts, are likely to have more wit than the serving man at Addle-gate.

Whereas he taxes me of adding to the Scripture, in that I said love only is the fulfilling of every commandment, I cited no particular Scripture, but spoke a general sense, which might be collected from many places. For seeing love includes faith, what is there that can fulfill every commandment but only love? And I meant, as any intelligent reader might apprehend, every positive and civil commandment, whereof Christ hath taught us that *man is the Lord.*[61] It is not the formal duty of worship, or the sitting still, that keeps the holy rest of Sabbath; but whosoever doth most according to charity, whether he works or works not, he breaks the holy rest of Sabbath least. So marriage being a civil ordinance made for man, not man for it, he who doth that which most accords with charity, first to himself, next to whom he next owes it, whether in marriage or divorce, he breaks the ordinance of marriage least. And what in religious prudence can be charity to himself, and what to his wife, either in continuing, or in dissolving the marriage-knot, hath been already oft enough discoursed. So that what St. Paul saith of circumcision,[62] the same I stick not to say of a civil ordinance, made to the good and comfort of man, not to his ruin; marriage is nothing, and divorce is nothing, but faith which works by love. And this I trust none can mistake.

Against the fifth argument, that a Christian in a higher order of priesthood than that Levitical, is a person dedicate to joy and peace, and therefore needs not in subjection to a civil ordinance, made to no other end but for his good (when without his fault he finds it impossible to be decently or tolerably observed) to plunge himself into immeasurable distractions and temptations, above his strength; against this he proves nothing, but gads into silly conjectures of what abuses would follow, and with as good reason might declaim against the best things that are.

Against the sixth argument, that to force the continuance of marriage between minds found utterly unfit and disproportional, is against nature, and seems forbid under that allegorical precept of Moses, *not to sow a field with divers seeds, lest both be defiled; not to plough with an ox and an ass together,*[63] which I deduced by the pattern of St. Paul's reasoning what was meant by not *muzzling the ox,*[64] he rambles over a long narration, to tell us that by the oxen are meant the preachers: which is not doubted. Then he demands, if this my reasoning be like St. Paul's. And I answer him, yes. He replies, that sure St. Paul would be ashamed to reason thus. And I tell him, no. He grants that place which I alleged, II Cor. 6, of unequal yoking, may allude to that of Moses, but says I cannot prove it makes to my purpose, and shows not first how he can disprove it. Weigh gentlemen, and consider, whether my affirmations, backed with reason, may hold balance against the bare denials of this ponderous confuter, elected by his ghostly patrons to be my copes-mate.[65]

Proceeding on to speak of mysterious things in nature, I had occasion to fit the language thereafter, matters not for the reading of this odious fool, who thus ever when he meets with aught above the cogitation of his breeding, leaves the noisome stench of his rude slot behind him, maligning that any thing should be spoke or understood above his own genuine baseness; and gives sentence that his confuting hath been employed about a frothy, immeritous, and undeserving discourse. Who could have believed so much insolence durst vent itself from out the hide of a varlet, as thus to censure that which men of mature judgment have applauded to be writ with good reason? But this contents him not, he fails not to rave in his barbarous abusiveness; and why? A reason befitting such an artificer, because he saith *the book is contrary to all human learn-*

ing; whenas the world knows, that all, both human and divine learning, 'til the canon law, allowed divorce by consent, and for many causes without consent. Next, he dooms it *as contrary to truth;* whenas it hath been disputable among learned men, ever since it was prohibited; and is by Peter Martyr thought an *opinion not impious, but hard to be refuted;* and by Erasmus deemed a doctrine *so charitable and pious, as, if it cannot be used, were to be wished it could;*[66] but is by Martin Bucer, a man of dearest and most religious memory in the Church, taught and maintained to be either most lawfully used, or most lawfully permitted. And for this, for I affirm no more than Bucer, what censure do you think, readers, he hath condemned the book to? To a death no less impious than *to be burned by the hangman.* Mr. Licenser, for I deal not now with this caitiff, never worth my earnest, and now not seasonable for my jest, you are reputed a man discreet enough, religious enough, honest enough, that is, to an ordinary competence in all these. But now your turn is, to hear what your own hand hath earned ye; that when you suffered this nameless hangman to cast into public such a despiteful contumely upon a name and person deserving of the Church and State equally to yourself, and one who hath done more to the present advancement of your own tribe than you or many of them have done for themselves, you forgot to be either honest, religious, or discreet. Whatever the State might do concerning it, supposed a matter to expect evil from, I should not doubt to meet among them with wise, and honourable, and knowing men. But as to this brute libel, so much the more impudent and lawless for the abused authority which it bears, I say again, that I abominate the censure of rascals and their licensers.

With difficulty I return to what remains of this ignoble talk, for the disdain I have to change a period more with the filth and venom of this gourmand, swelled into a confuter. Yet, for the satisfaction of others, I endure all this.

Against the seventh argument, that if the canon law and divines allow divorce for conspiracy of death, they may as well allow it to avoid the same consequence from the likelihood of natural causes.

First, he denies that the canon so decrees.

I answer, that it decrees for danger of life, as much as for adultery. *Decret. Gregor. l.* 4. tit. 19.[67] and in other places: and the best civilians who cite the canon law so collect, as *Schneidewin in Institut. tit. 10. p. 4. de divort.*,[68] and indeed who would have denied it, but one of a reprobate ignorance in all he meddles with.

Secondly, he saith, the case alters; for there the offender, *who seeks the life, doth implicitly at least act a divorce.*

And I answer, that here nature, though no offender, doth the same. But if an offender, by acting a divorce, shall release the offended, this is an ample grant against himself. He saith, *nature teacheth to save life from one who seeks it.* He saith, *that here they are both actors.* Admit they were, it would not be uncharitable to part them; yet sometimes they are not both actors, but the one of them most lamentedly passive. So he concludes, we must not take advantage of our own faults and corruptions to release us from our duties. But shall we take no advantage to save ourselves from the faults of another, who hath annulled his right to our duty? No, saith he, *let them die of the sullens, and try who will pity them.* Barbarian, the shame of all honest attorneys, why do they not hoist him over the bar and blanket him?[69]

Against his eighth argument, that they who are destitute of all marriageable gifts, except a body not plainly unfit, have not the calling to marry, and consequently married and so found, may be divorced: this, he saith, *is nothing to the purpose,* and not fit to be answered. I leave it therefore to the judgement of his masters.

Against his ninth argument, that marriage is a human society, and so chiefly seated in agreement and unity of mind; if therefore the mind cannot have that due society by marriage, that it may reasonably and humanly desire, it can be no human society, and so not without reason divorceable: here he falsifies, and turns what the position required of a reasonable agreement in the main matters of society into an agreement in all things, which makes the opinion not mine, and so he leaves it.

At last, and in good hour, we are come to his farewell, which is to be a concluding taste of his jabberment in law, the flashiest and the fustiest that ever corrupted in such an unswilled hogshead.

Against my tenth argument, as he calls it, but as I intended it, my other position, that divorce is not a thing determinable by a compulsive law, for that all law is for some good that may be frequently attained without the admixture of a worse inconvenience, but the law forbidding divorce never attains to any good end of such prohibition, but rather multiplies evil; therefore the prohibition of divorce is no good law. Now for his attorney's prise:[70] but first, like a right cunning and sturdy logician, he denies my argument, not mattering whether in the major or minor, and saith, *there are many laws made for good, and yet that good is not attained, through the defaults of the party, but a greater inconvenience follows.*

But I reply, that this answer builds upon a shallow foundation, and most unjustly supposes every one in default who seeks divorce from the most injurious wedlock. The default therefore will be found in the law itself: which is neither able to punish the offender but the innocent must withal suffer; nor can right the innocent in what is chiefly sought, the obtainment of love or quietness. His instances out of the common law are all so quite beside the matter which he would prove, as may be a warning to all clients how they venture their business with such a cock-brained solicitor. For being to show some law of England attaining to no good end, and yet through no default of the party, who is thereby debarred all remedy, he shows us only how some do lose the benefit of good laws through their own default. His first example saith, *It is a just law that every one shall peaceably enjoy his estate in lands or otherwise.* Does this law attain to no good end? The Bar will blush at this most incogitant woodcock. But see if a draft of Littleton will recover him to his senses. *If this man having fee-simple in his lands, yet will take a lease of his own lands from another, this shall be an estopple*[71] *to him in an assize*[72] *from the recovering of his own land.* Mark now, and register him. How many are there of ten thousand who have such a fee-simple in their sconce,[73] as to take a lease of their own lands from another? So that this inconvenience lights upon scarce one in an age, and by his own default; and the law of enjoying each man his own, is good to all others. But on the contrary, this prohibition of divorce is good to none, and brings inconvenience to numbers who lie under intolerable grievances without their own default, through the wickedness or folly of another; and all this iniquity the law remedies not, but in a manner maintains. His other causes are directly to the same purpose, and might have been spared, but that he is a tradesman of the law, and must be borne with at his first setting up, to lay forth his best ware, which is only gibberish.

I have now done that, which for many causes I might have thought could not likely have been my fortune, to be put to this under-work of scouring and unrubbishing the low and sordid ignorance of such a presumptuous lozel.[74] Yet Hercules had the labour once imposed upon him to carry dung out of the Augean stable. At any hand, I would be rid of him: for I had rather, since the life of man is likened to a scene, that all my entrances and exits might mix with such persons only whose worth erects them and their actions to a grave and tragic deportment, and not to have to do with clowns and vices.[75] But if a man cannot peaceably walk into the world, but must be infested, sometimes at his face with dorrs[76] and horse-flies, sometimes beneath with bawling whippets and shin-barkers, and these to be set on by plot and consultation with a junta[77] of clergymen and licensers, commended also and rejoiced in by those whose partiality cannot yet forgo old Papistical principles, have I not cause to be in such a manner defensive as may procure me freedom to pass more unmolested hereafter by those encumbrances, not so much regarded for themselves as for those who incite them? And what defence can properly be used in such a despicable encounter as this, but either the slap or the spurn? If they can afford me none but a ridiculous adversary, the blame belongs not to me, though the whole dispute be strewed and scattered with ridiculous. And if he have such an ambition to know no better who are his mates, but among those needy thoughts which, though his two faculties of serving man and solicitor should compound into one mongrel, would be but thin and meagre, if in this penury of soul he can be possible to have the lustiness to think of fame, let him but send me how he calls himself, and I may chance not fail to indorse him on the backside of posterity, not a golden, but a brazen ass.[78] Since my fate extorts from me a talent of sport, which I had thought to hide in a napkin, he shall be my *Batrachomuomachia,*[79] my Bavius,[80] my Calandrino,[81] the common adagy of ignorance and overweening. Nay, perhaps, as the provocation may be, I may be driven to curl up this gliding prose into a rough Sotadic,[82] that shall rhyme him into such a condition, as instead of judging good books to be burnt by the executioner, he shall be readier to be his own hangman. Thus much to this nuisance.

But as for the subject itself which I have writ and now defend, according as the opposition bears, if any man equal to the matter shall think it appertains him to take in hand this controversy, either excepting against aught written, or persuaded he can show better how this question, of such moment to be thoroughly known, may receive a true determination, not leaning on the old and rotten suggestions whereon it yet leans; if his intents be sincere to the public, and shall carry him on without bitterness to the opinion, or to the person dissenting, let him not, I entreat him, guess by the handling which meritoriously hath been bestowed on this object of contempt and laughter, that I account it any displeasure done me to be contradicted in print: but as it leads to the attainment of any thing more true, shall esteem it a benefit; and shall know how to return his civility and fair argument in such a sort, as he shall confess that to do so is my choice, and to have done thus was my chance.

The End.

Contemporary Pamphlets, 1644–45

William Prynne

Twelve Considerable Serious Questions

(1644)

William Prynne (1600–69) was the son of a gentleman farmer who worked land owned by Oriel College Oxford, from which Prynne graduated. He then studied law at Lincoln's Inn, and was admitted to the bar in 1628. Prynne, one of the most prolific pamphleteers in seventeenth century England, wrote more than 200 pamphlets, attacking stage plays, female masquers, bishops, Presbyterians, Jesuits, Levellers, Quakers, tithes, dueling, and drink (although he himself was very fond of ale). He was fundamentally nostalgic for the Protestantism of the Elizabethan era, and attacked any religious position that deviated from those early values. At the insistence of Archbishop Laud, the Star Chamber tried and convicted Prynne of sedition in 1633 and 1637, when his ears were chopped off, his nose slit, and his face branded. Sent into exile, he returned triumphantly in 1640 as a popular hero. He then wrote bitter tirades against Charles I, and attacked both the king and the Quakers as tools of the Jesuits (and therefore of the pope). In all his pamphlets, he annotated his work so extensively that he was nicknamed "Marginal" Prynne. In 1644, he was the lead prosecutor in the trial of Archbishop William Laud, who was thereafter beheaded. Prynne describes the trial in *Canterbury's Doome* (1645).

Twelve Considerable Serious Questions touching church government, published in September 1644, argued that the Independents were as dangerous a threat as the king. Thereafter, Prynne moved to a more centrist political position. He ultimately defended the joint sovereignty of Parliament and the monarchy, and opposed those who tried and executed the king. During the 1650s, Parliament commissioned him to write the official defense of the English civil war. After the Restoration, he supported the monarchy and was appointed the keeper of official records in the Tower of London.[1]

William Prynne, *Twelve Considerable Serious Questions touching chvrch government sadly propounded (out of a reall desire of vnitie and tranquillity in church and state) to all sober-minded Christians, cordially affecting a speedy settled reformation, and brotherly Christian vnion in all our churches and denominations, now miserably wasted with civill unnaturall warres, and deplorably lacerated with ecclesiasticall dissentions* (London: I. D. for Michael Sparke Senior, 1644)

10. Whether Independents can produce any one solid reason, why they ought not (in Point of Conscience) willingly to submit to a *Presbyteriall Government* in case it shall be established among us by the generall consent of the Synod, and Parliament, as most consonant to Gods word, the Lawes and Government, of our Realme? and if not, whether it will not be justly reputed an high degree of *Obstinacy, Singularity, Arrogancy, Selfe-ends,* and peremptory *Schisme* in them to oppose this forme of Governement, or demand a speciall exemption from it, for themselves alone? when as Papists, Anabaptists and all other Sects may claime the like exemption, upon the like grounds as they alleadge?

11. Whether that Independent Governement which some contend for, if positively and fully agreed on, and laid downe without disguises, and then duly pondered in the ballance of scripture or right reason, be not of its owne nature, a very Seminary of Schismes, and dangerous divisions in Church, state? a floud-Gate to let in an inundation of all manner of Heresies, Errors, Sects, Religions, distructive opinions, Libertinisme and lawlesnesse

among us, without any sufficient meanes of preventing or suppressing them when introduced? Whether the finall result of it (as Master [Roger] *Williams* in his late dangerous *Licentious Booke* [The Bloudy Tenent (1644)] determines) will not really resolve it selfe into this detestable conclusion. *That every man, whither he be Jew, Turk, Pagan, Papist, Arminian, Anabaptist, &c. ought to be left to his own free liberty of conscience, without any coertion or restraint, to embrace & publikely to professe what Religion, Opinion, Church, Government he pleaseth, & conceiveth to be truest, though never so erronious, false seditious, detestable in it selfe?*

And whither such a Government as this ought to be embraced much lesse established among us (the sad effects whereof we have already experimentally felt, by the late dangerous increase of many *Anabaptisticall, Antinomian, Heretica Atheisticall opinions, as of the souls mortality divorce at pleasure, &c.* lately Broached, Preached, Printed in this famous City, which I hope Our grand Councell will speedily and carefully suppresse, and by our devisions betweene some of our Commanders refusing to be *dependent* or subordinat one to another,) I referre to the judgement of all such who have any sparkes of love to God, Religion, their bleeding dying distracted native Country flaming in their brests, or any remainder of right reason residing in their braines.[2]

Herbert Palmer

The Glasse of Gods Providence

(1644)

Herbert Palmer (1601–47) was an ordained clergyman in the Church of England. As head of a parish in Canterbury, he was troubled by separatists and by the established clergy, and for a time was suspended. Subsequently named a "university preacher" in Cambridge, Palmer was entitled to preach anywhere and became well known as one of the finest preachers in England. Between 1643 and 1646, he preached several sermons before both houses of Parliament, including *The Glasse of Gods Providence* (1644). In part, this sermon explicated Psalm 99:8, emphasizing the evil and the good in human actions, and the generous mercy and just vengeance of God. Palmer was a member of the Westminster Assembly and helped draft its *Shorter Catechism* (1647). He designed an influential new form of catechetical instruction, based on a process of inquiry rather than simple declarations of belief. As a moral reformer, he advocated laws against clandestine marriages, drunkenness, and stage plays. Palmer was of extremely short stature, and may have been a dwarf. When he first preached to the French congregation in Canterbury, an elderly woman cried, "What will this child say to us?" Afterwards, she praised his "spiritual strength and vigour."[1]

Herbert Palmer, *The Glasse of Gods Providence Towards his Faithfull Ones. Held forth in a Sermon Preached to the two Houses of Parliament, at Margarets Westminster, Aug. 13. 1644 being an extraordinary Day of Humiliation. Wherein is discovered the great failings that the best are liable unto; upon which God is provoked sometimes to take Vengeance. The whole is applied specially to a more carefull observation of our late Covenant, and particularly against the ungodly Toleration pleaded for under pretence of Liberty of Conscience. By Herbert Palmer, B. D. Minister of Gods Word at Ashwell in Hertford-shire: A member of the Assembly of Divines* (London: Printed by G. M. for Th. Underhill at the Bible in Woodstreet, 1644)

Surely the *Extirpation of Heresie* and *Schisme,* (besides that *Popery* is abjured by name) and such an *universall Toleration,* and pretended *Liberty of Conscience,* are as *diametrically opposite* and *contradictory* one to the other, as *Light* is to *darknesse,* and *strict justice* to *licentious lawlesnesse.* If therefore you be true to your *Covenant,* your hand must needs be against such *Doctrines* and the *Promoters* of them. And those Clauses of [*whatsoever shall be found contrary to sound Doctrine and Power of Godlinesse*] doe lay yet a *stricter* bond upon you, to make you take great heed how you beare with *any opinion* or *opinionist* altogether. Though, if any such be found differing from the received opinions and practices, that are neither *Schismaticall* in disturbing the Churches Peace, nor *Opposite to sound Doctrine,* or the *Power of Godlinesse,* they may be born with, notwithstanding the Covenant. But I see not how it allowes *any* more. Onely still the *Wayes* of dealing with *opinions* and *opinionists,* who are not altogether to be borne, must be *sutable to the Nature of the opinions,* and of *those also that hold them,* and not in all *matters* nor to all *persons* alike; as was noted before. But against a *Toleration* in *generall,* even the *Covenant* it selfe, in that very Article hath a Reason sutable to the Text, *Lest we partake of other mens sins, and thereby be in danger to receive of their plagues,* saith the Covenant; which in the Language of the Text, is *Lest* GOD *take Vengeance on their Inventions,* and *ours* together. It is true that the name of *Conscience* hath an *awfull sound* unto a *Conscientious Eare*. But I pray, judge but in a few *Instances*, whether all *pretence* of Conscience ought to be a *sufficient plea* for *Toleration* and *Liberty?* 1. There be those that say their *Conscience* is against *all taking of an Oath before a Magistrate*. Will you allow an *Universall Liberty* of this? What then will become of all our *Legal* and *Judiciall* proceedings, which are confined to this *Way* of proofe; and so it was *by GOD appointed*, and hath been *by all Nations* practiced. 2. There be some that pretend *Liberty of Conscience* to *Equivocate in an Oath* even *before a Magistrate*, and to *elude all Examinations by Mentall Reservations*. Will you grant them *this* Liberty? Or can you, without *destroying all bonds of Civill Converse*, and wholly *overthrow* of all *Humane Judicature?* 3. If any plead Conscience for the Lawfulnesse of *Polygamy*; (or for divorce for other causes then Christ and His Apostles mention; Of which a *wicked booke* is abroad and *uncensured*, though *deserving to be burnt*, whose *Author* hath been so *impudent* as to *set his Name* to it, and,) or for Liberty to *marry incestuously*, will you grant a *Toleration* for all *this?* 4. If any say, Their *Conscience* allowes them not to *Contribute to your Just and Necessary Defence*, shall they be allowed *this* Liberty? Where then will your Armies be paid? 5. If others say, their Consciences allow not them to *beare Armes* for you, shall they have *altogether their Liberty?* (every one that will say so) How then shall your Armies be made up? 6. If any goe further, (as some doe in effect even in print,) and say their *Consciences* allow not any *Magistrates at all;* nor 7. *Propriety of goods:* Will you afford them their Liberty *herein?* What would become then of all *your own Authority*, and of all *Lawes*, and *Liberties of the Kingdome?* Or what *Bounds* or *Limits* can there be set to men *any Way*, if this opinion of *Liberty of Conscience*, as it is pleaded for, shall be admitted?[2]

[Anonymous]

An Answer to a Book, Intituled

The Doctrine and Discipline of Divorce, or, A Plea for Ladies and Gentlewomen, and all other Maried Women against Divorce (1644)

Milton's first edition of *The Doctrine and Discipline of Divorce* appeared on August 1, 1643. *An Answer to a Book, intituled, The Doctrine and Discipline of Divorce*—the only contemporary, full-length tract to engage with Milton's pamphlet and complete argument—was registered on October 31 and published on November 19. The tract was prefaced by an endorsement from the licenser and Independent divine, Joseph Caryl (1602–73), who sought "to preserve the strength of the Mariagebond and the Honour of that estate, against those sad breaches and dangerous abuses of it." Although Milton was convinced that Caryl collaborated in the pamphlet's authorship, no conclusive evidence has yet been found to assist in the positive identification of the writer or writers of *An Answer*. The tract was printed by G. M. [George Miller], who also produced another early attack on Milton's argument, Herbert Palmer's *The Glasse of Gods Providence Towards his Faithfull Ones* (registered November 7). Between 1644 and 1654, other men (including William Prynne, Daniel Featley, and Thomas Edwards) assailed Milton's position on divorce, but Palmer's sermon and the anonymous *Answer* are particularly important because they occasioned Milton's final divorce pamphlets, *Tetrachordon* and

Colasterion, which were published on the same day (March 4, 1645). *Tetrachordon* replies in learned, measured prose to Palmer and other prominent detractors. *Colasterion* castigates the "illiterat, and arrogant presumer" (YP 2:724) of *An Answer* with unremitting vituperation, demolishing his attack on *The Doctrine and Discipline of Divorce.*[1]

To preserve the strength of the Mariagebond and the Honour of that estate, against those sad breaches and dangerous abuses of it, which common discon[t]ents (on this side Adultery) are likely to make in unstaied mindes and men given to change, by taking in or grounding themselves upon the opinion answered, and with good reason confuted in this Treatise, I have approved the printing and publishing of it.

Novemb. 14 1644. Joseph Caryl.

Errata. In pag. 1. line 17. read *aut* for *and,* p. 2. l. 29. r. *Kens case* for *Keras case,* p. 9. l. 9. r. *to* for *as,* p. 12. l. 24. leave out *naturall* in the first place, p. 14. l. *ult,* r. *Obligee* for *Obligor.*[2]

An Answer to a Book, Intituled, THE Doctrine and Discipline of Divorce, _or,_ A Plea for Ladies and Gentlewomen, and all other Maried Women against Divorce. Wherein, Both Sexes are vindicated from all bondage of Canon Law, and other mistakes whatsoever: And the unfound Principles of the Author are examined and fully confuted by authority of Holy Scripture, the Laws of this Land, and sound Reason. Concil. Anglic. Anno 670. Can. 10. _Nullus conjugem propriam nisi (ut sanctum Evangelium docet,) fornicationis causa relinquat._

London, Printed by _G[eorge]. M[iller]._

For _William Lee_ at the Turks-Head in Fleet-street, next to the Miter Taverne. 1644.[3]

For our more orderly proceeding in this question of Divorce, *viz.* whether a man may divorce or put away his Wife for indisposition, unfitnesse, or contrariety of minde, we will do these three things.

1. Shew what the Doctrine or discipline of Divorce is.
2. Give some reasons why a man may not put away his wife for indisposition, unfitnesse, or contrariety of minde, although manifested in much sharpnesse.
3. We will answer the Arguments and Scriptures, which are brought by the Author of the Book, intitultd, *The Doctrine and Discipline of Divorce,* to prove that a divorce may lawfully be for contrariety of minds, &c.

Concerning the first thing, what Divorce is, or the Doctrine and discipline of it.

The word Divorce comes from the Latine word *divortium,* which comes *a divertendo aut divortendo,* to intimate that by divorce a woman is separated, divided, or turned aside from her husband: the Greek is *ἀποπομπή ex ἀποπέμπω, i.e. repudio, rectius ἀποστασίου, dicitur quod ab ἀπό & ἵστημι, i.e. sto, quasi dicas abscessio*. The Hebrew word is *Cherithuth* from *Chorath,*[4] which signifies a cutting off, dismembring, or separating, or *foedus icere;* but *Cherithuth* is *βιβλίον ἀποστασίου,* properly a Bill of divorce or parting. Thus concerning the word.

Now concerning the divorce it selfe, to shew what it is, we must consider it under a twofold notion.

First, as it hath been practised by the Jewes according as they thought directed by *Moses's* Law, and so Divorce was a free and a voluntary act of the Husband, made known by writing, whereby he did dismisse and for ever put away his Wife, and give her leave to marry to another man: To this purpose some of the Hebrew Rabbines have set down the form of the Bill of Divorce used amongst the Jewes: in effect thus.

I such an one (setting down his name, the day and year) do voluntarily, with the willingnesse of my soule without constraint, dismisse, leave, and put away, thou, even thou, (naming her name) which hast been my wife heretofore, but now I dismisse thee, that thou maist be free, and be married to whom thou wilt: And this is unto thee a writing of divorce, according to the law of Moses. Witnesse *R.* and *T.*

The Jewes require to make a lawfull divorce, that the man must put her away willingly, that it must be by writing, that he must put her quite out of his possession, that she be truly named in the deed of divorce, and that the deed of divorce be given to her either by himself or his Deputy before witnesse.

Thus of Divorce as practised by the Jewes in relation to *Moses's* Law.

In the second place we will consider of it as practised by the lawes of England.

And so Divorce is a sentence pronounced by an Ecclesiasticall Judge, whereby a man and woman formerly married, are separated or parted. *Cook lib. 7. Keras case.*

This Divorce is twofold. 1. There is a divorce *a vincule matrimonis* from the very bond of matrimony it selfe. 2. There is a divorce *tantum a mensa & thoro,* from bed and board only.

Concerning the first kinde of divorce from the very bond of matrimony it self: the cause of this: divorce must precede or go before marriage: amongst which are,

1. *Causa precontractus,* because the parties or one of them was contracted to another before: and so if a man marry one precontracted and have issue, its the fathers childe till divorce for precontract, and then is it *nullius filius,* a Bastard. *Cook lib. 6. 66. Dier 105.*
2. There is a divorce *a vinculo matrimonis, causa frigiditatis, vel causa impotentiae,* for cause of impotency to marriage duties: yet if after a man be divorced for impotency, and take another wife and have children by her, these shall not be Bastards, because a man may be *habilis & inhabilis diversis temporibus,* able and unable at divers times. *Cook lib. 5. 93. Dier fol. 178.*
3. There is a divorce *a vinculo matrimonis, causa minoris aetatis vel impubertatis,* because they are within age at the time of mariage: and so if two be married *infra anxos nubiles,* and after full age are divorced for the same, the woman may bring an Asise against the man, for land given her in frank-mariage, *Lib. Ass.*

> *19. An. plac. 2.* which proves the divorce is from the very bond of matrimony. Besides these there are divers other causes of divorce *a vinculo matrimonis,* as *causa affinitatis & causa consanguinitatis,* by reason of affinity and consanguinity or kindred, *Cook com. Littleton.*

So *causa prosessionis,* and *termino paschae 30 Edw. I. coram Rege,* there *William de Chadworths* case, how that he was divorced from his Wife, because he carnally knew the Daughter of his Wife before he married her mother: these are causes of divorce from the very bond of matrimony allowed on by the Common law; concerning which the Civill or Canon law makes some distinctions and additions. So in the case of divorce *causa impotentiae vel frigiditatis,* for impotency to mariage duties. Although *Justinian* (as some think discreetly) did will, that there should be three yeares triall of the disability: yet here the Canon law expects present proofe: yet some think this cause doth not dissolve from the very bond of matrimony, except the impotency or impediment can be proved to be before mariage, and not to fall out after: So of impotency the same they say, *Ut per ca matrimonium nunquam extitisse judicitur.* And concerning mariage of kindred in the line ascendant or discendant, it is counted so detestable, that *Bartel* sayes, they suffer confiscation of goods and deserve exile.

The Civill ad Canon law allow of divorce after a long time absence of either party, but they certainly agree not of the time of absence. So *Cod. lib. 5. tit. I. leg. 2, const. sponsa post biennium, & c.* allowed to marry after two years absence, but *tit.* 27. after three years, *leg.* 27. after four years. Others say the Civill law requires five years absence.

In Consil. Lateran. part. 50. cap. 23. There is an example of a Decree, upon a woman complaining her husband had been gone ten yeares, and it was commanded the parents of the husband should send for him home, and he in a long time came not; upon which the Bishop did pronounce a sentence of divorce, and gave the woman leave to marry, and the sentence was allowed of by the whole Councell.

So the Canon law decrees *causa 28. quest. I. cap. 4.* That if the wife refuse to dwell with her Christian husband, he may without any fault leave her.

Thus of the first kinde of divorce from the bond of matrimony it self, and this makes the children Bastards and bereaves the woman of her dower.

Secondly, there is a divorce *a mensa & thoro,* from bed and board only, and this is for some cause subsequent or during mariage, and not before mariage, as for adultery committed. Yet this being subsequent to the mariage, the bond of mariage by the law is not dissolved, but the freehold continues, the wife shall be indowed, and the children are mulier, and not Bastards.

Concerning the justnesse or conveniency of all these lawes in every thing, whether they will stand *in foro conscientiae* its not needfull now to dispute: our end being only a little to open the law of Divorce, that we may see what it is. And so now we leave this first thing what Divorce is, and the doctrine and discipline thereof, and come to the second thing.

And that is to prove that whatsoever other causes of Divorce may be allowed of, yet that disagreement of minde or disposition between husband and wife, yea though it shewes it selfe in much sharpnesie each to other, is not by the law of God allowed of for a just cause of divorce, neither ought to be allowed of by the lawes of man.

For the proof of this second thing propounded to be handled, to prove that Husbands and Wives ought not to be divorced for contrariety or unfitnesse of mindes or dispositions, although it should be manifested by much harsh cariage each to other, I shall as briefly as I can demonstrate the same.

Where the Scripture commands a thing to be done, it appoints when, how, and for what it shall be done: as in the case of death: when any one is by the law to dye, it sets down for what cause and fact: and so excommunication it teacheth when and for what. But now concerning Divorce for disagreement or contrariety of disposition, in regard there is between all maried people some contrariety or disagreement of mindes: and the Scriptures speak nothing to direct to what a measure of disagreement or contrariety it must grow to, before it shall be lawfull to divorce or part: therefore I conclude the Scripture allowes not of any divorce at all for disagreement, & c.

If it be not lawfull for a Husband to put away an Infidell wife who acknowledges not Christ, in case she be content to dwell with him: Then may not a man put away his wife for disagreement of mindes only: but the first is true, *ergo* the latter.

For the first part of the Argument the Apostle saith, *I Cor. 7. 13. If any brother hath a wife who is an Infidell, if she be content to dwell with him; let him not put her away.*

And for the second part, that if a man may not put away his wife who is an Infidell, much lesse may he put his wife away for disagreement of disposition, this seems clear: because difference in religion in its own nature, breeds as great a dislike and disagreement and greater than any naturall disagreement of disposition, constitution, or complexion whatsoever. Christ speaking of this difference, even between them of the nearest relation, saith, *The father shall be against the sonne, and the sonne against the father,* even to persecute with extremity: And that *the Disciples should be hated of all for Christs sake:* and yet I never heard of any that was hated of every man for his contrariety of naturall disposition.

So that if disagreement in religion be a greater cause of hatred and variance then disagreement of naturall dispositions and constitutions; and yet a man may not put away his wife for that disagreement, then much lesse for this.

The third Argument shall be from *Deut. 22. 13, 14, 15, & c.* There if a man shall take a Wife and hate her, and raise an ill report upon her, to the end that he might be rid of her: and if the report be found true she shall be stoned to death; but if it be not found true he shall not put her away all the dayes of his life: here although a man hates his Wife, so that he seeks by false reports to scandalize her, even to danger of her life, yet is not he permitted to put her away all the dayes of his life; and yet how great the disagreement of minde and disposition must of necessity be between such a man and his wife who so did hate her, let any man judge.

If every Christian ought to beare the burthens and infirmities of another Christian, to whom he is not bound by any civill relation;

much more is he to bear the burthen and infirmities of his Wife who is so neerly bound to him: but the first is true, *Gal. 6. 1. Ergo* the latter. But he that for infirmities or contrariety of minde, or the like, puts away his wife, doth not bear with her infirmities, and therefore he breaks the law of Christ.

If the Husband ought to love his Wife, as Christ doth his Church, then ought not a man to put away his Wife for weaknesse of nature, contrariety, or indisposition of minde. But the first is true, *Ergo* the latter.

For the first part, the words of *Paul Ephes. 5. 29. Husbands love your wives as Christ doth his Church.*

If any shall say, Similitudes hold not in every thing, and therefore *Paul* may not mean a man should love his Wife in perpetuity as Christ doth his Church, but for the sincerity, so long as she continues his wife.

Answ. Paul specifies wherein they should expresse their loves like to Christ, at least implicitely: that is, by passing by and healing the faults and infirmities of their Wives, as Christ gave himself, & c. that he might wash his Church, & c. And for the second part of the Argument its clear, because such love as is there required ought to hide and passe by faults, disagreement of minde, contrariety of disposition, & c.

The sixth Argument is from the expresse words of Christ, *Math. 5. 32.* where he being a preaching to his Disciples concerning the true sense of *Moses's* law (as it seemes) and of some addition thereto by his own Evangelicall precepts: he precisely tels them: *That whosoever puts away his wife except it were for* πορνεία, *scortatio, adultery, he commits adultery:* so that whether you make it a true interpretation of *Moses's* law against the glosses of others, or take it as a new precept belonging to the law of the Gospell, yet will it be an impregnable proofe against all effiminate and childish divorces, for disagreement and contrariety of mindes.

If any shall say, if Christs words hold universally and except no cause but adultery: then all other causes, as frigidity, mariage within degrees forbidden by *Moses, & c.* are no causes of divorce no more then contrariety of minde.

Christs speech holds universally according as he intended it, namely, to condemne all such grounds of divorce as were groundlesly practised amongst the Jewes, for every cause which they thought sufficient, and yet no wayes checks the law which forbids mariage within the degrees of affinity or consanguinity, or forbids other cause which makes mariage void *ipso facto;* or by due proofes may make void the mariage. If there be any other objections against this place, we shall refer them to what will afterwards be said in explication of this text, and of *Deut. 24. I.*

The seventh Argument is: If the Husband and Wife be by the Ordinance of God one flesh, then may they not separate or be separated from one another, except it be for some cause which either in it selfe or by consequence may justly be thought to be a just cause of dissolving the union of being one flesh. But the first is true, *Ergo,* also the latter.

For the first part, that the Husband and Wife are one flesh, *Paul* confirmes it, *Ephes. 5* and Christ himselfe *Matth. 19.*

And for the second part of the Argument as it depends upon the former, *viz.* if they be one flesh, then they ought not to separate or be separated. Its the Argument of Christ himselfe against the Pharisees, why divorce ought not to be for light causes, but for adultery only; because saith he, *they are no more two but one flesh,* therefore, *whomsoever God hath joyned together, let no man put asunder.*

Only as I intimated, such other causes may be allowed of as dissolves this union of being one flesh, either directly, or by consequence.

But sure contrariety of disposition and unfitnesse of minde can be no such thing as makes the Husband and Wife (being once by mariage one flesh) to be two againe.

In the next place I conceive something may be gathered to this purpose from the words of *Paul, I Cor. 7.* when speaking of mariage, he tels them, *such should have troubles in the flesh,* and not that freedome to serve God which the unmaried had: yet he concludes, he spared them, and would not forbid them for that cause to marry.

Now if troubles in the flesh comming by mariage which hinder the cheerfull service of God, be not a just cause to forbeare mariage: Then it would seem that to persons that are already maried and bound to each other by the union of one flesh, by covenant, by love, by the bonds of Christianity, although through the peevishnesse or ill dispositions of their natures, their troubles should increase to multitudes above what is ordinarie betwixt maried persons, yet ought they not to part and to marrie to others, because some sort and measure of troubles and discontent in mariage are inavoidable; and therefore where one is by mariage bound by so many bonds, he ought not to break the bonds to ease himself of disquietnesse and trouble which is inseparably incident to mariage, though not in that degree as he now lies under, and is subject to.

Yet am I not over confident of this Argument, but that with some colour of reason it may be evaded.

In the next place, if the Husband ought to love his Wife as himself, then may he not for discontent or disagreement put her away, no more then for some discontent or disquietnesse in himselfe, he may separate his soule from his body. But the first is true. *Ephes. 5. ult. Ergo* the latter.

Lastly, we may fetch an Argument from the inconveniencies that would follow if divorce were suffered, for this disagreement of disposition and unfitnesse of minde, as for example, it would be an occasion to the corrupt heart of man without any just cause at all, meerely for to satisfie his lust, to pretend causes of divorce when there is none; and to make quarrels and live discontentedly with his Wife, to the end he might have a pretence for to put her away: who sees not, how may thousands of lustfull and libidinous men would be parting from their Wives every week and marying others: and upon this, who should keep the children of these divorcers which sometimes they would leave in their Wives bellies? how shall they come by their Portions, of whom, or where? and how shall the Wife be endowed of her Husbands estate? Nay, commonly, to what reproach would the woman be left to, as being one left who was not fit for any ones company? and so who would venture upon her againe. And so by this means through her just cause of discouragement, she would probably hazard her self upon some dishonest and disgracefull course, with a hundred more the like inconveniencies, even to the overturning and overthrowing of all humane society, which would inevitably follow if this loose Doctrine of Divorce were once established by law.

To these Arguments we might adde the consent of Antiquity, who in this follow the direction and doctrine of Christ.

As *Concil. Tolet. 12. Can. 8. Preceptum Domini est, ut excepta causa fornicationis, uxor a viro dimitti non debeat. & c.* Its the command of the Lord, the Wife should not be put away but for fornication. So *Cod. lib. 3. tit. 38. leg. 11. const. Quis ferat, & c.* who can endure that Children from Parents, and Wives from Husbands should be separate?

So *Concil. Anglic. 670. Can. 10.* No man may put away his Wife, except as the Gospell teacheth for fornication. It is true, some of the Imperiall lawes allow Homicide, Sacriledge, Robbery, Manstealing, & c. for causes of divorce. *Cod. lib. 5. tit. 17. leg. 8.* but the Canon law decrees otherwise.

Divers other authorities might be alledged as to this point rightly agreeing, as *Greg. causa 29. quest. 7. cap. 19.* So *Zach. causa 29. quest. 2. cap. 2.* So *Justin Martyr Apol. pro Christianis sub initio. Tertullian* agrees *lib. de Monogamia.* As also the Confession of Saxony *Artic. 18.* Especially is *Erasmus* most cleare in this, in his Paraphrase upon the New Testament: And for our own Writers it is endlesse to name them being so numerous.

Thus have we briefly passed over the two first things propounded to be handled.

In the third and last place we come to answer the Book intituled, *The Doctrine and Discipline of Divorce,* which maintains the contrary, to what hath been here asserted, to answer which was the main thing intended in this Discourse.

So without any Preamble or Answer to the Introduction to this following Discours, we will presently come to the main Pillar upon which his whole Book is built, which is laid downe in these words.

That undisposition, unfitnesse, or contrariety of minde, arising from a cause in nature unchangeable, hindring and ever likely to hinder the main benefits of conjugall society, which are solace and peace, is a greater reason of divorce then naturall frigidity, especially if there be no children, and it be with consent.

This being that which all his insuing discourse is brought to prove, we shall first consider of the position it self, and then come to answer his reasons brought to defend the same.

This his Position or Ground-work as we conceive, may be divided into these four entire Propositions or Conclusions.

1. That there is in some men and women a disposition, unfitnesse, or contrariety of minde, arising from a cause unchangeable in nature.
2. That such a contrariety of disposition hinders the main benefit of mariage or conjugall society.
3. That solace and peace are the main and chiefe ends of mariage or conjugall society.
4. That such a contrariety of minde or disposition is a greater cause of divorce then naturall frigidity.

To the first we answer, that there is no such disposition in nature as is unchangeable, so teacheth Philosophy: That by the carefull use of diet and the help of Physick, there is no disposition or constitution but may be altered, if not altogether, yet in a great measure. And as Philosophy teacheth so, that it may be; so Naturall History teacheth, that sometime there is a change even in the naturall disposition, if not wholly, yet in part.

Suppose there were some disposition in nature altogether unchangeable, yet the Scripture teacheth, That by the grace of the Gospel, the Lionish dispositions shall so be changed that they shall be fit for the society of milder natures; and if so, it will follow, that if the disagreeing dispositions of a man & his Wife are from their own corruption and for want o'the grace of the Gospell, that they may not for this be separate the one from the other: for it is a rule in all lawes both Divine and just Humane lawes, that no man shall take advantage of his own corruption, to release himself from such bonds as God and Nature hath knit him in. So that here, unchangeablenesse of a corrupt disposition proceeding from a mans or womans own fault and corruption, will never be allowed for a just ground, for any man to seek a Divorce from his Wife, or the Wife from the Husband, but rather a Divorce or parting with their own corruption, which is the cause of all discord and disagreement.

2. To the second Position, that such a contrariety of disposition will hinder the maine ends and benefits of mariage or conjugall society.

We answer:

That if by contrarietie of minde is meant diversities of constitutions, then it is untrue: for the soft words and cariage of the patient man or woman, will so farre prevaile with the cholerick or sullen disposition of the other party, not only to a submission to the main conjugall and mariage duties, but even to ordinarie converse, as experience declareth, and *Salomon* teacheth, namely, that *soft words pacifie wrath,* which in effect is the same we speak.

If by contrarietie of minde or disposition he will mean some unheard of thing, which God and Nature hath planted on purpose in such a man and woman who afterwards shall marry, who shall hate one another with that mutuall antypathie as a man doth a Toad or Poyson; and this is not at all for any ill qualities that either sees in each other, but because they will hate each the other, as creatures between whom in nature cannot be any agreement. If he can finde such an example in the World, let him send his Book to them for to take the benefit of it.

If by your contrariety of disposition, you mean a sordid filthy sullen disposition, or other crabbed qualitie, kindled in each against the other after mariage, and increased by each mutuall provocaton; this is not naturall: no contrarietie in Nature, but a sinfull and corrupt aberration from Gods law and their owne duties, which they are bound to purge away and to amend; and so not being naturall or of nature, but corruption wilfully nourished, if this should hinder in any the main benefits of mariage, yet doth it make nothing to your purpose.

3. To your third Proposition, That solace and peace are the main benefits of conjuugall society.

We Answer.

That this is very true in a right sense. But that solace and peace which is contrary to discord and variance (in which sense you seem to take it) is not the main end of mariage or conjugall society, is very plain and apparent: nor yet the solace and content in the gifts of the minde of one another only, for then would it have been every wayes as much, yea more content and solace to *Adam;* and so consequently to every man, to have had another man made to him of his Rib in stead of *Eve:* this is apparent by experience, which shews, that man ordinarily exceeds woman in naturall gifts of minde, and in delectablenesse of converse; upon which we suppose it may be plainly concluded, that the solace and meetnesse of a helper to *Adam* which is spoken of, was not that which you seem to speak of as contrary to discord only, but is a solace and meetnesse made up chiefly as of different Sexes, consisting of Male and Female.

> To your fourth thing, that contrariety of disposition is a greater cause of divorce then naturall frigidity.

We Answer.

Contrariety of disposition or constitution is no cause at all of divorce (as shall be afterwards shewed in the Answer to your Arguments) or if it were a cause, yet not greater then naturall frigidity, as will appear. For,

1. Contrariety of minde or disposition, may easier, or at the least as easie in nature be taken away and cured, as naturall frigidity or coldnesse.
2. But secondly, to prove that contrarietie of disposition is not so great a cause of naturall divorce as naturall frigidity, I argue thus.

If contrariety of minde or disposition be not so great a cause to [h]ave maried pe[r]sons to burning in lust towards others, as naturall frigidity is, in the one maried partie, to leave the other to burn in lust to others, then is it not so great a cause of divorce as naturall frigiditie is. But the first is true, *Ergo* the latter.

For the first part of this Argument its apparent, for contrariety of dispositions is no cause of burning in lust towards others; because notwithstanding that, they may, and we see usually doe performe mariage duties each to other. But on the other side where naturall frigidity or coldnesse bears sway, [i.e.] an impotency to mariage duties, there the other partie is, as to burning in lust, as if they were not maried at all, or very little better, and for want of conjugall duties by their yoke-fellow, and an impotencie to the same, they are in a great measure as likey to burne in lust towards others as unmaried persons are; which such as have only a contrariety of minde or disposition properly so called are not likely so subject to.

As for the second part of the Argument, that if contrariety of mindes be not so great a cause of burning in lust as naturall frigidity, that then it is not so great a cause of divorce as naturall frigidity. This appears from what was said before, namely, because by the naturall frigidity of the one, the other is in its manner, as to mariage or mariage duties, as if they had no yoke-fellow, and so if the mariage it selfe be not void *ipso facto,* yet all law and reason must yield, that for the reason before cited he ought rather to be relieved by leaving his impotent yokefellow, then the other by leaving his or her wrangling yoke-fellow.

So much for to shew the error of your position, upon which all your following discourse is, or ought to be grounded.

Now to your reasons which are to prove contrariety of disposition a just cause of divorce; where we are to take notice, that you in your reasons go not about to prove your Position as you have laid it down, but only that contrarietie of minde is a just cause of divorce betweene maried persons, not taking notice whether it be unchangeable in nature, or whether it be a greater cause of divorce then naturall frigidity, or whether there be children between them, or consent, as he hath exprest himself in his Position.

We shall endeavour to trace you in the Roade you goe, only we shal be driven to contract or shorten your arguments for brevity sake.

But before we come to your particular Arguments, the Reader is to take notice of one thing, namely, that all his Arguments, to prove a man may put away his wife for disagreement of minde or disposition, except it be his Argument from *Deu. 24. I.* they prove as effectually, that the Wife may sue a Divorce from her Husband upon the same grounds.

Your first proofe is the institution of mariage Gen. 2. to make woman a meet help for man, because it was not good that man should be alone: whence you collect that a happy conversation by preventing lonelinesse, was the chiefest and noblest end of mariage; and in case this end cannot be found in mariage, there may be reliefe by parting.

We answer and tell you againe, that it is a happie or a pleasant conversation, made up by creating them male and female, and not simply as *Eve* was a fit conversing soule for *Adam,* as you afterward expresse it, for then would it have been more pleasant and beneficiall to *Adam* to have had another man created, then a woman.

> 2. What will follow upon this if it should be granted? will it follow, think you, that because the end of mariage is, that woman should bee a meet helpe to man, therefore if shee prove not so meet as is expected, he may then put her away and take another: I hope no: Such kind of reasoning deserves no answer at all. But now to his second Argument.

His second Argument is, *From the violence and cruelty which is in forcing the continuance of those maried persons together, whom God and nature in the gentlest ends of mariage never joyned.*

As for the phrase of the gentlest ends of mariage, its too abstruse and of no use, except it be as you think to please the Reader with a neet phrase.

And for the maine of your Argument, you take too much for granted: for though the case may be so, that some persons are joyned together in mariage neither by God nor Nature, *viz.* not allowing of it; yet that for disagreement of dispositions or contrarietie of mindes the mariage should be void, wee deny; for voide it must needs be, if it be neither of God nor Nature. Now where a thing is void *ipso facto,* there needs no legall proceeding to make it void. For clearing of this I hope you remember this distinction in our law, that some things are void, and some voidable by due processe of law. For example, if *John a Stiles* should enter into a bond of an hundred pound to *John a Nokes* with condition annexed, that if the Obligor did kill a third person before such a day, then the Obligation should be void. This Obligation being with a condition against law, is void by the very making of it, and the Obligor needs not to sue the Obliged in Chancery, to compell him to free him of the penaltie, because void in it self.

On the other side, some things are voidable, [i.e.] to be made void by the partie himself by Processe of law; as if *Titus* within the age of twenty one years makes a feoffement, levies a fine, or suffers a recovery of land to *Sempronius,* this is not simply void, but voidable: so that *Titus* when he comes to age, if the conveyance were by feoffement, he may remedie it by his Writ of *Dum fuit infra aetatem,* if it were by fine or recovery reverse them by error, because within age at the time. To apply it to your case, if men and women of disagreeing dispositions being joyned in mariage, the mariage is void, being neither of God nor Nature, then there needs no Divorce or legall proceeding to part them, and then it is nothing to the Title of your Book, being *The Doctrine and Discipline of Divorce,* which you pretend to handle, briefly when you have proved, that such men and women who are maried, and are of contrary dispositions or mindes, that their mariage is void, or not of God nor Nature, we will grant you the whole cotroversie, in the mean time it is too great a begging of the question.

In your prosecution of this Section, you are pleased to faine an Objection, *That the disposition ought to be knowne before mariage.*

You are pleased to answer, *That a discreet man being wary in this, yet may be mistaken;* for say you, *the sobrest and best governed men are least practised in these things.*

But how so? if sobrest and best governed I hope they are the better able to judge of the disposition and cariage of a Maid or Widow: But go on. You say, *Who knows not that the bashfull mutenesse of a Virgin may oft times hide all the unlivelinesse and naturall sloth, which is really unfit for conversation.*

Some are bashfull and mute indeed: but what of that? you speak of triall of them whether they are fit for conversation or no: if you would once tell what you mean by conversation, I doubt there is none so modest but you may make tryall of that: If you mean fit for discourse, and flexible to your desires, to go abroad or stay at home, & c. I know nothing of any modesty to hinder you, the tryall of these things before mariage, if you have so much time.

You adde, *That there is not that freenesse of accesse granted or presumed, as sufficeth to a perfect discerning till it be too late.*

Sir we beleeve you fain things to your self, to make good your Arguments. Kings and Princes indeed usually have little accesse to their Queen or Princesse before mariage; but for lower degrees, sure so much accesse is granted, without any immodestie to discerne what you speak of.

You further go on, and say, *That though they who have lived most loosely, prove most successefull in their matches, because their wilde affections unsetling at will have been as so many divorces to them to teach them experience: When as the sober man honouring the appearance of modesty, and hoping well of every sociall vertue under that veile, may easily chance to meet, if not with a body impenetrable, yet often with a minde to all other due conversation inaccessible.*

Modest men seldome deal with any, who as they are not of bodies impenetrable, so neither are they to all due conversation inaccessible. It is true, if every man were of your breeding and capacitie, there were some colour for this plea; for we believe you count no woman to due conversation accessible, as to you, except she can speak Hebrew, Greek, Latine, & French, and dispute against the Canon law as well as you, or at least be able to hold discourse with you. But other Gentlemen of good qualitie are content with meaner and fewer endowments, as you know well enough.

Very true it is, that it is not amisse, for men of the best capacities, learning, and breeding, that they should match with those of the best wits, qualitie, and breeding, and leave the duller Virgins for the simpler sort; there is enough to own them, and ordinarily they fall to their shares, and that it is not alwayes so, you have no need to attribute it to modestie, that men doe not try their Sweethearts wits before they have them: you know that may be done with modesty enough, although to try whether their bodies are impenitrable (as you call it) favours of the contrary.

Well, but you goe on to make up this your second Argument from the diverse evils that would follow if Divorce should not be suffered for contrarietie and disagreement of mindes.

The first you say, *Is an imputation upon God and his law, of dispensing with open and common adultery among his own people; which,* say you, *the rankest polititian would think it shame and dis-worship, that his lawes should countenance any such thing. But the shewing how this comes to passe, you say you will reserve to another place.*

We answer you, that we think this the fittest place for this Controversie, seeing you have named it here, and therefore shall free the law of God from any such imputation, and clear that here which you after bring from *Moses;* permitting divorce, and the sence of Christ in the Gospell.

Only first we shall speak to your phrase and manner of speaking, and then to the matter of it.

Your phrase is, *That such an imputation as would be cast upon the Law of God by this means, the rankest Polititian would think it shame and dis-worship that his lawes should be charged with any such thing.*

Is this the fine language that your Book is commended for: Good your worship look a little upon your Rhetorick in this one piece, shall I say of nonsense: however I am sure it is contrary to all lawes and customes of speaking. *Rankest Polititian.* Wonderfull!

What a Boarish Adjective you joyne with a Polititian. Polititian is a title worthie of honour and respect, and why you should so disgrace it with this homely language, I cannot imagine; except it be, because Polititians ordinarily differ from you in this your opinion. For although its likely some Polititians sometimes at a time of need are content to make use of others then their own wives, yet to be divorced from their own upon a little contrariety of mindes or dispositions, Polititians will not easily agree to it.

But to go on, *The rankest Polititian would think it shame his laws, &c.* His lawes; strange! Where were you bread? Sir, What are the lawes of your Common-wealth made only by one Polititian? sure that same is a barren Countrey of Noble and Learned men. And if it be not barbarous, yet is it a very harsh phrase, to call the lawes made in any Common-wealth, the lawes of the Polititians, much more of one only Polititian.

But peradventure you mean the King, and the lawes may be called his, you think.

If you do mean him, its no usuall phrase to call him Polititian without farther addition: or if it were, you know its no good sense in your own countrey, for I beleeve you are not to heare of, *Qui vulgus elegerit:* And if you meane of some other Countrey, write your Book in their language, for the English will but deride such language as this is.

Againe, *He would think it shame and dis-worship,* (say you) to what, say I? to his lawes: strange Philosophy! Are lawes now capable of shame and blushing? Speak a little plainer if you have any such point to broach.

But, peradventure you meane, the Polititian would think it shame and dis-worship. Well, but upon whom do you mean he thinks this shame and dis-worship will light? for you shew us not whether the Polititian would think this shame to redound to the lawes themselves, or to himself, or to a third person or thing, pray let's know the next time.

But againe, why shame and dis-worship? Do the lawes or the Polititian that makes them, use to be worshipped in your Common-wealth? Well, we leave the Gentleman of that worshipfull countrey, who looks for Good your Worship at every word, and *Utinam* they are not too worshipfull to be W.

Thus from your phrase we passe on to the matter, which should be put in here for the proofe of this first evill: namely, that denying of divorce for cause of contrarietie of minde and disposition, will cast an imputation upon the law of God, of dispensing and conniving with common and open adultery amongst his own people.

Well, how do you prove this? For the proofe of this we must be driven to bring in your Text of *Deut. 24. 1.* which as you say, *permits, nay, is a wise and pious law, that such who did not love their Wives for some displeasing naturall quality or unfitnesse in her, he should write her a Bill of Divorce:* so you speak *pag. 26.* compared with *pag. 10.* Now how this imputation will come to fall upon the law of God, I believe you mean thus. That for a man to divorce his Wife unjustly and to marrie another, is adultery: But the law of God allowes divorce unjustly, except disagreement of minde, or unpleasat naturall qualitie be a cause. *Ergo.*

In plaine tearms you mean God by *Moses* suffered men to put away their wives, if they found not love and favour in their eies; by reason of some unpleasing natural qualitie, (for so you are pleased to reade the Text of *Deut. 24. 1*) Now you infer, if *Moses* allowed this, and yet indeed it was not a just cause of divorce, then did God by *Moses's* law tolerate adulterie, in that tolerated a man or woman to marrie to another, whilest they were not lawfully parted from their first Husbands or Wives.

To take off this great Scare-crow and the maine Pillar which he trusts in to hold up his whole Book, or most part of it: it will be necessarie a little to consider of this Text of *Deut. 24. 1.* whether it doth indeed speak any such thing or no. Our English Translation hath it, If a man shall take a Wife and lie with her, and she finde not grace in his eyes because of some uncleannesse, let him write her a Bill of Divorce. So that it is for some uncleannesse, and not for some displeasing qualitie that is in her. According to our English: the French Bible agrees, *Pourtannt que il a trouve quelque laide tache in elle,* because he hath found in her some foule, unhonest, or abominable reproach, spot, or infamy; for so signifies *laide tache. Jeromes* Translation hath it, *Propter aliquans foeditatem,* filthinesse or shamefull thing. *Iunius* and *Tremelius* agrees.

A Translation according to the Septuagint printed at *Basil* hath it, *Quoniam invenit in ea foedam,* the Septuagint reads it *εὗρεν ἐν αὐτῇ ἄσχημον πρᾶγμα,* the Substantive *pragma,* is used, *Acts 5. 4.* to signifie *res*; and *I Cor. 6. 1. negotium,* businesse: *James 3. 16. opus* or work: and the Adjective is used by *Paul 1 Cor. 12. 23.* for *indecorus,* shamefull, dishonest, or unbeseeming: so signifying that they understood this place of *Deut. 24.* 1. to be meant of some shamefull or dishonest thing. So they which translate by the Septuagint have it, *rem turpem,* filthy thing. In the Hebrew it is *Gneruath Dabhar,*[5] the very same words which are used *Deut. 23. 14.* The Lord thy God walketh in thy Camp to deliver thee, therefore shall thy Campe be holy, that he see no *Gneruath Dabhar* in thee: that is, no uncleannesse or uncleane thing, as is apparant by the foregoing Verses: so here, if she finde not favour in her Husbands eyes because of some *Gneruath Dabhar,* some uncleannesse or uncleane thing. The Hebrewes themselves expound this Text, to be understood of a woman of evill condition, who is not modest according to the honest Daughters of Israel. So that here seems to be no ground for your understanding the Text to speak of any unpleasing naturall quality, when as indeed it speaks of uncleannesse: so that as we conceive, the maine Pillar of your Book is not able to hold up it self, much lesse will it serve for a prop to hold up the rest of your discourse.

But it may be demanded, what manner of uncleannesse this Text speaketh of; for it seems it cannot be meant of adulterie: for Christ speaking (as it seems) with a relation to this Text, *Matth 19.* saith, *Moses* indeed suffered you to put away your Wives, & c. But I say unto you, whosoever shall put away his Wife except it be for fornication, commits adulterie; so that which *Moses* suffered to put away Wives for, was aother cause then what Christ here speaks of, namely, fornication, which could not be that which *Moses* suffered putting away for, seeing Christ opposeth putting away for fornication to putting away by *Moses's* law.

To this we answer, that though it be little materiall to our point in hand, what uncleannesse this Text *Deut. 24. 1.* speaks of; whether it be a legall, ceremoniall, or a morall uncleannesse; for it sufficeth to our purpose, if it be not some unpleasing naturall qualitie, as this author hath affirmed: Yet we shall humbly propose to the judicious and learned with their favour, and under correction, what uncleannesse this Text of *Deut. 24.* speaks of.

Not proposing it as a sense infallible, but one which may be something probable.

And that is, that this Text *Deut. 24. 1.* speaks of an uncleannesse committed before mariage, which we usually call by the name of fornication; the same uncleannesse which is spoken of *Deut. 22. 13, 14, 15,* & c. Where it is said, *If a man take a wife and lye with her, and hate her, and shall say, I took this woman to wife, and when I came in unto her I found her not a maide;* and the Text goes on, and shewes what shall be done in this case.

This Text is doubtlesse to be understood of a man who takes a Wife and findes she hath committed follie before mariage, which we ordinarily call by the name of fornication. The same kinde of uncleannesse (under correction) may be here meant: that when a man marries a Wife and findes her not a Maide, but defiled, and to be uncleane by fornication committed before mariage.

Against this sense of the place we conceive there may be two strong objections made which we shall endeavour to answer, and so leave it to the consideration of the Reader.

The first Objection may be from that Text *Deut. 24. 12, 13,* &c. where the direction is there, that if it be found according to the complaint of her Husband, that she was not a Maide but defiled, that she should be stoned to death, and not be put away by Divorce; by the same reason, if this Text of *Deut. 24. 1.* speaks of that uncleannesse, she ought to be stoned to death, and not suffered to escape by Divorce.

To this we answer two things.

First that there was a twofold uncleannesse or defilement of Virgins by the law; the one was, when she consented not to the unclean[e]sse or defilement, but it was committed upon her by force, and this in the Maide did not deserve death, as is shewed *Deut. 22. 26.*

Secondly, there was a defilement with the consent of the Maide, and this seems to be distinguished by the law to be of two qualities.

1. The first was, when a man by intising words should tempt and intice a Maid to lye with her, and she upon his promises and inticements yielded to it, but presently after the fact did discover it to her father or kindred, to compell the same man to marrie her: and of this kind it seems is spoken of *Exod. 22. 16.* In this case the man was compellable to marry her, and so she was not in this case to be punished with death.

Secondly, there was another distinction of this defiling of a Virgin, *viz.* When the Maide consented to commit folly with any privately, and so as it proceeded from her whorish spirit principally, with a meer desire to commit filthinesse, as a comman Strumpet or Whore, and concealed this; so that the partie by her concealment could not be compelled to marrie her: and after, this defiled Virgin takes another man to Husband, and he findes her not a Maid, but to have committed follie in her fathers house, and never declared it, to the end the man who committed follie with her might be compelled to marrie: this (under favour) is that which *Deut. 22. 12, 13, 14,* & c. was to be punished with death, and a Divorce not to serve the turn.

But then for the uncleannesse, *Deut. 24.* 1. which a man found in his Wife, it might very well be, that a man ignorantly took such a woman to wife, as either had been ravished by force (as in the first sense) and so was defiled, or that had been defiled by the inticement of some man, of which fact she had made knowne to her father, to the end to compell him to marry her who defiled her, and her father upon knowledge of it utterly refused to give her to him to Wife, as *Exodus 22. 17.* and she after marries another who findes her defiled or uncleane is displeased therewith, so that she findes no favour in his eyes, he may not in this case prosecute her to the death, as in *Cap. 22.* but only divorce her, as *Cap. 24. 1. & 2.*

But secondly we answer, that in case it should be the same uncleannesse and defilement with that *Deut. 22. 11, 12,* & c. then we say it was left by the law to the choice of the man to prosecute her to death, as *Cap. 22.* or to Divorce her, as *Cap. 24.* And though I know this will sound very harsh and irreconcileable at the best: yet (under favour I conceive) I may as easily recocile these two places thus together, as Christs speech, *Matthew 5. 32.* can be reconciled to the law of adultery. For as I conceive, there is no man but will confesse that at that time when Christ spoke, the law of putting to death for adulterie was in force; and yet you see, *Matthew 5. 32.* he sayes not, he that prosecutes not his Wife to the death for being an Adulteresse, is guiltie: but whosoever puts away his Wife, except for fornication, he commits adulterie.

Now if there had been an absolute necessitie in the man to prosecute his Wife to death for adulterie, I suppose Christ would never have mentioned Divorce, for that which must of necessity have death. So it may seem it was left to the mercy of the Husband. The same I say to the reconciling the command of putting to death the defiled Virgin, *Deut. 22.* and divorcing her, *Cap. 24.*

It may further by [*sic*] objected, that it cannot be the same uncleannesse meant here which in *Chapter 22.* because there direction is given for a triall of the charge of uncleannesse laid to her, but not so here: and if upon triall there it be found a false charge he may not put her away all the dayes of his life.

To this we answer two things.

First it will not follow, but that the same triall ought to be in the *24 Chapter* as in the *22.* although not mentioned, yet to be understood; as well as the fathers dissent to the mariage of his Daughter to one who hath defiled her be not mentioned, *Deut. 22. 29.* yet is to be understood as well as it is *Exod. 22. 17.* where it is mentioned.

But suppose the same triall be not to be understood in the *24 Chapter* as in the *22.* yet will it not follow but that it may bee the same uncleannesse (onely differing in the consent of the Maide, &c.) for though it be the same uncleannesse, yet doth there not need that examination and tryall where onely a divorce is intended, as where death is intended.

But there seemes to be another great Objection against this sense of the word Uncleannesse, that it cannot be meant of fornicaton before mariage; because Christ speaking with relation to this Text, as it seemes, understood it otherwise then of fornication, as appeares by his conclusion, that whosoever should put away their Wives except for fornication, &c. So that it would seeme plaine CHRIST understood not this Text to bee meant of fornication, for he seemes to blame this putting away founded upon this Text, and yet allowes divorce for fornication.

For answer to this briefly, wee conceive the words fornication and adultery are used in the New Testament, if not reciprocally, yet at the least promiscuously: and that that by fornication is many times meant more then uncleannesse committed betweene unmaried persons: as *I Corinthians 5. 1.* there the word fornication is used and applyed to incest: And in *I Corinthians 10. 7.* Neither let us be fornicators, &c. being applyed to the Israelite *Numb. 25* who lay it is said, with the women of *Midian,* which seems to be no Maid, for the title Woman is seldome applyed to them: So *I Cor. 6.* he that commits fornication sins against his own bodie, is doubtlesse to be understood of adulterie as well as of uncleannesse between single persons, if it be not solely meant of adultery.

So then our answer is, that the word fornication is often used for adulterie, after mariage: and we conceive Christ intended it so, when he saith, *Whosoever shall put away his Wife, except for fornication,* &c. that is, for adultery, or defiling his mariage bed; and so Christ speaks not of the same uncleannesse *Moses* doth, although *Moses's* should be meant of fornication.

Thus you have our first answer to this your place of *Deut. 24.* I. that it is meant of uncleannesse, as the Originall and other languages reads it: and though we are not over confident of the kinde of uncleannesse whether it be fornication before mariage, as we have shewed, or some naturall, legall, or sinfull uncleannesse, it much matters not: this we only propose to the Readers consideration, upon triall to reject it, or receive it as he findes it upon examination.

But in case this answer fails; we have two other answers to your place of *Deut. 24.* I. only two Objections remain.

1. That Christ findes fault with this Divorce grounded upon *Moses's* law, and shewes it was not so from the beginning, nor ought not to be so now[:] which proves the divorce for uncleannesse *Deut. 24. I.* cannot be understood of fornication, or uncleannesse committed before mariage, for that was alwayes allowed of from the beginning as a just cause of divorce, and so seems to be now.

To this we only answer; that when either of these two are proved, we shall willingly let fall that interpretation; in the mean time we leave it to the considerate Reader.

2. But it may be further objected, that whatsoever it was that *Moses* allowed of Divorce for, whether for fornication before mariage, as is said before, or for some unpleasing naturall quality, as our Author would have it; yet the imputation of dispensing with common adultery is not taken away, in case it was not a just cause of divorce. For answer to this we come to our second answer to this place of *Deut. 24. I.*

In the second place we answer to *Deut. 24. I.* in case your reading should be found good to be of a displeasing naturall qualitie, and that they did unjustly put away by this law their wives: then we answer, this place of *Moses* permits no divorce at all; but was only a law made in favour of the woman who was unjustly put away, and a sufferer: in this case *Moses* provides, that though a woman should be wrongfully & by force be put away, yet he would by this law compell the Husband to give her a Bill of divorce, which should be a token to her father and her friends that it was the act of her husband to dismisse and put her away, and not her voluntary act: for which, had it been voluntary on her part, she would have been judged a Whore and a wandering Vagrant, and so would scarcely have been received into her fathers house: so that *Moses* may seem here not to give any law of divorce; but rather a law to compell such of the Jewes, who in their cruelty, and from the hardnesse of their hearts would unjustly and by force put away their wives, to make them a writing of divorce and to give it her, which should be a testimony for the woman after she departed, that she wandered not as a Whore or a Vagrant of her own minde from the company of her Husband, but it was his fact by force to put her away.

For the proofe of this sence of the place we conceive three things make to this purpose.

1. Because I finde no law of divorce allowing men to put away their wives before this law, (if in case this should be found to be such a law) and yet I finde divorce practised by the Jewes, therefore *Levit. 21. 14.* it is commanded to the Priest, that he shold not marry a Widow, or a woman that was divorced, which implies

there were some women divorced. Now if divorce was practised and no law allowing it, I have reason to think this place of *Deut. 24. I.* is a law to remedie the extremity of their unlawfull divorces, by compelling them to make a Bill in favour of the woman that was put away, and not a law either commanding or allowing the divorce it selfe.

2. It seemes to appear from the connexion of the words, hee shall give her a Bill of divorce, that when she is departed out of his house she may become the Wife of another man; so that the Bill seems meerly to be made for her benefit.
3. The Text here allowes the woman to marry againe, she being the suffering partie and unjustly put away; but he being the offending, it speaks nothing of allowing him to marrie againe; so it seems the provision of the Bill of Divorce was for her benefit only.

Against this the words of Christ will be objected, *Matth. 19.* and *Mark 10.* to the Pharisees, when they had asked, if a man might put away his Wife for every cause, *Matth. 19. 3.* Christ answers, That *God at the beginning made them Male and Female,* and *that a man shall forsake Father and Mother and cleave unto his Wife:* the Pharisees upon this, ask Christ, why *Moses* did command to give a writing of Divorce, and to put her away; then Christ answers, *Moses, because of the hardnesse of your hearts suffered you to put away your wives, but from the beginning it was not so.* So that some may say, Christ here seems to affirme not only the Bill of Divorce to be of *Moses,* but even the Divorce it self.

It appears not to be so, but rather that Christ answers the Pharisees according to their opinion of *Moses* law, and he grants them that in some sort *Moses* might be said to suff[e]r men to put away their Wives, because he commanded the Bill to be made in favour of the woman, the suffering party: but saith Christ, *from the beginning it was not so,* that men should put away their Wives as the Jewes did, neither was this Bill then invented: and this may seem to be the substance of Christs words.

We answer to your Text *Deut. 24.* I. in the third place, that if the other two satisfie not, then may that be a good positive law made by *Moses,* during the time of the Jewish politie or government, properly called Mosaicall: yet now Christ under the New Testament hath abolished that law to all his followers. To this purpose that of Christ *Matth. 5. 31, 32. It was said unto of old, that whosoever shall put away his Wife, let him give her a bill of divorce:* then Christ addes, *But I say unto you, whosoever shall put away his Wife except it be for cause of fornication, causeth her to commit adultery, and whosoever shall marry her that is divorced committeth adultery.* This place of our Saviour concerning divorce may seem not to be to the end to reforme the false glosses of the Pharisees concerning divorce, (as it is usually thought) but rather to shew the law of the Gospell to require more mutuall love and passing by injuries then the law: As who should say, under *Moses,* where there was many duties required; and yet through the darknesse of the d[i]spensation of heavenly things, there was little grace and power to performe what was required, then the law of Divorce did mercifully bear with the infirmities of people; and during the time of this dispensation, this law of Divorce was a good positive law: But now whosoever will be my follower and professe himself to have received the plenteous grace of the Gospell, he must be so farre from using hardship or unkindnesse to his Wife, or others to whom he is neerly bound, that he must not revenge wrong done from strangers & enemies, but pray for them, and blesse them; he must be so farre from turning his Wife out of doores for her ill cariage, yea although it should proceed to cursing and persecuting him, that he must use all mildnesse, and love, and godly means to reforme her; compare this with *verse 43, 44.* and indeed with all the latter part of the Chapter, and you will finde the drift of Christ, to give as it were new inlargements of lawes under the Gospell, requiring more spiritualness in observation, then the Mosaical government.

This interpretation I cannot conceive to be either contrary to the scope of Christ in this Chapter, which principally is, to shew that he came not to destroy the law but to fulfil it: nor is it contrary to any other sound and wholesome Doctrine laid downe in Scripture, neither opens any gap to any to throw away *Moses's* law, as not at all pertaining to us. I think there is none that thinks, but that there were given by *Moses,* not only ceremoniall Precepts, but even judiciall, to the Jewes, which for us to observe under the Gospell, would be so farre from piety, that it would be sinfull; and I know nothing why this law of Divorce may not be one.

Only one word to your corrupt and wicked glosse upon our Saviours words, *Matth. 19.* and *Mark 10.* where he tels the Pharisees, that whosoever should put away his Wife, except for fornication, he did commit adultery; you to put off the matter, as if Christs speech was never intended to forbid a Divorce, for your indisposition, unfitnesse, or contrariety of minde, but was only as you say, *That Christ here did only deale like a wise Physitian, administring one excesse against another to bring us to a perfect meane, and that where the Pharisees were strict, there Christ seemes to be remisse; and where they were too remisse he saw it needfull to seeme most severe: In one place,* say you, *he censures an unchaste look to be adultery already committed, and at another time he passeth over actuall adultery with lesse reproofe then for an unchaste look: So here,* say you, *he may be thought to give this rigid sentence against Divorce, not to cut off all remedy to a good man who consumes with a disconsolate matrimony, but to lay a bridle upon the bold abuser of these overweening Rabbies, &c.*

To this we answer, that this your glosse is not only intolerable abuse of Scripture, but smels very strongly of little lesse then blasphemie against Christ himself.

For what is it else, to say Christ was here most severe, where the Pharisees were most remisse, and that here he administred one excesse against another, &c. For though it should be found that Christ sometimes, to check the pride and hypocrisie of the Pharisies, should by his not affording them an answer seem remisse, where they were too severe, and so on the contrary. Yet that Christ should positively lay down a resolution, as one of his Precepts under the Gospell without any exception; and this his Precept to be an excesse to reduce the Pharisies to a mean, is too bold and dangerous an assertion for any man to venture upon.

And for your examples which you cite where Christ was one time remisse, and another time more severe against a lesse sinne, they are both utterly false; for in the one place Christ doth not say, that an unchaste look is adultery, but he that upon looking on a woman doth lust after her, he hath committed adultery in his heart, so that it is not the looking on her, but the lusting after her which is adultery, and that but of the heart neither: truely I finde not here an excesse, or too much severity in Christ, but fearfull audacity in you.

And for your other example of the woman taken in adultery, where he was more remisse, and gave her not so sharpe a reproof as here for an unchaste look; this is as false, for he bids her *goe away and sinne no more least a worse thing* then death by stoning *came to her;* and I hope this is severer then Christ speaks of the unchaste look, as you call it.

But to answer to what you chiefly intend, you are to know, Christ *Matthew 19.* doth not direct his speech concerning Divorce, as an excesse against the Pharisies tempting question only, but as a firme stable resolution of the Gospell: to clear this consider but two things.

1. That Christ before this time had given the same resolution to his Disciples *Matth. 5. 32.* where he spake principally to his Disciples, as appeares *Verse I.* And therefore it cannot be intended that Christ spake it to represse the pride and false glosses of the Pharisies only.
2. And secondly its apparant that Christ did intend otherwise then you say to contradict the Pharisees, for if he had only told them, that he which puts away his Wife except for fornication, committed adultery, this had been enough to have contradicted them: but he addes, that whosoever shall marry her who is put away otherwise, he commits adultery: And so I conclude, Christ intended this speech to his Disciples, as a direction bindig all Christians under the Gospell; and gave it not as an expressive resolution to represse and crosse the pride and false glosses of the Pharisies.

Now for the rest of your stuffe which fils many Pages about the sense of *Moses Deut. 24. 1.* and of Christ *Matth. 19.* and the opinions of other men upon the same, of which, some you approve, and some you confute, we conceive it needlesse to trace you, as thinking we have given you the true sense of *Moses* and Christ alreadie, to which we referre the triall of all which you are pleased to speak upon the same.

In briefe the summe of our answer to this place of *Deut. 24.* 1. for the lawfulnesse of putting away a mans Wife for some displeasing naturall qualitie, is, that first, that it speaks of Divorce for uncleannesse, and not for disagreement: or secondly, if it doth, it allowes not of the Divorce, but appoints the Bill in favour of the woman: or thirdly, if it allowes both, yet now is it altered by Christ under the Gospell.

If any shall think these answers to fall foul upon each other, we easily grant it, and say its usuall in this kinde; and besides we write not as Prophets but as men: and if any of the answers be to the point, and overthrow that which we conceived to be an error, its sufficient.

Your second evill which you say would follow, if Divorce were not lawfull for displeasing naturall qualities, &c. is, *That the Law and the Gospell would be subject to more then one contradiction, but to shew this you deferre it to another place.*

Answer. We shall take it here, and tell you, its no contradiction at all, that *Moses* should allow a Divorce and Christ deny it, if it could be proved: For there is a twofold cotradiction (as you know well enough;) one is, when the Gospell shall blame the Law for tolerating things contrary to it self, that one time it made a thing lawfull, at another time unlawfull; this is the contradiction you must speak of if you speak to the purpose, that the Gospel shall blame or contradict *Moses's* law, for maintaining contrarie things in it self.

Then secondly, there is a contradiction of the Gospell to the Law; that the Gospel counts some things under its dispensation to be altogether unlawfull to be done, which the Law allowed as lawfull and pious in the time of its dispensation: this kind of contradiction we grant there is betweene the Law and Gospel many times, but is nothing to your purpose at all: for example, Circumcision was a dutie of weight; now its a hainous crime: so Sacrifices, Offerings, Washings, and a hundred the like, and yet the Gospel blames not the Law for these things in the time of its dispensation: no more will it follow in case of Divorce, if it should be allowed then and denied now, except you can shew the first kinde of contradiction.

Your third evill which you say would follow if Divorce should be denied to such as are of contrariety of dispositions is, *That hereby the supreame dictate of Chariy, would bee many wayes violated and neglected.* But how is this done? You say, *we know Paul saith, it is better to marry then to burne:* tis true, *Paul* doth say so: what will follow of that? Is *Pauls* positive resolution become the supreame dictate of Charitie? else how followes it, the supreame dictate of Charitie is violated by denying Divorce on your grounds, because *Paul* saith *it is better to marry then to burne:* remember your self well, sure you think all Gospel you speak.

Well, what would you inferre from *Pauls* words, *it is better to marry then to burne?*

You say, *That mariage was given as a remedy of that trouble.* So say we; but yet not properly that ordination of mariage first in Paradise, for then was no such burning.

Well, go on; we ask you what this burning in lust is which *Paul* means: you are pleased to answer, *That, certainly not the meer motion of carnall lust not the meer goade of a sensitive desire, God doth not principally take care for such cattell.*

Truly you are apt to speake very high language: but what would follow if *Paul* should take care, not for the nourishment, but for the suppressing of a meer motion of carnall lust? Sure no evill.

Well, but we will have your advice positively, as well as negatively, what the Apostle means, when he sayes *it is better to marry then to burne.*

You say, *It is that desire which God put in Adam in Paradise, before he knew the sinne of incontinency: it was that desire, which God saw it was not good that man should be left alone, to burne in a longing to put off solitarinesse, by uniting another body, but not without a fit soule to his in the cheerfull society of wedlock.*

We pray you seriously to retract this sentence, and openly to confesse you were asleepe when you writ it.

We desire any indifferent man but to consider the scope of the Apostle in that Chapter of *I Cor. 7.* and to tell us if your exposition of these words, *it is better to marry then to burne,* be not such a meer trifling and abusing the Scripture as seldome is met with. This must needs be a just Paraphrase upon *Pauls* words if your exposition were sound.

I *Paul* am a Batchelour, and I never met with any fit and meet conversing soule, to fit my desire, to discourse and converse with me as I had when I was in *Adam;* but I speake to you Virgins and Widowes, although it be thus with me, yet it were good if you could remaine solitary without any fit conversing soule to discourse with you: but if you cannot live altogether alone all the dayes of your life (however I shift for my selfe) yet doe you marrie, *viz.* get some fit conversing soules, such an one as *Adam* thought of when he was alone in the Garden, and no bodie created but he. For it is better for you seeing you cannot live alwaies alone, to have some such fit conversing soule, to drive away the time with, then to pine away like a Dove in a Wildernesse, where there is none to beare her company. This is the effect of your exposition of *Paul,* when he saith, *it is better to marry then to burne:* the relating of which your exposition is enough to confute it and make it lighter then vanitie it self.

So we passe to your third Argument, the effect whereof seems to be this.

That the not allowing of divorce in case of contrariety of mindes and dispositions in maried persons, will be a ground or occasion of their desire after other persons, besides their own Wives; because when a man findes no contentment at home he is apt to looke for the same abroad.

We answer you, what if he do look abroad, so long as it is but to meet with a fit conversing soule, provided he meddles not with her bodie, let him recreate himself, its lawfull enough: tis your own doctrine, A fit conversing soule for man is the noblest end of mariage: Therefore I think we may without danger, let a mans reines loose to accomodate himself so, if his Wife hath not such a fit conversing soule as she should have, only let him remember to come home to her at night. If you should say, that you meane want of content at home will cause a man to lust unlawfully after the bodies of other mens Wives.

Wee answer you there is no congruitie in that sense with the rest of your Book: for according to your own Doctrine we may reason thus: That desire which is not satisfied at home by a mans own Wife, will break out towards other mens Wives; but the desire which is to be satisfied by a mans owne Wife is, that she be a fit conversing soule: *Ergo,* the not finding a man's Wife a fit conversing soule, will not endanger or stir up any other desires but to converse with the soules of other mens Wives; and thus we allow you to do and keep your own still.

But enough of this: only we desire the next time you write, to tell us the meaning of this fit conversing soule. We have heard that Angels converse with one another as they are Spirits; but for Husbands and Wives, though they ought not to love in word only, but in deed and in truth with the affections of the heart, yet we know no conversing with one another, but what is by words or actions.

Well you goe on and talk in this Section, *Of a man meeting instead of a sweet co-partner of pleasant society, it often happens, that young men, who have put their chiefe content in a contented mariage, yet they meet with an Image of earth and fleame.*

We confesse this is something a sad case: but yet I believe you speak but hyperbolically (as they use to say) for Women are usually more then earth and fleame, they have many times spirit enough to weare the Breeches, if they meet not with a rare Wit to order them. I wonder you should use such phrases; I know, nor heare of any Maids or Women that are all earth and fleame, much lesse Images of earth and fleame: If there be any such, yet you need take no thought for them, there are enough dull enough to own them; & for your self or any other who desire them, there are spirited Dames enough, who are something besides meere Images of earth and fleame.

Your fourth Argument is, *Because mariage is a Covenant, whose very being consists not in a forced cohabitation or a counterfeit performance of duties, but in unfeined love and peace.*

It is true, but how prove you by this, that if there be not found this peace and joy between maried persons, there may then be a Divorce: for where the chiefe end of a thing is not alwayes attained in its full measure, yet will it not be lawfull to seek a separation from it. Will you argue, that because *Heman Psal. 88*. found not that peace and solace which is the main end of communion with God, that therefore he might break off that communion. Or how think you; suppose you should covenant with a man at *Hackney,* that he should dwell in your house at Aldersgatestreet, & you in requital would dwel in his house at *Hackney* for a time; I doubt not but your main end in this your Covenant was your own solace, peace, and refreshing. Well, but suppose when you come there, the *Cavaliers* or other Souldiers should trouble you, and should be quartered there; who peradventure if they did not quite put you out, yet would lie in your most pleasant Chamber best scituate for your solace and refreshing; and divers other waies would annoy you; by meanes whereof you could not enjoy that pleasure and delight which you intended in your Covenant, when you changed houses with the other. Think you in this case it would be lawfull or accepted on by the other partie if now you should come to him and say; Sir, I covenanted for your house at *Hackney* for my own refreshing, comfort, and solace, but I am disturbed of it, I do not enjoy the end of my Covenant, give me my own house again, and go you live there. He would tel you, and so he might justly, stay Sir, take your own fortune, a bargain is a bargain, you must even stand to it. In the same case I suppose, though it be the end of mariage, that love and peace should be maintained; yet if it fall out otherwise they must be content.

But let us see your proofes to the contrarie: and that is say you, in such a case, where we finde not that content in mariage which was the end of it, but on the contrary vexation: *Paul* himselfe speaking of Mariage and Divorce, determines therein, that God hath called us to peace and not to bondage.

Well, we will examine what *Paul* makes for you, the place *I Cor. 7.* (though you seem loath to quote the place) where the Apostle speaks to Men and Women, who were Christians and had Infidels to their Husbands or Wives: And he tels them if any believer had a Wife who is an Infidell and yet she was content to dwell with him, that he should not put her away, &c. And then when he hath given the reason of it in the next Verse, he after tels them, that notwithstanding if in such a case the Infidell Husband or Wife will not dwell with their Christian Husband or Wife, but that they will depart and go away to live in some other place; a believer, saith *Paul,* is not in subjecftion in this case, but God hath called us to peace. Now what an argument will this be, if a Christian Husband hath an Infidell to his Wife, who out of spight and hatred to religion and to her Husband, and will depart and divorce her self, in such a case the Husband is not bound to follow her wandring about, to keep her company whether she resorts, on purpose from his companie. *Ergo,* will it follow that when a man dislikes his Wife, and she peradventure willing to live with him, yet he may by force against her will put her away: the truth is, this place makes quite against you as hath been shewed. But besides, you mistake the very Gramaticall sense, when you will bring in these words, God hath called us to peace, as a reason why the believing Husband may suffer his Wife being an Infidell to depart: for they rather seeme to be an Introduction to what he speaks after, how knowest thou O man whether thou shalt not save thy Wife, &c. As much as if he should say, though I tell you in the case before cited, a believer is not in subjection to his Wife, where there seems no means aileable with her to procure her cohabitation; yet sayes *Paul* I must tell you, God hath chiefly called us to peace, that is, he rather expects that as we are to follow peace with all men whatsoever, so especially with our Husbands and Wives, and to keep company and cohabitation together: and the Apostle saies in effect, I will give you a good reason for this; For how knowest thou O man, but that thou by dwelling and conversing with thy Wife, thou maist convert her and save her. So that it seems you are quite mistaken, in alledging this Text for your opinion.

Well, but have you any other Scriptures to prove this? Yes, say you, *For God himselfe commands by his law more then once, and by his Prophet Malachy, as Calvin and the best Interpreters reade, that he who hates his Wife let him divorce her, that is, say you, he who cannot love and delight in his Wife.*

We desire you to shew out of your new Scripture (if any such you have) where God in his Law commands, and that more then once, that he who hateth his Wife, should put her away; shew it but one time and we will yield you the whole controversie: If you meane *Deut. 24. 1.* that is but one place, and we have given you an answer to it.

And as for *Malachy,* although it be true, that some translations do reade it so, as *Jerome* and some Margents: yet why you should call these the best Interpreters of this Text, I know no reason, but because they agree with your opinion, which you dream to be the best. The last of our English Translations which other men count the best, hath it otherwise, *Mal. 2. 16.* and it saies, *for the Lord God of Israel saith, that he hateth putting away.* In the Hebrew it is, *Ci sane shallach, amar Jehovah Elohe Israel:*[6] which if your learning can make any other then a reason of what God had spoken before, you may peradventure make this place speak something for you. The truth is, this your reading is quite contrarie to the scope of the place; for God by his Prophet *Malachy* in the former verses vehemently complaines against the Jewes for dealing treacherouly with the Wives of their youths: Now how this was, although it be not so plain, yet it seems probable it was, by having of other lovers, and growing wearie of their own, and so a pretending some fault in them, to the end to put them away: Well saith God in the *16 Verse, The Lord God of Israel hateth this treachery of yours in seeking other lovers and being weary of your own wives put them away.* But on the other side, if your reading should be admitted, what a preposterous sense would here be; as if God should say, Oh you deceitfull Jewes, you treacherously deal with your own Wives, I pray let me heare no more of this treacherie; but this I command you, if you would faine be rid of them, do but hate them and then put them away, and then you are at libertie: And so God to prevent treacherie against mens wives, should command the greatest treacherie that can be devised.

In the prosecution of this reason you are pleased to say, *It is a lesse breach of wedlock to part with quiet consent betimes, then still to prophane that mystery of joy with a polluting sadnesse.*

Mysterie of joy, what language is this? is mariage now a Sacrament signifying joy? this I never heard of before: the Papists indeed make it a Sacrament, but not of joy, and yet I doubt they can say more for their opinion then you for yours.

But how a lesse breach of wedlock? is not wedlock quite broke by your divorce, though it should be with consent: but I am sure it is not quite broke by living sad and pensive lives; and yet their duties are to amend their faults which are the occasion of the sad living, and not to be separated from one anothers persons.

And whereas you say, *It is not the outward continuance of mariage which keeps the covenant of mariage whole, but whosoever doth most according to peace and love, whether in mariage or divorce, he breaks mariage least.*

We answer: this is a wilde, mad, and frantick divinitie, just like to the opinions of the Maids of Algate: Oh say they, we live in Christ, and Christ doth all for us; we are Christed with Christ and Godded with God, and at the same time we sin here, we joyned to Christ do justice in him, for our life is hid with God in Christ. So you, what, tell you of bearing the infirmities of your Wife, and so fulfill the law of Christ, and of giving honour to her as the weaker vessel: why you can do this when you have put her away, you do all in love and peace, you keep these Commandements well enough. Fie, fie, blush for shame, and publish no more of this loose Divinitie. But I would ask you a question or two.

May a man keep and maintaine that love which is required between maried persons towards her who was his Wife, but now is divorced from him. If not, why say you in effect, if there be but peace and love mariage is kept well enough, either by continuing in mariage or by divorce. If he may maintain that love to her that is divorced, this is just fast and loose, marry and hate, divorce and love: I will hate her now she is my Wife, but love her when my Concubine: So, so, you teach us good courteous Doctrine.

I ask you, whether mariage may continue after Divorce, if not, why say you in effect, that the mariage covenant is better kept by Divorce, so there be but love and peace, then by continuance in the sad companie of mariage. I grant according to the lawes of the kingdome there is a Divorce only *a mensa & thoro,* yet I believe they hardly allow that manifestation of love to each other which the covenant of mariage requires.

But let us see, have you any Scripture for this your new Gospell: yes, enough, say you, often repeated: yea, what is, that? The words of *Paul* forsooth, *Love only is the fulfilling of every commandement.*

You must remember you put in the word only, and so adde to the Scripture. But well it is true, the Scripture doth say, *love is the fulfilling of the law,* and so by consequence of every Commandement: but how this will make for your purpose I cannot yet possibly see. Sure I am *Paul* never intended to be a Patron of all injustice and injurie to be committed, under a fained pretence of keeping the same Commandements they broke, by a secret unknown love in their hearts. Its true indeed, he that doth unfeinedly love his Neighbour, he will honour his Parents, not commit murther, nor by adulterie defile his Neighbours Wife, or steale his goods; this is *Pauls* Doctrine. But *Paul* never taught, that a man might despise his Parents, murther, steale, and commit adulterie, and yet with a pretence of the grace of love earnestly burning in his heart, say he hath kept all the Commandements: No more doth he suffer a man to hate and put away his Wife with strife and variance, and tell him by the love and peace he had in his heart towards her, he had kept the Command of mariage unpoluted. *Pauls* intent in urging us so often with the dutie of love is, to put us in minde not to content our selves with the bare performance of duties to our Neighbour, without Christian love to their persons, he sayes *I Cor. 13. 2. If I give all my goods to the poore, and yet have no love, it profiteth not, &c.* But he never intended men should gape altogether upon this generall precept of love, and stick there, for *Paul* knew that would deceive thousands: therefore in the same place he descends to particulars, and thinks it not enough to bid them to love one another, but he bids to pay tribute to whom tribute belongs, and so keep the fifth Commandement: that they should owe nothing to man, and so keep the eight Commandement: *To walk honestly as in the day time, not in chambring and wantonnesse,* and so break the seventh Commandement; not in strife and envying, and so break the sixth Commandement: (this I speak according to the ordinary received opinion of ranking duties under each commandement, though I could never yet see how these duties can so well be brought in as being required in the 10 Commandements in a proper sense so to speak: its fit every Scripture should have its own weight and authority.) But to our purpose; as *Paul* is thus particular with the Romans, notwithstanding his generall precept of love; so if you will here bring in that love which is commanded between Husband and Wife, *Paul* means you shall expresse it, by covering or passing by a multitude of her faults, and by seeking to heale her errours; and by your meek, wise, and godly conversation towards her, labour to win her to God, and your self, and not most inhumanely hate her and put her away, and still say, you keepe the command of love. Thus of your fourth Argument.

The effect of your fifth Argument is, *That as the Priests of old were not to be long in sorrow, to the end they might execute their Priesthood rightly: So Christians now being Priests to God, dedicate to his service, they ought not by trouble and vexation of a disagreeing Wife to be hindred from serving God, but rather by divorce put her away, and so procure liberty to serve God.*

This argument is far fetched, yet is it not good for Ladies, nor scarce deserves any answer: but we tell you, most things concerning the priests were typicall, do you shew this to be the morall of this under the Gospel, that men might put away their Wives if they were cause of continuall heavinesse to them: how think you? might not many poor men by the same reason, who are by the providence of God compelled to labour, and so are hindred much from the cheerfull serving God in the things of his worship, which others have libertie in: may they not lawfully now leave their honest labour and fall to plunder or steal one hour or two in a day, and serve God cheerfully the rest? Why not, as well as when a man is by the providence of God maried to a yoke-fellow, which is in divers things cause of grief and vexation to him, therefore he may now break all bonds of law and providence, and under a pretence of serving God chearfully, he may unchristianly thrust his Wife out of dores with a bare Bill of Divorce in her hand to seek her living. For the rest of our discourse in this Division concerning divorce from Hereticks, we shall passe it over as nothing to our purpose, and so passe to your sixth Argument, the effect of which is.

That mariage which nature it selfe teacheth to be unlawfull, that may be destroyed or dissolved by divorce. But the mariage of persons of contrary mindes & dispositions, nature teacheth to be unlawfull. Ergo,

For the present we agree to the proposition, that such mariages as Nature it self teacheth to be unlawfull, may be dissolved by divorce.

But for the second part, that Nature teacheth such mariages to be unlawfull, as are made betwixt persons who are of a contrarie minde or disposition, this we utterly denie: and look for your proofs to the contrarie.

Well, you want not proofs, for you say, *Moses teacheth the Jewes that they should not sow their Vineyards with divers seeds, nor plough with an Oxe and an Asse together.*

Ho brave stuffe! but goe on; *Moses* teacheth so indeed: but how will you make this last to fit your shooe?

This you will do well enough, but how? *By following the example of Pauls reasoning,* say yo[u]. Well, lets see whether *Paul* or you are the best Logician. *Paul* reasons; doth God take care for Oxen and Asses how ill they yoke together, or is it spoke altogether for our sake? for our sakes doubtlesse: thus you would have *Paul* to reason for you: but the truth is, *Paul* doth reason thus, but it is in another case, the place is, *I Cor. 9*. Paul reasons thus; we that bestow our labour in preaching the Gospel, ought to be maintained thereby: and he proves it by familiar examples, that every one ought to be maintained by that which he takes paines in: as the Wayfaring man by travelling, the Vinedresser by planting, the Shepheard by looking to his flock; all these eat the fruit of their labour; and to put it out of doubt, *Paul* cites the Law of *Moses,* proving that not only Men, but even Beasts ought to eat the fruits of their labour, for it saith, *Thou shalt not muzle the mouth of the Oxe which treads out the corne.* Well, *Paul* goes on in his reasoning, lest any idle pated fellow should answer and say; *Paul,* what makes this for you, I hope you are no Oxe, neither do you tread out the corne. No, sayes *Paul,* that's true; but the force of my Argument is this, That God by *Moses* did not only intend in that speech, that Oxen should be fed, but it was with reference to other cases among the rest even for us Ministers of the Gospel, that we should not take pains in the Gospel, but should also be maintained thereby, as well as Oxen and other mean Callings are maintained by their labour: lo this is *Pauls* reasoning, and it is impregnable Logick: let's see how yours agrees. *Moses* tels the Jewes they should not plough with an Oxe and an Asse together, nor sow their field with divers seeds; *Ergo,* there being some other sense in this then meerly to take care for Oxen, &c. it will follow from hence, *that it is a foule incongruity and a great violence to the reverent secret of Nature, to force a mixture of mindes that cannot unite, and to sow the furrow of mans nativitie with seed of two incoh[e]rent and incombining dispositions.* Is this your reasoning like *Pauls,* as you promised: sure *Paul* would be ashamed to reason thus.

For although we believe there may be some typicall signification of that of *Moses,* yet that it should be yours is ridiculous. But you say, *Paul 2 Cor. 6.* alludes to that of *Moses,* and applies it to misyoking in mariage, as say you *by the Greek word is evident.*

To this we answer; that it may be likely both by the Greek word and English also, that *Paul* alludes to that in *Deuteronomy.* Yet that he applies it to mariage with Infidels you cannot prove, but rather to all needlesse conversation, but especially of companying with them in their service of Idols.

But suppose he did applie it to mariage with Infidels, and forbad it; yet you see after mariage is perfected and consummated, he will by no meanes allow of a Divorce if the Wife be but so much as content to live with her Husband, as was shewed upon *I Cor. 7.* And so this no waies makes for your purpose.

Now for that reverent expression of yours, *That it is a foule incongruity, and a great violence to the reverent secret of Nature, to force a mixture of mindes which cannot unite, and to sow the furrow of mans nativitie with the seed of two incoherent and incombining dispositions.*

This Court complement, so neatly and modestly drest, I believe deserves the pains of the best Ladie at Court to learn it. For answer to it being but a complement, for your forcing of a mixture of mindes that cannot unite; I know no bodie by force or fair means intends any such mixture in mariage: mindes are not capable of mixing but only agreeing and uniting; indeed you talk much of fit conversing soules, whether you mean by mixture or otherwise, it matters not, the language is too sublime and Angelicall for mortall creatures to comprehend it. And for your other phrase of *a great violence to the reverent secret of nature by sowing the furrow of mans nativitie, with the seed of two incoherent and incombining dispositions.*

This frothie discourse, were it not sugred over with a little neat language, would appear so immeritous and undeserving, so contrary to all humane learning, yea, truth and common experience it self, that all that reade it must needs count it worthie to be burnt by the Hangman.

For who ever thought before you, that the reverent sec[r]et of Nature, or the furrow of mans nativitie (so there was lawfull mariage preceded) might not be sowed by the seeds of such as are of diferent or uncombining disposition, if any such there be, without violence or foul incongruitie? If any think otherwise as you it seems doe; give advice that a Petition may be drawn, to have a Committee in every Countie of the Kingdome who shall carefully see to, and severely restraine the mariage of any two Men or Maids who differ in constitution, complexion, hair, countenance, or in disposition, lest this reverent secret of Nature be defiled and violated.

Your seventh Argument is, *The Canon law and Divines allow a Divorce where one of the parties conspires the death of the other: but sometimes through disagreement of dispositions, by a sad pensivenesse the life of one of the parties at least, is brought into danger,* Ergo *it seems a divorce ought in the latter case to be tolerated.*

To this I answer three things.

1. For the opinion of the Canon law, the whole bodie of it is not of your minde, for *Nichol. I. de matrim. Can. 6.* is contrarie, *quioquid mulier contrate cogit averit, non est excepta causa fornicationis rejicienda.* Whatsoever thy Wife conspires or plots against thee, there is no other cause of putting her away but fornication.

The case is not the like, betwixt the conspiring of one partie to kill the other, and your case: for where the one partie conspires to take away the life of the other, and the conspiration continues, there the offender doth implicitely at least act a Divorce; and though it should be true, that the partie grieved may in this case sue a Divorce, yet will it not follow in your case, that because a man may seek divorce from her who seeks his life, to the end to save his life, which Nature teacheth: therefore for disagreement of disposition, causing sadnesse, and wherein they are both actors, if not equals, there the Husband may will, she nill she, put her away; this is just a taking advantage of our own faults and corruptions, to release us from our duties.

But thirdly it would seem that there is no such cause meerly in Nature properly so called, that may cause such griefe as is destructive to the life: and if the cause be not in Nature, but in corruption, in pride, haughtinesse, sullennesse, &c. let them amend their faults, represse their pride and sullennesse, or else let them if they think best, die of the sullen disease, let them try who will pittie them.

The effect of your eighth Argument is this:

Those who are destitute of all mariage gifts, but only fitnesse of body, they have no calling to marry, and consequently if maried ought to be divorced: but facto some are. Ergo,

Briefly to this simple Argument, quite besides that which ought to be the scope of your Book, for what is here to contrariety of dispositions, now it is a disabilitie to all maried duties: This wavering & shaking in your opinion is not fit to be answered: for if it be a Lunatick *non compos mentis,* without any wit, a naturall Foole, which cannot count the daies in the week, or tell twenty, or measure a yard of cloath; you need not to inveigh against them, and you can seldome shew such an example: if Guardians doe sometime marrie such let the Lawyers alone with it, they know how to relieve the suffering partie well enough.

Mariage is a humane society, and so ought to have the consent of the minde; but if the minde cannot enjoy that in mariage which it may reasonably desire, it is no humane society. Ergo.

The consent of the minde ought to be had in mariage, or else it will hardly become a humane societie: but that after mariage the mindes of the Husband and Wife must in all things agree, or else the mariage becomes no humane societie, is a new principle unheard of till now, and so I leave it. As for the discourse of *Deut. 24. 1.* and Christs exposition to the Pharisees, we have spoken of it in answer to your second Argument.

Now a word to your last Argument and so farewell.

Every law is made for some good, which good may be attained unto without a greater inconvenience: but such is not the law that prohibits Divorce for disagreements of mindes and dispositions: Ergo, *it is not a just law.*

We denie this your Argument, and say, that there are many laws which are made for good, and yet that good is not attainable through the defaults of the partie, but a greater incovenience followes, and yet are indeed still just lawes.

I will give you two or three instances in our lawes of England. It is the righteous and just law of England, that every one shall peaceably enjoy his estate in lands or otherwise, accoriding to the goodnesse and latitude of his title: and I hope none will denie this to be a just law: yet see by the default of the partie how this may be evaded, and he fall into great inconvenience.

And so if a man having fee-simple in lands, and yet will take a lease from another of the same lands, this shall be an Estoppell to him in an Assise to recover his own land. *ter. leg. estop.*

So if a Daughter *mulier* will sue liverie of lands with her sister who is a Bastard, she shall not avoid it after by saying her sister was a Bastard not *mulier*.

So if a man had a rent, liberties, Common, &c. by prescription, and after takes a grant of the same from the King by Patent, that shall determine this prescription. *32 H. 8. Bro. tit. Estop. 200.*

So *37 H. 8. Bro. Estop. 218.* If two joyn tenants are, which hold of the King *in capite,* and the one release to the other in fee, and after both respite homage in the Exchequer, the other hath by this gained his moitie againe against the other, without any valuable considerations, by the default of the other.

So it is a just law in England, that no man shall be unjustly charged or taxed contrarie to the right, and what he is bound to doe.

Yet a man by his own fault may charge himselfe, or doe such things as the law will compell him to be charged, where before he was free.

For example. If a Towneship or a Corporation are bound to repaire or maintaine a Causey or a Bridge, and a private man where he is not bound will repaire this Bridge or Causey, time beyond the memorie of man, he shall then be compelled to repaire it for ever by the Law, and at the first he was compellable.

The end of citing these cases is to shew you the weaknesse of your reasons against the law of England which prohibits Divorce, for your pretended contrarietie of minde. For though it should be granted this law of prohibition of Divorce, the end of it could not be attained without a greater inconvenience: yet this inconvenience comming, arising and growing from the fault of the parties, and not from the Law; this Law of prohibiting Divorce shall remain (maugre the malice of all opposers) a just and a righteous law.[7]

FINIS.

Daniel Featley

The Dippers Dipt

(1645)

Daniel Featley (1578–1645), a theologian who helped prepare the Old Testament section of the King James Bible, held a variety of major religious appointments in the Church of England. He frequently argued the case for Protestantism in debates with Jesuit priests. He also argued the case against Arminian Protestants for being too close to Catholicism and against separatists for abandoning the Church of England, most famously in his debate with four Baptists at Southwark. He recorded that debate in *The Dippers Dipt, or the Anabaptists dunckt and plunged over head and ears* (1645). He was the only member of the Church of England in the Westminster Assembly, which was established to reform English Protestantism. Despite his participation there, he was regarded as hostile to Parliament and too sympathetic to the Laudian conservative religious agenda. In 1643, soldiers vandalized his church and killed two parishioners. Featley was then charged with instituting papist practices (including bowing at the name of Jesus and setting up a communion rail in his church), but the charges against him were narrowly voted down. The campaign against him continued, and later in 1643 Commons expelled him from the Westminster Assembly and had him imprisoned. *The Dippers Dipt,* his final work, was the most important of his prison writings. Featley argued against radical separatists, among whom he named Milton. *The Dippers Dipt* was attacked by a Baptist minister, Henry Denne, in

Antichrist Unmasked (1645). Featley died in 1645, worn down by controversy and confinement.[1]

Daniel Featley, *Καταβαπτισταὶ κατάπτυστοι,* ***The Dippers Dipt, or, The Anabaptists Duck'd and Plung'd over head and eares, at a Disputation in Southwark: together with a large and full discourse of their 1. Original. 2. Severall sorts. 3. Peculiar errours. 4. High attempts against the state. 5. Capitall Punishments, with an application to these times*** **(London: Printed for Nicholas Bourne… and Richard Royston, 1645)**

For they print not onely *Anabaptisme,* from whence they take their name; but many other most damnable doctrines, tending to carnall liberty, Familisme, and a *medley* and *hodg-podge* of all Religions. Witnesse the Book printed in 1644. called *The Bloodie Tenet,* which the Author affirmeth he wrote in Milke; and if he did so, he hath put much *Rats-bane* into it…Witnesse a Tractate of Divorce, in which the bonds of mariage are let loose to inordinate lust, and putting away wives for many other causes besides that which our Saviour onely approveth, namely, in the case of Adultery. Witnesse a Pamphlet newly come forth, intituled, *Mans Mortality,* in which the soul is cast into an Endymion sleep, from the houre of death to the day of Judgement. Witnesse a bold Libell offered to hundreds, and to some at the door of the house of Commons, called *The Vindication of the Royall Commission of King Jesus,* wherein the brazenfac'd Authour blusheth not to brand all the Reformed Churches, and the whole Christian world at this day which christen their children, and signe them with the seal of the Covenant, With the odious name of an *Antichristian faction.*[2]

Appendix

A Legacy of Reform, 1643–1973

The following selected list represents a range of documents that contribute to the long history of engagement with Milton's arguments for divorce reform, which would eventually become realized in England following the Archbishop of Canterbury's report on marriage and divorce, *Putting Asunder* (1966), and subsequent passage of the Divorce Reform Act (1969–73).

Contemporary Pamphlets, 1644–49

William Prynne, *Twelve Considerable Serious Questions* (1644)
Herbert Palmer, *The Glasse of Gods Providence* (1644)
[Anonymous], *An Answer to a book intituled, The Doctrine and Discipline of Divorce* (1644)
Daniel Featley, *The Dippers Dipt* (1645)
Ephraim Pagitt, *Heresiography* (1645)
Robert Baillie, *A Dissuasive from the Errours of the Time* (1645)
John Bachiler, "To the Impartial Reader" (1646)
Thomas Edwards, *Gangraena* (1646)
John Wilkins, *Ecclesiastes* (1646)
[Anonymous], *Little Non-Such* (1646)
[Anonymous], "A Catalogue of the Several Sects" (1647)
[Anonymous], "These Trades-men are Preachers" (1647)
[Anonymous], *A True and Perfect Picture* (1648)
Ministers of Christ, *A Testimony to the Truth* (1648)
T. C., *A Glasse for the Times* (1648)
Joseph Hall, *Resolutions and Decisions* (1649)

John Hakluyt, *The Metropolitan Nuncio* (1649)
Clement Walker, *Anarchia Anglicana* (1649)
Marchamont Nedham, *Mercurius Pragmaticus* (1649)
Christopher Wase, "The Return. To Her Highnesse" (1649)

Modern Documents, 1715–1973

William Fleetwood, *The Counsellor's Plea* (1715)
[Anonymous], *An Essay upon Divorcement* (1715)
Thomas Salmon, *A Critical Essay concerning Marriage* (1724)
William Kenrick, *Free Thoughts on Seduction, Adultery, and Divorce* (1771)
Thomas Jefferson, Notes regarding *Blair v. Blair* (1772)
Samuel Badcock, *Gentlemen's Magazine* 55 (1785)
A Civilian, "A Preface, Referring to Events of deep and powerful Interest at the present Crisis" (1820)
John Milton, *The Doctrine and Discipline of Divorce: in two books: also the Judgement of Martin Bucer, Tetrachordon, and an Abridgement of Colasterion* (1820)
[Anonymous], Review of the 1820 collection of Milton's divorce tracts, *The Monthly Review* 93 (September 1820)
William Carmichael Smyth, *Smyth v. Smyth, In the Consistory Court of London* (1826)
Justice James Hannen, *Durham v. Durham* (1885)
Michael Ramsey, *Putting Asunder* (1966)
House of Commons, Debates on the Divorce Reform Bill (1968–73)

Notes

Notes to Introduction

1. Direct quotations from Milton's divorce pamphlets in the introduction are from our editions of the tracts in this volume, *The Divorce Tracts of John Milton: Texts and Contexts.*

2. *A vinculo*: *a vinculo matrimonii* (from the bond of marriage). Divorce granted *a vinculo* means to be free of the bond of marriage with the right to remarry (Stephen, *New Commentaries on the Laws of England,* 2:311).

3. The standard modern edition of *The Doctrine and Discipline of Divorce* was prepared by Sir Ernest Sirluck, with preface and notes by Lowell Coolidge, in volume 2 of the *Complete Prose Works of John Milton,* cited throughout as YP. On the publication history of *The Doctrine and Discipline of Divorce,* see Parker, *Milton's Contemporary Reputation,* 270–77; and Lieb and Shawcross, appendix to *Achievements of the Left Hand,* 296–97. Four editions of *The Doctrine and Discipline of Divorce* were published between 1643 and 1645; the fourth (possibly the unauthorized work of a different printer) in 1645. Lowell Coolidge also prepared the preface and notes to *Colasterion* for YP. We are deeply indebted to the work of these scholars and to Arnold Williams, who prepared the preface and notes to *The Judgement of Martin Bucer* and *Tetrachordon* for YP.

4. Milton, *The Prose of John Milton,* includes the following texts: extracts from Milton's address to Parliament in the 1644 edition of *The Doctrine and Discipline of Divorce;* the complete 1643 first edition; and extracts from *The Judgement of Martin Bucer, Tetrachordon,* and *Colasterion.*

5. *An Answer* was registered October 31, 1644, licensed November 14, and printed in the interval between the publication of the second and third editions of *The Doctrine and Discipline of Divorce. An Answer,* however, addresses only Milton's 1643 text.

6. Prynne, *Twelve Considerable Serious Questions;* Palmer, *The Glasse of Gods Providence;* Featley, *The Dippers Dipt.*

7. On George Miller, see van den Berg and Howard, "G. M. Revealed," 242–52.

8. *A mensa et thoro:* from bed and board. A divorce granted *a mensa et thoro* means not a dissolution of the marriage, but a separation of the parties by act of law without permission to remarry (Stephen, *New Commentaries on the Laws of England,* 2:311).

9. Perkins, *The foundation of Christian religion,* 69; Stephen, *New Commentaries on the Laws of England,* 2:213.

10. Gouge, *Of domesticall duties,* 2.2:3.

11. Ames, *Conscience with the power and cases thereof,* A.8:209.

12. Beza, *De repudiis et divortiis,* 2.94.

13. Maresius, *Systema breve universae theologiae,* 631–32.

14. Milton, "I did but prompt the age," lines 9–11, in Shawcross, *Complete Poetry of John Milton;* hereafter cited as *CP* in the text.

15. Howard, "Milton's 'Divorcive' Liberties"; Achinstein, "'A Law in This Matter to Himself,'" 174–85; and Purkiss, "Whose Liberty?" 186–99.

16. Patrides, *John Milton: Selected Prose,* 71; hereafter cited as *SP* in the text.

17. Annabel Patterson, "Milton, Marriage and Divorce," in *A Companion to Milton,* ed. Thomas Corns, 279–93 (Oxford: Blackwell, 2001), 279.

18. Witte, *From Sacrament to Contract,* 165–93.

19. Calvin, *Institutes of the Christian Religion,* 3:19.15.

20. Patterson, "No Meer Amatorious Novel?" 87–101; Fallon, "The Spur of Self-Concernment," 220–42.

21. van den Berg, "Women, Children."

22. Fallon, "The Spur of Self-Concernment," 224.

23. Ibid., 230.

24. Anonymous, *An Answer,* i.

25. Parker, *Milton's Contemporary Reputation,* 18.

26. Palmer, *The Glasse of Gods Providence,* 56, 57.

27. Ibid., 56.

28. French, *Life Records of John Milton,* 2:107.

29. Prynne, *Twelve Considerable Serious Questions,* 6–7.

30. Parker, *Milton's Contemporary Reputation,* 92, 96.

31. Plomer, *Dictionary of Booksellers and Printers,* xiii.

32. Sirluck, introduction to YP, 2:142; Lewalski, *Life of John Milton,* 179, 598n90.

33. Eisenstein, *The Printing Press;* Darnton, *Literary Underground.*

34. Friest, *Governed by Opinion,* 87.

35. Dobrański, *Milton, Authorship,* 26.

36. Parker, *Milton's Contemporary Reputation,* 170–216.

37. Lieb and Shawcross, *Achievements of the Left Hand,* 374–75.

38. Luxon, *Single Imperfection,* 57–93.

39. *Obtunding:* blunting, deadening, and stultifying; *opiniastrous:* opinionated. "Obtunding" was used by James Joyce in *Ulysses,* but survives primarily as a medical term. "Opiniastrous" occurs only once in written English, in *Colasterion.*

40. Featley, *The Dippers Dipt,* xiii–xiv.

41. Witte, *From Sacrament to Contract;* Peters, *Marriage in Seventeenth-Century;* Stone, *Broken Lives.*

42. Ramsey, *Putting Asunder,* 61.

43. Mead, "Love's Labors," 79–82. See Confessore, "N.Y. Moves Closer," and Coontz, "Divorce, No-Fault Style." Both the news article and the subsequent op-ed column emphasize the financial effects of divorce on women and children.

Notes to *The Doctrine and Discipline of Divorce* (1st ed., 1643)

1. *Seasonable…the Reformation intended:* in July 1643, Parliament charged the Westminster Assembly to propose a reorganization of the Church of England (YP 2:217).

2. Milton anonymously published the first edition of this tract, which was printed on August 1. The printers, Thomas Paine and Matthew Simmons, were identified only by their initials. This reticence may indicate that the topic was incendiary. Milton may also have wanted to avoid any link between the argument and his separation from Mary Powell (ca. August 1642–October 1645).

3. Gen. 8:21; Matt. 15:19.

4. For the story of Jephthah and his daughter, see Judg. 11:30–40. Milton argues that Jephthah misinterpreted the law of God.

5. 1 Macc. 2:31–38. Milton argues against the Israelites' rigid interpretation of Sabbath proscriptions.

6. Matt. 5:31–32.

7. Gen. 2:18.

8. *Handed:* joined (first recorded use in *OED*). The image of Adam and Eve "hand in hand" is a recurrent image in *Paradise Lost.*

9. *Fadge together:* cobble separate pieces together.

10. Eccles. 5:13. The wise man is King Solomon, said to have written this book of the Bible.

11. Tertullian (ca. 160–230) and Jerome (ca. 320–420) were church authorities who exalted virginity and argued for a celibate clergy.

12. Subsequent church doctrine elevated marriage to a sacrament. Prior to 1753, however, a free exchange of vows—whether promised openly or in secret—could also create a valid marriage. The Marriage Act of 1753 (popularly known as Lord Hardwicke's Act) stated that only weddings preceded by banns and conducted in church, in accordance with *The Book of Common Prayer,* were legal. Only Jews and Quakers were exempted. Nonconforming, civil contract marriages were not permitted until the Dissenters' Marriage Act of 1836.

13. John Selden, *Uxor Ebraica,* makes a similar connection between divorce law and natural law: "The question of married women and

marriage generally (as well as many other questions of greatest importance) among Hebrews, according to their commentaries, is subject to a tripartite law: Natural Law, the Law of Nations, and Civil Law" (1).

14. Milton attacks continental Protestant nations for subjecting marriage to legal regulations, against the internal law of conscience.

15. From Justinian through Constantine, Roman laws that permitted divorce remained in effect (YP 2:238n).

16. Church scholars.

17. *Hugo Grotius:* Grotius was a Dutch legal scholar, theologian, and statesman, famous for his studies of natural law, international law, and the Bible.

18. A marriage contract unconsummated due to either party's physical incapacity could be nullified (YP 2:240n).

19. Gen. 2:18.

20. Matt. 11:30.

21. Matt. 11:16–19; Luke 7:31–35.

22. This is the crux of Milton's argument.

23. *Reclaims:* denies.

24. Milton argues that no law, whether secular or religious, should act against its own purposes.

25. Gen. 2:18. The Hebrew phrase *ezer k'negdo* means literally "a help beside and/or against him."

26. *Complexion:* disposition.

27. *Reprobates:* those who reject the call of God (Calvin).

28. Milton follows common Protestant theory that the home is the foundation of the state.

29. Canon law permitted annulment on grounds of impotence if it began before marriage and lasted at least three years (YP 2:248n).

30. Human seed was compared to the heavenly "fifth essence," a theory that originated in Aristotle's *On the Generation of Animals* (YP 2:248n).

31. Milton quotes the marriage ceremony in *The Boke of Common Praier* (YP 2:248n).

32. *Disappointing of an impetuous nerve:* physical impotence.

33. *Disworship:* dishonor.

34. 1 Cor. 7:9.

35. Cf. 1 Cor. 9:9: "Doth God take care for oxen?"

36. Song of Sol. 8:6–7.

37. See Plato's *Symposium,* book 1 (YP 2:252n).

38. Gen. 2:18–24.

39. Cf. Mal. 2:16. Milton explicates this text in chapter 6 of the 1644 edition. *Avera,* a Hebrew word meaning "hateful sin against God or man," is a possible source for Milton's phrase, "turning aside from a mistaken object."

40. *Fleam:* Phlegm, the "humour," or fluid in the body associated with dullness.

41. *Mutin:* mutiny.
42. Eccles. 9:9.
43. Mal. 2:13–15.
44. Rom. 13:10.
45. *Disbanded:* sent away.
46. 1 Tim. 4:1–3.
47. *Some of the circumcision:* Jewish converts to Christianity.
48. Acts 10:9–28.
49. 1 Cor. 7:14.
50. *Antagony:* antagonism.
51. Theodore Beza, commentator on 1 Corinthians.
52. The Code of Justinian and canon law permitted divorce for physical frigidity, a reason Milton labels cold-hearted or frigid (YP 2:269n).
53. *Sublunary:* transitory, material (part of the temporal world under the moon).
54. *Respectless:* disregarding.
55. 1 Cor. 9:8–10.
56. Num. 30:6–15.
57. See below, "*Omitted pa.* 19. *lin.* 28," at the end of Milton's tract. That alternate phrase also appears in the 1644 edition, p. 27.
58. *First table:* the first commandment, "Remembre the Sabbath daie, to kepe it holy." Cf. Exod. 20:8.
59. *Astriction:* obligation, bond.
60. Article 25 in the *Thirty-Nine Articles* of the Church of England expressly denies that marriage is a sacrament (YP 2:277n).
61. *Fanatic dreams:* radical sects. Anabaptists believed in adult baptism, opposed Lutheran theology, and advocated separation of church and state. The Family of Love practiced free love because they saw God in all things. Antinomians believed that truth was revealed and known by inspiration rather than external law.
62. *Inconcileable:* irreconcilable.
63. *Alphabetical servility:* servile obedience to the letter of the law (YP 2:280n).
64. Matt. 5:28.
65. Mark 5:28.
66. John 8:3–11.
67. *Countersway:* opposing force.
68. Matt. 5:17–20.
69. Lev. 20:10; Deut. 22:22.
70. Gal. 3:24.
71. See below, "*Omitted pa.* 24. *lin.* 22," at the end of Milton's tract. Milton's 1643 edition prints that passage on unnumbered pages [49–50] at the end of the pamphlet. The passage illustrates Milton's revisions already in progress and appears thereafter in the 1644 edition, p. 34 (YP 2:285n).

72. In the second edition, Milton will add a lengthy discussion of dispensation and secret marriages.

73. Gen. 42:18.

74. Milton omits this sentence in 1644 and shifts the emphasis of his argument away from this concept (YP 2:303n).

75. Hab. 1:13.

76. In the second edition, Milton will expand his discussion of the Law and the Gospel.

77. No one during Milton's time—not even major talmudic commentators—seemed to understand precisely the Hebrew phrase *ervath davar,* "an unclean thing," as grounds for divorce in Deuteronomy 24:1. The talmudic dispute about this passage is recorded in Tractate Gittin 93b. The School of Hillel, which would predominate, maintained that the emphasis should be placed on the word "thing," and that a wife could therefore be divorced for any unpleasing trait; the School of Shammai, on the other hand, emphasized "uncleanness" and thus upheld adultery as the sole grounds for divorce. In the 1644 edition of *The Doctrine and Discipline of Divorce,* Milton's translation of *ervath davar* as "nakedness of ought, or any real nakedness" incorporates the ideas of both Hillel (unpleasantness) and Shammai (sexual dysfunction).

78. Milton modifies this sentence in the second edition to claim his translation is preferable to that of the King James Version of the Bible.

79. Matt. 5:31: "It hathe bene said also, Whosoever shal put away his wife, let him give her a testimonial of divorcement."

80. Matt. 19:8.

81. Mark 10:5.

82. *Impression:* stress, emphasis.

83. In the second edition, Milton extends this paragraph to discuss Christ's revision of the law.

84. Matt. 19:16–22.

85. *Screws him up higher:* tunes him (like a stringed instrument) to a higher pitch (YP 2:308n).

86. Gen. 2:24.

87. Gen. 2:18.

88. *Individually:* indivisibly.

89. In the second edition, Milton adds a further argument based on Plato's *Laws.*

90. Matt. 19:4–5.

91. Milton expands this argument in the second edition.

92. Matt. 5:19.

93. Calvin argues that the first four verses of Deuteronomy 24 are a unit, the first three setting forth the conditions of the fourth (YP 2:313n).

94. Milton reiterates and expands this argument in the second edition.

95. Gen. 2:2–3; Exod. 20:8–11.

96. In the second edition, Milton adds a brief discussion of Luke 16.

97. The Jewish law of divorce required that a husband initiate a bill of divorce in the presence of two witnesses, and that the bill be delivered to the wife (YP 2:317n).

98. *Court-leet:* a minor district court. Milton uses the term contemptuously (YP 2:318n).

99. *They...in Egypt:* David Paraeus (1548–1622) was a noted Calvinist scholar who taught at Heidelberg (cited in YP 2:31n). Paraeus cites Egyptian custom in his commentary on Matthew 5:32.

100. Gen. 3:24; *Paradise Lost* 12.641–44.

101. William Perkins (1558–1602) was a widely admired Puritan teacher and writer. Perkins distinguished between Mosaic law and rabbinical interpretation in *A Godly and Learned Exposition* (1608) (YP 2:320n).

102. Lev. 20:10.

103. Milton follows Perkins, one of many Puritans who argued that money-lending (although legal in England) violated the law of God.

104. *Circumcised:* limited, circumscribed.

105. Acts 15:22–29.

106. *Fall:* fail. Milton corrected this typographical error in the 1644 edition.

107. Rom. 13:1: "For there is no power but of God: & the powers that be, are ordeined of God."

108. Many Reform Protestants charged that the papacy owned brothels in Rome (YP 2:322n).

109. In the second edition, Milton expands his defense of the law.

110. This is the first mention in this tract of a woman's right to petition for divorce. Milton will amplify that concern in *Tetrachordon* within the context of his reading of Genesis 1:27: "Thus God created the man in his image; in the image of God created he him: he created them male and female."

111. In the second edition, Milton adds a passage that argues strongly that woman was made for man, and is subordinate to man.

112. Although there were different Protestant interpretations of the Eucharist, all agreed with Milton that the Catholic literal reading of these words was incorrect.

113. *Amuses:* confuses, bewilders.

114. *Mezentius:* Mezentius was an Etruscan despot who would "link dead bodies with the living, fitting hand to hand and face to face" (Vergil, *Aeneid,* 8.485–88, cited in YP 2:327n).

115. In the second edition, Milton adds comments on the daily sorrow of unhappy marriages.

116. *Common expositors:* Reform interpreters of the Bible.

117. *Uneasy:* difficult.

118. Matt. 19:9.

119. John 13:34.

120. Col. 3:14.

121. *Halted:* failed.

122. In the second edition, Milton expands his passionate denunciation of unhappy marriage.

123. Milton continues to argue, in the second edition, that Moses set forth a foundation for divorce that was not contradicted by Christ, and that hatred in marriage is a greater evil than adultery.

124. Matt. 5:28.

125. *Tympany:* malignancy.

126. Num. 5:27.

127. *Ordalium:* Trial by ordeal, abolished in England in 1215, but used in European witchcraft prosecutions on the Continent (YP 2:336n).

128. *Exasperated:* made more severe.

129. In the second edition, Milton expands his redefinition of "fornication" and gives his interpretation of the woman taken in adultery (John 8:3–11).

130. *Fleshly accustoming:* habitual intimacy.

131. Matt. 81:12–13; Luke 15:4–6.

132. *Obduring:* stubbornness, resistance. According to the *OED,* this is the earliest occurrence of the word.

133. Milton adapts the image of the Gordian knot (cut by Alexander the Great) to argue that charity can cut through doctrinal disputes better than any sword.

134. *Revolve:* ponder, consider.

135. *Boisterous:* stiff, unyielding.

136. "The gifts of God are of two sorts, some are general, some are Proper. General gifts are such as God giveth generally to all, & these may be obtained, if they be asked according to God's word, lawfully, Jam. 1.5.... Proper gifts are those which are given only to some certain men: of which sort is the gift of continence, & such like, which though they be often and earnestly asked, yet they are seldom or never granted unto some men" (William Perkins, *Christian Economy,* cited in YP 2:341n).

137. *A bolt overshot...:* Milton seems to refer to the bolt of a lock, which when forced may become stuck and useless (YP 2:342n).

138. *Supportless:* intolerable, insupportable.

139. *Mystery:* secret purpose. See 2 Thess. 2:7 (suggested in YP 2:342n).

140. *Casuisting:* deliberating in the manner of a casuist. A casuist (often a theologian) studies and resolves matters of conscience or doubtful questions regarding duty and conduct.

141. In the second edition, Milton inserts into this sentence a long section on the power of the Christian magistrate to grant a divorce in cases of "hatred."

142. *Anne of Cleves:* Anne of Cleves was the fourth wife of Henry VIII.

143. Rather than make a virtue of necessity, they made a necessity of virtue.

144. *Tongue-fence:* debate.

145. Pope Clement VII delegated Cardinals Campeggio and Wolsey to consider the plea of Henry VIII that his marriage to Catherine of Aragon be annulled. The grounds for the plea were that she had been married to the king's deceased older brother, so her marriage to Henry VIII was incestuous.

146. *Familiary:* domestic.

147. *Appeached:* questioned, proved false.

148. Plutarch cites this remark in his Life of Aemilius Paulus (YP 2:348n).

149. *Feed gamester:* hired attorney. Milton believed that divorce should be a private, not a legal, proceeding.

150. Milton omits the preceding paragraph in the second edition.

151. In the second edition, Milton begins his peroration at this point.

152. Milton follows William Perkins in arguing that divorce should be a private, family matter rather than a legal proceeding (YP 2:353n).

153. "To throw the mountain of Sinai upon him" echoes the Babylonian Talmud, Shabbos 2:88b (which comments on Mishnah 7 by way of Exodus 19:17, "they stood at the bottom of the mount"): "R. Abdimi b. Hama b. Hasa said 'This teaches that the Holy One, blessed be He, overturned the mountain upon them like an [inverted] cask, and said to them, 'If ye accept the Torah, 'tis well, if not, there shall be your burial'" (Babylonian Talmud, Tractate Shabbos 2, Mishnah 88b, 415).

154. Mal. 2:14–16.

155. Eccles. 7:16.

156. *Atoms:* motes of dust.

157. Luke 13:16.

158. Matt. 9:13.

159. Matt. 22:40.

160. 1 Cor. 15:27; 1 Tim. 1:5.

161. See note 57 above.

162. *Politician:* Milton almost always uses this word in a derogatory sense (YP 2:285n).

163. Milton elsewhere accused the Roman Catholic Church of plotting with Austria.

164. See note 71 above.

Notes to *The Doctrine and Discipline of Divorce* (2nd ed., 1644)

1. Milton revised the subtitle of his tract. The first edition (1643) had emphasized "Christian freedom, guided by the rule of charity" and the recovery of "lost" meanings of Scripture (presumably by his own

interpretations). In this edition, Milton shifts the weight of his argument to the relationship between Law and Gospel—a combined legal and theological purpose—hence the dedication to "the Parliament of *England* with the Assembly." The addition of Westminster Assembly, which was charged by Parliament to restructure church government, suggests that Milton is making a strategic decision to seek support from that appointed group as well as from Parliament as a whole.

2. This addition to the subtitle rebukes Milton's opponents, those who condemn divorce as "sin" despite the Old Testament Law of God and the New Testament Gospel of Christ. The meaning of Law (Hebrew Bible) and Gospel (New Testament) is developed in Milton's expanded text.

3. Milton has organized this much longer second edition of his tract into two books, each divided into chapters.

4. Milton adds this verse from Scripture to rebuke those who attacked his work without reading it, and to suggest that he is carefully replying to those who wrote or spoke against him.

5. Unlike the first edition, this text is explicitly directed to Parliament and to the Westminster Assembly, which was considering reforms of the English church (YP 2:217).

6. Ezek. 2:8–3:3. Ezekiel learns the will of God by eating a scroll.

7. *Concoction:* digestion.

8. This image of Error is derived from Spenser's *Faerie Queene* 1.1.18–24.

9. *Humour and innovation:* Milton rejects the suggestion that his argument is merely personal (based on his own "humour") or novel ("innovation").

10. *7th son of a 7th son:* proverbial; a man said to be destined for greatness.

11. Deut. 24:1. Milton connects Jewish law to statutory law, thus placing marital law within a civil framework.

12. Josiah (ca. 640–609 BCE) was king of Judah during a time of Deuteronomic reform and is credited by some historians with establishing Jewish Scripture in written form. He recovered a book of the law. According to midrashic legend, the book he recovered and published was Deuteronomy, the last of the five books of Moses. See 2 Chron. 34–35.

13. Phil. 1:18.

14. Milton mingles the classic myth of "Truth, the daughter of Time" with the Christian ceremony of "churching" (of the mother). In Milton's version, Truth (like Minerva) has no mother, but only a father, Time, who is "churched."

15. Until 1680, "Patriots" referred to those who supported the country and Parliament against the king and court.

16. *By-ends:* covert purpose.

17. Cf. Milton's Sonnet 11, replying to those who condemned his argument for divorce as licentious.

18. *Megrim:* migraine.

19. *Assyrian Blasphemer:* Sennecherib, king of Assyria (704–681 BCE), laid siege to Jerusalem (2 Kings 17–19). According to Herodotus, Sennecherib's invasion of Egypt failed when the gods sent an army of mice to eat the bowstrings and quivers of the Assyrian army. The Egyptians then erected in the temple of Vulcan a statue of the pharoah holding a mouse, with the following inscription: "Look on me, and learn to reverence the gods" (Herodotus, *Histories* II).

20. *Belawgiven:* legislated to.

21. Paul, in 2 Thessalonians 2:3–4, condemns "the son of perdition, Who opposeth and exalteth himself above all that is called God."

22. Israelites, whose "hardness of heart" prompted the Mosaic law of divorce (see Matt. 19:8 and Mark 10:5).

23. Milton attacks the pope ("Antichrist") and papal dispensations that permitted close relatives to marry.

24. Matt. 12:1–14, 15:1–20, 23:1–33; Mark 2:23–26, 7:1–23; Luke 6:1–11, 11:37–54.

25. *Straiter:* tighter, more burdensome.

26. *Indifferent:* neither good nor evil.

27. *Over-front:* confront.

28. *Adversary:* Satan (whose name means "adversary" in Hebrew).

29. Col. 2:21.

30. 1 Cor. 16:14.

31. Rom. 13:10.

32. *Economical:* domestic.

33. Matt. 5:17–19; Deut. 24:1 states the law.

34. Edward the Confessor reigned from 1002 until 1066, when the Normans invaded and conquered England.

35. *In what calends:* when.

36. *Masorah:* marginal notes compiled by rabbinical scholars; concordance.

37. *Synagogue of Ezra, School at Tiberias:* famous centers of scholarship.

38. *Norman Isles:* Channel Islands.

39. The Emperor Constantine was said to have been born in Britain.

40. St. Willibrod (ca. 657–ca. 738); Winifrede of Devon refers to St. Boniface (680–755), a Benedictine monk.

41. Alcuin was a famous English scholar in the court of Charlemagne; John Wycliffe (1320–84) was an English Protestant reformer.

42. *Medulla:* the "marrow" or digest of a subject.

43. *Another tongue:* Latin.

44. *Outlandish:* foreign.

45. Hugo Grotius was a Dutch legal scholar, theologian, and statesman, famous for his studies of natural law, international law, and the Bible. Paul Fagius was a German Protestant minister who was invited to England by Henry VIII and became the Reader in Hebrew at Cambridge University.

46. *Lin:* cease, desist.

47. Cf. Gen. 8:21 and Matt. 15:19.

48. For the story of Jephthah and his daughter, see Judges 11:30–40. Milton argues that Jephthah misinterpreted the law of God.

49. 1 Macc. 2:31–38. Milton argues against the Israelites' rigid interpretation of Sabbath proscriptions.

50. Matt. 5:31–32.

51. Gen. 2:18.

52. *Handed:* joined (first recorded use in *OED*). The image of Adam and Eve "hand in hand" is a powerful motif in *Paradise Lost.*

53. *Fadge together:* cobble separate pieces together.

54. Eccles. 5:13. The wise man is King Solomon, said to have written this book of the Bible.

55. *Element:* letter.

56. Tertullian (ca. 160–230) and St. Jerome (ca. 320–420), church authorities who exalted virginity and argued for a celibate clergy.

57. Subsequent church doctrine elevated marriage to a sacrament (YP 2:237n).

58. Continental Protestant churches did not consider marriage a sacrament and did not follow canon law.

59. Milton attacks continental Protestant nations for subjecting marriage to legal regulations, against the internal law of conscience.

60. From Justinian through Constantine, Roman laws that permitted divorce remained in effect (YP 2:240n).

61. *Fathers then living:* church scholars.

62. *Period:* goal.

63. Gen. 2:18.

64. Matt. 11:30.

65. Matt. 11:16–19; Luke 7:31–35.

66. Matt. 5:18.

67. Matt. 19:3–9.

68. The planetary tables of Copernicus were named "Protenic" for his patron, Duke Albert of Prussia, and were superseded by those of Kepler in 1627. *Wide expositors* refers to false biblical interpreters.

69. *Sounds:* means.

70. Deut. 23:14; Isa. 20:4; 1 Sam. 20:30. "Nakedness" is an accurate translation of *ervath,* meaning "groin." "Ought" renders *davar,* meaning either "thing" or "word." *Ervath davar* (literally "groin thing/word") could refer to nakedness of either body or mind.

71. *Reclaims:* denies.

72. Milton argues that no law, whether secular or religious, should act against its own purpose.

73. Gen. 2:18. *Ezer k'negdo,* "a help beside and/or against him." Milton's subsequent assertion that "a meet and happy conversation is the

chiefest and the noblest end of marriage" blunts the oppositional edge to the original Hebrew phrase.

74. *Conversation:* intimacy.

75. Four major Protestant authorities. David Paraeus (1548–1622) was a Calvinist scholar who taught at Heidelberg; Andrew Rivetus (1572–1651) taught at Leiden and Breda.

76. *Complexion:* disposition.

77. *Reprobates:* those who reject the call of God (Calvin).

78. Milton follows common Protestant theory that the home is the foundation of the state.

79. *Stews:* brothels.

80. Canon law permitted annulment on grounds of impotence if it began before marriage and lasted at least three years (YP 2:248n).

81. Human seed was compared to the heavenly "fifth essence," a theory that originated in Aristotle's *On the Generation of Animals* (YP 2:248n).

82. Milton quotes the marriage ceremony in *The Boke of Common Praier* (1552).

83. *Disappointing of an impetuous nerve:* physical impotence.

84. *Ingenuous:* noble.

85. The Yale Press editor, Lowell W. Coolidge, suggests that this clause was added to the second edition because Milton was aware that the vignette of the unhappy man might seem personal and self-serving (YP 2:2494n).

86. *Disworship:* dishonor (YP 2:250n).

87. 1 Cor. 7:9.

88. Cf. 1 Cor. 9:9: "Doth God take care for oxen?"

89. Song of Sol. 8:6–7.

90. *Provender:* possibly an error. Lowell W. Coolidge suggests "provendered," a word Milton uses elsewhere (YP 2:252n). Another possible meaning might be "fodder" (as in feeding a flame).

91. See Plato's *Symposium,* book 1 (YP 2:252n).

92. Gen. 2:18–24.

93. Alternate reading in 1644: "mutuall."

94. Mal. 2:16. Milton explicates this text in chapter 6. "Turning aside" is a literal translation of *avera,* the Hebrew word for "a hateful sin against God or man."

95. *Fleam:* phlegm, the "humour" or fluid in the body associated with dullness.

96. *Mutin:* mutiny.

97. *Anteros:* the figure of reciprocated love in Plato's *Phaedrus,* 255d. In later allegories, Eros (Love) cannot exist without his younger brother, Anteros.

98. *Obvious and suborned:* common and false.

99. *Apogaeum:* apogee. In Ptolemaic astronomy, the point in the orbit of a heavenly body when it is farthest from Earth.

100. *Personated:* counterfeit, false.

101. *Braids:* strings of his bow.

102. *Amatorious novel:* love story.

103. Cf. "sea of glass" in Revelations 4:6 and 15:2.

104. Eccles. 9:9.

105. Mal. 2.16. The Hebrew text could be translated as either "God hates divorce" or "he who hates, let him divorce" because *ki sane sholayach* could mean either "because he hates sending away" or "that he sends away the hated one." Milton entertains both translations of this verse in *Tetrachordon,* but leans toward the first, which connotes a hatred of divorce, because that tract, like the text of Malachi, calls for humane treatment of the divorced woman.

106. Maimonides, *Guide to the Perplexed* (ca. 1190), trans. Johann Buxtorf (1629). Moses Maimonides (1135–1204) was a Jewish rabbi, physician, and philosopher, who lived in southern Spain, Morocco, and Egypt.

107. *Grind in the mill…servile copulation:* directly echoes Maimonides' language in his *Book of Women* and in his Code of Jewish Law, popularly known today as the Mishneh Torah, originally compiled (ca. 1170–80). Both Milton and his contemporary John Selden (1584–1654) conducted thorough studies of Jewish marital law, consulting texts such as the talmudic Tractate Gittin, which glosses Maimonides's Code. Selden, the leading Hebrew scholar in seventeenth century England, wrote *Uxor Ebraica* [*The Hebrew Wife*] (1646), a study of Jewish marriage law.

108. *Mourns:* longs.

109. Rom. 13:10.

110. Milton refers to the Protestant doctrine of "the priesthood of all believers."

111. *The [English Prose] Works [of Mr. John Milton]* (London, 1697) prints "cheerishness," the only instance of that word recorded in the *OED.*

112. Mal. 2:13.

113. *Disbanded:* sent away (YP 2:260n).

114. 1 Tim. 4:1–3.

115. *Some of the circumcision:* Jewish converts to Christianity.

116. Acts 10:9–28.

117. 1 Cor. 7:14.

118. *Done:* thoroughly.

119. *Aversation:* turning away from; avoidance.

120. 2 Cor. 6:17. See also Isa. 52:11.

121. Deut. 7:3.

122. Job 2:9–10.

123. Exod. 4:25, 18:2; Num. 12:3.

124. Gen. 21:1–14.

125. 2 Sam. 6:20–23.

126. The sucking-fish (*Echenis remora*), a small fish supposedly capable of stopping a ship from moving. See Pliny, *Natural History*, 32.i, cited in YP 2:264n.

127. *Antagony:* antagonism.

128. Theodore Beza wrote an important commentary on 1 Corinthians (YP 2:266n).

129. 1 Cor. 7:12: "If anie brother have a wife, that beleveth not, if she be content to dwell with him, let him not forsake her."

130. Matt. 7:6, 18:17, 10:14.

131. The Code of Justinian and canon law permitted divorce for physical frigidity, a reason Milton labels "cold-hearted" or "frigid" (YP 2:269n).

132. *Sublunary:* transitory, material (part of the temporal world "under the moon").

133. *Respectless:* regardless.

134. 1 Cor. 9:8–10.

135. 1 Cor. 7:3. "Benevolence" in Hebrew directly connotes sexual intercourse.

136. Reform Protestants excluded Ecclesiasticus from the canon of Scripture, but Milton here praises the author's wisdom.

137. *Elemental crasis:* blend of elements.

138. Milton avoids speculating on the validity of astrology to explain why one person is attracted to another.

139. *Odyssey*, 17.218: "God brings like unto like" (cited in YP 2:271n).

140. Num. 30:6–15.

141. Cf. Matt. 12:8–13; Mark 2:27–28; and Luke 6:5–10 for examples of lawful breaking of Sabbath restrictions.

142. *First table:* the first commandment, "Remember keep holy the Sabbath day." See Exod. 20:8.

143. *Astriction:* obligation, bond.

144. Article 25 in the Thirty-Nine Articles of the Church of England expressly denies that marriage is a sacrament (YP 2:277n).

145. Acts 15:6–11.

146. *Fanatic dreams:* radical sects. Anabaptists believed in adult baptism, opposed Lutheran theology, and advocated separation of church and state. The Family of Love practiced free love because they saw God in all things. Antinomians believed in the truth of inspiration rather than external law.

147. Several defenses of these sects had been published after the first edition of Milton's tract. The addition of this parenthetical clause in the second edition suggests he may have become more sympathetic to them.

148. *Inconcileable:* irreconcilable.

149. *Alphabetical servility:* servile obedience to the letter of the law (YP 2:280n).

150. *Reprove:* reject.

151. Matt. 5:32.

152. Exod. 20:10.

153. Mark 2:27.

154. *Pall, mitre, ordination, induction, keys:* Milton claims priestly authority as a man of faith, whose claim to authority does not need the warrant of ecclesiastical garb, rituals, or symbols.

155. Matt. 5:28.

156. John 8:3–11.

157. *Countersway:* opposing force.

158. Matt. 5:17–20.

159. Luke 16:17, 18.

160. Lev. 20:10; Deut. 22:22.

161. Gal. 3:24.

162. Lowell W. Coolidge notes that Milton always uses "politician" in a derogatory sense (YP 2:284n).

163. Milton was suspicious that the Roman Catholic Church was plotting with Austria.

164. Rom. 3:20.

165. *Flies:* moths.

166. Deut. 7:1–2.

167. *Villenage:* the tenure by which a feudal villein held or occupied his land; tenure of lands by bond-service rendered to the lord or superior (*OED*).

168. *Manumitted:* that which has been manumitted or released from service (*OED*).

169. *Diagonial:* diametrically opposed.

170. *His:* Milton is not gendering sin masculine. The pronoun "its" was not in common use until later in the seventeenth century.

171. See Pareus, in his commentary on 1 Corinthians: "For the remedy of divorce did not so much help the hardheartedness of men as the misery of wives."

172. Matt. 23:23.

173. Matt. 27:11–24.

174. *Beelzebub:* prince of devils (Matt. 12:24).

175. Lev. 19:17.

176. Prov. 26:28, 29:5.

177. 1 Sam. 2:22–24.

178. 1 Sam. 3:14. Hophni and Phineas were the sons of Eli.

179. Rom. 7:7.

180. Rev. 22:11.

181. Rom. 13:4.

182. *Graduating:* progressing toward.
183. Hosea 1:2–3.
184. *Savourily:* heartily.
185. Manasseh was king of Judah. See 2 Kings 22:11.
186. Exod. 24:17.
187. *Connivent:* dormant.
188. *Oscitant:* yawning, drowsy.
189. Lev. 6:13.
190. Jacobus Arminius led a Dutch Protestant sect that opposed the Calvinist doctrine of predestination and affirmed a belief in free will. To reject free will, he argued, was to make God the author of evil.
191. In Hesiod's *Theogony,* Epimetheus opens Pandora's box and lets evil loose in the world.
192. *Insulsity:* stupidity.
193. *Except against:* take exception to, reject.
194. 1 Cor. 7:9.
195. Gen. 18:23–25.
196. Ps. 119:138, 140.
197. 2 Tim. 2:13.
198. Matt. 5:48.
199. *Covert:* justification.
200. *Eleusinian Mysteries:* secret Greek rites to worship Demeter and Persephone.
201. Gal. 2:16.
202. *Shewbread:* the twelve loaves of bread used in Sabbath rituals were eaten only by rabbis.
203. Matt. 12:3–4; Mark 2:25–26; Luke 6:3–4.
204. James 1:17.
205. Luke 11:12.
206. Num. 11:31–33.
207. 1 Sam. 8:1–9.
208. Ps. 19:7; Prov. 22:20–21.
209. Matt. 19:6.
210. Secret marriages were valid, but strongly condemned by the church.
211. Gen. 17:10–14.
212. *Scapes:* omissions.
213. Mark 16:16.
214. Matt. 19:11; 1 Cor. 7:7; Acts 15:10.
215. Col. 3:5.
216. Rom. 11:6.
217. *Extravagance:* deviation.
218. Prov. 30:21–23. Milton cites this verse to document the assertion that a calamitous and odious woman may be discarded. In *Tetrachordon*

he translates the same proverb as "a hated or hateful woman" (YP 2:623). The Hebrew *s'nuah* could mean either "one who is hated" or "one who is characterized by hate."

219. Matt. 5:31.

220. *Impression:* stress, emphasis (YP 2:307n).

221. 1 Tim. 1:5–8.

222. Matt. 19:16–22.

223. Gen. 2:24.

224. Gen. 2:18.

225. *Individually:* indivisibly.

226. Matt. 19:4–5.

227. Matt. 19:11–12.

228. Calvin insists that the first four verses of Deuteronomy 24 are a unit, the first three setting forth the conditions of the fourth (YP 2:313n).

229. Rom. 3:8.

230. Euripides, *Medea,* lines 1978–80: "I know to what bad things I go, but louder than all thought doth cry Anger, which maketh man's worse misery."

231. See Aristotle, *Nicomachean Ethics,* 3.5.

232. Plutarch criticized Pompey for yielding to the popular demand that he fight Caesar at Pharsalia. Brutus was persuaded to assassinate Caesar.

233. Plutarch celebrates the determination, and the victories, of Themistocles and Fabius, who maintained their strategies despite popular disapproval.

234. 1 Sam. 3:12–13.

235. Matt. 27:22–26.

236. Gen. 2:2–3; Exod. 20:8–11.

237. Luke 16:17–18.

238. The Jewish law of divorce required a bill of divorce initiated by the husband, the signatures of two witnesses, and the delivery of the bill to the wife (YP 2:317n). Selden, a noted scholar and polymath, was one of the English antiquaries Milton here cites.

239. William Perkins (1558–1602). Milton uses Perkins's works whenever he can to support his argument.

240. *Court-leet:* a minor district court (YP 2:318n). Milton uses the word contemptuously.

241. Gen. 3:24. Milton understands the richness of the Hebrew verb *hamishapeches,* "ever-turning" or "turning every which way," in direct reference to the flaming sword that guards the garden of Eden, a sword that always permits the possibility of reentry.

242. Lev. 20:10.

243. Rom. 6:23.

244. *Circumcised:* limited, circumscribed (YP 2:321n).

245. *A politic law:* all editions after 1644, following the uncorrected state of sig. 1, read "Apostolic law" (YP 2:321n).

246. Acts 15:22–29.

247. Protestants often claimed that the papacy owned brothels or profited from taxes paid by brothels in Rome (YP 2:322n).

248. Milton borrows this phrase from Cicero, *De officiis,* 3.6 (YP 2:323n).

249. Luke 16:1–8.

250. *Person:* personify.

251. Be allowed to build up a debt he cannot pay.

252. When Antiochus IV attempted to invade Egypt, Gaius Popilius halted him by drawing a circle around him and ordering him not to step outside it until he had accepted the terms imposed by the Roman Senate. This incident is the origin of the proverbial "line in the sand." See Polybius, *Histories,* 39.27 (cited in YP 2:323n).

253. Beza's commentary on Matthew 19:8 notes that Moses mandated giving a divorce to rejected wives to protect them from cruel husbands (YP 2:324n).

254. 1 Tim. 2:12.

255. Prov. 12:3, 10:13, 21:19.

256. Prov. 27:16.

257. Esther 1:10–22.

258. Protestants rejected transubstantiation, the Catholic doctrine that consecrated bread and wine were the body and blood of Christ, and regarded the Eucharist as the body of Christ only at the liturgical moment (Lutherans) or as only a symbol of Christ's body (Calvinists). Despite differences, all Protestants agreed with Milton that the Catholic literal reading of these words was incorrect.

259. *Alleging:* pleading, urging as a reason.

260. *Amuses:* confuses.

261. *Mezentius:* Mezentius was an Etruscan despot who "would even link dead bodies with the living, fitting hand to hand and face to face" (Virgil, *Aeneid,* 8.485–88; cited in YP 2:327n).

262. Josephus, *Antiquities of the Jews,* 15:7. In *The Tragedie of Mariam* (1613), Lady Elizabeth Cary dramatized Salome's radical claim that a woman should be able to initiate divorce proceedings.

263. Placidia threatened to divorce Constantius unless he removed an infidel magician from Ravenna. The magician was executed, and the divorce averted.

264. *Palisadoes:* fence made of stakes.

265. *Common expositors:* Protestant biblical commentators.

266. *Uneasy:* difficult (YP 2:329n).

267. Matt. 19:9.

268. John 13:34.

269. Col. 3:14.

270. *Halted:* fell short.

271. *Vacation:* void, cessation.

272. *Sanguify:* generate blood. In Renaissance medical theory, the liver generated blood and impurities were then removed by the spleen. Milton compares the will to the spleen, and understanding to the liver.

273. Matt. 8:26; Mark 4:39; Luke 8:24.

274. Rom. 7:7.

275. Origen (ca. 185–253 BCE), an important early Christian writer. Eusebius reports that Origen castrated himself because he interpreted Matthew 19:12 literally: "For there are some chaste, which were so borne of their mothers bellie: and there be some chaste, which be made chaste by men: & there be some chaste, which have made them selves chaste for the kingdome of heaven. He that is able to receive this, let him receive it" (Matt. 19:12). See Eusebius, *Ecclesiastical History,* 6.8.1–3 (YP 2:334n). Origen's rejection of such literal interpretation renders the story unlikely.

276. Milton's commentary on Judges 19:2 provides ample evidence of his use of a Hebrew Rabbinic Bible, the *Buxtorf Biblia Sacra* (1619), given to Milton in 1623 by his tutor, Thomas Young.

277. Matt. 5:28.

278. For Jewish tests, see Numbers 5:11–31.

279. England abolished trial by ordeal in 1215.

280. *Exasperated:* made more severe.

281. John 8:3–11.

282. "In such cases" (1 Cor. 7:15).

283. Demetrius, *On Style,* 301 (YP 2:388n). The work is of uncertain authorship and date.

284. *Fleshly accustoming:* habitual intimacy.

285. Matt. 18:12–13; Luke 15:4–6.

286. *Obduring:* stubbornness.

287. Alexander the Great cut the Gordian knot with his sword when no one could untangle it.

288. *Revolve:* consider.

289. *Boisterous:* strict, unyielding (YP 2:341n).

290. *Trading lust:* commercial sex.

291. *Supportless yoke:* unbearable burden.

292. *Mystery:* secret purpose (YP 2:342n).

293. *Ordinances:* decrees by God, dispensations, ceremonial observances; also, established principles of civil government (*OED*). It is not clear which meaning Milton intends. Throughout the tracts, Milton engages both sacred and secular connotations. Unlike the Sabbath, an ordinance made for God, marriage is a dispensation made for man.

294. English consistory courts sometimes permitted divorce with-

out permission to remarry. Milton advocated the continental Protestant reforms of marital law that allowed divorce and remarriage.

295. *Merely:* entirely.

296. *Equal:* worthy.

297. *Twist a rope of sand:* proverbial metaphor for trying to do the impossible. George Herbert uses this metaphor in "The Collar" to describe his struggles with his own priestly calling (Herbert, *English Poems*). Contrast the "rope of sand" image to the "line in the sand" referenced in the account of Antiochus IV.

298. Ocnus was condemned to weave a rope of straw, which an ass continually ate. See Propertius, *Elegies* 4.3.21–22; cited in YP 2:346n).

299. *Allusion:* comparison.

300. *Recollecting:* removing.

301. *In diameter against:* diametrically opposed to.

302. In *Gorgias,* Socrates argues that justice is inherent in things and opposes Callicles's contention that justice is mere convention (YP 2:346n).

303. The marriage of Henry VIII and his fourth wife, Anne of Cleves, was annulled in 1540. Henry claimed that his "misliking" of her before and after the wedding made it impossible to consummate the marriage.

304. 1 Cor. 11:3.

305. *Masters of tongue-fence:* lawyers.

306. Cardinal Campeggio and Cardinal Wolsey were delegated by Pope Clement VII to hear Henry's plea to annul his marriage to Catherine of Aragon.

307. Milton is enraged that the king had to expose his queen's fault in order to win an annulment.

308. *Appeached:* impeached, questioned.

309. *Aemilius Paulus,* in Plutarch, *Lives of the Noble Greeks* (YP 2:350n).

310. *Feed gamester:* paid attorney. "Masters of tongue-fence" and "gamester" voice Milton's contempt for divorce attorneys in court proceedings.

311. *Tuition:* protection.

312. John Selden was a leading jurist, historian, and Hebrew scholar. His *Of the Law of Nature and of Nations* was published in 1640. Selden wrote 27 legal works—the majority of which deal with some aspect of Jewish law—and argued that natural law begins with the seven Noachite laws of the Hebrew Bible (YP 2:350n).

313. *Sumless sums:* endless summaries.

314. Johannes Gratian and Peter Lombard were twelfth century clerics, allegedly brothers of Peter Comestor, who wrote a history of Scholastic philosophy. This supposed kinship united the three major Fathers of canon law, theology, and biblical scholarship.

315. *Tubalcain:* teacher of brass and ironworkers (see Gen. 4:22).
316. *Amerced:* punished.
317. Luke 12:13–14.
318. John 8:3–11.
319. *Cockering:* coddling.
320. Gal. 3:24–25.
321. Mal. 2:14–16.
322. Eccles. 7:16.
323. *Atoms:* specks of dust.
324. Luke 13:16.
325. Matt. 9:13.
326. Matt. 22:40.
327. 1 Cor. 15:27; 1 Tim. 1:5.

Notes to *The Judgement of Martin Bucer* (1644)

1. Bucer's *De Regno Christi* was published posthumously in 1557. It was written in 1550, when Bucer was Regius Professor of Divinity at Cambridge. Martin Bucer was, after Martin Luther and Philip Melancthon, the most influential German Protestant reformer. Bucer was invited to England by Archbishop Cranmer in 1548, and died in 1551. King Edward VI, the frail son of Henry VIII and Jane Seymour (who died 12 days after giving birth to him), died in 1553.

2. Milton composed this translation between May and July 1644 to support his arguments in *The Doctrine and Discipline of Divorce.* He had discovered support in the writings of Hugo Grotius and Paulus Fagius in time to cite them in the second edition of that tract, but then found the arguments of Martin Bucer useful enough to warrant publication in a separate translation. Although Milton's name is not on the title page, he signed the prefatory letter to Parliament, thereby forgoing anonymity.

3. This tract was licensed by John Downham. In the postscript to the tract, Milton outlines the basis for his protest against licensing in *Areopagitica,* published a few months later.

4. Matthew Simmons is here listed by name, not just by initials, as a condition of the license to print the tract.

5. Simon Grynaeus (1493–1541), German Reform theologian and teacher at Basel. Milton translates only a portion of a letter prefatory to Bucer's *Scripta Anglicana* [English Letters] (1577). All the tributes printed by Milton are taken from this source.

6. Sir John Cheke (1514–57), classical scholar at Cambridge University. He helped frame the laws of the Church of England after Edward VI rejected the canon law system of the Catholic Church.

7. Milton refers to Cheke's longer account of Bucer's death and burial.

8. Johann Sturm (1507–89), humanist educator and reformer, taught at Strasburg. Milton's spelling indicates the English pronunciation of the city's name.

9. *Sutt'ly:* subtly.

10. Here Milton cites Theodore Beza's *Icones* (Geneva, 1551), a set of profiles of exemplary religious leaders. Beza (1519–1605) was a French Protestant theologian who succeeded John Calvin in Geneva.

11. *Diets:* assemblies.

12. Milton omits Beza's account of his conversion to Protestantism.

13. John Foxe's *Acts and Monuments,* known as the *Book of Martyrs,* compiled a record of Protestants executed in England during the reign of Queen Mary, who succeeded her brother Edward VI. The book was published in at least seven editions before Milton wrote this tract.

14. Andrew Perne (1519–89), Catholic administrator at Cambridge, preached the sermon when Bucer and Fagius were exhumed and condemned as heretics and later presided over the Cambridge University Senate when their earlier honors were restored in 1560.

15. Cardinal Reginald Pole (1500–58) was chancellor of Cambridge University.

16. This tribute blends statements from the *Historia Vera* [True Histories] of Conradus Hubertus and Foxe's *Acts and Monuments.*

17. George Acworth (d. 1578), elected Public Orator at Cambridge in 1559, gave the oration restoring honors to Bucer and Fagius.

18. Nicholas Carr (1524–68) was Regius Professor of Greek at Cambridge; Walter Haddon (1516–72) was Regius Professor of civil law at Cambridge; and Matthew Parker (1504–75) was Archbishop of Canterbury (1559–75) during the reign of Queen Elizabeth I.

19. *Jacobus Verheiden:* Dutch biographer of Protestant divines.

20. Peter Martyr (1500–62) was an Italian friar who became a leading Protestant Reformer and was Regius Professor of Divinity at Oxford University (1548–53). Conradus Hubertus was secretary to Martin Bucer and editor of *Scripta Anglicana.*

21. *Unanimous:* like-minded.

22. Johann Sleidan (1506–56) was a German jurist, diplomat, and historian, and professor of law at Strasburg. Jacobus Thuanus (Jacques Aujguste de Thou) (1553–1617) was a French historian.

23. Thuanus, *Historia* (1626), does not name the witness.

24. In Ezra 10:1–44, the Jews returning from captivity pledged to divorce their foreign wives. Recalcitrant husbands were later forced to do so (Neh. 13:23–30).

25. *Warrantable:* trustworthy.

26. *Natureless:* unnatural, artificial.

27. Johann Oporinus (1507–68) was Bucer's Swiss printer.

28. Matthaus Zell (1477–1548) and Kaspar Heid (1494–1552) were leading Reformers in Strasburg; Capito (Wolfgang Fabricius Koepfel, 1472–1541) was a famous Hebrew scholar and colleague of Martin Bucer; Mathis Pfarrer (1485–1568) was elected mayor of Strasburg seven times; and Jakob Sturm (1489–1553) was Strasburg's greatest statesman and a Reform leader.

29. Hugo Grotius published his annotations on the Gospels in 1641.

30. The first edition of *The Doctrine and Discipline of Divorce* was published anonymously.

31. *Ails:* troubles.

32. Milton added his initials to the title page of subsequent editions, and his full name to the prefatory letter to Parliament.

33. Frederick II (1482–1556), termed "the wise," became a Protestant in 1546 and sought Fagius's help to establish Protestantism as the official faith of the Palatinate.

34. *Donative:* given or presented (*OED*).

35. *Obvious:* frequent.

36. *Prejudicating:* prejudging.

37. *Authentic:* original.

38. *That good Prince:* Edward VI. In order to convey the tenor of Bucer's respect for King Edward, which Milton's text emulates, "Prince" is capitalized in this tract.

39. *Unadequate:* not equal in magnitude or fitness (*OED*).

40. *Attaint:* to accuse or condemn (*OED*).

41. *Appeachment:* criminal charge.

42. Milton mocks the process that his critics would have to undertake to impeach the arguments of Bucer and Fagius.

43. *Qualify:* mollify.

44. *Intermit:* stop.

45. Milton's summary of each chapter and other additions to Bucer's text are italicized.

46. Bucer argued that marriage was a civil institution, not a sacrament.

47. *Judicature:* court system.

48. A new edition of the legal codes of Justinian was published in Geneva (1594–95).

49. *Antichrists:* popes.

50. *Laws of Antichrist:* canon law.

51. *Rack:* instrument of torture.

52. This selective affirmation of Old Testament laws is common among Protestant Reform writers.

53. The Code of Justinian provides that the state can restore to a husband a wife detained by her parents, a father cannot compel his son to take a wife, and a daughter cannot be forced to marry a madman.

54. Milton omits the rest of this sentence, which argues that marriage is valid after carnal intercourse.

55. *Imperial laws:* laws of the Roman Empire.

56. Milton adds the phrase "as they call it."

57. *They:* guardians of marriage.

58. *Contemned:* disregarded.

59. *Austin:* Saint Augustine.

60. Jerome defends Fabiola against the sin of remarriage by praising her subsequent life of penance and charity. The Yale editor argues that Bucer misrepresents Jerome (YP 2:448n).

61. Paul, 1 Cor. 7:9.

62. *Equal:* fair-minded.

63. Milton omits a paragraph concerning "the vigor of the Gospel."

64. Milton omits a paragraph about Jerome's reluctant endorsement of remarriage.

65. Cyprian (d. 258) was an early apologist for Christianity.

66. Gelasius was an early pope (492–96); Epiphanius was bishop of Constantia, island of Cyprus (310–20).

67. As pope, Leo the Great (440–46) asserted Rome's authority over the entire clergy.

68. Milton omits a long passage arguing that the church fathers permitted divorce because of human weakness.

69. Milton omits a paragraph in which Bucer, although admiring the church fathers, privileges Scripture over their opinions.

70. Milton abbreviates Bucer's scriptural citations. Milton also omits a passage in which Bucer identifies the biblical sources of the church fathers' opinion that remarriage after divorce was prohibited except in cases of fornication.

71. "The I. axiom that Christ could not condemn of adultery that which he once commanded" (Milton's note).

72. Milton abbreviates the biblical passage.

73. Milton omits Bucer's argument that hate-filled husbands and wives become murderers and liars.

74. "The second Axiom" (Milton's note).

75. "Axiom 4" (Milton's note).

76. Matt. 5:34 (Milton's note).

77. Milton quotes these passages, amplifying Bucer's references to them.

78. Milton omits a paragraph concerning desertion as grounds for divorce in 1 Corinthians 7.

79. Milton supplies this passage.

80. Milton adds this reference.

81. Milton omits three paragraphs concerning continuous cohabitation.

82. Bucer lists murder, witchcraft, plotting against the state, robbery, and sacrilege.

83. *Appeached:* accused (*OED*).
84. Milton adds this sentence.
85. According to Bucer's summary of Roman law, a woman could divorce her husband on four grounds: (1) failing to defend her against malicious gossip, (2) failing to defend her reputation for chastity, (3) accusing her of adultery without proof, and (4) having an affair and refusing to end it. A man could divorce his wife on four grounds: (1) adultery, (2) abortion, (3) consorting with other men, and (4) bigamy.
86. Milton adds this sentence.
87. *Donatio propter nuptias:* gift on account of marriage.
88. Added by Milton. The correct reference is 1 John 3:15.
89. *Misbeliever:* non-Christian.
90. *Conversation:* relationship.
91. Milton added the passage in italics.
92. *Depravation:* moral deterioration.
93. Added by Milton.
94. Added by Milton.
95. Reference added by Milton.
96. *Enthrall:* enslave.
97. *Epitomized:* paraphrased, summarized.
98. *Mere Englishman:* someone who only reads English.

Notes to *Tetrachordon* (1645)

1. *Tetrachordon* is a Greek word meaning "four-stringed," and refers to a Greek musical scale of four tones.
2. Euripides, *Medea,* 2.298–301, "For if thou bring strange wisdom unto dullards / Useless thou shalt be counted and not wise / And, if thy fame outshine those heretofore / Held wise, thou shalt be odious in men's eyes," (YP 2:578n1). Milton's text varies slightly from the Loeb edition. The passage may also be translated more freely: "If you introduce ingenious novelties to dim-wits, they will think that you're fundamentally good for nothing and hardly intelligent; whereas if you are regarded as superior to those in a community who have a reputation for sophisticated knowledge, you will be hated." Modern texts do not place the comma in the fourth line, as Milton's original title-page does: "κρείσσων νομισθεὶς ἐν πόλει, λυπρὸς φανῇ." Ancient Greek had no punctuation. The flow of the original verse suggests that "in a community" is ambiguous, attached both to those "who have a reputation" and to "you will be hated." Milton's comma emphasizes the link to those with reputation in the community.
3. The year 1645 is new style. The absence of a printer's name and a publisher's name indicates this work was not licensed or registered.
4. *Information:* formation.

5. The Solemn Covenant (1643) taken by Parliament, The Westminster Assembly, and all English citizens (including Milton).

6. *Maritime law:* law pertaining to shipping. Milton is comparing his statement of purpose in the introduction to declaring the cargo of his ship at customs.

7. *Fraughtage:* cargo.

8. *Gnostics:* a term used in the seventeenth century to mean false prophets or Roman Catholics, who followed others rather than reasoning independently.

9. *Vulgar:* common people.

10. In a sermon to Parliament, Herbert Palmer attacked Milton's divorce tract. The sermon was published as *The Glasse of God's Providence towards His Faithfull Ones* (November 1644).

11. *Was by him made no scruple:* he had no qualms about it.

12. *Special day of humiliation:* August 13, 1644, the day on which Herbert Palmer preached his sermon vilifying Milton.

13. *Martin Bucer:* Milton's publication of extracts of Martin Bucer's work concerning divorce was published on August 6, 1644.

14. *Best and purest times of Edward the sixth:* Edward VI was revered by Protestants as a pious and godly king of England (1547–53). During the first three years of his reign, under the Protectorate of his uncle, Edward Seymour, Duke of Somerset, there was no censorship, and religious writing flourished. It was during his reign that Martin Bucer came to England from Germany.

15. *Choler:* bile was one of the "four humours" of early physiology supposed to cause irascibility of temper (*OED*).

16. Milton is listed as "J. M." on the title page of the 1644 edition of *The Doctrine and Discipline of Divorce.*

17. Milton argues that Herbert Palmer was a chief author of *Scripture and Reason Pleaded for Defensive Armes* (1643).

18. *Phylactery:* a reminder; a religious observance or profession of faith; an ostentatious or hypocritical display of piety or rectitude, a mark of Pharisaism; a burdensome traditional observance. *To make broad the phylactery* (from Matt. 23:5): to vaunt one's righteousness. This instance marks the first recorded use of this sense of the word in the *OED.*

19. *Addicted:* avowed.

20. Dr. Daniel Featley wrote *The Dippers Dipt* (1645), which attacked Anabaptists for permitting divorce and derided Milton's tract "in which the bonds of marriage are let loose to inordinate lust."

21. *Dippers:* the Anabaptists believed, among other things, in baptism by full immersion.

22. *Prelatical:* relating to priests, a word with decided derogatory connotations in Protestant England. Milton wrote pamphlets against a clerical hierarchy.

23. *Apostemated:* abcessed.

24. *Ever made the worse cause seem the better:* related in Plato's *Apology,* I. Socrates's skill at argument made him able to make what was the worse of two positions appear best.

25. *Fifth Monarchy:* see Dan. 2:44. The Fifth Monarchy Men were a sect who believed in the imminent coming of Christ.

26. Prov. 2:2–3.

27. In 1535, an English law authorized a commission to draft a new ecclesiastical code to replace the canon law of the Roman Catholic Church.

28. *Want:* lack.

29. *Meer show of wisdom:* Col. 2:23.

30. *Dead letter:* see 2 Cor. 3:6.

31. *Solon and Epaminondas...for whom it was made:* in *De inventione,* Cicero does not so much defend Epaminondas as point out a possible way in which he could be defended.

32. *Belly-doctrines:* Rom. 16:18.

33. *David in the shewbread:* 1 Sam. 21:2–6.

34. *Hezekiah in the Passover:* 2 Chron. 30:18–19.

35. *Hermaphrodite:* the idea that man was originally created as an hermaphrodite is advanced by Aristophanes in Plato's *Symposium,* and can also be found in Genesis 1:27, "Male and female created he them." An Agadic Midrash on that passage suggests that man was originally created with two faces (one male, the other female), which were later divided.

36. *He not for her, but she for him:* echoed in *Paradise Lost* 4:299, "He for God only, she for God in him."

37. *Priority:* privileges associated with being first created.

38. *Catharist:* ascetic. Catharists believed that all forms of life were sacred, so no living thing should be killed. Moreover, they believed that all pain should be endured or disregarded.

39. *Fond:* foolish.

40. Eph. 5:23–25.

41. *Penuriously:* cheaply, narrowly.

42. *Deportments:* behavior.

43. *Noah and his sons:* Gen. 9:1.

44. *Philo... barrenness away:* Philo argues that the purpose of marriage is procreation, and thus a man can divorce a barren woman.

45. *Carvillius... Dionysius and Gellius:* Dionysius of Halicarnassus in *Roman Antiquities* (2.25) and Aulus Gellius in *Noctes Atticae* (4.3) both relate this story. The Yale editors shows that Milton followed Dionysus (YP 2:593).

46. *School doctors:* Dionysus and Gellius both held that procreation was more important than spousal love. Dionysus noted that he was hated for that opinion (YP 2:593n).

47. *Antichrist who forbids to marry:* an attack on Catholic clerical celibacy.

48. *Cooking:* alteration. See Luke 11:11–13: "If a sonne shal aske bread of any of you that is a father, wil he give him a stone? or if he ask a fishe, wil he for a fishe give him a serpent? If he aske an egge, wil he give him a scorpion? If ye then which are evil, can give good giftes unto your children, how muche more wil your heavenlie Father give the holie Gost to them, that desire him?"

49. *Austin:* Saint Augustine in *De genesi ad litteram* (A Literal Interpretation of Genesis).

50. *Our writers:* Protestant writers.

51. *Peculiar:* particular.

52. *I was... before him:* Prov. 8:30.

53. *Gravest Proverbs:* Prov. 5:18–19.

54. *Jupiter... unloved race:* see Pindar's second *Pythian Ode* for the tale of Ixion.

55. *Delusive:* deceptive, beguiling.

56. *Conjunctive:* closely united.

57. *Isidore of Seville:* the bird lays eggs but does not brood them in the usual way. The ostrich was said to leave its eggs in the sun to hatch (*Etymologies,* book 12, 7:20).

58. *Incontinence:* lack of control.

59. *Adamantine:* unbreakable rock.

60. *Concupiscence:* lust.

61. *Carnal acrimony:* acrimony used in the sense of sharpness; hence, lust.

62. *Sty of an ingrateful... holy or human:* See John Milton, *A Masque Performed at Ludlow Castle* (1634), lines 68–77.

63. *Lees:* dregs.

64. *Abstersive:* cleansing, purging.

65. *David Pareus,* (1548–1622), a German Protestant theologian, quotes the Hebrew, Septuagint Greek, and Luther's German version of this text in his commentary on Genesis, *In Genesin* (Geneva, 1614).

66. *Treatably:* deliberately, distinctly, with clear utterance; without haste or violence, gently, easily, moderately (*OED*).

67. *Irreprehensible:* not reprehensible or blameworthy; not liable to blame or reproof; irreproachable (*OED*).

68. *Benignity:* kindly feeling and its manifestation; kindness of disposition, or of manner (*OED*).

69. *Consanguinity:* shared blood, kinship.

70. *Prejudicant:* prejudiced.

71. *Socinians:* supposedly believed that Adam was created entirely ignorant, and acquired knowledge by eating of the fruit of the tree of knowledge.

72. *Desertrice:* female deserter. This is the only example given in the *OED.*

73. *Capernaitans:* people of Capernaum, lacking faith (see Matt. 11:23 and Luke 10:15).

74. 2 Thess. 2:7.

75. Milton cites *In Genesin,* col. 420, in which Pareus quotes John Chrysostom's homily 5 on the Gospel of John. Milton makes use of *In Genesin* throughout *Tetrachordon.*

76. *Consectary:* following by consequence.

77. *Form:* see Aristotle's *Art of Logic.*

78. *Kindlyness:* according to nature.

79. *Individual:* indivisible.

80. *Mutual benevolence:* see Pareus, *In Genesin,* col. 416.

81. *Catholickly:* universally.

82. William Ames (1576–1633), Puritan theologian and author of *The Marrow of Sacred Divinity* (London, 1643). He moved to the Netherlands and was quickly recognized as a champion of hard-line Calvinism.

83. *Hemingius:* Niels Hemmingsen (1513–1600) was a Danish theologian and author of *Libellus de conjugio, repudio, et divortio* (Leipzig, 1578).

84. Phillip Melanchthon (1497–1560) was a disciple of Luther. Desidirius Erasmus (1469?–1536) was a Dutch humanist and devout Catholic who criticized some of the abuses of the Catholic Church, for which he was adopted by the Protestant cause.

85. *Punctually:* precisely.

86. Hemming, *De conjugio,* col. 993.

87. *Joseph and Mary:* according to Catholic tradition, Joseph and Mary never consummated their marriage.

88. A frequent statement in the *Justinian institutiones juris civilis* (Geneva, 1594–95). Emperor Justinian I (483–565) compiled the *Corpus juris civilis,* a comprehensive rewriting of Roman law that is still the basis of Western civil law. The *Institutes,* a textbook on legal principles, is one part of the *Corpus.*

89. *Justinian:* Roman emperor (527–65). His reign is chiefly remembered for the creation of the Justinian code, a codification of imperial law that served as the basis for continental law.

90. *Tribonian:* Tribonianus (d. ca. 543–45) was head of the council that Justinian appointed to codify the law.

91. *Comment:* comment upon.

92. Gerardus Tuningus wrote a commentary on the *Institutes* of Justinian. See *In quatuor libros institutionum juris civilis divi Justiniani commentarius,* title x, "De Nuptiis."

93. *Pandects out of Modestinus:* Herrenius Modestinus (fl. 222–44) was a Roman legal authority. The *Pandects* are a compilation of Roman legal opinions.

94. *Hylas:* companion of Hercules. Hylas drowned at Cios. See Theocritus, *Idyll* 13.

95. *Consectary:* effect, consequence.

96. *Sciential:* scientific.

97. *Pusillanimity:* cowardliness.

98. Franciscus Vatablus (d. 1547) was a French Hebrew scholar who compiled a set of notes on the Old Testament.

99. Theodore Beza (1519–1605), a French Protestant theologian and scholar, was a disciple of Calvin. Beza attacked Vatablus in *Icones.*

100. Franciscus Junius (1545–1602) was a Protestant theologian who tried to reconcile Calvinists, Lutherans, and Roman Catholics. He is best known for his translation of the Hebrew Bible into Latin.

101. John Calvin (1509–64), leader of Protestants in Geneva and author of *The Institutes of the Christian Religion.*

102. John Diotati (1576–1649), leader of the Italian Protestant congregation in Geneva and noted biblical scholar, was the uncle of Charles Diodati, Milton's close friend.

103. *Atchievement:* escutcheon or ensign armorial, granted for a great accomplishment.

104. There were three opinions about the authorship of Malachi: (1) it was written by an angel, (2) it was written by Ezra, and (3) the author lived in the time of Ezra and Nehemiah.

105. *Author of Ecclesiasticus...Ptolemaeus Euergetes:* Jesus Sirach is credited with authoring the apocryphal book of Ecclesiasticus, but the preface says he translated his grandfather's Hebrew text into Greek during the reign of Ptolemy Eurgetes (246–221 BCE).

106. *Startling:* fickle.

107. *Juris Civilis, Pandects,* 1.3.33–35. Custom is observed as law "in those matters which have not come down in writing."

108. *Euclides:* Euclid was the author of the standard text on geometry.

109. Here Milton demonstrates an awareness of the divisions of Jewish law. Statutes (for example, kosher laws) are both inexplicable and immutable. Judgments (*mishpoatim*) are precedent based and can be emended.

110. Milton consolidates several biblical texts, omitting some words and phrases.

111. *Slug:* be lazy.

112. *Coy:* hidden.

113. *Cullen, or of Lovain:* Cologne and Louvain were the locations of prominent Catholic schools of divinity.

114. *Phimostomus:* not necessarily linked to either of those schools; Milton appears to have been guessing.

115. The three phrases mean "out of good faith"; "what is more just, is better"; "so among good men the good will be done."

116. *Scotisms:* teachings of Duns Scotus (ca. 1265–1308), a medieval philosopher.

117. *Lumbard:* Peter Lombard (ca. 1100–60) was the author of the *Sententiae,* a guide to theology.

118. *Abraham and Lot:* Gen. 13:6–12.

119. *Paul and Barnabas:* Acts 15:37–40.

120. Luke 13:15–16.

121. *Sottish:* foolish, doltish, stupid (*OED*).

122. Roman law provided that an insolent freed slave could be returned to slavery by a judge.

123. *Donations:* means by which a giver was allowed to recover a gift if the receiver was unable to fulfill the terms of the gift.

124. *Rescript:* the reply sent by a Roman emperor to a magistrate or other person consulting him on a doubtful point of law or as to the action to be taken in particular circumstances (*OED*).

125. Antoninus Pius (86–161) was a Roman emperor. His rule (138–61) was marked by peace, except for unrest in Britain.

126. Roman law provided that cruel masters could be forced to sell their slaves.

127. Milton argues from omission, citing unnamed authorities who argue that divorce is implicitly allowed for a wronged wife.

128. *Rahab:* ancestor of Jesus (Matt. 1:5) who protected Joshua's spies in Jericho (Josh. 2:1–21).

129. *Amerced:* fined.

130. *Shekels of silver:* an ancient unit of weight of the Babylonians, hence also of the Phoenicians, Hebrews, and others.

131. *Remitments:* payments.

132. Horse-traders were traditionally regarded as deceptive.

133. *Bereaved his morsel:* denied his treat.

134. Milton consistently argues for reading the law "charitably" rather than narrowly.

135. Eph. 5:23.

136. Mal. 2:15.

137. *Monks and canonists:* being unmarried, monks and canon lawyers (who were priests) should not judge marriages.

138. *Session:* court.

139. *Stand fast . . . bondage:* Gal. 5:1.

140. *Sack:* dry Spanish wine.

141. *Canary:* wine made in the Canary Islands.

142. *Tun:* a cask for storing alcoholic beverages.

143. These references have not been located.

144. *Talmud:* commentary, derived from the Hebrew tradition of Old Testament commentary.

145. *Elements:* first principles.

146. *Analytics:* systematic logic.

147. Luke 14:2–4.

148. *Eusebius:* Eusebius Pamphili (260?–341?), bishop of Caesarea in Palestine, the "father of church history," was an early Christian chronicler, chiefly remembered for his *Ecclesiastical Histories* (ca. 303).

149. *Council of Trent:* the nineteenth ecumenical council opened at Trent on December 13, 1545, and closed on December 4, 1563. Its goals were to define doctrine so that effective disputation with heretics could become possible, and to introduce reforms that might satisfy Protestants.

150. *Marinaro:* Antonius Marianarius was a Carmelite who died in 1570.

151. *Carmelite:* an enclosed, Catholic order of mendicant friars founded in the twelfth century by Saint Bertold on Mount Carmel in Israel.

152. Reginald Pole (1500–58) opposed Henry VIII and became papal legate under Mary Tudor.

153. *German colloquy:* this story is from Paulo Sarpi's *The History of the Council of Trent* (1619).

154. *Cracked cymbals:* 1 Cor. 13:1.

155 . Horace, *Epistles* 1.16.40–45 (Milton's translation).

156. Matt. 5:17–19.

157. *Pentheus... Thebes:* from Euripides' *Bacchae*. Pentheus is unaware of where he is, or what he is doing.

158. Johannes Maldonatus (1534?–83), a Jesuit exegete, was attacked unsuccessfully in 1574 as a heretic by professors of the Sorbonne.

159. *Scribes and Pharisees:* Pareus, in his commentary on St. Matthew, attacks Anabaptists and Jesuits for doubting the perfection of biblical law.

160. *Until all were fulfilled:* Matt. 5:18.

161. *Burdensome:* Burdensomeness.

162. *Fish:* squid, which escapes from adversaries by shooting a cloud of ink.

163. *Punishment of adultery:* John 8:3–11.

164. Matt. 22:17–21.

165. *Austin:* from Saint Augustine's *De conjugiis adulterinis ad pollentium,* 1.13. An English translation was published in London, 1550, entitled *A worke of the Holy bishop S. Augustine concerning adulterous marriages.*

166. *Tertullian... Marcion:* Tertullian (ca. 155–230), Latin church father. This passage refers to his *Adversus Marcionem,* 4.34.

167. *Against Herod... out of Josephus:* see Josephus, *Antiquitates Judaicae,* 4.253.

168. The Hebrew word for "divorce" is not a verb, but rather a noun phrase, *safer k'ritut* (a book of cutting off). This book was later called a *get,* or a bill of divorce, and was subject to many laws as to its composition and delivery, codified in the talmudic Tractate Gittin. Like a summons, the get must be delivered directly into the woman's hands.

169. *Hilary:* Hilarius, pope from 461–68. See Erasmus, *Omnia opera,* 5.317.

170. *Ethics of Aristotle:* Aristotle, *Nichomachean Ethics,* 5.9.11396.

171. Josephus, *Antiquitates Judaicae,* 4.253.

172. Philo of Alexandria (20 BCE–50 CE) was a Hellenized Jew who blended Hebrew mystical thought with Greek philosophy.

173. *Syriac translator:* Martinus Trostius translated the New Testament from Syriac (now commonly called Aramaic) into Latin in 1621.

174. John Cameron (ca. 1579–1623) was a Scottish theologian and moderate Calvinist who taught at Saumur (the French Protestant seminary) and at the University of Glasgow.

175. *Materious:* consisting of matter; significant or important (*OED*).

176. *Docible:* easily taught or managed.

177. *Prodigy:* monstrosity.

178. *Laxative:* relaxing.

179. *Juris Civilis, Institutes,* book 1, title 1.

180. Rom. 7:7.

181. Rom. 3:8.

182. Matt. 12:39; Mark 8:12; Luke 11:29.

183. *Glossists:* commentators.

184. *Endamage:* damage.

185. Cicero, *Letters to Atticus,* 2.1.

186. *Romulean circumscriptions . . . hard success:* Romulus built walls around Rome. When his brother Remus leaped over the wall, Romulus killed him.

187. *Predicament:* category or quality of being.

188. *Philistean foreskins:* 1 Sam. 18:25–27.

189. *Ingots:* a mass (usually oblong or brick-shaped) of cast metal, especially of gold or silver.

190. Andraeus Rivetus (1572–1651) was a French Protestant theologian, who wrote a tract on divorce because of adultery.

191. In his *Commentary on Matthew,* Pareus notes that Paul permits divorce in cases of an infidel spouse's desertion.

192. *Manumise:* to free a slave.

193. Saint Augustine, *Confessions,* 11.12.

194. *Libanius the Sophist . . . apostate:* the story of Libanius and Julian the Apostate is taken from Theodoret, *Ecclesiastical History,* 3.18.

195. *Scheme:* rhetorical flourish.

196. *Ananias and Sapphira:* Acts 5:1–10.

197. Justin Martyr (ca. 100–65) was a Christian apologist who wrote 140 years after Pentecost.

198. *Manured:* handled (maneuvered).

199. *Begirting:* surrounding, encompassing, enclosing. Milton's use here is cited in the *OED.*

200. *Postillers:* commentators.

201. *Tetrarch:* in Roman eras, the ruler of one of four divisions of a country or province; at a later time, this term was applied more generally to subordinate rulers, especially in Syria.

202. *Gnomologies:* collections of adages or brief wise sayings.

203. *Masorites:* Jewish scholars who were particularly literal in their interpretation.

204. *Fardel:* bundle, parcel.

205. *Vendible:* current, accepted, acceptable. Milton's use here is cited in the *OED*.

206. 1 Cor. 7:10–16.

207. Martin Bucer, *In sacra Quatuor Evangelia Ennarrationes,* 197: "If therefore for any cause she cannot be a wife, as we have certainly shown, who does not see that this responsc of Christ does not fit, so that she cannot be put away."

208. *Cast:* condemn.

209. *Syriacisms:* words in Greek style, Hebrew style, Syriac style.

210. *Filing:* shaping.

211. *Scholiaze:* to write scholia, comment. Milton is the only example cited in the *OED*.

212. *Hebraizes:* uses language in a manner typical of Hebrew, simultaneously signifying word and thing.

213. *Equipollent:* equal in power, effectiveness, or validity.

214. *Claudius divorced Messalina:* Claudius, emperor of Rome (10–54 CE), was generally reported to have had his third wife, Valeria Messalina, killed because of her infidelity. He divorced his first two wives.

215. *Stews:* brothels.

216. *Austin... expounded it:* Saint Augustine, *De Sermone Domini in Monte* (Concerning the Lord's Sermon on the Mount).

217. *Joseph sought to put away his betrothed wife privately:* when he discovered that Mary was pregnant, Joseph tried to spare her public humiliation and probable death without himself being party to breaking the law.

218. *Prevalent:* powerful.

219. *Vertumnian:* Vertumnus was the Roman god of seasons.

220. *Gabardine:* a type of cloth.

221. *Alphabets:* the letter of the law.

222. Freidrich Spanheim (1600–49) was a German Calvinist theologian at Geneva and Leiden.

223. *Choleric:* chronic anger, supposed to occur as a result of an excess of choler, or yellow bile.

224. *Parricide:* murdering one's father. According to German legend, the murderer was sewn in a sack with a snake, a cock, an ape, and a dog, and the sack was then sunk in the sea.

225. *Amuse:* bewilder.

226. Matt. 19:24.

227. *Anomalies:* discrepancies.

228. *Obliquities:* deviations.

229. Milton offers an astrological reading of Nature.

230. Peter Martyr's commentary on Paul's First Epistle to the Corinthians (1567). Petrus Martyrus Vermilius (1500–62) was a converted Augustinian friar, later Regius Professor of Divinity at Oxford (1548–53).

231. *Maugre:* despite.

232. *Caiaphas:* John 18:14.

233. Beza, *Tractatio de repudiis et divortiis.*

234. *Supererogations:* the performance of good works beyond what God commands or requires that are held to constitute a store of merit, which the church may dispense to others to make up for their deficiencies. This use cited in *OED*.

235. "Matthaeus Monachus" was Matthew Paris (d. 1259), whose three-volume manuscript, *Chronica Maiora,* includes a discussion of the Greek concept of marriage. John Leunclavius (1533–93) was a classicist and historian best known for his knowledge of Ottoman history.

236. Theodore Balsamon (d. ca. 1200) was a Byzantine commentator on canon law.

237. Theodotus of Ancyra (d. 446) was a theologian and bishop.

238. *Dissentanie:* disagreeing, discordant (*OED*).

239. *Tax and taile:* obligation.

240. One of the conflicts in early Christianity was whether Gentiles could be Christians, or if they had to first become Jews. It was eventually decided that the Jewish laws requiring circumcision and forbidding the ingestion of some animals—most notably, perhaps, pork—did not apply to Christians.

241. Cameron, *Myrothecium Evangelicum.*

242. *Gerard:* Johan Gerhard (1582–1637) was a German theologian.

243. *Brabbles:* arguments.

244. Matt. 18:15–17.

245. *Inartificial:* not according to the art of logic.

246. *Vulgar:* ignorant.

247. The story is told in the Second Apology, and cited by Eusebius in his *Ecclesiastical History.*

248. *Carthaginian phrase:* Tertullian, born in Carthage.

249. See Origen's commentary on Matthew 14 and 24 (328 CE).

250. Lucius Caelius Lactantius (ca. 240–ca. 320), a Christian apologist and author of *Divine Institutiones* (303–11), was noted for his elaborate rhetorical style.

251. *Council of Eliberis in Spain:* Elvira, near Granada, ca. 313.

252. *Council Neocaesarea:* ca. 316.

253. *Laic:* one of the laity; a layman or lay person; one who is not an ecclesiastic.

254. *Council of Nantes:* ca. 1110.

255. Daniel Chamier (d. 1621) was a French Protestant theologian.

256. Epiphanius (d. 535) was Patriarch of Constantinople.

257. *Ambrose:* (ca. 340–97) was bishop of Milan (374–97) and one of the most illustrious fathers and doctors of the church.

258. *Knacks:* tricks, taunts, toys.

259. *Council of Agatha:* Agde in Languedoc, 506.

260. Theodosius served as a Roman general under Flavius Valentinianus, known as Valentinian I, and became emperor after Valentinian's death in 375.

261. Procopius of Caesarea was considered the last great Roman historian. His *Secret History,* discovered in the Renaissance and edited by Niccolo Alamanni (Lyons, 1623), attacked Justinian I and related salacious details about the empress Theodora.

262. Photius (ca. 815–97), Patriarch of Constantinople, was the chief author of the schism between the East and West.

263. Leo VI, "the Wise," was a Byzantine emperor (886–912) who modernized both the law code of Justinian and canon law. He tried unsuccessfully to heal the schism between East and West.

264. Agathias (ca. 536–82) was a Greek poet and lawyer who completed Procopius's history of the reign of Justinian.

265. Alaricus was king of the Visigoths, ca. 370–410; Theodoric (ca. 454–526) was king of the Ostrogoths and leader of the invasion that, in 476, conquered Rome.

266. *Corpulent:* large, bulky, material.

267. *Decretals:* decrees.

268. Gregory I, "the Great" (ca. 540–604), who left a monastery to become pope (590–604), was one of the six Latin fathers of the church. He sent Augustine of Canterbury to England to convert the Anglo-Saxons.

269. *Eldest horn:* first sign of his coming.

270. Alexander III, who succeeded his brother, Leon VI, as pope (1159–81), was best known for upholding the doctrine of papal supremacy against Frederick Barbarossa and Henry II.

271. Frederick Barbarossa (1152–90) was a German emperor and opponent of Alexander III.

272. *Henry II... Becket:* Henry II's quarrel with Thomas Becket, Archbishop of Canterbury, over the rights of the clergy culminated in Becket's murder in the Canterbury Cathedral. Henry, although he had not participated in the murder, bore some responsibility for the act.

273. *Corpus Juris Canonici, Emendatum et Notis Illustratum Gregorii* 13, col. 588 (Lyons, 1591). Title 19 permits divorce (i.e., separating from bed and board) on several grounds: plotting against a spouse's life, witchcraft, adultery, heresy, and infidelity (YP 2:706n).

274. *Balaams:* Num. 23 and 24; Rev. 2:14.

275. *Bed and board... sacrament:* church law permitted separation from "bed and board" without the right to remarry.

276. *Oblation:* gift or contribution made to the church.

277. John Wycliffe (ca. 1320–84), "the Morning Star of the Reformation," was an English theologian and early proponent of reform in the Roman Catholic Church. Wycliffe and his Bohemian follower, John Huss (ca. 1369–1415), anticipated many of Luther's teachings.

278. Hennigus Arnisaeus of Halberstad (d. ca. 1636) was a German jurist and author of a treatise on marriage law, *De jure connubiorum* (Frankfurt, 1613).

279. Johannes Corasius (Jean de Coras) (1513–72) was a French jurist who participated in the trial of Martin Guerre, and a Protestant who was murdered in prison after the St. Bartholomew's Day Massacre.

280. Martin Luther (1483–1546) was a German theologian credited with starting the Protestant Reformation by nailing his 95 Theses to the church door in Wittenberg on the eve of All Saints, 1517. The Theses dealt with the sale of indulgences, but the debate rapidly expanded to include clerical celibacy, the Eucharist, the sacraments, and papal infallibility.

281. *Dutch:* Deutsch, that is, German.

282. *Send away... in her stead:* a reference to the story told in the biblical book Esther, where the queen disobeys her husband and is dismissed. The king then chooses Esther as his new wife.

283. 1 Cor. 13:3.

284. *To some unlawful thing:* Milton quotes "De conjugio," *Loci communes theologici,* 724–25, by Philip Melanchthon (1497–1560), who was Luther's closest associate.

285. This parenthetical phrase may not be as impressive as Milton would wish. Simple reference to dates will point out that Erasmus died in 1536, and the Protestant Reformation is generally accepted to have started in 1517. Thus, although Protestantism did expand rapidly out of Germany, it was not as widespread as might be suggested by Milton's comment.

286. *Dr. Rainolds:* John Rainoldes (1549–1607) was an Elizabethan rhetorician and churchman.

287. Paulus Fagius (1504–49) was a German reformist and scholar who came to England in 1548 at the invitation of Thomas Cranmer, Archbishop of Canterbury. Earlier in his career, Fagius had been invited by Frederick II "the Wise" (1482–1556) to establish Protestantism in the Palatine.

288. The German city of Strassburg was a center of Reformation activity.

289. Matthaus Zell (1477–1548) was a Reformation leader in Strassburg. Kaspar Heid (1494–1552) was his co-worker, as was Wolfgang Fabricius Koepfel (1472–1541). Koepfel (Capito) was also a famous Hebrew scholar, teacher of Fagius, and co-author with Bucer of the *Confessio oder Bekantnus,* the articles of faith of Strassburg, Constance, Lindau, and Memmingen (YP 2:433n)

290. *We teach...pious Caesars:* from Bucer's *Scripta Anglicana* (English Writings).

291. *Peter Martyr:* Saint Peter of Verona (1206–52), Dominican preacher and Grand Inquisitor in Italy.

292. *Because it was...yet so rife?:* from Peter Martyr's *In selectissimam D. Pauli priorem ad Corinthios Epistolam* (Selected Decretals on St. Paul's First Epistle to the Corinthians).

293. Wolfgang Musculus (1497–1563), a converted Benedictine monk, who visited England in 1548.

294. *Gualter of Zuric:* Rudolph Walther (1519–86) was a classical scholar and follower of Ulrich Zwingli (1484–1531), leader of the Protestant Reformation in Switzerland and founder of the Swiss Reformed churches.

295. *Hemingius:* Neils Hemmingsen was the author of *Libellus de conjugo, repudio et divortio* (1572).

296. *Equipollent:* of equal power, equivalent.

297. Aegidius Hunnius the Elder (1550–1603), Doctor of Wittenberg, opposed Catholics and Calvinists. Milton quotes from *Commentarius in Evangelium de Jesu Christo Secundum Matthaeum* (Commentary on the Gospel of Jesus Christ according to Matthew).

298. Felix Bidenbach (1564–1612) was a German theologian best known for his two works on marriage. Milton cites Bidenbach's *De causis matrimonialibus tractatus* (Concerning the Causes of Matrimony).

299. Burchard Harbart (1546–1614) was a German Lutheran theologian who served as dean of the theology faculty at the University of Leipzig. Milton refers to him as "Harbardus, an author not unknown," and Arnisaeus may refer to him as "Borch." The Yale editor was unaware of Harbart (YP 2:712n).

300. *Wigandus:* Johann Wigand (1523–87) was a Lutheran minister.

301. Benedictus Aretius (1505–74) was a Swiss theologian and author of *Problema theologica* (Theological Issues) (Mainz, 1574).

302. *Alciat of Milan:* Andraeus Alciatus of Milan (1492–1550) was an Italian jurist who wrote commentaries on the Justinian code, but who is best known for his *Emblemata liber* (1531), a book of emblems that was frequently reprinted.

303. Isidore (560–636), archbishop of Seville for more than 30 years, was a Spanish theologian whose encyclopedic *Etymologies* (1470) established him as the most learned man of his era.

304. Christophorus Helvicus, *The Theatre of History* (1609).

305. Matthew Wesenbeck (1531–96) was a Flemish jurist and author of *Pandectas juris civilis* (Pandects of Civil Law) (Lyon, 1583).

306. Hugo Grotius (1583–1645) was the foremost legal theorist of Europe. Milton cites his *Annotationes in libros evangeliorum* (Annotations on the Books of the Evangelists) (Amsterdam, 1641).

307. Thomas Cranmer (1489–1556) served as Archbishop of Canterbury (1533–56) and invited learned Protestants to England, including Martin

Bucer. Cranmer was influential in crafting the *Book of Common Prayer* (1552).

308. Walter Haddon (1516–1572) was Regius Professor of civil law at Cambridge.

309. Sir John Cheke (1514–57) was a notable English humanist, tutor to Edward VI, and first professor of Greek at Cambridge. Milton praises him in his eleventh sonnet, "A book was writ of late call'd *Tetrachordon*."

310. *Peculiar:* chosen.

311. *Pledged:* certified, guaranteed.

312. These corrections are part of Milton's text.

Notes to *Colasterion* (1645)

1. *Colasterion:* place (or instrument) of punishment.

2. *Nameless:* anonymous.

3. *Queries:* William Prynne, *Twelve Considerable Serious Questions Touching Church Government* (1644).

4. *Jolly:* bold.

5. Milton was disappointed with Prynne.

6. *Subitanes:* sudden. Sarcastic reference to Prynne's word in the opening of *Twelve Considerable Serious Questions:* "Having neither *leisure* nor *opportunity* to debate the late *unhappy differences* sprung up amongst us touching *church governance*" (2).

7. Prynne filled the wide margins of his text with biblical quotations.

8. Edmund Bonner (1500–69) became bishop of London in 1540 and was known as "bloody Bonner" for burning Protestants during the reign of Queen Mary.

9. *Creeded:* believed.

10. In fact, Milton anonymously published the 1643 edition of *The Doctrine and Discipline of Divorce* and signed only his initials to the 1644 text.

11. *Judicature:* system of courts and laws.

12. *Wind egg:* imperfect or unproductive egg. The *OED* cites Milton's use of this metaphor.

13. *Pack of heads:* other writers, including Herbert Palmer, who attacked Milton's pamphlet.

14. *Legers:* residents.

15. See John 5:2–4. Bethesda was a place where lame beggars lay.

16. *Champarty:* a combination or conspiracy to do ill.

17. No one has identified the clergyman who helped prepare for publication *An Answer to a Book Intituled the Doctrine and Discipline of Divorce* (1644), the primary object of Milton's wrath in *Colasterion.*

18. Joseph Caryl (1620–73) was a preacher, a member of the Westminster Assembly, and the government licenser of religious books, including *An Answer.*

19. *Stale:* decoy.
20. *Salvo jure:* legal exception.
21. Caryl published his lectures on the book of Job in 1643.
22. *Edomitish:* of Ps. 137:7.
23. The enraged Ajax whipped a ram, thinking it was Ulysses (Sophocles, *Ajax,* 1–333).
24. *An Answer* often cites cases from the *First Part of the Institutes of the Lawes of England; or, A Commentarie upon Littleton, not the name of a Lawyer onely, but of the Law it self* (1628), an important legal text by Sir Edward Coke.
25. *Handsel:* down-payment.
26. *Dormitory:* resting place.
27. *Battery:* assault.
28. *Major:* major premise in a logical argument.
29. *Opiniastrous:* portmanteau word combining "opinionated" and "disastrous."
30. 1 Cor. 7:12.
31. Prov. 30:21–23, 21:9, 21:19.
32. *Curvet:* leap.
33. Sir Thomas Littleton (ca. 1402–81) wrote *Treatise on Tenures* (London, 1481), the first printed book on English law.
34. Toledo was famous for sword-making.
35. *Temperature:* temperament.
36. It was the goal of medical practitioners to treat disease by correcting any imbalance in the four humours of the body. The humours were also the basis of mental states and temperament, which were not so amenable to treatment.
37. *Austin:* Saint Augustine.
38. *Rusticity:* lack of culture; ignorance.
39. Professional handbook written by Thomas Powell (London, 1623).
40. *John-a-Noaks and John-a-Stiles:* common names used in legal disputes.
41. *John Dory:* hero of a popular ballad.
42. *Obtunding:* deadening.
43. *Feoffment:* giving a person a fief or fee. In law, transferring ownership of property by "livery of seisin"—that is, handing over a key or other token object; now a written deed is required (*OED*).
44. *Hoyden:* rude, ignorant person.
45. *Larder:* pantry. May suggest the occupation of the author of *An Answer* as butler, steward, or valet.
46. *Points:* laces to fasten clothing.
47. *Fox... brain-worm:* allusions to the title character, a swindler, in Ben Jonson's *Volpone* (1607) and the servant Brain-worm in *Every Man in His Humour* (1601). These plays were published in Jonson's *Workes* (London, 1616).
48. *Endighter:* accuser (*OED*).

49. *Institution:* Gen. 2:18, the foundational text of marriage.
50. 1 Kings 7:21.
51. Matt. 5:39–40.
52. *Black jack:* large leather jug.
53. *Voiding:* clearing the table.
54. *Tressle:* set of wooden legs, often in an X-shape, supporting a flat surface, such as a table (*OED*).
55. *Bayard:* arrogant ignoramus.
56. Psalm 88, attributed to Heman.
57. *I change houses*... *my bargain: An Answer* refers to Milton's house in Aldersgate.
58. Alludes to the plot of *Andria,* the first play by P. Terence (P. Terentius Afer), first performed in Rome (170 BCE).
59. *Pragmatics and folk-mooters:* officious meddlers and provincial politicians.
60. Women Antinomians, who followed John Eaton, a curate near Aldgate.
61. Matt. 12:8; Mark 2:27–28; Luke 6:5.
62. Gal. 5:6.
63. Deut. 22:9–10.
64. 1 Cor. 9:8–10.
65. *Copes-mate:* adversary.
66. *The Common Places [of] Doctor Peter Martyr,* trans. Anthonie Marten (London, 1583), and Erasmus, *Annotations on 1 Corinthians* (Basel, 1519).
67. The Gregorian rules permit a man to leave a wife who conspires to murder him.
68. Johann Schneidewin (1519–68) was a noted professor of law at Wittenberg. His commentary on the Institutes of Justinian was published in Strasburg (1580).
69. *Blanket him:* toss him in a blanket (a tavern game).
70. *Prise:* rebuke.
71. *Estopple:* obstruction.
72. *Assize:* stature, statutory measure.
73. *Sconce:* jocular term for the top of the head; hence, "head" or ability, sense, wit (*OED*).
74. *Lozel:* worthless person.
75. See Shakespeare, *As You Like It,* 2.8.47.
76. *Dorrs:* hornets or bees.
77. *Junta:* with reference to Spain or Italy, a deliberative or administrative council or committee (*OED*).
78. *Brazen ass:* Apuleius, *The XI Bookes of the Golden Ass,* trans. William Adlington (1566).
79. *Batrachomuomachia:* a parody of the *Iliad,* attributed by Plutarch (*Moralia,* 1572) to Pigres of Helicarnassus.

80. Bavius (d. 35 BCE) was a Roman critic who belittled Virgil and Horace. Virgil retaliated in *Eclogues* 3.90 and Horace in *Epodes* 10.

81. *Calandrino:* simpleton in Boccaccio's *Decameron.*

82. *Into a rough Sotadic:* Sotades (third century BCE) was a Greek poet who wrote obscene satirical verse and is credited with inventing the palindrome. After he attacked the incestuous marriage of Ptolemy II, Sotades was shut up in a leaden box and dumped into the sea.

Notes to Prynne, *Twelve Considerable Serious Questions* (1644)

1. This introduction draws on the biographical entry for Prynne in the online *Oxford Directory of National Biography* (2004–07), prepared by William Lamont.

2. *EEBO*, 6–7.

Notes to Palmer, *The Glasse of Gods Providence* (1644)

1. This introduction draws on the biographical entry for Palmer in the online *Oxford Directory of National Biography* (2007–07), prepared by Jacqueline Eales, and S. Clark, "The Life of Master Herbert Palmer," in *A generall martyrologie* (London, 1641), 416–40. Eales quotes Clark, "The Life," 421.

2. *EEBO*, 56–57.

Notes to *An Answer* (1644)

1. This introduction draws upon the following sources: Parker, *Milton's Contemporary Reputation*; Parker, *Milton: A Biographical Commentary*; Sirluck, introduction to YP 2; Shawcross, "A Survey"; van den Berg and Howard, "G. M. Revealed."

2. This information is printed on the page before the title page of *An Answer.*

3. The source for our transcription of *An Answer* is *Tracts by Milton and Relating to Him: 1641–1681.* This unique Bridgewater volume may be the earliest gathering of Milton's writings on divorce and significant responses to them. The Huntington Library's copy (shelfmark RB 46430) includes no information about the book's publication history. The volume includes the following pamphlets: Milton's *Of Reformation Touching Church Discipline* (1641); *An Argument or, Debate in Law of the Great Question Concerning the Militia* by J. M. [John Marsh] (1642); *Tyrannicall-Government Anatomized: or, a Discourse Concerning Evil-Councellors. Being the Life and Death of John the Baptist* by George Buchanan (1642); Milton's *The Doctrine and Discipline of Divorce* (1643); the consequent

An Answer (1644); Milton's *The Judgement of Martin Bucer* (1644), *Colasterion* (1645), *Tetrachordon* (1645), and *The Tenure of Kings and Magistrates* (1649); concluding with *Mr. John Milton's Character of the Long Parliament and Assembly of Divines in MDCXLI omitted in his other works and never before printed* (1681), one of Milton's texts that was erroneously identified (by Wing, no. T3590) as "Mr. John M. Hon's character of the Long Parliament," supposedly by Sir James Tyrrell. The Bridgewater Library collection (which includes the Ellesmere Chaucer) was begun by Sir Thomas Egerton and was completed by Francis Egerton, First Earl of Ellesmere (d. 1857). Henry Huntington purchased the Bridgewater Library for $1 million in 1917. See **Collier,** *A Catalogue Bibliographical.* The pamphlet also includes the following title at the top of the first page of text: "An Answer to a Book, intituled, *The Doctrine and Discipline of Divorce restored to the good of both Sexes from the bondage of the Canon Law.*"

4. *Cherithuth... Chorath:* these two words should read as *qeritut* and *qorat*. The author of *An Answer* may have used *th* for *t* due to Sefardic (Eastern) teachers.

5. *Gneruath Dabhar:* This should read as *ervath davar.*

6. *Ci sane shallach, amar Jehovah Elohe Israel:* ki sane shalach, amar Jehovah Elohe Yisroel.

7. *EEBO*, Wing A3304.

Notes to Featley, *The Dippers Dipt* (1645)

1. This introduction draws on the biographical entry for Daniel [Fairclough] Featley in the online *Oxford Directory of National Biography* (2004–07), prepared by Arnold Hunt.

2. *EEBO*, xiii–xiv.

Selected Bibliography

Abbott, Mary. *Life Cycles in England, 1560–1720: Cradle to Grave*. New York: Routledge, 1996.

Achinstein, Sharon. "'A Law in This Matter to Himself': Contextualizing Milton's Divorce Tracts." In *The Oxford Handbook of Milton*, ed. Nicholas McDowell and Nigel Smith, 174–85. Oxford: Oxford University Press, 2009.

———. *Milton and the Revolutionary Reader*. Princeton, N.J.: Princeton University Press, 1994.

Aers, David, and Bob Hodge. "'Rational burning': Milton on Sex and Marriage." In *Milton Studies*, vol. 12, ed. James D. Simmonds, 3–33. Pittsburgh: University of Pittsburgh Press, 1979.

Alblas, Jacques B. H. "Milton's *The Doctrine and Discipline of Divorce*: The Unknown Dutch Translation (1655) Discovered." *Milton Quarterly* 28, no. 2 (1994): 35–39.

Ames, William. *Conscience with the power and cases thereof*. London, 1639.

Anonymous, *An Answer to a Book, Intituled, the Doctrine and Discipline of divorce,* OR, *A Plea for Ladies and Gentlewomen, and all other Maried Women against Divorce. Wherein, Both Sexes are vindicated from all bondage of Canon Law, and other mistakes whatsoever: And the unfound Principles of the Author are examined and fully confuted by authority of Holy Scripture, the Laws of this Land, and sound Reason* (London, 1644). *Source:* Henry E. Huntington Library and Art Gallery, Wing A3304; *EEBO*.

———. *A Directory for publique worship of God throughout the three kingdoms of England, Scotland, and Ireland together with an ordinance of Parliament for the taking away of the Book of common-prayer, and for establishing and observing of this present directory throughout the kingdom of England and dominion of Wales*. London, 1645.

———. Review of 1820 collection of Milton's divorce tracts, *The Monthly Review* 93 (September 1820).

Anonymous [John Milton]. *An Essay upon Divorcement: writ for the good of both sexes. Shewing the lawfulness and unlawfulness, the conveniences and inconveniences of divorce: with a peremptory conclusion... upon Sir Geo. Downing and Mrs. Forester, petitioning for a divorce.* London, 1715.

Apuleius. *The XI Bookes of the Golden Ass.* Trans. William Adlington. London, 1566.

Aristotle. *Nicomachean Ethics.* Oxford: Clarendon Press, 1894.

Badcock, Samuel. *Gentlemen's Magazine* 55 (1785).

Barker, Arthur E. "Christian Liberty in Milton's Divorce Pamphlets." *Modern Language Review* 35 (1940): 153–61.

Beza, Theodore. *De repudiis et divortiis.* Geneva, 1582.

———. *Icones.* Geneva, 1580.

———. *Tractatio de repudus et divortus* (Treatise on Annulments and Divorces). Geneva, 1596.

Biberman, Matthew. "Milton, Marriage and a Woman's Right to Divorce." *Studies in English Literature, 1500–1900* 39 (1999): 131–53.

Bidenbach, Felix. *De causis matrimonialibus tractatus* (Concerning the Causes of Matrimony). Frankfurt, 1608.

Blum, Abbe. "The Author's Authority: *Areopagitica* and the Labour of Licensing." In *Re-Membering Milton: Essays on the Texts and Traditions,* ed. Mary Nyquist and Margaret Ferguson, 74–96. New York: Methuen, 1987.

Boke of Common Praier, The. London, 1552.

Booty, John E., ed. *The Book of Common Prayer, 1559: The Elizabethan Prayer Book.* Charlottesville, Va.: Published for the Folger Shakespeare Library by the University Press of Virginia, 1976.

Boyette, Purvis E. "Milton's Divorce Tracts and the Law of Marriage." *Tulane Studies in English* 17 (1969): 73–92.

Bucer, Martin. *De regno Christi.* 1557. STC (2nd ed.): 3965. *Early English Books Online.*

———. *In sacra quatuor evangelia enarrationes.* Basel, 1536.

Cable, Lana. *Carnal Rhetoric: Milton's Iconoclasm and the Poetics of Desire.* Durham, N.C.: Duke University Press, 1995.

———. "Coupling Logic and Milton's Doctrine of Divorce." In *Milton Studies,* vol. 15, ed. James D. Simmonds, 143–59. Pittsburgh: University of Pittsburgh Press, 1981.

Calvin, John. *Institutes of the Christian Religion*. 1599. Trans. Henry Beveridge. Chicago: Encyclopædia Britannica, Inc., 1990.

Cameron, John. *Myrothecium Evangelicum*. Geneva, 1632.

Campbell, Gordon. *A Milton Chronology*. New York: St. Martin's Press, 1997.

Cary, Lady Elizabeth (Tanfield), Viscountess Falkland. *The Tragedie of Mariam, the faire queen of Jewry*. London, 1613.

———. *Tragedy of Mariam: The Fair Queen of Jewry, with The Lady Falkland: Her Life*. Ed. Barry Weller and Margaret Ferguson. Berkeley and Los Angeles: University of California Press, 1994.

Cicero, Marcus Tullius. *De officiis*. London: W. Heinemann, 1913.

Civilian, A. "A Preface, Referring to Events of deep and powerful Interest at the present Crisis." *The Doctrine and Discipline of Divorce: in Two Books: also the Judgement of Martin Bucer; Tetrachordon; and an abridgement of Colasterion v–xv, by John Milton*. London: Printed for Sherwood, Neely, and Jones, Paternoster-Row, 1820.

Coke, Sir Edward. *First Part of the Institutes of the Lawes of England; or, A Commentarie upon Littleton, not the name of a Lawyer onely, but of the Law it self*. London, 1628.

Collier, John Payne. *A Catalogue Bibliographical and Critical of Early English Literature: Forming a portion of the library at Bridgewater house, the property of the Rt. Hon. Lord Francis Egerton*. London, 1837.

Confessore, Nicholas. "N.Y. Moves Closer to No-Fault Divorce." *New York Times*, June 15, 2010.

Coontz, Stephanie. "Divorce, No-Fault Style." *New York Times*, June 16, 2010.

Corns, Thomas N. *Uncloister'd Virtue: English Political Literature, 1640–1660*. Oxford: Clarendon Press, 1992.

Corns, Thomas N., ed. *A Companion to Milton*. Oxford: Blackwell, 2001.

Cressy, David. *Birth, Marriage, and Death*. Oxford: Oxford University Press, 1997.

Cressy, David, and Lori Anne Ferrell, eds. *Religion and Society in Early Modern England: A Sourcebook*. New York: Routledge, 1996.

Danielson, Dennis, ed. *The Cambridge Companion to Milton*. 2nd ed. Cambridge: Cambridge University Press, 1999.

Darnton, Robert. *The Literary Underground of the Old Regime*. Cambridge, Mass.: Harvard University Press, 1982.

Davies, Horton. *Worship and Theology in England.* Princeton, N.J.: Princeton University Press, 1961–75.

Demetrius. *On Style.* Trans. W. Rhys Roberts. Cambridge, Mass.: Harvard University Press, 1932.

Dewey, Frank L. *Thomas Jefferson, Lawyer.* Charlottesville: University Press of Virginia, 1986.

Dobranski, Stephen B. *Milton, Authorship, and the Book Trade.* Cambridge: Cambridge University Press, 1999.

Dobranski, Stephen B., and John P. Rumrich, eds. *Milton and Heresy.* Cambridge: Cambridge University Press, 1998.

Eisenstein, Elizabeth. *The Printing Press as an Agent of Change.* 2 vols. Cambridge, Mass.: Harvard University Press, 1979.

Erasmus, Desiderius. *Omnia opera.* Basel, 1540.

Euripides. *Medea.* Ed. and trans. Denys and Michael Page. Oxford: Clarendon Press, 1938.

Eusebius, Bishop of Caesarea. *Ecclesiastical History.* London, 1636.

Fallon, Stephen. "The Metaphysics of Milton's Divorce Tracts." In *Politics, Poetics, and Hermeneutics in Milton's Prose,* ed. David Loewenstein and James Grantham Turner, 69–83. Cambridge: Cambridge University Press, 1990.

———. "The Spur of Self-Concernment: Milton in His Divorce Tracts." In *Milton Studies,* vol. 38, *John Milton: The Writer in His Works,* ed. Michael Lieb and Albert C. Labriola, 220–42. Pittsburgh: University of Pittsburgh Press, 2000.

Featley, Daniel. *The Dippers Dipt; or, The Anabaptists Duck'd and Plung'd over head and eares, at a Disputation in Southwark: together with a large and full discourse of their 1. Original. 2. Severall sorts. 3. Peculiar errours. 4. High attempts against the state. 5. Capitall Punishments, with an application to these times.* London, 1645.

Fish, Stanley. *How Milton Works.* Cambridge, Mass.: Harvard University Press, 2001.

Fleetwood, William. *The Counsellor's Plea for the Divorce of Sir G. D. and Mrs. F.* London, 1715.

French, J. Milton, ed. *The Life Records of John Milton.* 5 vols. New Brunswick, N.J.: Rutgers University Press, 1949–58.

Friest, Dagmar. *Governed by Opinion: Politics, Religion and the Dynamics of Communication in Stuart London, 1637–1645.* London: I. B. Tauris, 1997.

The Geneva Bible: A facsimile of the 1560 edition. Madison: University of Wisconsin Press, 1969.

Gibson, Colin S. *Dissolving Wedlock.* London: Routledge, 1994.

Gouge, William. *Of domesticall duties.* London, 1634.

Halkett, John. *Milton and the Idea of Matrimony: A Study of the Divorce Tracts and "Paradise Lost."* New Haven: Yale University Press, 1970.

Haller, William. "Hail Wedded Love." *ELH* 13 (1946): 79–97.

Haller, William, and Malleville Haller. "The Puritan Art of Love." *Huntington Library Quarterly* 5 (1942): 235–72.

Hannen, Sir James. *Durham v. Durham* [1885] 10 PD 10, 1 TLR 338.

Hansard. House of Commons Official Report. Divorce Reform Bill Debate. April 25, 1969.

Haskin, Dayton. "Choosing the Better Part with Mary and with Ruth." In *Of Poetry and Politics: New Essays on Milton and His World,* ed. P. G. Stanwood, 153–69. Binghamton, N.Y.: Medieval and Renaissance Texts and Studies, 1995.

Hatten, Charles. "The Politics of Marital Reform and the Rationalization of Romance in *The Doctrine and Discipline of Divorce.*" In *Milton Studies,* vol. 27, ed. James D. Simmonds, 95–113. Pittsburgh: University of Pittsburgh Press, 1991.

Hawkes, David. "The Politics of Character in John Milton's Divorce Tracts." *Journal of the History of Ideas* 62, no. 1 (2001): 141–60.

Hemmingsen, Niels. *Libellus de conjugio, repudio, et divortio.* Leipzig, 1578.

Herbert, George. *The English Poems of George Herbert.* Ed. C. A. Patrides. London: Dent, 1974.

Herodotus. *The Landmark Herodotus: The Histories.* Ed. Robert Stassler. New York: Random House, 2007.

"Historical Perspective on Divorce and Remarriage." *Presbyterian Church in America.* PCAnet, 21 August 2003. <http://www.pcanet.org/history/>.

Homer. *The Iliad.* Trans. Robert Fitzgerald. New York: Anchor Books, 1974.

———. *The Odyssey.* Trans. Robert Fitzgerald. New York: Anchor Books, 1963.

House of Commons. Divorce Reform Bill Debates. London, 1968–73.

Howard, W. Scott. "Milton's 'Divorcive' Liberties: Ecclesiastical, Domestic or Private, Civil and Cosmological." *Early Modern Literary Studies* 10, no. 1, 2004. http://purl.oclc.org/emls/10-1/howamilt.htm.

Huguelet, T. L. "The Rule of Charity in Milton's Divorce Tracts." In *Milton Studies,* vol. 6, ed. James D. Simmonds, 199–214. Pittsburgh: University of Pittsburgh Press, 1974.

Hutchinson, F. E., ed. *The Poetry of George Herbert.* Oxford: Clarendon Press, 1941.

Jefferson, Thomas. Notes regarding *Blair v. Blair* (1772). Library of Congress, Thomas Jefferson papers.

Jenkins, Hugh. "Jefferson (Re)Reading Milton." *Milton Quarterly* 32 (1998): 32–38.

Johns, Adrian. *The Nature of the Book: Print and Knowledge in the Making.* Chicago: University of Chicago Press, 1998.

Johnson, James T. *A Society Ordained by God: English Puritan Marriage Doctrine in the First Half of the Seventeenth Century.* Nashville: Abingdon Press, 1970.

Jonson, Ben. *Works.* Ed. C. H. Herford and Percy and Evelyn Simpson. Oxford: Clarendon Press, 1926–52.

Josephus, Flavius. *Antiquitates Judaicae.* 1558. Ed. and trans. Steve Mason. Leiden: Brill, 2000.

Kahn, Victoria. "'The Duty to Love': Passion and Obligation in Early Modern Political Theory." *Representations* 68 (1999): 84–107.

Kenrick, William. *Free Thoughts on Seduction, Adultery, and Divorce.* London, 1771.

Kirby, R. Kenneth. "Milton's Biblical Hermeneutics in *The Doctrine and Discipline of Divorce.*" *Milton Quarterly* 18, no. 4 (1984): 116–25.

Kranidas, Thomas. "The Colasterion: Milton's Plural Adversary." *Prose Studies* 19, no. 3 (1996): 275–81.

Lewalski, Barbara. *The Life of John Milton: A Critical Biography.* Oxford: Blackwell, 2000.

Lieb, Michael, and John T. Shawcross, eds. *Achievements of the Left Hand: Essays on the Prose of John Milton.* Amherst: University of Massachusetts Press, 1974.

Loewenstein, David, and James Grantham Turner, eds. *Politics, Poetics and Hermeneutics in Milton's Prose.* Cambridge: Cambridge University Press, 1990.

Luxon, Thomas. *Single Imperfection: Milton, Marriage, and Friendship.* Pittsburgh: Duquesne University Press, 2005.

Magro, Maria. "Milton's Sexualized Woman and the Creation of a Gendered Public Sphere." *Milton Quarterly* 35, no. 2 (2001): 98–112.

Maimonides, Moses. *Mishneh Torah.* Jerusalem: Feldheim, 1974–75.

Maresius, Samuel. *Systema breve universae theologiae.* London, 1659.

Marten, Anthonie, trans. *The Common Places [of] Doctor Peter Martyr.* London, 1583.

Martin, Catherine Gimelli, ed. *Milton and Gender.* Cambridge: Cambridge University Press, 2004.

Peter Martyr. *In selectissimam D. Pauili priorem ad Corinthios Epistolam* (Selected Decretals on St. Paul's First Epistle to the Corinthians). Tiguri, 1551.

Masson, David. *The Life of John Milton: Narrated in Connexion with the Political, Ecclesiastical, and Literary History of His Time.* 7 vols. London, 1859–94.

Mazzola, Elizabeth. *The Pathology of the English Renaissance: Sacred Remains and Holy Ghosts.* Boston: Brill, 1998.

McCready, Amy. "Milton's Casuistry: The Case of *The Doctrine and Discipline of Divorce.*" *Journal of Medieval and Renaissance Studies* 22, no. 3 (1992): 393–428.

McKenzie, D. F. "The London Book Trade in 1644." In *Making Meaning: Printers of the Mind and Other Essays,* ed. Peter McDonald and Michael Suarez, 126–43. Amherst: University of Massachusetts Press, 2002.

McKerrow, Ronald B. *A Dictionary of Printers and Booksellers in England, Scotland and Ireland, and of Foreign Printers of English Books, 1557–1640.* London: Printed for the Bibliographical Society by Blades, East and Blades, 1910.

Mead, Rebecca. "Love's Labors: Monogamy, Marriage, and Other Menaces." *The New Yorker,* August 11, 2003, 79–82.

Melanchthon, Philip. *Loci communes theologici.* Basel, 1561.

Milton, John. *Colasterion: A Reply to a Nameless Answer against The Doctrine and Discipline of Divorce. Wherein The trivial Author of that Answer is discovered, the Licenser conferred with, and the Opinion which they traduce defended.* London, 1645.

———. *The Complete Poetry of John Milton.* Ed. John T. Shawcross. New York: Doubleday, 1971.

———. *The Complete Prose Works of John Milton.* 8 vols. Ed. Don M. Wolfe et al. New Haven: Yale University Press, 1953–82.

———. *The Doctrine and Discipline of Divorce: in Two Books: also The Judgement of Martin Bucer; Tetrachordon; and an abridgement of*

Colasterion, v–xv. London: Printed for Sherwood, Neely, and Jones, Paternoster-Row, 1820.

———. *The Doctrine and Discipline of Divorce: Restored to the good of both sexes, From the bondage of Canon Law, and other mistakes, to Christian freedom, guided by the Rule of Charity. Wherein also many places of Scripture have recovered their long-lost meaning. Seasonable to be now thought on in the Reformation intended,* London, 1643.

———. *The Doctrine & Discipline of Divorce Restored to the good of both Sexes, From the bondage of Canon Law, and other mistakes, to the true meaning of Scripture in the Law and Gospel compared. Wherein also are set down the bad consequences of abolishing or condemning of Sin, that which the Law of God allows, and Christ abolished not. Now the second time revised and much augmented, In Two Books: To the Parliament of England with the Assembly.* London, 1644.

———. *An Essay upon Divorcement,* 1715. *See* Anonymous [John Milton] entry.

———. *John Milton: Selected Prose.* Ed. C. A. Patrides. Columbia: University of Missouri Press, 1985.

———. *The Judgement of Martin Bucer, Concerning Divorce, Written to Edward the sixth, in his second Book of the Kingdom of Christ. And now Englished. Wherein a late Book restoring the Doctrine and Discipline of Divorce is here confirmed and justified by the authority of Martin Bucer.* London, 1644.

———. *A Masque Performed at Ludlow Castle.* London, 1634.

———. *Paradise Lost.* Ed. Alastair Fowler. London: Longman, 1971.

———. *The Prose of John Milton.* Ed. J. Max Patrick. New York: New York University Press, 1968.

———. *The Prose Works.* London, 1797. *Early English Books Online,* Wing M2086. New Haven: Yale University Library.

———. *Tetrachordon: expositions upon The four chief places in Scripture, which treat of Marriage, or nullities in Marriage. Wherein the Doctrine and Discipline of Divorce, as was lately published, is confirmed by explanation of Scripture, by testimony of ancient Fathers, of civil laws in the Primitive Church, of famousest Reformed Divines, And lastly, by an intended Act of the Parliament and Church of England in the last year of Edward the Sixth* (London, 1645). *Source:* British Library, Wing (2nd ed.), M2184, Thomason E.271[12]; *EEBO.*

———. *Tracts by Milton and Relating to Him: 1641–1681.* Bridgewater volume. Huntington Library, shelfmark RB 46430.

[John Milton]. *An Essay upon Divorcement: writ for the good of both sexes. Shewing the lawfulness and unlawfulness, the conveniences and inconveniences of divorce: with a peremptory conclusion... upon Sir Geo. Downing and Mrs. Forester, petitioning for a divorce.* London, 1715.

Nyquist, Mary. "The Genesis of Gendered Subjectivity in the Divorce Tracts and in *Paradise Lost.*" In *Re-membering Milton: Essays on the Texts and Traditions,* ed. Mary Nyquist and M. W. Ferguson, 99–127. New York: Methuen, 1987.

———. "Gynesis, Genesis, Exegesis, and the Formation of Milton's Eve." In *Cannibals, Witches, and Divorce: Estranging the Renaissance,* ed. Marjorie Garber, 147–208. Baltimore: The Johns Hopkins University Press, 1987.

Owen, Eivion. "Selden and Milton on Divorce." *Studies in Philology* 43 (1946): 233–57.

Oxford English Dictionary. Oxford: Oxford University Press, 2009.

Palmer, Herbert. *The Glasse of Gods Providence Towards his Faithfull Ones. Held forth in a Sermon Preached to the two Houses of Parliament, at Margarets Westminster, Aug. 13.1644. being an extraordinary Day of Humiliation. Wherein is discovered the great failings that the best are liable unto; upon which God is provoked sometimes to take Vengeance. The whole is applied specially to a more carefull observation of our late Covenant, and particularly against the ungodly Toleration pleaded for under pretence of Liberty of Conscience.* London, 1644.

———. *Scripture and Reason Pleaded for Defensive Armes.* London, 1643.

Pareus, David. *In Genesin*. Geneva, 1614.

Parker, William Riley. *Milton: A Biographical Commentary*. 2nd ed. Rev. ed. Gordon Campbell. Oxford: Oxford University Press, 1996.

———. *Milton's Contemporary Reputation.* 1940. New York: Haskell House, 1971.

Patterson, Annabel. "Milton, Marriage and Divorce." In *A Companion to Milton,* ed. Thomas Corns, 279–93. Oxford: Blackwell, 2001.

———. "No Meer Amatorious Novel?" In *John Milton,* ed. Annabel Patterson, 87–101. New York: Longman, 1992.

Perkins, William. *The foundation of Christian religion.* Cambridge, 1618.

Perlette, John. "Milton, Ascham and the Rhetoric of the Divorce Controversy." In *Milton Studies,* vol. 10, ed. James D. Simmonds, 195–215. Pittsburgh: University of Pittsburgh Press, 1977.

Peters, Belinda. *Marriage in Seventeenth-Century English Political Thought*. New York: Palgrave Macmillan, 2004.

Phillips, Roderick. *Putting Asunder: A History of Divorce in Western Society*. Cambridge: Cambridge University Press, 1988.

Pindar. *Works. Greek and English*. Ed. and trans. William H. Race. Cambridge, Mass.: Harvard University Press, 1997.

Plato. *The Collected Dialogues*. Ed. Edith Hamilton and Huntington Cairns. Princeton, N.J.: Princeton University Press, 1961.

Plomer, Henry R. *A Dictionary of the Booksellers and Printers Who Were at Work in England, Scotland and Ireland from 1641 to 1667*. London: Printed for the Bibliographical Society by Blades, East and Blades, 1907.

Plutarch. *The Lives of the Noble Grecians and Romans*. Trans. John Dryden. Ed. Rev. Arthur Hugh Clough. Chicago: Encyclopedia Britannica, 1952.

Polybius. *The Histories*. 6 vols. London: W. Heinemann, 1922–27.

Poole, Kristen. *Radical Religion from Shakespeare to Milton*. Cambridge: Cambridge University Press, 2000.

Potts, James B., Jr. "Milton and Augustine: The Rule of 'Charity.'" *Explorations in Renaissance Culture* 16 (1990): 101–10.

Powell, Chilton L. *English Domestic Relations, 1487–1653*. New York: Columbia University Press, 1917.

Propertius, Sextus. *Elegiae*. Ed. and trans. G. P. Gould. Cambridge, Mass.: Harvard University Press, 1990.

Prynne, William. *Twelve Considerable Serious Questions touching church government sadly propounded (out of a reall desire of unitie and tranquillity in church and state) to all sober-minded Christians, cordially affecting a speedy settled reformation, and brotherly Christian union in all our churches and denominations, now miserably wasted with civill unnatuall warres, and deplorably lacerated with ecclesiasticall dissentions*. London, 1644.

Purkiss, Diane. "Whose Liberty? The Rhetoric of Milton's Divorce Tracts." In *The Oxford Handbook of Milton*, ed. Nicholas McDowell and Nigel Smith, 186–99. Oxford: Oxford University Press, 2009.

Ramsey, Michael. *Putting Asunder: A Divorce Law for Contemporary Society. The Report of a Group Appointed by the Archbishop of Canterbury in January, 1964*. London: SPCK, 1966.

Rosenblatt, Jason P. "Milton's Chief Rabbi." In *Milton Studies*, vol. 24, ed. James D. Simmonds, 43–71. Pittsburgh: University of Pittsburgh Press, 1988.

Salmon, Thomas. *A Critical Essay concerning Marriage*. London, 1724.

Sánchez, Reuben. "'The Middling Temper of Nourishment': Biblical Exegesis and the Art of Indeterminate Balance in *Tetrachordon*." *Milton Quarterly* 29, no. 1 (1995): 1–12.

Schocket, Gordon J. *Patriarchalism in Political Thought: The Authoritarian Family and Political Attitudes Especially in Seventeenth Century England*. Oxford: Blackwell, 1975.

Selden, John. *De iure naturali & gentium*. London, 1640.

———. *Uxor Ebraica* [*The Hebrew Wife*]. London, 1646.

Shakespeare, William. *As You Like It*. Ed. Juliet Dusinberre. Arden Shakespeare, 3rd ser. London: Arden Shakespeare, 2006.

Shanley, Mary Lyndon. "Marriage Contract and Social Contract in Seventeenth Century English Political Thought." *Western Political Quarterly* 32, no. 1 (1979): 79–91.

Shawcross, John T. *John Milton: The Self and the World*. Lexington: The University Press of Kentucky, 1993.

———. "A Survey of Milton's Prose Works." In *Achievements of the Left Hand: Essays on the Prose of John Milton*, ed. Michael Lieb and John T. Shawcross, 291–391. Amherst: University of Massachusetts Press, 1974.

Shoulson, Jeffrey S. *Milton and the Rabbis: Hebraism, Hellenism, and Christianity*. New York: Columbia University Press, 2001.

Sirluck, Ernest. Introduction to *The Complete Prose Works of John Milton*, vol. 2, ed. Douglas Bush, 1–216. New Haven: Yale University Press, 1959.

Smith, David. L. "Divorce and Remarriage: From the Early Church to John Wesley." *Trinity Journal* 11, no. 2 (1990): 131–42.

Smyth, William Carmichael. *An Appeal to the King's Most Excellent Majesty, and to the British Nation*. London, 1830.

———. *In the Consistory Court of London: 1st session, Easter Term, 14th April 1826: Smyth against Smyth*. London, 1826.

Sophocles. *Ajax*. Trans. F. Storr. Cambridge, Mass.: Harvard University Press, 1912–13.

Spenser, Edmund. *The Faerie Queene*. Ed. A. C. Hamilton, Hiroshi Yamashita, Toshiyuki Suzuki, and Shohachi Fukuda. 2nd ed. New York: Pearson Longman, 2006.

Stephen, Henry John. *New Commentaries on the Laws of England: Partly Founded on Blackstone*. 4 vols. London: Henry Butterworth, 1842.

Stone, Lawrence. *Broken Lives: Separation and Divorce in England, 1660–1857.* Oxford: Oxford University Press, 1993.

———. *The Family, Sex and Marriage.* New York: Harper and Row, 1977.

———. *The Road to Divorce: England, 1530–1987.* Oxford: Oxford University Press, 1990.

Svendsen, Kester. "Science and Structure in Milton's Doctrine of Divorce." *PMLA* 67 (1952): 435–45.

Theodoret. *Ecclesiastical History.* Saint-Omer, 1612.

Thirty-Nine Articles. London, 1571.

Thompson, Claude A. "'Coded' Signatures: A Printer's Clue to the Bibliographical Tangle of *The Doctrine and Discipline of Divorce* (1644)." *Papers of the Bibliographical Society of America* 8 (1974): 297–305.

Tuningus, Gerardus. *In quatuor libros institutionum juris civilis divi Justiniani commentarius.* Leyden, 1618.

Turner, James G. *One Flesh: Paradisal Marriage and Sexual Relations in the Age of Milton.* Oxford: Oxford University Press, 1987.

Urban, David V. "'Out of His Treasurie Things New and Old.'" In *Milton's Legacy*, ed. Kristin A. Pruitt and Charles W. Durham, 208–19. Selinsgrove, Pa.: Susquehanna University Press, 2005.

Valbuena, Olga. "Milton's 'Divorsive' Interpretation and the Gendered Reader." In *Milton Studies,* vol. 27, ed. James D. Simmonds, 115–36. Pittsburgh: University of Pittsburgh Press, 1992.

———. *Subjects to the King's Divorce: Equivocation, Infidelity, and Resistance in Early Modern England.* Bloomington: Indiana University Press, 2003.

van den Berg, Sara. "Women, Children, and the Rhetoric of Milton's Divorce Tracts." *Early Modern Literary Studies* 10, no. 1, 2004. http://purl.oclc.org/emls/10 1/bergmilt.htm.

van den Berg, Sara, and W. Scott Howard. "G. M. Revealed: Printer of the First Attacks on *The Doctrine and Discipline of Divorce.*" *Milton Quarterly* 38, no. 4 (2004): 242–52.

Wheeler, C. B. "Milton's Doctrine and Discipline of Divorce." *Nineteenth Century* 61 (1907): 127–35.

Witte, John, Jr. *From Sacrament to Contract: Marriage, Religion, and Law in the Western Tradition.* Louisville, Ky.: Westminster John Knox Press, 1997.

Zagorin, Perez. *Milton: Aristocrat and Rebel: The Poet and His Politics.* New York: D. S. Brewer, 1992.

Index